Fifteenth Edition

Illinois SCHOOL LAW SURVEY

2018 - 2020

Brian A. Braun

ILLINOIS ASSOCIATION
OF SCHOOL BOARDS

2921 Baker Drive
Springfield, Illinois 62703-5929

One Imperial Place
1 East 22nd Street
Lombard, Illinois 60148-6120

March 2018

ISBN: 978-1-880331-35-4

CAUTIONARY NOTE

Illinois School Law Survey provides answers to general questions regarding statutes and case law in force and reported as of January 1, 2018 and administrative rules in effect as of December 15, 2017. *Illinois School Law Survey* is not intended to provide advice in the handling of specific situations. Because the law is in a state of continual change, the reader should treat this publication as a source of instruction in the basic principles of school law and as a guide to matters meriting further study or the assistance of legal counsel.

Finally, *Illinois School Law Survey* generally excludes laws that are unique to Chicago Public School District 299.

Comments and suggestions for improvements to *Illinois School Law Survey* may be addressed to either the author or to the Communications Department of the Illinois Association of School Boards.

THE AUTHOR

Brian Braun, of Champaign, has been an attorney with the firm of Miller, Tracy, Braun, Funk & Miller, Ltd. since 1983. He was an attorney on the staff of the Illinois Association of School Boards (IASB) from 1977 to 1983 and a language arts teacher in DuPage County from 1969 until 1977. He was born in Chicago and raised in Glencoe, Illinois, where he attended the Glencoe Public Schools and New Trier High School. He is a graduate of the University of Illinois College of Communications and the DePaul University College of Law.

Mr. Braun has lectured on school law and labor relations at a number of Illinois colleges and universities, was a member of the Board of Directors of the National Council of School Attorneys (1991-1995) and is a past chairman of the executive committee of the Illinois Council of School Attorneys. In November 1996, Brian Braun received the Harold P. Seamon Award from IASB for distinguished service to public education.

Mr. Braun and his wife, Terre, a kindergarten teacher at Westview Elementary School in Champaign, have three adult children, David, who practices law with Mr. Braun; Aaron, who is the rabbi at Northbrook Community Synagogue; and Max, who is a digital analyst with V.S.A. Partners in Chicago. Mr. Braun and his wife have six grandchildren, Samantha and Ari, children of David and Sadie Braun; and Aidan, Lily, Jonah, and Jack, children of Aaron and Marina Braun.

AUTHOR'S ACKNOWLEDGEMENTS

Many thanks to those who have been mentors, colleagues, and friends. A special thank you to Jerry Glaub, longtime director of communications and deputy executive director at IASB, without whom this project would have been impossible at its inception and to my son, David Braun, who has assisted in the preparation of the *Survey* since the Tenth Edition, and who I hope will someday take over the task of writing this book.

For Terre, my children, daughters-in-law, and grandchildren, who will always mean everything to me.

Brian A. Braun
Champaign, Illinois
March 1, 2018

HOW TO USE *ILLINOIS SCHOOL LAW SURVEY*

In addition to simply reading the text from front to back, the user of *Illinois School Law Survey* has two ways to locate desired information. The Table of Contents on pages vi through viii lists the broad topics covered in each chapter. In many cases, these topic headings lead directly to the desired information.

However, any legal question probably relates to several topics, and information can show up under any number of different headings. (Seniority rights of teachers, for example, may be discussed under teacher employment as well as under collective bargaining.) Moreover, broad topic headings often will not describe or suggest a particular question or narrow point of law. The user interested either in a narrow topic or in one with multiple facets should use the Quick Reference Index beginning on page 406. This alphabetical list of topics includes references too narrow to be listed in the Table of Contents and shows whether the topic is discussed at more than one place in the text.

The reader also will find a table of court cases arranged in alphabetical order by name of plaintiff beginning on page 379. All court decisions cited in the book are listed in the table with a full legal reference. At the end of each case citation is listed the question(s) where the case is cited in the text.

The Table of Cases serves two purposes. The user who knows only a case name will be able to find a full citation and a list of applicable questions and answers. Also, where an answer cites a court decision, the reader can use the table to find other questions and answers related to the same decision.

Packaged with this Fifteenth Edition of the *Illinois School Law Survey* is a unique code for access to the digital version that includes the entire text of the book's 27 chapters and Table of Cases. Plus, it provides direct links from the Contents to reach relevant questions and answers, as well as links in the Quick Reference Index to easily navigate to relevant question numbers on a narrow topic.

Moreover, the digital version provides special advantages for legal research. Anyone who is reasonably skilled in navigating the web should find the digital version particularly productive and efficient. It links to all Illinois statutes and administrative rules. It also carries nearly all of the federal statutes and rules plus most court decisions cited in the book, compiled and annotated by legal publisher LexisNexis.

Access to the digital version will be available at *http://lawsurvey.iasb.com* until publication of the next edition.

QUESTION NUMBERS

The number to the left of the colon in each question number reflects the chapter number, 1 through 27. Questions within each chapter are numbered to the right of each colon; that is, 1:10, 1:20, 1:25, 2:10, 2:15, and so on.

While questions are presented in numerical sequence, intervals between numbers are variable. Questions in the first edition were numbered at intervals of 10, leaving room for the insertion of new questions as needed in subsequent editions.

CONTENTS

UNDERSTANDING LEGAL REFERENCES

All legal references in this book are cited in standard forms that employ numerous abbreviations. In order to retrieve legal source materials, therefore, the lay reader must (a) understand the abbreviations used in the legal citations; and (b) know where to find the legal publications cited.

An explanation of abbreviations used in this book is provided on page xii.

Citations involving statutes may be the easiest for the lay reader to locate. Law libraries and most attorneys and courthouses will have current statutes available — the *United States Code* and the *Illinois Compiled Statutes.* Numbering of chapters and sections are relatively easy to comprehend.

Administrative regulations may be the most difficult materials to locate in hard copy. The *Illinois Administrative Code* is a publication that is not always found in a law office or courthouse. However, the Code is available on the website of the Joint Committee on Administrative Rules (JCAR). JCAR provides a link to the complete Code, along with a search engine, at *http://www.ilga.gov/commission/jcar/.* Rules also may be obtained from the administrative agency that issued the regulation in question.

Federal rules are found in *Federal Rules Digest* and *Code of Federal Regulations*.

READING CASE CITATIONS

Publications that report court decisions are found in law libraries. In Illinois, law libraries are maintained by most universities and colleges and can be found in most county courthouses. Many lawyers maintain small law libraries.

Court cases are cited by case name, which is printed in italics. Case citations following each case name reveal which court decided the case and in what year. Case citations also tell where to find the case cited. The format for most case citations is as follows:

- The first number refers to the volume of the set of books in which the case can be found.
- The second reference is to the set of books in which the case can be found.
- The next reference is to the edition of that set of books.
- The final reference is to the page on which the case cited can be found in the volume and set.

For example, 23 Ill. App. 3d 196 means the case referred to can be found in volume 23 of *Illinois Appellate Reports, Third Edition* on page 196.

Knowing the edition is important, because cases are reported chronologically. New editions of various reporters are issued randomly whenever the publishers think the volume numbers have gotten too high. Thus, when the publishers thought the volume numbers were getting too high in *Illinois Appellate Reports*, they simply went from volume 351 Ill. App. to volume 1 Ill. App. 2d. Thus, knowing the volume and page number is not enough to find a case easily unless you know the edition number, too.

Cases are frequently reported in more than one set of books. Thus, the same case may be found in *Supreme Court Reporter*, in United States Reports, and in Lawyers' Edition. Wherever possible we have given multiple citations for each case.

SPECIAL NOTICE:

The case citation system in Illinois has changed since the Twelfth Edition of the *Survey* was published in 2012. Cases cited and decided since that publication date follow a new format adopted by the Illinois Supreme Court. This format change does not affect citations for cases that were reported before the change. In the new format:

- The first number is the year the decision was rendered.
- The second reference is the court that rendered the decision.
- The last number is the docket number or in the case of appellate decisions, the last six digits of the docket number of the case.

STATE COURTS

Cases which have been tried in the Illinois state court system are identifiable by their citations. There are three levels of courts in Illinois. The lowest is the circuit court, which is the trial level. Circuit court decisions are not generally reported, and have very little precedential value.

A party may appeal an adverse circuit court decision to the appropriate Illinois appellate court as a matter of right. There are five geographically determined Illinois appellate courts, which are designated by district numbers one through five. The First District Appellate Court hears Cook County appeals and the Second District Appellate Court covers Lake County and the northwestern part of the state. The Third and Fourth Districts hear north central and south central appeals, and the Fifth District hears cases originating in circuit courts located in the southern third of the state.

All Illinois appellate court citations are cited to one of the three editions of *Illinois Appellate Reports* — Ill. App. or Ill. App. 2d or Ill. App. 3d. Each appellate court citation also gives the reader information in a parenthetical notation about which appellate court decided the case cited and when it was decided. For example, (5th Dist. 1990) means the Fifth District Appellate Court decided the case in 1990.

A party may ask the Illinois Supreme Court to review an adverse appellate court decision. The Illinois Supreme Court may accept or reject most appeals at its pleasure. The reader can determine whether the Illinois Supreme Court has rendered a decision in a case, because all such cases are cited to *Illinois Appellate Reports*. If a case has a citation to Ill. or Ill. 2d, the reader will know the decision referred to was rendered by the Illinois Supreme Court.

FEDERAL COURTS

The federal court system is also three-tiered. Usually, in education law, lawsuits dealing with federal Constitutional questions are brought in federal court and questions which deal with state law are brought in state court.

The federal court system starts with a federal district court. There are three federal district courts in Illinois, designated as the Northern District, Central District, and Southern District. Federal District Court decisions are reported in a set of books called *Federal Supplement*. If the reader sees a citation to F. Supp., it means the case cited was decided by the lowest federal court, a federal district court.

A party may appeal an adverse federal district court decision to the appropriate federal circuit court of appeals as a matter of right. There are eleven federal circuit courts of appeals across the nation. All Illinois cases are heard by the Seventh Circuit Court of Appeals. All federal court of appeals cases are cited in this text to *Federal Reporter.* Therefore, if the reader sees a citation to F. or F. 2d, this means the case cited was decided by a federal appeals court. Each court of appeals citation includes a parenthetical notation designating the court of appeals which rendered the decision and the year the decision was rendered. For example, (7th Cir. 1990) means the Seventh Circuit Court of Appeals decided the case in 1990.

A party may ask the United States Supreme Court to review an adverse decision rendered by a court of appeals. In most cases, the Supreme Court may review a decision or deny the right to review at its pleasure. All cases referred to in this text decided by the Supreme Court are cited to *Supreme Court Reporter*. Therefore, if the reader sees a citation to S. Ct., this means the case was decided by the United States Supreme Court.

REFERENCE LINKS IN DIGITAL VERSION

The digital version of *Illinois School Law Survey* makes it easy to locate legal references cited herein from a web browser. In addition to the text of the publication, the digital version carries hyperlinks to most of the cited legal references. Each legal citation is linked directly to the full text of the cited material, including state and federal laws, administrative rules, and court decisions. The digital version of the *Survey* provides an "all-in-one" reference work.

Links to court cases and federal statutes and regulations are compiled for the *Survey* by LexisNexis Legal Publishers. For Illinois statutes, the digital version links to the *Illinois Compiled Statutes*, which are located on the website of the Illinois General Assembly. Reference links to the *Illinois Administrative Code* go to the website of the Joint Committee on Administrative Rules.

Links to the bylaws and policies of the Illinois High School Association (IHSA) cited in Chapter 27 go to the IHSA website where the sources are provided. Decisions rendered by the Illinois Educational Labor Relations Board (IELRB) are cited as PERI – *Public Employee Reporter for Illinois* — and go to the IELRB website.

A few court cases are not available in the digital version, including some trial court decisions identified with docket numbers and some recent decisions not yet published at press time.

ABBREVIATIONS USED IN LEGAL CITATIONS

2d — second edition
3d — third edition
A. — *Atlantic Reporter*
ALR — *American Law Reporter*
aff'd. — affirmed
app. — appeal
art. — article
BNAC — Bureau of National Affairs
c. — chapter
C.D. Ill. — Central District of Illinois, refers to the federal district court in Illinois in which the case was tried. Federal district courts are identified in parentheses by state and region within the state; i.e., M.D. Pa. for Middle District of Pennsylvania, and year (M.D. Pa. 1992).
cert. — certiorari (the word is used in this text to describe a request to the United States Supreme Court to review an adverse court of appeals decision)
cert. den. — certiorari denied (means the U.S. Supreme Court declined to review the case)
C.F.R. — *Code of Federal Regulations*
Cir. — circuit
C.J.S. — Corpus Juris Secundum (a legal encyclopedia)
Cmwlth. — Commonwealth
Const. — Constitution
D.C. — District Court or District of Columbia
D.C. Cir. — U. S. Court of Appeals for the District of Columbia Circuit
den. — denied
E.D. — Eastern District
eff. — effective
et al. — in the name of a case, "et al." means there are other parties who are referred to collectively
et seq. — et sequentes (and the following)
et ux. — and wife
ex rel. — on behalf of, for the use of, or on the relation of
F. — *Federal Reporter*
F.E.P. — *Fair Employment Practice Cases*
Fed.R.Civ.P. — *Federal Rules of Civil Procedure*
Fla. Cir. Ct. — Florida Circuit Court
F.R.D. — *Federal Rules Digest*
F. Supp. — *Federal Supplement*
IELRB — Illinois Educational Labor Relations Board
ILCS — *Illinois Compiled Statutes*
IL — *Illinois Reports* (newer citation format)
Ill. — *Illinois Reports*
Ill. Admin. Code — *Illinois Administrative Code* (also known as *Code of Illinois Rules* and cited in that form as "CILR")
IL App — *Illinois Appellate Reports* (newer citation format)
Ill. App. — *Illinois Appellate Reports*
Ill. Const. — *Illinois Constitution*
Ill. Dec. — *Illinois Decisions*
in re — in the matter of, petition of, or application of
Ind. — *Indiana Reports*
La. App. — *Louisiana Courts of Appeal Reporter*
L. Ed. — *Lawyers' Edition*
LEXIS — Lexis on line service
M.D. — Middle District
Minn. Sup. Ct. — Minnesota Supreme Court
N.D. — Northern District
N.E. — *Northeastern Reporter*
N.J. — *New Jersey Reports*
no. — number
N.W. — *Northwestern Reporter*
N.Y. — *New York Reporter*
N.Y.S. — *New York Supplement*
Ohio Misc. — *Ohio Miscellaneous*
op. — opinion
P. — *Pacific Reporter*
P.A. — Public Act
Pa. Super. — Pennsylvania Superior Court
Pa. Cmwlth. — *Pennsylvania Commonwealth Court Reports*
PERI — *Public Employee Reporter for Illinois*
reh. — rehearing
rem. — remand or remanded (returned to a lower court)
rev. — reversed
S. Ct. — *Supreme Court Reporter*
S.D. — Southern District
S.E. — *Southeastern Reporter*
So. — *Southern Reporter*
sec. — section
Slip op. — Slip opinion (an opinion which is so new it is not yet published in law reporters)
sub nom. — sub nominee (in the name of)
sugg. — suggestion
supp. — supplemented
S.W. — *South Western Reporter*
Tex. Ct. App. — Texas Court of Appeals
U.S. — *United States Reports*
U.S.C. — *United States Code*
U.S.L.W. — *United States Law Week*
Va. App. — *Virginia Court of Appeals Reports*
vac. — vacated
Wash. — *Washington Reports*
Wash. Super. Ct.—Washington Superior Court
W.D. — Western District
WL — *Westlaw and Code of Federal Regulations*.

1: CONTROL OF ILLINOIS PUBLIC SCHOOLS

FEDERAL GOVERNMENT

1:10 Is education a state or federal function?

Early in the 19th century there was little state involvement in education. Later, education became almost entirely a function of state or local government. In the 20th century, the state has assumed responsibility for the regulation of education. The Illinois State Constitution establishes a system of public schools, whereas the U.S. Constitution makes no mention of education. Ostensibly, therefore, education is a responsibility of the state.

Since the 1950s, however, the federal government has assumed a more aggressive role in the regulation of schools by imposing requirements upon the states. Federal laws, such as the 1964 Civil Rights Act and its amendments and the Individuals with Disabilities Education Act, have greatly changed education in the last 60 years.

1:20 What federal agency is responsible for the administration of federal programs for public schools?

The U.S. Department of Education is the principal federal agency that regulates public schools.

20 U.S.C. 3411

STATE GOVERNMENT

1:30 Are public school districts governmental entities?

The Illinois Constitution provides:

"A fundamental goal of the People of the State is the educational development of all persons to the limits of their capacities.

"The State shall provide for an efficient system of high quality public educational institutions and services. Education in public schools through the secondary level shall be free. There may be such other free education as the General Assembly provides by law.

"The State has the primary responsibility for financing the system of public education."

Ill. Const. art. X, sec. 1

Board of Education of Community Consolidated School District 606, Tazewell County v. Board of Education of Community Unit District 124 of Mason and Tazewell Counties, 11 Ill. App. 2d 408, 137 N.E. 2d 721 (3rd Dist. 1956)

O'Connor v. Board of Education of School District No. 23, 645 F. 2d 578 (7th Cir. 1981) cert. den. 102 S. Ct. 641, 454 U.S. 1084, 70 L. Ed. 2d 619 (1981), on rem. 545 F. Supp. 376

1:40 Are all the laws that govern Illinois public schools found in the Illinois School Code?

The laws of Illinois are published in the Illinois Compiled Statutes which can be found online at *www.ilga.gov*. Many of the laws affecting education are contained in Chapter 105, which is commonly called the "School Code." The laws of Illinois were reorganized in 1993. Before January 1, 1993, Illinois laws were organized as Illinois Revised Statutes. In Illinois Revised Statutes, the School Code was Chapter 122.

Many chapters in addition to Chapter 105 of the Illinois Compiled Statutes directly affect or regulate schools. For example, elections are administered by laws contained in Chapter 10. The Educational Labor Relations Act and other labor matters are found in Chapter 115, the Open Meetings Act is included in Chapter 5, pensions laws are in Chapter 40, and various laws relating to records are contained in Chapter 50.

Many other chapters of the Illinois Compiled Statutes are relevant to schools. Various state agencies have rules and regulations that are found in the Illinois Administrative Code. There are also numerous federal laws that apply to schools.

1:45 Where can I access Illinois State Board of Education rules that affect public schools?

The Illinois Administrative Code can be accessed online at *www.ilga.gov*. Rules adopted by the Illinois State Board of Education are found in Title 23.

23 Ill. Admin. Code

1:50 What is the difference between the terms "common schools," "free schools," and "public schools"?

The terms common schools, free schools, and public schools are used interchangeably in the School Code.

105 ILCS 5/1-3

SCHOOL DISTRICTS

1:60 What are "county school units"?

The territory in each county, exclusive of charter districts that are required to appoint their own school treasurers, constitutes a county school unit. County school units of less than two million inhabitants are known as Class I county school units, and county school units of two million or more inhabitants are known as Class II county school units.

105 ILCS 5/5-1

1:70 What types of school districts are there in Illinois?

The numerous school district designations in Illinois vary mostly in name and reflect, not important legal distinctions, but different statutory terminology in use at the time different school districts were organized. Many of the statutes under which Illinois school districts were first organized have since been repealed. Among the variations in district type that reflect important legal distinctions:

1) Unit districts, which were created under various designations, provide education for kindergarten through grade 12. Elementary districts (grades K-8) and high school districts (grades 9-12) create a dual structure.

2) Charter districts, originally created under charters granted by the state, typically are governed by special sections of the School Code. Schools in the City of Chicago, for example, are governed by Article 34 of the School Code.

105 ILCS 5/11E-10
105 ILCS 5/12-1
105 ILCS 5/12-10
105 ILCS 5/32-1.1
105 ILCS 5/33-1
105 ILCS 5/34-2

SCHOOL BOARDS

1:80 What is a school board?

The term "school board" refers to the governing body of any school district created under the authority of the School Code, including boards of school directors and boards of education. The majority of school boards are governed by Article 10 of the School Code. However, the boards of some larger school districts and some special charter districts are governed by Articles 32, 33, and 34 of the School Code.

105 ILCS 5/10-1 et seq.
105 ILCS 5/32-1 et seq.
105 ILCS 5/33-1 et seq.
105 ILCS 5/34-1 et seq.

Board of Education of Bremen High School District No. 228 v. Mitchell, 387 Ill. App. 3d 117, 899 N.E. 2d 1160, 326 Ill. Dec. 509 (1st Dist. 2008)

1:90 Are school boards created by the state Constitution?

No, the Illinois Constitution does not refer to local school boards. They are creations of state statutes.

1:100 Do school districts or their governing bodies have inherent powers?

A school board is a creation of the state, and creations of the state are without inherent power. A school board may exercise only those powers that the legislature has specifically granted, or those powers that are reasonably implied from a specified power, to achieve the purposes that the legislature has assigned to them.

Goedde v. Community Unit School District No. 7, Macoupin County, 21 Ill. App. 2d 79, 157 N.E. 2d 266 (3rd Dist. 1959)

1:110 What kinds of school boards are there in Illinois?

The majority of school boards are governed by Section 10-10 of the School Code that requires each to have seven members elected for terms of four years. There are numerous exceptions allowed or required by law, however

1) A 2005 amendment to the School Code allows a board of education or board of school directors to appoint a non-voting student member to the board. The student member may not participate in or attend closed sessions;

2) Sections 10-1 and 10-3 provide for a three-member board of school directors in school districts with fewer than 1,000 inhabitants, except that a consolidated district must have a board of seven directors;

3) A law enacted in 2006 (Section 11E-10 et. seq.) permits the creation, conversion, or combination of certain school districts and defines the composition of the resulting school boards;

4) Section 32-1.1 authorizes school boards of charter districts with 100,000 to one million inhabitants to

expand from seven members to 11 members unless the district's original charter or other special law provides otherwise;

5) Article 34 provides for a seven-member board of education appointed by the mayor in Chicago;

6) Section 32-1.5 authorizes the voters of special charter districts to elect a school board of three, five, or seven members;

7) Section 32-3.2 requires certain special charter districts in cities of more than 45,000 inhabitants to have 11 members appointed by the mayor; and

8) Section 33-1 authorizes special charter districts in cities of 100,000 to 500,000 inhabitants to elect seven-member boards of education, with members serving five-year terms. The same boards are authorized by Section 33-1a to adopt an alternative arrangement, subject to voter approval at a referendum, electing three board members at large and four members from school board districts that are substantially equal in population.

The school boards of special charter districts, which predate most of the laws creating school boards, operate under provisions of their own state charters unless they have chosen to adopt Article 10 of the School Code or have selected one of the other options available in Articles 32 or 33.

105 ILCS 5/10-1
105 ILCS 5/10-3
105 ILCS 5/10-10
105 ILCS 5/11E-10
105 ILCS 5/11E-55
105 ILCS 5/32-1 et seq.
105 ILCS 5/33-1
105 ILCS 5/34-3

1:120 May citizens claim that an improper type of school board exists in a given school district?

When a petition signed by 10 percent or 1,500 legal voters, whichever is less, is submitted to a regional superintendent of schools, the regional superintendent must take a special census of the school district to determine if the district has the proper type of school board, a board of school directors, or a board of education. The expenses of this census are to be borne by the school district involved.

If the census shows that the proper type of board does not exist, then the regional superintendent is required to immediately notify the school district and to certify to the proper election authorities that an election shall be held at the next general election in order to select the appropriate and entirely new board of the type legally required for a given school district.

105 ILCS 5/3-14.16

STATE BOARD OF EDUCATION

1:130 How was the State Board of Education created?

The State Board of Education was created by the Illinois Constitution, which provides in part:

"There is created a State Board of Education to be elected or selected on a regional basis. The number of members, their qualifications, terms of office and manner of election or selection shall be provided by law. The Board, except as limited by law, may establish goals, determine policies, provide for planning and evaluating education programs and recommend financing. The Board shall have such other duties and powers as provided by law.

"The State Board of Education shall appoint a chief state educational officer."

Ill. Const. art. X, sec. 2

1:140 How are members of the Illinois State Board of Education selected?

Members of the State Board of Education are appointed by the Governor with the advice and consent of the Senate. The State Board consists of eight members and a chairperson. Members are appointed pursuant to statutorily defined geographic areas of representation. Three members (including the chairperson) are appointed as at-large members.

Before a 2004 change in the statute that governs State Board membership, no more than five members of the State Board could have been from one political party. The party membership limitation in the composition of the State Board now provides that of the four members excluding the chairperson whose terms expire in 2007, no more than two of those members may be from one political party and of the four members whose terms expire in 2009 and every four years thereafter, no more than two of those members may be from one political party. Members of the State Board serve for staggered four-year terms that expire in January of odd numbered years. Before the 2004 change in the statute State Board members served staggered six-year terms.

105 ILCS 5/1A-1
105 ILCS 5/1A-2

1:150 What are the qualifications for membership on the State Board of Education?

The members of the State Board of Education must be citizens of the United States and residents of the State of Illinois and are selected on the basis of their knowledge of or interest and experience in problems of public education. No member of the State Board may be gainfully employed or administratively connected with any public school system nor have any interest in or benefit from funds provided by the State Board of Education to an institution of higher learning, public or private, within Illinois nor shall they be members of a school board or board of school trustees of a public or nonpublic school, college, university, or technical institution within Illinois.

105 ILCS 5/1A-2

Hoskins v. Walker, 57 Ill. 2d 503, 315 N.E. 2d 25 (1974)

1:160 Are State Board of Education members compensated?

State Board of Education members are reimbursed for all ordinary and necessary expenses incurred in performing their duties as members of the board. They receive no other compensation. Expenses must be approved by the State Board and must be consistent with the laws, policies, and requirements of the State of Illinois regarding such expenditures. Any member may include in his or her claim for expenses $50 per day for meeting days.

105 ILCS 5/1A-2

1:170 How is a vacancy on the State Board of Education created?

A vacancy on the State Board of Education is created when a member

1) Dies;

2) Files a written resignation with the Governor;

3) Is adjudicated to be a person under legal disability under the Probate Act or a person subject to involuntary admission under the Mental Health and Developmental Disabilities Code;

4) Ceases to be a resident of the region from which he or she was appointed;

5) Is convicted of an infamous crime, or of any offense involving a violation of his or her duties under the School Code; or

6) Fails to maintain the qualifications for membership as provided in Section 1A-2.

105 ILCS 5/1A-2

105 ILCS 5/1A-2.1

405 ILCS 5/3-700 et seq.

755 ILCS 5/11a-1 et seq.

1:180 How may a member of the Illinois State Board of Education be removed from office?

The Governor may remove a member of the State Board of Education for incompetence, neglect of duty, or malfeasance in office.

Ill. Const. art. V, sec. 10

105 ILCS 5/1A-2.1

1:190 What are the qualifications for the office of State Superintendent of Education?

A 2004 change in the relevant statute links the term of the contract of the State Superintendent of Education to the term of the Governor.

The State Board of Education determines the qualifications of and appoints the State Superintendent. The Governor may suggest a State Superintendent who serves at the pleasure of the State Board and pursuant to a performance contract linked to statewide student performance and academic improvement within Illinois schools.

The State Superintendent must, at a minimum, be appointed at the beginning of each term of a Governor after that Governor has made appointments to the State Board. The first State Superintendent contract after the change in the statute must expire no later than February 1, 2007 and subsequent contracts must expire no later than February 1, each four years thereafter. The State Superintendent cannot be a member of the State Board.

The State Board establishes the compensation for the State Superintendent and establishes the duties, powers, and responsibilities of the office.

105 ILCS 5/1A-4(B)

1:200 What are the duties and authorities of the State Superintendent of Education?

The State Superintendent of Education is the chief administrative officer of the State Board of Education and as such, is responsible for the supervision and evaluation of all public schools, for enacting and enforcing rules governing the operation of public schools, and for carrying out the policies of the State Board of Education.

105 ILCS 5/1A-4

105 ILCS 5/2-2 et seq.

1:210 What types of school district recognition does the State Board of Education grant?

There are four recognition categories:

1) Fully recognized

2) On probation

3) Recognized pending further review

4) Non-recognized.

A school or district that meets the requirements imposed by law, including the requirements established by the State Board pursuant to Section 2-3.25 of the School Code, is fully recognized.

A school or district is to be placed on probation if it

1) Exhibits deficiencies that present a health hazard or a danger to students or staff;

2) Fails to offer required coursework;

3) Employs personnel who lack the required qualifications and who are not in the process of attaining such qualifications;

4) Fails or refuses to serve students according to relevant legal and/or regulatory requirements; and/or

5) Prolongs or repeats instances of noncompliance to a degree that indicates an intention not to comply with relevant requirements.

A school or district shall be recognized pending further review if it exhibits areas of noncompliance that are not serious enough to warrant probation and may be corrected prior to the end of the school year following the school year in which they were identified. A district must be recognized pending further review whenever one or more of the district's schools are first removed from full recognition, whether recognized pending further review or placed on probation. The district shall subsequently be placed on probation if the instances of noncompliance cited for one or more schools have not been corrected within the time allowed.

The recognition status of a district or a school may be changed by the State Board of Education at any time to reflect information confirmed during compliance monitoring or by any other means.

The superintendent of a district that is recognized pending further review or in which one or more schools are recognized pending further review may, within 30 days after receipt of notification to this effect, request a conference at which representatives of the district will have an opportunity to discuss compliance issues with representatives of the State Board of Education.

The State Superintendent must schedule a conference with the superintendent of a district that is placed on probation at which representatives of the district will discuss compliance issues with representatives of the State Board of Education. Within 60 days following this conference, the school district must submit to the regional superintendent of schools and the State Superintendent of Education a corrective plan that conforms to the requirements of the law. It must be signed by the secretary of the local board of education (showing the board adopted a resolution) if it relates to noncompliance at the district level and by the district superintendent and each principal if it relates to noncompliance at one or more schools.

The State Superintendent of Education must respond to the submission of a plan within 15 days after receiving it and may consult with the regional superintendent of schools to determine the appropriateness of the actions proposed by the district to correct the cited deficiencies. The State Superintendent must approve a plan if it specifies steps to be taken by the district that are directly related to the area or areas of noncompliance cited and provides evidence that the district has the resources and the ability to take the steps described without giving rise to other issues of compliance that would lead to probationary status, and if it specifies a timeline for correction of the cited deficiencies that is demonstrably linked to the factors leading to noncompliance and is no longer than needed to correct the identified problems.

If a district's plan is not approvable because it fails to meet the requirements above, the State Superintendent shall notify the district. If no plan is submitted, or if no approvable plan is received within 60 days after the district's conference with the State Board, the status of the district, or of the affected school or schools, as applicable, shall be changed to "non-recognized."

The superintendent of a district that is non-recognized, or in which one or more schools are non-recognized, may request a conference with representatives of the State Board of Education within 15 days after receipt of notification to this effect.

If a conference is requested by a superintendent on behalf of a non-recognized school or district and the areas of concern are not resolved, the State Superintendent shall furnish the school board with a Notice of Opportunity for Hearing. The school board may submit an appeal by adopted board resolution within 15 days after receipt of the notice. The appeal must identify the specific findings with which the district disagrees. The district will be given a hearing in accordance with the State Board's rules for Contested Cases and Other Formal Hearings. A final decision shall be rendered by the State Board of Education. If no conference is requested, the district shall be deemed not to intend to appeal the non-recognition.

Neither a district nor a school may be non-recognized without first having been placed on probation. A district that is non-recognized, or in which one or more schools are non-recognized, is subject to state aid penalties.

105 ILCS 5/2-3.25f
105 ILCS 5/18-8.05 (A)(3)(a)
23 Ill. Admin. Code 1.20
23 Ill. Admin. Code 475.10 et seq.

REGIONAL GOVERNANCE

1:220 What is an educational service region?

An educational service region is a county or a group of counties administered for educational purposes by a regional superintendent of schools.

105 ILCS 5/3A-1 et seq.

1:222 What is the difference between an educational service region and a regional office of education?

There is no difference. The terms are synonymous.

105 ILCS 5/3-0.01
105 ILCS 5/3-2.5

1:230 How are regional superintendents of schools selected?

Regional superintendents of schools are elected pursuant to general election laws by popular vote from all counties comprising the educational service region served.

105 ILCS 5/3A-6

1:240 What is the difference between a county superintendent of schools, a regional superintendent of schools, and a regional superintendent?

These terms refer to the same elective office and are interchangeable, although as the service areas of the superintendents have been consolidated over time to encompass multiple counties, the term "county superintendent of schools" is being used less frequently.

105 ILCS 5/3-0.01

1:250 What are the qualifications for regional superintendent of schools?

No one is eligible to file a petition of candidacy for the office of regional superintendent of schools at any primary or general election, or to enter into the duties of this office either by election or appointment, unless possessing the following qualifications:

1) Is of good character;

2) Has a master's degree;

3) Has earned at least 20 semester hours of credit in professional education at the graduate level;

4) Holds a valid all-grade supervisory certificate, limited supervisory certificate, life supervisory certificate, or an administrative certificate;

5) Has had at least four years of experience in teaching; and

6) Was engaged for at least two years of the previous four years in full-time teaching or supervising in the common public schools or serving as a county or regional superintendent of schools for an educational service region in Illinois.

A candidate for office must file a statement of economic interests and if elected must take an oath of office, post a bond of no less than $12,000, and may not practice any other profession during the term of office.

5 ILCS 420/1-101 et seq.

105 ILCS 5/3-1

105 ILCS 5/3A-6

1:255 May a regional superintendent provide for shared services among school districts?

A 2011 statute permits the regional superintendent of schools, at the request of a school district, to present to the school district possible services and functions that multiple schools may share or consolidate. Services and functions may include, but are not limited to, bidding and purchasing, office functions such as payroll and accounting, information technology, professional development, grant writing, food service management, or administrative positions. Regional superintendents of schools may share best financial practices with school districts that are exploring new methods to become more financially efficient.

Nothing in the statute exempts school districts that make use of such services from other statutes that may apply (such as the bidding statute).

105 ILCS 5/3-15.14a

LOCAL-MUNICIPAL GOVERNMENT

1:260 May any other unit of local government regulate a school district?

The operation of public schools is a state function and not a function of local government. Local governmental entities may not regulate the operation of a school district.

Ill. Const. art. VII, sec. 1

Ill. Const. art. VII, sec. 10

Board of Education of Minooka Community High School District No. 111 Grundy, Kendall and Will Counties v. Carter, 119 Ill. App. 3d 857, 458 N.E. 2d 50, 75 Ill. Dec. 882, (3rd Dist. 1983)

Board of Education of School District No. 150 v. City of Peoria, 76 Ill. 2d 469, 394 N.E. 2d 399, 31 Ill. Dec. 197 (1979)

Board of Education of the City of Rockford v. Page, 33 Ill. 2d 372, 211 N.E. 2d 361 (1965)

Board of Education of School District 33 v. City of West Chicago, 55 Ill. App. 2d 401, 205 N.E. 2d 63 (2nd Dist. 1965)

1:270 May school districts enter into cooperative agreements with units of local government?

The Illinois Constitution allows intergovernmental cooperative agreements, providing in part:

"Units of local government and school districts may contract or otherwise associate among themselves, with the State, with other states and their units of local government and school districts, and with the United States to obtain or share services and to exercise, combine, or transfer any power or function, in any manner not prohibited by law or by ordinance. Units of local government and school districts may contract and otherwise associate with individuals, associations, and corporations in any manner not prohibited by law or by ordinance. Participating units of government may use their credit, revenues, and other resources to pay costs and to service debt related to intergovernmental activities.

"Officers and employees of units of local government and school districts may participate in intergovernmental activities authorized by their units of government without relinquishing their offices or positions.

"The State shall encourage intergovernmental cooperation and use its technical and financial resources to assist intergovernmental activities."

Ill. Const. art. VII, sec. 10

5 ILCS 220/1 et seq.

Village of Elmwood Park v. Forest Preserve District of Cook County, 21 Ill. App. 3d 597, 316 N.E. 2d 140 (1st Dist. 1974)

1:280 How is fire protection for school sites provided?

If the location of any public school building is not within any municipality or fire protection district, fire protection service is provided by the municipality or fire protection district that maintains the facility for firefighting equipment that is closest to the school site. The school district must pay to the municipality or fire protection district the reasonable cost of such service.

105 ILCS 5/16-10

STATE ACADEMIC STANDARDS

1:300 What factors are considered in the establishment of state recognition standards for student performance and school improvement?

The standards include, but are not necessarily limited to, state assessment of student performance, local assessment results, student attendance rates, retention rates, expulsion rates, and graduation rates.

105 ILCS 5/2-3.25

1:305 What authority does the State Superintendent of Education have to intervene in a low performing school?

From any funds appropriated to the State Board of Education for the purposes of intervening in low-performing schools, the State Superintendent may, in his or her discretion, select school districts and schools from the lowest five percent in terms of performance in the state in which to directly or indirectly intervene. Intervention may take the form of a needs assessment or additional, more intensive intervention as determined by the State Superintendent. Expenditures from funds appropriated for this purpose may include, without limitation, contracts, grants, and travel to support the intervention.

105 ILCS 5/2-3.154

1:310 Does the State Board of Education have authority to collect school information from a school district to determine its level of recognition?

The State Board is authorized to collect information, data, test results, student performance, and school improvement indicators with respect to school recognition standards, student performance, and school improvement.

105 ILCS 5/2-3.25b

1:320 What is state academic early warning and watch status?

Those schools that do not meet standards of academic performance and improvement for two consecutive annual calculations are placed on academic early warning status for the next school year. Schools on academic early warning status that do not meet adequate yearly progress criteria for a fourth annual calculation are placed on initial academic watch status. The watch and warning standards are likely to change as the federal Every Student Succeeds Act is actualized in Illinois.

105 ILCS 5/2-3.25d

1:330 What is required of a school district that has a school or schools placed on academic watch status?

A school district with a school or schools on academic watch status must submit a revised school improvement plan listing the district's expectations for removing each school in the district from watch status and for improving student performance in the school. The improvement plan must be developed in consultation with the staff of the affected school and approved by the school board. The revised improvement plan must be submitted to the State Board of Education for approval and must have specific measurable outcomes for improving student performance so that performance meets adequate yearly progress criteria as specified by the State Board.

The State Board of Education, when moneys are available, administers a grant program that provides two-year grants to school districts on the academic watch list and other school districts that have the lowest achieving students, as determined by the State Board. In order to receive a grant a school district must establish an accountability program that involves the use of statewide testing standards and local evaluation measures. The grant is automatically renewed when achievement goals are met.

105 ILCS 5/2-3.25d

1:335 Are any school districts relieved of quality review and school improvement plan requirements?

If a school district has completed school improvement plans in all required curricular areas and if in any two of the three most recent school years the composite assessment test scores of the students at a school within the district places the school in the "exceeds standards" category or within the top 15 percent of the "meets standards" categories established by the State Board of Education, that school is exempt for the next two succeeding school years from all requirements relating to the school improvement plan and from quality review visits.

105 ILCS 5/2-3.25k

1:360 What may happen to a school or school district that fails to make reasonable efforts to implement an approved improvement plan?

The school or school district may suffer loss of state funds by school district, attendance center, or program as the State Board of Education deems appropriate.

105 ILCS 5/2-3.25f

Texas v. United States, 118 S. Ct. 1257, 523 U.S. 296, 140 L. Ed. 2d 406 (1998)

1:370 What penalties may the State Board of Education impose on a school or school district that has been on academic watch status for more than three years?

The School Code requires the State Board of Education to choose a sanction. School board members may be removed from office, and an independent authority may be appointed to operate the school or school district for purposes of improving pupil performance and school improvement. The State Board of Education may non-recognize the school or school district and reassign its students or direct the reassignment or replacement of school district personnel who are relevant to the failure to meet adequate yearly progress criteria. If a school district is non-recognized in its entirety, it is automatically dissolved under a procedure established by law.

There are constitutional questions about certain aspects of this legislation because it may not be consistent with provisions of the federal Voting Rights Act. Moreover, how the courts will interpret sanctions that are in conflict with other School Code provisions or collectively bargained agreements is also uncertain.

105 ILCS 5/2-3.25f (2)

105 ILCS 5/3-14.28

Texas v. United States, 118 S. Ct. 1257, 523 U.S. 296, 140 L. Ed. 2d 406 (1998)

WAIVER OF STATE REQUIREMENTS

1:380 May the State Board of Education grant waivers from the requirements of the School Code or from State Board administrative rules and regulations?

A school district, or governing board or administrative district of a joint agreement, or the regional superintendent of schools on behalf of schools and programs operated by the regional office of education, may petition the State Board of Education for a waiver or modification of the mandates of the School Code or from the administrative rules and regulations of the State Board. Waivers or modifications may be requested when a school district demonstrates that it can address the intent of the rule or mandate in a "more effective, efficient, or economical manner or when necessary to stimulate innovation or improve student performance."

105 ILCS 5/2-3.25g

Reece, et al. v. Board of Education of the City of Chicago, et al., 328 Ill. App. 3d 773, 767 N.E. 2d 395, 262 Ill. Dec. 935 (1st Dist. 2002)

1:382 Are there rules, regulations, or laws from which waivers cannot be requested or granted?

Waivers cannot be requested and will not be granted from laws, rules, and regulations pertaining to special education, teacher certification, or teacher tenure and seniority, Section 5-2.1 of the School Code (eligibility of voters in school elections), or from compliance with the Every Student Succeeds Act. On and after a school district's evaluation implementation date, a school district cannot waive or seek a modification of a mandate regarding the requirements for student performance data to be a significant factor in teacher or principal evaluations or for the four rating categories and any previously granted waiver or modification from such requirements terminates.

105 ILCS 5/2-3.25g

1:384 How does a waiver applicant request a waiver?

The applicant must approve the waiver request following a public hearing on the application and plan. Notice of the time, date, place, and general subject matter of the public hearing must be posted on the waiver applicant's website at least 14 days before the hearing. The waiver request must be submitted to the State Board of Education within 15 days of approval by the school board, joint agreement, or regional superintendent of schools. The hearing must give educators, parents, and students an opportunity to provide testimony to the school board. The application submitted to the State Board must include a description of the public hearing which includes the means of notice of public hearing, the number of people in attendance, the number of people who spoke as proponents or opponents of the waiver, a brief description of their comments, and whether there were any written statements submitted.

If the applicant is a joint agreement or a school board, the public hearing must be separate from the time period established by the school board for public comment on other matters. If a physical education waiver or modification is sought the hearing must be held on a day other than the day on which a regular meeting of the school board or joint agreement is held. Until 2006, all such hearings required a special meeting of the school board.

The hearing must be preceded by at least one notice published in a newspaper of general circulation in the school district (a newspaper in each member district if the applicant is a joint agreement or regional superintendent of schools, except that a notice appearing in a newspaper "generally circulated in more than one school district" fulfills this requirement "with respect to all the affected districts") that sets forth the time, date, place, and general subject matter of the hearing. The published notice must appear at least seven days prior to the hearing.

The applicant must provide written notice to the affected exclusive bargaining agent at least seven days before the hearing of the applicant's intent to seek approval of a waiver or modification and of the hearing. The eligible applicant must also notify in writing the affected State legislators representing the eligible applicant's territory of its intent to seek approval of a waiver or modification and of the hearing to be held.

There are additional rules in the relevant statute that govern waivers involving increased fees for driver education or subcontracting driver education.

105 ILCS 5/2-3.25g

1:386 How are waivers approved?

Following the receipt of waiver request, the State Board of Education has 45 days to review the request. If the State Board fails to disapprove a request, the request is deemed granted. Any request disapproved by the State Board may be appealed to the General Assembly by the requesting school district.

105 ILCS 5/2-3.25g

1:388 For how long are approved waivers effective?

An approved waiver or modification may remain in effect for a period not to exceed five school years and may be renewed upon application by the applicant.

If neither the State Board of Education nor the General Assembly disapproves, the change is granted.

105 ILCS 5/2-3.25g

CHARTER SCHOOLS

1:500 What is a charter school?

A charter school is a public, nonsectarian, nonreligious, non-home based, nonprofit school. A charter school is organized and operated as a nonprofit corporation or other discrete, legal, nonprofit entity authorized under the laws of the state of Illinois. A charter school may be established by creating a new school or converting an existing public school or attendance center to charter school status. Charter schools are exempt from some, but not all, School Code requirements otherwise applicable to public schools. Over time, more School Code requirements have been made applicable to charter schools than were applicable when the first charter schools were established in the 1990s.

In the 2010s, some charter schools began adding virtual schooling to their curricula. Virtual schooling is teaching courses online with online instructors, rather than with the instructor and student being at the same physical location.

105 ILCS 5/27A-5

1:510 How is a charter school created?

A proposal to establish a charter school may be initiated by individuals or organizations meeting certain statutory requirements. The proposal is submitted to the local school board for consideration. The school board is required to convene a public meeting within 45 days of receipt of a charter school proposal and to evaluate the proposal in relation to statutory guidelines. The school board must file a report with the State Board of Education granting or denying the proposal. If the school board approves the proposal, a contract is developed and submitted to the State Board of Education for certification.

A charter school may be created if a charter school proposal has been certified by the State Board of Education and thereafter a petition of five percent or more of the voters of a school district or districts is circulated. Certification and properly completed petitions result in a referendum on the question of the establishment of a charter school. If the referendum question carries, the State Board of Education is required to approve the charter within seven days after certification by the State Board that the proposition received a majority of the votes cast.

In 2011, the General Assembly created the State Charter School Commission that has statewide chartering jurisdiction and authority. The commission consists of nine members appointed by the State Board of Education. Members of the commission serve four-year terms, although the terms of six of the initial appointees were shorter to create staggered terms of service.

105 ILCS 5/27A-6
105 ILCS 5/27A-6.5
105 ILCS 5/27A-7
105 ILCS 5/27A-7.5
105 ILCS 5/27A-8

Board of Education of Woodland Community Consolidated School District No. 50 v. Illinois State Charter School Commission, 2016 IL App (1st) 151372 60 N.E. 3d 107, 406 Ill. Dec. 205

1:520 Is an appeal available if the local school board denies a charter school proposal?

The State Charter School Commission may reverse a local board's denial if it finds the charter school proposal is in compliance with statutory requirements and is in the best interests of students. If the Commission reverses the local board, the Commission acts as the authorized chartering entity for the charter school, performing all functions under the charter school statute otherwise performed by the local school board.

The State Board will withhold from funds otherwise due the school district any funds authorized for the charter school and pay those amounts to the charter school.

105 ILCS 5/27A-9

Board of Education of Woodland Community Consolidated School District No. 50 v. Illinois State Charter School Commission, 2016 IL App (1st) 151372 60 N.E. 3d 107, 406 Ill. Dec. 205

Board of Education of Rich Township High School District No. 227 v. Illinois State Board of Education, 2011 IL App. (1st) 110182, 965 N.E. 2d 13, 358 Ill. Dec. 285

1:530 With which laws must a charter school comply?

A charter school must comply with the School Code requirements for

1) Criminal history records checks;

2) Section 24-24 of the School Code regarding the discipline of students;

3) The Tort Immunity Act;

4) Section 108.75 of the General Not For Profit Corporation Act of 1986 regarding indemnification of officers, directors, employees, and agents;

5) The Abused and Neglected Child Reporting Act, including the 2017 amendment concerning prevention of neglect and abuse;

6) The Illinois School Student Records Act;

7) State goals, standards, and assessments established in Section 2-3.64 of the School Code;

8) Before a 2009 amendment to the Illinois Educational Labor Relations Act, charter schools, subcontractors of instructional services, contract schools, and contract turnaround schools were exempt from the bargaining obligations that apply to all other Illinois public schools;

9) Beginning in 2016, truancy laws (including chronic truancy reporting laws); and

10) Beginning in 2017, statutory requirements regarding the employment of social workers;

In addition, a charter school must comply with all federal laws that would be otherwise applicable to a public school and all federal and state laws and constitutional provisions prohibiting discrimination on the basis of disability, race, creed, color, gender, national origin, religion, ancestry, marital status, or need for special education services.

105 ILCS 5/10-20.60
105 ILCS 5/10-21.9

105 ILCS 5/24-24
105 ILCS 5/26-18
105 ILCS 5/27A-4 (a)
105 ILCS 5/27A-5 (g)
105 ILCS 5/27A-5.5
105 ILCS 10/1 et seq.
115 ILCS 5/1 et seq.
325 ILCS 5/1 et seq.
745 ILCS 10/1-101 et seq.
805 ILCS 105/108.75

1:540 Is there a limit on the number of charter schools that may operate in the state at any one time?

The total number of charter schools operating at any one time may not exceed 120. Not more than 70 may operate in Chicago (except that there is a provision that allows five charter schools exclusively for re-enrolled high school dropouts), not more than 45 in the remainder of the state with not more than one charter school that has been initiated by a school board or by intergovernmental agreement between or among school boards operating at any one time in the school district where the charter school is located.

105 ILCS 5/27A-4(b)

1:550 May an existing private, parochial, or non-public school be approved as a charter school?

No.

105 ILCS 5/27A-4(c)
105 ILCS 5/27A-6.5(a)

1:560 May two or more school boards issue a charter to a single shared charter school?

Yes.

105 ILCS 5/27A-4(e)

1:570 Who may enroll in a charter school?

Enrollment is open to any pupil who resides within the geographic boundaries of the area served by the local school board. There is a limited statutory exception that applies to Chicago alone.

105 ILCS 5/27A-4(d)

1:580 May children be assigned and required to attend a charter school?

No.

105 ILCS 5/27A-4(g)

1:590 May teachers or non-certificated employees be assigned to a charter school?

A school board may not require any employee to be employed in a charter school.

105 ILCS 5/27A-4(f)

1:600 What elements must be included in a charter school proposal?

The following elements must be included in a charter school proposal:

1) The name of the proposed charter school, which must include the words "Charter School."

2) The age or grade range, areas of focus, minimum and maximum numbers of pupils to be enrolled in the charter school, and any other admission criteria that would be legal if used by a school district.

3) A description of and an address for the physical plant in which the charter school will be located.

4) The mission statement of the charter school, which must be consistent with the General Assembly's declared purposes.

5) The goals, objectives, and pupil performance standards to be achieved by the charter school.

6) In the case of a proposal to establish a charter school by converting an existing public school or attendance center to charter school status, evidence that the proposed formation of the charter school has received the required approval from certified teachers, parents, and guardians.

7) A description of the charter school's educational program, pupil performance standards, curriculum, school year, school days, and hours of operation.

8) A description of the charter school's plan for evaluating pupil performance, the types of assessments that will be used to measure pupil progress towards achievement of the school's pupil performance standards, the timeline for achievement of those standards, and the procedures for taking corrective action in the event that pupil performance at the charter school falls below those standards.

9) Evidence that the terms of the charter as proposed are economically sound for both the charter school and the school district, a proposed budget for the term of the charter, a description of the manner in which an annual audit of the financial and administrative operations of the charter school including any services provided by the school district are to be conducted, and a plan for the displacement of pupils, teachers, and other employees who will not attend or be employed in the charter school.

10) A description of the governance and operation of the charter school, including the extent and nature of parental, professional educator, and community involvement in the governance and operation of the charter school.

11) An explanation of the relationship that will exist between the charter school and its employees, including evidence that the terms and conditions of employment have been addressed with affected employees and their recognized representative, if any. However, a bargaining unit of charter school employees shall be separate and distinct from any bargaining units formed from employees of the school district in which the charter school is located.

12) An agreement between the parties regarding their respective legal liability and applicable insurance coverage.

13) A description of how the charter school plans to meet the transportation needs of its pupils, and a plan for addressing the transportation needs of low-income and at-risk pupils.

14) The proposed effective date of the charter; provided that the first day of the first academic year and the first day of the fiscal year of the charter school shall be no earlier than August 15 and no later than September 15.

15) Any other information reasonably required by the State Board of Education.

105 ILCS 5/27A-7

1:610 For what term is a charter granted?

For charters granted before January 1, 2017, a charter could be granted for a period not less than five and not more than 10 school years. For charters granted on or after January 1, 2017, a charter must be granted for a period of five school years. For charters renewed before January 1, 2017, a charter may be renewed in incremental periods not to exceed five school years. For charters renewed on or after January 1, 2017, a charter may be renewed in incremental periods not to exceed five school years; however, the Commission may renew a charter only in incremental periods not to exceed five years. Renewals and charters require the school to meet certain statutory requirements.

105 ILCS 5/27A-9

1:620 Who may teach in a charter school?

A charter school teacher is not required to meet every certification condition otherwise required of teachers in Illinois public schools.

Charter school teachers must either be fully certificated or have

1) A bachelor's degree from an accredited institution of higher learning;

2) Been employed for at least five years in an area requiring application of the person's education;

3) Passed the tests of basic skills and subject matter knowledge required in the School Code; and

4) Demonstrated continuing evidence of professional growth that includes but is not limited to successful teaching experience, attendance at professional meetings, membership in professional organizations, additional credits earned at institutions of higher learning, travel specifically for educational purposes, and reading of professional books and periodicals.

105 ILCS 5/27A-10(c)

1:630 When may a charter school teacher resign?

A charter school teacher may resign only if notice of resignation is given to the charter school's governing body at least 60 days before the end of the school term and the resignation must take effect immediately upon the end of the school term.

105 ILCS 5/27A-10(d)

1:640 Is a school board required to grant a leave of absence for a teacher to teach in a charter school?

Yes. A school board must grant a teacher's leave of absence request for up to five years if the teacher accepts employment in a charter school. At the end of the authorized leave of absence the teacher must return to the district or resign. If the teacher returns to the district he or she must be assigned to a position that requires teacher certification and qualification. The tenure and retirement benefits of a teacher who is granted a leave of absence to teach in a charter school may not be affected by the leave of absence.

105 ILCS 5/27A-10(b)

2: SCHOOL BOARDS

SCHOOL BOARD STRUCTURE

2:10 How is the membership of an Illinois school board structured?

Most Illinois school boards consist of seven members elected at large. School districts with less than 1,000 inhabitants that were not created under Section 11E of the School Code are governed by three-member boards of school directors unless the voters in the district petition the board and vote in a general election to increase the number of board members to seven. Charter district boards also may have more or fewer than seven members, depending upon the section of the School Code that governs.

A 2005 amendment to the School Code allows a board of education or board of school directors (including a charter school board) to appoint a non-voting student member to the board. The student member may not participate in or attend closed sessions.

There also are exceptions to the at-large provision. The boards of many school districts must guarantee representation to unincorporated areas or ensure that congressional townships have proper representation. The constitutionality of these provisions has not been tested and these requirements vary with type of district, when the district was created, and how resident population is distributed.

105 ILCS 5/10-1
105 ILCS 5/10-10
105 ILCS 5/11E-55

2:20 Are all school boards elected?

The Chicago Board of Education is appointed by the mayor of Chicago. Special charter districts may have an appointed school board if such a procedure is set forth in the original charter and the charter has not been amended.

105 ILCS 5/9-1 et seq.
105 ILCS 5/32-1.5 et seq.
105 ILCS 5/34-3 et seq.
Latham v. Board of Education of Chicago, 31 Ill. 2d 178, 201 N.E. 2d 111 (1964)

2:25 What are the territorial representation requirements that apply to Illinois school boards?

The General Assembly drastically changed the law governing the creation, conversion, and combination of school districts in 2006. Except after an election to have representation at large as provided in 105 ILCS 5/10-10.5(b) for community unit school districts formed before January 1, 1975 and for combined school districts formed before July 1, 1983, the following provisions apply:

1) If the territory of the district is greater than two congressional townships or 72 square miles, then not more than three board members may be selected from any one congressional township, except that congressional townships of less than 100 inhabitants are not considered for the purpose of this mandatory board representation.

2) If in a community unit school district or combined school district at least 75 percent but not more than 90 percent of the population is in one congressional township, then four board members are selected from the congressional township and three board members are selected from the rest of the district, except that if in the community unit school district or combined school district more than 90 percent of the population is in one congressional township, then all board members may be selected from one or more congressional townships.

3) If the territory of any community unit school district or combined school district consists of not more than two congressional townships or 72 square miles, but consists of more than one congressional township or 36 square miles outside of the corporate limits of any city, village, or incorporated town within the school district, then not more than five board members may be selected from any city, village, or incorporated town in the school district.

105 ILCS 5/9-12
105 ILCS 5/10-10
105 ILCS 5/10-10.5
105 ILCS 5/10-16

2:27 How does a school board subject to representation requirements become an at-large board?

A unit school district formed prior to 1975 or a combined school district formed before July 1, 1983 or a community consolidated school district may elect its school board at-large and without regard to intra-district representation requirements if the matter is submitted to voters and a majority of those voting in the election in each congressional township, including any township of less than 100 inhabitants, vote in favor of the proposition.

The school board may cause the matter to be placed on the ballot, or the matter may be placed on the ballot by petition of the lesser of 2,500 or five percent of the school district's registered voters.

105 ILCS 5/10-10.5

2:30 May school board members be elected from representative districts rather than at-large?

A school board may, by resolution, or must if petitioned by the lesser of 2,500 or five percent of the district's registered voters, submit to election the question of electing school board members by representative districts rather than at-large.

105 ILCS 5/9-22

2:40 If the voters approve the election of school board members by representative districts, how are the representative districts formed?

The at-large school board must divide the school district into seven school board districts, each of which must be compact and contiguous and substantially equal in population to each other district. The terms of office of the board members incumbent at the time the proposition to elect from representative districts is adopted expire on the day of the next regular school election, at which time one member is elected from each school board district.

In districts that have four-year terms, those members first elected from representative districts must, by lot, determine three to serve for two years and four to serve for four years. Their successors serve four-year terms.

In school districts that have six-year school board terms, those members first elected from representative districts must, by lot, determine three to serve two-year terms, two to serve four-year terms, and two to serve six-year terms. Their successors serve six-year terms.

105 ILCS 5/9-22

2:45 How are representative districts altered to reflect changes in population patterns?

The school board must reapportion the representative districts to reflect the results of each decennial census. The reapportionment plan must be approved by a majority of the board not less than 90 days before the last date for filing nominating petitions for the next board election in the year following the census. The school board also must, publicly by lot, divide the representative districts into two groups providing staggered terms. Board members from one group of districts will be elected for terms of four years, four years, and two years, while those from the other group will be elected for terms of two years, four years, and four years.

105 ILCS 5/9-22

2:50 What is a school board member's term of office?

The standard term of office for a school board member is four years. A school board may, by resolution, submit to the voters the question of increasing the term of office to six years.

Under certain circumstances a school board member's term of office may be less than four years. During the transition period from November to April elections in 1999 and 2001, some school board members served less than four-year terms of office.

A school board member also may be appointed and/or elected to less than a full term to fill a vacancy on the board.

105 ILCS 5/9-5
105 ILCS 5/10-10

2:60 How many times may a school board member be elected?

There is no limit to the number of terms to which a school board member may be elected.

105 ILCS 5/9-1

VACANCIES

2:70 What acts create a vacancy on a school board?

Elective offices become vacant within the meaning of the School Code, unless the context indicates otherwise, on the happening of any of the following events before the expiration of the term of the office:

1) Death of the incumbent;

2) Resignation in writing filed with the secretary or clerk of the board;

3) Becoming a person under legal disability;

4) Ceasing to be an inhabitant of the district from which the member was elected;

5) Conviction of an infamous crime, or of any offense involving a violation of official oath;

6) Removal from office;

7) The decision of a competent tribunal declaring the election void; or

8) Ceasing to be an inhabitant of a particular area from which the member was elected, if the residential requirements are violated.

105 ILCS 5/10-10

105 ILCS 5/10-10.5

105 ILCS 5/10-11

105 ILCS 5/11E-35

105 ILCS 5/20-6

Lutkauskas v. Ricker, 2013 IL App (1st) 121112, 998 N.E. 2d 549, 376 Ill. Dec. 7

2:74 What are the infamous crimes that would prevent a person from holding public office in Illinois?

Illinois courts have defined infamous crimes as felonies involving conduct that is inconsistent with commonly accepted principles of honesty and decency or that involve moral turpitude. Generally, the courts have held that if the crime is one for which a penitentiary sentence could be imposed it is an infamous crime. Certain misdemeanors of sufficient seriousness or import may be infamous crimes.

The vacancy occurs upon the public official's conviction in a trial court whether or not an appeal is filed or pending.

Ill. Const. art. XII, sec. 1

5 ILCS 280/1

10 ILCS 5/29-15

People ex rel. Keenan v. McGuane, 13 Ill. 2d 520, 150 N.E. 2d 168 (1958)

2:80 If a school board member's conviction of an infamous crime is reversed, is the member's school board seat restored to him?

Any elected official of any school district convicted in any court of the State of Illinois or of the United States of a felony, bribery, perjury, or other infamous crime is, upon conviction, ineligible to continue in office. If a final order reverses the conviction, eligibility to hold the office is restored, and the officer is reinstated for the duration of the term of office remaining.

Upon the conviction and ineligibility of any person, a successor is chosen to fill the vacancy. The successor holds office for the remainder of the term or until a final order reversing the conviction is entered, whichever occurs first.

5 ILCS 280/1

2:85 Which public body has authority to determine whether or not a vacancy exists on a school board?

The school board has authority to determine whether or not the facts occasioning a vacancy exist, but removal of a board member who disputes the facts requires a quo warranto proceeding brought either in court by a party with standing or by the state's attorney.

10 ILCS 5/25-3

People ex rel. Ballard v. Niekamp, 2011 IL App (4th) 100796, 961 N.E. 2d 288, 356 Ill. Dec. 192

Brown v. Johnson, 362 Ill. App. 3d 413, 839 N.E. 2d 634, 298 Ill. Dec. 311 (1st Dist. 2005)

2:100 How is a vacancy on a school board filled?

The procedure for filling a vacancy on a board of school directors is set forth in Section 10-4 of the School Code and differs somewhat from the procedure for filling a board of education vacancy as set forth in Section 10-10.

When a vacancy occurs on a board of directors, the remaining directors must, within 30 days, fill the vacancy by appointment until the next regular school election. If they fail to do so, the regional superintendent must fill the vacancy by appointment within 30 days. If the regional superintendent fails to fill the vacancy, it is filled at the next regularly scheduled election.

When a vacancy occurs on a board of education, the remaining members must notify the regional superintendent of the vacancy within five days of its occurrence. The school board then fills the vacancy by appointment until the next regular school election, at which election a successor is elected to serve the remainder of the unexpired term.

However, if the vacancy occurs with less than 868 days remaining in the term, or if the vacancy occurs less than 88 days before the next regularly scheduled election for the vacant office, then the person so appointed serves the remainder of the unexpired term, and no election to fill the vacancy is held.

Should a board of education fail to act within 45 days after the vacancy occurs, the regional superintendent must, within 30 days after the remaining members have failed to fill the vacancy, fill the vacancy by appointment.

105 ILCS 5/10-4

105 ILCS 5/10-10

2:110 What qualifications must a person have to be appointed to fill a school board vacancy?

To be appointed to fill a school board vacancy, a person must have the same qualifications as the person to be replaced. On the date of appointment, the appointee must be at least 18 years of age, a resident of the state and the district for at least one year preceding appointment, a registered voter, not a school trustee or school treasurer, and shall not be a child sex offender as defined in Section 11-9.3 of the Criminal Code.

Whether elected or appointed by the remaining members or the regional superintendent, the successor must be an inhabitant of the particular area from which the predecessor was elected if residential requirements apply.

105 ILCS 5/9-12
105 ILCS 5/10-4
105 ILCS 5/10-10
105 ILCS 5/10-10.5
105 ILCS 5/10-11
720 ILCS 5/11-9.3

2:115 When a school board's membership must include representation of particular congressional townships or unincorporated areas, must the person selected to fill a vacancy live in the same township or unincorporated area as the predecessor?

The answer to this question turns on which ballot format applies. If ballot format 5 is applicable, a person filling such a board vacancy must live in the same congressional township as his or her predecessor. Ballot format 5 is for school boards that must have four members from the district's most populous township and three members from the rest of the district.

If ballot format 4 applies, the successor need not be from the same township as his or her predecessor, but the successor's residency must not cause the board to have more than three members from any one township. Format 4 is for boards that may have no more than three members from any one township.

105 ILCS 5/10-10
105 ILCS 5/10-10.5
105 ILCS 5/10-11

SCHOOL BOARD POWERS AND DUTIES

2:130 Who holds the authority to establish rules and regulations in school districts?

School boards. Illinois law provides that school boards are to adopt and enforce all necessary rules for the management and government of the public schools of their district. The rules adopted by a school board are to be filed for public inspection in the administrative office of the district.

105 ILCS 5/10-20.5

Veazey v. Rich Township High School District 227, 2016 IL App (1st) 151795, 59 N.E. 3d 857, 406 Ill. Dec. 79

Board of Education of Bremen High School District No. 228 v. Mitchell, 387 Ill. App. 3d 117, 899 N.E. 2d 1160, 326 Ill. Dec. 509 (1st Dist. 2008)

Board of Education of City of Chicago v. Chicago Teachers' Union, Local 1, 89 Ill. App. 3d 861, 412 N.E. 2d 587, 45 Ill. Dec. 236 (1st. Dist. 1980), rev. on other grounds 88 Ill. 2d 63, 430 N.E. 2d 1111 58 Ill. Dec. 860

Beck v. Board of Education of Harlem Consolidated School District No. 122, 27 Ill. App. 3d 4, 325 N.E. 2d 640 (2nd Dist. 1975) aff'd. 63 Ill. 2d 10, 344 N.E. 2d 440 (1976)

2:135 What is the distinction between "school board powers" and the powers of a school board member?

A school board has powers set forth in the law. A school board member acting as an individual has none of those powers.

2:140 May a school board member acting alone exercise the powers granted to a school board?

A school board may act only at a legal meeting when a quorum is present and after a requisite number of "yea" votes is counted on a properly presented and seconded motion on an issue properly within the powers of the board.

105 ILCS 5/10-12

Bunsen v. County Board of School Trustees of Lake County, 48 Ill. App. 2d 291, 198 N.E. 2d 735 (2nd Dist. 1964)

2:144 Is a school board member who acts or speaks as an individual about school district matters vulnerable to a defamation suit?

A school board member who acts or speaks as an individual about school district matters probably has no protection from suit. School board members are protected from liability when acting "during the formal legislative process" at school board meetings, but may not have protection when speaking in other contexts.

A speaker, whether or not a government official, who is motivated by a genuine desire to petition the government for action, is immune from liability for his or her otherwise defamatory actions. The only exception is when the speaker's actions were not genuinely aimed at procuring favorable government action.

775 ILCS 110/15

Sandholm v. Kuecker, et al., 405 Ill. App. 3d 835, 942 N.E. 2d 544, 347 Ill. Dec. 341 (2nd Dist. 2010)

Meyer v. McKeown, 266 Ill. App. 3d 324, 641 N.E. 2d 1212, 204 Ill. Dec. 593, (3rd Dist. 1994)

2:150 May a board member visit schools of the district to ensure their proper functioning?

A board of education is directed by law to "maintain" schools. In 2010, the legislature amended the applicable School Code provision, which used to read "visit, inspect and maintain" by deleting the references to "visit and inspect." Although boards routinely delegate the "visit and inspect" duty to employees, it also is lawful for a board to include school visits and inspections as part of a properly convened meeting (even after the statutory change).

Unless so directed by official action of the board, however, the individual board member is free to visit and inspect schools only in accordance with board policies regulating public visitation. The individual board member may not assume powers or duties belonging to the full board, and has only the same rights and powers as other citizens when the board is not in session.

105 ILCS 5/10-20.6

105 ILCS 5/24-25

2:160 Where are the powers of a school board enumerated in the law?

School board powers are enumerated in the School Code at Sections 10-20 et seq., Sections 10-22 et seq. ,and 10-23 et seq. The listing of school board powers is not exclusive and a school board may "exercise all other powers not inconsistent with this Act that may be requisite or proper for the maintenance, operation, and development of any school or schools under the jurisdiction of the board."

105 ILCS 5/10-20 et seq.

105 ILCS 5/10-22 et seq.

105 ILCS 5/10-23 et seq.

Board of Education of Bremen High School District No. 228 v. Mitchell, 387 Ill. App. 3d 117, 899 N.E. 2d 1160, 326 Ill. Dec. 509 (1st Dist. 2008)

2:163 May a school board delegate its powers?

A school board is responsible for exercising its powers in accordance with the law. A school board is empowered to decide who is entitled to attend school, employ teachers, select textbooks, approve contracts, dismiss teachers, expel students, and to make numerous other decisions. In each case, the board's decision must be recorded in the minutes of a meeting as a motion or resolution adopted by a formal vote.

A school board may delegate to the superintendent the authority necessary to exercise certain of the board's powers. Some powers of the board are not delegable, including the powers to dismiss teachers or expel students, for example. When powers are delegated, the person to whom they are delegated may be held responsible for the reasonable use of that authority.

A board that wishes to give its superintendent authority for the exercise of board powers needs to (a) be sure the superintendent understands the board's aims and standards, (b) devise a means for periodically checking to see that its powers are being used reasonably, and (c) be prepared to take formal action supporting the superintendent's decisions on these matters when they come to the board in the form of recommendations.

105 ILCS 5/10-22.1 et seq.

105 ILCS 5/10-23 et seq.

Board of Education of Rockford School District No. 205 v. The Illinois Educational Labor Relations Board, 165 Ill. 2d 80, 649 N.E. 2d 369, 208 Ill. Dec. 313 (1995)

2:165 What is the difference between school board policies and administrative procedures?

School board policies are the pronouncements of the school board that govern the school district. Policies may be broad and general or narrow and specific.

Administrative procedures describe how the school district will go about adhering to board policies. Administrative procedures must be consistent with board policy, picking up where the policies leave off and filling in the specific details not contained in the policies. Policies are usually rules that are adopted by the board; administrative procedures are rules created by administrators.

School board policies and administrative procedures that affect the wages, hours, or terms and conditions of employment of the members of a bargaining unit may have to be bargained before they can be implemented.

2:167 Must a school district's administrative procedures be adopted by the school board in order to have legal effect?

No, although the administration must have some authority from the board to create rules, regulations, or procedures. The safer practice would be for a board to specifically empower its administrators to act. Such authority might be specific to the task at hand, or it might be a general grant of authority.

In the absence of a specific board authorization, an administrative rule, regulation, or procedure probably binds the board and the district when the board has knowledge of the rule, regulation, or procedure and fails to take action to amend or repeal it.

2:170 May a school board reverse a previously adopted official act?

In most cases a school board may revoke or rescind a previous action. Excepted are situations when the prior act has vested rights in third parties that would be prejudiced if the board's original action were reversed.

City of Kankakee v. Small, 317 Ill. 55, 147 N.E. 404 (1925)

People ex rel. MacMahon v. Davis, 209 Ill. App. 117 (1st Dist. 1918), rev. 284 Ill. 439, 120 N.E. 326 (1918)

People v. Trustees of Schools, 42 Ill. App. 60 (2nd Dist. 1891)

2:180 Are the actions of a prior school board binding on a successor school board?

A school board is a continuing entity. While the individual membership of the board may change, the board itself is ongoing. The lawful acts of a prior school board bind a successor school board unless the act of the prior board is reversible and the successor board votes to reverse.

City of Kankakee v. Small, 317 Ill. 55, 147 N.E. 404 (1925)

People ex rel. MacMahon v. Davis, 209 Ill. App. 117 (1st Dist. 1918), rev. 284 Ill. 439, 120 N.E. 326 (1918)

2:190 What happens if a local school board fails to forward reports required by law?

If the trustees of schools of any township in Class II county school unit, or any school district that forms a part of a Class II county school unit but that is not subject to the jurisdiction of the trustees of schools of any township in which the district is located, or any school district in the case of any Class I county school unit fail to prepare and forward, or cause to be prepared and forwarded, to the regional superintendent of schools reports required by the School Code, the regional superintendent is required by law to furnish such information or to employ a person to furnish such information as far as is practicable. Such a person shall have access to the books, records, and papers of the school district to enable him or her to prepare the reports required by law, and the school district is required to permit such person to examine its books, records, and papers at a time and place that may be desired for this purpose.

The regional superintendent is authorized by law to bill the district for such services in an amount to cover the cost of the preparation of the reports if an external person is employed to prepare them.

105 ILCS 5/3-7

105 ILCS 5/3-15.1

2:200 Are school boards authorized to pay membership dues to professional organizations or associations?

A school board is authorized to pay both state and national association membership dues to school associations that benefit students.

A school board may also form, join, and provide for the expenses of associations of Illinois school boards formed for the purpose of conducting county or regional school board institutes and otherwise disseminating and interchanging information regarding school board problems, duties, and responsibilities. There are statutory requirements that must be met by any such organization in order to qualify to receive financial support from school districts.

105 ILCS 5/10-22.40

105 ILCS 5/23-1 et seq.

2:210 May a school board appoint committees?

A school board may appoint committees to research and make recommendations to the board. A school board may not give up its non-delegable decision-making authority to a committee. It is unclear whether or not the PERA (evaluation) committee and the Joint Committee mandated in 2011 by Senate Bill 7 are or are not school board committees, although the State Board of Education and at least some of the unions affected have initially argued they are not committees of the board.

105 ILCS 5/24-12

105 ILCS 5/24A-1 et seq.

Thomas v. Board of Education of Community Unit School District of Pope County, 117 Ill. App. 3d 374, 453 N.E. 2d 150, 721 Ill. Dec. 845 (5th Dist. 1983)

Elder v. Board of Education of School District 127 1/2 of Cook County, 60 Ill. App. 2d 56, 208 N.E. 2d 423 (1st Dist. 1965)

Lindblad v. Board of Education of Normal School District, 221 Ill. 261, 77 N.E. 450 (1906)

2:220 May a citizen (or group of citizens) compel a school board to act if the board fails to do what it is required to do by law?

A citizen or group of citizens can sue to compel a school board to do what it is required to do by law. The legal proceeding is called a writ of mandamus. To be entitled to this extraordinary relief, a plaintiff must establish a clear right to the relief requested, a clear duty of the defendant to act, and clear authority in the defendant to comply with the writ when issued. A writ will not issue when its effect would be to substitute the court's judgment or discretion for that of the school board.

Clarke v. Community Unit School District 303, __ Ill. App. 3d __, 971 N.E. 2d 1163, 361 Ill. Dec. 341 (2nd Dist. 2012)

2:225 Who can sue if a school board misappropriates public funds?

Taxpayers have direct standing to enjoin the misuse of public funds. That standing allows challenges to illegal board votes.

Veazey v. Rich Township High School District 227, 2016 IL App (1st) 151795, 59 N.E. 3d 857, 406 Ill. Dec. 79

3: SCHOOL BOARD MEMBERSHIP

QUALIFICATIONS

3:10 What are the qualifications for school board membership?

In order to qualify for school board membership, an individual must be, in each case as of the date of election: a United States citizen, a resident of the state of Illinois and of the school district for at least one year preceding election, at least 18 years of age, a registered voter, not a school trustee, and not a child sex offender as defined in Section 11-9.3 of the Criminal Code.

Illinois law also prohibits a person who has been convicted of an "infamous crime" from holding public office unless the person has had such right restored by law. An infamous crime is generally defined as one for which a penitentiary sentence could be imposed.

A school board member may not hold an incompatible office. Certain types of school districts have additional residency requirements. Additional residential requirements apply to persons appointed to fill school board vacancies.

5 ILCS 280/1
10 ILCS 5/29-15
105 ILCS 5/9-12
105 ILCS 5/10-3
105 ILCS 5/10-10
105 ILCS 5/10-10.5
720 ILCS 5/11-9.3
People ex rel. Keenan v. McGuane, 13 Ill. 2d 520, 150 N.E. 2d 168 (1958)

3:15 May a postal employee run for election to a school board?

Federal law prohibits postal employees from running in partisan elections. School board elections once were, but are no longer, explicitly non-partisan.

5 U.S.C. 7323(a)

3:17 Must school board members receive training?

Each voting member of a school board elected or appointed for a term beginning after June 13, 2011, or in each other case by June 13, 2012, or the first year of his or her first term, must complete a minimum of four hours of professional development leadership training covering topics in education and labor law, financial oversight and accountability, and fiduciary responsibilities of a school board member. The school board member's actual and necessary expenses for such training may be paid by the school district.

Each school district must maintain on its internet website, if any, the names of all voting members of the school board who have successfully completed the training.

105 ILCS 5/10-16a

3:20 What does residence mean in the context of qualification for school board membership?

Residence is physical presence in a particular place with intention to remain permanently.

Stein v. County Board of School Trustees of DuPage County, 40 Ill. 2d 477, 240 N.E. 2d 668 (1968)

INCOMPATIBILITY

3:30 What is meant by the term "incompatibility of offices?"

When two public offices are deemed incompatible under the law, it means that an individual may not hold those two offices simultaneously. Offices are incompatible when, because of the duties of either office, a conflict of interest may arise; or when the duties of one office are such that the holder cannot in every instance faithfully perform the duties of the other. A public official who accepts a second office that is incompatible constructively resigns or vacates the first office.

Ill. Const. art. IV, par. 2(e)
Ill. Const. art. VI, par. 13(b)
105 ILCS 5/3-2
105 ILCS 5/5-3
105 ILCS 5/8-1
People ex rel. Black v. Dukes, 108 Ill. App. 3d 965, 439 N.E. 2d 1305, 64 Ill. Dec. 497 (3rd Dist. 1982) vac. 96 Ill. 2d 273, 449 N.E. 2d 856, 70 Ill. Dec. 509 (1983)
People ex rel. Myers v. Haas, 145 Ill. App. 283 (1st Dist. 1908)

3:40 What public offices are incompatible with school board membership?

The following offices are incompatible with school board membership by reason of the listed authority:

1) By reason of state Constitutional prohibition, certain elective offices in the judicial, executive, or legislative branches of government are incompatible with membership on a school board. These incompatible offices include all classes of judges, such elected statewide officers as governor, attorney general, and secretary of state. Other offices must be examined case by case.

2) By reason of statutory prohibitions, a school board member may not serve simultaneously as a school trustee, or member of a regional board of school trustees, Cook County school treasurer, regional superintendent of schools, or member of the State Board of Education. A school board member elected to the board of a community college district may serve only the remainder of the unexpired school board term while serving on the community college board.

In addition, the Illinois Attorney General's office has at various times issued opinions that the following offices are incompatible with school board membership: board of review member, county zoning board of appeals member, township assessor, township school trustee, and village president. Many other elective offices are incompatible with school board membership.

In a city, village, or unincorporated town with fewer than 2,500 inhabitants, an alderman of the city or a member of the board of trustees of a village or incorporated town, during the term of office for which he or she is elected may also serve on a school board, regional board of school trustees, board of school directors, or board of school inspectors.

Because there are necessary interactions between a high school district and an underlying elementary district, an individual's membership on both boards creates a compatibility problem.

Persons sometimes serve in incompatible positions because no one raises the compatibility issue or, for various political reasons, it is not addressed by persons who might otherwise prevent an individual from holding incompatible offices.

Ill. Const. art. IV, par. 2(e)
Ill. Const. art. VI, par. 13(b)
50 ILCS 105/0.01
50 ILCS 105/1
50 ILCS 105/1.2
50 ILCS 105/1.3
50 ILCS 105/2
50 ILCS 105/2a
105 ILCS 5/3-2
105 ILCS 5/5-3
105 ILCS 5/6-3
105 ILCS 5/8-1
110 ILCS 805/3-7

People ex rel. Smith v. Wilson, 357 Ill. App. 3d 204, 828 N.E. 2d 1214, 293 Ill. Dec. 716 (3rd Dist. 2005)

People ex rel. Black v. Dukes, 108 Ill. App. 3d 965, 439 N.E. 2d 1305, 64 Ill. Dec. 497 (3rd Dist. 1982) vac. 96 Ill. 2d 273, 449 N.E. 2d 856, 70 Ill. Dec. 509 (1983)

People ex rel. Myers v. Haas, 145 Ill. App. 283 (1st Dist. 1908)

COMPENSATION AND EXPENSES

3:50 May a school board compensate its members for services rendered?

No member of a school board may be compensated for services rendered except the secretary or clerk of the board, who may be paid an amount to a limit specified by statute.

105 ILCS 5/10-10
105 ILCS 5/10-22.32
105 ILCS 5/22-1

3:60 May a school board member be advanced expenses to attend meetings?

A school board may advance its members the actual and necessary expenses incurred in attending the following meetings:

1) Meetings sponsored by the State Board of Education or the Regional Superintendent of Schools.

2) Meetings sponsored by the Illinois Association of School Boards.

3) Meetings sponsored by a national organization in the field of public school education.

Authorized expenses are those reasonably anticipated to be incurred on the days necessary for travel to and from, and for attendance at, such meetings including meals, lodging, transportation, parking, and tips. Entertainment expenses (plays or concerts, for example) are not generally reimbursable.

If moneys are so advanced, the member to whom money is advanced must submit an itemized verified expense voucher showing the amount of his or her actual expenditures, with receipts attached where possible. When moneys are advanced but not required for such actual reasonable expenses, the member must refund the excess amount. The member may be reimbursed if the actual reasonable expenses exceed the amount advanced.

105 ILCS 5/10-22.32
105 ILCS 5/23-1

3:65 Are there limitations on expense reimbursements for school board members and school officials?

Beginning on January 1, 2017, each school board is required to adopt a resolution to regulate the reimbursement of all travel, meal, and lodging expenses of officers and employees. The resolution must include the types of official business for which travel, meal, and lodging expenses are allowed; the maximum allowable reimbursement for travel, meal, and lodging expenses; and a standardized form for submission of travel, meal, and lodging expenses supported by the minimum documentation required under the Act. There is a procedure allowing approval of expenses that exceed the maximum upon a roll call vote of the school board. The Act prohibits reimbursement for entertainment expenses.

50 ILCS 150/10
50 ILCS 150/15
50 ILCS 150/20

3:70 May a school board member receive reimbursement for actual expenses incurred by a non-member spouse who accompanies him to a school board function?

No.

105 ILCS 5/10-22.32

3:80 May a school board member receive lost wages as a school board expense?

No.

105 ILCS 5/10-22.32

3:85 Must a school board member's employer provide time off for the board member to attend board meetings?

A school board member is entitled, on the day and time of an official meeting, to absent himself from any services or employment in which he or she is then engaged or employed, for a period of time in which the official meeting is held plus necessary traveling time to and from the meeting. "Official meeting" means any gathering of the public body in which a quorum of the members are expected to attend and which is to be held for the purpose of discussing public business.

The school board member cannot be liable to any penalty for being absent from work, except that the employer may deduct an amount of compensation from the board member's wages for the period of absence. The school board member must inform the employer in advance of his or her intent to absent himself from employment for attendance at the meeting.

50 ILCS 115/1

DISCLOSURE OF ECONOMIC INTERESTS

3:90 Which school district personnel are required to file economic interest statements?

Each school board member must file annually an economic interest statement. Each person employed by a school district in a position that requires that person to hold administrative certification or chief business official endorsement must file; and each school employee who functions as the head of a department and who exercises similar authority and has direct supervisory authority over or direct responsibility for the formulation, negotiation, or execution of contracts in the amount of $1,000 or greater; or who has authority to issue or promulgate rules and regulations within areas under the authority of the school district; or who has supervisory authority for 20 or more employees is also required to file an economic interest statement each year.

Anyone working for the school district as an independent contractor need not file an economic interest statement.

5 ILCS 420/4A-101 (f)
5 ILCS 420/4A-101 (i)
5 ILCS 420/4A-105
105 ILCS 5/9-10
Havens v. Miller, 102 Ill. App. 3d 558, 429 N.E. 2d 1292, 57 Ill. Dec. 929 (1st. Dist. 1981)

3:100 When must an economic interest statement be filed?

A person required to file an economic interest statement must do so upon initial appointment or employment and by May 1 of each year unless he or she has already filed a statement in that calendar year.

A candidate for elective office must file an economic interest statement no later than the end of the period during which nominating papers can be filed, if he or she has not already filed a statement in relation to the same unit of government within a year preceding such action.

5 ILCS 420/4A-105

Miceli v. Lavelle, 114 Ill. App. 3d 311, 448 N.E. 2d 989, 70 Ill. Dec. 111 (1st. Dist. 1983)

Allen v. Love, 112 Ill. App. 3d 338, 445 N.E. 2d 514, 68 Ill. Dec. 66 (1st Dist. 1983)

3:110 What are the penalties for failure to file an economic interest statement?

Persons who fail to meet the May 1 filing deadline are subject to late filing penalties ranging from a late filing fee of $15 until May 15, to $100 per day from May 15 until May 31. Failure to file by May 31, or willful filing of a false or incomplete economic interest statement, is a Class A misdemeanor and may cause forfeiture of office or employment. However, any filing within 30 days of actual notice of failure to file bars forfeiture of office or employment.

If the failure to file resulted from not being included for notification by the school district and a statement is filed within 30 days of actual notice of the failure to file, no fine or forfeiture of office results. The Secretary of State provides the Attorney General with the names of persons who failed to file a statement and the county clerk provides the State's Attorney of the county of the entity for which the filing of economic interest is required with the name of persons who failed to file.

5 ILCS 420/4A-101

5 ILCS 420/4A-107

Miceli v. Lavelle, 114 Ill. App. 3d 311, 448 N.E. 2d 989, 70 Ill. Dec. 111 (1st. Dist. 1983)

Allen v. Love, 112 Ill. App. 3d 338, 445 N.E. 2d 514, 68 Ill. Dec. 66 (1st Dist. 1983)

3:115 How is notice given regarding failure to file or obligation to file the statement of economic interests?

The county clerk notifies elected officials who fail to meet the May 1 filing deadline.

In addition, the superintendent of each school district must certify to applicable county clerks, no later than February 1 of each year, the names and addresses of employees who are required to file the statement of economic interests. Certification must include a separate alphabetized list of the covered employees by the county in which the employees reside.

The county clerk notifies no later than April 1 those persons whose names are included on the lists that they must file the statement of economic interests by May 1.

5 ILCS 420/4A-106

3:120 Must a school board candidate disclose campaign contributions?

If a school board candidate accepts campaign contributions of any kind or makes campaign expenditures of any kind in an aggregate amount exceeding $3,000 during any 12-month period, the candidate is subject to disclosure and filing requirements. The provisions of the applicable statutes include keeping a detailed account of every contribution in excess of $20, including the name and address of the person making the contribution and the date on which it was made.

10 ILCS 5/9-1 et seq.

INTEREST IN CONTRACTS

3:130 What is the Corrupt Practices Act?

The Corrupt Practices Act provides in part:

"No person holding any office, either by election or appointment under the laws or Constitution of this State, may be in any manner financially interested, directly in his or her own name or indirectly in the name of any other person, association, trust, or corporation, in any contract or the performance of any work in the making or letting of which such officer may be called upon to act or vote."

The Act contains exceptions similar in type to those contained in the School Code conflict of interest provisions applicable to school board members.

50 ILCS 105/3

105 ILCS 5/10-9

Brown v. Kirk, 33 Ill. App. 3d 477, 342 N.E. 2d 137 (5th Dist. 1975), rev. on other grounds 64 Ill. 2d 144, 355 N.E. 2d 12 (1975)

3:140 What interest may a school board member have in a school contract?

A school board member is prohibited from having any interest directly or indirectly in any contract, work, or business of the school district or in the sale of any article to the school district. A school board member has no conflict merely by being an employee of a business that does business with the school district "provided the board member has no financial interest other than as an employee." A school board member is prohibited from purchasing any school district property, except a school board member may purchase a house constructed by the school district's vocational education students if the property is to be used as the board member's primary residence and if the sale is as otherwise provided for in the law.

These prohibitions are subject to certain limited exceptions. The exceptions permit certain small contracts to be let ($1,000 or less), and allow a limited business relationship with the school district if certain procedures are followed and the school board member owns less than a 7 1/2 percent interest in the company desiring to do business with the school district. If materials, merchandise, property, services, or labor to be provided under a contract are not available from any other person, firm, association, partnership, corporation, or cooperative association in the district, a contract may be let in which a school board member would otherwise have an impermissible interest if the aggregate amount of all such contracts let to the school board member does not exceed $5,000 in any fiscal year.

105 ILCS 5/5-22
105 ILCS 5/10-9

3:145 Is it a conflict of interest for an elected public school official to be employed as a substitute teacher in the same school district in which he or she is an elected official?

Whether or not service as a substitute teacher results in a conflict depends upon the amount of salary earned by the board member. The statute provides the amount "of the contract" must be less than $1,000. However, because there are appearances of impropriety inherent in any situation wherein a school board member seems to personally benefit from service on the board and practical conflicts are inevitable when a principal or other mid-level administrator is called upon to supervise or direct his or her employer, service by a board member in any capacity as an employee of the school district is unwise.

105 ILCS 5/10-9

3:147 May a school board member receive insurance coverage from the school district if he or she is a dependent of an employee of the school district?

Yes. The coverage received must be given as part of the benefit package of the employee.

105 ILCS 5/10-22.3a

3:150 May a school board member avoid conflict of interest by abstaining on the vote to award a contract in which he or she is interested?

If the award of a contract would otherwise result in a conflict of interest, the conflict is not cured by a school board member's abstention on the vote or absence from the meeting when the vote is taken.

105 ILCS 5/10-9

3:160 Is it a conflict of interest for a school board member to be married to a person employed by the district that the school board member serves?

This has been a controversial area of the law. It is probably not a conflict of interest if the employee was hired by the school district before the school board member was seated. A conflict of interest may result if the spouse of a school board member is hired during the school board member's term of office and the school board member influences the hiring decision.

50 ILCS 105/3
105 ILCS 5/10-9
Veazey v. Rich Township High School District 227, 2016 IL App (1st) 151795, 59 N.E. 3d 857, 406 Ill. Dec. 79
Hollister v. North, 50 Ill. App. 3d 56, 365 N.E. 2d 258, 8 Ill. Dec. 20 (4th Dist. 1977)
Illinois v. Simpkins, 45 Ill. App. 3d 202, 359 N.E. 2d 828, 3 Ill. Dec. 969 (5th Dist. 1977)
Shoresman v. Burgess, 412 F. Supp. 831 (N.D. Ill. 1976)

3:170 May a school board member or school employee have a financial interest in the books, apparatus, or furniture used in the district?

No state, county, township, or school officer or teacher may be interested in the sale, proceeds, or profits of any book, apparatus, or furniture used or to be used in any school with which such officer or teacher may be connected, except when the interest of the teacher is based upon authorship or development of instructional materials listed with the State Board of Education and adopted for use by a school board. Each teacher having an interest in instructional materials must file an annual statement so certifying with the secretary of the school board.

No employee or officer of a school district, special education joint agreement, office of a regional superintendent of schools, or the State Board of Education may have a direct or indirect financial interest in any agreement between the entity of which the person is an employee or officer and any corporation, organization, or other entity that collects or participates in the collection of payments from private health care benefit plans or federally funded health care programs.

105 ILCS 5/14-7.04(b)
105 ILCS 5/22-5

3:175 Can a teacher copyright and thereby own curriculum materials he or she develops?

A teacher might be able to copyright a curriculum or other teaching materials. To enforce the copyright (sue for copyright infringement), the teacher must register it with the United States Copyright Office. Copyright protection does not extend to any idea, procedure, process, system, method of operation, concept, principle, or discovery, regardless of the form in which it is described, explained, illustrated, or embodied in such work. It is not the idea that is protected, but rather the original expression of the idea.

To prevail in a copyright infringement action, the plaintiff must show that the form of words in which he or she embodied his or her ideas was copied.

17 U.S.C. 411(a)

105 ILCS 5/ 22-5

Brooks-Ngwenya v. Indianapolis Public Schools, 564 F. 3d 804 (7th Cir. 2009)

RESIGNATIONS

3:180 When a school board member resigns, when is the resignation effective?

A school board member's resignation, once tendered, is final and is effective when filed with the school board secretary or clerk.

105 ILCS 5/10-11

Cole v. McGillicuddy, 21 Ill. App. 3d 645, 316 N.E. 2d 109 (1st Dist. 1974)

Allen v. Powell, 42 Ill. 2d 66, 244 N.E. 2d 596 (1969)

3:185 When does the resignation of a public official take effect?

Although a resignation once tendered is effective on receipt and may not be thereafter withdrawn, a resignation specifying a future effective date does not take effect until the date specified. A vacancy does not exist in the office resigned until the future effective date contained in the resignation, although for certain purposes a time period triggered by the resignation may begin at the time the resignation is tendered no matter when the resignation may be effective.

10 ILCS 5/25-1

105 ILCS 5/10-11

Cole v. McGillicuddy, 21 Ill. App. 3d 645, 316 N.E. 2d 109 (1st Dist. 1974)

Allen v. Powell, 42 Ill. 2d 66, 244 N.E. 2d 596 (1969)

REMOVAL AND FORFEITURE

3:190 May a regional superintendent of schools remove a school board member from office?

A regional superintendent of schools may remove a school board member from office for willful failure to perform official duties. A regional superintendent may not remove a school board member from office for any other cause.

105 ILCS 5/3-15.5

Texas v. United States, 118 S. Ct. 1257, 523 U.S. 296, 140 L. Ed. 2d 406 (1998)

East St. Louis Federation of Teachers Local 1220, American Federation of Teachers, AFL-CIO v. East St. Louis District Financial Oversight Panel, 178 Ill. 2d 399, 687 N.E. 2d 1050, 227 Ill. Dec. 568 (1997)

People ex rel. Kolker v. Blair, 8 Ill. App. 3d 197, 289 N.E. 2d 688 (5th Dist. 1972)

People ex rel. Howard v. Harris, 164 Ill. App. 136 (3rd Dist. 1911)

3:193 May a school board member be removed from office for failure to attend meetings?

The regional superintendent of schools is empowered to remove a school board member from office for "willful failure to perform official duties." Regional superintendents have seldom exercised this power.

105 ILCS 5/3-15.5

3:195 May voters remove a school board member from office by recall petition or election?

No. Neither may a board member be removed from office by his or her fellow board members. The board may publicly censure one of its members by voting to do so, but other than possibly embarrassing the member being censured, the vote has no other weight.

5 ILCS 420/4A-107

105 ILCS 5/3-15.5

105 ILCS 5/10-10 et seq.

720 ILCS 5/33-3

3:196 What course of action is available to a citizen who believes a member of a school board is not legally qualified to hold office?

The school board has the authority to determine that a vacancy exists, but if the declaration of vacancy is challenged by a sitting board member then the board lacks authority to remove the board member. A registered voter who is a resident of the area represented by the board member may petition the court using a quo warranto proceeding to challenge the board member's right to hold office. Such a person or anyone else may also request that the attorney general or local state's attorney intervene or initiate proceedings.

10 ILCS 5/25-3

3:198 May a school board member continue to hold office when called to active military service?

There is no means in Illinois law to remove such a member from office, but members of the military (including members of the National Guard) who are serving on active duty for a period expected to last more than 270 days must obtain permission from the Secretary of the Army, Air Force, Navy, or Coast Guard, as appropriate, in order to continue to hold office. The relevant regulation also prohibits such persons from being nominees or candidates for office.

10 U.S.C. 973

Department of Defense Directive 1344.10

3:200 Under what circumstances does a school board member forfeit office?

A school board member forfeits office if convicted of official misconduct.

Official misconduct occurs when a board member, acting in an official capacity, intentionally or recklessly fails to perform any mandatory duty as required by law; knowingly performs an act he or she knows is forbidden by law to perform; intends to obtain a personal advantage for self or another by performing an act in excess of lawful authority; or solicits or knowingly accepts for the performance of any act a fee or reward that he or she knows is not authorized by law.

A school board member also forfeits office when he or she willfully violates any of the laws governing a school district's working cash fund. Board members may also lose their seats under a number of other circumstances, including conviction of certain crimes, failure to maintain residency in the district, or failure to perform certain required acts.

105 ILCS 5/10-11

105 ILCS 5/20-1 et seq.

720 ILCS 5/33-3

3:210 May a school board member be subject to a fine for willfully violating any laws governing the operation of Illinois public school districts?

Under some conditions, fines against school board members may be assessed. For example, Illinois law provides that any member of a board of school directors or board of education of any school district, or any other person holding any office, trust, or employment under any school district, who willfully violates any of the provisions of the School Code governing a working cash fund is guilty of a business offense and fined not exceeding $10,000, and forfeits the right to the office, trust, or employment and is "removed therefrom."

Any member or other person is liable for any sum that may be unlawfully diverted from the working cash fund or otherwise used, to be recovered by a school district or by any taxpayer in the name and for the benefit of the school district in an appropriate civil action.

105 ILCS 5/20-6

105 ILCS 5/22-1 et seq.

GIFT BAN ACT

3:300 What is the State Gift Ban Act and to whom does it apply?

In 2003, The General Assembly repealed the 1998 State Gift Ban Act and replaced it with a similar statute, The State Officials and Employees Ethics Act, which includes gift ban provisions. The Act restricts receipt of gifts by public officials and employees. The Act applies to school board members, administrators, teachers, and all other full or part-time certificated and full or part-time non-certificated employees of the school district. It also applies to the spouse and the immediate family.

5 ILCS 430/1-5 et seq.

5 ILCS 430/10-10

Flynn v. Ryan, 199 Ill. 2d 430, 771 N.E. 2d 414, 264 Ill. Dec. 710 (2002)

3:310 What is a gift as defined by the State Gift Ban Act?

The definition of gift is broad. A gift is any "gratuity, discount, entertainment, hospitality, loan, forbearance, or other tangible or intangible item having monetary value including but not limited to, cash, food and drink, and honoraria for speaking engagements related to or attributable to government employment or the official position" of a school employee or member of a school board.

5 ILCS 430/1-5

3:320 Who is a gift giver under the State Gift Ban Act?

The statute defines gift givers as prohibited sources. "Prohibited source" means any person or entity who:

1) Is seeking official action by the member or officer or in the case of an employee, by the employee or by the member, officer, state agency, or other employee directing the employee;

2) Does business or seeks to do business with the member or officer or in the case of an employee, with the employee or with the member, officer, state agency, or other employee directing the employee;

3) Conducts activities regulated by the member or officer or in the case of an employee, by the employee or by the member, officer, state agency, or other employee directing the employee;

4) Has interests that may be substantially affected by the performance or non-performance of the official duties of the member, officer, or employee; or

5) Is registered or required to be registered with the Secretary of State under the Lobbyist Registration Act, except that an entity not otherwise a prohibited source does not become a prohibited source merely because a registered lobbyist is one of its members or serves on its board of directors.

5 ILCS 430/1-5

3:330 What gifts are not prohibited by the State Gift Ban Act?

There are 12 types of gifts that are permitted under the Act. Each of the exceptions is mutually exclusive and independent of one another. They are:

1) Opportunities, benefits, and services that are available on the same conditions as for the general public.

2) Anything for which the officer, member, or employee pays the market value.

3) Any (i) contribution that is lawfully made under the Election Code or under the Act or (ii) activities associated with a fundraising event in support of a political organization or candidate.

4) Educational materials and missions. This exception may be further defined by rules adopted by the appropriate ethics commission.

5) Travel expenses for a meeting to discuss state business. This exception may be further defined by rules adopted by the appropriate ethics commission.

6) A gift from a relative, meaning those people related to the individual as father, mother, son, daughter, brother, sister, uncle, aunt, great aunt, great uncle, first cousin, nephew, niece, husband, wife, grandfather, grandmother, grandson, granddaughter, father-in-law, mother-in-law, son-in-law, daughter-in-law, brother-in-law, sister-in-law, stepfather, stepmother, stepson, stepdaughter, stepbrother, stepsister, half brother, half sister, and including the father, mother, grandfather, or grandmother of the individual's spouse and the individual's fiancé or fiancée.

7) Anything provided by an individual on the basis of a personal friendship unless the member, officer, or employee has reason to believe that, under the circumstances, the gift was provided because of the official position or employment of the member, officer, or employee and not because of the personal friendship. In determining whether a gift is provided on the basis of personal friendship, the member, officer, or employee must consider the circumstances under which the gift was offered, such as

(i) The history of the relationship between the individual giving the gift and the recipient of the gift, including any previous exchange of gifts between those individuals;

(ii) Whether to the actual knowledge of the member, officer, or employee the individual who gave the gift personally paid for the gift or sought a tax deduction or business reimbursement for the gift; and

(iii) Whether to the actual knowledge of the member, officer, or employee the individual who gave the gift also at the same time gave the same or similar gifts to other members, officers, or employees.

8) Food or refreshments not exceeding $75 per person in value on a single calendar day; provided that the food or refreshments are (i) consumed on the premises from which they were purchased or prepared or (ii) catered. "Catered" means food or refreshments that are purchased ready to eat and delivered by any means.

9) Food, refreshments, lodging, transportation, and other benefits resulting from the outside business or employment activities (or outside activities that are not connected to the duties of the officer, member, or employee as an office holder or employee) of the officer, member, or employee, or the spouse of the officer, member, or employee, if the benefits have not been offered or enhanced because of the official position or employment of the officer, member, or employee, and are customarily provided to others in similar circumstances.

10) Intra-governmental and inter-governmental gifts. For the purpose of this Act, "intra-governmental gift" means any gift given to a member, officer, or employee of a state agency from another member, officer, or employee of the same state agency; and "inter-governmental gift" means any gift given to a member, officer, or employee of a state agency, by a member, officer, or employee of another state agency, of a federal agency, or of any governmental entity.

11) Bequests, inheritances, and other transfers at death.

12) Any item or items from any one prohibited source during any calendar year having a cumulative total value of less than $100.

5 ILCS 430/10-15

3:340 What is the penalty for violation of the Gift Ban Act?

A person who intentionally violates any gift ban is guilty of a business offense and subject to a fine of at least $1,001 and up to $5,000. Any person who intentionally makes a false report alleging a violation of any provision of the Act to an ethics commission, an inspector general, the state police, a state's attorney, the attorney general, or any other law enforcement official is guilty of a Class A misdemeanor.

An ethics commission may levy an administrative fine of up to $5,000 against any person who violates this Act, who intentionally obstructs or interferes with an investigation conducted under this Act by an inspector general, or who intentionally makes a false, frivolous, or bad faith allegation. In addition to any other penalty that may apply, whether criminal or civil, a state employee who intentionally violates any provision of Section 5-15, 5-20, 5-30, 5-35, 5-40, or 5-50, Article 10, Article 15, or Section 20-90 or 25-90 of the State Officials and Employees Ethic Act is subject to discipline or discharge by the appropriate ultimate jurisdictional authority.

5 ILCS 430/5-5
5 ILCS 430/5-20
5 ILCS 430/5-30
5 ILCS 430/5-35
5 ILCS 430/5-40
5 ILCS 430/5-50
5 ILCS 430/10-10 et seq.
5 ILCS 430/15-10 et seq.
5 ILCS 430/20-90
5 ICLS 430/25-90
5 ICLS 430/50-5

4: SCHOOL ELECTION PROCEDURES

GENERAL ELECTION LAWS

4:10 What types of elections involve public school districts?

Elections conducted by public school districts include the election of school board members and various public policy propositions, such as to increase authorized property tax rates, issue bonds, consolidate districts, create single-member school board districts, or deactivate a high school. A school election also may involve an advisory question placed before the voters.

4:20 What laws govern the election of school board members?

School board elections except those involving school districts that have adopted Article 33 of the School Code are consolidated elections governed by the general election laws of the state. Provisions peculiar to school boards are found in the School Code.

10 ILCS 5/1-1 et seq.
105 ILCS 5/9-1 et seq.
105 ILCS 5/33-1 et seq.

4:30 When are school board members elected?

From 1981 until 1998, school board members were elected in odd numbered years in a nonpartisan election held on the first Tuesday after the first Monday in November. Beginning in 1999, school board members have been elected in odd-numbered years on the first Tuesday in April (Consolidated Election).

School districts that have adopted Article 33 of the School Code elect school board members on the first Tuesday in April in odd-numbered years (Consolidated Election) and the third Tuesday in March in even-numbered years (General Primary Election).

10 ILCS 5/2A-1.1(b)
10 ILCS 5/2A-1.2 (4)
10 ILCS 5/2A-1.2 (12)
105 ILCS 5/33-1 et seq.

4:40 What laws govern the holding of a school district referendum on a public policy issue, such as a proposition to increase tax rates, issue bonds, or consolidate districts?

Article 28 of the Election Code sets forth the general election laws governing all public policy referendums. Article 9 of the School Code addresses some specific requirements of school district referendums.

However, school boards may place on the ballot only those public policy questions authorized by statute. Such authorization is found at several locations in the School Code, including Article 17 (increases in authorized tax rates), Article 19 (issuance of building bonds), and Article 20 (working cash fund bonds). Authority for elections on school district reorganization and consolidation are found in Articles 7, 7A, 11A, 11B, and 11D.

To place a proposition on the ballot at a referendum, a school board must adopt a resolution citing the specific authorizing statute.

10 ILCS 5/28-1
105 ILCS 5/9-1

4:50 When may public policy issues be placed on the ballot?

A public policy referendum may be held only on any of the four scheduled election dates in each two-year election cycle. In even-numbered years, those dates are the third Tuesday in March (General Primary) and the first Tuesday after the first Monday in November (General Election).

In odd-numbered years, regular election dates are the last Tuesday in February (Consolidated Primary) and the first Tuesday in April (Consolidated Election).

There are three exceptions to this schedule that may apply in different circumstances:

1) A proposition may not be placed on the ballot at any regular election where there is no contest for a public office on the ballot in at least one precinct within the school district.

2) A school board may petition the circuit court for an emergency election where the board believes it cannot reasonably wait until the next regular election date.

3) Not more than three propositions (other than propositions submitted by backdoor referendum) may be submitted to the voters of a school district at the same election.

10 ILCS 5/2A-1.1
10 ILCS 5/2A-1.2(f)
10 ILCS 5/2A-1.4
10 ILCS 5/28-1

4:55 When must a school board submit a public policy advisory referendum to vote at a regularly scheduled election?

Whenever a petition regarding a question of public policy is submitted to a school board signed by a number of voters residing in the school district equal to at least eight percent of the votes cast for the candidates for Governor in the preceding gubernatorial election, the board must cause the question to be submitted to the voters.

New legislation passed in 2011 permits a school board to authorize an advisory question of public policy be placed on the ballot at the next regularly scheduled election (except a consolidated primary election) by vote of a majority of the members of the school board.

The result of an advisory referendum is not binding on the school board.

10 ILCS 5/28-2
10 ILCS 5/28-6
105 ILCS 5/9-1.5

ELECTION AUTHORITY

4:60 Who is in charge of conducting elections?

The Illinois State Board of Elections has general supervision over the administration of registration and election laws of the state.

Local elections are conducted by an election authority designated by statute. In most locales, the election authority is the county clerk. In a number of cities, a Municipal Board of Election Commissioners is the election authority. In DuPage County, a County Board of Election Commissioners is the election authority.

The election authority is responsible for voter registration, determining polling places, publishing notices, printing ballots, absentee voting, and other mechanics of running the election.

10 ILCS 5/1-3
10 ILCS 5/1A-1 et seq.

4:70 Does the school board have any duties related to the conduct of school elections?

The school board has no duties directly relating to the conduct of any election. Prior to a 2013 change in the relevant laws, members of the school board made up an electoral board to hear and rule on objections to candidate nominating petitions and voter petitions and the school board secretary or clerk served as the local election official. Nominating petitions are now filed with county clerk or county board of election commissioners and objections are heard by the County Officers Electoral Board.

10 ILCS 5/1-3
10 ILCS 5/10-9
10 ILCS 5/22-17
105 ILCS 5/9-1.1
105 ILCS 5/9-2(d)
105 ILCS 5/9-10

4:80 What are the election duties of the school board secretary?

Duties of the school board secretary, in the capacity of local election official, are set out in Article 9 of the School Code and various sections of the Election Code. The secretary's duties have been greatly reduced by legislation enacted in 2013, which shifted numerous responsibilities from the school board secretary to the county clerk or county board of election commissioners.

Current duties of the board secretary include

1) Publish a legal notice of the time and place for filing nominating papers with the county clerk or county board of election commissioners for the biennial school board election (an optional duty);

2) Receive voter petitions and school board resolutions calling for propositions to be placed on the ballot at a regular election; and

3) Certify to the election authority any public policy propositions that are to appear on the ballot, including the wording of the proposition as taken from the school board resolution or voter petition.

10 ILCS 5/10-1 et seq.
10 ILCS 5/17-22
105 ILCS 5/9-1.5

ELECTION OF SCHOOL BOARD MEMBERS

4:90 What effect does consolidation of school districts have on the election of board members?

When a school district will cease to exist by consolidation, annexation, or otherwise within six months after a regular school board election date, no election of school board members is held on that date and any board member whose term would otherwise terminate is continued until the old district ceases to exist.

Under certain circumstances relating to the consolidation, creation, and/or combination of school districts, a new school board may be elected at the same time the district's structural change is being voted on.

105 ILCS 5/10-10
105 ILCS 5/11E-55
105 ILCS 5/11E-70

4:100 Is the procedure for running for the school board in a newly organized school district's first election the same as when running for an existing school board?

The procedures are the same except that in a newly created district's first election, the regional superintendent of schools, rather than the school board secretary, performs all of the duties (if any) of the local election official.

105 ILCS 5/9-10

CANDIDATE NOMINATIONS

4:110 How does a school board candidate acquire a place on the ballot?

To be placed on the ballot, a candidate must cause to be filed a nominating petition and a statement of candidacy with the county clerk or county board of election commissioners. The statement of candidacy must include a receipt showing that a statement of economic interests has been timely filed with the county clerk.

5 ILCS 420/4A-101 et seq.
105 ILCS 5/10-10

4:120 When may a school board candidate circulate a nominating petition to gather signatures?

A school board candidate may cause to be circulated a petition no earlier than 90 days preceding the last day for the filing of the petition (196 days before the election).

10 ILCS 5/10-4

4:130 During what time frame must a school board candidate file his or her nominating petition?

A candidate for school board must cause his or her nominating petition and statement of candidacy to be filed no more than 113 days nor less than 106 days before the date of the election.

10 ILCS 5/10-6(2)
105 ILCS 5/9-10

4:140 With whom does a school board candidate file a nominating petition?

A school board candidate must cause his or her nominating petition to be filed with the county clerk or the county board of election commissioners. The county clerk or county board of election commissioners must, within seven days of filing the nominating petition or on the last day for filing the petition, whichever is earlier, acknowledge to the petitioner in writing the acceptance of the nominating petition.

105 ILCS 5/9-10

4:150 What information is required on a petition of candidacy for school board?

A petition must include

1) A statement of candidacy;
2) The name of the school district;
3) The name and place of residence of the candidate with specified street and number;
4) Whether the candidate is seeking a full term or is seeking to fill a partial term caused by a board vacancy;
5) The date of the election;
6) The number of voter signatures required;
7) The notarized signature of the petition circulator; and
8) A receipt from the county clerk showing the candidate has timely filed a statement of economic interests.

School board nominating petitions must be on sheets of uniform size, and must contain the circulator's affidavit and a statement of an individual's candidacy.

10 ILCS 5/10-5
105 ILCS 5/9-10
Klingelmueller v. Haas, 111 Ill. App. 3d 88, 443 N.E. 2d 782, 66 Ill. Dec. 856 (3rd Dist. 1982)

4:160 How many signatures are required on a school board candidate nominating petition?

Nominating petitions for board of education candidates must be signed by at least 50 registered voters who reside in the school district or 10 percent of the registered voters who reside in the school district, whichever is less. Nominating petitions for school directors must be signed by at least 25 registered voters who reside in the school district or 5 percent of the voters who reside in the school district, whichever is less.

105 ILCS 5/9-10

4:165 How must a candidate's name be listed on a nominating petition?

In the designation of the name of a candidate on a petition for nomination, the candidate's given name or names, initial or initials, a nickname by which the candidate is commonly known, or a combination thereof may be used in addition to the candidate's surname.

If a candidate has changed his or her name, whether by a statutory or common law procedure in Illinois or any other jurisdiction, within three years before the last day for filing the petition, then the candidate's name on the petition must be followed by "formerly known as (list all prior names during the three year period) until name changed on (list date of each such name change)" and the petition must be accompanied by the candidate's affidavit stating the candidate's previous names during the period specified and the date or dates each of those names was changed.

Failure to meet these requirements is grounds for denying certification of the candidate's name for the ballot, but these requirements do not apply to name changes resulting from adoption to assume an adoptive parent's or parents' surname, marriage to assume a spouse's surname, or dissolution of marriage or declaration of invalidity of marriage to assume a former surname.

No other designation, such as a political slogan, as defined by Section 7-17 of the Election Code, title or degree, or nickname suggesting or implying possession of a title, degree or professional status, or similar information may be used in connection with the candidate's surname.

105 ILCS 5/9-10

4:170 Must a candidate for school board declare a political party affiliation?

School board candidates are not required to declare political party affiliation.

4:180 May a school board candidate be required to sign a loyalty oath in order to file a nominating petition?

While a signed loyalty oath is required by the Election Code for filing a school board candidate's nominating petition, this requirement is unconstitutional and is, therefore, unenforceable. A school board candidate's nominating petition may not be refused for a candidate's failure or refusal to sign a loyalty oath.

Communist Party of Illinois v. Ogilvie, 357 F. Supp. 105 (N.D. Ill. 1972)

CANDIDATE WITHDRAWAL

4:190 May a school board candidate run for both a full term and a partial term created by a board vacancy?

No. A candidate for either a board of education or board of school directors who has filed nominating petitions for both a full term and a partial term at the same election must withdraw one petition or the other, in writing, within five business days following the last day for filing petitions.

10 ILCS 5/10-7
105 ILCS 5/9-10

4:200 How may a school board candidate withdraw his or her candidacy and have his or her name removed from the ballot?

A candidate may withdraw by filing a written request signed by the candidate and acknowledged before an officer qualified to take acknowledgment of deeds not later than the date for certification of candidates for the ballot. Filing is to be made at the county clerk or county board of election commissioners. If a request for withdrawal is received after the date for certification of candidates, then the votes for the withdrawn candidate are invalid and are not reported by the election authority.

10 ILCS 5/10-7

OBJECTIONS TO NOMINATING PETITIONS

4:210 Who determines whether a candidate's nominating papers meet legal requirements?

The county clerk or county board of election commissioners who receives and files nominating papers makes an initial determination as to whether the papers are in apparent conformity with the law. A 2016 amendment to Section 9-10 of the School Code limited the scope of the authority of the election official to make this determination. Before 2013, this duty was vested in the school board secretary.

105 ILCS 5/9-10
Haymore v. Orr, 385 Ill. App. 3d 915, 897 N.E. 2d 337, 325 Ill. Dec. 89 (1st Dist. 2008)

4:215 What authority does the county clerk or county board of election commissioners have for accepting or rejecting a candidate's nominating papers?

Whether the county clerk or county board of election commissioners has the authority to reject a candidate's nominating papers depends on the nature of the deficiency. Nominating papers that are in apparent conformity with the law are valid unless a proper objection is filed. Relying on prior case authority and "concerns for public policy," an Illinois appellate court held that a local election official has the affirmative duty to refuse to certify nominating petitions that do not apparently conform to the mandatory requirements of the Election Code. The court concluded that there must be "a gatekeeper to turn away nominating papers that do not even purport to conform to the law. We believe that the local election official serves this function."

10 ILCS 5/10-3.1 et seq.

105 ILCS 5/9-10

Haymore v. Orr, 385 Ill. App. 3d 915, 897 N.E. 2d 337, 325 Ill. Dec. 89 (1st Dist. 2008)

North v. Hinkle, 295 Ill. App. 3d 84, 692 N.E. 2d 352, 229 Ill. Dec. 579 (2nd Dist. 1998)

4:220 Is it possible to challenge a school board candidate's nominating petitions on the grounds that signatures are invalid or were improperly gathered or that other information contained in the petition is incorrect?

The election official has no authority to question the accuracy or truthfulness of information contained in a nominating petition. However, candidate nominating petitions are open to public inspection and any legal voter of the district may file a written objection with the county clerk or the county board of election commissioners or the State Board of Elections within five business days after the last day for filing nominating petitions. The objector's petition must state fully the nature of the objection, the interest of the objector, and the relief requested.

10 ILCS 5/10-7

10 ILCS 5/10-8

4:230 Who hears objections to school board candidate nominating petitions?

The County Officers Electoral Board (COEB) hears challenges to school board candidate nominating petitions. The COEB is composed of the county clerk, or an assistant designated by the county clerk, the state's attorney of the county or an assistant state's attorney designated by the state's attorney, and the clerk of the circuit court, or an assistant designated by the clerk of the circuit court, of the county.

The county clerk or his or her designee is the chairperson, except that in any county which has established a county board of election commissioners that board must constitute the county officers electoral board ex-officio. If a school district is located in two or more counties, the county officers electoral board of the county in which thc principal office of the school district is located hears and passes on objections to nominations of candidates for school district office in that school district.

10 ILCS 5/10-9

4:240 What procedures are used by the County Officers Electoral Board for hearing objections to nominating petitions?

When the election official receives an objection to a nominating petition, the official must send a copy of the objection pursuant to statutory delivery requirement to the candidate. The original objection is sent to the chairperson of the County Officers Electoral Board (COEB) by registered mail, noting the day and hour the objector's petition was received.

The chairperson of the COEB must call a meeting of the COEB to hold a hearing on the objector's petition. The hearing must be held not less than three nor more than five days after the chairperson receives the secretary's notice of objection. A hearing notice must be sent to the objector and to the candidate(s) named in the objection by registered mail and the chairperson of the COEB must cause the sheriff to serve the parties with notice.

Following a hearing to consider the objection, the COEB must render a timely decision in writing. The decision of the COEB is subject to appeal to the circuit court within five days of the COEB's decision. If no court challenge is filed within the five-day period, the COEB must send a copy of its decision to the school board secretary by registered or certified mail.

10 ILCS 5/10-8 et seq.

Schumann v. Kumarich, 102 Ill. App. 3d 454, 430 N.E. 2d 99, 58 Ill. Dec. 157 (1st Dist. 1981)

Gilbert v. Municipal Officers' Electoral Board of Deerfield, 97 Ill. App. 3d 847, 423 N.E. 2d 952, 53 Ill. Dec. 283 (2nd Dist. 1981)

People ex rel. Talerico v. Lata, 96 Ill. App. 2d 34, 238 N.E. 2d 217 (1st Dist. 1968)

CERTIFICATION OF CANDIDATES

4:250 When do election officials certify school board candidates?

The county clerk or county board of election commissioners must certify candidates to the election authority not less than 68 days before the election, directing the election authority to place the names of candidates on the official ballot in the same manner as presented on the certification.

10 ILCS 5/10-15

4:260 What determines the format of the school board election ballot?

Ballots for school board elections are prescribed in the School Code, which provides for differing formats that conform to differing residential restrictions on school board membership. Ballot formats include those for boards with members elected entirely at large, as well as for those with restrictions on the number of members that may be elected from less populous congressional townships and unincorporated areas.

105 ILCS 5/9-12 et seq.
105 ILCS 5/9-22

4:265 How do election officials determine the territorial residential qualifications that apply to candidates for election?

The territorial residential qualifications that pertain to school board membership are usually those established at the most recent consolidation or reorganization. The easiest way to determine the school district's ballot format is to look at the ballot format from the most recent election.

4:270 What determines the order of names on a school board election ballot?

Candidates' names appear on the ballot in the order filed with the county clerk or county board of election commissioners. The relevant election official must conduct a lottery to establish the order of candidates' names in the event of simultaneous filings. Simultaneous filings are those petitions filed by persons standing in line at the normal opening hour of the office on the first day for filing and those petitions received in the first mail delivery of the day or those petitions filed in the last hour before the filing deadline.

Where residency restrictions call for a ballot format that groups candidates by area of residence, the order in which petitions are filed or selected by lottery establishes the order in which candidates groupings appear on the ballot.

105 ILCS 5/9-11.1 et seq.

4:275 Is the election official required to use any particular lottery procedure in determining the order of candidates' names in the event of simultaneous filings?

Simultaneous filings of candidate nominating petitions for the same office occur only at 8 a.m. on the first day of filing, and in the last hour of filing on the last day of filing. The lottery system to be used by the State Board of Elections, the election authority, or the local election official to break ties resulting from simultaneous filings must be approved by the State Board of Elections. The Election Code requires election officials to use a lottery approved by the State Board of Elections. Board of Elections Rule 201.40 describes an approved lottery procedure that, summarized briefly, provides the following:

1) The names of all candidates who filed simultaneously for the same office shall be listed alphabetically and shall be numbered consecutively commencing with the number one, which is assigned to the candidate whose name is listed first on the alphabetic list, however, candidates filing a group petition for the same office are treated as one in the alphabetical listing, using the name of the first candidate for that office to appear on the petitions as the name to be included in the alphabetical list.

2) All ties will be broken by a single drawing. A number is placed in a container representing each number assigned to each candidate as provided for above. For example, if there are five candidates involved in the lottery, the numbers one through five are placed in a container.

3) Numbers in the container are thoroughly shaken and mixed and then drawn one at a time. The candidate or group of candidates whose position on the alphabetical list corresponds to the first number drawn is certified ahead of the other candidates. The candidate whose position on the list corresponds to the second number drawn is certified second, and so on.

A separate but identical procedure is used in the event of simultaneous filings for a separate election to fill an unexpired term.

10 ILCS 5/10-6.2
105 ILCS 5/9-11.1
26 Ill. Admin. Code 201.40

4:280 Are write-in candidates permitted at a school board election?

Voters may write in and cast votes for persons not listed on the ballot. However, write-in votes are not counted unless the candidate has filed with the election authority a notarized declaration of intent to run as a write-in candidate not later than 61 days prior to the election.

Further, when an objection to a candidate's nominating papers is sustained under Section 10-10 of the Election Code after the 61st day before the election, then write-in votes are counted for that candidate if he or she has filed a notarized declaration of intent to be a write-in candidate for that office with the election authority not later than seven days prior to the election.

10 ILCS 5/10-10
10 ILCS 5/17-16.1
10 ILCS 5/18-9.1

PUBLIC POLICY ELECTIONS

4:290 How does a school board get a public policy issue on the ballot?

A school board must pass a proper resolution at an official board meeting that a question be submitted to the voters in a referendum at a regularly scheduled election. The resolution must be adopted at least 79 days prior to the date of the regularly scheduled election. The resolution must state the regular election at which the referendum will be submitted to the voters.

The school board secretary is responsible for certifying the question to be submitted at the referendum to the county clerk or county board of election commissioners at least 68 days before the election. This certification must include the form of the referendum question, the date the school board adopted the resolution, and a certified copy of the resolution passed by the school board.

10 ILCS 5/10-15
10 ILCS 5/28-1 et seq.

4:300 How many separate propositions may a school board have placed on the ballot at any one election?

Not more than three public policy questions other than backdoor referendums may be submitted to referendum at the same election.

105 ILCS 5/28 1 et seq.

4:310 How are voter-initiated petitions, including backdoor referendums and advisory referendums, placed on the ballot?

Except under certain conditions specified in statute, a voter-initiated petition must be filed with the school board secretary at least 92 days before the regularly scheduled election. The board secretary must certify the question to be placed on the ballot to the county clerk at least 68 days prior to the regularly scheduled election.

10 ILCS 5/10-15
10 ILCS 5/28-2
10 ILCS 5/28-5
Ayers v. Martin, 233 Ill. App. 3d 397, 584 N.E. 2d 1028, 165 Ill. Dec. 594 (4th Dist. 1991)

4:313 What information must be provided in the publication of a notice of a resolution that may be subject to backdoor referendum?

The publication of the resolution must include a notice of the specific number of voters required to sign a petition requesting that the public question be submitted to the voters, the time within which the petition must be filed, and the date of the prospective referendum.

In addition, when a resolution for issuing working cash fund bonds is published, the recording officer of the district (presumably the board secretary) must provide a petition form to any individual requesting one.

10 ILCS 5/28-2(f)
105 ILCS 5/20-7

4:315 Is it possible to challenge a voter-initiated petition on the grounds that signatures are invalid or were improperly gathered or that other information contained in the petition is incorrect?

The local election official has no authority to question the accuracy or truthfulness of information contained in a voter-initiated petition.

The school board lacks standing to challenge the accuracy or truthfulness of information contained in a voter-initiated petition. However, such petitions are open to public inspection and any legal voter of the district may file a written objection with the county clerk or county board of election commissioners five days after the last day for filing voter-initiated petitions. The objector's petition must state fully the nature of the objection, the interest of the objector and the relief requested. Such objections frequently challenge whether the petitions contain the required number of valid signatures by identifying some signatures as forgeries, those of non-residents, unregistered voters, or identify technical errors in the execution of the petitions.

The objections are heard and ruled upon by the County Officers Electoral Board in generally the same manner as objections to candidate nominating petitions.

10 ILCS 5/10-8 et seq.
10 ILCS 5/28-3

4:320 What is an emergency referendum?

An "emergency referendum" is a referendum conducted on other than a regularly scheduled election date. Whenever any public question is to be submitted pursuant to law, whether by action of the governing body of a school district, by petition, or by court order, the governing body of the school district whose powers or duties are directly affected by the result of the vote on the public question may petition the circuit court for an order declaring such proposition to be an emergency and fixing a date other than a regularly scheduled election date on which a special referendum election shall be held for the submission of the public question.

The petition must set forth the public question and the action taken that requires the submission of the question, the next regularly scheduled election at which the proposition could otherwise be placed on the ballot, the estimated costs of conducting a separate special election, and the reasons why an emergency exists to justify the special election prior to the next ensuing regular election. The petition must be approved by a majority of the members of the school board.

The court must conduct a hearing on the petition. Any resident of the area in which the referendum is to be conducted may oppose the petition. The court may approve the petition for an emergency referendum only upon a finding, supported by the evidence, that the referendum is necessitated by an imminent need for approval of additional authority in order to maintain the operations or facilities of the school district and that such need is due to circumstances beyond the control of the governing body.

10 ILCS 5/2A-1.4

4:330 What information must be provided on the ballot and in a notice of election increasing a district's tax rate?

In addition to the notice requirements of the general election law, whenever a proposition to increase a school tax rate is submitted to be voted upon by the voters of any district, the notice of such election must include an estimate of the approximate amount of taxes extendible under the maximum rate then in force and an estimate of the approximate amount of taxes extendible under the proposed increased rate, such amounts being computed upon the last known full, fair cash value; provided that any error, miscalculation, or inaccuracy in computing the amounts does not invalidate or affect the validity of any rate so increased.

The school board must make such estimate, and the secretary must certify such amount to the election authority as part of the certification of the proposition as required by the general election law. The estimate must appear on the ballot on which the proposition is printed but must not appear as a part of the proposition.

In addition, where the proposition is to authorize or increase a tax rate, the notice of election and the form of ballot must include:

1) The geographic or other common name of the school district by which it is commonly known and referred to, as well as the number of the district;

2) The maximum rate at which such tax may be levied if the proposition is approved;

3) The total dollar amount of the most recently approved annual budget of the district, what the total dollar amount of that budget would be if increased by the amount of additional tax that may be levied if the proposition is approved, and what the percentage increase in that annual budget would be if the total dollar amount were increased by that amount of additional tax; and

4) If the proposition is to increase the annual rate of an existing tax levied by the district, then the annual rate at which the tax is currently levied and the percentage of increase between the maximum rate at which such tax may be levied if the proposition is approved and the annual rate at which such tax currently is levied.

105 ILCS 5/9-11
105 ILCS 5/17-3.4

ADVOCACY AND ELECTIONEERING

4:340 May a school board use school district funds to inform voters of its reason for seeking a tax rate increase, bond issue, or other public policy question?

The school board has an obligation to present voters with the facts so they might arrive at informed judgments. On the other hand, public funds belong to all the electorate — opponents as well as proponents — and cannot be used to represent just one side or to finance a campaign to influence the outcome of the referendum. A school board should exercise extreme caution when expending money (including printing and mailing costs) on issues related to a referendum.

An electioneering communication is any communication that refers to a clearly identified question of public policy that will appear on the ballot, as opposed to communications that suggest that voters register or vote (without reference to a specific issue).

If a school district engages in electioneering and expends more than $3,000 in a 12-month period for electioneering communications, it will be considered a local political committee and must register consistent with the requirements of the Election Code.

Public funds must not be used to urge any elector to vote for or against any candidate or proposition or be appropriated for political campaign purposes. Although there is some disagreement regarding this issue among attorneys with reasonable interpretations of relevant law, there is probably no prohibition on the use of public funds for dissemination of factual information relative to any proposition appearing on an election ballot.

There is an Illinois appellate decision supporting the legality of the expenditure of public funds to employ a public relations consultant to promote a school board's plan to raze a building and build a new one. Whether the case has broad applicability is uncertain.

5 ILCS 430/1-5 et seq.

10 ILCS 5/9-25 et seq.

Peraica et. al v. Riverside Brookfield School District, 2013 IL App (1st) 122351, 999 N.E. 2d 399, 376 Ill. Dec. 516

Citizens Organized to Save the Tax Cap v. State Board of Elections, et al., 392 Ill. App. 3d 392, 910 N.E. 2d 605, 331 Ill. Dec. 196 (1st Dist. 2009)

Ryan v. Warren Township High School District No. 121, 155 Ill. App. 3d 203, 510 N.E. 2d 911, 109 Ill. Dec. 843 (2nd Dist. 1987)

Citizens to Protect Public Funds v. Board of Education of Parsippany-Troy Hills, 13 N.J. 172 (1953)

Elsenau v. City of Chicago, 334 Ill. 78, 165 N.E. 129 (1929)

4:350 May a school board use district funds to disseminate printed information regarding a public policy question on the ballot?

Yes, so long as the printed information presents the facts, both pro and con, and does not urge voters to vote for or against the issue.

10 ILCS 5/9-25 et seq.

Citizens to Protect Public Funds v. Board of Education of Parsippany-Troy Hills, 13 N.J. 172 (1953)

Elsenau v. City of Chicago, 334 Ill. 78, 165 N.E. 129 (1929)

4:360 May supporters of a school board referendum urge voters to support the ballot proposition?

Yes, provided that:

1) No public funds are used by supporters of such an effort;

2) Any individual or organization that accepts or expends $3,000 or more in supporting or opposing a school referendum organizes as a "local political committee" under the Election Code; and

3) The school board and school employees, in their official capacities, treat proponents and opponents with an equal hand.

10 ILCS 5/9-1 et seq.

10 ILCS 5/9-25 et seq.

Citizens to Protect Public Funds v. Board of Education of Parsippany-Troy Hills, 13 N.J. 172 (1953)

Elsenau v. City of Chicago, 334 Ill. 78, 165 N.E. 129 (1929)

4:370 What is required of a local political committee?

Such a committee must file a statement of organization and must report contributions and expenditures. Forms are obtained from and filed with the county clerk. Obligations are set forth in publications issued by the State Board of Elections.

10 ILCS 5/9-1 et seq.

10 ILCS 5/9-10

4:380 What legal requirements apply to the literature of a political committee?

Any literature issued by the school board should be clearly identified as to source and purpose. It should be made clear that the political literature of a citizens committee was not financed with public funds.

People v. White, 116 Ill. 2d 171, 506 N.E. 2d 1284, 107 Ill. Dec. 229 (1987)

4:385 May a candidate for public office distribute anonymous campaign literature?

Any political committee that makes expenditure for a pamphlet; circular; handbill; internet or telephone communication; radio, television, or print advertisement; or other communication directed at voters and mentioning the name of a candidate in the next upcoming election is required to ensure that the name of the political committee paying for any part of the communication, including its preparation and distribution, is identified within the communication as the payer. This provision does not apply to items that are too small to contain the required disclosure.

Any political committee that makes an expenditure for a pamphlet; circular; handbill; internet or telephone communication; radio, television, or print advertisement; or other communication directed at voters and mentioning the name of a candidate in the next upcoming election, without that candidate's permission, and advocating for or against a public policy position must ensure that the name of the political committee paying for any part of the communication, including, but not limited to, its preparation and distribution, is identified clearly within the communication.

Disclosure is not required on any telephone communication using random sampling or other scientific survey methods to gauge public opinion for or against any candidate or question of public policy.

10 ILCS 5/9-9.5

People v. White, 116 Ill. 2d 171, 506 N.E. 2d 1284, 107 Ill. Dec. 229 (1987)

4:390 May a local political committee of citizens assign poll watchers to polling places on Election Day?

Yes, each organization of proponents and opponents of a ballot proposition that has registered with the election authority at least 40 days before the election is entitled to have one poll watcher per precinct. Each poll watcher must be registered to vote in Illinois and must have obtained necessary credentials from the election authority or the State Board of Elections. Credentials must be available for distribution at least two weeks before the election.

10 ILCS 5/17-23

DETERMINING ELECTION RESULTS

4:400 Who canvasses an election?

Prior to 2005, school boards conducted the election canvass. An amendment to the relevant statutes in 2004 provides that the election authority (county clerk or board of election commissioners) conducts the canvass. For a short time during the period 2005-2008, there was confusion as to whether the school board or the election authority was responsible for the canvass because the legislature had initially failed to change all the relevant statutes necessary to effect the change.

10 ILCS 5/1-8
10 ILCS 5/17-22
10 ILCS 5/22-17 et seq.

4:405 Where candidates for the school board must be grouped into residential areas, may the election authority select winners in a manner that ensures all seats are filled?

Generally, the election authority must seat candidates in order from the highest vote getter on the ballot to the lowest vote getter. Where seating a high vote getter would exceed the maximum number of board members who may be elected from a particular geographic area, the election authority must skip that candidate and go to the next highest vote getter.

However, where a ballot includes an unexpired term, the unexpired term must be filled first and independently of the full terms.

10 ILCS 5/22-17
105 ILCS 5/9-12
105 ILCS 5/10-10

4:410 What steps must be taken by a successful write-in candidate and by the election authority prior to seating a winning write-in candidate?

Election statutes are silent with respect to the seating of successful write-in candidates in a school board election. However:

1) Every school board member must have a statement of economic interests on file with the county clerk.

2) Statutes governing the seating of successful write-in candidates at primary and consolidated elections call for the filing of a statement of candidacy and a receipt for the filing of an economic interests statement for the office sought. The statement of candidacy provides a notarized affirmation that legal qualifications are met.

5 ILCS 420/4A-101 et seq.
10 ILCS 5/7-60 et seq.

4:415 What steps must be taken to determine the winner in the event of a tie vote among two or more school board candidates?

The election authority has the duty of breaking the tie in order to declare a winner. However, the law is unclear as to how such ties are to be broken. Presumably any lottery method would be acceptable if it is a fair and impartial method of random selection. The lottery prescribed by the State Board of Elections for determining ballot order of names in the event of simultaneous filings would be such a method.

10 ILCS 5/10-6.2
10 ILCS 5/22-17 et seq.
105 ILCS 5/9-11.1
26 Ill. Admin. Code 201.40

4:420 On what bases are school board elections invalidated?

The mandatory requirements of the election laws must be met or an election will be set aside. Whether a provision of election law is mandatory or not is subject to the following analysis:

1) Does the statutory scheme expressly or impliedly provide that the failure to follow the provision will render an election void?

2) Does the failure interfere with the result of the election?

3) Was any person legally eligible to vote not permitted to vote?

4) Was any person voting not a resident of the territory sought to be organized?

5) Were the polling places chosen for any improper motive?

6) Was there fraud in, or resulting from, the selection of the polling places?

Jones v. Municipal Officers Electoral Board, 122 Ill. App. 3d 926, 446 N.E. 2d 173, 61 Ill. Dec. 684 (1st Dist. 1983).

Madden v. Schumann, 105 Ill. App. 3d 900, 435 N.E. 2d 173, 61 Ill. Dec. 684 (1st Dist. 1982)

Schumann v. Kumarich, 102 Ill. App. 3d 454, 430 N.E. 2d 99, 58 Ill. Dec. 157 (1st Dist. 1981)

Havens v. Miller, 102 Ill. App. 3d 558, 429 N.E. 2d 1292, 57 Ill. Dec. 929 (1st Dist. 1981)

Goble v. Board of Education of Iuka Community Consolidated School District No. 7, Marion County, 83 Ill. App. 3d 284, 404 N.E. 2d 343, 38 Ill. Dec. 919 (5th Dist. 1980)

Menssen v. Eureka Unit District No. 140, 70 Ill. App. 3d 9, 388 N.E. 2d 273, 26 Ill. Dec. 649 (4th Dist. 1979)

Gibson v. Kankakee School District No. 111, 34 Ill. App. 3d 948, 341 N.E. 2d 447 (3rd Dist. 1975)

Gann v. Harrisburg Community Unit School District, 73 Ill. App. 2d 103, 218 N.E. 2d 833 (5th Dist. 1966)

4:430 What oath of office is required of school board members?

Each school board member, before taking his or her seat on the board, must take an oath of office, administered as determined by the board, in substantially the following form:

"I, (name of member or successful candidate), do solemnly swear (or affirm) that I will faithfully discharge the duties of the office of member of the Board of Education of (name of school district), in accordance with the Constitution of the United States, the Constitution of the State of Illinois, and the laws of the State of Illinois, to the best of my ability.

"I further swear (or affirm) that: I shall respect taxpayer interests by serving as a faithful protector of the school district's assets; I shall encourage and respect the free expression of opinion by my fellow board members and others who seek a hearing before the board, while respecting the privacy of students and employees; I shall recognize that a board member has no legal authority as an individual and that decisions can be made only by a majority vote at a public board meeting; and I shall abide by majority decisions of the board, while retaining the right to seek changes in such decisions through ethical and constructive channels."

105 ILCS 5/10-16.5

VOTING

4:500 Who is eligible to vote in elections of school board members and on public policy issues placed on the ballot by a school board?

To vote in a school board election or public policy referendum presented by a school board, an individual must be registered to vote from a residence within the boundaries of the school district.

In school board elections where board membership is at-large, the voter may vote for as many seats as are up for election. The same is true where the number of board members elected from particular townships or incorporated areas is regulated by law. In the latter case, a voter may vote for more candidates than may be lawfully elected from a particular geographic area.

In a school district where board members are elected from board member districts, the school district is divided into seven voting districts of substantially equal population. Voters living within each voting district elect one school board member from among candidates running from residencies within that voting district.

10 ILCS 5/6-27

105 ILCS 5/9-12 et seq.

105 ILCS 5/9-22

105 ILCS 5/10-10.5

105 ILCS 5/11E-55

105 ILCS 5/12-2

5: SCHOOL BOARD OFFICERS

ELECTED OFFICERS

5:10 What officers must a school board elect?

The School Code requires boards of school directors to elect a president and a clerk. Boards of education must elect a president, vice president, and a secretary. The secretary need not be a member of the school board, but all other board officers must be members.

No other officers are required by the School Code, but additional offices may be created by vote of the school board.

105 ILCS 5/10-5

105 ILCS 5/10-13 et seq.

5:20 May school board officers be elected by secret ballot?

The Open Meetings Act requires the election of school board officers by open vote at a public meeting. The voting may not be done by any form of secret ballot.

5 ILCS 120/1

People ex rel. Hopf v. Barger, 30 Ill. App. 3d 525, 332 N.E. 2d 649 (2nd Dist. 1975)

5:30 For how long are school board officers elected?

Officers of boards of education serve two-year terms unless the school board adopts a resolution and policy fixing the term at one year. Illinois law does not specify a term of office for officers of boards of directors. In such districts, officers' terms may be fixed by board resolution.

105 ILCS 5/10-5

105 ILCS 5/10-13 et seq.

5:35 When are school board officers elected?

Officers are elected at the school board's organizational meeting following the seating of members elected at each biennial election in odd-numbered years. Boards that opt for one-year terms must also elect officers in the even-numbered years.

105 ILCS 5/10-5

105 ILCS 5/10-16

5:40 Who serves as the president of the school board in the absence of the elected president?

The vice president of the school board performs the duties of the president if there is a vacancy in the office or in the president's absence or inability to act.

105 ILCS 5/10-13 et seq.

5:43 What are the duties of a school board president?

The president presides at board meetings. In addition, Illinois laws impose the following duties on the president:

1) Sign official district documents requiring the president's signature, including the minutes of board meetings and the certificate of tax levy; and

2) Call special meetings of the board.

The school board may also enact policies that impose additional duties on the president.

The president is also entitled to vote on all matters and, under some rules of order, is permitted to make and second motions and engage in discussion.

10 ILCS 5/10-9

105 ILCS 5/10-6

105 ILCS 5/10-7

105 ILCS 5/10-13

105 ILCS 5/10-16

5:45 What are the duties of a school board secretary?

Duties imposed upon the secretary by law include:

1) Keep and maintain minutes of meetings and related records safe and easily accessible;

2) Attest to the authenticity of official school board documents, such as minutes of meetings, resolutions, and records of all types and prepare an annual report to the treasurer;

3) Receive written resignations of board members; and

4) Receive voter petitions and school board resolutions calling for propositions to be placed on the ballot at a regular election and certify to the election authority any propositions that are to appear on the ballot, including the wording of the proposition as taken from the school board resolution or voter petition.

The school board also may enact policies that impose additional duties on the secretary. A secretary who is a member of the board is entitled to vote on all matters before the board and may make or second motions and participate in discussion.

105 ILCS 5/9-2(d)
105 ILCS 5/10-7
105 ILCS 5/10-8
105 ILCS 5/10-10
105 ILCS 5/10-11
105 ILCS 5/10-14

5:50 May school board officers be paid for their services?

Only the secretary of a board of education may be compensated. Other officers of the board may not be paid for their services.

105 ILCS 5/10-14

5:60 Are there limitations on compensation of the board secretary?

The secretary of the board of education, whether a member of the board of education or not, may be paid. The rate of pay must be set by the board of education at least 180 days before the beginning of the secretary's term of office.

If the secretary is a member of the board, the rate of pay may not exceed the statutory limit set forth in the School Code. There is no statutory limit on the compensation for a secretary who is not a member of the board.

50 ILCS 145/2
105 ILCS 5/10-14

5:65 May a school board elect a district employee to serve as board secretary?

Yes, although this is probably not a good practice. A board secretary is elected for a fixed term. A board is very limited in its ability to supervise, discipline, or dismiss an elected secretary. A way to avoid the conflict is to elect a board member as secretary and then appoint an employee to assist. An employee in this capacity serves at the pleasure of the board.

5:70 Who serves as board secretary or clerk in the absence of the elected secretary or clerk?

If a clerk or secretary is absent from a board meeting or refuses to perform the duties of the office, a secretary or clerk pro tempore must be appointed by the remaining board members.

105 ILCS 5/10-14

5:75 May a school board officer be removed from office for failure to attend meetings?

No. However, the statutes that provide for the election of school board officers also allow the appointment of pro tempore officers in the absence, inability to act, or incapacity of the elected officer.

105 ILCS 5/10-13 et seq.

TREASURERS

5:80 What is a school treasurer?

The school treasurer is the only lawful custodian of school funds; is responsible for all receipts, disbursements, and investments of school funds; and pays orders issued by the school board.

105 ILCS 5/8-1 et seq.

5:90 How is a school treasurer elected or appointed?

In Class I county school units (all counties other than Cook), each school board either

1) Elects one of its members to serve as treasurer without salary for a period of one year; or

2) Appoints a non-member as treasurer and fixes compensation. The appointed treasurer (non-member of the board) serves at the pleasure of the board.

In Class II county school units (Cook County), the trustees of schools appoint a township treasurer unless the Class II county school unit is no longer subject to the jurisdiction and authority of the trustees of schools, which may occur in a number of different ways pursuant to a complicated statutory scheme.

105 ILCS 5/5-1
105 ILCS 5/8-1 et seq.

5:95 What qualifications are required of a school district treasurer?

Illinois statutes provide various sets of qualifications for school treasurers, depending upon the source and manner of appointment:

1) A treasurer who is a member of the school board has no required qualifications other than election by vote of the board for a term of one year. This option of electing a board member as treasurer is available to school boards in all counties other than Cook, as well as to any

Cook County school board that has withdrawn from the jurisdiction of the township trustees and township school treasurer under Section 5-1(b) of the School Code.

2) A treasurer who is not a member of the school board must be at least 21 years old, of approved integrity and, if appointed for the first time after October 1, 1977, must have a financial background or related experience or 12 semester hours of credit of college level accounting. This option of appointing a treasurer who meets these qualifications is available to school boards in all counties other than Cook, as well as to any Cook County school board that has withdrawn from the jurisdiction of the township trustees and township school treasurer under Section 5-1(b) of the School Code.

3) A township school treasurer appointed by township trustees in Cook County must be a resident of the township and neither a trustee nor member of a school board. If appointed for the first time after August 14, 1989, the individual must be a certified public accountant or certified school business official or have experience as a Cook County township school treasurer prior to July 1, 1989.

4) A treasurer appointed by a Cook County school board that was under the jurisdiction of a township treasurer at the time that office was abolished in the township under Section 5-1(c) of the School Code must be neither a school board member nor district superintendent and, if appointed for the first time after August 14, 1989, must be a certified public accountant or certified school business official or have experience as a Cook County township school treasurer prior to July 1, 1989.

105 ILCS 5/5-1(b)
105 ILCS 5/5-1(c)
105 ILCS 5/8-1

5:100 May the county treasurer be designated the treasurer of a school district?

Yes.

Ill. Const. art. VII, sec. 4(e)

5:105 Is the school treasurer required to post a bond?

The school treasurer is required to post two types of bonds. The first is a surety bond that every school treasurer must post "before entering upon his or her duties." The bond must provide a penalty of 25 percent of "all bonds, notes, mortgages, moneys, and effects of which the treasurer has custody at any time." The penalty may be increased or decreased to accommodate changes in the value of financial instruments under the treasurer's control, but it can never be less than the 25 percent requirement. The bond must be approved by the governing school board or by the township trustees in Class II counties (Cook) for school districts under the jurisdiction of township trustees. The bond must then be filed with the regional superintendent of schools.

The second bond is required before the treasurer can accept possession of the proceeds of a bond issue and will normally be required before bond counsel will give approval to the issuance of bonds. This bond must be equal to 25 percent of the amount of the bond issue and must be approved by the governing school board or board of township trustees.

The treasurer's bond requires a calculation of the highest amount that is likely to be under the treasurer's control at any one time. This bond, however, need not duplicate coverage of the special bond required for a bond issue.

105 ILCS 5/8-2
105 ILCS 5/19-6

5:110 How is a vacancy in the office of school treasurer filled?

In Class I county school units and Class II county school units no longer within the jurisdiction of the trustees of schools and township treasurer, when a vacancy occurs in the office of school treasurer by death, resignation, or removal from office, the school board appoints a new treasurer.

In Class II county school units still within the jurisdiction of the trustees of schools, the trustees of schools elect a treasurer to fill the unexpired term.

105 ILCS 5/8-1

5:120 How is the school treasurer paid?

In Class I county school units, a school board may elect one of its members as school treasurer to serve without compensation or appoint a non-member and fix compensation.

In Class II county school units no longer within the jurisdiction of the trustees of schools and township treasurer, the school board appoints the treasurer who may not be its superintendent of schools and fixes compensation unless the treasurer is a school board member, in which case he or she shall perform his or her duties without compensation.

In Class II county school units still within the jurisdiction of the trustees of schools, the trustees appoint a school treasurer and fix compensation. The treasurer so appointed cannot be a trustee or school board member.

Compensation for a school treasurer must be fixed prior to the appointment of the treasurer and may not be decreased during the treasurer's term of office.

105 ILCS 5/5-1
105 ILCS 5/8-1
105 ILCS 5/8-3

5:130 Who is responsible for checking a school treasurer's books?

The regional superintendent of schools is required to examine all books, accounts, and vouchers of every school treasurer in the region at least once each year. If any irregularities are found, the regional superintendent is required to report the irregularities at once in writing to the trustees of Class II county school units, or to the respective school boards of those school districts that form a part of a Class II county school unit but that are not subject to the jurisdiction of the trustees of schools of any township in which any such district is located, or to the respective school boards of districts in Class I county school units. The trustees or the school board is required to take immediate action as the case demands.

The regional superintendent is also required to examine all notes, bonds, mortgages, and other evidence of indebtedness that the township or school treasurer holds officially, and if any of the papers are found not to be in proper order or the securities are insufficient, the regional superintendent is required to report the problem in writing to the board of trustees.

105 ILCS 5/3-14.11

5:140 When may a school treasurer be removed from office?

In Class I county school units (all counties except Cook) and in Class II county school units (Cook County) that are no longer subject to the jurisdiction of the trustees of schools and township treasurer, an appointed school treasurer serves at the pleasure of the school board and may be removed by the board at any time for cause. The School Code does not provide a method to remove an elected school treasurer from office during the treasurer's one-year term.

In Class II county school units still within the jurisdiction of the trustees of schools, the trustees of schools may remove a school treasurer from office for cause.

105 ILCS 5/8-1

Hertel v. Boismenue, 229 Ill. 474, 82 N.E. 298 (1907)

6: SCHOOL BOARD MEETINGS

PUBLIC MEETINGS

6:10 What is a meeting under Illinois law?

The Open Meetings Act defines a meeting as any gathering, whether in person or by video or audio conference, telephone call, electronic means (such as without limitation, electronic mail, electronic chat, and instant messaging) or other means of contemporaneous interactive communication, of a majority of a quorum of the members of a public body held for the purposes of discussing public business.

The definition of "public body" includes committees and subcommittees of the school board, an ethics commission acting under the State Officials and Employees Ethics Act, as well as the school board itself.

The provisions of the Open Meetings Act do not apply to collective bargaining negotiations or grievance arbitrations.

5 ILCS 120/1.02

115 ILCS 5/18

Board of Regents of the Regency University System v. Reynard, et al., 292 Ill. App. 3d 968, 686 N.E. 2d 122, 227 Ill. Dec. 66 (4th Dist. 1997)

Nabhani v. Coglianese, 552 F. Supp. 657 (N.D. Ill. 1983)

People ex rel. Difanis v. Barr, 83 Ill. 2d 191, 414 N.E. 2d 731, 46 Ill. Dec. 678 (4th Dist. 1980)

People ex rel. Cooper v. Carlson, 28 Ill. App. 3d 569, 328 N.E. 2d 675 (2nd Dist. 1975)

6:12 What training on the Open Meetings Act is required of school board members?

A 2011 change in the Open Meetings Act requires that each school board member successfully complete an electronic training curriculum developed and administered by the Public Access Counselor in the office of the Illinois Attorney General.

For members of the school board who were on the board on January 1, 2012, the training must be completed by January 1, 2013. For members new to a board after January 1, 2012, training must be completed not later than the 90th day after the date the member takes the oath of office.

Each member successfully completing the electronic training curriculum must file a copy of the certificate of completion with the public body. Completing the required training as a member of the board satisfies the requirements with regard to the member's service on a committee or subcommittee of the board and the member's ex officio service on any other public body.

The failure of one or more members of the board to complete the training does not affect the validity of an action taken by the board.

An elected or appointed member of a public body who has successfully completed the required training and filed a copy of the certificate of completion with the public body is not required to subsequently complete the training.

5 ILCS 120/1.05

6:15 Must a school board comply with the Open Meetings Act?

School boards are governed by the notice and conduct of meeting provisions of the Open Meetings Act.

5 ILCS 120/1 et seq.

105 ILCS 5/10-6

105 ILCS 5/10-16

6:20 Are school board meetings open to the public?

A school board meeting must be convenient and open to the public unless

1) The purpose of the meeting is collective bargaining negotiations or grievance arbitration; or

2) The school board excludes the public by voting to convene in closed session for one or any combination of the permissible reasons for closed session.

The provisions for exceptions to open meetings requirements are strictly construed against closed meetings.

5 ILCS 120/1

5 ILCS 120/2 et seq.

115 ILCS 5/18

Gerwin v. Livingston County Board, 345 Ill. App. 3d 352, 802 N.E. 2d 410, 280 Ill. Dec. 485 (4th Dist. 2003)

6:30 May school boards or school board members hold unofficial meetings to discuss school business?

No. It is public policy in Illinois that public business is to be conducted in public, and both the actions and deliberations of public bodies are to be conducted in public. The conduct of school business is limited to official meetings of the school board or its committees.

A discussion of school business by a majority of a quorum — three members of a seven-member school board — would be a violation of the Open Meetings Act as would a meeting held by a majority of a quorum of a committee of a public body at which school business was discussed.

5 ILCS 120/1

105 ILCS 5/10-6

105 ILCS 5/10-16

Board of Regents of the Regency University System v. Reynard, et al., 292 Ill. App. 3d 968, 686 N.E. 2d 122, 227 Ill. Dec. 66 (4th Dist. 1997)

Illinois News Broadcasters Association v. City of Springfield, 22 Ill. App. 3d 226, 317 N.E. 2d 288 (4th Dist. 1974)

6:35 Does the Open Meetings Act apply to school board committee meetings?

The Open Meetings Act applies to all school board committees. Committees appointed by or wholly composed of faculty or administration are not generally school board committees and, therefore, are not subject to the Open Meetings Act. Whether any particular school board created or endorsed committee is or is not subject to the Open Meetings Act is a fact question that requires an analysis of the duties, purpose, and structure of the committee.

5 ILCS 120/1.02

115 ILCS 5/18

Board of Regents of the Regency University System v. Reynard, et al., 292 Ill. App. 3d 968, 686 N.E. 2d 122, 227 Ill. Dec. 66 (4th Dist. 1997)

People ex rel. Difanis v. Barr, 83 Ill. 2d 191, 414 N.E. 2d 731, 46 Ill. Dec. 678 (1980)

Rockford Newspapers, Inc. v. Northern Illinois Council on Alcoholism and Drug Dependence, 64 Ill. App. 3d 94, 380 N.E. 2d 1192, 21 Ill. Dec. 16 (2nd Dist. 1978)

Pope v. Parkinson, 48 Ill. App. 3d 797, 363 N.E. 2d 438, 6 Ill. Dec. 756 (4th Dist. 1977)

6:37 Are meetings of persons who have been elected to a school board but not yet seated subject to the Open Meetings Act?

No. Persons who have been elected to a public body are not members of the public body and cannot conduct business until they are seated.

5 ILCS 120/1.02

105 ILCS 5/10-16

6:40 Are school staff meetings subject to the Open Meetings Act?

Staff meetings involving teachers, administrators, or other employees are not subject to the Open Meetings Act even when such meetings are held to prepare presentations for the school board.

People ex rel. Cooper v. Carlson, 28 Ill. App. 3d 569, 328 N.E. 2d 675 (2nd Dist. 1975)

6:42 Are meetings of the Senate Bill 7 or PERA joint committees subject to the Open Meetings Act?

Senate Bill 7 (P.A. 97-08) and the Performance Evaluation Reform Act (PERA, P.A. 96-186) require the formation of committees to perform certain tasks required by the underlying legislation. In 2016 the Public Access Counselor issued a non-binding opinion holding that the Senate Bill 7 committee is subject to the Open Meetings Act.

2014 PAC 27532 (September 8, 2016)

6:45 May school board members use the internet between meetings to communicate among themselves or with administrators?

A 2006 amendment to the Open Meetings Act clarified that electronic gatherings of a public body must comply with the Open Meetings Act. Under the amendment, a meeting is any ". . .gathering whether in person or by video or audio conference, telephone call, electronic means (such as, without limitation, electronic mail, electronic chat, and instant messaging) or other means of contemporaneous interactive communication of a majority of a quorum of the members of a public body held for the purposes of discussing public business."

The discussion of substantive topics by board members or the superintendent in email messages, by use of text messaging, or in chat rooms violates the open meeting requirements of the Open Meetings Act.

School officials should refrain from conducting school business by email or on the web. Internet communication should be limited to reminders of meeting times, dates, and places and communications among persons constituting less than a majority of a quorum of the board or any committee thereof.

No person should have any expectation of privacy with respect to email or any other internet communication.

5 ILCS 120/1.02

6:47 Are school board member cell phone or computer records public records within the meaning of the Freedom of Information Act?

The Freedom of Information Act defines records as "all records, reports, forms, writings, letters, memorandums, books, papers, maps, photographs, microfilms, cards, tapes, recordings, electronic data processing records, electronic communications, recorded information, and all other documentary materials pertaining to the transaction of public business, regardless of physical form or characteristics, having been prepared by or for, or having been or being used by, received by, in the possession of, or under the control of any public body."

The Public Access Counselor in the office of the Illinois Attorney General has issued a binding opinion concluding that where, how, or on what device a record was created is not determined by whether a record is a public record, but rather whether that record "was prepared by or used by one or more members of the public body in conducting the affairs of government." The Public Access Counselor held that if a member of a public body sent or received communications on personal electronic devices during a meeting or study session then those communications are public records, even though the records were never possessed, used, or received by the public body.

5 ILCS 140/2(c)

City of Champaign v. Madigan, 2013 IL App (4th) 120662, 992 N.E. 2d 627, 372 Ill. Dec. 787

Public Access Opinion No. 11-06

6:50 May citizens make audio or video tape recordings of school board meetings?

Citizens may tape, film, or use other means of recording the activities at open school board meetings. School boards may adopt reasonable rules to govern the making of such recordings.

5 ILCS 120/2.05

6:60 What is the penalty for violation of the Open Meetings Act?

Any person, including the State's Attorney of the county in which the school district is located, may bring a civil action in circuit court alleging a violation of the Open Meetings Act. Circuit courts are authorized to award attorney fees and costs to a successful complainant. The court may provide such other relief as it may deem appropriate. The school board may be ordered to open a future meeting or meetings to the public or to make available to the public all or parts of the minutes of the improperly closed session.

The court has the power to declare null and void any final action taken at an illegal meeting, and may enjoin the school board from future violations of the Open Meetings Act.

5 ILCS 120/3

Bromberek School District No. 65 v. Sanders, 174 Ill. App. 3d 301, 528 N.E. 2d 1336, 124 Ill. Dec. 228 (1st Dist. 1988) app. den. 124 Ill. 2d 553, 535 N.E. 2d 912, 129 Ill. Dec. 147 (1989)

6:62 How are Open Meetings Act violations enforced?

The most common means of enforcement is the issuance of a binding opinion. But the relevant law also allows that when there is a violation, or when there is probable cause to believe that there will be a violation, any person, including the State's Attorney of the county in which such noncompliance may occur, may bring a civil action in the circuit court for the judicial circuit in which the alleged noncompliance has occurred or is about to occur, or in which the affected public body has its principal office, prior to or within 60 days of the meeting alleged to be in violation of this Act or, if facts concerning the meeting are not discovered within the 60-day period, within 60 days of the discovery of a violation by the State's Attorney or, if the person timely files a request for review, within 60 days of the decision by the Attorney General to resolve a request for review by a means other than the issuance of a binding opinion.

http://foia.ilattorneygeneral.net/bindingopinions.aspx

5 ILCS 120/3

6:70 Are individuals subject to criminal charges for Open Meetings Act violations?

Violation of the Open Meetings Act by an individual is a Class C misdemeanor, punishable by a fine of up to $1,500 and/or up to 30 days in jail.

5 ILCS 120/3

730 ILCS 5/5-4.5-65

CALLING MEETINGS

6:80 When must a newly constituted board of education first meet?

Within 28 days after each election of members, a school board must organize by electing its officers and fixing a time and place for regular meetings.

105 ILCS 5/10-16

6:90 When may a school board hold meetings?

Meetings of school boards must be public and held at times and places convenient to the public.

A school board may hold regular meetings at such times as it designates in the annual notice of its regular meetings. Special meetings may be called by the president or any three members of a board of education or any two members of a board of school directors.

Public notice of all meetings must be given and no official business may be transacted except when a quorum of members is present at a regular or a special meeting.

Meetings subject to the Open Meetings Act may not be held on legal holidays except when a regular meeting date falls on a legal holiday.

5 ILCS 120/2.01 et seq.

105 ILCS 5/10-16

6:100 How must a school board give notice of its regular meetings?

A school board is required to give notice of all regular meetings of the board. At the beginning of each calendar or fiscal year, the school board must give public notice of the schedule of all its regular meetings for the year. The schedule must state the times, dates, and places of the meetings and must be posted at the principal office of the district, or, if there is no such office, at the building in which the meeting is to be held.

If the school district has a website maintained by its full-time staff, it must post notice of all its regular meetings on the website. Notice of an annual schedule of meetings must remain on the website until a new public notice of the schedule of regular meetings is approved. Any notice of a regular meeting must remain posted until the meeting is concluded. A failure to post on its website the required notice of meeting or agenda does not invalidate any meeting or any actions taken at the meeting.

5 ILCS 120/2.02 et seq.

105 ILCS 5/10-16

Argo High School Council of Local 571, I.F.T., A.F.T., A.F.L.-C.I.O. v. Argo Community High School District 217, 163 Ill. App. 3d 578, 516 N.E. 2d 834, 114 Ill. Dec. 679 (1st Dist. 1987)

6:102 Is a school board required to post an agenda before its meetings?

Except for meetings held in the event of a bona fide emergency, or with respect to open meetings to be reconvened within 24 hours, or when the time and place of a reconvened meeting is given at the original meeting and there is no change in the agenda, a school board must post an agenda at least 48 hours in advance of the holding of a meeting.

The agenda must be posted at the principal office of the school board and at the location where the meeting is to be held. If the school district has a website that the full-time staff maintains, it must post the agenda of its regular meetings on its website and each agenda must remain on the website until the meeting it concerns is concluded. A failure to post on its website the required agenda does not invalidate any meeting or any actions taken at the meeting.

The agenda must include the general subject matter of any resolution or ordinance that will be the subject of final action at the meeting. The public body conducting a public meeting shall ensure that at least one copy of any requested notice and agenda for the meeting is continuously available for public review during the entire 48-hour period preceding the meeting. Posting of the notice and agenda on a website that is maintained by the public body satisfies the requirement for continuous posting. If a notice or agenda is not continuously available for the full 48-hour period due to actions outside the control of the public body, then that lack of availability does not invalidate any meeting or action taken at a meeting.

5 ILCS 120/2.02

6:104 May a school board hold a closed session at a meeting for which its agenda does not include notice of closed session?

Yes, provided both the public meeting and the closed session are otherwise in compliance with the provisions of the Open Meetings Act.

5 ILCS 120/2a

Wyman v. Schweighart and the City of Champaign, 385 Ill. App. 3d 1099, 904 N.E. 2d 77, 328 Ill. Dec. 315 (4th Dist. 2008) 4 N.E. 2d 434, 128 Ill. Dec. 252 (5th Dist. 1989) app. den. 126 Ill. 2d 558, 541 N.E. 2d 1106, 133 Ill. Dec. 668 (1990)

Gosnell v. Hogan, 179 Ill. App. 3d 161, 534 N.E. 2d 434, 128 Ill. Dec. 252, (5th Dist. 1989) app. den. 126 Ill. 2d 558, 541 N.E.2d 1106, 133 Ill. Dec. 668 (1990)

6:110 How does a school board change its schedule of regular meeting dates?

A school board may change the dates of its regularly scheduled meetings by giving 10 days' notice in a manner set forth by statute.

5 ILCS 120/2.02

5 ILCS 120/2.03

Argo High School Council of Local 571, I.F.T., A.F.T., A.F.L.-C.I.O. v. Argo Community High School District 217, 163 Ill. App. 3d 578, 516 N.E. 2d 834, 114 Ill. Dec. 679 (1st Dist. 1987)

6:120 How does a school board call a special meeting?

Special meetings may be called by the president or by any three members of a board of education or any two members of a board of school directors.

Board members must be given notice of special meetings in writing, stating the time, place, and purpose of the meeting.

Public notice must be given and an agenda of the meeting posted at least 48 hours in advance of a special meeting. Notice also must be given to any news medium that has provided necessary information in the same manner as is given to members of the board.

Special meeting notices must include an agenda.

5 ILCS 120/2.02

105 ILCS 5/10-6

105 ILCS 5/10-16

Argo High School Council of Local 571, I.F.T., A.F.T., A.F.L.-C.I.O. v. Argo Community High School District 217, 163 Ill. App. 3d 578, 516 N.E. 2d 834, 114 Ill. Dec. 679 (1st Dist. 1987)

6:130 May a school board adjourn a meeting to another meeting?

A meeting may be adjourned to another meeting as many times as the school board deems necessary so long as the school board complies with the provisions of the Open Meetings Act with respect to each reconvened meeting.

Public notice, including an agenda, must be given for each reconvened meeting unless the original meeting was open to the public and is to be reconvened within 24 hours. Public notice also is not required when an announcement of the time and place of the reconvened meeting was made at the original public meeting and there is no change in the agenda.

5 ILCS 120/1 et seq.

NOTICE OF MEETINGS

6:140 How must public notice of school board meetings be given?

Public notice must be given by posting a copy of the notice at the principal office of the school board or, if no such office exists, at the building in which the meeting is to be held. The board must supply copies of the notice of its regular meetings, and of the notice of any special, emergency, rescheduled, or reconvened meeting, to any news medium that has filed an annual request for notice. Any such news medium must also be given the same notice of all special, emergency, rescheduled, or reconvened meetings in the same manner as is given to members of the school board provided such news medium has given the school board an address or telephone number within the territorial jurisdiction of the school board at which such notice may be given.

Public notice must include an agenda in the case of a regular, special, rescheduled, or reconvened meeting. An agenda for a regular meeting must be posted at the principal office of the school board and at the location where the meeting is to be held.

If the school district has a website that the full-time staff maintains, it must post the agenda of its regular meetings on its website and each agenda must remain on the website until the meeting it concerns is concluded. A failure to post on its website the required notice of meeting does not invalidate any meeting or any actions taken at the meeting.

The agenda must include the general subject matter of any resolution or ordinance that will be the subject of final action at the meeting. The public body conducting a public meeting shall ensure that at least one copy of any requested notice and agenda for the meeting is continuously available for public review during the entire 48-hour period preceding the meeting. Posting of the notice and agenda on a website that is maintained by the public body satisfies the requirement for continuous posting. If a notice or agenda is not continuously available for the full 48-hour period due to actions outside the control of the public body, then that lack of availability does not invalidate any meeting or action taken at a meeting.

5 ILCS 120/2.02

6:145 When a statute requires that a school board give notice, what form must the notice take?

In some cases, the relevant statute establishes a form of notice and defines the terms under which the notice is legally sufficient. The Truth in Taxation Act requires a precise form of notice. In other cases, the relevant statute merely requires that notice be given. In such cases, the form of the notice need only be sufficient to provide notice to the public. In any instance when the provision of notice is required, the school official should obtain a certificate of publication that specifies that the newspaper conforms to the requirements of the Notice by Publication Act and that shows when the notice was published. Notices must be published for three consecutive weeks.

35 ILCS 200/18-80

715 ILCS 5/1 et seq.

6:150 May a school board hold an unscheduled emergency meeting without notice?

In a bona fide emergency, notice requirements may be waived. However, notice must be given as soon as practicable prior to such meeting to any news media that have filed annual requests for meeting notices. One Illinois appellate court has held that "emergency" means a sudden and serious event or unforeseen change in circumstances that calls for immediate action to avert, control, or remedy harm or an urgent need for relief or help.

5 ILCS 120/2.02

Board of Education of the City of Chicago v. Illinois State Board of Education, 2017 IL 161147 App (1st), 78 N.E. 3d 1080, 413 Ill. Dec. 804

Laukhuf v. Board of Education of School District No. 140, et al., 02 CH 59 (Cir. Ct. of the 11th Judicial Circuit, Woodford County)

6:160 What must a school board include in its meeting agenda?

The content of a school board meeting agenda is at the discretion of the board except that the agenda must include the subject matter of any resolution that will be the subject of final action at the meeting. The Open Meetings Act requires only that an agenda be included with the public notice of special meetings, rescheduled regular meetings, and reconvened meetings for which public notice is required and that an agenda be posted 48 hours prior to a regular meeting.

5 ILCS 120/2.02

6:165 May a school board conduct business not listed on its agenda at a regular, special, rescheduled, or reconvened meeting?

At a special meeting or a rescheduled or reconvened meeting that requires an agenda, the school board may transact only the business that is germane to items listed on the agenda. Action taken on any item not identified on the agenda may be held invalid by a court.

At a regular meeting, the school board may discuss items not listed on its agenda, but one Illinois appellate court has held a board may not take action on items not specifically listed in its agenda. The court decided that while the Open Meetings Act permits "the consideration of" items not specifically set forth in the agenda, that phrase "permits deliberations and discussion and not actions taken." A 2012 change in the relevant statute requires that the pre-meeting agenda list any resolution to be considered at a board meeting.

5 ILCS 120/2.02

Rice v. Board of Trustees of Adams County, 326 Ill. App. 3d 1120, 762 N.E. 2d 1205, 261 Ill. Dec. 278 (4th Dist. 2002)

CLOSED MEETINGS

6:170 When may a school board hold a closed meeting?

The Open Meetings Act requires all meetings of school boards to be open meetings. Meetings or portions of regular or special board meetings may be closed to the public only under the exceptions provided for in the Act. The only exceptions are for collective bargaining negotiations and grievance arbitrations that are exempt from the provisions of the Open Meetings Act. The following are closed meeting exceptions:

1) The appointment, employment, compensation, discipline, performance, or dismissal of specific employees of the public body or legal counsel for the public body, including hearing testimony on a complaint lodged against an employee of the public body or against legal counsel for the public body to determine its validity.

2) Collective negotiating matters between the public body and its employees or their representatives or deliberations concerning salary schedules for one or more classes of employees.

3) The selection of a person to fill a public office, as public office is defined in the Open Meetings Act; or to fill a vacancy in a public office when the public body is given the power to appoint under law; or the discipline, performance or removal of the occupant of a public office when the public body is given power to remove the occupant under law.

4) Evidence or testimony presented in open hearing, or in closed hearing where specifically authorized by law, to a quasi-adjudicative body as defined in the Open Meetings Act, provided that the body prepares and makes available for public inspection a written decision setting forth its determinative reasoning.

5) The purchase or lease of real property for the use of the public body.

6) The setting of a price for the sale or lease of property owned by the public body.

7) The sale or purchase of securities, investments, or investment contracts.

8) Emergency security procedures and the use of personnel and equipment to respond to actual danger to the safety of employees, students, staff, the public, or public property.

9) Student disciplinary cases.

10) The placement of individual students in special education programs and other matters relating to individual students.

11) Litigation, when an action against, affecting, or on behalf of the particular public body has been filed and is pending before a court or administrative tribunal, or when the public body finds that an action is probable or imminent, in which case the basis for the finding must be recorded and entered into the minutes of the closed meeting.

12) The establishment of reserves or settlement of claims as provided in the Local Governmental and Governmental Employees Tort Immunity Act, if otherwise the disposition of a claim or potential claim might be prejudiced, or the review or discussion of

claims, loss or risk management information, records, data, advice or communications from or with respect to any insurer of the public body or intergovernmental risk management association or self-insurance pool of which the public body is a member.

13) Self-evaluation, practices and procedures, or professional ethics, when meeting with a representative of a statewide association of which the public body is a member.

14) Discussion of minutes of meetings lawfully closed under the Open Meetings Act, whether for purpose of approval by the body of the minutes or semi-annual review of the minutes.

15) Meetings between internal or external auditors and school board audit committees, finance committees, and their equivalents when the discussion involves internal control weaknesses, identification of potential fraud risk areas, known or suspected frauds, and fraud interviews conducted in accordance with generally accepted U.S. auditing standards.

5 ILCS 120/2

115 ILCS 5/18

Illinois Attorney General Public Access Opinion 16-007

Illinois Attorney General Public Access Opinion 17-004

Wyman v. Schweighart and the City of Champaign, 385 Ill. App. 3d 1099, 904 N.E. 2d 77, 328 Ill. Dec. 315 (4th Dist. 2008)

Galena Gazette Publications, Inc. v. County of Jo Daviess, 375 Ill. App. 3d 338, 872 N.E. 2d 1049, 313 Ill. Dec. 660 (2nd Dist. 2007).

Henry v. Anderson, 356 Ill. App. 3d 952, 827 N.E. 2d 522, 292 Ill. Dec. 993 (4th Dist. 2005)

People ex rel. Ryan v. Villa Park, 212 Ill. App. 3d 187, 570 N.E. 2d 882, 156 Ill. Dec. 406 (2nd Dist. 1991)

6:172 Who may be present during a properly convened closed session?

Members of the public body have a right to be present in a closed session because there is no authority for a public body to exclude one of its members and no means to enforce such exclusion. The public body has authority to decide who, besides its members, may enter a properly convened closed session.

Wyman v. Schweighart and the City of Champaign, 385 Ill. App. 3d 1099, 904 N.E. 2d 77, 328 Ill. Dec. 315 (4th Dist. 2008)

6:174 If a school board votes to enter a closed session, what may be discussed in the closed session?

A school board's discussion in closed session is limited to those matters that are germane to the motion to enter the closed session. Once the board is properly in closed session, in order to consider any other matter that might be properly discussed in closed session the board must exit the closed session, return to open session, and vote in public to re-enter closed session for a different purpose.

5 ILCS 120/2a

Galena Gazette Publications, Inc. v. County of Jo Daviess, 375 Ill. App. 3d 338, 872 N.E. 2d 1049, 313 Ill. Dec. 660 (2nd Dist. 2007).

Henry v. Anderson, 356 Ill. App. 3d 952, 827 N.E. 2d 522, 292 Ill. Dec. 993 (4th Dist. 2005)

6:176 Must a school board keep a verbatim record of its closed sessions?

A school board must keep a verbatim record of all its closed meetings in the form of an audio or video recording. Written minutes are also required.

Closed session minutes may be kept confidential, but the board must review the entire body of its closed session written minutes every six months to determine if there is a continuing need for confidentiality as to all or any part of those minutes.

A school board's failure to strictly comply with the semi-annual review of closed session minutes does not cause the minutes or the verbatim record to become public or available for inspection in any judicial proceeding other than a proceeding involving an alleged violation of the Act if the school board, within 60 days of discovering its failure to strictly comply, reviews the closed session minutes and determines and thereafter reports in open session that either the need for confidentiality still exists as to all or part of the minutes or verbatim record; or that the minutes or recordings or portions thereof no longer require confidential treatment and are available for public inspection.

5 ILCS 120/2.06 (a)

5 ILCS 120/2.06 (d)

105 ILCS 5/10-7

6:177 Under what circumstances may the verbatim record be destroyed?

The verbatim record may be destroyed without notification to or the approval of the Records Commission or the State Archivist under the Local Records Act no less than 18 months after the completion of the meeting recorded, but only after

1) The school board approves the destruction of a particular recording; and

2) The school board approves minutes of the closed meeting that meet the written minutes requirements of the Open Meetings Act.

5 ILCS 120/2.06(c)

6:178 Under what circumstances may a verbatim record be made public?

Courts have authority to examine closed session minutes in camera (privately) in deciding litigable issues. Courts also have authority to require school board members to testify about what occurred in closed session, and may order the release to the public of closed session minutes.

Unless the school board has made a determination that the verbatim recording no longer requires confidential treatment or otherwise consents to disclosure, the verbatim record of a meeting closed to the public is not open for public inspection or subject to discovery in any administrative proceeding other than one brought to enforce the Open Meetings Act.

In the case of a civil action bought to enforce the Act, the court, if the judge believes such an examination is necessary, may conduct such in camera examination of the verbatim record as it finds appropriate in order to determine whether there has been an Open Meetings Act violation.

In the case of a criminal proceeding, the court may conduct an examination in order to determine what portions, if any, must be made available to the parties for use as evidence in the prosecution. Any such initial inspection must be held in camera.

If the court determines that a complaint or suit brought for noncompliance under the Open Meetings Act is valid it may, for the purposes of discovery, redact from the minutes of the meeting closed to the public any information deemed qualified under the attorney-client privilege. The provisions of this subsection of the Open Meetings Act do not supersede the privacy or confidentiality provisions of state or federal law.

In all other cases, minutes of meetings closed to the public are available only after the school board determines that is no longer necessary to protect the public interest or the privacy of an individual by keeping them confidential.

5 ILCS 120/2.06(e) et seq.

5 ILCS 120/3(b) et seq.

5 ILCS 140/11(d), (f)

Bobkoski v. Board of Education of Cary Consolidated School District 26, 141 F.R.D. 88 (N.D. Ill. 1992)

Illinois Educational Labor Relations Board v. Homer Community Consolidated School District No. 208, 160 Ill. App. 3d 730, 514 N.E. 2d 465, 112 Ill. Dec. 802, aff'd. 132 Ill. 2d 29, 547 N.E. 2d 182, 138 Ill. Dec. 213 (1989)

6:179 Under what circumstances may an individual board member inspect closed session minutes or recordings?

Normally, an individual board member acting alone has no greater authority than a member of the public. But a 2016 amendment to the Open Meetings Act made an exception that provides that access to verbatim recordings are provided to duly elected officials or appointed officials filling a vacancy of an elected office in a public body. Access is available in the public body's main office or official storage location, in the presence of a records secretary, an administrative official of the public body, or any elected official of the public body. No verbatim recordings can be recorded or removed from the office or official storage location, except by vote of the public body or by court order.

5 ILCS 120/2.06

6:180 What final actions of a school board may be taken in closed session?

None. All final actions of a school board must be taken in open session. There is, however, a Public Access Counselor opinion that finds that when a public body reaches a consensus on a matter in closed session and then fails to take action on the subject of the consensus in open session, the consensus constitutes final action.

5 ILCS 120/2

Public Access Opinion No. 12-013

6:190 May a school board poll its members or take a straw vote in closed session?

A school board may poll its members or take a preliminary vote in closed session so long as the final vote is taken in open session.

Board of Education of Springfield School District No. 186 v. Attorney General of Illinois, 2017 IL 120343, 77 N.E. 3d 625, 413 Ill. Dec. 20

Jewell v. Board of Education DuQuoin Community Unit Schools, 19 Ill. App. 3d 1091, 312 N.E. 2d 659 (5th Dist. 1974)

6:200 What procedure is required to enter closed session?

A school board must, by roll call vote in open session, pass a motion to go into closed session. The vote of each member must be publicly disclosed and recorded. The motion to close must include a legally sufficient reason for the closed session and must be entered in board minutes. Only those topics specified in the vote to close may be deliberated during the closed session.

5 ILCS 120/2a

Wyman v. Schweighart and the City of Champaign, 385 Ill. App. 3d 1099, 904 N.E. 2d 77, 328 Ill. Dec. 315 (4th Dist. 2008)

6:210 If a school board meeting is to consist entirely of a closed session, must a board give notice?

Yes. Such a meeting presumably would be either a special meeting or a reconvened meeting stemming from a formal vote of the board at an earlier public meeting. Notice requirements for special or reconvened meetings would apply.

A public vote to go into closed session is required at the opening of the special or reconvened meeting or during the original adjourned meeting.

5 ILCS 120/2.02

6:220 With respect to the term "employment," what may a school board discuss in closed session?

A school board may meet in closed session to consider the employment of individual employees (or legal counsel). A school board may also meet in closed session to consider the performance of specific employees. The term "employment" does not include matters of policy or matters involving classifications of employees. Such matters that relate to collective bargaining may fall under the collective bargaining exception.

Even when discussion of employment may be held in closed session, final action must be taken in open session.

5 ILCS 120/2

People v. Board of Education of District 170 of Lee and Ogle Counties, 40 Ill. App. 3d 819, 353 N.E. 2d 147 (2nd Dist. 1976)

6:225 May a school board insist that complaints against employees be heard only in closed session?

Yes. A school board may vote to meet in open or, on a permissible subject, in closed session. A permissible subject for a closed meeting is for the school board to hear testimony on a complaint lodged against an employee to determine its validity.

With respect to any alleged right to criticize an employee in public at a school board meeting, the School Code allows a school board to establish reasonable rules governing public comment at its meetings. A school board probably cannot prevent a person who wishes to publicly complain about an employee from using a school board meeting as a forum for the complaint.

5 ILCS 120/2

105 ILCS 5/10-16

Leventhal v. Vista Unified School District, 973 F. Supp. 951 (D.C. So. Cal. 1997)

Stachura v. Truszkowski, 763 F. 2d 211 (6th Cir. 1985)

6:226 What effects are there to public disclosure of the causes for an employee's dismissal?

Public employees have constitutionally protected liberty interests in personal reputation, integrity, and the right to have access to future employment opportunities. When a school board seeks to dismiss an employee for causes that may impugn his or her reputation or character, and makes the stigmatizing charges public, the employee must be provided a hearing at which he or she has the opportunity to refute the charges.

If a school district places stigmatizing charges in an employee's personnel record, it has publicized the charges. If the employee disputes the accuracy of the charges, the employer must provide the employee with a "name-clearing" hearing.

Donato v. Plainview-Old Bethpage Central School District, 96 F. 3d 623 (2nd Cir. 1996) cert. den. 117 S. Ct. 1083, 519 U.S. 1150, 137 L. Ed. 2d 218

Hayes v. Phoenix Talent School District, 893 F. 2d 235 (9th Cir. 1990)

Brandt v. Board of Co-op Educational Services, Third Supervisory District, Suffolk County, New York, 820 F. 2d 41, app. after rem. 845 F. 2d 416 (2nd Cir. 1988)

Bishop v. Wood, 96 S. Ct. 2074, 426 U.S. 341, 48 L. Ed. 2d 864 (1976)

Board of Regents of State Colleges v. Roth, 92 S. Ct. 2701, 408 U.S. 564, 33 L. Ed. 2d 548 (1972)

6:227 May a school board censure one of its members for disclosing confidential information from a closed meeting?

A school board has no explicit power to censure or otherwise sanction one of its members. Neither is a school board explicitly prohibited from doing so. A censure resolution has no legal or practical effect except to publicly embarrass the censured party.

Swanson v. Board of Police Commissioners, 197 Ill. App. 3d 592, 555 N.E. 2d 35, 144 Ill. Dec. 138 (1990), cert. den., 133 Ill. 2d 874 (1990)

6:228 May a school board meet in a closed session to discuss a complaint about the conduct or performance of a board member?

There is no relevant provision in the Open Meetings Act that would permit a board to hold such a meeting in closed session. A board may discuss a complaint against an employee of the public body in closed session, but not a complaint against or about one of its members.

A board might use the self-evaluation exception to get into closed session to air such issues. The self-evaluation exception allows a board to go into closed session for "self evaluation, practices and procedures or professional ethics, when meeting with a representative of a statewide association of which the public body is a member."

5 ILCS 120/2 (1)
5 ILCS 120/2 (16)

CONDUCTING MEETINGS

6:230 What rules of procedure must a school board follow with respect to the conduct of school board meetings?

School boards are not required to follow any particular rules of procedure in the conduct of their meetings. The School Code authorizes school boards to adopt rules and regulations for the management and governance of the schools. Rules adopted by a school board must be made available for public inspection in the administrative office of the school district.

105 ILCS 5/10-20.5

6:233 Must a school board's rules of procedure be in writing?

In order to have any legal effect, rules must be in writing and available for public inspection. Moreover, written rules of procedure increase the likelihood that all members of the public body will understand and abide by them and decrease the opportunity for misunderstanding and legal challenges to board actions.

105 ILCS 5/10-20.5

6:235 Must a school board abide by any rules of procedure that it has adopted?

A public body may formally change its own rules or may temporarily suspend them. Decisions regarding rules and whether they are changed or suspended are made by majority vote of the public body. Rules that are required by law (for example, the minimum number of votes required to discharge a tenured teacher) may not be changed.

6:240 Must a school board allow time for public comment at a school board meeting?

At each public meeting of the school board, employees, and members of the public must be afforded time, subject to reasonable constraints, to comment or ask questions of the board.

105 ILCS 5/10-6
105 ILCS 5/10-16

6:244 May a school board establish a rule limiting the time for public comment?

A school board may establish reasonable time, place, and manner of speech rules that restrict public comment. A school board may establish a uniform time limit for persons who wish to address the board. Two- or three-minute time limits have survived challenge. A school board may not establish rules that address the content of speech.

Kindt v. Santa Monica Rent Control Board, 67 F. 3d 266 (9th Cir. 1995)
Collinson v. Gott, 895 F. 2d 994 (4th Cir. 1990)
Jones v. Heyman, 888 F. 2d 1328 (11th Cir. 1989)

6:245 May a school board limit a speaker who becomes repetitious, unruly, or profane?

The presiding officer may cut off a speaker who becomes unduly repetitious or drones on and on about matters of little public concern. A school official contemplating cutting off such a speaker should be careful that the decision is based on the repetitiousness or relevancy of the speech, and not disagreement with its content.

Profanity restrictions are content based. A school board's ability to control such speech is limited to a situation that the decision maker reasonably perceives as a threat or actually disrupts the orderly and fair progress of the discussion.

Surita, et al., v. Hyde, et al., 665 F. 3d 860 (7th Cir. 2011)
Kindt v. Santa Monica Rent Control Board, 67 F. 3d 266 (9th Cir. 1995)
Collinson v. Gott, 895 F. 2d 994 (4th Cir. 1990)
White v. City of Norwalk, 900 F. 2d 1421 (9th Cir. 1990)
Rosenfeld v. New Jersey, 92 S. Ct. 2479, 408 U.S. 901, 33 L. Ed. 2d 321 (1972) on rem. *State of New Jersey v. Rosenfeld,* 303 A. 2d 889 (N.J. 1973)

6:250 What is a quorum of a school board?

For a seven-member board, a quorum is four and a majority of a quorum is three. For a five-member board or board committee a quorum is three. For a three-member board or board committee, two members is a quorum and two members is also a majority of a quorum.

5 ILCS 120/1.02
105 ILCS 5/10-6
105 ILCS 5/10-12

6:260 May a school board adjourn a meeting when a quorum is not present?

If a quorum is not present at a special or regularly scheduled meeting, those members present, by a majority vote, may adjourn the meeting to a specific time and place, provided the date to which the adjournment is taken is prior to the date of the next regularly scheduled board meeting.

5 ILCS 120/2.02

6:270 May school board officers vote on motions?

Any school board member, including the president, vice president, secretary, or clerk (provided they are members of the board), may make motions, second motions, participate in debate, and vote.

On any motion requiring a record of the voting, the vote of the president and each other officer must be recorded as yes, no, abstain, or absent.

105 ILCS 5/10-7

6:280 How many members of a school board must vote for a measure in order for it to carry?

A quorum of the school board must be present to have an official meeting and to conduct business. No vote, except a vote to adjourn, has any weight and effect without a quorum present.

Unless otherwise provided by law (for example, the Open Meetings Act requires that three votes are necessary to carry a motion of a five person committee of the board), a motion is decided by a majority of the votes cast. A tie vote defeats the motion.

The following actions require an affirmative vote by a majority of the entire school board (four votes for a seven-member board) regardless of how many members are present at the meeting at which the vote is taken:

1) A motion to dismiss a tenured teacher.

2) A petition to the circuit court for an emergency election.

3) A motion to lay off employees by reason of reduction in force.

4) Adoption of a supplemental budget following a successful referendum.

The following require an affirmative vote of two-thirds of the entire school board (five votes for a seven-member board) regardless of how many members are present at the meeting at which the vote is taken:

1) The sale of school real estate or improvements thereon.

2) A property or equipment lease agreement for a term longer than 10 years.

3) Lease of school property to another governmental body.

4) Lease of a school building.

5) Exchange of building sites.

6) Request for waiver of the administrative cost cap.

5 ILCS 120/1.02
105 ILCS 5/5-22
105 ILCS 5/10-12
105 ILCS 5/10-22.11
105 ILCS 5/10-22.12
105 ILCS 5/24-12

6:285 What does it mean to "record the yeas and nays?"

The School Code requires that "On all questions involving the expenditure of money, the yeas and nays shall be taken and entered on the records of the proceedings of the board." When the school board votes on motions such as the approval of bills for payment or the approval of a contract, the minutes of the meeting must show how each member voted.

105 ILCS 5/10-7

6:286 What is a consent agenda?

A consent agenda is a listing of usually routine and uncontroversial board meeting agenda items on which the board intends to take action, but about which board members do not believe explanation or discussion will be necessary. Consent agenda items are voted on by the board with a single motion to approve all the items on the agenda. The advantage of a consent agenda is that it expedites meetings by relieving the board of the burden of voting on routine matters one by one.

However, placement of an item on the consent agenda does not eliminate any requirement for a super-majority vote or a recording of the yeas and nays. Moreover, a member of the board should be allowed to remove any item from the consent agenda for separate discussion and vote. The board should be cautious about the inclusion of items in a consent agenda that require explanation, with respect to items likely to draw comment from board members or members of the public, or with respect to items that require a roll call vote or more than a simple majority of a quorum.

105 ILCS 5/10-7

6:287 Must a school board use a roll call vote when voting to approve the items on a consent agenda?

If any item on the consent agenda requires that yeas and nays be taken and entered into the minutes, then a roll call vote is required. If any item on the consent agenda requires approval by a super-majority, then that standard would be required for the entire consent agenda. For that reason, any item requiring a super-majority probably should not appear on a consent agenda.

6:290 How is a vote of present or abstain counted?

When a statute requires concurrence of a majority of the members of a decision-making body and a member passes, abstains or does not vote, that member is deemed to have concurred with the majority of those who voted. If the statute requires an affirmative vote of a majority, then nothing less than a majority of yeas or nays is required.

Lake County Forest Preserve District v. Northern Trust Bank, 207 Ill. App. 3d 290, 565 N.E. 2d 715, 152 Ill. Dec. 182 (2nd Dist. 1990)

Prosser v. Village of Fox Lake, 91 Ill. 2d 389, 438 N.E. 2d 134, 63 Ill. Dec. 396 (1982)

6:295 May a member of a public body cast a vote by proxy?

The Open Meetings Act requires that public business be conducted openly. A proxy vote is in conflict with the legislative purpose of the Act.

5 ILCS 120/1 et seq.
105 ILCS 5/10-12

6:297 May a school board hold a meeting via telephone conference call or can a single member call in and participate electronically?

If a quorum of the members of the school board is physically present at an open meeting, a majority of the public body may allow a member of that body to attend the meeting by video or audio conference if the member is prevented from physically attending because of personal illness or disability, employment purposes or the business of the public body, or a family or other emergency. If a member wishes to attend a meeting by audio or video conference, the member must notify the recording secretary or clerk of the public body before the meeting unless advance notice is impractical.

A majority of the school board may allow a member to attend a meeting by other means only in accordance with and to the extent allowed by rules adopted by the board. The rules must conform to the requirements above and may further limit the extent to which attendance by other means is allowed and may provide for the giving of additional notice to the public or further facilitate public access to meetings.

5 ILCS 120/7

Freedom Oil Company v. Illinois Pollution Control Board, 275 Ill. App. 3d 508, 655 N.E. 2d 1184, 211 Ill. Dec. 801 (4th Dist. 1995)

6:299 What notice must a school board give the public of the business it is conducting?

In addition to agenda and posting requirements, every final action "shall be preceded by a public recital of the nature of the matter being considered and other information that will inform the public of the business being conducted." The recital must include the key terms of a proposed public contract or agreement so that a member of the public can discern the essence of the contract or agreement. The document need not be read word for word into the record, but enough detail must be provided such that a person in the audience would know what action was being taken and the essential terms of that action.

5 ILCS 120/2(e)

Allen, et al. v. Clark County Park District Board of Commissioners, 2016 IL App (4th) 150963, 67 N.E. 3d 536, 409 Ill. Dec. 324

Board of Education of Springfield School District No. 186 v. Attorney General of Illinois, 2017 IL 120343, 77 N.E. 3d 625, 413 Ill. Dec. 20

MINUTES

6:300 How should minutes be recorded?

The secretary or clerk must keep a record of the official acts of the school board in a punctual, orderly, and reliable manner. The minutes must be signed by the president and the secretary or clerk of the board.

The minutes, whether of open or closed session, must minimally include the date, time, and place of the meeting; list board members present or absent and whether the members were physically present or present by means of video or audio conference; and give a summary of discussion on all matters proposed, deliberated, or decided and a record of any votes taken. The minutes must record all motions, identify the board members making the motion and the second, and show the result of the voting.

In addition to the requirement that written minutes be kept, a verbatim record must be made of all closed sessions.

On all matters involving the expenditure of money, the yeas and nays must be recorded (a roll call vote is required).

5 ILCS 120/2.06
105 ILCS 5/10-7
105 ILCS 5/10-14
Davis-El v. O'Leary, 626 F. Supp. 1037 (N.D. Ill. 1986)

6:305 Must a public body give official approval to the minutes of its meetings?

A public body must approve its open meeting minutes within 30 days of the meeting or at the public body's second subsequent regular meeting, whichever is later. For all practical purposes, minutes are official as soon as the secretary types them into a readable form. In fact, the secretary's handwritten notes or tape recordings may be considered official for some purposes if that is all that is available, or if a court orders an investigation of what actually happened at a meeting.

However, Illinois law recognizes the approval process gives the public body an opportunity to correct any errors that the secretary might have made in recording what happened at the meeting. The Open Meetings Act provides "the minutes of meetings open to the public shall be available for public inspection within 10 days of the approval of such minutes by the public body."

5 ILCS 120/2.06(b)

6:307 Must the minutes be read aloud at a public meeting before the public body approves them?

No. An acceptable and more common practice is to provide each member of the public body with a copy of the minutes for review and to adopt a motion to "approve the minutes as written and distributed."

6:310 May a school board amend its minutes after official approval?

A school board may amend its minutes or other official record after approval in order to make the minutes or record conform to the facts. This may be done at any time by formal board action.

However, alteration of the minutes will not suffice to change the outcome of a vote, or otherwise reverse or alter a previous act. Rather, a legally sufficient vote of the school board reversing the previous act or vote is required.

Menssen v. Eureka Unit School District 140, 70 Ill. App. 3d 9, 388 N.E. 2d 273, 26 Ill. Dec. 649 (1979)

6:315 Must a public body make the minutes of its public meetings available for public inspection and copying?

Yes. The Open Meetings Act provides "the minutes of meetings open to the public shall be available for public inspection within seven days of the approval of such minutes by the public body." If the school district has a website that is maintained by its full-time staff, it must post its open session minutes on the website within seven days of their approval by the school board. Minutes must remain posted for at least 60 days after their initial posting. The statute on website posting does not specifically so provide, but it is likely that a failure to post will not invalidate any meeting or action taken at a meeting.

The Freedom of Information Act provides that public records, including the minutes of public meetings, must be made available to the public for copying as well as inspection.

5 ILCS 120/2.06(b)
5 ILCS 140/3(a)

7: SCHOOL DISTRICT RECORDS

APPLICABLE STATUTES

7:10 Which statutes govern access to school district records?

With respect to inspection, school district records that were prepared or received prior to July 1, 1984, are governed by the Local Records Act; reports and records prepared or received on or after July 1, 1984, are governed by the Freedom of Information Act.

Student records are regulated by the Illinois Student Records Act and the federal Family Educational Rights and Privacy Act.

The records of school employees are regulated by the state Personnel Record Review Act.

20 U.S.C. 1232g
5 ILCS 140/1 et seq.
50 ILCS 205/15
105 ILCS 10/1 et seq.
820 ILCS 40/2 et seq.
Spinelli v. Immanuel Evangelical Lutheran Congregation, Inc., 144 Ill. App. 3d 325, 494 N.E. 2d 196, 98 Ill. Dec. 269 (2nd Dist. 1986), aff'd. in part, rev. in part 118 Ill. 2d 389, 515 N.E. 2d 1222, 113 Ill. Dec. 915 (1987)

7:12 Which school district records covered by the Local Records Act are available for public access and inspection?

The Local Records Act requires the maintenance of certain school district financial records and allows public access and inspection of those records. The Local Records Act applies to records prepared or received by a school district before July 1, 1984.

50 ILCS 205/3a

7:20 When may school officials destroy school district records?

The Local Records Act provides, "All public records made or received by, or under the authority of, or coming into the custody, control, or possession of any officer or agency shall not be mutilated, destroyed, transferred, removed, or otherwise damaged or disposed of, in whole or in part, except as provided by law."

"Public record" is defined broadly. The Act provides such records may be destroyed only with the authorization of the Local Records Commission. Minutes and other records must be retained in perpetuity unless the school board seeks authorization from the Local Records Commission to destroy them. Whether such authorization is granted will most likely depend upon the age and nature of the records.

50 ILCS 205/2
50 ILCS 205/4
50 ILCS 205/10

7:30 For how long must a school board keep state aid records?

A school board must keep records to substantiate its state aid claims for at least three years.

105 ILCS 5/10-20.1

PERSONNEL RECORDS

7:40 Do school district employees have a right to inspect their school district personnel records?

School employees may have the right to access their personnel records if a collective bargaining agreement so provides or pursuant to the Illinois Personnel Record Review Act.

The Act applies to school districts having five or more employees. Under the Act, an employee may inspect most personnel documents dated July 1, 1984 or later that have been or are intended to be used for employment, promotion, transfer, additional compensation, discharge, or discipline.

820 ILCS 40/0.01 et seq.
Spinelli v. Immanuel Evangelical Lutheran Congregation, Inc., 144 Ill. App. 3d 325, 494 N.E. 2d 196, 98 Ill. Dec. 269 (2nd Dist. 1986), aff'd. in part, rev. in part 118 Ill. 2d 389, 515 N.E. 2d 1222, 113 Ill. Dec. 915 (1987)

7:50 What procedures govern the inspection of personnel records?

The procedures governing the inspection of employee records may be covered in a local employee collective bargaining agreement. Rules regarding inspection of personnel records are subject to bargaining when a recognized bargaining unit is involved.

In other cases, the procedures that may be used are contained in the Personnel Record Review Act.

820 ILCS 40/0.01 et seq.

7:55 What information about a teacher's qualifications is a school required to give a parent who requests such information?

Any school district that receives federal funds must notify the parents of each student attending any school receiving funds that the parents may request, and the district will provide the parents on request and in a timely manner information regarding the professional qualifications of the student's classroom teachers including at a minimum:

1) Whether the teacher has met state licensing criteria for the grade levels and subject areas in which the teacher provides instruction;

2) Whether the teacher is teaching under emergency or other provisional status through which state qualification or licensing criteria have been waived;

3) Whether the teacher is teaching in the field of discipline of the certification of the teacher; and

4) Whether the child is provided services by paraprofessionals and, if so, their qualifications.

A school is required to provide parents with notice of the level of achievement of their child on each of the state academic assessments required under federal law and is required to timely notify parents when their child has been assigned, or has been taught for more than four weeks by a teacher who is not highly qualified.

20 U.S.C. 6312(e)

7:60 What parts of an employee's personnel record may a school board withhold from inspection?

Provided an applicable collective bargaining agreement does not provide to the contrary, a school board may withhold from inspection and copying

1) Letters of reference;

2) Any portion of a test document, except that the employee may see a cumulative total test score for either a section or the entire test document;

3) Materials that are used by the school board for management planning including, but not limited to, judgments, external peer review, documents, or recommendations concerning future salary increases and other wage treatments, school board bonus plans, promotion and job assignments, or other comments or ratings used for a school board's planning purposes;

4) Information of a personal nature about a person other than the employee if disclosure of the information would constitute a "clearly unwarranted invasion of the other person's privacy; unless the disclosure is consented to in writing by the individual subjects of the information;"

5) Any records relevant to any pending claim between the school board and the employee that might be discovered in a legal proceeding;

6) Investigatory or security records maintained by the school board to investigate criminal conduct by an employee or other activity by the employee that could reasonably be expected to harm school property, operations, or business, or could by the employee's activity cause the school board financial liability unless and until the school board takes adverse personnel action based on information in that record; and

7) Performance evaluations.

820 ILCS 40/7
820 ILCS 40/10
820 ILCS 40/11

7:70 May an employee copy the contents of his or her personnel file?

An employee may obtain copies of non-confidential information contained in his or her personnel file. A school board may charge a copying fee not to exceed the cost of duplication.

820 ILCS 40/3

7:80 Are employee personnel records subject to public access and inspection?

Employee personnel records are exempt from the requirements of laws granting public access to and inspection of school district records except as such records bear on the public duties of the employee. The exemption is permissive, however, and may be waived by the employee. Performance evaluations may not be disclosed, although the exclusive bargaining representative may have effective access to summative ratings when examining groupings in conjunction with a reduction in force.

An employee's employment contract is a public record bearing on the public duties of a public employee and is not exempt from disclosure. To the extent that a personnel file contains both private information of the type ordinarily intended to be protected and information that bears on public duties, a trial court must determine through an in camera inspection of the file whether the requested information is exempt as a clearly unwarranted invasion of personal privacy and whether the presence of exempt private information can be cured through redaction.

5 ILCS 140/7
5 ILCS 140/11

Gekas v. Williamson, 393 Ill. App. 3d 573, 912 N.E. 2d 347, 332 Ill. Dec. 161 (4th Dist. 2009)

Stern v. Wheaton-Warrenville Community Unit School District 200, 233 Ill. 2d. 396, 910 N.E. 2d 85, 331 Ill. Dec. 12 (2009)

Reppert v. Southern Illinois University, 375 Ill. App. 3d 502, 874 N.E. 2d 905, 314 Ill. Dec. 540 (4th Dist. 2007)

Copley Press, Inc. v. Board of Education for Peoria School Dist. No. 150, 359 Ill. App. 3d 321, 834 N.E. 2d 558, 296 Ill. Dec. 1. (3rd Dist. 2005)

Lieber v. Board of Trustees of Southern Illinois University, 176 Ill. 2d 401, 223 Ill. Dec. 641, 680 N.E. 2d 374 (1997).

7:90 May a school board make employee disciplinary records public over the employee's objections?

A school board may not divulge a disciplinary report, letter of reprimand, or other disciplinary action to a third party other than the employee's labor organization or the employee's representative unless advance written notice is provided to the employee by first class mail to the employee's last known address.

However, advance written notice to the employee is not required under any of these conditions:

1) The employee has specifically waived the requirement of written notice as part of a written and signed employment application.

2) The disclosure is ordered in a legal proceeding or arbitration.

3) The information is requested by a government agency as a result of a claim by an employee or in connection with a criminal investigation by a governmental agency.

If the school district receives a Freedom of Information Act request for a disciplinary report, letter of reprimand, or other employee disciplinary action, it may provide notification to the employee by first class mail or by electronic mail, if available.

820 ILCS 40/7(1)

7:100 Are school boards restricted in what information may be collected and inserted in employee personnel records?

An employer may not gather or keep records of employee associations, political activities, publications, communications, or non-employment activities unless the employee submits the information in writing or authorizes the employer in writing to keep or gather the information.

These prohibitions do not apply to activities that occur on the employer's premises or during working hours that interfere with the performance of the employee's duties or the duties of other employees or activities, regardless of when and where occurring, that constitute criminal conduct or may reasonably be expected to harm the employer's property, operations, or business, or could, by the employee's action, cause the employer financial liability.

The employer must purge from an employee's file records relating to a Department of Children and Family Services investigation that results in an unfounded report.

820 ILCS 40/9

820 ILCS 40/13

7:110 What happens if a school district or a vendor inadvertently discloses employee or retiree private information such as Social Security numbers or health insurance elections?

The Personnel Record Review Act does not address this question. However, the federal Health Insurance Portability and Protection Act of 1996 (HIPPA) prohibits the disclosure of individually identifiable health information to another person, but employment records held by a covered entity in its role as employer are specifically excluded from HIPPA protection.

To prevail on a negligence claim, the employee must show the employer or the vendor had a duty to protect the information. The Personal Information Protection Act requires only that any data collector that maintains computerized data that includes personal information that the data collector does not own or license notify the owner or licensee of the information of any breach of security immediately following discovery if the personal information was, or reasonably believed to have been, acquired by an unauthorized person.

Except when the disclosure causes actual damages resulting from purely economic injury, it is unlikely that a plaintiff can recover for disclosure of private information.

42 U.S.C. 1320d-6

815 ILCS 530/1 et seq.

Cooney, et al. v. Chicago Public Schools, 407 Ill. App. 3d 358, 943 N.E. 2d 23, 347 Ill. Dec. 733 (1st Dist. 2010)

7:120 What is meant by the prohibition against keeping records as to employee associations?

A school board is prohibited from keeping records of employee activities or associations when these activities or associations are not related to the employee's job. The prohibition is intended to prevent the accumulation and retention of information as to non-job-related employee politics, religion, affiliation, and belief.

820 ILCS 40/9

7:130 Under what circumstances must a school board delete disciplinary information from an employee personnel file?

Disciplinary reports, letters of reprimand, or other disciplinary records that are more than four years old must be deleted from a personnel file when the contents of the personnel file are provided to third parties except in conjunction with a legal proceeding or arbitration.

The relevant law does not require that such material be removed from the file. The retention of old employee disciplinary records is necessary to establish patterns of behavior or conduct and old material should not be removed from an employee file unless the material is found to be false or the material is so old that it is clearly no longer relevant.

820 ILCS 40/8

7:140 May an employee remove material from his or her personnel file?

Except in the case of Department of Children and Family Service investigations that have been returned unfounded, an employee does not have a statutory right to remove material from his or her employer-maintained personnel file.

820 ILCS 40/6
820 ILCS 40/13

7:150 What are the employee's rights if the employee disagrees with information contained in his or her personnel file?

In the event an employee disagrees with some portion of the contents of his or her personnel file, the employee may submit a written statement and the employer is required to attach the statement to the disputed portion of the file.

820 ILCS 40/6

STUDENT RECORDS

7:160 What is the purpose of the Student Records Act?

The purpose of the Student Records Act is to establish a degree of privacy and confidentiality with regard to student records. It gives parents and students limited access to student records, the right to inspect and copy the contents of the records, and the right to challenge material contained in them. The Act restricts who may have access to student records and what may be disclosed from them.

105 ILCS 10/1 et seq.

7:165 May a teacher permit students to grade each other's papers?

Probably. The United States Supreme Court has held that a student assignment, as soon as it is peer-graded by another student, does not satisfy the definition of "education records" within the Family Educational Rights and Privacy Act (FERPA). Thus, FERPA is not violated by such grading or by calling out the scores.

The court held that education records under FERPA are records containing information directly related to a student, which are maintained by an educational agency or institution or by a person acting for such agency or institution, and concluded that the word "maintained" suggests FERPA records will be kept in a filing cabinet in a records room at the school or on a permanent secure database, perhaps even after the student is no longer enrolled. The court also held that the phrase "acting for" connotes agents of the school, such as teachers, administrators, and other school employees. The court held FERPA implies that education records are institutional records kept by a single central custodian, such as a registrar, not individual assignments handled by many student graders in their separate classrooms.

How an Illinois court examining the same question would interpret the subject under the Illinois Student Records Act is uncertain.

20 U.S.C. 1232g
105 ILCS 10/1 et seq.
Falvo v. Owasso Independent School District, 122 S. Ct. 934, 543 U.S. 426, 151 L. Ed. 2d 896 (2002)

7:170 What are student records within the meaning of the Student Records Act?

A student record is any writing or other recorded information created on or after January 1, 1975 concerning a student and by which a student may be individually identified, maintained by a school or at its direction or by an employee of a school, regardless of how or where the information is stored. The Student Records Act applies to the records of current students and students previously enrolled. Orders of protection must be kept in a student's record.

Records maintained by a school employee for his or her personal use are not covered by the Act if those records are destroyed no later than the student's graduation or permanent withdrawal from school.

105 ILCS 10/1 et seq.

750 ILCS 60/222(f)

Lindeman v. Kelso School District No. 458, 127 Wash. 2d 526, 111 P. 3d 1235 (2005)

Falvo v. Owasso Independent School District, 122 S. Ct. 934, 543 U.S. 426, 151 L. Ed. 2d 896 (2002)

Sieck v. Oak Park-River Forest High School District No. 200, 807 F. Supp. 73 (N.D. Ill. 1992)

7:171 Are emails among school officials about a student records within the meaning of the Student Records Act?

Yes. Emails and other electronic records fall within the definition of records in the Student Records Act, although some email may be ephemeral and a school district might argue such email is not "maintained."

105 ILCS 10/2(d)

7:172 Are the records of a police officer who works at school student records?

Student records do not include information maintained by law enforcement professionals working in the school.

105 ILCS 10/2(d)

7:180 What is a student records custodian?

Each public school must designate an official records custodian who is responsible for the maintenance, care, and security of all student records regardless of whether or not the records are in his or her personal custody or control. The custodian must take all reasonable measures to prevent unauthorized access to, or dissemination of, student records. School boards must take reasonable measures to assure persons affected by the Student Records Act are informed of their rights and obligations.

105 ILCS 10/3 et seq.

Human Rights Authority of the State of Illinois Guardianship and Advocacy Commission by Aune v. Miller, 124 Ill. App. 3d 701, 464 N.E. 2d 833, 79 Ill. Dec. 929 (3rd Dist. 1984)

7:190 Does federal law govern student records?

The federal Family Educational Rights and Privacy Act (FERPA) regulates student records. Its provisions are similar to those of the Illinois Student Records Act.

20 U.S.C. 1232

7:200 Who has the right to access, inspect, and copy student records?

Parents and any person designated a representative by a parent have rights of access, inspection, and copying with regard to both permanent and temporary student records. Students have a right to access, inspect, and copy their permanent records and may be permitted access to their temporary records. The following categories of persons are also permitted access:

1) Employees or officials of the school district or the State Board of Education who have a current educational or administrative interest in the student;

2) The records custodian of another school in which the student has enrolled or will enroll;

3) Any person for research, statistical reporting, or planning purposes, provided it is permissible and undertaken in accordance with the Family Educational Rights and Privacy Act;

4) Persons designated by court order;

5) Persons required by state or federal law;

6) Juvenile authorities when necessary for the discharge of their official duties who request information prior to the adjudication of the student and who certify in writing that the information will not be disclosed to any other party except as provided under law or order of court. "Juvenile authorities" means a judge of the circuit court and members of the staff of the court designated by the judge; parties to the proceedings under the Juvenile Court Act of 1987 and their attorneys; probation officers and court appointed advocates for the juvenile authorized by the judge hearing the case; any individual, public, or private agency having custody of the child pursuant to court order; any individual, public, or private agency providing education, medical, or mental health service to the child when the requested information is needed to determine the appropriate service or treatment for the minor; any potential placement provider when such release is authorized by the court for the limited purpose of determining the appropriateness of the potential placement; law enforcement officers and prosecutors; adult and juvenile prisoner review boards; authorized military personnel; and individuals authorized by court;

7) Appropriate persons in connection with an emergency if the knowledge of such information is necessary to protect the health or safety of the student or other persons;

8) A governmental agency or social service agency contracted by a governmental agency in furtherance of an investigation of a student's school attendance pursuant to the compulsory student attendance laws provided

that the records are released to the employee or agent designated by the agency;

9) Reciprocal reporting committee members under narrow circumstances specified in the Student Records Act;

10) With parental consent, the Illinois Department of Public Aid under narrow circumstances related to the collection of school lunch information; and

11) To the State Board of Education or another state government agency or between or among state government agencies in order to evaluate or audit federal or state programs or perform research and planning, but only to the extent that the release, transfer, disclosure, or dissemination is consistent with the federal Family Educational Rights and Privacy Act.

20 U.S.C. 1221 et seq.
20 U.S.C. 1232(g)
34 C.F.R. 99.31 (a)(5)
34 C.F.R. 99.8(c)
105 ILCS 10/5 et seq.
105 ILCS 5/10-20.14
105 ILCS 5/22-35
23 Ill. Admin. Code 375.20
Ibata v. Board of Education of Edwardsville CUSD 7, et al., 365 Ill. App. 3d 1056, 851 N.E. 2d 658, 303 Ill. Dec. 471 (5th Dist. 2006)

7:204 May law enforcement officers or the state's attorney gain access to student records without a court order?

The relevant statutes are unclear as to the answer to this question. It was probably the legislative intent of a 1998 amendment to the Student Records Act that law enforcement officers and officers of the court have access to permanent and temporary student records without a court order. However, the express language of Sections 5 and 6 of the Act prevent the disclosure of temporary records without a court order.

34 C.F.R. 99.31 (a)(5)
34 C.F.R. 99.8(c)
105 ILCS 10/4 (f)
105 ILCS 10/6(a)(6.5)

7:206 May school officials disclose student records in response to a subpoena?

It is common for school officials to receive requests for student records in connection with civil suits and in custody disputes. Student records may not be disclosed (even in response to a subpoena) by school officials except under circumstances authorized by the Student Records Act. Usually, disclosure requires either consent from one parent or the adult student, or if consent cannot be obtained, a court order. A 2013 amendment to the Juvenile Court Act explicitly provides that a subpoena is not a court order and should not be treated as such for purposes of inspection of juvenile records.

105 ILCS 10/6
705 ILCS 405/1-8

7:207 May school officials disclose student records to the school's attorneys without parental notice?

School officials may release student records without parental notice to the school's attorneys in conjunction with proceedings regarding a student's special education placement and almost certainly with regard to any other matter in which a legal opinion is sought or when litigation is contemplated.

Ibata v. Board of Education of Edwardsville CUSD 7, et al., 365 Ill. App. 3d 1056, 851 N.E. 2d 658, 303 Ill. Dec. 471 (5th Dist. 2006)

7:208 May school officials use a video recording of a student for disciplinary purposes?

This question usually arises when a disciplinary event is captured on a video camera that is programmed to continuously record in a public place, such as a hallway or on a school bus. Whether the video can "be used" is a complicated question that turns on whether or not the video is a student record and if so, for whom it is a student record. The video is probably not a student record for students who appear on the video in the background and who are not involved in the incident. The video is a student record for any student school officials seek to discipline as a result of the incident and it may be a student record for certain witnesses. School officials must have appropriate consent from all the students for whom the video is a student record in order to "disclose the contents" of the video. Video editing software is readily available that may make it possible to redact certain images so as to resolve records issues.

105 ILCS 10/6
Bryner v. Canyons School District, 351 P. 3d 852 (Utah Ct. App. 2015)
Timothy S. Wachter letter, Chief Privacy Officer, U.S. Department of Education, December 7, 2017

7:210 When do parental rights to access student records end?

All rights and privileges held by the parent with respect to accessing student records become exclusively those of the student on the student's 18th birthday, when the student is legally emancipated, upon graduation from high school, marriage, or entry into military service.

105 ILCS 10/2(g)

7:220 When a parent, representative, or student requests to inspect and copy student records, how promptly must the records be produced?

Access must be granted within a reasonable time, but in no case later than 10 business days after the date of receipt of the request by the official records custodian. Under certain circumstances specified in the statute the time for response may be extended for an additional five business days.

105 ILCS 10/5(c)

7:230 What student records may be withheld from parental or student access?

A parent or student may be denied access to confidential letters and statements of recommendation furnished in connection with applications for employment or admission to a post-secondary educational institution, or the receipt of an honor or honorary recognition, provided that the letters and statements are not used for purposes other than those for which they were specifically intended and were either

1) Placed in a school student record prior to January 1, 1975; or

2) The student waives access after being advised of the right to obtain the names of persons making the confidential recommendations.

A respondent named in an order of protection must be denied access to information contained in his or her child's student records.

Communications otherwise protected by law as privileged or confidential, including but not limited to information communicated in confidence to a physician, psychologist, or other psychotherapist, or information that is communicated by a student or parent in confidence to school personnel may also be withheld.

105 ILCS 10/5(e)

750 ILCS 60/222(f)

John K. v. Board of Education for School District No. 65, Cook County, 152 Ill. App. 3d 543, 504 N.E. 2d 797, 105 Ill. Dec. 512 (1st Dist. 1987) app. den. 115 Ill. 2d 542, 511 N.E. 2d 429, 110 Ill. Dec. 457 (1987)

7:240 May a student's school records or report card be withheld from the student or parent as a disciplinary measure?

No.

105 ILCS 10/8

7:250 What must be contained in a parent and student notification of student records rights?

School districts must notify students and parents of their rights to inspection and copying under the Student Records Act when the student enrolls or transfers. The notification must contain the following information:

1) The types of information contained in the permanent and temporary records of students;

2) The right to inspect and copy permanent and temporary records;

3) The cost of copying such records;

4) The right to control access and release of student records;

5) The right to request a copy of information released;

6) The rights and procedures for challenging the contents of student records, including under a procedure contained in rules, the right to remove certain college entrance examination scores;

7) The persons, agencies, or organizations having access to student records without parental consent;

8) The right to copy student records or information contained in a student record that is proposed to be destroyed or deleted and the school's schedule for reviewing and destroying such information;

9) The categories of information the school has designated as "directory information" and the right of parents to prohibit the release of such information;

10) A statement informing the parents that no person may condition the granting or withholding of any right, privilege, or benefits or make as a condition of employment, credit, or insurance the securing by any individual of information from a student's temporary record that such individual may obtain through the exercise of any right secured under the Act or these regulations;

11) The right of parents to inspect and challenge the information contained in a student record forwarded to another school district; and

12) The student record policies of the school district that are not included in the Act.

The principal of each school or his or her designee must inform staff of their Student Records Act responsibilities.

34 C.F.R. 99.3

105 ILCS 10/3

23 Ill. Admin. Code 375.30

7:260 What are student permanent records?

Student permanent record means the "minimum personal information necessary to a school in the education of the student and contained in a school student record." A permanent record must include the student's name, birth date and place, address, grades and grade level, parents' names and addresses, attendance records, gender, place of birth, grades, class rank, graduation date, grade level achieved, scores on college entrance examinations (except that a parent may request removal from an academic transcript any score received on a college entrance examination), scores received on all state assessment tests administered at the high school level, accident reports, health records, and the records pertaining to any release of permanent record information.

Honors and awards received, information about participation in school-sponsored activities or athletics, or offices held in school-sponsored organizations may be included in the student's permanent record. No other information may be included in a student's permanent record.

105 ILCS 10/2(e)
23 Ill. Admin. Code 375.10

7:270 What are student temporary records?

Student temporary record means all information contained in a school student record but not contained in the student permanent record. A temporary record may include family background information; intelligence test scores; aptitude test scores; scores received on all state assessment tests administered at the elementary grade levels (kindergarten through eighth); reports of psychological evaluations including information on intelligence, personality and academic information obtained through test administration, observation or interview; elementary and secondary achievement level test results; participation in extracurricular activities including any offices held in school-sponsored activities; honors and awards received; teacher anecdotal records; other disciplinary information; special education records, 504 plans, or information from non-educational person, agencies, or organizations; and other information of clear relevance to the education of the student.

A student's temporary record must include information regarding a record of release of temporary record information; scores received on the state assessment tests administered in the elementary grade levels (i.e., K-8); a completed home language survey form; information regarding serious infractions (i.e., those involving drugs, weapons, or bodily harm to another) that resulted in expulsion, suspension, or the imposition of punishment or sanction; information provided under Section 8.6 of the Abused and Neglected Child Reporting Act [325 ILCS 5/8.6]; any biometric information that is collected; and health-related information and accident reports.

105 ILCS 10/2(f)
105 ILCS 10/4 (c), (d)
23 Ill. Admin. Code 375.10
John K. v. Board of Education for School District No. 65, Cook County, 152 Ill. App. 3d 543, 504 N.E. 2d 797, 105 Ill. Dec. 512 (1st Dist. 1987) app. den. 115 Ill. 2d 542, 511 N.E. 2d 429, 110 Ill. Dec. 457 (1987)

7:280 For how long must a school preserve a student's permanent record?

A student's permanent record must be maintained by a school for a minimum of 60 years after the student has transferred, graduated, or otherwise permanently withdrawn from school.

105 ILCS 10/4(e)

7:290 For what period may a school retain a student's temporary record?

A student's temporary record must be maintained for not less than five years after the student has transferred, graduated, or otherwise withdrawn from school.

105 ILCS 10/4(f)

7:300 What directory information contained in student records may be made public by a school district?

Directory information is the student's name, address, gender, grade level, and birth date and place, and parents' names, mailing addresses, electronic mail addresses, and telephone numbers. Photographs, videos, or digital images used for informational or news-related purposes (whether by a media outlet or by the school) of a student participating in school or school-sponsored activities, organizations, and athletics that have appeared in school publications, such as yearbooks, newspapers, or sporting or fine arts programs, except that: No photograph highlighting individual faces can be used for commercial purposes, including solicitation, advertising, promotion or fundraising without the prior, specific, dated, and written consent of the parent or student, as applicable. No image on a school security video recording may be designated as directory information.

Directory information includes academic awards, degrees, and honors; information in relation to school-sponsored activities, organizations, and athletics; major field of study; and period of attendance in the school.

No student Social Security number or student identification (ID) or unique student identifier can be designated as directory information. Directory information may be released to the general public, unless a parent requests that any or all the directory information not be released on his/her child. School districts shall notify parents annually of the information that is considered to be directory information and of the procedures to be used by parents to request that specific information not be released.

34 C.F.R. 99.3
105 ILCS 10/6(e)
23 Ill. Admin. Code 375.80

7:305 Must schools make student directory information available to military recruiters?

Beginning July 1, 2002, schools must provide military recruiters the same access to students and to directory information about the students as is provided to colleges or prospective employers unless the school board has adopted a policy denying or restricting access by military recruiters.

10 U.S.C. 503
20 U.S.C. 7908

7:307 From whom must directory information be withheld?

A school district, including its agents, employees, student or alumni associations, or any affiliates may not provide a student's name, address, telephone number, social security number, email address, or other personal identifying information to a business organization or financial institution that issues credit or debit cards.

105 ILCS 5/10-20.38

7:310 What notice must be given to parents before a school releases student records to another school district?

No information from student records may be released to another school unless otherwise permitted by the Student Records Act or unless the parents receive prior written notice of the nature and substance of the information proposed to be released. Also, prior to the release of school records, the parents must be given an opportunity to inspect and copy the records and challenge their contents.

105 ILCS 10/5(b)
23 Ill. Admin. Code 375.70

7:320 Does the Illinois Freedom of Information Act provide public access to student records?

The Freedom of Information Act provides that information prohibited from disclosure by state or federal law is exempt from access under the Act. Therefore, access to student records is not possible under the Act.

5 ILCS 140/7
5 ILCS 140/7.5
105 ILCS 10/6

Bowie v. Evanston Community Consolidated School District No. 65, 165 Ill. App. 3d 101, 522 N.E. 2d 669, 119 Ill. Dec. 7 (1st Dist. 1988) app. allowed 122 Ill. 2d 570, 530 N.E. 2d 239, 125 Ill. Dec. 211, aff'd. 128 Ill. 2d 373, 538 N.E. 2d 557, 131 Ill. Dec. 182 (1989)

7:330 Must a school maintain a record of the information that is released from a student record?

A record of any information released from a student record must be made and kept as a part of the student record. The record of release must be maintained for the life of the student record and is available only to the parent, student, and the official records custodian. Each record of release must include

1) The nature and substance of the information released;

2) The name and signature of the official records custodian releasing the information;

3) The name of the person requesting the information, the capacity in which the request has been made, and the purpose of the request;

4) The date of the release; and

5) A copy of consent to the release.

Except for parents and students, no person to whom information is released, and no person designated a representative by a parent, may permit any other person to have access to information without a prior consent of the parent.

105 ILCS 10/6(c), (d)

7:340 May a school district restrict parental access to student psychological reports or do parents have a right to review raw material?

Parents may review any material contained in student records, including material upon which further conclusions are drawn and any raw psychological data. The school or the parent may elect to have present at the time of review a qualified professional to assist in the interpretation of raw data.

105 ILCS 10/5(a), (b)

John K. v. Board of Education for School District No. 65, Cook County, 152 Ill. App. 3d 543, 504 N.E. 2d 797, 105 Ill. Dec. 512 (1st Dist. 1987) app. den. 115 Ill. 2d 542, 511 N.E. 2d 429, 110 Ill. Dec. 457 (1987)

7:350 May parents challenge the contents of a student's records?

Parents may challenge the accuracy, relevance, or propriety of any entry in a student record except

1) Academic grades;

2) The name and contact information for the official records custodian; and

3) References to expulsions or out of school suspensions if the challenge is made at the time the student's records are forwarded to another school to which the student is transferring. There are hearing procedures by which disputed information may be removed from a student record as a result of parental challenge.

Parents may insert in their child's school student record a statement of reasonable length setting forth their position on any disputed information contained in the record. The school must include a copy of this statement in any subsequent dissemination of the information in dispute.

105 ILCS 10/7

23 Ill. Admin. Code 375.90

7:360 What are the hearing procedures for student record challenges?

Each school board must establish administrative procedures for parents to challenge the content of student records. The procedural aspects of the policy must include at minimum: The request for a hearing be submitted in writing to the school district's official records custodian and must contain notice of the specific entry or entries to be challenged and the basis of the challenge. The challenge procedures must include an initial informal conference with the parents, within 15 school days of receipt of the request for a hearing.

If the challenge is not resolved by the informal conference, formal procedures follow. A hearing officer, who is not employed in the attendance center in which the student is enrolled, is appointed by the school. The hearing officer must notify parents and school officials of the time and place and conduct a hearing no later than 15 days after the informal conference unless an extension of time is agreed upon by the parents and school officials.

At the hearing each party has the rights outlined in Section 7 of the Student Records Act. A verbatim record of the hearing must be made by a tape recorder or a court reporter. A typewritten transcript may be prepared by either party in the event of an appeal of the hearing officer's decision, however a typewritten transcript is not required in an appeal. The written decision of the hearing officer must, no later than 10 school days after the conclusion of the hearing, be transmitted to the parents and the school district. It shall be based solely on the information presented at the hearing and shall be one of the following: To retain the challenged contents of the student record; to remove the challenged contents of the student record; or to change, clarify, or add to the challenged contents of the student record.

Any party shall have the right to appeal the decision of the local hearing officer to the Regional Superintendent within 20 school days after the decision is transmitted. If the parent appeals, the parent must inform the school and within 10 school days the school must forward a transcript of the hearing, a copy of the record entry in question, and any other pertinent materials to the Regional Superintendent. The school may initiate an appeal by the same procedures. Upon receipt of the documents, the Regional Superintendent must examine the documents and record to determine whether the school district's proposed action in regard to the student's record is in compliance with the rules and law, make findings, and issue a written decision to the parents and the school within 20 school days of the receipt of the appeal documents. If the subject of the appeal involves the accuracy, relevance, or propriety of any entry in special education records, the Regional Superintendent should seek advice from special education personnel who were not authors of the entry, and whose special education skills are relevant to the subjects of the entry in question. The school is responsible for implementing the decision of the Regional Superintendent. Final decisions of the Regional Superintendent may be appealed to the circuit court of the county in which the school is located.

105 ILCS 10/7

23 Ill. Admin. Code 375.90

7:370 What are a school board's duties with respect to maintenance of the records of students not enrolled in school on or after the enactment of the Student Records Act (March 24, 1976)?

Schools are not required to separate permanent and temporary records, or to destroy records according to any statutorily established schedule for students not enrolled in school on or after the effective date of the Student Records Act (March 24, 1976).

However, the parents of a student not enrolled in school on or after March 24, 1976, may request a school board to comply with the Student Records Act with respect to their child's records, and the school board must honor this request.

105 ILCS 10/4(i)

7:380 How often must a school district review the contents of student records?

Each school district is required to review student records periodically as necessary, but not less than once every four years or upon a student's change in attendance center, whichever occurs first.

The purpose of review is to verify entries and eliminate or correct out-of-date, misleading, inaccurate, unnecessary, or irrelevant information.

105 ILCS 10/4(g)
23 Ill. Admin. Code 375.40 (b)

7:390 What is the penalty for violation of the Student Records Act?

Any person who is aggrieved by any violation of the Student Records Act may seek injunctive relief. Any person who is injured by a willful or negligent violation of the Act may sue for damages. Costs and attorneys' fees are available to a successful plaintiff in either cause.

The State Board of Education or designated state's attorneys also may seek injunctive relief to secure compliance with the Act.

Willful failure to comply with any provision of the Act is a petty offense, except that willful or malicious falsification of student records is a Class A misdemeanor. A Class A misdemeanor is punishable by a determinate sentence of less than one year, and a fine not to exceed $2,500 may be imposed.

Absent proof of malice, no cause of action or claim for relief, civil or criminal, is possible against any school, employee, or official of a school, or person acting at the direction of a school for any statement made or judgment expressed in any entry to a school student record of a type that does not violate the Act or the regulations issued by the State Board of Education.

105 ILCS 10/9
730 ILCS 5/5-4.5-55
John K. v. Board of Education for School District No. 65, Cook County, 152 Ill. App. 3d 543, 504 N.E. 2d 797, 105 Ill. Dec. 512 (1st Dist. 1987) app. den. 115 Ill. 2d 542, 511 N.E. 2d 429, 110 Ill. Dec. 457 (1987)

FREEDOM OF INFORMATION ACT

7:400 What are records within the meaning of the Freedom of Information Act?

The Freedom of Information Act (FOIA) defines public records broadly and the Act contains a statement that all records in the custody or possession of a public body are presumed to be open to inspection or copying. If a school district claims a record is exempt from disclosure, it has the burden of proving by clear and convincing evidence that it is exempt. The definition of public records includes all records, reports, forms, writings, letters, memorandums, books, papers, maps, photographs, microfilms, cards, tapes, recordings, electronic data processing records, electronic communications, recorded information, and all other documentary materials pertaining to the transaction of public business regardless of physical form or characteristics having been prepared by or for or having been used by, received by, in the possession of, or under the control of the school district.

To qualify as a public record, a communication must first pertain to business or community interests as opposed to private affairs, and then the courts determine if the communication has been prepared by a public body, for a public body, used by the public body, received by a public body, possessed by a public body, or controlled by a public body.

An individual member of a school board is not a "public body" within the meaning of FOIA, but messages sent or received by an individual member become records of the public body when such messages are transmitted to enough members of a public body to constitute a quorum for that particular public body.

Text messages, social media posts, and emails sent to or among school board members may be public records if they meet the public body and public record requirements, no matter where the school board member is physically located when they are sent or received, and even though the board member is using his or her personal electronic equipment to communicate.

5 ILCS 140/1.2
5 ILCS 140/2(c)
5 ILCS 140/7
5 ILCS 140/7.5
Hites v. Waubonsee Community College, 2016 IL App (2d) 150836, 56 N.E. 3d 1049, 404 Ill. Dec. 636
City of Champaign v. Madigan, 2013 IL App (4th) 120662, 992 N.E. 2d 627, 372 Ill. Dec. 787
Kenyon v. Garrels, 184 Ill. App. 3d 28, 540 N.E. 2d 11, 132 Ill. Dec. 595 (4th Dist. 1989)

7:401 Must a public body search its database records to find records in response to a Freedom of Information Act request?

School officials need not create a new database or reorganize its method of archiving data, but if the school district already stores records in its database, searching that database does not involve the creation of a new record. A database is an aggregation of data, not a discrete document. School officials must perform database searches in response to Freedom of Information Act (FOIA) requests. Sorting a database to make information intelligible does not create a new record. Fields of records are subject to FOIA discovery. School officials may even be compelled to turn over an entire database to the extent the information in it is not exempt from disclosure.

Hites v. Waubonsee Community College, 2016 IL App (2d) 150836, 56 N.E. 3d 1049, 404 Ill. Dec. 636

7:402 What is a public body under the Freedom of Information Act?

To determine whether an entity is a public body, the courts use a three-part test. The court will consider whether the entity has a legal existence independent of government resolution, the nature of the functions performed by the entity, and the degree of government control exerted.

Better Government Association v. Illinois High School Association, 2016 IL App (1st) 151356, __ N.E. __, __ Ill. Dec. __

Rockford Newspapers, Inc. v. Northern Illinois Council on Alcoholism and Drug Dependence, 64 Ill. App. 3d 94, 380 N.E. 2d 1192, 21 Ill. Dec. 16 (2nd Dist. 1978)

7:405 Who is a Freedom of Information officer?

Each public body (school district) must designate one or more officials or employees to act as its Freedom of Information officer or officers. Except in instances when records are furnished immediately, Freedom of Information officers, or their designees, shall receive requests submitted to the public body under FOIA, ensure that the public body responds to requests in a timely fashion, and issue FOIA responses.

Freedom of Information officers must develop a list of documents or categories of records that the public body must immediately disclose upon request.

Upon receiving a request for a public record, the Freedom of Information officer must

1) Note the date the public body receives the written request;

2) Compute the day on which the period for response will expire and make a notation of that date on the written request;

3) Maintain an electronic or paper copy of a written request, including all documents submitted with the request until the request has been complied with or denied; and

4) Create a file for the retention of the original request, a copy of the response, a record of written communications with the requester, and a copy of other communications.

Freedom of Information officers must, by July 1, 2010, successfully complete an electronic training curriculum developed by the Attorney General's Public Access Counselor and thereafter successfully complete an annual training program. Thereafter, whenever a new Freedom of Information officer is designated by a public body, that person must successfully complete the electronic training curriculum within 30 days after assuming the position. Successful completion of the required training curriculum within the periods provided is a prerequisite to service as a Freedom of Information officer.

5 ILCS 140/3.5

7:410 Who has the right to inspect and copy school board records under the Freedom of Information Act?

Any person may access, inspect, or copy school board public records. A person is any "individual, corporation, partnership, firm, organization, or association, acting individually or as a group."

5 ILCS 140/2(b)

7:415 May a member of the public request public records from a school board member?

The Freedom of Information Act requires the disclosure of the records of public bodies, not the records of individual members. School board records, including information pertaining to an individual board member, must be obtained by filing a request with the school district, not with the individual member. It is possible that records that a member of a public body believes are personal (including electronic messages) are discoverable under certain circumstances if those messages pertain to the business of the public body on which the member serves.

5 ILCS 140/3(a)

Quinn v. Stone, 211 Ill. App. 3d 809, 570 N.E. 2d 676, 156 Ill. Dec. 200 (1st Dist. 1991) app. den. 141 Ill. 2d 559, 580 N.E. 2d 133, 162 Ill. Dec. 507 (1991)

7:420 May a school board limit public access to school board records to residents of the school district?

No. Access to public records may not be limited based on residency or any other criterion.

5 ILCS 140/2

7:430 What must be contained in Freedom of Information Act notice to the public?

A school board must prominently display at each of its administrative or regional offices, make available for inspection and copying, and send through the mail if requested to do so, the following:

1) A brief description of the school district, including but not be limited to, a short summary of its purpose, a block diagram giving its functional subdivisions, the total amount of its operating budget, the

number and location of all of its separate offices, the approximate number of full- and part-time employees, and the identification and membership of any board, commission, committee, or council that operates in an advisory capacity relative to the operation of the school board, or that exercises control over its policies or procedures, or to which it is required to report.

2) A brief description of the methods whereby the public may request information and public records, a directory designating the Freedom of Information officer or officers, the address where requests for public records should be directed, and any fees allowable under the Act.

If the school district maintains a website, this information must be posted there.

5 ILCS 140/4

7:435 Must a school board maintain a list of records it maintains?

A school board must maintain and make available for inspection and copying a reasonably current list of all types or categories of records under its control that were prepared or received after July 1, 1984. The list must be reasonably detailed in order to aid persons in obtaining access to the public records. A school board must also furnish upon request a description of the manner in which public records stored by means of electronic data processing may be obtained in a form comprehensible to persons lacking knowledge of computer language or printout format.

5 ILCS 140/5

7:440 May a school board adopt rules regulating the time and place at which citizens may have access to public records?

A school board may promulgate rules regulating the times and places where publicly accessible records will be made available, the person from whom the records may be obtained, and rules or regulations pertaining to both the availability of district records and the procedures to access the records.

5 ILCS 140/3(h)

7:445 How can a school district deal with repeated requests from the same person?

The relevant statute (which was amended in 2011) defines a recurrent requester as a person who, in the 12 months immediately preceding the request, has submitted to the same public body a minimum of 50 requests for records, a minimum of 15 requests for records within a 30-day period, or a minimum of seven requests for records within a seven-day period. Requests made by news media and non-profit, scientific, or academic organizations are not considered in calculating the number of requests made in the time periods when the principal purpose of the requests is to access and disseminate information concerning news and current or passing events, for articles of opinion or features of interest to the public, or for the purpose of academic, scientific, or public research or education.

"Request" means a written document (or oral request, if the public body chooses to honor oral requests) that is submitted to a public body via personal delivery, mail, fax, email, or other means available to the public body and that identifies the particular public record the requester seeks. One request may identify multiple records to be inspected or copied.

A public body must respond to a request from a recurrent requester within 21 business days after receipt. The response must provide to the requester an estimate of the time required by the public body to provide the records requested and an estimate of the fees to be charged, which the public body may require the person to pay in full before copying the requested document;, deny the request pursuant to one or more of the exemptions allowed in the law; notify the requester that the request is unduly burdensome and extend an opportunity to the requester to attempt to reduce the request to manageable proportions; or provide the records requested.

Within five business days after receiving a request from a recurrent requester, the public body must notify the requester that the public body is treating the request as a request from a recurrent requester, of the reasons why the public body is treating the request as such, and that the public body will send an initial response within 21 business days after receipt. The public body shall also notify the requester of the proposed responses that can be asserted. Unless the records are exempt from disclosure, a public body must comply with a request within a reasonable period considering the size and complexity of the request.

5 ILCS 140/3(g)
5 ILCS 140/3.2

7:450 What records are exempt from public access and inspection under the Freedom of Information Act?

The Freedom of Information Act exempts numerous records from public access and copying. When a request is made to inspect or copy a public record that contains information that is exempt from disclosure, but also contains information that is not exempt from disclosure, the school district may elect to redact the information that is exempt. The school district must make the remaining information available for inspection and copying. The Freedom of Information Act

(FOIA) exempts numerous records from public access and copying. Some of the most common categories of records that are exempt include the following:

1) Information specifically prohibited from disclosure by federal or state law or rules and regulations implementing federal or state law.

2) Private information unless disclosure is required by another FOIA provision, a state or federal law, or a court order.

3) Personal information contained within public records, the disclosure of which would constitute a clearly unwarranted invasion of personal privacy, unless the disclosure is consented to in writing by the individual subjects of the information. "Unwarranted invasion of personal privacy" means the disclosure of information that is highly personal or objectionable to a reasonable person and in which the subject's right to privacy outweighs any legitimate public interest in obtaining the information. The disclosure of information that bears on the public duties of public employees and officials shall not be considered an invasion of personal privacy. It is likely that teacher, principal, and superintendent performance evaluations are exempt from disclosure because of an exemption provided in the 2010 Race to the Top legislation in Section 24A-7.1 of the School Code. It is also likely that other certified employee evaluations (assistant principals, for example) are covered by this exemption.

4) Records in the possession of any public body created in the course of administrative enforcement proceedings, but only to the extent that disclosure would

a) Interfere with active administrative enforcement proceedings conducted by the public body that is the recipient of the request;

b) Create a substantial likelihood that a person will be deprived of a fair trial or an impartial hearing;

c) Unavoidably disclose the identity of a confidential source; confidential information furnished only by the confidential source; or persons who file complaints with or provide information to administrative, investigative, law enforcement, or penal agencies; except that the identities of witnesses to traffic accidents, traffic accident reports, and rescue reports shall be provided by agencies of local government, except when disclosure would interfere with an active criminal investigation conducted by the agency that is the recipient of the request;

d) Disclose unique or specialized investigative techniques other than those generally used and known or disclose internal documents of correctional agencies related to detection, observation, or investigation of incidents of crime or misconduct, and disclosure would result in demonstrable harm to the agency or public body that is the recipient of the request;

e) Endanger the life or physical safety of law enforcement personnel or any other person; or

f) Obstruct an ongoing criminal investigation by the agency that is the recipient of the request.

5) Preliminary drafts, notes, recommendations, memorandums, and other records in which opinions are expressed, or policies or actions are formulated, except that a specific record or relevant portion of a record shall not be exempt when the record is publicly cited and identified by the superintendent.

6) Trade secrets and commercial or financial information obtained from a person or business where the trade secrets or commercial or financial information are furnished under a claim that they are proprietary, privileged, or confidential, and that disclosure of the trade secrets or commercial or financial information would cause competitive harm to the person or business, and only insofar as the claim directly applies to the records requested.

7) All trade secrets and commercial or financial information obtained by a public body, including a public pension fund, from a private equity fund or a privately held company within the investment portfolio of a private equity fund as a result of either investing or evaluating a potential investment of public funds in a private equity fund. The exemption contained in this item does not apply to the aggregate financial performance information of a private equity fund, or to the identity of the fund's managers or general partners. The exemption contained in this item does not apply to the identity of a privately held company within the investment portfolio of a private equity fund, unless the disclosure of the identity of a privately held company may cause competitive harm. A person or business may consent to disclosure.

8) Proposals and bids for any contract, grant, or agreement, including information which if it were disclosed would frustrate procurement or give an advantage to any person proposing to enter into a contractor agreement with the body, until an award or final selection is made. Information prepared by or for the body in preparation of a bid solicitation shall be exempt until an award or final selection is made.

9) Valuable formulae, computer geographic systems, designs, drawings, and research data obtained or produced by any public body when disclosure could reasonably be expected to produce private gain or public loss. The exemption for "computer geographic systems" does not extend to requests made by news media when the requested information is not otherwise exempt and the only purpose of the request is to access and disseminate information regarding the health, safety, welfare, or legal rights of the general public.

10) The following information pertaining to educational matters:

a) Test questions, scoring keys, and other examin--ation data used to administer an academic examination.

b) Information received by a primary or secondary school under its procedures for the evaluation of faculty members by their academic peers.

c) Information concerning a school or university's adjudication of student disciplinary cases, but only to the extent that disclosure would unavoidably reveal the identity of the student.

d) Course materials or research materials used by faculty members.

11) Architects' plans, engineers' technical submissions, and other construction-related technical documents for projects not constructed or developed in whole or in part with public funds and the same for projects constructed or developed with public funds, including but not limited to power generating and distribution stations and other transmission and distribution facilities, water treatment facilities, airport facilities, sport stadiums, convention centers, and all government owned, operated, or occupied buildings, but only to the extent that disclosure would compromise security.

12) Minutes of meetings of public bodies closed to the public as provided in the Open Meetings Act until the public body makes the minutes available to the public under Section 2.06 of the Open Meetings Act.

13) Communications between a public body and an attorney or auditor representing the public body that would not be subject to discovery in litigation, and materials prepared or compiled by or for a public body in anticipation of a criminal, civil or administrative proceeding upon the request of an attorney advising the public body, and materials prepared or compiled with respect to internal audits of public bodies.

14) Records relating to a public body's adjudication of employee grievances or disciplinary cases; however, this exemption shall not extend to the final outcome of cases in which discipline is imposed.

15) Administrative or technical information associated with automated data processing operations, including but not limited to software, operating protocols, computer program abstracts, file layouts, source listings, object modules, load modules, user guides, documentation pertaining to all logical and physical design of computerized systems, employee manuals, and any other information that, if disclosed, would jeopardize the security of the system or its data or the security of materials exempt under this section.

16) Records relating to collective negotiating matters between public bodies and their employees or representatives, except that any final contract or agreement shall be subject to inspection and copying.

17) Test questions, scoring keys, and other examination data used to determine the qualifications of an applicant for a license or employment.

18) The records, documents, and information relating to real estate purchase negotiations until those negotiations have been completed or otherwise terminated. With regard to a parcel involved in a pending or actually and reasonably contemplated eminent domain proceeding under the Eminent Domain Act, records, documents, and information relating to that parcel shall be exempt except as may be allowed under discovery rules adopted by the Illinois Supreme Court. The records, documents, and information relating to a real estate sale shall be exempt until a sale is consummated.

19) Any and all proprietary information and records related to the operation of an intergovernmental risk management association or self-insurance pool or jointly self-administered health and accident cooperative or pool. Insurance or self-insurance (including any intergovernmental risk management association or self-insurance pool) claims, loss or risk management information, records, data, advice, or communications.

20) Information that would disclose or might lead to the disclosure of secret or confidential information, codes, algorithms, programs, or private keys intended to be used to create electronic or digital signatures under the Electronic Commerce Security Act.

21) Vulnerability assessments, security measures, and response policies or plans that are designed to identify, prevent, or respond to potential attacks upon a community's population or systems, facilities, or installations, the destruction or contamination of which would constitute a clear and present danger to the health or safety of the community, but only to the extent that disclosure could reasonably be expected to jeopardize the effectiveness of the measures or the safety of the personnel who implement them or the public. Information exempt under this item may include such things as details pertaining to the mobilization or deployment of personnel or equipment, to the operation of communication systems or protocols, or to tactical operations.

22) Library circulation and order records identifying library users with specific materials under the Library Records Confidentiality Act.

23) Information the disclosure of which is exempted under the State Officials and Employees Ethics Act.

24) Information contained in a local emergency energy plan submitted to a municipality in accordance with a local emergency energy plan ordinance that is adopted under Section 11-21.5-5 of the Illinois Municipal Code.

25) Information prohibited from being disclosed by the Personnel Record Review Act.

26) Information prohibited from being disclosed by the Illinois School Student Records Act.

27) Information exempt from disclosure under Section 5-1014.3 of the Counties Code or Section 8-11-21 of the Municipal Code.

28) Names and addresses or other personal information of minors who are participants and registrants in programs of park districts, forest preserve districts, conservation districts, recreation agencies, and special recreation associations, or the same information if the program is "targeted primarily to minors.

29) Certain records requested by a person in a county jail or committed to the Department of Corrections.

A public record that is not in the possession of a public body but is in the possession of a party with whom the agency has contracted to perform a governmental function on behalf of the public body, and that directly relates to the governmental function and is not otherwise exempt under FOIA is a public record of the public body.

There are numerous other categories of information that are exempted from disclosure under the Act.

5 ILCS 140/1

5 ILCS 140/3(f)

5 ILCS 140/7

5 ILCS 140/7.5

50 ILCS 205/3a

105 ILCS 10/1 et seq.

105 ILCS 5/24A-7.1

Copley Press, Inc. v. Board of Education for Peoria School Dist. No. 150, 359 Ill. App. 3d 321, 834 N.E. 2d 558, 296 Ill. Dec. 1. (3rd Dist. 2005)

Lieber v. Board of Trustees of Southern Illinois University, 176 Ill. 2d 401, 223 Ill. Dec. 641, 680 N.E. 2d 374 (1997)

Illinois Educational Labor Relations Board v. Homer Community Consolidated School District No. 208, 160 Ill. App. 3d 730, 514 N.E. 2d 465, 112 Ill. Dec. 802, aff'd. 132 Ill. 2d 29, 547 N.E. 2d 182, 138 Ill. Dec. 213 (1989)

Bowie v. Evanston Community Consolidated School District No. 65, 165 Ill. App. 3d 101, 522 N.E. 2d 669, 119 Ill. Dec. 7 (1st Dist. 1988) app. allowed 122 Ill. 2d 570, 530 N.E. 2d 239, 125 Ill. Dec. 211, aff'd. 128 Ill. 2d 373, 538 N.E. 2d 557, 131 Ill. Dec. 182 (1989)

Hamer v. Lentz, 132 Ill. 2d 49, 547 N.E. 2d 191, 138 Ill. Dec. 222 (1989)

7:455 Does the adjudication exemption in the Freedom of Information Act allow school officials to withhold information obtained in a grievance or disciplinary investigation?

A 2016 Third District opinion found that a complaint or grievance "is part of an investigatory process that is separate and distinct from a disciplinary adjudication" (which is exempt). The court concluded that "adjudication is a formalized legal process that results in a final and enforceable decision."

Peoria Journal Star v. City of Peoria, 2016 IL. App. (3d) 140838, 52 N.E. 3d 711, 402 Ill. Dec. 790

7:460 May school officials disclose free and reduced lunch information?

Information obtained from applications for free and reduced-price lunches can be disclosed with parental consent. Otherwise, federal law severely limits disclosure to enforcement agencies and for other specific purposes.

42 U.S.C. 1758(b)(6)(A)

7:470 Must a school board comply with a request to make public the names and salaries of its employees?

The names and salaries of school board employees are public record and available for public inspection.

5 ILCS 140/2(c)

People ex rel. Recktenwald v. Janura, 59 Ill. App. 3d 143, 376 N.E. 2d 22, 17 Ill. Dec. 129 (1st Dist. 1978)

Stein v. Howlett, 52 Ill. 2d 570, 289 N.E. 2d 409 (1972)

7:480 How quickly must a school board respond to a Freedom of Information Act request?

A school board must either comply with the request or deny the request for public records within five working days after the request has been received. A request may be either fully or partially fulfilled or denied.

If a school board fails to respond to a written request within five working days after it is received, the request is deemed denied.

5 ILCS 140/3(d)

7:485 How is a Freedom of Information Act request for commercial purposes treated differently?

"Commercial purpose" means the use of any part of a public record or records, or information derived from public records, in any form for sale, resale, or solicitation or advertisement for sales or services. Requests made by news media and non-profit, scientific, or academic organizations are not considered to be made for a "commercial purpose" when the principal purpose of the request is to access and disseminate information concerning news and current or passing events, for articles of opinion or features of interest to the public or for the purpose of academic, scientific, or public research or education.

A public body has 21 working days from receipt to respond to a request for records to be used for a commercial purpose. The response must provide to the requester an estimate of the time required by the public body to provide the records requested and an estimate of the fees to be charged, which the public body may require the person to pay in full before copying the requested documents, deny the request pursuant to one or more of the exemptions set out in the Freedom of Information Act (FOIA), notify the requester that the request is unduly burdensome and extend an opportunity to the requester to attempt to reduce the request to manageable proportions, or provide the records requested.

Unless the records are exempt from disclosure, a public body must comply with a request within a reasonable period considering the size and complexity of the request, and giving priority to records requested for non-commercial purposes. It is a violation of FOIA for a person to knowingly obtain a public record for a commercial purpose without disclosing that it is for a commercial purpose, if requested to do so by the public body.

5 ILCS 140/2(c-10)
5 ILCS 140/3.3

7:490 May a school board extend the time to respond to a Freedom of Information Act request beyond five days?

A school board may extend the time limit to respond to a request to access or copy school records for not more than an additional five business days from the original due date for any of the following reasons:

1) The requested records are stored in whole or in part at other locations than the office having charge of the requested records.

2) The request requires the collection of a substantial number of specified records.

3) The request is couched in categorical terms and requires an extensive search for the records responsive to it.

4) The requested records have not been located in the course of routine search and additional efforts are being made to locate them.

5) The requested records require examination and evaluation by personnel having the necessary competence and discretion to determine if they are exempt from disclosure or should be revealed only with appropriate deletions.

6) The request for records cannot be complied with by the school board within the time limits prescribed without unduly burdening or interfering with the operation of the school.

7) There is a need for consultation, which shall be conducted with all practicable speed, with another public body or among two or more components of a public body having a substantial interest in the determination or in the subject matter of the request.

When additional time is required for any of the above reasons, the school board must notify the person making the request by letter within the five days after receipt of the request the reasons for the extension and the date by which the records will be forthcoming.

Failure to respond within the time permitted for extension is considered a denial of the request. A public body that fails to respond to a request within the time permitted for extension but thereafter provides the requester with copies of the requested public records cannot impose a fee for those copies. A public body that requests an extension and subsequently fails to respond to the request cannot treat the request as unduly burdensome.

5 ILCS 140/3(e)
5 ILCS 140/3(f)

7:500 What appeal is available to the public following denial of a request to inspect and copy public records?

A person whose request to inspect or copy a public record is denied by a public body may file a request for review with the Attorney General's Public Access Counselor (PAC) not later than 60 days after the date of the final denial. The request for review must be in writing, signed by the requester, and include a copy of the request for access to records and any responses from the public body.

A public body that receives a request for records and asserts that the records are exempt must within the time periods provided for responding to a request, provide written notice to the requester, and under certain very narrow circumstances, to the PAC of its intent to deny the request in whole or in part. The notice must include a copy of the request for access to records, the proposed response from the public body, and a detailed summary of the public body's basis for asserting the exemption.

Upon receipt of a notice of intent to deny from a public body, the PAC must determine whether further inquiry is warranted. Within five working days after receipt of the notice of intent to deny, the PAC must notify the public body and the requester whether further inquiry is warranted. If the PAC determines that further inquiry is warranted, there are procedures in the law regarding the review of denials, including the production of documents, that are applicable to the inquiry and resolution of a notice of intent to deny. Times for response or compliance by the public body under of the Freedom of Information Act (FOIA) shall be tolled until the PAC concludes the inquiry.

Upon receipt of a request for review, the PAC determines whether further action is warranted. If the PAC determines that the alleged violation is unfounded, he or she must so advise the requester and the public body and no further action is undertaken. In all other cases, the PAC must forward a copy of the request for review to the public body within seven working days after receipt and must specify the records or other documents that the public body must furnish to facilitate the review. Within seven working days after receipt of the request for review, the public body must provide copies of records requested and must otherwise fully cooperate with the PAC. If a public body fails to furnish specified records, or if otherwise necessary, the Attorney General may issue a subpoena to any person or public body having knowledge of or records pertaining to a request for review of a denial of access to records. To the extent that records or documents produced by a public body contain information that is claimed to be exempt from disclosure under Section 7 of FOIA, the PAC must not further disclose that information.

Within seven working days after it receives a copy of a request for review and request for production of records from the PAC, the public body may, but is not required to, answer the allegations of the request for review. The answer may take the form of a letter, brief, or memorandum. The PAC must forward a copy of the answer to the person submitting the request for review, with any alleged confidential information to which the request pertains redacted from the copy. The requester may, but is not required to, respond in writing to the answer within seven working days and must provide a copy of the response to the public body.

In addition to the request for review, and the answer and the response thereto, if any, a requester or a public body may furnish affidavits or records concerning any matter germane to the review.

Unless the PAC extends the time by no more than 21 business days by sending written notice to the requester and the public body that includes a statement of the reasons for the extension in the notice, or decides to address the matter without the issuance of a binding opinion, the Attorney General must examine the issues and the records, make findings of fact and conclusions of law, and issue to the requester and the public body an opinion in response to the request for review within 60 days after its receipt. The opinion is binding upon both the requester and the public body, subject to administrative review under Section 11.5 of FOIA.

In responding to any request, the Attorney General may exercise his or her discretion and choose to resolve a request for review by mediation or by a means other than the issuance of a binding opinion. The decision not to issue a binding opinion is not reviewable.

Upon receipt of a binding opinion concluding that a violation of FOIA has occurred, the public body must either take necessary action immediately to comply with the directive of the opinion or must initiate administrative review under Section 11.5 of FOIA. If the opinion concludes that no violation of the Act has occurred, the requester may initiate administrative review under Section 11.5.

A public body that discloses records in accordance with an opinion of the Attorney General is immune from all liabilities by reason thereof and shall not be liable for penalties under this Act.

If the requester files suit under Section 11 of FOIA with respect to the same denial that is the subject of a pending request for review, the requester must notify the PAC, and the PAC must take no further action with respect to the request for review and must so notify the public body.

The Attorney General may also issue advisory opinions to public bodies regarding compliance with FOIA. A review may be initiated upon receipt of a written request from the head of the public body or its attorney, which shall contain sufficient accurate facts from which a determination can be made. The PAC may request additional information from the public body in order to assist in the review.

A public body that relies in good faith on an advisory opinion of the Attorney General in responding to a request is not liable for penalties under this Act, so long as the facts upon which the opinion is based have been fully and fairly disclosed to the PAC.

5 ILCS 140/9.5

7:505 What is the penalty for a public body's refusal to comply with a binding opinion?

The requester may file suit if the public body does not file for administrative review or comply within 35 days after the binding opinion is served on the public body. The enforcement remedies include fines of not less than $2,500 and not more than $5,000 for each offense and the possibility of a $1,000 a day fine under certain limited circumstances.

5 ILCS 140/11
5 ILCS 140/11.6

7:510 What are the procedural requirements necessary to deny a request to inspect and copy records?

A school board may refuse a request to inspect and copy records when an exemption is provided in the law or when responding would be unduly burdensome. When a request is denied, the school board must notify the person making the request in writing of the decision to deny; the reasons for the denial, including a detailed factual basis for the application of any exemption claimed; and the name and title or position of each person responsible for the denial.

The notice also must inform the person of his or her right to review by the Public Access Counselor (PAC) and provide the address and phone number for the PAC and each notice of denial must inform the person of his or her right to seek judicial review in a circuit court of proper jurisdiction.

When a request for school district records is denied on the grounds the records are exempt under the Freedom of Information Act, the notice of denial must specify the exemption claimed to authorize the denial and the specific reasons for the denial including a detailed factual basis and a citation to supporting legal authority.

Copies of each denial issued by a school board must be retained in a single, central office file that is open to the public. The file must be indexed according to the type of exemption and, to the extent feasible, according to the type of records that have been requested.

5 ILCS 140/9

7:520 Is any further appeal available to an individual denied access to public records following appeal to the school board president?

Any person who has been denied access to inspect or copy public records and who has exhausted administrative remedies may file suit in the circuit court of the county where the school district is located. An advisory opinion issued by the Attorney General's Public Access Counselor is not subject to review. A binding opinion is subject to review.

5 ILCS 140/11

Garlick v. The Office of the Public Access Counselor, 2013 IL App (1st) 122444, 4 N.E. 3d 503, 378 Ill. Dec. 620

Brown v. Grosskopf, 2013 IL App (4th) 120402, 984 N.E. 2d 1167, 368 Ill. Dec. 697

7:530 Does the Freedom of Information Act require a school board to create or maintain any specific records?

The Act does not require a school board to create or maintain any record not otherwise required by law, rule, or regulation, or maintained at the discretion of the school board.

5 ILCS 140/1

Heinrich v. White, 2012 IL App (2d) 110584, 975 N.E. 2d 726, 363 Ill. Dec. 700

7:540 What is the penalty for violation of the Freedom of Information Act (FOIA)?

If, after a suit is filed, a court determines that a public body willfully and intentionally failed to comply with FOIA, or otherwise acted in bad faith, the court must also impose upon the public body a civil penalty of not less than $2,500 nor more than $5,000 for each occurrence. In assessing the civil penalty, the court must consider in aggravation or mitigation the budget of the public body and whether the public body has previously been assessed penalties for FOIA violations.

5 ILCS 140/11(j)

7:550 How can one find Freedom of Information Act opinions issued by the Illinois Attorney General?

Illinois Attorney General opinions interpreting FOIA are available on the Attorney General's website: *http://foia.ilattorneygeneral.net/bindingopinions.aspx*

15 ILCS 205/7(g)

PERSONAL INFORMATION PROTECTION ACT

7:600 Which information is protected "personal information" under the Personal Information Protection Act?

Personal information under the Personal Information Protection Act includes, when combined with identifiers described in the Act, certain health insurance and/or medical information, Social Security number, driver license number or state identification number, credit card number when combined with access information, and certain biometric data. Personal information does not include publicly available information that is lawfully made available to the general public from federal, state, or local government records.

815 ILCS 530/5

7:610 What is a data breach under the Personal Information Protections Act?

"Breach of the security of the system data" or "breach" means unauthorized acquisition of computerized data that compromises the security, confidentiality, or integrity of personal information maintained by the school district. "Breach of the security of the system data" does not include good faith acquisition of personal information by an employee or agent of the school district for a legitimate purpose of the school district, provided that the personal information is not used for a purpose unrelated to the school district's business or subject to further unauthorized disclosure.

815 ILCS 530/5

7:620 What happens if a school district has a security breach?

If a school district has a breach of security system data within the meaning of the Personal Information Protection Act, it is required to comply with certain notice requirements to persons affected by the breach and under certain circumstances is required to notify the Attorney General.

815 ILCS 530/12

8: CHANGING SCHOOL DISTRICT BOUNDARIES AND TERRITORY

DISTRICT CONSOLIDATION

8:10 May two or more entire elementary districts or two or more entire high school districts combine to form a new district?

Yes. Any contiguous territory having an equalized assessed valuation of at least $5,000,000 and a population of not less than 1,500 and not more than 500,000 may be formed into a combined school district. A petition calling for the combination of districts must be filed by the school boards of each district affected or by 10 percent of the legal voters residing in each district affected. The petition must be filed with the regional superintendent of the region in which the greater portion of the equalized assessed valuation of the territory described in the petition is located.

The petition must be approved by the regional superintendent after a hearing on the petition and by the State Superintendent of Education and thereafter (only after approval has been obtained) the proposal placed on the ballot at an election in the affected territory. The proposed combination of districts must be approved by a majority of voters of each district who vote on the proposition in the election.

105 ILCS 5/7-1
105 ILCS 5/7-4
105 ILCS 5/7-7.7
105 ILCS 5/11E-5 et seq.

8:15 What is a "Committee of Ten"?

A petition calling for the creation, formation, or conversion of a school district must provide for a committee of 10 petitioners to represent the interests of all petitioners. The committee is authorized, for example, to amend the petition within certain parameters.

A Committee of Ten also is called for in detachment and annexation petitions.

105 ILCS 5/7-2b
105 ILCS 5/11E-35

8:20 May new community consolidated or community high school districts be formed?

All statutory references to the creation of community consolidated school districts were removed from the School Code by the General Assembly. It is possible for two or more contiguous unit school districts — or one or more unit school districts and one or more high school districts — all of which are contiguous, to dissolve and form a single new high school district and one or more new elementary districts. New legislation in 2013 allows the formation of a new district from non-contiguous districts under very limited circumstances. It is not possible under other circumstances to form a new high school district.

A single unit school district may not, for example, divide into high school and elementary districts. Almost all the existing community consolidated and township high school districts were formed before statutory restrictions were enacted limiting the formation of such districts.

105 ILCS 5/10-21.5
105 ILCS 5/11E-30
Board of Education of Hamilton County Community Unit School District No. 10, Hamilton County v. Regional Board of School Trustees of Jefferson and Hamilton Counties, 121 Ill. App. 3d 848, 460 N.E. 2d 100, 77 Ill. Dec. 241 (5th Dist. 1984)

8:30 What kind of school district may be newly created under current law?

Any type of school district except a community consolidated district may be newly created, although some types of school districts may be newly created only under very limited circumstances.

105 ILCS 5/7-1 et seq.
105 ILCS 5/11E-15
105 ILCS 5/11E-20
105 ILCS 5/11E-25
105 ILCS 5/11E-30

8:33 What is a unit school district?

A unit school district is one that offers education for all children in grades kindergarten through 12 who live within the territory of the district.

8:36 What is a dual district?

A dual district is an area served by two separate school districts, one an elementary district providing education through eighth grade and the second a high school district providing education from grades 9-12. Boundaries of the elementary district and high school district may be coterminous but often are not. One high school district may cover all or some of the same geographic area as two or more elementary districts. Or an elementary district may serve portions of the same area served by two or more high school districts.

8:40 How is a community unit district created?

Creation of a community unit school district begins with the filing of a petition with the regional superintendent of schools and concludes with approval of the voters and election of a new school board. The petition may be filed by the boards of education of each of the school districts wholly or partially included in the territory described in the petition, or the petition may be filed by a specified number of voters residing in the affected school districts. The petition must be approved by the regional superintendent and State Superintendent of Education.

At the election, the proposition must be approved by a majority of the votes cast in each of the affected school districts. (The proposition loses if it is defeated by a majority of the votes cast in any one of the affected school districts, even if it receives a majority of the votes in all of the districts combined.)

The School Code sets forth specific requirements for (a) the territory to be included in the proposed unit district; (b) signatures required on the petition; (c) the filing of the petition; (d) hearing procedures; (e) the referendum on the proposal; and (f) the election of a new school board.

105 ILCS 5/11E-25

Adsit v. Sanders, 157 Ill. App. 3d 416, 510 N.E. 2d 547, 109 Ill. Dec. 679(4th Dist. 1987), app. dismissed 117 Ill. 2d 541, 517 N.E. 2d 1083, 115 Ill. Dec. 397 (1987)

8:45 What happens to the debt of the previously existing school districts when a new school district is formed?

Subject to the terms and provisions below, whenever a new district is created under any of the provisions of Article 11E of the School Code, the outstanding bonded indebtedness is treated as provided in that section and in Section 19-29. The tax rate for bonded indebtedness is determined as provided in Section 19-7 of the School Code, and, notwithstanding the creation of any such district, the county clerk or clerks must annually extend taxes, for each outstanding bond issue against all of the taxable property that was situated within the boundaries of the district, as those boundaries existed at the time of the issuance of the bond issue, regardless of whether the property is still contained in that same district at the time of the extension of the taxes by the county clerk or clerks.

For a unit district formation, whenever a part of a district is included within the boundaries of a newly created unit district, the regional superintendent of schools must cause an accounting to be had between the districts affected by the change in boundaries as provided for in Article 11C. Whenever the entire territory of two or more school districts is organized into a unit district pursuant to a petition filed under Article 11E, the petition may provide that the entire territory of the new unit district must assume the bonded indebtedness of the previously existing school districts. In that case, the tax rate for bonded indebtedness is determined in the manner provided in Section 19-7 of the School Code, except that the county clerk annually extends taxes for each outstanding bond issue against all the taxable property situated in the new unit district as it exists after the organization.

For a high school-unit conversion, unit to dual conversion, or multi-unit conversion, upon the effective date of the change as provided in Section 11E-70, each newly created elementary district receives all of the assets and assumes all of the liabilities and obligations of the dissolved unit district forming the boundary of the newly created elementary district.

Notwithstanding any contrary requirement, upon the stipulation of the school board of the school district serving a newly created elementary district for high school purposes and either (i) the school board of the unit district prior to the effective date of its dissolution or (ii) thereafter the school board of the newly created elementary district and with the approval in either case of the regional superintendent of schools of the educational service region in which the territory described in the petition filed under this Article or the greater percentage of equalized assessed valuation of the territory is situated; the assets, liabilities, and obligations of the dissolved unit district may be divided and assumed between and by the newly created elementary district and the school district serving the newly created elementary district for high school purposes, in accordance with the terms and provisions of the stipulation and approval. In this event, the provisions of Section 19-29 are applied to determine the debt incurring power of the newly created elementary district and of the school district serving the newly created elementary district for high school purposes.

Without regard to whether the receipt of assets and the assumption of liabilities and obligations of the dissolved unit district are determined, the tax rate for bonded indebtedness is determined in the manner provided in Section 19-7, and, notwithstanding the creation of this new elementary district, the county clerk or clerks annually extends taxes for each outstanding bond issue against all of the taxable property that was situated within the boundaries of the dissolved unit district as those boundaries existed at the time of the issuance of the bond issue, regardless of whether the property was still contained in that unit district at the time of its dissolution and regardless of whether the property is contained in the newly created elementary district at the time of the extension of the taxes by the county clerk or clerks.

105 ILCS 5/11C-1 et seq.
105 ILCS 5/11E-35
105 ILCS 5/11E-105
105 ILCS 5/19-7
105 ILCS 5/19-29

8:47 What rights do teachers have in a dissolution or consolidation?

When dissolution and annexation become effective for purposes of administration and attendance, the positions of tenured teachers in the district being dissolved are transferred to an annexing district or districts. The rights of affected teachers are governed by Section 24-11 of the School Code. In the event that the territory is added to two or more districts, the decision on which positions are to be transferred to which annexing districts must be made giving consideration to the proportionate percentage of pupils transferred and the annexing districts' staffing needs, and the transfer of specific individuals into such positions must be based upon the request of those teachers in order of seniority in the dissolving district. The tenure status of any teacher thereby transferred to an annexing district is not lost and the different school board is subject to the School Code with respect to the transferred teacher in the same manner as if the teacher was that district's employee and had been its employee during the time the teacher was actually employed by the school board of the dissolving district from which the position was transferred.

105 ILCS 5/7-10.5

8:50 Who may vote in an election to organize a community unit school district?

Only those residents in the territory described in the petition for organizing a community unit school district may vote in such an election. The proposition must be approved by a majority of the votes cast in each of the affected school districts, not merely by a majority of the votes cast in the total combined territory.

105 ILCS 5/11E-65

8:60 What assistance does the State Board of Education provide to a school district considering consolidation?

The State Board of Education Department of School District Organization assists school districts in studying school district organizational problems. It provides consultation to school districts considering consolidation.

105 ILCS 5/2-3.35

8:70 How does school district reorganization affect state aid?

The state provides financial incentives to encourage school district consolidation. For fixed specified periods of time after a reorganization, the state may provide additional supplementary state aid (or evidence-based funding) to newly reconfigured districts. The supplementary aid wholly or partially offsets the costs incurred by a district in acquiring another district's deficits and differences in financial structure and partially offsets the costs associated with merging the teacher salary schedules of combining school districts. The schedule of payments takes into account the size of the resulting school district and provides larger incentives to newly created districts with the highest student average daily attendance.

105 ILCS 5/11E-135

BOUNDARY CHANGES

8:80 How may school district boundaries be changed?

School district boundaries may be changed by detachment, annexation, division, dissolution, or any combination thereof. The regional board(s) of school trustees is authorized to change the boundaries when petitioned under certain circumstances. In 2017, the legislature revised process under which boundary changes occur.

105 ILCS 5/7-1
105 ILCS 5/7-2a
105 ILCS 5/7-2b
105 ILCS 5/7-2.4

8:90 May a school district be entirely dissolved?

Yes. Upon petition by a majority of the legal resident voters residing in the district proposed to be dissolved, or by a petition filed by the board of education of the school district seeking dissolution, the regional board of school trustees may dissolve a school district and annex its territory to another district or districts.

105 ILCS 5/7-2a

8:95 For purposes of detachment and dissolution what is a legal resident voter?

Legal resident voter is a person who is registered to vote at the time a circulated petition is filed and when the regional board of school trustees renders a decision, at the address shown opposite his or her signature on the petition, and resides in the detaching territory or dissolving school district.

105 ILCS 5/7-01b

8:100 What is detachment and annexation?

Detachment is the removal of a portion of the territory of a school district. Annexation is the addition of territory to a school district. Detachment and annexation, therefore, is the removal of territory from one school district and the addition of it to the territory of another school district.

105 ILCS 5/7-1 et seq.

8:105 Do provisions for dissolution, detachment, and annexation apply to all school districts in Illinois?

Yes. However, statutory procedures for detachment and annexation involving a special charter district differ somewhat from the procedures applicable for other districts. Procedures that apply to special charter districts are addressed beginning with question 8:300.

NON-CHARTER DISTRICT DETACHMENT AND ANNEXATION

8:110 May territory be detached and annexed to a school district if the resulting district is not compact and contiguous?

In most cases, school district boundaries resulting from detachment and annexation must be compact and contiguous, although a school district may have "highly irregular" boundaries and still be compact and contiguous if children residing therein can reasonably avail themselves of school. In general, corridors are compact and contiguous; islands are not. New legislation in 2013 allows the creation of a new school from non-contiguous territory under very limited circumstances.

105 ILCS 5/11E-20

People on rel. Community Unit School District No. 1, Macon and DeWitt Counties v. Decatur School District No. 61, 45 Ill. App. 2d 33, 194 N.E. 2d 659 (3rd Dist. 1963)

Streator Township High School District No. 40 v. County Board of School Trustees of Livingston County, 14 Ill. App. 2d 251, 144 N.E. 2d 531 (2nd Dist. 1957)

People ex rel. Warren v. Drummet, 415 Ill. 411, 114 N.E. 2d 364 (1953)

People ex rel. McLain v. Gardner, 408 Ill. 228, 96 N.E. 2d 551 (1951)

People v. Deatherage, 401 Ill. 25, 81 N.E. 2d 581 (1948)

People ex rel. Bartlett v. Vass, 325 Ill. 64 (1927)

8:120 What is the effective date of change for the change of boundaries of a school district?

In the event that the granting of a petition has become final, through failure to seek administrative review, by the final decision of a court on review if no further appeal is taken, or upon certification of election results in the event of a dissolution, the change in boundaries becomes effective the following July 1. The school boards of the districts as they existed prior to the change exercise the same power and authority over the affected territory until that date, unless accelerated or postponed by stipulation of the school boards of each detaching or dissolving and annexing school district and approval by the regional board of school trustees with which the original petition is required to be filed.

New legislation in 2013 allows the effective date for the reorganization of two or more school districts to be conditional on the award of a construction grant provided the voters approve a referendum containing the condition.

105 ILCS 5/7-9

8:130 When do school board members' terms of office expire after the annexation of the school district from which they were elected?

Upon the close of the current school year during which any school district is annexed to another school district, the terms of office of the school board members of the annexed school district are terminated and the school board of the annexing district performs all of the duties and has all of the powers of the school board of the annexed district.

105 ILCS 5/7-12

8:140 What happens to the assets and liabilities of an annexed district?

The annexing district, as it is constituted on and after the time of annexation, usually receives all the assets and assumes all the obligations and liabilities, including the bonded indebtedness, of the original annexing district and of the district annexed. In certain dissolutions and under certain conditions in the case of a detachment-annexation, the bonded indebtedness does not become the obligation of the annexing district but remains the obligation of the taxable property that was situated within the boundaries of the dissolved district at the time of the issuance of each bond issue. The territory of the dissolved district does not assume the bonded indebtedness of the annexing district unless the school board of the dissolved district votes before dissolution to assume the debt.

When two or more school districts receive territory from a dissolved school district, the regional board of school trustees has authority to divide the assets and liabilities of the dissolved school district. As a practical matter, however, the division of assets and liabilities of the dissolved district is generally resolved by intergovernmental agreement between the annexing districts. The intergovernmental agreement is usually ratified by the regional board of school trustees.

105 ILCS 5/7-11
105 ILCS 5/7-12
105 ILCS 5/7-14

Board of Education of Community Unit School District No. 325, Peoria County v. Board of Education of Special Charter School District No. 150, Peoria County, 2 Ill. App. 3d 643, 276 N.E. 2d 732 (3rd Dist. 1971)

8:143 What method is used to determine an annexing district's share of bonded debt that accompanies territory detached from another district?

The amount of bonded debt accompanying annexed territory is prorated based on the equalized assessed valuation (EAV) of the annexed territory as a percentage of the total EAV of the original detaching district.

105 ILCS 5/7-14
105 ILCS 5/19-29

8:145 Are state financial incentives provided to offset the cost to an annexing district of absorbing non-certificated personnel?

No state incentives are provided to offset the costs of absorbing non-certificated personnel. The lack of incentives can be an important deterrent when there are large differences between the salaries and benefits paid to non-certificated employees in the two districts affected.

105 ILCS 5/18-8.05

DETACHMENT AND ANNEXATION PETITIONS

8:150 How frequently may a petition for detachment be submitted?

Any territory involved in a detachment or dissolution proceeding that is not approved may not be involved in another boundary change proceeding for at least two years after final determination of the first proceeding, unless during the two-year period a petition filed is substantially different than any other previously filed petition during the previous two years, or if a school district involved is placed on the academic watch status or financial watch list, or if the first petition was brought under School Code Section 7-2b (a petition by voters to make the boundaries of an annexing elementary or high school district coterminous). The two-year period is counted beginning from the date of a final administrative decision after all appeal timelines have run, upon final court order after all appeal timelines have run, or upon the certification of the election results in the event of a dissolution. The two-year period is two calendar years.

105 ILCS 5/7-8

Helmig v. Regional Board of School Trustees, 286 Ill. App. 3d 220, 675 N.E. 2d 966, 221 Ill. Dec. 542 (3rd Dist. 1997)

Board of Education of Community Unit School District No. 300, Kane, Cook, McHenry and Lake Counties v. County Board of School Trustees of Kane County, 60 Ill. App. 3d 415, 376 N.E. 2d 1054, 17 Ill. Dec. 725 (2nd Dist. 1978)

Hall Township High School District No. 502 Bureau County v. School Trustees of Bureau County, 80 Ill. App. 2d 475, 225 N.E. 2d 228 (3rd Dist. 1967)

Board of Education of Consolidated School District No. 138 of Winnebago County v. County Board of School Trustees of Winnebago County, 37 Ill. App. 2d 166, 185 N.E. 2d 374 (2nd Dist. 1962)

8:160 May a detachment petition be filed when a school district affected by the petition has a bond referendum pending?

No. When notice of a bond issue election has been published, no petition affecting the boundaries of the school district may be filed pending defeat of the bond issue proposal, issuance of the bonds, a board resolution abandoning its plan to issue bonds, or the elapse of 75 days following the election, whichever comes first. This prohibition applies only to the first such election called in any calendar year, and the period of the prohibition may be affected if the district is involved in a legal boundary dispute at the time the election notice is published.

105 ILCS 5/7-3

8:165 May a detachment and annexation petition be withdrawn after filing to allow students to be sent to another school on a tuition basis?

At any time prior to the granting of a petition for detachment and annexation of non-coterminous territory, the Committee of Ten that petitioned the annexation and detachment may amend the petition to withdraw the detachment and annexation proposal and substitute a proposal to require the school district from which the territory would have been detached to pay the per capita tuition costs for each pupil residing in the non-coterminous territory to attend the school in the school district to which the territory would have been annexed.

105 ILCS 5/7-2b

8:170 May a petitioner remove his or her name from an annexation or detachment petition?

A petitioner may have his or her name removed from a detachment or annexation petition at any time prior to final determination by the regional board of school trustees.

Konald v. Board of Education of Community Unit School District No. 220, 114 Ill. App. 3d 512, 448 N.E. 2d 555, 69 Ill. Dec. 837 (2nd Dist. 1983)

Board of Education of Avoca School District No. 37, Cook County, v. Regional Board of School Trustees of Cook County, 82 Ill. App. 3d 1067, 403 N.E. 2d 578, 38 Ill. Dec. 347 (1st Dist. 1980)

Board of Education of Metropolis Community High School District No. 20, Massac County v. County Board of School Trustees, Massac County, 34 Ill. App. 3d 901, 341 N.E. 2d 10 (5th Dist. 1976)

8:175 May a petition for detachment be modified by the court on review?

The reviewing court may not modify the petition. The Administrative Review Law only authorizes the reviewing court to affirm or reverse the decision of the regional board of school trustees, nothing more.

105 ILCS 5/7-6(d)

Board of Education of Indian Prairie Community Unit School District No. 204 v. Regional Board of School Trustees of Will County, et al., 393 Ill. App. 2d 561, 913 N.E. 2d 630, 332 Ill. Dec. 698 (3rd Dist. 2009)

REGIONAL BOARD OF SCHOOL TRUSTEES

8:180 With what body is a detachment or annexation petition filed?

A detachment or annexation petition is filed with the appropriate regional board of school trustees.

105 ILCS 5/7-1 et seq.

105 ILCS 5/7-2a

8:200 What happens following the filing of a detachment and annexation petition?

The secretary of the regional board of school trustees or designee, the chief administrative officer of an educational service center or designee, or the person designated by the trustees of schools in an educational service region with 2 million or more inhabitants receive the filing of the petition, make a validity determination, publish the notice, conduct the hearing, and issue the final order. Upon the filing of a petition with the secretary of the regional board of school trustees under the provisions of Section 7-1 of the School Code, the secretary causes a copy of the petition to be given to the president of the school board of each detaching or dissolving and annexing school district and causes a notice to be published once in a newspaper having general circulation within the area of the detaching or dissolving and annexing territory described in the petition.

105 ILCS 5/7-6

Board of Education of Rockford School District No. 205 Winnebago and Boone Counties v. Hearing Board of Counties of Boone and Winnebago, 152 Ill. App. 3d 936, 505 N.E. 2d 32, 105 Ill. Dec. 906 (2nd Dist. 1987) app. den. 115 Ill. 2d 535, 511 N.E. 2d 425, 110 Ill. Dec. 453 (1987)

Phillips v. Special Hearing Board of Boone and Winnebago Counties, 154 Ill. App. 3d 799, 504 N.E. 2d 1251, 105 Ill. Dec. 733 (2nd Dist. 1986) app. den. 115 Ill. 2d 550, 511 N.E. 2d 436, 110 Ill. Dec. 464 (1987)

Board of Education of Niles Township High School District 219, Cook County v. Regional Board of School Trustees of Cook County, 127 Ill. App. 3d 210, 468 N.E. 2d 1247, 82 Ill. Dec. 467 (1st Dist. 1984)

8:210 Who bears the burden of proof in a detachment or annexation proceeding?

The petitioners bear the burden of proof in a detachment or annexation proceeding.

Rhinehart v. Board of Education of Bloomington School District No. 87, McLean County, 132 Ill. App. 2d 1078, 271 N.E. 2d 104 (4th Dist. 1971)

8:220 What factors must regional boards consider in ruling on detachment petitions?

The regional board of school trustees must consider the ability of the districts affected to meet statutory standards of recognition, and whether the detaching district will be able to remain financially healthy after annexation. It must also consider what is best for the pupils in the entire area, as well as for the school districts affected by the petition. The overall benefit to the annexing district and detachment area must clearly outweigh the detriment to the losing district and surrounding community as a whole. There must not be serious harm done to the financial or educational resources of either district.

105 ILCS 5/7-2.6

Board of Education, Joliet Township High School District No. 204 v. The Board of Education, Lincoln Way Community High School District No. 210, et al. 231 Ill. 2d 184, 897 N.E. 2d 756, 325 Ill. Dec. 217 (2008)

Carver v. Bond / Fayette / Effingham Regional Board of School Trustees, 203 Ill. App. 3d 799, 561 N.E. 2d 135, 148 Ill. Dec. 829 (5th Dist. 1991) app. allowed 136 Ill. 2d 542, 567 N.E. 2d 329, 153 Ill. Dec. 375, aff'd. 146 Ill. 2d 347, 586 N.E. 2d 1273, 167 Ill. Dec. 1 (1992)

Board of Education of Golf School District No. 67 v. Regional Board of School Trustees of Cook County, 89 Ill. 2d 392, 433 N.E. 2d 240, 60 Ill. Dec. 443 (1982)

Board of Education of Pearl City Community Unit School District No. 200 v. Regional Board of School Trustees of Stephenson County, 98 Ill. App. 3d 599, 424 N.E. 2d 808, 54 Ill. Dec. 58 (2nd Dist. 1981)

Board of Education of Jonesboro Community Consolidated School District v. Regional Board of School Trustees of Union County, 86 Ill. App. 3d 230, 407 N.E. 2d 1084, 41 Ill. Dec. 586 (5th Dist. 1980)

Richmond v. County Board of School Trustees of Whiteside County, 93 Ill. App. 2d 142, 235 N.E. 2d 657 (3rd Dist. 1968)

Sesser Community Unit District No. 196, Franklin County v. County Board of School Trustees of Franklin County, 74 Ill. App. 2d 152, 219 N.E. 2d 364 (5th Dist. 1966)

Board of Education of Community Unit School District No. 323, Winnebago and Stephenson Counties v. County Board of School Trustees of Winnebago and Stephenson Counties, 19 Ill. App. 2d 196, 153 N.E. 2d 378 (2nd Dist. 1958)

Oakdale Community Consolidated School District No. 1 v. County Board of School Trustees, 12 Ill. 2d 190, 145 N.E. 736 (1957)

People v. Deatherage, 401 Ill. 25, 81 N.E. 2d 581 (1948)

8:230 May a regional board of school trustees amend a detachment or annexation petition?

No. In ruling on a detachment or annexation petition, a regional board of school trustees may allow or deny a petition but cannot modify it.

Board of Education of Wellington Community Unit School District No. 7 of Iroquois County v. County Board of School Trustees of Vermilion County, 13 Ill. App. 2d 561, 142 N.E. 2d 742 (3rd Dist. 1957)

Trico Community Unit School District No. 176 v. County Board of School Trustees, 8 Ill. App. 2d 494, 131 N.E. 2d 829 (5th Dist. 1956)

Oakdale Community Consolidated School District No. 1, v. County Board of School Trustees of Randolph County, 12 Ill. App. 2d 260, 139 N.E. 2d 795 (4th Dist. 1956)

8:240 May a detachment petition be granted solely based on expanded educational opportunities for a student?

When there are no countervailing factors, and when the best interests of the children involved are served by the detachment, the courts usually apply the "whole child" and "community of interest" tests.

The "whole child" test considers whether or not there will be increased participation in school activities by the students and their families and how the educational, social, and extracurricular needs of the student can best be satisfied. The "community of interest" test considers whether the detachment area is identified with the school district and community to which annexation is sought.

Carver v. Bond / Fayette / Effingham Regional Board of School Trustees, 203 Ill. App. 3d 799, 561 N.E. 2d 135, 148 Ill. Dec. 829 (5th Dist. 1991) app. allowed 136 Ill. 2d 542, 567 N.E. 2d 329, 153 Ill. Dec. 375, aff'd 146 Ill. 2d 347, 586 N.E. 2d 1273, 167 Ill. Dec. 1 (1992)

Fixmer v. Regional Board of School Trustees of Kane County, 146 Ill. App. 3d 660, 497 N.E. 2d 152, 100 Ill. Dec. 272 (2nd Dist. 1986)

City National Bank of Kankakee v. Schott, 113 Ill. App. 3d 388, 447 N.E. 2d 478, 69 Ill. Dec. 261 (3rd Dist. 1983)

Granfield v. Regional Board of School Trustees of Bureau County, 108 Ill. App. 3d 703, 438 N.E. 2d 497, 64 Ill. Dec. 246 (3rd Dist. 1982)

Board of Education of Golf School District No. 67 v. Regional Board of School Trustees of Cook County, 89 Ill. 2d 392, 433 N.E. 2d 240, 60 Ill. Dec. 443 (1982)

Board of Education of Community High School District No. 154, McHenry County v. Regional Board of School Trustees of McHenry County, 84 Ill. App. 3d 501, 405 N.E. 2d 495 (2nd Dist. 1980)

Burnidge v. County Board of School Trustees of Kane County, 25 Ill. App. 2d 503, 167 N.E. 2d 21 (3rd Dist. 1960)

8:250 What is the benefit-detriment analysis?

The benefit-detriment analysis is used to determine whether the benefit derived from the annexation of the affected territory will outweigh the detriment to the losing district, the territory, and the community as a whole.

Carver v. Bond/Fayette/Effingham Regional Board of School Trustees, 203 Ill. App. 3d 799, 561 N.E. 2d 135, 148 Ill. Dec. 829 (5th Dist. 1991) app. allowed 136 Ill. 2d 542, 567 N.E. 2d 329, 153 Ill. Dec. 375, aff'd. 146 Ill. 2d 347, 586 N.E. 2d 1273, 167 Ill. Dec. 1 (1992)

Burnidge v. County Board of School Trustees of Kane County, 25 Ill. App. 2d 503, 167 N.E. 2d 21 (3rd Dist. 1960)

People v. Deatherage, 401 Ill. 25, 81 N.E. 2d 581 (1948)

8:260 May the regional board of school trustees consider parental preference and convenience in deciding a petition for detachment and annexation?

While they may be treated as one factor in ruling on the detachment petition, parental preference and convenience alone are usually insufficient to support a detachment and annexation petition.

Carver v. Bond/Fayette/Effingham Regional Board of School Trustees, 203 Ill. App. 3d 799, 561 N.E. 2d 135, 148 Ill. Dec. 829 (5th Dist. 1991) app. allowed 136 Ill. 2d 542, 567 N.E. 2d 329, 153 Ill. Dec. 375, aff'd. 146 Ill. 2d 347, 586 N.E. 2d 1273, 167 Ill. Dec. 1 (1992)

Eble v. Hamilton, 52 Ill. App. 3d 550, 367 N.E. 2d 788 (3rd Dist. 1977)

Ottawa Township High School District No. 140 of LaSalle County v. County Board of School Trustees, 106 Ill. App. 2d 439, 246 N.E. 2d 138 (3rd Dist. 1969)

Burgner v. County Board of School Trustees of Peoria County, 60 Ill. App. 2d 267, 208 N.E. 2d 54 (3rd Dist. 1965)

Trico Community Unit School District No. 176 v. County Board of School Trustees, 8 Ill. App. 2d 494, 131 N.E. 2d 829 (4th Dist. 1956)

8:270 What considerations apply to detachment and annexation petitions involving territory where no students reside?

In detachment and annexation hearings concerning property that is either uninhabited and/or in which no students reside, it is the duty of the regional board of school trustees to determine whether the annexation would be beneficial to the educational welfare of any pupils who might later reside in that area. Educational welfare is to be determined by considering whether or not the territory involved is part of an integral or main activity of the community served by the receiving school district, the residential potential of the tract of land involved, and the distance students would travel along and across any heavily traveled roads in order to attend school.

Pontiac Township High School District No. 90 v. Regional Board of School Trustees for Livingston County, 183 Ill. App. 3d 885, 539 N.E. 2d 885, 132 Ill. Dec. 322 (4th Dist. 1989)

City National Bank of Kankakee v. Schott, 113 Ill. App. 3d 388, 447 N.E. 2d 478, 69 Ill. Dec. 261 (3rd Dist. 1983)

Rhinehart v. Board of Education of Bloomington School District No. 87, McLean County, 132 Ill. App. 2d 1078, 271 N.E. 2d 104 (4th Dist. 1971)

Board of Education of Springfield School District No. 186 v. Scott, 105 Ill. App. 2d 192, 244 N.E. 2d 821 (4th Dist. 1969)

8:280 Who may appeal an annexation, detachment, or dissolution decision of a regional board of school trustees?

Any resident, petitioner, or school board entitled to receive a certified copy of the Regional Board of School Trustees' order may appeal a dissolution with 10 days after a copy of the decision sought to be reviewed was served certified mail, return receipt requested upon the resident, petitioner, or school board. An appeal may also be timely filed within 35 days of the decision in the case of a change of boundaries petition.

105 ILCS 5/7-1
105 ILCS 5/7-7
105 ILCS 5/7-11

8:290 What happens if an annexation, detachment, or dissolution decision of a regional board of school trustees is appealed?

If a decision of a regional board of school trustees is appealed, the complaint for judicial review operates as a stay of enforcement, and there is no enforcement of the decision until there is final disposition of the review. This means the entire matter of the dissolution, detachment, or annexation is in limbo until all appeals have been exhausted.

105 ILCS 5/7-7
105 ILCS 5/7-11

8:295 What happens if the regional board of school trustees fails to act on a detachment, annexation, division, or dissolution petition?

If within 12 months after a petition is submitted under Section 7-1 of the School Code the regional board of school trustees fails to approve or deny the petition, the petitioners may submit a copy of the petition directly to the State Superintendent of Education for approval or denial.

105 ILCS 5/7-6 (1)

CHARTER DISTRICT DETACHMENT AND ANNEXATION

8:300 How is a petition for annexation to or detachment of territory from a charter district filed?

A request for annexation or detachment of territory may be initiated by any district affected by the filing of a petition signed by the school board and by a petition signed by 25 percent or 1,000 of the legal voters of the district, whichever is less, or by a petition signed by 50 percent of the legal voters residing in any territory requesting to be annexed or detached, or if there are no legal voters residing within the territory proposed to be detached or annexed, the petition may be signed by 50 percent of the owners of real estate of record.

There is a provision that permits the attachment of land by petition only to a special charter school district located in a special charter city under very narrow conditions specified in the statute.

65 ILCS 5/1-1-1 et seq.

105 ILCS 5/7-2.3 et seq.

Schreiber v. County Board of School Trustees of Peoria County, 31 Ill. 2d 121, 198 N.E. 2d 848 (1964)

People on rel. Community Unit School District No. 1, Macon and DeWitt Counties v. Decatur School District No. 61, 45 Ill. App. 2d 33, 194 N.E. 2d 659 (3rd Dist. 1963)

8:310 With what body is a charter district detachment or annexation petition filed?

A petition for detachment of territory from a special charter district with annexation to another school district, for detachment of territory from a school district with annexation to a special charter district, or for dissolution of a school district with annexation to a special charter district, must be filed with the governing body of the special charter district, and a certified copy must be sent to each other detaching, dissolving, or annexing school district and to the regional board of school trustees of the region in which the regional superintendent has supervision and control of the detaching or dissolving district. A petition for such annexation or detachment of territory must be filed by the school board of the detaching or dissolving district, by a majority of the legal resident voters in the dissolving district, or by two-thirds of a combination of the legal resident voters and the owners of record of any real estate with no legal resident voters in any territory proposed to be detached. If any of the territory proposed to be detached contains real estate with no legal resident voters, petitioners must deliver the petition by certified mail, return receipt requested, to all owners of record of any real estate with no legal resident voters. Any owner of record of real estate with no legal resident voters in any territory proposed to be detached may either sign the petition in person and before the circulator as described in Section 7-1 of the School Code or return the petition with his or her notarized signature to be included as a petitioner. No person may sign a petition in the capacity of both a legal resident voter and owner of record. If there are no legal resident voters within the territory proposed to be detached, then the petition must be signed by all of the owners of record of the real estate of the territory. Where there is only one school building in an approved operating school district, the building and building site may not be included in any detachment proceeding.

65 ILCS 5/1-1-1 et seq.

105 ILCS 5/7-2.4

8:320 What happens following the filing of a charter district detachment and annexation petition?

If no objection is filed with the regional board of school trustees or the governing body of the special charter district within 30 days after the filing of the petition, the dissolution or detachment takes effect subject however to stay rules in the event of appeal and other statutory timelines. If an objection is filed, the regional board of school trustees and the school district must appoint a hearing board. The regional board of school trustees appoints two members and the school board appoints two members. These four members meet and appoint three more members who reside outside the area to be detached or annexed.

105 ILCS 5/7-2.5 et seq.

105 ILCS 5/7-9

Board of Education of Rockford School District No. 205 Winnebago and Boone Counties v. Hearing Board of Counties of Boone and Winnebago, 152 Ill. App. 3d 936, 505 N.E. 2d 32, 105 Ill. Dec. 906 (2nd Dist. 1987), app. den. 115 Ill. 2d 535, 511 N.E. 2d 425, 110 Ill. Dec 453 (1987)

Board of Education of Rockford School District No. 205 Winnebago and Boone Counties v. Regional Board of School Trustees of Boone and Winnebago Counties, 135 Ill. App. 3d 486, 481 N.E. 2d 1266, 90 Ill. Dec. 355 (2nd Dist. 1985)

Board of Education of Niles Township High School District 219, Cook County v. Regional Board of School Trustees of Cook County, 127 Ill. App. 3d 210, 468 N.E. 2d 1247, 82 Ill. Dec. 467 (1st Dist. 1984)

8:330 What factors must the hearing board consider in ruling on petitions?

The hearing board must consider: (a) the school needs and conditions of the territory in the area within and adjacent to the area to be attached or detached and the ability of the districts affected to meet the standards of recognition as prescribed by the State Board of Education, (b) the division of funds and assets that will result from any change of boundaries, (c) the will of the people of the area affected, and (d) the best interests of the schools of the area and the educational welfare of the pupils.

105 ILCS 5/7-2.6

First National Bank of Elgin v. West Aurora School District 129, 200 Ill. App. 3d 210, 558 N.E. 2d 686, 146 Ill. Dec. 723 (2nd Dist. 1990)

Desmond v. Regional Board of School Trustees, Malta Community Unit School District No. 433, 183 Ill. App. 3d 316, 538 N.E. 2d 1350, 131 Ill. Dec. 794 (2nd Dist. 1989), app. den. 127 Ill. 2d 614, 545 N.E. 2d 108, 136 Ill. Dec. 584 (1989)

Phillips v. Special Hearing Board of Boone and Winnebago Counties, 154 Ill. App. 3d 799, 504 N.E. 2d 1251, 105 Ill. Dec. 733 (2nd Dist. 1986) app. den. 115 Ill. 2d 550, 511 N.E. 2d 436, 110 Ill. Dec. 464 (1987)

City National Bank of Kankakee v. Schott, 113 Ill. App. 3d 388, 447 N.E. 2d 478, 69 Ill. Dec. 261 (4th Dist. 1983)

Wirth v. Green, 96 Ill. App. 3d 89, 420 N.E. 2d 1200, 51 Ill. Dec. 642 (3rd Dist. 1981)

Board of Education of Springfield School District No. 186, Sangamon County v. Scott, 105 Ill. App. 2d 192, 244 N.E. 2d 821 (4th Dist. 1969)

Board of Education of City of Bloomington, McLean County v. County Board of School Trustees of McLean County, 77 Ill. App. 2d 368, 222 N.E. 2d 343 (4th Dist. 1966)

Horth v. Board of Education of School District No. 205, Winnebago County, 42 Ill. App. 2d 65, 191 N.E. 2d 601 (2nd Dist. 1963)

8:340 What is the effective date of change for the creation or change of boundaries of a charter school district?

When a petition is filed for the change in boundaries of a charter school district, the commencement of any action for judicial review acts as a stay of enforcement, and no further proceedings may be had until final disposition of the review. A petition for rehearing operates as a stay until the hearing board enters its final order on the petition for rehearing.

In the event that the granting of a petition has become final, through failure to seek administrative review, by the final decision of a court on review if no further appeal is taken, or upon certification of election results in the event of a dissolution, the change in boundaries becomes effective the following July 1. The school boards of the districts as they existed prior to the change exercise the same power and authority over the territory until that date, unless accelerated or postponed by stipulation of the school boards of each detaching or dissolving and annexing school district and approval by the regional board of school trustees with which the original petition is required to be filed.

105 ILCS 5/7-2.6
105 ILCS 5/7-2.7
105 ILCS 5/7-9

9: CONTROL AND USE OF SCHOOL PROPERTY

ACQUISITION AND OWNERSHIP

9:10 What was the original source of school property in Illinois?

The Northwest Ordinance in 1787 set aside the sixteenth section (640 acres) in every congressional township for the maintenance of public schools. This land was used for school sites or, more often, for rental or sale with proceeds used to support the schools. Common school land today is defined as "the sixteenth section in every township and the sections and parts of sections granted in place of all or part of the sixteenth section."

1 U.S. Land Laws 852
105 ILCS 5/15-1

9:20 Who holds title to public school property?

Public school property is actually state property. Prior to 1993, title to most school property was held by boards of township school trustees in Class II counties (Cook) and by regional boards of school trustees in Class I counties (all other counties). School boards could hold title to certain property acquired by gift or legacy or property acquired for vocational training projects.

As a result of legislation enacted in 1993, school boards outside Cook County hold title to real property formerly held by the regional board of school trustees, as well as real or personal property acquired from a direct grant, gift, donation, or legacy to the board. Also, in Cook County, certain school districts may, by resolution, withdraw from the jurisdiction of the trustees of schools and thereby acquire title to real property.

Title to public school property in Chicago is held by the city.

105 ILCS 5/5-1
105 ILCS 5/5-21
105 ILCS 5/10-22.35b
105 ILCS 5/10-23.3
105 ILCS 5/16-1
105 ILCS 5/34-20

9:30 Are school districts subject to local zoning laws?

For many years prior to a 2016 change in the relevant statute, there was uncertainty as the application of local zoning ordinances to school districts. The change mandates that a school district is subject to, and its school board must comply with, any valid local government zoning ordinance or resolution that applies where the pertinent part of the building, structure, or site owned by the school district is located.

65 ILCS 5/11-13-1
105 ILCS 5/10-22.10
105 ILCS 5/10-22.13a
105 ILCS 5/10-22.35A
City of Waukegan v. Illinois E.P.A., 339 Ill. App. 3d 963, 791 N.E. 2d 635, 274 Ill. Dec. 543 (2nd Dist. 2003)
City of Joliet v. Snyder, 317 Ill. App. 3d 940, 741 N.E. 2d 1051, 251 Ill. Dec. 873 (3rd Dist. 2000)
Wilmette Park District v. Village of Wilmette, 112 Ill. 2d 6, 490 N.E. 2d 1282, 96 Ill. Dec. 77 (1986)
City of Des Plaines v. Metropolitan Sanitary District of Greater Chicago, 48 Ill. 2d 11, 268 N.E. 2d 428, (1971)
Heft v. Zoning Board of Appeals of Peoria County, 31 Ill. 2d 266, 201 N.E. 2d 364 (1964)

9:35 Which school property is exempt from local property taxes?

All property of schools, not sold or leased or otherwise used with a view to profit, is exempt from local property taxes, whether owned by an Illinois resident or a non-resident or by a corporation incorporated in any state. Any property of schools on which the schools are located and any other property of schools (including property the school leases) used by the schools exclusively for school purposes is exempt.

35 ILCS 200/15-35

9:40 How may a school board acquire property?

A school board may acquire school property by purchase or lease; condemnation; grant, gift, donation, devise, or bequest; or by receipt of a beneficial interest from a trust.

50 ILCS 605/1 et seq.
65 ILCS 5/11-78-1 et seq.
105 ILCS 5/10-22.12
105 ILCS 5/10-22.35A
105 ILCS 5/10-23.6

9:44 May a school board purchase real property with a contract for deed?

A school board may purchase school sites or sites for office facilities by contracting for the deed. The contract may not exceed 10 years in length and installment payments on the contract must be made from the operations and maintenance fund.

105 ILCS 5/10-22.35a

105 ILCS 5/17-7

9:46 May a school board enter into a lease-purchase agreement for school buildings or grounds?

A school board may lease school buildings and/or grounds for up to 10 years, or may enter into a 99-year lease with a two-thirds vote of the full membership of the school board (five votes on a seven-member board). A school board may levy a tax at a rate up to .05 (.10 with voter approval) to pay the rent on such a lease.

If the school board takes title to the property at the end of the lease period, however, the acquisition of title calls into question whether or not the payment contract that the parties called a lease actually was a lease, or rather was a contract for deed or some other financing arrangement.

105 ILCS 5/10-22.12

105 ILCS 5/17-2.2c

9:50 May a school board exercise power of eminent domain?

In appropriate circumstances, a school district may benefit from acquisition of private property by eminent domain. Eminent domain involves the taking of private property by the government (in this case a school district) for just compensation, but without the consent of the owner. Sometimes price is agreed upon by the government entity and the owner, but more often the courts determine fair market value. The Illinois Constitution provides in pertinent part:

"Private property shall not be taken or damaged for public use without just compensation as provided by law. Such compensation shall be determined by a jury as provided by law."

Ill. Const. art. I, sec. 15

Scheller v. Trustees of Schools, Township 41 North, 67 Ill. App. 3d 857, 384 N.E. 2d 971, 24 Ill. Dec. 104 (2nd Dist. 1978)

County Board of School Trustees of DuPage County v. Boram, 26 Ill. 2d 167, 186 N.E. 2d 275 (1962)

9:60 How is the price determined when property is acquired by eminent domain?

The courts establish the price to be paid when the governmental unit and the property owner cannot agree upon a price. Fair market value is the price standard applied. Fair market value is established by competent evidence.

105 ILCS 5/16-6

Chicago in Trust for Schools v. Albert J. Schorsch Realty Co., 6 Ill. App. 3d 1074, 287 N.E. 2d 93 (1st Dist. 1972)

Board of Junior College District 515 v. Wagner, 3 Ill. App. 3d 1006, 279 N.E. 2d 754 (1st Dist. 1971)

9:70 May a school board acquire property that is not contiguous to school grounds for use as a playground or athletic field?

Yes. Property acquired by a school board for use as playgrounds, recreational fields, or athletic fields need not be contiguous to any school grounds.

105 ILCS 5/16-7

9:80 May a school board purchase land located outside the boundaries of its school district?

Under certain conditions, a school district may have statutory authority to purchase land outside the boundaries of its school district. Such authority is frequently required to accommodate the school building requirements of joint agreements and cooperative education arrangements.

105 ILCS 5/10-22.31b

105 ILCS 5/10-23.6

105 ILCS 5/22-16

9:90 May a municipality transfer real estate to a school district?

Yes. The corporate authority of municipalities includes the power to transfer all of the rights, title, and interest held by it to a school district.

50 ILCS 605/2

9:100 May a school district require a land developer to set aside property for school purposes?

A school district has no direct means to require a developer to set aside land. A municipality may require a developer to set aside land and/or money for school purposes by passing an ordinance to that effect.

55 ILCS 5/5-1041.1

65 ILCS 5/11-12-5.1

Krughoff v. Naperville, 68 Ill. 2d 352, 369 N.E. 2d 892, 12 Ill. Dec. 185, (1977)

Board of Education School District No. 68 DuPage County v. Surety Developers, Inc., 24 Ill. App. 3d 638, 321 N.E. 2d 99 (2nd Dist. 1974)

Board of Education Community Consolidated School District No. 59, Cook County v. E.A. Herzog Construction Co., 29 Ill. App. 2d 138, 172 N.E. 2d 645 (1st Dist. 1961)

DISPOSING OF SCHOOL PROPERTY

9:110 Who has power to decide that a school site is unnecessary, unsuitable, or inconvenient for a school building?

A school board may decide when a site or building has become unnecessary, unsuitable, or inconvenient for use as a school. By resolution adopted by at least two-thirds of its membership, a school board may elect to sell, enter into a contract for deed, or convey a site under a seller-will-finance agreement.

50 ILCS 605/0.01 et seq.
105 ILCS 5/5-22

9:120 Under what conditions may a school board deactivate its high school or elementary school and send its students to another school district?

There is a statutory process whereby a school district may deactivate its high school or elementary school facility and pay tuition to send its students to another school district. The process requires voter approval and is subject to numerous statutory limitations and conditions.

105 ILCS 5/10-22.22b

9:130 May one school district sell school land to another school district?

If a school board decides a schoolhouse site, with or without a building, is of no further use to the district and agrees on a price with the school board of another school district within or next to the boundaries of the site, it may, after complying with statutory procedures, transfer the use of the site to the purchasing district.

105 ILCS 5/5-24
105 ILCS 5/16-3

9:135 May a school district donate land to another governmental entity?

An Illinois school district may donate a school building and site to another Illinois governmental entity provided both units of government comply with requisite statutory procedures. The process requires a resolution approved by at least two-thirds of the board members.

50 ILCS 605/0.01 et seq.
105 ILCS 5/5-22
105 ILCS 5/5-24

9:140 How may a school board offer real estate for public sale?

School real estate may be sold by auction or sealed bid, with or without a minimum selling price. If the school board specifies a minimum selling price and the price is not met, or no bids are received, a real estate broker may be employed pursuant to statutory terms. If at any time the school board lowers the minimum selling price, a new auction or sealed bid procedure must follow. The school board may increase the minimum selling price without repeating the public sale procedures.

105 ILCS 5/5-22

9:142 How may a school board sell a building trades house?

Building trades houses must be sold in the same manner as other school district real estate is sold. Any board member may purchase a building trades house for use as the board member's primary place of residence if the purchase occurs on the same basis as would be applicable to any other person that would be entitled to purchase the property.

After provision has been made for the payment of all school expenses, a school board may appropriate from the educational fund, use school funds, or borrow funds for the purchase of real estate and for the improvement by construction of buildings or other structures, or improved real estate in a deteriorated or uninhabitable condition, for vocational and other educational training of pupils. A school board may, when authorized by a resolution receiving a two-thirds majority vote, acquire title to the real estate in the name of the school district and sell and convey it; but no such property may be bought or used as a schoolhouse or for permanent use as school property. Such property purchased and improved must be sold or otherwise disposed of within five years from the date of its acquisition. Not more than one piece of real estate to be improved and one piece of improved real estate in a deteriorated or uninhabitable condition may be purchased for each secondary school or area vocational center that offers vocational training within the school district for any such purpose in any one calendar year, unless additional properties are examined and approved by the regional superintendent in the county in which the district is located, for larger training programs necessitating more property to accommodate larger student enrollments. No such real estate may be acquired for any such purpose by means of eminent domain proceedings.

If the school board does not hold legal title to the school site or other school property that is to be used for vocational or educational training, then upon the adoption of a resolution by two-thirds of the board members of the district requesting the conveyance of a school site or other school property or a portion thereof, the trustees of schools or other school official having legal title to the property must convey the property to the school district as provided in Section 5-21 of the School Code.

The sale of the house by the district must comply with the requirements of Section 5-22 of the School Code. A 2016 amendment to Section 5-22 allows the school board to hire a licensed real estate broker to sell the property for a commission not to exceed 7 percent, provided the property is listed on a multiple listing service for at least 14 calendar days and sold within 120 days.

105 ILCS 5/5-21
105 ILCS 5/5-22
105 ILCS 5/10-9
105 ILCS 5/10-23.3

9:145 Must a school district selling property notify a buyer of hazardous materials in school buildings and on school grounds?

In most cases, a school district selling real property must disclose to the buyer the presence of hazardous materials on the property. A disclosure statement is required by law to identify the existence of asbestos or certain underground storage tanks, for example.

15 U.S.C. 2642 et seq.
42 U.S.C. 11022
Bonnell v. Regional Board of School Trustees of Madison County, 258 Ill. App. 3d 485, 630 N.E. 2d 547, 196 Ill. Dec. 612 (5th Dist. 1994)

9:150 May the citizens of a school district initiate the sale of school land?

Citizens may petition a school board to sell school buildings and grounds to another school district or other municipality. The petition must be signed by at least 10 percent of the voters of the district. Upon receipt of the petition, the school board must adopt a resolution for the sale, fix the price, and order the school board secretary to certify the proposition to the election authorities for submission to the voters.

105 ILCS 5/5-24
105 ILCS 5/15-7

9:160 If a school board decides to close a school building and sell the property, may the land be sold separately from the building?

Title to any building erected on school grounds may be disposed of separately from the site upon which it is located.

Miner v. Yantis, 410 Ill. 401, 102 N.E. 2d 524 (1952)

9:165 How may the school board take payment for real estate?

The school board may take cash, may enter into a contract for deed, mortgage, or sell on the basis of another seller-financed basis as determined by the school board.

105 ILCS 5/5-22

9:170 May a school board exchange school property for other property?

By a two-thirds majority vote of its members, a school board may exchange a school site or a site with a building on it for another site. To do so, the school board must file a Certificate of Findings and Declarations with the Recorder of Deeds and comply with other statutory procedures.

105 ILCS 5/5-23

9:180 How may a school board use the proceeds from the sale of school property?

A school board must use the proceeds from the sale of school sites, buildings, or other real estate first to pay the principal and interest on any outstanding bonds on the property being sold. After all such bonds have been retired, the proceeds from the sale may be used for any authorized purpose and may be deposited into any district fund.

105 ILCS 5/5-22

9:190 May a school board lease school property to a third party?

A school board may lease school property to another school district, municipality, not-for-profit school organization, suitable lessee for educational purposes, another governmental body, or for any other purpose that serves the interests of the community. The permissible terms of the initial lease vary according to the type of lessee.

A referendum is required for leasing to a private not-for-profit school organization for use in the care of the trainable and educable mentally handicapped or for the education of the gifted.

A lease for a permissible term in excess of 10 years or the modification of a lease whose unexpired term is in excess of 10 years requires a vote of two-thirds of the full membership of the school board.

105 ILCS 5/10-22.11 et seq.

SCHOOL BUILDINGS

9:200 May a school board construct school buildings?

A school board is authorized to build or purchase a building for school classroom or instructional purposes upon voter approval at a referendum. A board also may issue bonds to finance construction upon voter approval.

105 ILCS 5/10-22.36
105 ILCS 5/19-1 et seq.

9:202 Is a referendum required to build a school office or to move a school building?

Before a 2001 amendment to Section 10-22.36 of the School Code, a referendum may have been necessary, although in practice some school districts were building without a referendum. The 2001 amendment provides it is no longer necessary to obtain voter approval to build a school office building or to move a school building.

105 ILCS 5/10-22.35A
105 ILCS 5/10-22.36

9:210 May a school board accumulate operating funds for the purpose of constructing a school building?

A building intended for classroom or instructional use may be constructed only after voter approval at a referendum unless the building is being leased by the school district or is purchased with funds derived from the sale or disposal of other buildings, land, or structures of the school district or with funds received as a grant under the School Construction Law or as gifts or donations, provided that no funds to complete such a building other than lease payments are derived from the district's bonded indebtedness or its tax levy.

Voter approval is also required for the accumulation of funds in the operations and maintenance fund.

105 ILCS 5/10 22.36
105 ILCS 5/17-5.1

9:215 Must a school district make its facilities handicapped accessible?

New building construction and alterations that affect the usability of the facility or a part of it must be handicapped accessible if first occupancy is after January 26, 1993. There is no requirement that existing facilities be altered to be handicapped accessible unless a student's Individualized Education Program, 504 plan, an accommodation for a handicapped employee, or some other specific accommodation so requires.

42 U.S.C. 12201 et seq.

9:220 Is a school board authorized to build an athletic stadium or arena for spectator sports?

A school board may issue revenue bonds to build an athletic stadium or arena and has wide authority to operate, control, and manage it. Funds to retire the bonds are acquired through charges and fees for the use of the facility.

105 ILCS 5/19a-1 et seq.

STATE CONSTRUCTION AID

9:230 Does the state of Illinois offer financial assistance to public school districts in the construction of school facilities?

For school districts that qualify and when moneys are appropriated by the legislature for this purpose, the state offers assistance in the building of school facilities. The Capital Development Board distributes and administers assistance funds.

30 ILCS 390/1 et seq.
30 ILCS 420/3 et seq.
105 ILCS 5/35-1
105 ILCS 230/5-10

9:240 What is the Illinois Capital Development Board?

The Illinois Capital Development Board is a state agency that administers distribution of funds for school sites, buildings, and equipment subject to statutory limitations. The State Board of Education establishes eligibility standards and priorities and notifies the Capital Development Board of approved construction projects.

20 ILCS 3105/1 et seq.

30 ILCS 390/1 et seq.

9:250 How does a school district get a Capital Development Board grant?

A school district may apply to the State Board of Education for a school construction project grant. A school district must establish eligibility for such a grant by submitting a District Facility Plan, subject to review and approval by the State Board of Education.

The facilities plan must include an assessment of present and future district facility needs as required by present and anticipated educational programming; the availability of local financial resources including current revenues, fund balances, and unused bonding capacity; a fiscal plan for meeting present and anticipated debt service obligations; and a maintenance plan and schedule that contain necessary assurances that new, renovated, and existing facilities are being or will be properly maintained.

If a district that applies for a grant has no unused bonding capacity or if its unused bonding capacity is less than the cost of the project that the district would be required to finance with non-grant funds, the application and facility plan submitted by the district must provide an estimate of the project cost the district proposes to finance by the issuance of bonds.

20 ILCS 3105/1

105 ILCS 230/5-20

9:255 What is a construction debt service grant?

School districts that have issued approved construction bonds are eligible to apply for debt service grants. If awarded, a debt service grant is equal to 10 percent of the principal amount of approved school construction bonds issued by the district times the grant index for the district.

Debt service grants can be used by the district to retire principal of approved school construction bonds, restructure debt service on such bonds, or to abate the property taxes levied for the district's bond and interest fund by an amount identical to the amount of the debt service grant.

105 ILCS 230/5-45

9:260 How are the building needs of school districts prioritized?

Under a 1997 amendment to the School Code, the State Board of Education establishes eligibility standards for school construction project grants and debt service grants. The Capital Development Board establishes project standards for all school construction project grants.

The State Board of Education prioritizes projects as follows:

1) Replacement or reconstruction of school buildings destroyed or damaged by flood, tornado, fire, earthquake, mine subsidence, or other disasters either man-made or produced by nature;

2) Projects designed to alleviate a shortage of classrooms due to population growth or to replace or rehabilitate aging school buildings;

3) Projects resulting from inter-district reorganization of school districts contingent on local referendums;

4) Replacement, rehabilitation, or reconstruction of school facilities determined to be severe and continuing health or life safety hazards;

5) Alterations necessary to provide accessibility for qualified individuals with disabilities;

6) Other unique solutions to facility needs.

The Capital Development Board considers the current average daily attendance in the district and its attendance areas and the probable average daily attendance for the succeeding five years in light of the growth trend of the district, the effect of slum clearance and large-scale housing projects, the pattern of attendance between private and public schools and plans for the curtailment or additions to private school facilities in the area, and any other factors bearing upon the probable continuing building needs of the district. It also determines the number of available classrooms that meet the minimum requirements specified by the State Board of Education. It proceeds on the assumption that each district needs one classroom for every 32 pupils in average daily attendance in grades K-6, one classroom for each 28 students in average daily attendance in grades 7-9, and one classroom for every 25 students in average daily attendance in grades 10-12.

105 ILCS 5/35-6 et seq.

105 ILCS 230/5-25

105 ILCS 230/5-30

9:265 What is the school construction grant index?

The grant index is a figure for each school district equal to one minus the ratio of the district's equalized assessed valuation per pupil in average daily attendance to the equalized assessed valuation of the district in the 90th percentile for all districts of the same category. For the purpose of calculating the grant index school districts are grouped into two categories, Category I and Category II.

Category I consists of elementary and unit school districts. The equalized assessed valuation per pupil in average daily attendance for each school district in Category I shall be computed using the grades K-8 average daily attendance figures. A unit school district's Category I grant index is used for projects or portions of projects constructed for elementary school pupils.

Category II consists of high school and unit school districts. The equalized valuation per pupil in average daily attendance of each school district in Category II is computed using grades 9-12 average daily attendance figures. A unit school district's Category II grant index is used for projects or portions of projects constructed for high school pupils.

The changes made by a 2001 amendment to the grant index statute applies to all grants made on or after July 26, 2001 except for grants not yet made on July 26, 2001, but made in fiscal year 2001 and for grants made in fiscal year 2002, the grant index for a school district is the greater of (i) the grant index as calculated under the new law on or after July 26, 2001 or (ii) the grant index as calculated under the old law . The grant index is no less than .35 and no greater than .75 for each district except that a district whose equalized assessed valuation per pupil in average daily attendance is at the 99th percentile and above for all districts of the same type receives a grant index of zero.

105 ILCS 230/5-5

9:266 What is a school construction project?

A school construction project in the context of school construction grants is the acquisition, development, construction, reconstruction, rehabilitation, improvement, architectural planning, and installation of capital facilities consisting of buildings, structures, durable equipment, and land for educational purposes.

105 ILCS 230/5-5

9:267 What is a school maintenance project?

A school maintenance project in the context of school construction grants is a project other than a school construction project intended to provide maintenance or upkeep of buildings or structures for educational purposes but does not include ongoing operational costs.

105 ILCS 230/5-5

9:268 What is a school maintenance project grant?

The State Board of Education can make grants to school districts from the School Infrastructure Fund for school maintenance projects. No one grant for one fiscal year can exceed $50,000, but a school district can receive grants for more than one project during one fiscal year. A school district must provide local matching funds in an amount equal to the amount of the grant. There is grant entitlement.

The State Board of Education will adopt rules to implement the grants. The rules specify (i) the manner of applying for grants; (ii) project eligibility requirements; (iii) restrictions on the use of grant moneys; (iv) the manner in which school districts must account for the use of grant moneys; and (v) any other provision that the State Board determines to be necessary or useful for the administration of this section. The rules specify the methods and standards used by the State Board to prioritize applications.

School maintenance projects are prioritized in the following order:

1) Emergency projects;
2) Health/life safety projects;
3) State Program priority projects;
4) Permanent improvement projects;
5) Other projects.

School maintenance grants have not been funded in recent years.

105 ILCS 230/5-100

9:270 What qualifications must a school district meet in order to receive assistance from the Capital Development Board?

No school district is entitled to have a building acquired or constructed by the Capital Development Board (CDB) unless:

1) The CDB determines the district will require, in addition to its present classrooms and those for which funds have been provided by the district, classrooms for at least 110 pupils in average daily attendance in grades 9-12 and 200 pupils in average daily attendance in grades K-12 at the beginning of the ensuing fall school term and the need for such additional classrooms will continue through five ensuing school years.

2) The district has either reduced its bonding power to less than $5,000 or will have done so in complying with the provisions of this requirement.

3) The school board has been authorized to levy a special tax sufficient in amount to provide the rent for the facilities to be so provided, but the CDB may approve an application for the construction of a classroom in a district contingent upon compliance with this provision within 60 days after such approval.

105 ILCS 5/35-7

9:280 May the Capital Development Board lease facilities to school districts?

The Capital Development Board may lease facilities to school districts.

105 ILCS 5/22-17

105 ILCS 5/35-5(c)

105 ILCS 5/35-5(i)

9:290 If a school district is to build a facility with Capital Development Board assistance, who has control over site selection?

The Capital Development Board may reject any site selected by a school board if the site does not meet minimum engineering and construction standards.

20 ILCS 3105/10.16

BUILDING CONTRACTORS

9:300 Must a school district pay "prevailing wages" to workers on a construction contract?

Laborers, workers, and mechanics employed by or on behalf of a school district, its contractors, or subcontractors to perform construction work including any maintenance, repair, assembly, or disassembly work performed on equipment whether owned, leased, or rented must be paid not less than the hourly wage generally prevailing for similar work in the area. A school district employer need not pay prevailing wages to its own employees.

The school district must ascertain the prevailing rate of wages on a per-hour basis or ask the Department of Labor to ascertain the rate. The school district must specify in its resolution and call for bids that the prevailing hourly rate will be paid for each worker, and must stipulate in the contract that all workers must be paid no less than such prevailing rate. The school district must require contractors to include in their bonds provisions to guarantee the payment of prevailing wage rates.

The school district has an obligation to inform contractors and subcontractors of possible rate revisions. This obligation is met by inserting into each contract a notice that rates are subject to revision and are available on the Department of Labor's official website at *www.state.il.us/agency/idol/publicb/publicb.htm*.

820 ILCS 130/1 et seq.

People ex rel. Bernardi v. Roofing Systems, Inc., 101 Ill. 2d 424, 463 N.E. 2d 123, 78 Ill. Dec. 945 (1984)

Beaver Glass and Mirror Company, Inc. v. Board of Education of Rockford School District No. 205, Winnebago County, 59 Ill. App. 3d 880, 376 N.E. 2d 377, 17 Ill. Dec. 378 (2nd Dist. 1978)

City of Monmouth v. Payes, 39 Ill. App. 2d 32, 188 N.E. 2d 48 (2nd Dist. 1963)

Bradley v. Casey, 415 Ill. 576, 114 N.E. 2d 681 (1953)

9:302 What is the meaning of "public works" as that term is used in the Prevailing Wage Act?

Public works means all fixed works constructed or demolished by any public body, other than work done directly by any public utility company, whether or not done under public supervision or direction, or paid for wholly or in part out of public funds. The relevant statute includes a list of statutes by which funding for public works might be obtained and provides that if funds are used from the listed sources the project is "public works."

820 ILCS 130/2

9:305 Must a school board require a building contractor or subcontractor to supply a performance bond to guarantee construction work?

A school district must require every contractor to supply and deliver a bond for work costing over $5,000. A bank letter of credit is not sufficient surety unless the funding that supports the project that the bond would otherwise insure does not include moneys received from state or federal sources and the contract is under $100,000. The amount of the bond may be established by the school board and among other conditions must be conditioned upon the completion of the contract, the payment of material used in the work, and for all labor performed in the work whether by the contractor, subcontractor, or otherwise.

30 ILCS 550/0.01 et seq.

9:310 Is school district property subject to a mechanic's lien?

No. School district real estate is not subject to a mechanic's lien. Subcontractors may acquire a mechanic's lien on the money, bonds, or warrants due or that may become due.

770 ILCS 60/23

Board of Education of School District No. 108, Tazewell Co. for Use of A.Y. McDonald Manufacturing

Company v. Collum, 77 Ill. App. 2d 479, 222 N.E. 2d 804 (3rd Dist. 1966)

Spaulding Lumber Company v. Brown, 171 Ill. 487, 49 N.E. 725 (1898)

BUILDING SAFETY

9:320 Is school district property subject to any laws regarding safety?

School building construction and maintenance are subject to State Board of Education regulations contained in the School Building Code and the Health Life Safety Code. Schools also are subject to the occupational safety standards of the Illinois Department of Labor. Other safety standards applicable to schools include various environmental requirements, such as asbestos abatement and safe drinking water, traffic safety, and the common law "duty of care" owed to students while on school premises.

23 Ill. Admin. Code 180.10 et seq.

9:330 What is the Health Life Safety Code?

The Health Life Safety Code is a document prepared by the State Board of Education with the advice of the Department of Public Health, the Capital Development Board, and the State Fire Marshal to "conserve the health and safety and general welfare of the pupils," school personnel, and others who use public school facilities.

105 ILCS 5/2-3.12

23 Ill. Admin. Code 180.10 et seq.

Board of Education of City of Rockford v. Page, 33 Ill. 2d 372, 211 N.E. 2d 361 (1965)

Board of Education of School District No. 33, DuPage County v. City of West Chicago, 55 Ill. App. 2d 401, 205 N.E. 2d 63 (2nd Dist 1965)

9:337 What is a Safety Survey Report?

School buildings must be surveyed by an architect or engineer who, upon completion of the survey, issues a Safety Survey Report to the local school board. The survey is generally required on a 10-year cycle. The report contains prioritized recommendations and, upon approval of the regional superintendent of schools and the State Superintendent of Education, may require a local school board to make corrections.

105 ILCS 5/2-3.12

9:340 Who is responsible for school inspections under the School Building Code?

The regional superintendent of schools is charged with the responsibility to inspect the plans and specifications for the heating, ventilating, lighting, seating, water supply, toilets, and fire safety of all the public school rooms and buildings within his or her region to ensure compliance with the School Building Code. The State Fire Marshal or a qualified fire official to whom the State Fire Marshal has delegated his or her authority is authorized to conduct up to two routine fire safety checks per year and an annual fire safety inspection of each school building. If the regional superintendent of schools does not approve or deny plans submitted to him within 30 days, the school board may submit the plans or specifications directly to the State Superintendent of schools for approval or denial.

If a municipality or, in the case of an unincorporated area, a county or, if applicable, a fire protection district wishes to perform new construction inspections under the jurisdiction of a regional superintendent, then the entity must register this wish with the regional superintendent. These inspections must be based on the building code authorized in Section 2-3.12 of the School Code. The inspections must be at no cost to the school district.

105 ILCS 5/2-3.12

105 ILCS 5/3-14.20

105 ILCS 5/3-14.21

9:345 What agencies have authority to inspect school cafeterias for health and safety?

The county health department has such authority. The regional superintendent does not have exclusive authority to conduct inspections for sanitation or health control.

Macon County v. Board of Education of Decatur School District No. 61, 165 Ill. App. 3d 1, 518 N.E. 2d 653, 116 Ill. Dec. 31 (4th Dist. 1987) app. den. 119 Ill. 2d 558, 517 N.E. 2d 1246, 119 Ill. Dec. 387 (1988)

9:350 Can a regional superintendent of schools condemn a school building?

If a regional superintendent of schools believes a school building to be unsafe, he or she may request the Department of Public Health, the State Fire Marshal, or the supervising architect to inspect public school buildings and temporary school facilities that appear to him to be unsafe, unsanitary, or unfit for occupancy. These officials must inspect, and if in their opinion, the buildings or temporary facilities are unsafe, unsanitary, or unfit for occupancy, they must state in writing in what particular the facilities are deficient. Upon receiving the statement, the regional superintendent must condemn the building or temporary facility and notify the school board in writing stating the reasons for the condemnation.

105 ILCS 5/3-14.22

9:355 What happens if a school district does not correct deficiencies identified in a life-safety report?

If a regional superintendent determines that a school board has failed in a timely manner to correct urgent items identified in a previous life-safety report or as otherwise previously ordered by the regional superintendent, the superintendent can order the school board to adopt and submit a plan for the immediate correction of the building violations.

The plan must be adopted after the conduct of a public hearing by the school board. The hearing must be preceded by notice published at least seven days before the hearing in a newspaper of general circulation within the school district.

If the deficiencies are not corrected by the next annual inspection, the state can withhold general state aid or evidence-based funding. State aid or evidence-based funding sufficient to correct the violations may be withheld and remitted to the regional superintendent who has the power to contract on behalf of the school board to cause repairs to be made that will correct the violations.

105 ILCS 5/3-14.21

9:360 Which standards control fire prevention and safety for public school buildings, those of the State Fire Marshal or the Illinois State Board of Education?

The State Board of Education School Building Code applies. The State Fire Marshal's Grey Book does not apply.

Board of Education of Minooka Community High School District No. 111 Grundy, Kendall and Will Counties v. Carter, 119 Ill. App. 3d 857, 458 N.E. 2d 50, 75 Ill. Dec. 882, (3rd Dist. 1983)

9:361 Does the School Building Code prevent fire inspections by agencies other than the State Board of Education or the Regional Superintendent of Schools?

No. The regulating statutory provision, a political battleground, has been amended numerous times, each time changing the agencies having authority to conduct fire inspections. A 2005 amendment authorizes the State Fire Marshal or "a qualified fire official to whom the State Fire Marshal has delegated his or her authority" to conduct safety checks. The amendment also requires that if a fire official notifies the school district that corrective action must be taken, the school board has one year to take such action, except that violations that present an imminent danger must be corrected immediately.

Schools may be investigated pursuant to Section 9 of the Fire Investigation Act and by other agencies that may have jurisdiction. Such investigations must be coordinated with the regional superintendent of schools and the School Building Code must be used as the standard for compliance.

105 ILCS 5/2-3.12

105 ILCS 5/3-14.21

425 ILCS 25/9

9:365 Are sprinkler systems required in schools?

Sprinkler systems are required in all new public school buildings, building additions, and remodeling projects involving 50 percent or more of a school building. An addition of less than 7,200 square feet to an existing building may be equipped with an automatic fire detection system in lieu of a sprinkler system.

30 ILCS 805/8.15

105 ILCS 5/22-23

HEALTH AND SAFETY

9:370 What is the Illinois Health and Safety Act?

The Health and Safety Act requires employers, including school districts, to provide employees with a safe workplace. It is administered by the Illinois Department of Labor (IDOL), which has enacted rules implementing the statute. Employers are required, among other things, to (a) post notices of employee rights under the act, including the right to file complaints with the Department of Labor; (b) submit to IDOL inspections and provide access to requested information and records; and (c) keep records of injuries arising in the workplace.

820 ILCS 225/1 et seq.

9:375 May a school board designate smoking areas in its school buildings for its employees who smoke?

No. Federal law requires that a school district prohibit smoking in every indoor, enclosed school facility that is owned, leased, or contracted for and utilized for the provision of routine and regular kindergarten, elementary, and secondary education and library services to students. A school district that violates the law risks loss of federal funds.

The School Code requires schools to prohibit the use of tobacco on school property when the property is being used for any school purpose. The school board may not authorize or permit any exception or exemption from the prohibition at any place or at any time. The tobacco ban includes all events or activities or other use of school property that the school board or school officials authorize or permit on school property including interscholastic or extracurricular activities or other events sponsored by the school board in which students participate. The ban includes cigarettes, cigars, or tobacco in any other form including loose, cut, shredded, ground, powdered, compressed, or leaf tobacco that is intended to be placed in the mouth without being smoked.

20 U.S.C. 6082
20 U.S.C. 7181 et seq.
105 ILCS 5/10-20.5b

9:380 Is a school board required to provide crossing guards for students walking to and from school?

No. However, a school board may employ persons to direct traffic on school grounds, or on or along streets and highways within a radius of one mile from school grounds. If a board elects to hire crossing guards, the cost may be shared with any unit of local government.

105 ILCS 5/10-22.28a

9:381 May a municipality that has shared the cost of providing crossing guards unilaterally decide to stop doing so?

Yes. While the School Code permits school districts to share the cost of crossing guards with other units of local government, there is no means by which a school district can compel a unit of local government to share in the cost.

9:390 May a school board establish a school safety patrol?

Yes. Student participation requires written parental consent.

105 ILCS 5/10-22.28

9:400 May a school district install traffic signals at crossings where students walk to and from school?

A school board may acquire, install, operate, and maintain traffic signals outside city, village, or incorporated town limits and within a one-mile radius of school grounds, subject to certain statutory limitations.

105 ILCS 5/10-22.28a

9:405 Are school buildings required to maintain defibrillators?

Each public school must have a plan to respond to medical emergencies and, except with respect to very narrow exceptions not relevant for most schools, must have a defibrillator on site at each school building containing a gym on the following schedule:

For school districts with four or fewer buildings containing gyms, one must have a defibrillator by July 1, 2006; a second by July 1, 2007; a third by July 1, 2008; and its fourth by July 1, 2009.

For school districts with more than four buildings containing gyms, 25 percent must have a defibrillator by July 1, 2006; 50 percent by July 1, 2007; 75 percent by July 1, 2008; and 100 percent by July 1, 2009.

A school district is not liable for civil damages for any act or omission involving the use of the defibrillator except for willful or wanton misconduct if the school district complies with the Physical Fitness Facility Medical Emergency Preparedness Act.

210 ILCS 74/1 et seq.
410 ILCS 4/30 (c)

9:410 What is the purpose of the Asbestos Abatement Act?

The purpose of the Illinois Asbestos Abatement Act is to provide for the identification, containment, or removal of those asbestos materials that constitute a significant health hazard to students, school personnel, parents, or visitors in the public elementary and secondary schools of the state of Illinois.

15 U.S.C. 2641 et seq.
105 ILCS 105/1 et seq.

9:415 Must a school district use "green" cleaning supplies?

A law enacted in 2007 requires that all public elementary and secondary schools and all non-public such schools with 50 or more students must purchase and use environmentally sensitive cleaning products "when it is economically feasible." Adopting a green cleaning policy is not economically feasible under the law when it would result in an increase in the cleaning costs of the school.

The law allows schools to deplete their current supply stocks and implement the requirement in the following school year.

105 ILCS 140/10 et seq.

USE OF SCHOOL FACILITIES

9:420 May a school district hold a child's parents financially responsible for damage the child does to school property?

A civil suit under common law may be instituted. Recovery is also possible pursuant to the Parental Responsibility Act, under which a school district may hold a minor's parents responsible for actual damages or for the willful or malicious acts of a minor, to a maximum of $20,000, for injury to persons or school property for a first act or occurrence and $30,000 if a pattern or practice of willful or malicious acts by a minor exists for a separate act or occurrence in addition to court costs and attorney fees. A minor in this context is any unemancipated person who is over 11 but not yet 19 years of age and who lives with his or her parents or legal guardian.

The Parental Responsibility Act permits the recovery of attorney fees for successful plaintiffs who are not governmental entities and reasonable attorney fees up to $15,000 if the plaintiff is a governmental unit.

740 ILCS 115/3

740 ILCS 115/5

9:430 May a school board allow an outside organization to use school facilities during non-school hours?

A school board may permit use of school facilities by outside organizations during non-school hours and if it determines to do so, must adopt a policy governing such use. The policy must prohibit use if it would interfere with school functions or the safety of students or school personnel or if the use would affect the property or liability of the school district.

Statutory authority exists for use for religious meetings, Sunday schools, evening schools, literary societies, and for such other meetings as the school board deems proper.

A school board that permits use must be cautious that it does not engage in viewpoint discrimination because if a group can prove it was denied use or otherwise discriminated against on the basis of its viewpoint, the group might be able prevail in a lawsuit. Viewpoint discrimination might be evidenced by refusal to allow use or it might be evidenced in rules or fees that are charged for one kind of activity but not for another.

Restrictions that slip from neutral time, place, and manner concerns into concerns about content are never permissible. The government cannot impose financial burdens on speakers or groups based on the content of their speech.

105 ILCS 5/10-20.41

105 ILCS 5/10-22.10

Surita, et al., v. Hyde, et al., 665 F. 3d 860 (7th Cir. 2011)

Faith Center Church Evangelistic Ministries v. Glover, 462 F. 3d 1194 (9th Cir. 2006)

Resnick v. East Brunswick Township Board of Education, 77 N.J. 88, 389 A. 2d 944 (1978)

Board of Education of the City of Chicago v. Crilly, 312 Ill. App. 177, 37 N.E. 2d 873 (1941)

9:432 May a school district determine which groups are given access to school facilities?

If a school district allows use of its facilities generally, it may not discriminate among users on the basis of the content of the speech of a potential user. A school may have the ability to deny use to a student group only if recognition would "materially and substantially interfere with the school's overarching mission to educate its students."

Faith Center Church Evangelistic Ministries v. Glover, 462 F. 3d 1194 (9th Cir. 2006)

Christian Legal Society v. Walker, 453 F. 3d 853 (7th Cir. 2006)

Hsu v. Roslyn Union Free School District No. 3, 85 F. 3d 839 (2nd Cir. 1996)

Hurley v. Irish American Gay, Lesbian and Bisexual Group of Boston, 115 S. Ct. 2338, 515 U.S. 557, 132 L. Ed. 2d 487 (1995)

Lamb's Chapel v. Center Moriches Union Free School District, 113 S. Ct. 2141, 508 U.S. 384, 124 L. Ed. 2d 352 (1993)

9:434 May school officials ban an unruly individual from entering upon school grounds?

Because school buildings are public places and because the activities that occur at school are important to society, the removal of individuals from school grounds should be a last resort.

To remove a student from access to school facilities for up to two years requires a lawful expulsion hearing before the school board and a carefully worded expulsion motion.

To ban a member of the community from access to extracurricular activities for up to one year also requires a board hearing pursuant to statute. To attach conditions to the access of a member of the public to school grounds or to ban a member of the public requires a written notice to the person school officials seek to restrict or ban.

Except where the School Code defines a procedure that must be followed, because a member of the public does not have a protected liberty interest in accessing school grounds, a school board need not provide due process in connection with its imposition of a ban from school grounds.

105 ILCS 5/10-22.6

105 ILCS 5/24-24

720 ILCS 5/21-5

Hannemann v. Southern Door County School District, 673 F. 3d 746 (7th Cir. 2012)

9:440 May or must a school board charge fees to outside organizations for the use of school facilities?

A school board may establish fees for the use of school facilities, but is not required to do so. However, any fees not applied equally to all organizations must be structured by some reasonable classification, such as with lower fees or no fees for school-related groups (e.g., PTA, band boosters) or not-for-profit groups. Fees structured to discriminate against groups espousing unpopular views, for example, may be subject to challenge on constitutional grounds.

105 ILCS 5/10-22.10

SAFETY DRILL REQUIREMENTS

9:600 What types of safety drills are required by law?

During each academic year each school building must conduct a minimum of three school evacuation drills, one of which must include the participation of the local fire department or fire district, a minimum of one bus evacuation drill, and one severe weather and shelter-in-place drill. A school district must include in its curriculum bus riding safety instruction.

Each school must conduct an annual law enforcement drill to address a school shooting incident. The school administrator and local law enforcement agency must set, by mutual agreement, a date for the drill.

With respect to evacuation drills, each local fire department or fire district is required to contact the appropriate school administrator or designee no later than September 1 each year to arrange for participation in the school evacuation drill. Each school administrator or designee is required to contact the responding local fire official no later than September 15 each year to propose to the local fire official four dates in the month of October, during at least two different weeks of October, on which the drill shall occur. The fire official may choose any of the four available dates, and if he or she does so, the drill shall occur on that date.

The school administrator or designee and the local fire official may also, by mutual agreement, set any other date for the drill, including a date outside of the month of October.

If the fire official does not select one of the four offered dates in October or set another date by mutual agreement, the requirement that the school include the local fire service in one of its mandatory school evacuation drills is waived.

Upon the participation of the local fire service, the appropriate local fire official shall certify that the school evacuation drill was conducted.

When scheduling the school evacuation drill, the school administrator or designee and the local fire department or fire district may, by mutual agreement on or before September 14, choose to waive the provisions relating to the scheduling (not the requirement that they occur) of drills.

105 ILCS 128/20

9:610 Must a school review its safety plans?

Each school district, through its school board or the board's designee, must conduct a minimum of one annual meeting at which it reviews each school building's emergency and crisis response plans, protocols, and procedures and each building's compliance with the school safety drill programs. The purpose of this annual review is to review and update the emergency and crisis response plans, protocols, and procedures and the school safety drill programs of the district and each of its school buildings.

Each school board or the board's designee is required to participate in the annual review and to invite each of the following parties to the annual review and provide each party with a minimum of 30 days' notice before the date of the annual review:

1) The principal of each school within the school district or official designee.

2) Representatives from any other education-related organization or association deemed appropriate by the school district.

3) Representatives from all local first responder organizations to participate, advise, and consult in the review process, including, but not limited to the appropriate local fire department or district; the appropriate local law enforcement agency; the appropriate local emergency medical services agency if the agency is a separate, local first responder unit; and any other member of the first responder or emergency management community that has contacted the superintendent or designee during the past year to request

involvement in a school's emergency planning or drill process.

The school board or its designee may also choose to invite to the annual review any other persons whom it believes will aid in the review process, including, but not limited to, any members of any other education-related organization or the first responder or emergency management community.

Upon the conclusion of the annual review, the school board or the board's designee must sign a one-page report, which may be in either a check-off format or a narrative format, that summarizes the recommended changes to the existing school safety plans and drill plans; lists the parties that participated in the annual review, and includes the annual review's attendance record; certifies that an effective review of the emergency and crisis response plans, protocols, and procedures and the school safety drill programs of the district and each of its school buildings has occurred; states that the school district will implement those plans, protocols, procedures, and programs, during the academic year; and includes the authorization of the school board or the board's designee.

The school board or its designee must send a copy of the report to each party that participates in the annual review process and to the appropriate regional superintendent of schools. If any of the participating parties have comments on the certification document, those parties must submit their comments in writing to the appropriate regional superintendent. The regional superintendent maintains a record of these comments. The certification document may be in a check-off format or narrative format, at the discretion of the district superintendent.

The review must occur at least once during each calendar year, at a specific time chosen at the school district superintendent's discretion.

105 ILCS 128/25

OTHER CONTROL ISSUES

9:650 When is it unlawful for a child sex offender to be near schoolchildren?

It is unlawful for a child sex offender (the relevant law contains a lengthy and detailed definition of the term "child sex offender") to knowingly be present in any school building, on real property comprising any school, or in any conveyance owned, leased, or contracted by a school to transport students to or from school or a school-related activity when persons under the age of 18 are present in the building, on the grounds or in the conveyance, unless the offender is a parent or guardian of a student attending the school and the parent or guardian is:

1) Attending a conference at the school with school personnel to discuss the progress of his or her child academically or socially;

2) Participating in child review conferences in which evaluation and placement decisions may be made with respect to his or her child regarding special education services; or

3) Attending conferences to discuss other student issues concerning his or her child such as retention and promotion and notifies the principal of the school of his or her presence at school or unless the offender has permission to be present from the superintendent or the school board.

If permission is granted, the superintendent or school board president must inform the principal of the school where the sex offender will be present. Notification includes the nature of the sex offender's visit and the hours in which the sex offender will be present in the school. The sex offender is responsible for notifying the principal's office when he or she arrives on school property and when he or she departs from school property. If the sex offender is to be present in the vicinity of children, the sex offender has the duty to remain under the direct supervision of a school official.

It is also unlawful for a child sex offender to knowingly loiter within 500 feet of a school building or real property comprising any school while persons under the age of 18 are present in the building or on the grounds, unless the offender is a parent or guardian of a student attending the school and is conferencing as defined in the statute or has permission to be present from the superintendent or the school board. It is unlawful for a child sex offender to knowingly reside within 500 feet of a playground, child care institution, day care center, part-day child care facility, day care home, group day care home, or a facility providing programs or services exclusively directed toward persons under 18 years of age. Nothing prohibits a child sex offender from residing within 500 feet of a playground or a facility providing programs or services exclusively directed toward persons less than 18 years of age if the property is owned by the child sex offender and was purchased before July 7, 2000. Nothing prohibits a child sex offender from residing within 500 feet of a child care institution, day care center, or part-day child care facility if the property is owned by the child sex offender and was purchased before June 26, 2006. Nothing prohibits a child sex offender from residing within 500 feet of a day care home or group day care home if the property is owned by the child sex offender and was purchased before August 14, 2008.

It is unlawful for a child sex offender to knowingly reside within 500 feet of the victim of the sex offense unless the property in which the child sex offender resides is owned by the child sex offender and was purchased before August 22, 2002 or if the victim of the sex offense is 21 years of age or older.

It is unlawful for a child sex offender to knowingly communicate, other than for a lawful purpose under Illinois law, using the internet or any other digital media, with a person under 18 years of age or with a person whom he or she believes to be a person under 18 years of age, unless the offender is a parent or guardian of the person under 18 years of age.

It is unlawful for a child sex offender to knowingly operate, manage, be employed by, volunteer at, be associated with, or knowingly be present at any (i) facility providing programs or services exclusively directed toward persons under the age of 18; (ii) day care center; (iii) part-day child care facility; (iv) child care institution; (v) school providing before- and after-school programs for children under 18 years of age; (vi) day care home; or (vii) group day care home. This does not prohibit a child sex offender from owning the real property upon which the programs or services are offered or upon which the day care center, part-day child care facility, child care institution, or school providing before- and after-school programs for children under 18 years of age is located, provided the child sex offender refrains from being present on the premises for the hours during which the programs or services are being offered or the day care center, part-day child care facility, child care institution, or school providing before- and after-school programs for children under 18 years of age, day care home, or group day care home is operated.

A child sex offender may be present in a school building to vote if his or her polling place is located in the building.

It is unlawful for a child sex offender to knowingly reside within 500 feet of a school building or the real property comprising any school that persons under the age of 18 attend unless the property is owned by the child sex offender and was purchased before July 7, 2000. The 500-foot distance is measured from the edge of the property of the school building or the edge of the real property comprising the school that is closest to the edge of the property of the child sex offender's residence or where he or she is loitering.

There are other prohibitions listed in the relevant law (720 ILCS 5/11-9.3). A child sex offender who violates any provision of the above law is guilty of a Class 4 felony.

720 ILCS 5/11-9.3
730 ILCS 5/5-4.5-45

9:660 What is a "safe school zone?"

A safe school zone is an area that encompasses any of the following places during regular school hours or within 60 minutes before or after the school day or 60 minutes before or after a school-sponsored activity:

1) Any school property, ground, or street.

2) Any sidewalk or public way immediately adjacent to school property.

3) Any public right-of-way situated immediately adjacent to school property.

The safe school zone does not include any portion of the highway not actually on school property.

720 ILCS 5/21-5.5

9:670 What is criminal trespass to a safe school zone?

A state statute effective January 1, 2012 provides that "A person commits the offense of criminal trespass to a safe school zone when he or she knowingly:

"(1) enters or remains in a safe school zone without lawful business, when as a student or employee, who has been suspended, expelled, or dismissed for disrupting the orderly operation of the school, and as a condition of the suspension or dismissal, has been denied access to the safe school zone for the period of the suspension or in the case of dismissal for a period not to exceed the term of expulsion, and has been served in person or by registered or certified mail, at the last address given by that person, with a written notice of the suspension or dismissal and condition; or

"(2) enters or remains in a safe school zone without lawful business, once being served either in person or by registered or certified mail that his or her presence has been withdrawn by the school administrator, or his or her designee, and whose presence or acts interfere with, or whenever there is reasonable suspicion to believe, such person will disrupt the orderly operation, or the safety, or peaceful conduct of the school or school activities."

Conduct protected by the Illinois Educational Labor Relations Act or any other law applicable to labor relations, as well as conduct protected by the First Amendment to the Constitution of the United States or Article I of the Illinois Constitution, including the exercise of free speech, free expression, and the free exercise of religion or expression of religiously based views is excluded.

Criminal trespass to a safe school zone is a Class A misdemeanor.

720 ILCS 5/21-5.5

9:690 May a person bring a gun onto school property if he or she has a "concealed carry" permit?

The Illinois concealed carry law provides that "a licensee under this Act shall not knowingly carry a firearm on or into any building, real property, and parking area under the control of a public or private elementary or secondary school."

The law allows an exception for the license holder to store the weapon or ammunition concealed in a case within the vehicle.

430 ILCS 66/65

10: THE EDUCATIONAL PROGRAM

CURRICULAR AUTHORITY

10:10 What authority does a school board have to establish curriculum?

The School Code mandates certain courses of study for all pupils in Illinois public schools. School boards may set requirements in excess of those mandated by the state.

105 ILCS 5/10-20.8

105 ILCS 5/27-1 et seq.

Leebaert v. Harrington, 332 F. 3d 134 (2nd Cir. 2003)

People ex rel. McKeever v. Board of Education of Drummer Township High School, 176 Ill. App. 491 (3rd Dist. 1912)

10:20 Who has authority to determine appropriate class size?

Except with respect to special education, and unless a collective bargaining agreement provides otherwise, the school board has authority to determine appropriate class size. Class size is, however, a mandatory subject of bargaining, and a school board decision affecting class size may trigger a demand to bargain from affected employee bargaining units.

Board of Education Decatur District No. 61 v. Illinois Educational Labor Relations Board, 180 Ill. App. 3d 770, 536 N.E. 2d 743, 129 Ill. Dec. 693 (4th Dist. 1989)

10:30 Who establishes requirements for high school graduation?

The school board has the authority to establish the requirements for high school graduation. However, by law, those requirements must include the following core curriculum:

Each pupil entering the 9th grade in the 2008-2009 school year or a subsequent school year must, in addition to other course requirements, successfully complete all of the following courses:

1) Four years of language arts;

2) Two years of writing intensive courses, one of which must be English and the other of which may be English or any other subject. When applicable, writing-intensive courses may be counted towards the fulfillment of other graduation requirements;

3) Three years of mathematics, one of which must be Algebra I and one of which must include geometry content;

4) Two years of science;

5) Two years of social studies, of which at least one year must be history of the United States or a combination of history of the United States and American government; and

6) One year chosen from (i) music, (ii) art, (iii) foreign language, which includes American Sign Language, or (iv) vocational education.

The requirements do not apply to pupils with disabilities whose course of study is determined by an Individualized Education Program and are subject to the provisions of Section 27-22.05 of the School Code, which allows for vocational and technical education substitutions.

State law also requires a student to acquire 16 units in grades 9-12 (for four-year high schools) and 12 units in grades 10-12 (for three-year high schools). Students also must receive instruction in the principles of representative government and other specified related subjects.

The Administrative Code section cited below contains a list of courses in addition to those cited here and in some cases the standards for fulfilling course requirements.

Students who seek admission to any Illinois public community college, college, or university must have completed four years of English; three years each of social studies, mathematics, and science; and two years of music, art, or a foreign language.

A school board may not require a student to meet occupational standards for graduation unless the student is voluntarily enrolled in a job training program.

105 ILCS 5/10-20.31

105 ILCS 5/27-1 et seq.

105 ILCS 5/27-22

105 ILCS 5/27-22.05

23 Ill. Admin. Code 1.440

10:34 May a school board establish a community service requirement for high school graduation?

A school board may establish a community service requirement for graduation provided the requirement has an educational objective and is not otherwise suspect by reason of constitutional infirmity.

A school board contemplating a service requirement should be careful that the requirement does not infringe on student right to free speech and free exercise of religion and that the service requirement is not onerous.

Herndon v. Chapel Hill-Carrboro City Board of Education, 89 F. 3d 174 (4th Cir. 1996)

Immediato by Immediato v. Rye Neck School District, 73 F. 3d 454 (2nd Cir. 1996) cert. den. 117 S. Ct. 60, 519 U.S. 813, 136 L. Ed. 2d 22 (1996)

10:36 May a school board award a diploma to a veteran who did not complete high school?

Upon request, the school board of any district that maintains grades 10-12 may award a diploma to any honorably discharged veteran who served in the armed forces of the United States during World War II, the Korean Conflict, or the Vietnam Conflict, and resided within an area currently within the district, and left high school before graduating to serve in the armed forces of the United States and has not received a high school diploma.

105 ILCS 5/22-27

10:40 May a school board grant academic credit on the basis of a proficiency exam?

A school board may, by policy, determine to allow or prohibit proficiency credit. The School Code requires students to "successfully complete" those courses required for high school graduation and probably does not contemplate exemption by proficiency examination except where expressly allowed.

105 ILCS 5/27-22

23 Ill. Admin. Code 1.460

10:45 Under what circumstances may a school board grant high school credit to an elementary school student?

Notwithstanding any other provision in the School Code, the school board of a school district that maintains any of grades 9-12 may adopt a policy under which a student enrolled in grade 7 or 8 who is enrolled in the unit school district or would be enrolled in the high school district upon completion of elementary school, whichever is applicable, may enroll in a course required under Section 27-22 of the School Code (the section of the School Code that defines the courses required for high school graduation), provided that (i) the course is offered by the high school that the student would attend; and (ii) the student participates in the course at the location of the high school, and the elementary student's enrollment in the course would not prevent a high school student from being able to enroll; or (iii) the student participates in the course where the student attends school as long as the course is taught by a certified high school teacher who teaches in a high school of the school district where the student will attend when in high school and no high school students are enrolled in the course.

A school board that adopts such a policy must grant academic credit to an elementary school student who successfully completes the high school course, and that credit shall satisfy the requirements of Section 27-22 of the School Code for that course.

A school board must award high school course credit to a student transferring to its school district for any course that the student successfully completed pursuant to the above, unless evidence about the course's rigor and content shows that it does not address the relevant Illinois Learning Standard at the level appropriate for the high school grade during which the course is usually taken, and that credit shall satisfy the requirements of Section 27-22 of the School Code for that course.

A student's grade in any course successfully completed under this section must be included in his or her grade point average in accordance with the school board's policy for making that calculation.

105 ILCS 5/27-22.10

10:50 May a student, by demonstrating proficiency, become exempt from state-required instructional programs?

Until 2010, only the state's consumer education laws permitted an exemption based on proficiency. The relevant statute was amended in 2010 to eliminate the proficiency exemption.

105 ILCS 5/27-12.1

10:55 May a school board award academic credit for foreign language proficiency?

A school board may award credit to high school students who have studied a foreign language in an approved ethnic school or may grant one year of high school foreign language credit to any student who has graduated from elementary school and who can demonstrate proficiency in a foreign language. Foreign language includes American Sign Language.

105 ILCS 5/2-3.44 et seq.

105 ILCS 5/10-22.43 et seq.

DRIVER EDUCATION

10:60 Is driver education a required course for high school students?

School districts are required by law to offer driver education to high school students but students are not required by law to take the course.

105 ILCS 5/27-23

105 ILCS 5/27-24.2

Acorn Auto Driving School, Inc. v. Leyden High School District No. 212, 27 Ill. 2d 93, 187 N.E. 2d 722 (1963)

10:62 May a student be permitted to receive credit by demonstrating proficiency in behind-the-wheel driver education?

Prior to 2008 it was possible for a school district to adopt a policy to permit proficiency examinations for the practice driving part of driver's education after three hours of behind-the-wheel instruction. Proficiency examinations are no longer authorized. To receive state aid, a school district must provide at least 30 hours of classroom instruction and at least six hours or practice driving in a car having dual operating controls under individual instruction.

105 ILCS 5/27-24.3
625 ILCS 5/6-408.5

10:65 Must a school district provide driver education for parochial, private, and home school students residing in the district?

A school district must provide classroom driver education for each student attending any public or non-public high school in the district receiving a passing grade in at least eight courses during the previous two semesters prior to enrolling in a driver education course, or the student must not be permitted to enroll in the course; provided that the local superintendent of schools (with respect to a student attending a public high school in the district) or chief school administrator (with respect to a student attending a non-public high school in the district) may waive the requirement if the superintendent or chief school administrator, as the case may be, deems it to be in the best interest of the student.

The course of instruction required of each eligible student at the high school level shall consist of a minimum of 30 clock hours of classroom instruction and a minimum of six clock hours of individual behind-the-wheel instruction in a dual control car on public roadways taught by a driver education instructor endorsed by the State Board of Education.

A student may be allowed to begin the classroom instruction part of driver education prior to reaching age 15 if the student will be eligible to complete the entire course within 12 months after being allowed to begin classroom instruction.

The school district may charge a reasonable fee, not to exceed $50, to students who participate in driver education, unless a student is unable to pay, in which event the fee for such a student must be waived.

105 ILCS 5/27-24.2
625 ILCS 5/6-408.5

10:68 May a school district contract out driver education?

Before a 2017 change in the law a school district had to seek a waiver to contract out driver education. Now, a school district may offer a driver education course by contracting with a commercial driver training school to provide both the classroom instruction part and the practice driving part or either one without having to request a modification or waiver, if the school district approves the action during a public hearing on whether to enter into a contract with a commercial driver training school. The public hearing must be held at a school board meeting prior to entering into a contract. If a school district chooses to approve a contract with a commercial driver training school, then the district must provide evidence to the State Board of Education that the commercial driver training school with which it will contract holds a license issued by the Secretary of State under the Illinois Vehicle Code and that each instructor employed by the commercial driver training school to provide instruction to students served by the school district holds a valid teaching license.

105 ILCS 5/2-3.25g
625 ILCS 5/6-401 et seq.
23 Ill. Admin. Code 252.10 et seq.
23 Ill. Admin. Code 252.20(e)

10:70 May a dropout obtain driver education?

There are statutory obstacles that must be overcome for a dropout who is under 18 to obtain a certificate of completion of a driver-training program. A dropout must have a waiver from the superintendent of schools or

1) Be enrolled in a GED program (high school equivalency);

2) Be enrolled in an alternative education program;

3) Have a GED certificate;

4) Prior to dropping out received a passing grade in at least eight courses during the two previous semesters last ending prior to requesting a certificate of completion; or

5) Have the written consent from the dropout's parents or guardians and the regional superintendent of schools.

625 ILCS 5/6-408.5

10:75 May a school dropout obtain a driver license?

The Motor Vehicle Code contains provisions that are intended to prevent a dropout from obtaining a driver license. The driver license law is enforced through use of a school district reporting scheme (required by the

School Code) that delivers the names of dropouts to the Secretary of State.

The reporting requirement seems to conflict with School Student Records Act privacy requirements. Under the relevant reporting provision, school officials are required to provide in October, January, April, and July to the regional superintendent and to the Secretary of State a list of pupils, excluding transferees, who have been expelled or have withdrawn or who have left school and have been removed from the regular attendance rolls during the period of time school was in regular session from the time of the previous quarterly report.

The list must include the names and addresses of pupils formerly in attendance, the names and addresses of persons having custody or control of such pupils, the reason, if known, such pupils are no longer in attendance, and the date of removal from the attendance rolls.

The list must also include the names of pupils whose withdrawal is due to extraordinary circumstances, including but not limited to economic or medical necessity or family hardship, as determined by the criteria established by the school district; pupils who have re-enrolled in school since their names were removed from the attendance rolls; any pupil certified to be a chronic or habitual truant, as defined in Section 26-2a of the School Code; and pupils previously certified as chronic or habitual truants who have resumed regular school attendance. The regional superintendent is required to inform the county or district truant officer who investigates.

Each school district must establish, in writing, a set of criteria for use by the local superintendent of schools in determining whether a pupil's failure to attend school is the result of extraordinary circumstances, including but not limited to economic or medical necessity or family hardship.

If a pupil re-enrolls in school after his or her name was removed from the attendance rolls or resumes regular attendance after being certified a chronic or habitual truant, the pupil must obtain and forward to the Secretary of State, on a form designated by the Secretary of State, verification of his or her re-enrollment. The verification may be in the form of a signature or seal or in any other form determined by the school board.

20 U.S.C. 1232g
34 C.F.R. 99
105 ILCS 5/26-3a
105 ILCS 10/1 et seq.
625 ILCS 5/6-107

OTHER SCHOOL PROGRAMS

10:80 Who is eligible for a GED?

Regional superintendents and the Illinois Community College Board administer a high school diploma equivalency testing program (Test of General Educational Development — GED) and "alternative methods of credentialing." An individual is eligible to apply to the regional superintendent for the region in which he or she resides if he or she is a person who is 17 years of age or older, has maintained residence in the state of Illinois, and is not a high school graduate or a person who is successfully completing an alternative education program under Section 2-3.81, Article 13A, or Article 13B of the School Code, or a person who is enrolled in a youth education program sponsored by the Illinois National Guard.

For GED eligibility, residence is the abode the applicant considers his or her home. Applicants may provide as sufficient proof of such residence and as an acceptable form of identification a driver's license, valid passport, military ID, or other form of government-issued national or foreign identification that shows the applicant's name, address, date of birth, signature, and photograph or other acceptable identification as may be allowed by law or as regulated by the Illinois Community College Board. The regional superintendent determines if the applicant meets statutory and regulatory state standards. The applicant is charged a test fee and is notified of results in writing.

Beginning in January 2018, The Illinois Community College Board (ICCB) established alternative methods of credentialing for the issuance of high school equivalency certification. In addition to high school equivalency testing, the following alternative methods of receiving a high school equivalency credential are available:

1) A qualified candidate may petition to have his or her high school transcripts evaluated to determine what the candidate needs to meet criteria as established by the ICCB;

2) A qualified candidate may petition to have his or her post-secondary transcripts evaluated to determine what the candidate needs to meet criteria established by the ICCB; or

3) A qualified candidate may petition to have his or her foreign high school or post-secondary transcripts evaluated to determine what the candidate needs to meet criteria established by the ICCB.

The ICCB has guidelines for competency-based high school equivalency programs.

Any applicant who has attained the age of 17 years and maintained residence in the state of Illinois and is not a high school graduate, any person who has enrolled in a youth education program sponsored by the Illinois National Guard, or any person who has successfully completed an alternative education program under Section 2-3.81, Article 13A, or Article 13B of the School Code is eligible to apply for a high school equivalency certificate (if he or she meets the requirements prescribed by the Illinois Community College Board) upon showing evidence that he or she has completed, successfully, the high school level GED tests, administered by the United States Armed Forces Institute, official GED centers established in other states, or at Veterans' Administration Hospitals or the office of the State Superintendent of Education administered for the Illinois State Penitentiary System and the Department of Corrections. An applicant must apply to the regional superintendent of the region wherein he or she has maintained residence, and upon payment of the established fee the regional superintendent must issue a high school equivalency certificate, and immediately thereafter certify to the ICCB the score of the applicant and such other and additional information as may be required by the ICCB. Any applicant who has been out of school for at least one year may request the regional superintendent of schools to administer the restricted GED test upon written request of:

1) The director of a program who certifies to the Chief Examiner of an official GED center that the applicant has completed a program of instruction provided by such agencies as the Job Corps, the Postal Service Academy, or apprenticeship training program;

2) An employer or program director for purposes of entry into apprenticeship programs; or

3) Another State Department of Education in order to meet regulations established by that Department of Education, a post-high school educational institution for purposes of admission, the Department of Professional Regulation for licensing purposes, or the Armed Forces for induction purposes.

The regional superintendent must administer the test and the applicant must be notified in writing that he or she is eligible to receive the Illinois High School Equivalency Certificate upon reaching age 17, provided he or she meets the standards established by the ICCB.

Any GED test administered to an applicant who does not speak and understand English may at the discretion of the administering agency be given and answered in any language in which the test is printed. The regional superintendent of schools may waive any fees in case of hardship.

105 ILCS 5/2-3.81
105 ILCS 5/3-15.12
105 ILCS 5/13A-1 et seq.
105 ILCS 5/13B-1 et seq.

10:90 May a school board make sex education a required course offering?

A school board may not require a pupil to take or participate in a sex education class if the pupil's parent or guardian submits a written objection to the school district. A student may not be disciplined by reason of the parental objection. In 2013, the legislature amended the sex education statute and added criteria for the "classes that teach sex education or discuss sexual intercourse in grades 6-12."

105 ILCS 5/27-9.1 et seq.

Brown v. Hot, Sexy and Safer Productions, Inc. 68 F. 3d 525 (1st Cir. 1995) cert. den., 116 S. Ct. 1044, 516 U.S. 1159, 134 L. Ed. 2d 191 (1996)

Bergstrand v. Rock Island Board of Education, School District No. 41, 161 Ill. App. 3d 180, 514 N.E. 2d 256, 112 Ill. Dec. 790 (3rd Dist. 1987)

10:93 Must a student who objects be excused from participating in science projects that involve dissection of animals?

No. Illinois law permits school officials to excuse an objector, but does not require that an objector be excused. When considering an objection, school officials lack authority to consider the merits of the objection. If electing to excuse a student, school officials have authority to assign an alternative non-punitive project intended to convey similar knowledge. The relevant law prevents school officials from penalizing or discriminating against a student who refuses to perform, participate in, or observe dissection.

105 ILCS 112/5 et seq.

10:100 May a school board require its students to receive instruction on disease?

A student is not required to take or participate in instruction on disease if the student's parent or guardian submits written objections on constitutional grounds. A student may not be disciplined by reason of the parental objection.

105 ILCS 5/27-11

10:110 Must boards of education provide special programming for gifted or talented children?

No. Such a requirement previously existed in article 14A of the School Code but the mandatory gifted program was repealed in 2003 because funding was not available. In 2005, article 14A was restored as an optional program. In 2010, a funding request procedure was added, but funds are dispersed only "if available." The statute establishes requirements that must be met by school districts that seek funding for gifted education if and when funds are available.

105 ILCS 5/14A-15
105 ILCS 5/14A-30

10:120 Under what conditions may a child be excused from the daily physical education requirement?

Physical education is required three days per five-day week, A child may be excused from physical education when an appropriate excuse is submitted by a doctor, parent, or guardian.

In addition, a school board may excuse a pupil on an individual basis in grade 11 and 12 who requests to be excused if the student is an ongoing participant in interscholastic athletics or in order to enroll in a class that if not taken would prevent the student from graduating or result in the student's being denied admission to the institution of higher learning of the student's choice.

A student in grades 9-12 may be excused on an individual basis upon request if (1) the student is enrolled in a for-credit marching band program; (2) if the student is enrolled in a Reserve Officer's Training Corps (ROTC) program sponsored by the school district; or (3) under conditions specified in the statute for special education students. A school board may also, on a case-by-case basis, excuse pupils in grades 7-12 who participate in an interscholastic or extracurricular athletic program from engaging in physical education courses.

Under conditions specified in the law, vocational, or technical education courses may be substituted for physical education.

105 ILCS 5/27-6
105 ILCS 5/27-22.05

10:130 May a school district offer a summer school program?

A school board may operate a summer school program. Tuition may be charged in an amount not to exceed the per capita cost of the program. A school board may give regular school credit for satisfactory completion of summer school courses that are approved for credit by the State Board of Education. A statutory funding formula provides limited funds under narrow circumstances to support summer school programs.

The school board may require the attendance at summer school of academically at-risk students. Written notice requiring attendance sent to the parent or guardian of the student not later than the close of the school term immediately preceding the summer term is required.

105 ILCS 5/10-22.33A
105 ILCS 5/10-22.33B
105 ILCS 5/18-4.3
105 ILCS 5/26-1

10:140 When is a school district required to provide transitional bilingual education?

Every school age child of limited English speaking ability must be provided a program in transitional bilingual education (or, under certain circumstances, a transitional instructional program in his or her own language) for a period of three years or until the child learns sufficient English language skills to allow him to perform successfully in classes taught in English, whichever occurs first.

105 ILCS 5/14B-1 et seq.

Teresa P. v. Berkeley Unified School District, 724 F. Supp. 698 (N.D. Cal. 1989)

Castenada v. Pickard, 648 F. 2d 989 (5th Cir. 1981)

10:145 What notice must a school district provide to the parents of a child enrolled in bilingual education?

No later than 30 days after the beginning of the school year or 14 days after the enrollment of any child in a program in transitional bilingual education during the middle of a school year, the school district in which the child resides must notify by mail the parents or legal guardian of the child that their child has been enrolled in a program in transitional bilingual education. The notice must contain all of the following information in simple, nontechnical language:

1) The reasons why the child has been placed in and needs the services of the program.

2) The child's level of English proficiency, how this level was assessed, and the child's current level of academic achievement.

3) The method of instruction used in the program and in other available offerings of the district, including how the program differs from those other offerings in content, instructional goals, and the use of English and native language instruction.

4) How the program will meet the educational strengths and needs of the child.

5) How the program will specifically help the child to learn English and to meet academic achievement standards for grade promotion and graduation.

6) The specific exit requirements for the program, the expected rate of transition from the program into the regular curriculum, and the expected graduation rate for children in the program if the program is offered at the secondary level.

7) How the program meets the objectives of the child's Individualized Education Program (IEP), if applicable.

8) The right of the parents to decline to enroll the child in the program or to choose another program or method of instruction, if available.

9) The right of the parents to have the child immediately removed from the program upon request.

10) The right of the parents to visit transitional bilingual education classes in which their child is enrolled and to come to the school for a conference to explain the nature of transitional bilingual education.

The notice must be in writing in English and in the language of which the child of the parents so notified possesses a primary speaking ability. Any parent whose child has been enrolled in a program in transitional bilingual education shall have the absolute right to immediately withdraw his or her child from said program by providing written notice of such desire to the school authorities of the school in which his or her child is enrolled or to the school district in which his or her child resides.

20 U.S.C. 6312(g)
105 ILCS 5/14C-4

10:150 How are school district work experience programs limited by child labor laws?

Child labor laws regulate the work that may be performed by minors. Generally, minors below age 14 are subject to stringent regulation and are, in most cases, prohibited from employment. The employment of minors between the ages of 14 and 16 is permitted in limited circumstances. The child labor laws state at what age minors may be employed in specific occupations, how many hours a day they may work, and cover many other work related subjects.

820 ILCS 205/1

10:155 May a school district require a student to meet occupational standards?

A school board may not require a student to meet occupational standards for grade level promotion or graduation unless the student is voluntarily enrolled in a job-training program.

105 ILCS 5/2-3.128
105 ILCS 5/10-20.31

10:160 May a school board establish a full-day kindergarten?

A school board may provide a full-day or half-day kindergarten. However, if a full-day program is offered, a half-day program must also be offered as an alternative for parents.

105 ILCS 5/10-22.18
105 ILCS 5/10-22.19a
Morgan v. Board of Education of Trico Community Unit School District 176, 22 Ill. App. 3d 241, 317 N.E. 2d 393 (5th Dist. 1974)

10:165 May a school establish a summer kindergarten?

A school board may establish, maintain, and operate, in connection with the kindergarten program of the school district, a summer kindergarten program that begins two months before the beginning of the regular school year and a summer kindergarten program for grade one readiness for those pupils making unsatisfactory progress during the regular kindergarten session that continues for two months after the regular school year.

The summer kindergarten program may be held within the school district or, pursuant to a contract that must be approved by the State Board of Education, may be operated by two or more adjacent school districts or by a public or private university or college. Transportation costs for students attending a summer kindergarten program are not reimbursed by the state.

105 ILCS 5/10-20.37

10:170 May a school board establish a before or after school day care center?

There is statutory authorization for the establishment of before or after school programs for grades K-6. The school district may charge parents of participating students a fee not to exceed the cost of the program. The program may include time for homework, physical exercise, afternoon nutritional snacks, and educational offerings that are in addition to those offered during the regular school day.

The schedule of these programs may follow the work calendar of the local community rather than the regular school calendar. Programs must be coordinated by teachers or persons who meet the requirements for supervising day care centers.

105 ILCS 5/10-22.18b

10:180 If a school board chooses to establish a before- or after-school day care center, must it provide transportation for the students?

The parents or guardians of the participating students are responsible for the transportation of the students to and from a before- or after-school day care center operated by a school district.

105 ILCS 5/10-22.18b

10:190 May a school board offer adult education classes?

A school board may establish classes for the instruction of persons 21 years of age and over and of persons less than 21 and not otherwise in attendance in public school. A statutory funding formula provides limited funds to support such programs. If a school board establishes an adult education program, it must provide transportation and child care. A school board may establish a tuition charge for persons enrolled who are not subject to state reimbursement not to exceed the per capita cost of the classes.

105 ILCS 5/10-22.20

10:200 May a school district operate a nursery school?

School districts maintaining grades 1-8 or 1-12 may establish nursery schools for the instruction of children between the ages of 2 and 6 years if sufficient funds obtained from sources other than local district taxes are available to pay the costs of the nursery school.

105 ILCS 5/10-23.2

10:210 May school boards enter into joint agreements with other school districts or agencies to provide educational programs?

Two or more educational agencies, including school districts, may establish an educational joint agreement or cooperative by agreeing in writing to work together to provide some educational program. Common examples are vocational and special education cooperatives. In some cases, a new joint agreement school district results from the cooperative effort, and in some cases an existing school district becomes the administrative district for the resulting cooperative and, as a result, no new entity is formed. Some cooperative agreements require voter approval.

School districts with small high schools also may agree to jointly operate a cooperative attendance center.

105 ILCS 5/10-22.22c
105 ILCS 5/10-22.31 et seq.

10:215 What is a dual credit course?

Secondary schools and community colleges sometimes allow high school students to take courses for which they receive both high school and college credit. There is no specific statutory authority for such courses, but in practice they exist and are accepted almost everywhere. Sometimes there are bargaining issues because the teachers of such courses are not members of the bargaining unit and therefore their employment is subcontracting.

105 ILCS 5/2-3.66b (f)
105 ILCS 5/2-3.144
105 ILCS 10-21.4
110 ILCS 27-1 et seq.

10:220 May a school district and a park district operate a joint recreational program?

Park districts have authority to develop, operate, finance, and participate in joint recreational programs with school districts and to enter into joint agreements.

70 ILCS 1205/8-18
70 ILCS 1205/9.1-5 et seq.

THE SCHOOL YEAR AND DAY

10:230 What is the minimum number of days in a school year?

Each school board is required by law to annually prepare a calendar for the school term that specifies both the opening and closing dates of the term. The calendar must provide a minimum term of at least 185 days that generally includes five emergency days and four teachers' institute days in order to ensure 176 days of actual pupil attendance. Any teachers' institute day not used for an institute (for teachers or educational support personnel) or used as a parental institute increases the minimum term of 176 pupil attendance days by the number of unused teacher institute days.

The adoption of a school calendar may have collective bargaining implications with respect to recognized bargaining units. The calendar for the school term and any changes must be submitted to and approved by the regional superintendent of schools before the calendar or changes may take effect.

105 ILCS 5/10-19
105 ILCS 5/10-22.18d
105 ILCS 5/24-1

Board of Education Arbor Park School District No. 145, Cook County v. Ballweber, 105 Ill. App. 3d 412, 434 N.E. 2d 448, 61 Ill. Dec. 295 (1st Dist. 1981) aff'd. 96 Ill. 2d 520, 451 N.E. 2d 858, 71 Ill. Dec. 704 (1982)

Miller v. School District No. 189 East St. Louis, 26 Ill. App. 3d 172, 325 N.E. 2d 43 (5th Dist. 1975)

10:240 What is an "institute day"?

An "institute day" is any educational gathering, demonstration of methods of instruction, or visitation of schools or other institutions or facilities held or approved by the regional superintendent. Teacher "institutes" may include in-service training workshops or equivalent professional education experiences. Under circumstances provided for in the law, a school district may have up to two parental institute days in any given year instead of teacher institute days. A 2011 change in the law allows use of these days for educational support personnel workshops.

105 ILCS 5/3-11

105 ILCS 5/10-22.18d

Miller v. School District No. 189, East St. Louis, 26 Ill. App. 3d 172, 325 N.E. 2d 43 (5th Dist. 1975)

10:242 May an employee be docked pay for failure to attend an institute?

The days in any school year spent by teachers or educational support personnel at a teachers institute or equivalent professional educational experience held under the direction of the county superintendent of schools must, by law, be considered time expended in the service of the district and no deduction from wages may be made for attendance.

The school employer may make a pro-rata deduction from the salary of any teacher or educational support employee who fails or refuses to attend an institute unless, in the case of educational support personnel, they are exempt from attending. School boards are required to close schools for county institutes.

105 ILCS 5/24-3

10:245 What is a parental institute day?

A school district may use up to two teacher institute days to conduct parental institutes for the parents and guardians of students. Parental institute days require the consent of the district's in-service advisory committee or, if the district does not have an in-service advisory committee, parental institute days must be approved by the district's teachers.

Parental institute days may be held during that period of the day that is not part of the regular school day and may be held on Saturday. A school district may establish reasonable fees, not to exceed the cost of holding the parental institute, but must waive the fee for parents or guardians who cannot afford the fee.

105 ILCS 5/10-22.18d

10:250 When may institute days be used?

A regional superintendent of schools may arrange for or conduct district, regional or county institutes or equivalent professional educational experiences not more than four days annually. Of those four days, two days may be used as a teacher's workshop when approved by the regional superintendent, up to two days may be used for conducting parent-teacher conferences, or up to two days may be used as parental institute days under conditions specified in the law. A school district may use one of its institute days on the last day of the school term. Institute days may be held on consecutive or separate days at the option of the regional superintendent of schools.

105 ILCS 5/3-11

105 ILCS 5/10-22.18d

10:270 What is the minimum school day?

A school day must consist of no less than five clock hours under the direct supervision of teachers in order to meet State Board of Education standards and to qualify as a full day of school in calculating state aid entitlements. Some exceptions are authorized.

105 ILCS 5/18-8.05

10:280 What are the exceptions to the minimum five clock hour school day?

There are five exceptions:

1) Two and one half hours may be counted as a half-day for students in grades 2-12.

2) Four clock hours may be counted as a day of attendance for first-graders and full-day kindergartners.

3) Two clock hours may be counted as a half-day of attendance for first graders and full-day kindergartners.

4) One clock hour may count as a half-day of attendance for handicapped children below the age of six who cannot attend a two-hour session because of handicap or immaturity.

5) There are exceptions available under a specific and complicated statutory scheme for in-service training programs for teachers and that permit scheduling of parent-teacher conferences in partial and full day increments.

Before June 30, 2013, when the exception was removed, days of attendance could be less than five clock hours on the opening and closing days of the school term.

Four clock hours may be counted as a day of attendance upon certification by the regional superintendent and approval of the State Superintendent of Education.

105 ILCS 5/18-8.05 (F) (2) et seq.

23 Ill. Admin. Code 1.420

TESTING AND REPORTING

10:290 May a school district require minimum competency testing?

Minimum competency testing is standardized testing to measure the acquisition of skills at or beyond a certain defined minimum standard. The use of minimum competency testing is within the discretionary authority of a school board.

105 ILCS 5/2-3.42
105 ILCS 5/10-20.25
105 ILCS 5/14-6.01

10:300 What student performance assessments are required by law?

The State Board of Education (ISBE) establishes standards and assesses the performance of students. To some extent, ISBE's testing decisions and authority are driven by the requirements of federal law. There is state legislation governing local testing requirements intended to result in the state and ISBE's compliance with federal requirements. ISBE has repeatedly introduced new testing legislation and the legislature has approved changes in testing procedures frequently since the mid-1990s.

Beginning with the 1998-1999 school year, the state assessment identifies pupils in the third or fifth grades who do not meet state standards. If, by performance of the state assessment or local assessments or by teacher judgment, a student's performance is determined to be two or more grades below current placement the student must be provided a remediation program (with an emphasis on reading and mathematics if the student has performed below grade level for two consecutive school years) developed by the district in consultation with the parents or guardians.

20 U.S.C. 9622
105 ILCS 5/2-3.64
105 ILCS 5/2-3.64a-5

10:301 How are special education and transitional bilingual education students tested?

Every Individualized Education Program of a special education student must identify the components of the state test that are appropriate for the student and which are not. Students who are in transitional bilingual education program participate in the state tests. The State Board of Education prescribes alternate assessments for students for whom the state test is inappropriate.

105 ILCS 5/2-3.64

10:302 What is state achievement assessment?

State student achievement testing has taken many different forms in recent years, including the Prairie State Achievement Test and Partnership for Assessment of Readiness for College and Careers (PARCC). The State Board of Education establishes academic standards and determines the form of the statewide test that is administered to certain students annually and that measures student achievement.

Each student, except a student whose Individualized Education Program identifies the examination as inappropriate for the student, is required to take the examination.

105 ILCS 5/2-3.64

10:303 May a student be denied a high school diploma by reason of a poor score on the state achievement test?

Not by reason of having obtained a poor score. A student may not be denied a diploma if he completes all other applicable high school graduation requirements. But most students are required to take the test in order to receive their diplomas.

A student cannot be awarded a regular high school diploma without taking the state achievement test unless the student is exempted from taking the test because the student's Individualized Education Program identifies the test as inappropriate for the student, or the student is exempt due to the student's lack of English language proficiency, or the student is enrolled in a program of adult and continuing education, or the school district is not required to test the student for purposes of accountability under No Child Left Behind (the reference to No Child Left Behind remains in the relevant statute) or the student is otherwise identified by the State Board of Education through rules as being exempt from the test.

105 ILCS 5/2-3.64

10:304 May a special education student be required to take the state achievement test?

The test may not be required by school officials unless the student's Individualized Education Program (IEP) identifies the test as appropriate. But the law allows students whose IEPs do not require the test to take it if such students elect to do so. The State Board of Education has the authority to develop rules and regulations governing the administration of alternative tests prescribed within each student's Individualized Education Program that are appropriate to the disability of each student.

105 ILCS 5/2-3.64

10:305 Must students enrolled in transitional bilingual education take the state achievement test?

Students enrolled in bilingual education must participate in state testing. At a local school district's discretion, certain qualifying bilingual education students may take an accommodated test.

105 ILCS 5/2-3.64

10:310 What must a school board report publicly with respect to the performance of the district's schools and students?

Each school district must submit to parents, taxpayers of the district, the Governor, the General Assembly, and the State Board of Education a school report card assessing the performance of its schools and students and it must report some expenditures. The reporting requirement is mandated by both state and federal law. The report card must describe the performance of students by school attendance center and must describe the district's use of financial resources. The report card must specify the amount of money the district receives from all sources, including without limitation subcategories specifying the amount from local property taxes, the amount from general state aid, the amount from other state funding, and the amount from other income. Beginning in 2017, student attendance rates and additional financial information are reported. Many other items must be reported because the statute requires they be reported.

The report card must be presented at a regular school board meeting, must be made available to a newspaper of general circulation serving the district, and must be sent home to parents. The report card must be posted on the school district's website, if the district maintains a website. If the district posts the report card on its website, the district shall send a written notice home to parents stating the report card is available on the website, giving the url of the website, that a printed copy of the report card will be sent to parents upon request, and the telephone number that parents may call to request a printed copy of the report card. The report card must include indicators of parental involvement in each attendance center.

The report card form is prepared by the State Board of Education and is disseminated prior to October 31 in each school year.

105 ILCS 5/10-17a

20 U.S.C. 6311(h)(2)

10:315 May a parent require that a child be excused from school testing for religious or moral reasons?

A federal law requires that no student be compelled to submit to a survey, analysis, or evaluation that reveals information concerning:

1) Political affiliations;

2) Mental and psychological problems potentially embarrassing to the student or his or her family;

3) Sex behavior and attitudes;

4) Illegal, anti-social, self-incriminating, and demeaning behavior;

5) Critical appraisals of other individuals with whom the respondents have close family relationships;

6) Legally recognized privileged or analogous relationships, such as those of lawyers, physicians, and ministers; or

7) Income (other than that required by law to determine eligibility for participation in a program or for receiving financial assistance under such program).

20 U.S.C. 1232h(b)

Fields v. Palmdale School District, 427 F. 3d 1197 (3rd Cir. 2005)

C.N. v. Ridgewood Board of Education, 430 F. 3d 159 (3rd Cir. 2005)

10:317 Could state-mandated achievement tests be required of students attending private schools?

If the legislature so determined, the tests could be required of all students, public, and private.

Ohio Association of Independent Schools v. Goff, 92 F. 3d 419 (6th Cir. 1996)

GRADES AND GRADING

10:320 Who has final authority to determine whether a student is promoted or retained at grade level?

Except in the case of a student who has been found to be in need of special education, a school board has general authority to determine retention and promotion.

A 1997 amendment to the School Code prohibits social promotion of students and prevents promotion based upon age or any other social reason not related to the academic performance of the student. Decisions to retain or promote must be based on successful completion of the curriculum, attendance, performance on the Illinois Goals and Assessment Program tests (IGAP), the Iowa Test of Basic Skills, other testing or other criteria established by the school board.

Students who do not qualify for promotion must be provided remedial assistance which may include, but is not limited to, a summer bridge program of not less than 90 hours, tutoring, increased or concentrated instructional time, modification of instructional materials, and retention in grade. Each school district must have a promotion-retention policy in place by not later than September 1, 1998.

105 ILCS 5/10-20.9a

Morgan v. Board of Education of Trico Community Unit School District 176, 22 Ill. App. 3d 241, 317 N.E. 2d 393 (5th Dist. 1974)

10:330 May a school district adopt a policy permitting student grade reduction for disciplinary infractions or for excessive absences?

This area of school law is unsettled. Some courts have allowed policies that tie grade reductions to disciplinary infractions or excessive absences, and some have not. Whether or not any such policy is permissible will depend upon the terms of the policy and the facts relating to its implementation. A student challenging a grade reduction probably cannot make a claim of constitutional deprivation, but can make a viable claim if the student was not provided appropriate procedural due process or by claiming the rule is arbitrary and capricious.

Grade reduction policies are fairly common and usually go unchallenged. A school district that has such a policy should be forewarned, however, that if challenged, defending the policy will be expensive and the outcome uncertain.

State ex rel. Barno v. Crestwood Board of Education, 134 Ohio App. 3d 494, 731 N.E. 2d 701 (Ohio Ct. of App. 2007)

Dunn and McCullough v. Fairfield Community High School District No. 225, 158 F. 3d 962 (7th Cir. 1998)

Hamer v. Board of Education of Township High School District 113, 66 Ill. App. 3d 7, 383 N.E. 2d 231, 22 Ill. Dec. 755 (2nd Dist. 1978)

Knight v. Board of Education of Tri-Point Community Unit School District 6J, 38 Ill. App. 3d 603, 348 N.E. 2d 299 (4th Dist. 1976)

10:340 Can a non-custodial parent require a school district to report student progress?

In the absence of a court order to the contrary, upon the request of either parent of a pupil whose parents are divorced, a school board must mail all correspondence and reports that are furnished to one parent to the other parent.

105 ILCS 5/10-21.8

Crowley v. McKinney, 400 F. 3d 965 (7th Cir. 2005), cert. den. 126 S. Ct. 750, 546 U.S. 1033, 163 L. Ed. 2d 573 (2005)

EDUCATIONAL MATERIALS

10:350 What statutory authority is given a school board with respect to the adoption of textbooks?

A school board has statutory authority to adopt such printed instructional materials as are needed in the schools. Publishers are required to meet certain state standards. A record of the adoption of texts and other print materials must be filed with the regional superintendent of schools.

105 ILCS 5/2-3.155

105 ILCS 5/28-21

10:360 Do citizens have a right to inspect instructional materials?

State law provides that any member of the public may inspect all text and instructional material used in the public schools. The term "instructional material" includes both printed and non-print materials that are used in the educational process.

Federal law requires that parents be permitted to inspect instructional materials including teacher's manuals, films, tapes, or other supplementary material that is to be used in connection with any "survey, analysis or evaluation." Neither law permits parental inspection of test questions.

20 U.S.C. 1232h

105 ILCS 5/28-19.1 et seq.

10:370 May a school board charge a rental fee for textbooks?

A school board may purchase textbooks and rent them or resell them to students.

105 ILCS 5/10-22.25

105 ILCS 5/28-8

Hamer v. Board of Education, School District No. 109, Lake County, 9 Ill. App. 3d 663, 292 N.E. 2d 569 (2d Dist. 1977)

10:380 Under what circumstances must a school district provide free textbooks to all its students?

Whenever petitioned by five percent or more of the voters, a school board must submit to the voters at a general election the question of whether to furnish free school textbooks.

105 ILCS 5/28-14 et seq.

10:390 Must a school board provide textbooks at no charge to children whose parents are unable to pay for them?

A school board must provide at no charge textbooks for children whose parents are unable to afford them. The definition of which parents cannot afford textbooks for their children includes, but is not limited to, those whose children are living in households eligible for free breakfast or lunch programs.

The law provides that a school district that establishes a process for the determination of eligibility for waiver of fees that is completely independent of a student's application for, eligibility for, or participation in a federally funded, school-based child nutrition program may provide for fee waiver verification no more often than every 60 calendar days. Information obtained during the independent fee waiver verification process indicating that the student does not meet free lunch or breakfast eligibility guidelines may be used to deny the waiver of the student's fees, provided that any information obtained through this independent process for determining or verifying eligibility for fee waivers must not be used to determine or verify eligibility for any federally funded, school-based child nutrition program.

105 ILCS 5/10-20.13

105 ILCS 5/28-19.2

Latham v. Board of Education of City of Chicago, 31 Ill. 2d 178, 201 N.E. 2d 111 (1964)

10:400 May a school board order the removal of books from the school curriculum or the school library, or may the school board block the acquisition of books because school officials determine the ideas contained in the books are offensive?

School boards have broad authority to manage the schools, including the authority to select or remove textbooks from the curriculum and to determine courses of study. The First Amendment imposes limitations on the discretion of a school board to remove library books from the schools or to otherwise limit student access to ideas.

105 ILCS 5/10-20.8

Kreimer v. Bureau of Police for the Town of Morristown, 958 F. 2d 1242 (3rd Cir. 1992)

Board of Education of Island Trees Union Free School District No. 26 v. Pico, 102 S. Ct. 2799, 457 U.S. 853, 73 L. Ed. 2d 435 (1982)

10:410 May school officials limit the content of postings on school social media sites?

Schools that have social media websites with provisions for public postings have created either a public forum or a limited public forum, depending on whether the website is completely open or subject to certain limiting rules. School officials may establish reasonable rules regarding such postings such as prohibiting obscenity or off-topic comments, but must be mindful that attempts to limit content critical of school officials or school policy will run afoul of the First Amendment. Moreover, such rules must be written with care because the courts will hold school officials to the limits of their own rules.

Davison v. Loudoun County Board of Supervisors, U.S. District Court for the Eastern District of Virginia 2016

Rosenberger v. Rector and Visitors of the University of Virginia, 115 S. Ct. 2510, 515 U.S. 819, 132 L. Ed. 2d 700 (1995)

Perry Education Association v. Perry Local Educators' Association, 103 S. Ct. 948, 460 U.S. 37, 74 L. Ed. 2d 794 (1983)

ALTERNATIVE LEARNING OPPORTUNITIES

10:500 What is the Alternative Learning Opportunities Law?

The Alternative Learning Opportunities Law was enacted by the Illinois General Assembly in 2001 in order to provide students at risk of academic failure with the education and support services needed to meet Illinois Learning Standards and to complete their education in an orderly, safe, and secure learning environment. The law became effective January 1, 2002.

105 ILCS 5/13B-1 et seq.

10:505 Who may operate alternative learning opportunity programs?

School districts may establish alternative learning opportunities programs or may contract with regional offices of education, intermediate service centers, public community colleges, non-profit or for-profit education providers, youth service agencies, community-based organizations, or other appropriate entities to establish alternative learning opportunities programs. Districts may individually operate alternative learning opportunities programs or may collaborate with two or more districts or one or more regional offices of education or both or with intermediate service centers to create and operate alternative learning opportunities programs.

105 ILCS 5/13B-20.10

10:510 What kinds of programs may be available under the alternative learning opportunities law?

Alternative learning opportunities programs may include evening high school; in-school tutoring and mentoring programs; in-school suspension programs; high school completion programs to assist high school drop-outs in completing their education; support services; parental involvement programs; and programs to develop, enhance, or extend the transition for students transferring back to the regular school program, an adult education program, or a post-secondary education program.

105 ILCS 5/13B-20.5

10:515 What is the meaning of "support services" in the alternative learning opportunities law?

Support services includes alcohol and drug rehabilitation; individual, group, and family counseling;

mentoring; tutoring; school physicals; health and nutrition education; classroom aides; career counseling; child care; and any other social, health, or supplemental service approved as part of the student success plan that is required by students for their academic success.

105 ILCS 5/13B-15.20

10:520 With whom may school districts contract for alternative learning opportunity services?

School districts may contract with health, mental health, or human service organizations, workforce development boards or agencies, juvenile court services, juvenile justice agencies, juvenile detention programs, programs operated by the Department of Corrections, or other appropriate agencies or organizations to serve students whose needs are not being met in the regular school program by providing alternative learning opportunities.

105 ILCS 5/13B-20.15

10:525 Which students are eligible for alternative learning services?

Students in grades 4-12 who meet enrollment criteria established by the school district and who meet the definition of "student at risk of academic failure" are eligible to participate. All rights granted to a student's parent or guardian become exclusively those of the student upon the student's 18th birthday.

105 ILCS 5/13B-20.25

10:530 Who is a "student at risk of academic failure" within the meaning of the Alternative Learning Opportunities law?

A student at risk of academic failure is a student at risk of not meeting the Illinois Learning Standards or not graduating from elementary school or high school and who demonstrates a need for educational support or social services beyond that provided by the regular school program. Such students are eligible for services up to the age of 21.

105 ILCS 5/13B-15.20

10:535 May a special education student be enrolled in alternative learning opportunities program?

Any enrollment of a special education student in an alternative learning opportunities program must be done only if included in the student's Individualized Education Program. The student's Individualized Education Program must be implemented in the program by appropriately certified personnel.

105 ILCS 5/13B-60.20

10:540 How is a student enrolled in an alternative learning opportunities program?

A school district that operates an alternative learning opportunities program shall ensure that parents and guardians are aware of the program and the services that the program offers. A student may be enrolled in the program only upon the request of the student or the student's parent or guardian and may remain in the program only with the consent of the student's parent or guardian.

Before being enrolled in an alternative learning opportunities program, the student and each of his or her parents or guardians shall receive written notice to attend a conference to determine if the student would benefit from attending an alternative learning opportunities program. The conference must provide all of the information necessary for the student and parent or guardian to make an informed decision regarding enrollment in an alternative learning opportunities program. The conference must include a discussion of the extent to which the student, if enrolled in the program, may participate in school activities.

No student shall be enrolled in an alternative learning opportunities program without the consent of the student's parent or guardian.

105 ILCS 5/13B-60.5
105 ILCS 5/13B-60.10
105 ILCS 5/13B-60.15

10:545 What is a "student success plan?"

A student success plan is a plan based on an assessment of the student's educational and social functioning and skills that establishes goals and objectives for satisfactory performance in an alternative learning opportunities program. The plan must:

1) Specify the curriculum and instructional methods to be used in improving the student's educational performance;

2) Outline the support services needed to remove barriers to learning;

3) Specify, when appropriate, the career development experiences the student will receive to enhance his or her career awareness;

4) Set objectives to ensure a successful transition back to the regular school program or to post-secondary educational options; and

5) Outline the student's responsibilities under the plan.

A student success plan must be developed for each student enrolled in an alternative learning opportunities program. The student and his or her parent or guardian must be afforded an opportunity to participate in the development of the plan.

105 ILCS 5/13B-15.15
105 ILCS 5/13B-60.25

10:550 How many days and hours of attendance are required in an alternative learning opportunities program?

An alternative learning opportunities program must provide students with at least the minimum number of days of pupil attendance required under Section 10-19 of the School Code and the minimum number of daily hours of schoolwork required under Section 18-8.05 of the School Code, except the State Board may approve exceptions to these requirements if the program meets all of the following conditions:

1) The district plan establishes that a program providing the required minimum number of days of attendance or daily hours of schoolwork would not serve the needs of the program's students.

2) Each day of attendance may provide no fewer than three clock hours of schoolwork, as defined under of 18-8.05 of the School Code.

3) Each day of attendance that provides fewer than five clock hours of schoolwork must also provide supplementary services, work-based learning, student assistance programs, counseling, case management, health and fitness programs, or life-skills or conflict resolution training, in order to provide a total daily program to the student of five clock hours. A program may claim general state aid for up to two hours of the time each day that a student is receiving supplementary services.

4) Each program must provide no fewer than 174 days of actual pupil attendance during the school term; however, approved evening programs that meet the requirements of Section 13B-45 of the School Code may offer less than 174 days of actual pupil attendance during the school term.

105 ILCS 5/13B-45

10:555 Where is an alternative learning program located?

A school district must consider offering an alternative learning opportunities program on-site in the regular school. An alternative learning opportunities program may be provided at facilities separate from the regular school or in classrooms elsewhere on school premises.

105 ILCS 5/13B-20.30

10:560 Must a school district provide transportation to an alternative learning program site?

School districts that are required to provide transportation must provide transportation for students enrolled in alternative learning opportunities programs. Other school districts must provide transportation to the same extent they provide transportation to other students. A school district may collaborate with the regional superintendent of schools to establish a cooperative transportation agreement among school districts in the region to reduce the costs of transportation and to provide for greater accessibility for students attending alternative learning opportunities programs.

105 ILCS 5/13A-9
105 ILCS 5/13B-20.35

10:565 What must a school district show to be eligible for alternative learning program funding?

To be eligible for funding, an alternative learning opportunities program must provide evidence of an administrative structure, program activities, program staff, a budget, and a specific curriculum that is consistent with Illinois Learning Standards but may be different from the regular school program in terms of location, length of school day, program sequence, pace, instructional activities, or any combination of these.

Before receiving state funds for an alternative learning opportunities program, a school district must adopt policies and guidelines for the admission and transfer of students to the program and for transitioning students as appropriate back to the regular school program in a manner consistent with guidelines provided by the State Board of Education. A school district must adopt policies and procedures for the establishment of a new alternative learning opportunities program or for securing state approval for an existing program.

Any district that plans to establish an alternative learning opportunities program must notify the State Superintendent of Education before enrolling students in the program. To apply for funding to establish or maintain an alternative learning opportunities program, a school district must initiate a planning process to specify the type of program needed by the district.

Before submission of the district plan, the school district or consortium may apply for a one-year planning grant. The planning process may involve key education and community stakeholders, such as teachers, administrators, parents, interested members of the community, and other agencies or organizations as appropriate.

105 ILCS 5/13B-25.5
105 ILCS 5/13B-25.10
105 ILCS 5/13B-25.15

10:570 What must be contained in a school district's alternative learning opportunities plan?

The district plan must be updated annually and submitted to the State Board of Education. It must be consistent with the school district's overall mission and goals and aligned with the local school improvement plans of each participating school. The district plan must include all of the following:

1) A description of the program, including the students at risk of academic failure to be served, evidence of need, program goals, objectives, and measurable outcomes.

2) A staffing plan, including the experiences, competency, and qualifications of certified and non-certificated staff and emphasizing their individual and collective abilities to work with students at risk of academic failure.

3) A description and schedule of support services that will be available to students as part of their instructional program, including procedures for accessing services required for students on an as-needed basis.

4) How the district will use grant funds to improve the educational achievement of students at risk of academic failure.

5) A detailed program budget that includes sources of funding to be used in conjunction with alternative learning opportunities grant funds and a plan for allocating costs to those funds.

6) A plan that outlines how funding for alternative learning opportunities will be coordinated with other state and federal funds to ensure the efficient and effective delivery of the program.

7) A description of other sources of revenue the district will allocate to the program.

8) An estimate of the total cost per student for the program and an estimate of any gap between existing revenue available for the program and the total cost of the program.

9) A description of how parents and community members will be involved in the program.

10) Policies and procedures used by the district to grant credit for student work satisfactorily completed in the program.

11) How the district will assess students enrolled in the program, including how statewide testing for students in alternative learning opportunities settings will be addressed.

12) How students will be admitted to the program and how students will make an effective transition back to the regular school program, as appropriate.

13) All cooperative and intergovernmental agreements and subcontracts with eligible entities.

105 ILCS 5/13B-25.20
105 ILCS 5/13B-25.30

10:575 Under what circumstances may approval of an alternative learning opportunities program be revoked?

The State Board of Education may suspend or revoke approval of an alternative learning opportunities program under any one of the following conditions:

1) A failure to meet educational outcomes as enumerated in alternative learning opportunities law and as specified in the alternative learning opportunities grant agreement for a period of two or more consecutive years.

2) A failure to comply with School Code requirements.

3) A failure to comply with the terms and conditions of the alternative learning opportunities grant.

4) A failure to maintain financial records according to generally accepted accounting procedures as specified by the State Board.

105 ILCS 5/13B-30.20

10:600 What is a remote educational program?

A remote educational program is one delivered to students in the home or other location outside of a school building. A student may participate in the program only after the school district, under an adopted school board policy, and a person authorized to enroll the student under Section 10-20.12b of the School Code (residency) determine that a program will best serve the student's individual learning needs. The adopted school board policy must include, but need not be limited to, all of the following:

1) Criteria for determining that a program will best serve a student's individual learning needs. The criteria must include consideration of, at a minimum, a student's prior attendance, disciplinary record, and academic history.

2) Any limitations on the number of students or grade levels that may participate in a program.

3) A description of the process that the school district will use to approve participation in the program. The process must include without limitation a requirement that, for any student who qualifies to receive special education services, the student's participation in the program receive prior approval from the student's Individualized Education Program (IEP) team.

4) A description of the process the school district will use to develop and approve a written remote educational plan that meets this law's clock hour requirements.

5) A description of the system the school district will establish to calculate the number of clock hours a student is participating in instruction in accordance with the program.

6) A description of the process for renewing a program at the expiration of its term.

7) Such other terms and provisions as the school district deems necessary to provide for the establishment and delivery of a program.

The school district must establish the program's curriculum is aligned to state learning standards and that the program offers instruction and educational experiences consistent with those given to students at the same grade level in the district. The program must be delivered by instructors that meet the following qualifications:

1) They are certificated under Article 21 of the School Code;

2) They meet applicable highly qualified criteria under federal law; and

3) They have responsibility for planning instruction, diagnosing learning needs, prescribing content delivery through class activities, assessing learning, reporting outcomes to administrators and parents and guardians, and evaluating the effects of instruction.

During the period of time from and including the opening date to the closing date of the regular school term of the school district established in Section 10-19 of the School Code, participation in a program may be claimed for general state aid purposes on any calendar day, notwithstanding whether the day is a day of pupil attendance or institute day on the school district's calendar or other provision of law restricting instruction on that day. If the district holds year-round classes in some buildings, the district must classify each student's participation in a remote educational program as either on a year-round or non-year-round schedule for purposes of claiming general state aid. Outside of the regular school term of the district, the program may be offered as part of any School Code authorized summer school program.

Each student participating in a program must have a written remote educational plan that has been approved by the school district and a person authorized to enroll the student under Section 10-20.12b. The school district and the person authorized to enroll must approve any amendment to a remote educational plan.

The remote educational plan must include, but is not limited to, all of the following:

1) Specific achievement goals for the student aligned to state learning standards.

2) A description of all assessments that will be used to measure student progress, which must indicate the assessments that will be administered at an attendance center within the school district.

3) A description of the progress reports that will be provided to the school district and the person or persons authorized to enroll the student.

4) Expectations, processes, and schedules for interaction between a teacher and student.

5) A description of the specific responsibilities of the student's family and the school district with respect to equipment, materials, phone and internet service, and any other requirements applicable to the home or other location outside of a school building necessary for the delivery of the program.

6) If applicable, a description of how the program will be delivered in a manner consistent with the student's IEP or plan to ensure compliance with Section 504 of the Rehabilitation Act.

7) A description of the procedures and opportunities for participation in academic and extracurricular activities and programs within the school district.

8) The identification of a parent, guardian, or other responsible adult who will provide direct supervision of the program. The plan must include an acknowledgment by the parent, guardian, or other responsible adult that he or she may engage only in non-teaching duties not requiring instructional judgment or the evaluation of a student. The plan must designate the parent, guardian, or other responsible adult as non-teaching personnel or volunteer personnel under Section 10-22.34 of the School Code.

9) The identification of a school district administrator who will oversee the program for the school district and who may be contacted by the student's parents with respect to any issues or concerns with the program.

10) The term of the student's participation in the program, that may not extend for longer than 12 months, unless the term is renewed.

11) A description of the specific location or locations in which the program will be delivered. If the program is to be delivered to a student in any location other than the student's home, the plan must include a written determination by the school district that the location will provide a learning environment appropriate for the delivery of the program. The location or locations in which the program will be delivered is deemed a long-distance teaching reception area under Section 10-22.34 of the School Code.

12) Certification by the school district that the plan meets all other requirements of this section.

Students participating in the program must be enrolled in a school district attendance center pursuant to the school district's enrollment policy or policies. A student participating in a program must be tested as part of all assessments administered by the school district pursuant to Section 2-3.64 of the School Code at the attendance center in which the student is enrolled and in accordance with the attendance center's assessment policies and schedule. The student must be included within all adequate yearly progress and other accountability determinations for the school district and attendance center under state and federal law.

The term of a student's participation in a program may not extend for longer than 12 months, unless the term is renewed by the school district. The district may only renew a student's participation in a remote educational program following an evaluation of the student's progress in the program, a determination that the student's continuation in the program will best serve the student's individual learning needs, and an amendment to the student's written remote educational plan addressing any changes for the upcoming term of the program.

A school district may, by resolution of its school board, establish a remote educational program. Days of attendance by students in a meeting the requirements of the law may be claimed by the school district and shall be counted as schoolwork for general state aid purposes in accordance with and subject to the limitations of Section 18-8.05 of the School Code.

The impact of remote educational programs on wages, hours, and terms and conditions of employment of educational employees within the school district are subject to local collective bargaining agreements.

The use of a home or other location outside of a school building for a remote educational program shall not cause the home or other location to be deemed a public school facility.

A remote educational program may be used, but is not required, for instruction delivered to a student in the home or other location outside of a school building that is not claimed for general state aid purposes under Section 18-8.05.

School districts that adopt a policy for a remote educational program must submit to the State Board of Education (ISBE) a copy of the policy and any amendments thereto, as well as data on student participation in a format specified by ISBE.

105 ILCS 5/10-29

11: STUDENTS AND PARENTS

COMPULSORY ATTENDANCE

11:10 What are the ages of compulsory school attendance in Illinois?

Before 2004, the compulsory school age was seven to 16. From 2004 to 2014 the compulsory school age was seven to 17. Beginning with the 2014-2015 school year the age for compulsory attendance is six (on or before September 1) to 17 (unless the child has already graduated from high school).

105 ILCS 5/13-3

105 ILCS 5/26-1

Chicago Board of Education v. Terrile, 47 Ill. App. 3d 75, 361 N.E. 2d 778, 5 Ill. Dec. 455 (1st Dist. 1977)

Scoma v. Chicago Board of Education, 391 F. Supp. 452 (N.D. Ill. 1974)

11:20 What is the minimum age for kindergarten attendance?

Any child who will be five on or before September 1 of any school year may attend school at the beginning of the school term. Based on an assessment of a child's readiness, a school district may permit a child to enter at a younger age.

105 ILCS 5/10-20.12

Morrison by Morrison v. Chicago Board of Education, 188 Ill. App. 3d 588, 544 N.E. 2d 1099, 136 Ill. Dec. 324 (1st Dist. 1989)

Morgan v. Board of Education of Trico Community Unit School District No. 176, 22 Ill. App. 3d 241, 317 N.E. 2d 393 (5th Dist. 1974)

11:30 Do compulsory attendance laws require that children attend kindergarten?

No. Kindergarten attendance is optional.

105 ILCS 5/26-1

Morgan v. Board of Education of Trico Community Unit School District No. 176, 22 Ill. App. 3d 241, 317 N.E. 2d 393 (5th Dist. 1974)

11:40 Under what circumstances is a child of compulsory school age exempt from compulsory attendance?

A child is exempt from public school attendance under the following circumstances:

1) If the child attends a private or parochial school where instruction is in the English language;

2) If the child is physically or mentally unable to attend school when the disability is certified by a physician licensed in Illinois to practice medicine in all its branches, a chiropractic physician licensed under the Medical Practice Act of 1987, an advanced practice nurse who has a written collaborative agreement with a collaborating physician that authorizes the nurse to perform health examinations, a physician assistant who has been delegated the authority to perform health examinations by his or her supervising physician, a Christian Science practitioner residing in the state and listed in the Christian Science Journal, or is excused for temporary absence for cause by the principal or teacher of the school that the child attends;

3) If the child is necessarily and lawfully employed consistent with child labor laws, the child may be excused from school by the regional superintendent of schools or the superintendent of the public school which the child should be attending, and upon approval in either instance of the child's school board;

4) If the child is over 12 and under 14 years of age the child must be excused to attend confirmation classes;

5) A child must be excused if the tenets of his or her religion prohibit secular activity on a particular day or days or at a particular time of day;

6) If the child is 16 or older and submits to the school district evidence of necessary and lawful employment pursuant to 3) above and is enrolled in a graduation incentives program under Section 26-16 of the School Code or an alternative learning opportunities program as provided in Article 13B of the School Code.

7) If the child is in grade 6-12 for the purpose of sounding Taps at an Illinois military honors funeral for a deceased veteran.

8) Under certain circumstances, five days during a school year if the child's parent is an active member of the "uniformed services."

105 ILCS 5/13B-1 et seq.

105 ILCS 5/26-1

105 ILCS 5/26-16

People v. Berger, 109 Ill. App. 3d 1054, 441 N.E. 2d 915, 65 Ill. Dec. 600 (2nd Dist. 1982)

Morton v. Board of Education of City of Chicago, 69 Ill. App. 2d 38, 216 N.E. 2d 305 (1st Dist. 1966)

People ex rel. Latimer v. Board of Education of City of Chicago, 394 Ill. 228, 68 N.E. 2d 305 (1946)

11:42 What responsibilities apply to school officials with respect to missing children?

Upon notification by the Illinois State Police of a child's disappearance, the school in which the child is currently or was previously enrolled must flag the record of the child in such a manner that whenever a copy of information regarding the record is requested, the school is alerted that the record is that of a missing person. "Missing person" in this context means a person 17 years old or younger reported to any law enforcement authority as abducted, lost, or a runaway.

The school must immediately report to the State Police any request concerning flagged records or knowledge as to the whereabouts of any missing person. Upon notification by the State Police the missing person has been recovered, the school must remove the flag from the student's record.

325 ILCS 50/5
325 ILCS 55/5

11:44 Who is a drop out?

A dropout is any child enrolled in grades 9-12 whose name has been removed from the district enrollment roster for any reason other than the student's death, extended illness, removal for medical noncompliance, expulsion, aging out, graduation, or completion of a program of studies and who has not transferred to another public or private school and is not known to be home schooled by his or her parents or guardians or continuing school in another country.

105 ILCS 5/25-2a

11:45 May school officials advise failing students to drop out?

No. Senate Bill 100 (P.A. 99-456) prohibits school officials from advising or encouraging students to drop out due to behavioral or academic difficulties.

105 ILCS 5/10-22.6(h)

11:46 How must school officials report student drop-outs and withdrawals?

Beginning in July 2007, the clerk or secretary of the school board must furnish quarterly on the first school day of October, January, April, and July to the regional superintendent and to the Secretary of State a list of pupils, excluding transferees, who have been expelled or have withdrawn or who have left school and have been removed from the regular attendance rolls during the period of time school was in regular session from the time of the previous quarterly report.

The list must include the names and addresses of pupils formerly in attendance, the names and addresses of persons having custody or control of such pupils, the reason, if known, such pupils are no longer in attendance and the date of removal from the attendance rolls.

The list shall also include the names of: pupils whose withdrawal is due to extraordinary circumstances, including but not limited to economic or medical necessity or family hardship, as determined by the criteria established by the school district; pupils who have re-enrolled in school since their names were removed from the attendance rolls; any pupil certified to be a chronic or habitual truant, as defined in Section 26-2a; and pupils previously certified as chronic or habitual truants who have resumed regular school attendance. The regional superintendent shall inform the county or district truant officer who investigates.

Each local school district must establish, in writing, a set of criteria for use by the local superintendent of schools in determining whether a pupil's failure to attend school is the result of extraordinary circumstances, including but not limited to economic or medical necessity or family hardship.

If a pupil re-enrolls in school after his or her name was removed from the attendance rolls or resumes regular attendance after being certified a chronic or habitual truant, the pupil must obtain and forward to the Secretary of State, on a form designated by the Secretary of State, verification of his or her re-enrollment. The verification may be in the form of a signature or seal or in any other form determined by the school board.

105 ILCS 5/26-2a
105 ILCS 5/26-3a

11:47 What records must school officials obtain from students who seek to register for school?

For every child enrolled in a particular elementary or secondary school or preschool, the school must notify in writing the person enrolling the student that within 30 days he or she must provide either a certified copy of the student's birth certificate or other reliable proof, as determined by the State Police, of the student's identity and age and an affidavit explaining the inability to produce a copy of the birth certificate. Other reliable proof of the student's identity and age may include a passport, visa, or other governmental documentation of the child's identity.

When the person enrolling the child provides the school or other entity with a certified copy of the child's birth certificate, the school or other entity shall promptly make a copy of the certified copy for its records and return the original certified copy to the person enrolling the child. Once a school or other entity has been provided with a certified copy of a child's birth certificate, the school or other entity need not request another such certified copy with respect to that child for any other year in which the child is enrolled in that school or other entity.

Upon the failure of a person enrolling a student to comply with the above, the school must immediately notify the Illinois State Police or local law enforcement agency of such failure, and must notify the person enrolling the student in writing that he or she has 10 additional days to comply. The school must immediately report to the State Police any affidavit that appears inaccurate or suspicious in form or content.

Within 14 days after enrolling a transfer student, the elementary or secondary school must request directly from the student's previous school a certified copy of his or her record. The requesting school must exercise due diligence in obtaining the copy of the record requested. Any elementary or secondary school requested to forward a copy of a transferring student's record to the new school must comply within 10 days of receipt of the request unless the record has been flagged because the student is a missing person, in which case the copy shall not be forwarded and the requested school shall notify the State Police or local law enforcement authority of the request.

325 ILCS 50/5
325 ILCS 55/5

TRUANCY

11:50 What is a truant?

A truant is a child subject to compulsory school attendance who is absent from school without valid cause for a school day or any portion of a school day.

105 ILCS 5/26-2a
705 ILCS 405/3-1
People v. R.G., 131 Ill. 2d 328, 546 N.E. 2d 533, 137 Ill. Dec. 588 (1989)
In Interest of Burr, 119 Ill. App. 2d 134, 255 N.E. 2d 57 (4th Dist. 1969)

11:55 What student absences are permitted by law?

The School Code provides the valid causes for absence are illness, observance of a religious holiday, death in the immediate family, family emergency, and includes such other situations beyond the control of the student as determined by the board of education in each district, or such other circumstances which cause reasonable concern to the parent for the safety or health of the student. "Religion" for the purposes of truancy law, includes all aspects of religious observance and practice, as well as belief.

105 ILCS 5/26-2a

11:60 What duty does a school district have to notify parents of a student absence?

If a child in grades K-8 is absent from school, and there is no record the absence is for a valid cause and there is no notification the absence has been authorized, the school must, within two hours after the first class in which the child is enrolled, make a reasonable effort to telephone and notify the parent, legal guardian, or other person having legal custody of the child of the child's absence from school.

105 ILCS 5/26-3b

11:70 What is the penalty for encouraging truancy?

Any person who has custody or control of a child subject to compulsory attendance who knowingly or willfully permits the child to persist in truancy, if convicted, is guilty of a Class C misdemeanor and may be subject to up to 30 days imprisonment and/or a fine of up to $1,500. Any person who willfully induces or attempts to induce any child to be absent from school or who knowingly employs or harbors any child who is unlawfully absent from school for three consecutive school days, if convicted, is guilty of a Class C misdemeanor. Any person who prevents or interferes with a child's attendance at school by threat, menace, or intimidation is guilty of a Class A misdemeanor. A Class A misdemeanor is punishable by imprisonment for a term up to a year and a fine not to exceed $2,500.

In any such proceeding against parents or guardians the school district must demonstrate it has attempted to counsel the student and the person(s) having custody and control of the student and has provided support services, alternative programs, and other school resources in an effort to correct the truant behavior.

105 ILCS 5/22-12
105 ILCS 5/26-8 et seq.
730 ILCS 5/5-4.5-55
730 ILCS 5/5-4.5-65

11:80 Who has jurisdiction to act with respect to truant minors?

Under given circumstances a school district, the school district truant officer, the regional superintendent of schools, the state's attorney and/or the Illinois Department of Children and Family Services may have jurisdiction.

105 ILCS 5/26-2a et seq.
305 ILCS 5/1-1 et seq.
705 ILCS 405/3-1 et seq.

11:90 What is a chronic or habitual truant?

A chronic or habitual truant is a child subject to compulsory attendance laws who is absent without valid cause from school for five percent or more of the previous 180 regular attendance days.

105 ILCS 5/26-2a

11:100 What restrictions are placed on a school district in dealing with a chronic or habitual truant?

Compulsory attendance laws provide a school district may take no punitive action against a chronic or habitual truant for truancy until the district has made available to the student all support services and other school resources in order to correct the chronic or habitually truant behavior.

105 ILCS 5/26-12

11:110 How are truant officers appointed?

Truant officers are appointed in one of two ways. A school board may appoint a truant officer and fix and pay his or her salary from school district funds. The regional superintendent of schools is required to appoint a truant officer for those districts that fail to appoint. The person appointed receives such compensation as may be fixed by the county board and is paid by the county. The county truant officer's appointment must be approved by a circuit judge.

105 ILCS 5/3-13
105 ILCS 5/26-5
Burris v. Board of Education, 221 Ill. App. 397 (4th Dist. 1920)

RIGHT TO ATTEND SCHOOL

11:120 Who is authorized to establish school attendance boundaries?

A school district with two or more attendance centers at the same grade level may establish attendance boundaries for each attendance center. A school board may not cause students to be segregated between two or more elementary schools on the basis of such factors as race, color, creed, national origin, sex, religion, or other constitutionally-impermissible factor. In the absence of such factors, the establishment of school attendance zones is a discretionary power of a school board and neither students nor their parents may require the school board to assign them to any particular attendance center.

105 ILCS 5/10-21.3
Tometz v. Board of Education Waukegan City School District No. 61, 39 Ill. 2d 593, 237 N.E. 2d 498 (1968)

11:125 Who controls the transfer of students from attendance center to attendance center within a school district?

Each school board is required to establish and implement a policy governing the transfer of a student from one attendance center to another within the school district upon the request of the student's parent or guardian. Any request by a parent or guardian to transfer his or her child from one attendance center to another within the school district pursuant to Section 1116 of the federal Elementary and Secondary Education Act of 1965 must be made no later than 30 days after the parent or guardian receives notice of the right to transfer pursuant to that law. A student may not transfer to any of the following attendance centers, except by change in residence if the policy authorizes enrollment based on residence in an attendance area or unless approved by the board on an individual basis:

1) An attendance center that exceeds or as a result of the transfer would exceed its attendance capacity.

2) An attendance center for which the board has established academic criteria for enrollment if the student does not meet the criteria, provided that the transfer must be permitted if the attendance center is the only attendance center serving the student's grade that has not been identified for school improvement, corrective action, or restructuring under Section 1116 of the federal Elementary and Secondary Education Act.

3) Any attendance center if the transfer would prevent the school district from meeting its obligations under a state or federal law, court order, or consent decree applicable to the school district.

20 U.S.C. 6311 (d) (1) (D)
105 ILCS 5/10-21.3a

11:126 May a student transfer from a dangerous school to a less dangerous school?

A 2004 amendment to the School Code requires each school board to have a policy governing the transfer of students within a school district from "a persistently dangerous school" to another public school in the district that is not persistently dangerous. To be persistently dangerous, a school must meet all of the following criteria for two consecutive years:

1) Have greater than 3 percent of the students enrolled in the school expelled for violence-related conduct.

2) Have one or more students expelled for bringing a firearm to school as defined in 18 U.S.C. 921 which defines firearm as "any weapon (including a starter gun) which will or is designed to or may readily be converted to expel a projectile by the action of an explosive; the frame or receiver of any such weapon; any firearm muffler or firearm silencer; or any destructive device. Such term does not include an antique firearm." Destructive device is also defined at 18 U.S.C. 921 as any explosive, incendiary, or poison gas, bomb, grenade, rocket having a propellant charge of more than four ounces, missile having an explosive or incendiary charge of more than one-quarter ounce, mine, or device similar to any of the devices described in the preceding clauses.

3) Have at least 3 percent of the students enrolled in the school exercise the individual option to transfer schools pursuant to the immediately following paragraph:

A student may transfer from one public school to another public school in that district if the student is a victim of a violent crime as defined in Section 3 of the Rights of Crime Victims and Witnesses Act. The violent crime must have occurred on school grounds during regular school hours or during a school-sponsored event. Transfers must be made in compliance with federal law.

18 U.S.C. 921
20 U.S.C. 6311 (d) (1) (D)
105 ILCS 5/10-21.3a
725 ILCS 120/3 et seq.

11:140 Under what circumstances must a school district deny enrollment to a student who resides in the school district?

A school district must deny enrollment in its secondary schools to any child above the age of 19 years who has dropped out of school and who could not, because of age and lack of credits, attend classes during the normal school year and graduate before his or her 21st birthday. A district may, at the district's option, enroll the child in an alternative learning opportunity program established under Article 13B of the School Code.

To deny enrollment the school district must schedule a hearing "as required in cases of expulsion." If as a result of the hearing the child is denied enrollment, the school district must provide counseling to the child and direct him to alternative educational programs that lead to graduation or receipt of a GED.

A school or school district may deny enrollment to a student 16 or older for one semester for failure to meet minimum academic standards if all of the following conditions are met:

1) The student achieved a grade point average of less than "D" (or its equivalent) in the semester immediately prior to the current semester.

2) The student and the student's parent or guardian are given written notice warning that the student is failing academically and is subject to denial from enrollment for one semester unless a "D" average (or its equivalent) or better is attained in the current semester.

3) The parent or guardian is provided with the right to appeal the notice as determined by the State Board of Education in accordance with due process.

4) The student is provided with an academic remediation plan and academic remediation services.

5) The student fails to achieve a "D" average (or its equivalent) or better in the current semester.

A school or school district may deny enrollment to a student 16 or older for one semester for failure to meet minimum attendance standards if all the following conditions are met:

1) The student was absent without valid cause for 20 percent or more of the attendance days in the semester immediately prior to the current semester.

2) The student and the student's parent or guardian are given written notice warning that the student is subject to denial from enrollment for one semester unless the student is absent without valid cause less than 20 percent of the attendance days in the current semester.

3) The student's parent or guardian is provided with the right to appeal the notice, as determined by the State Board of Education in accordance with due process.

4) The student is provided with attendance remediation services including, without limitation, assessment, counseling, and support services.

5) A student is absent without valid cause for 20 percent or more of the attendance days in the current semester.

A school or school district may not deny enrollment to a student (or re-enrollment to a drop out) who is at least 16 but not more than 19 for one consecutive semester for failure to meet academic or attendance standards.

No child may be denied enrollment or re-enrollment in violation of the Individuals with Disabilities Education Act (IDEA) or the Americans with Disabilities Act (ADA).

Re-enrolled student means a dropout who has re-enrolled full time in a public school. Each school district is required to identify, track, and report on the educational progress and outcomes of re-enrolled students as a subject of the district's required reporting on all enrollments. A re-enrolled student who again drops out may not be counted again against the district's dropout rate performance measure.

20 U.S.C. 1400 et seq.
42 U.S.C. 12101 et seq.
105 ILCS 5/13B-1 et seq.
105 ILCS 5/26-2

11:145 Should school officials deny enrollment to migrant children who are in the country illegally?

No. Such children are entitled to the same access to educational opportunity as are children who are United States citizens. The immigration status of parents and or their children is not relevant to the enrollment decision. School officials should make a determination regarding where the child resides (to ascertain whether or not the child resides in the district) in the same manner it would make such inquiry with regard to any other child seeking to enroll. School officials may not make inquiry into the immigration status of parents or their children. Some such children may be homeless.

Residence in the school district is the basis for tuition free enrollment determinations for foreign exchange students and illegal aliens.

Plyler v. Doe, 102 S. Ct. 2382, 457 U.S. 202, 72 L. Ed. 2d 786 (1981) reh. den.103 S. Ct. 14, 458 U.S. 1131, L. Ed. 2d (1982)

11:160 May a student be excluded from school because she is pregnant?

A school board may not exclude a student because of pregnancy. A school district is required to provide home instruction, correspondence courses, or other courses of instruction for students who are unable to attend school because of pregnancy and for up to three months following the birth of a child or miscarriage.

105 ILCS 5/10-22.6a
105 ILCS 5/26-1

11:170 May a school district discipline a student because she is pregnant out of wedlock?

No, and neither may the school discriminate in any other way against her.

20 U.S.C. 1681
Wort v. Vierling, 778 F. 2d 1233 (7th Cir. 1985)

STUDENT RESIDENCY AND TUITION

11:180 Is a child living in a school district necessarily entitled to tuition-free enrollment in the schools of the district where he or she lives?

A child is entitled to tuition-free enrollment in the school district wherein he or she resides. Residency, in this context, has a specific meaning in the law. A child is presumed to be a resident of the school district wherein the persons who have legal custody of him reside. After a divorce, a child is presumed to reside with the custodial parent. A school district has a duty to charge tuition to non-resident pupils.

105 ILCS 5/10-20.12a
105 ILCS 5/10-20.12b
105 ILCS 5/10-22.5
Martinez Morales v. Bynum, 103 S. Ct. 1838, 461 U.S. 321, 75 L. Ed. 2d 879 (1983)
Kraut v. Rachford, 51 Ill. App. 3d 206, 366 N.E. 2d 497, 9 Ill. Dec. 240 (1st Dist. 1977)
Turner v. Board of Education North Chicago Community High School District 123, 54 Ill. 2d 68, 294 N.E. 2d 264 (1973)

11:185 For purposes of school attendance, what is residence?

Residence is physical presence with an intention to remain on a permanent basis.

Mina ex rel. Anghel v. Board of Education for Homewood-Flossmoor, 348 Ill. App. 3d 264, 809 N.E. 2d 168, 284 Ill. Dec. 46, (1st Dist. 2004)
Connelly v. Gibbs, 112 Ill. App. 3d 257, 445 N.E. 2d 477, 68 Ill. Dec. 29 (1st Dist. 1983)

11:190 For purposes of establishing a student's residency, what does "legal custody" mean?

Legal custody means one of the following:

1) Custody exercised by a natural or adoptive parent with whom the student resides;

2) Custody granted by order of a court of competent jurisdiction to a person with whom the pupil resides for reasons other than to have access to the educational programs of the school district;

3) Custody exercised under a statutory short-term guardianship for reasons other than to have access to the educational programs of the school district;

4) Custody exercised by an adult caretaker relative who is receiving aid under the Illinois Public Aid Code for the pupil who resides with the adult caretaker relative for purposes other than to have access to the educational programs of the school district;

5) Custody exercised by an adult who demonstrates that, in fact, he or she has assumed and exercises legal responsibility for the pupil and provides the pupil with a regular fixed nighttime abode for purposes other than to have access to the educational programs of the school district.

If a pupil's change of residence is due to the military service obligation of his or her legal custodian, then, upon the written request of the custodian, the residence of the pupil is, for the duration of the custodian's military service obligation to be the same as the residence of the pupil immediately before the change of residence caused by the military service obligation. No fees, costs, or tuition may be charged. A school district is not responsible for transportation.

105 ILCS 5/10-20.12b

755 ILCS 5/11-5.4

11:192 What should school officials do when divorced biological parents disagree about an educational decision or the physical custody of the child?

Divorced parents are frequently at odds about decisions affecting their child. These disagreements may surface at school when the parents disagree about visitation (who should be allowed to pick up the child after school or which bus route the child should ride), how and with whom educational information should be shared, and who has decision-making authority when the parents disagree. Sometimes, the child becomes a pawn in a parental dispute and school officials are unwilling participants in the conflict.

Non-biological parents (second spouses) usually have no independent decision-making authority in the instance of a divorce. Therefore, even though the second spouse may be a primary care-giver, school officials should be careful to obtain authority for decisions or directions from a party with the appropriate legal ability to do so. Usually, the order issued at the time of the divorce (and orders subsequently modifying it) provide guidance as to the proper course of action to be taken by school officials.

Divorce documents are public records and school officials can, and should, obtain copies of such records when disputes arise. It is not uncommon for custody orders to undergo multiple modifications during the period of a child's minority, and school officials should be careful to obtain the most recent order. When it is apparent divorced parents are disagreeing, school officials should obtain information necessary to educational decision-making at the time of the child's registration, and should not wait until a dispute arises.

More difficult are instances when there is no court order to guide school officials. This frequently occurs when there is only one legally acknowledged biological parent (child born out of wedlock). Decisions in these cases are fact-driven.

Navin v. Park Ridge School District No. 64, 270 F. 3d 1147 (7th Cir. 2001)

Pauley v. Anchorage School District, 31 P. 3d 1284 (Alaska 2001)

11:195 May a school district waive tuition for a non-resident student?

In most cases, a school district need not admit a non-resident pupil and may require the student to attend school in the school district in which he or she resides.

A school district may permit a student from an adjacent school district to attend its schools tuition free when requested for the student's health and safety by the student or parent, and when both school districts involved determine that the student's health and safety will be served by the enrollment. Neither school district is required to alter its existing transportation services as a result of such an agreement.

If, at the time of enrollment, a dependent of United States military personnel is housed in temporary housing located outside of a school district, but will be living within the district within 60 days after the time of initial enrollment, the dependent must be allowed to enroll and must not be charged tuition. Any United States military personnel attempting to enroll a dependent must provide proof that the dependent will be living within the district within 60 days after the time of initial enrollment. Proof of residency may include, but is not limited to, post-marked mail addressed to the military personnel and sent to an address located within the district, a lease agreement for occupancy of a residence located within the district, or proof of ownership of a residence located within the district.

If a pupil lives outside the school district but the pupil's change of residence from a residence within the school district was due to the military service obligation of his or her legal custodian, then, upon the written request of the custodian, the residence of the pupil is, for the duration of the custodian's military service obligation to be the same as the residence of the pupil immediately before the change of residence caused by the military service obligation. No fees, costs, or tuition may be charged. A school district is not responsible for transportation

In other circumstances, if the school district elects to admit a non-resident pupil, it has a duty to charge tuition and may not waive tuition charges except in circumstances authorized by statute. Some school districts have sought and received waivers of their statutory obligations under the residency requirements, but school officials who seek such a waiver should be mindful of their bargaining obligations, the political consequences of the request, and the possibility that the request is granted.

105 ILCS 5/10-20.12a

105 ILCS 5/10-20.12b

105 ILCS 5/10-22.5a

IRS Publication 970

Cohen v. Wauconda Community Unit School District No. 118, 779 F. Supp. 88 (N.D. Ill. 1991)

11:200 What is the amount of tuition for a non-resident pupil?

A school board has a duty to charge non-resident pupils tuition in an amount not to exceed 110 percent of the per capita cost of maintaining the schools of the district for the preceding school year. Per capita costs are computed by dividing the total cost of conducting and maintaining the schools of the district by the average daily attendance, including tuition pupils.

105 ILCS 5/10-20.12a

11:205 If a school district finds that an enrolled student is a non-resident, how can the student be required to pay tuition or be removed from school?

Once a child has been enrolled in the school district the child must be provided due process before he or she can be charged tuition or barred from attendance. To charge tuition, the school board must notify the person who enrolled the student by certified mail of the amount of tuition due and the specific reasons why the board believes the pupil is non-resident. Within 10 calendar days of the receipt of the notice the person who enrolled the student may request a hearing before the school board to review the determination. Within 10 calendar days after the receipt of the request, the school board must notify by certified mail the person requesting the hearing of the time and place of the hearing that must be held not less than 10 nor more than 20 calendar days after the notice of hearing is given.

The board or a hearing officer designated by it must conduct the hearing. The board and the person who enrolled the pupil may be represented at the hearing by representatives of their choice. The person who enrolled the pupil has the burden of going forward with the evidence. If the hearing is conducted by a hearing officer, the hearing officer, within five calendar days after the conclusion of the hearing shall send a written report of his or her findings by certified mail to the board and to the person who enrolled the pupil. The person who enrolled the pupil may, within five calendar days after receiving the findings, file written objections to the findings with the school board by sending the objections by certified mail addressed to the district superintendent.

Whether the hearing is conducted by the school board or a hearing officer, the school board shall, within 30 calendar days after the conclusion of the hearing decide whether the pupil is a resident of the district and the amount of any tuition required to be charged as a result of the pupil's attendance in the schools of the district. The school board must send a copy of its decision within five calendar days to the person who enrolled the pupil by certified mail.

If a hearing is requested, the pupil may, at the request of the person who enrolled the pupil, continue attendance at the schools of the district pending the decision of the school board following the hearing. However, attendance of the pupil in the schools of the district does not relieve any person who enrolled the pupil of the obligation to pay the tuition charged for attendance if ultimately the decision is that the pupil is a non-resident of the district.

In 2016, the General Assembly added an appeal from a board residency hearing to the regional superintendent of schools and added significant procedural requirements to the introduction of evidence at a residency hearing.

If a pupil is determined to be a non-resident of the district for whom tuition is required to be charged, the school board must refuse to permit the pupil to continue attending the schools of the district unless the required tuition is paid for the pupil.

105 ILCS 5/10-20.12b

Mina ex rel. Anghel v. Board of Education for Homewood-Flossmoor, 348 Ill. App. 3d 264, 809 N.E. 2d 168, 284 Ill. Dec. 46, (1st Dist. 2004)

11:210 What is the penalty for providing false information regarding the residency of a pupil?

A person who knowingly or willfully provides false information to a school district regarding the residency of a pupil for the purpose of enabling the pupil to attend any school in the district without the payment of a non-resident tuition charge commits a Class C misdemeanor (not more than 30 days in jail and/or a fine not to exceed $1500).

105 ILCS 5/10-20.12b

730 ILCS 5/5-4.5-65

Jones v. Chicago Board of Education, 2013 WL 39357799 (opinion withdrawn) 2013 IL App (1st) 122437 (not reported)

11:215 If a child begins a school term enrolled in a school district, may the child complete the school term in that district even if the child moves out of the district during the school term?

If a student becomes non-resident during a school term, the child must be permitted to attend school in the school district in which the child was originally enrolled and cannot be charged tuition for the remainder of the school term in which the child became non-resident.

105 ILCS 5/10-20.12a

11:220 Can residence of a child for school purposes be established by the temporary transfer of custody of the child to a relative?

The facts surrounding any temporary transfer of custody will determine whether or not residency has been established. The mere creation of a guardianship, transfer of custody, or change of address is not sufficient to establish residence for school attendance purposes.

105 ILCS 5/10-20.12b

Israel S. By Owens v. Board of Education of Oak Park and River Forest High School District 200, Cook County, 235 Ill. App. 3d 652, 601 N.E. 2d 1264, 176 Ill. Dec. 566 (1st Dist. 1992)

Kraut v. Rachford, 51 Ill. App. 3d 206, 366 N.E. 2d 497, 9 Ill. Dec. 240 (1st Dist. 1977)

Turner v. Board of Education North Chicago Community High School District 123, 54 Ill. 2d 68, 294 N.E. 2d 264 (1973)

11:225 Which school district must pay for a child's educational costs if the child is in a residential program?

Except in the case of special education students, and unless otherwise agreed by the parties involved and unless educational services are not otherwise provided for, if an Illinois student under the age of 21 is enrolled in a residential program, the child's education is provided by the school district in which the residential facility is located and paid for by the school district in which the child resides.

105 ILCS 5/10-20.12a

105 ILCS 5/14-7.05

Carbondale Community High School District No. 165 v. Herrin Community Unit School District No. 4, 303 Ill. App. 3d 656, 708 N.E. 2d 844, 237 Ill. Dec. 41 (5th Dist. 1999)

HOMELESS CHILD

11:230 Must a school district enroll a homeless child regardless of the child's residency?

"Homeless child" is broadly defined in state law to include (but is not limited to) a child or youth who has a primary nighttime abode that is:

• A supervised publicly or privately operated shelter designed to provide temporary living accommodations;

• An institution that provides temporary residence for a person intended to be institutionalized; or

• A public or private place not designed or ordinarily used as a regular sleeping accommodation for human beings.

Under federal law, "homeless children and youths" also includes those who are sharing the housing of other persons due to loss of housing, economic hardship, or a similar reason; are living in motels, hotels, trailer parks, or camping grounds due to the lack of alternative adequate accommodations; are living in emergency or transitional shelters; are abandoned in hospitals; and children and youths who are living in cars, parks, public spaces, abandoned buildings, substandard housing, bus or train stations, or similar settings.

The parents of a homeless child have the option of:

1) Continuing the child's education in the school of origin for as long as the child remains homeless or if the child becomes permanently housed until the end of the academic year during which the housing was acquired, or

2) Enrolling the child in any school that non-homeless students who live in the attendance area in which the child is actually living are eligible to attend.

42 U.S.C 11301 et seq.

42 U.S.C. 11431 et seq.

42 U.S.C. 11434a

105 ILCS 45/1-5

105 ILCS 45/1-10

11:232 May a school district provide financial assistance to an at-risk or homeless child?

A 2017 change in the law expressly allows, under specified circumstances, a school district to expend funds to assist children who are homeless or at risk of becoming homeless.

105 ILCS 45/1-17

11:235 Must a school district provide transportation for a homeless child?

If a child becomes homeless or if a homeless child changes temporary living arrangements and if the child's parents or guardians decide to continue the child's education in the school of origin, the parents or guardians must provide or attempt to provide or may authorize relatives, friends, or a shelter to provide the child with transportation. If transportation is not provided in this manner it must be provided:

1) If the homeless child continues to live in the school district in which the school of origin is located, the child's transportation to and from the school of origin must be provided by the school district in which the school of origin is located.

2) If the homeless child's living arrangements in the school district of origin terminate and the child,

though continuing his or her education in the school of origin, begins living in another school district, the responsibility and the cost of providing the child with transportation to and from the school of origin shall be apportioned between the two districts unless the districts cannot agree on the apportionment in which case the costs shall be shared equally.

42 U.S.C. 11431 et seq.
105 ILCS 45/1-15

11:237 How are disputes regarding homeless children resolved?

Each regional superintendent appoints an ombudsperson for homeless children, provides resource information, and resolves disputes at schools relating to the rights of homeless children under Education for Homeless Children Act. If a school denies a homeless child enrollment or transportation, it must immediately refer the child or his or her parent or guardian to the ombudsperson and provide the child or his or her parent or guardian with a written statement of the basis for the denial. The child must be admitted and transported to the school chosen by the parent or guardian until final resolution of the dispute. The ombudsperson must convene a meeting of all parties and attempt to resolve the dispute within five school days after receiving notice of the dispute, if possible.

Whenever a child and his or her parent or guardian who initially share the housing of another person due to loss of housing, economic hardship, or a similar hardship continue to share the housing, a school district may, after the passage of 18 months and annually thereafter, conduct a review as to whether the hardship continues to exist. The district may, at the time of review, request information from the parent or guardian to reasonably establish the hardship, and sworn affidavits or declarations may be sought and provided. If, upon review, the district determines that the family no longer suffers such hardship, it may notify the family in writing and begin the process of dispute resolution as set forth in the Education for Homeless Children Act. Any change required as a result of this review and determination is effective solely at the close of the school year. Any person who knowingly or willfully presents false information regarding the hardship of a child in any review under this law is guilty of a Class C misdemeanor.

Any party to a dispute under the Education for Homeless Children Act may file a civil action in a court of competent jurisdiction to seek appropriate relief. In any civil action, a party whose rights under this Act are found to have been violated can recover reasonable attorney's fees and costs.

If a dispute arises, the school district must inform parents and guardians of homeless children of the availability of the ombudsperson, sources of low-cost or free legal assistance, and other advocacy services in the community.

105 ILCS 45/1-25

HEALTH EXAMINATION AND IMMUNIZATION

11:240 At what grade levels are students required to show proof of health examination and immunization?

Proof of health examination and proof of immunization against preventable communicable disease are required upon entry to kindergarten or the first grade level a school offers, prior to entrance into nursery school, upon entering sixth and ninth grades, and upon first entry into any school. The Department of Health rules regarding required immunizations cited below as Administrative Code references were amended in February 2017.

An eye examination performed during the previous year by an optometrist or a physician licensed to practice medicine in all its branches is required of each child upon entry in kindergarten or first entry into school. If a child fails to provide proof by October 15, the school may hold the child's report card until one of the following occurs: 1) the child presents proof of a completed eye examination, or 2) the child provides proof that an eye examination will take place within 60 days after October 15. The Department of Public Health has established by rule a waiver for children who show an undue burden or a lack of access to an eye doctor. A student may not be excluded from school for failure to comply with eye examination requirements.

Each child in the second and sixth grades is required to have a dental examination. Each child must present proof of having been examined by a dentist before May 15 of the school year. If a child in the second or sixth grade fails to provide proof by May 15, the school may hold the child's report card until one of the following occurs: 1) the child presents proof of a completed dental examination, or 2) the child provides proof that a dental examination will take place within 60 days after May 15. The Department of Public Health has established by rule a waiver for children who show an undue burden or a lack of access to a dentist. Each school is required to give notice of the dental examination requirement to the parents and guardians of students at least 60 days before May 15 of each school year.

Tuberculosis examinations are required by the Department of Public Health when the child involved resides in an area that has a high incidence of tuberculosis.

Until June 30, 2015, if the student is an out-of-state transfer student and does not have the proof required before October 15 of the current year or whatever date is set by the school district, then he or she may only attend classes if he or she has proof that an appointment for the required vaccinations has been scheduled with a party authorized to submit proof of the required vaccinations. If the proof of vaccination required is not submitted within 30 days after the student is permitted to attend classes, then the student is not permitted to attend classes until proof of the vaccinations has been properly submitted. No school district or employee of a school district is held liable for any injury or illness to another person that results from admitting an out-of-state transfer student to class that has an appointment scheduled.

105 ILCS 5/27-8.1

77 Ill. Admin. Code 665.210

77 Ill. Admin. Code 665.240

11:242 May a required student health exam be performed by someone other than a physician?

Yes. Physicians licensed to practice medicine in all of its branches, advanced practice nurses who have a written collaborative agreement with a collaborating physician that authorizes them to perform health examinations, or physician assistants who have been delegated the performance of health examinations by their supervising physician are authorized by statute to perform the examinations.

105 ILCS 5/27-8.1

11:250 May a school board exclude a student for failure to show proof of immunization?

If a child does not present proof of health examination and immunizations by October 15 of a year in which such proof is required, the school board is required to suspend the child from school. There are limited statutory medical and/or constitutional circumstances and until June 1, 2015, an exception for out of state transfer students under which the October 15 deadline may be extended for a particular child.

105 ILCS 5/27-8.1

11:252 May a school board establish a date earlier than October 15 for proof of immunization?

Yes, provided the school district gives notice of the requirement at least 60 days prior to the established earlier date.

105 ILCS 5/27-8.1(5)

11:255 May a child be exempted from immunizations or health examinations for religious reasons?

Children whose parents or guardians object to health examinations or immunizations on religious grounds may be exempted from examinations or immunizations on presentation to the local school authority a signed statement of objection.

105 ILCS 5/27-8.1 (8)

STUDENT FEES

11:260 May a school district charge student fees?

No fees may be charged that would have the effect of abridging a student's right to a free appropriate public education. Reasonable fees may be charged for services and activities that are tangential to the educational program; however, a school board must waive fees for those unable to pay. Book and towel rental fees have been held permissible. Tuition fees are not permissible.

105 ILCS 5/10-20.13

105 ILCS 5/10-22.25

Hamer v. Board of Education, School District No. 109, Lake County, 9 Ill. App. 3d 663, 292 N.E. 2d 569 (2d Dist. 1977)

Polzin v. Rand, McNally & Co., 250 Ill. 561, 95 N.E. 623 (1911)

11:270 May a school district charge a fee for driver education?

A school district may charge up to $50 for district residents between the ages of 15 and 21 years who take part in the driver education course. However, the fee must be waived for any such resident who is unable to pay, regardless of whether the individual is in school or out of school. A school district may increase this fee to an amount not to exceed $250 by school board resolution following a public hearing on the increase, which increased fee must be waived for students who participate in the course and are unable to pay for the course. The public hearing must be announced on the district's website at least 14 days prior to the hearing and in a newspaper of general circulation at least seven days before the hearing. The notices must include the amount of the fee increase.

When space permits, the district also may provide driver education for residents above age 55 who have never been licensed to drive and may charge a fee not to exceed actual costs.

105 ILCS 5/2-3.25(g) (c-5)

105 ILCS 27-24.2

23 Ill. Admin. Code 252.10 et seq.

11:275 May a school district allow the use of credit cards in the payment of student fees?

Yes. Use of credit cards for payment is permissible at the option of the school district.

105 ILCS 5/10-23.11

STUDENT INSURANCE

11:280 Must a school board provide health insurance for student athletes?

The law requires school districts to provide catastrophic accident insurance coverage for high school students who participate in IHSA sanctioned events. The coverage requirement is in addition to any other coverage (health insurance, for example) that may be prudent.

A school board may provide accident and health insurance on a group or individual basis, or through nonprofit hospital service corporations or medical service plan corporations, or both, for its pupils who are injured while participating in any athletic activity under the jurisdiction of, or sponsored or controlled by, the district. The cost of the insurance, when paid from the funds of the district, must, to the extent there is sufficient money to do so, be paid from money derived from athletic activities. To the extent that money derived from athletic activities is insufficient, the cost may be paid from the educational fund.

105 ILCS 5/22-15

Frederich v. Board of Education of Community Unit School District No. 304, 59 Ill. App. 3d 49, 375 N.E. 2d 141, 10 Ill. Dec. 510 (2nd Dist. 1978)

STATUS OF MINORS

11:290 What is an emancipated minor?

An emancipated minor is a person 16 to 18 years old who has demonstrated the ability and capacity to manage his or her own affairs and to live wholly or partially independent of parents or guardians. Such an individual may petition a circuit court for a declaration of complete or partial emancipation. Marriage emancipates a minor for most purposes in the law.

750 ILCS 30/2 et seq.

Kowalski v. Liska, 78 Ill. App. 3d 64, 397 N.E. 2d 39, 33 Ill. Dec. 706 (1st Dist. 1979)

11:295 May an emancipated minor establish residence in a school district other than that in which his or her parents reside?

An emancipated minor may establish his or her own residence.

750 ILCS 30/2 et seq.

11:300 May minors buy tobacco products?

State law prohibits the purchase of tobacco or tobacco products in any form (including alternative nicotine products) by minors under 18 years of age. There is an exception for minors involved in "sting" operations. The statute also prohibits persons who have reached majority from buying tobacco for minors. The law does not prohibit the possession of tobacco products by minors, but does prohibit the possession of alternate nicotine product by minors.

720 ILCS 675/1

720 ILCS 675/1.5

CHILD ABUSE AND NEGLECT

11:310 What is an "abused" child?

An "abused child" is a child whose parent or immediate family member, or any person responsible for the child's welfare, or any individual residing in the same home as the child, or a paramour of the child's parent does any of the following:

1) Inflicts, causes to be inflicted, or allows to be inflicted upon such child physical injury, by other than accidental means, that causes death, disfigurement, impairment of physical or emotional health, or loss or impairment of any bodily function;

2) Creates substantial risk of physical injury to such child by other than accidental means that would be likely to cause death, disfigurement, impairment of physical or emotional health, or loss or impairment of any bodily function;

3) Commits or allows to be committed any sex offense against such child, and extending the Criminal Code definitions of sex offenses to include children under 18 years of age;

4) Commits or allows to be committed an act or acts of torture upon such child; or

5) Inflicts excessive corporal punishment.

6) Commits or allows to be committed the offense of female genital mutilation against the child.

7) Causes to be sold, transferred, distributed, or given to such child under 18 years of age a controlled substance as defined in Section 102 of The Illinois Controlled Substances Act in violation of Article IV of the Illinois Controlled Substances Act or in violation of

the Methamphetamine Control and Community Protection Act except for substances prescribed in accordance with the Act and dispensed in a manner that substantially complies with the prescription.

8) Commits or allows to be committed the offense of involuntary servitude, involuntary sexual servitude of a minor, or trafficking in persons.

A minor is not considered abused for the sole reason that the minor has been relinquished in accordance with the Abandoned Newborn Infant Protection Act.

325 ILCS 5/3

11:320 What is a "neglected" child?

A "neglected child" is any child who is not receiving the proper or necessary nourishment or medically indicated treatment, including food or care not provided solely on the basis of present or anticipated mental or physical impairment, as determined by a physician acting alone or in consultation with other physicians or otherwise is not receiving the proper or necessary support, education as required by law, or medical or other remedial care recognized under state law as necessary for a child's well-being, or other care necessary for his or her well-being, including adequate food, clothing, and shelter; or who is subjected to an environment that is injurious insofar as the child's environment creates a likelihood of harm to the child's health, physical well-being, or welfare and the likely harm to the child is the result of a blatant disregard of parent or caretaker responsibilities; or who is abandoned by his or her parents or other person responsible for the child's welfare without a proper plan of care.

A child is not neglected for the sole reason that the child's parent or other person responsible for the child's welfare has left the child with an adult relative for any period of time or because the child has been relinquished in accordance with the Abandoned Newborn Infant Protection Act.

325 ILCS 5/3

11:330 Are school personnel responsible for reporting suspected cases of child abuse or neglect?

All school personnel are required to report any suspected child abuse or neglect directly to the Illinois Department of Children and Family Services (DCFS) by telephoning a toll-free number to a DCFS central register. Administrators, teachers, and non-certified personnel are all mandated reporters. School board members who become aware of child abuse (as defined by law) at a board meeting must direct the superintendent to comply with the law regarding the reporting of child abuse.

Within one year of initial employment and at least every five years thereafter, school personnel must complete mandated reporter training by a provider or agency with expertise in recognizing and reporting child abuse.

Any person required by law to report child abuse and neglect who willfully fails to report is guilty of a Class 4 felony.

The statutory requirement that school officials report child abuse does not create a duty to the abused child enforceable under Illinois tort law unless the violation also breaches a common law duty of care. A school district with unique knowledge that one of its teachers or students poses a particular threat to another student may acquire a duty to protect.

325 ILCS 5/3

325 ILCS 5/4.02

325 ILCS 5/7

Doe-2 v. McLean County Unit District No. 5, 593 F. 3d 507 (7th Cir. 2010)

11:332 Under what circumstances do police officials become involved in a DCFS investigation?

When a DCFS report alleges the death of a child; serious injury to a child including, but not limited to, brain damage, skull fractures, subdural hematomas, and internal injuries; torture of a child; malnutrition of a child; or sexual abuse to a child, including, but not limited to, sexual intercourse, sexual exploitation, sexual molestation, and sexually transmitted disease in a child age 12 and under, DCFS is required, within 24 hours, to notify local law enforcement and the office of the state's attorney of the involved county of the receipt of any report alleging any of the above. Such oral reports made by DCFS must be confirmed in writing within 24 hours of the oral report.

325 ILCS 5/7

11:333 Can DCFS compel the suspension of a school employee during an abuse or neglect investigation?

A 2017 change in the relevant statute may encourage DCFS staff to make recommendations, but DCFS does not have the authority to compel school officials to impose a disciplinary response or any particular disciplinary response.

325 ILCS 5/7.4 (c-10)

11:335 May school officials independently determine the credibility of abuse and neglect rumors before making a hotline report?

Although a school official may initially investigate the credibility of any rumors of abuse or neglect, whether there is reasonable cause to report the allegations is an objective determination. For purposes of the reporting act, the issue of whether school personnel have reasonable cause to report suspected allegations of abuse is determined by the objective belief of a reasonable person, not the subjective belief of school personnel.

Doe v. Dimovski, 336 Ill. App. 3d 292, 270 Ill. Dec. 618, 783 N.E. 2d 193 (2nd Dist. 2003) pet. for leave to appeal den. 204 Ill. 2d 658, 792 N.E. 2d 306, 275 Ill. Dec. 75 (2003)

Lipscomb v. Sisters of St. Francis Health Services, Inc., 343 Ill. App. 3d 1036, 799 N.E. 2d 293, 278 Ill. Dec. 575 (1st Dist. 2003) pet. for leave to appeal den. 207 Ill. 2d 605, 807 N.E. 2d 976, 283 Ill. Dec. 135 (2004)

11:340 What information must be included in a report of child abuse or neglect?

All reports from educational employees required by law to report cases of child abuse or neglect must include, when known, the name and address of the child and his or her parents or other persons having his or her custody, the child's age, the nature of the child's condition including any evidence of previous injuries or disabilities, and any other information that the person reporting believes might be helpful in establishing the cause of such abuse or neglect and the identity of the person believed to have caused the abuse or neglect.

325 ILCS 5/7

11:350 What action may be taken against a school employee who files a report of child abuse or neglect that turns out to be false?

School personnel are granted broad immunities against civil and criminal claims when they file a report of suspected child abuse or neglect in good faith, even if the report proves groundless. Such immunities are not available, however, to the individual who knowingly files a false report.

325 ILCS 5/4
325 ILCS 5/9

STUDENT TRANSPORTATION

11:360 For which students must a school board provide free transportation to and from school?

Community consolidated, community unit, consolidated, consolidated high school, optional elementary unit districts, combined high school-unit districts and combined school districts (if the combined district includes a district that was previously required to provide free transportation), and any newly created elementary or high school districts resulting from a high school-unit conversion, a unit-to-dual conversion, or a multi-unit conversion (if the newly created district includes any area that was previously required to provide transportation) are required to provide free transportation for students residing 1.5 miles or more from any school to which they are assigned for attendance, unless adequate public transportation is available.

Charter districts, elementary school districts, community high school districts, township high school districts, and certain unit districts are not required to provide free transportation (although almost all do).

105 ILCS 5/29-3

11:365 When a school district is obligated to provide transportation, must the district transport the student the full distance, door to door, from home to school and back?

No. The school district may establish bus routes that pick up students from and deliver students to specified pick up points not more than 1.5 miles from the students' homes. A school district must be careful to meet its duty to protect the safety of the students in establishing bus stops and bus routes.

105 ILCS 5/29-3

Garrett v. Grant School District No. 124, 139 Ill. App. 3d 569, 487 N.E. 2d 699, 93 Ill. Dec. 874 (2nd Dist. 1985)

Posteher v. Pana Community Unit School District, 96 Ill. App. 3d 709, 421 N.E. 2d 1049, 52 Ill. Dec. 186 (4th Dist. 1981)

Katamay v. Chicago Transit Authority, 53 Ill. 2d 27, 289 N.E. 2d 623 (1972)

Sims v. Chicago Transit Authority, 351 Ill. App. 314, 115 N.E. 2d 96 (1st Dist. 1953), rev. on other grounds 4 Ill. 2d 60, 122 N.E. 2d 221 (1954)

11:370 For purposes of requiring a school board to bus students to and from school, how is the 1.5-mile minimum distance measured?

The 1.5-mile minimum distance is measured from the exit of the property where the student resides to the point where pupils are normally unloaded at the school attended. The distance is measured by determining the shortest distance on normally traveled roads or streets.

105 ILCS 5/29-3

11:380 When must a school board provide free transportation for students living less than 1.5 miles from school?

A school board must provide free transportation for students living less than 1.5 miles from school when conditions are such that walking, either to or from the school to which a pupil is assigned for attendance or to or from a pick-up point or bus stop, constitutes a serious hazard to the safety of the pupil due to vehicular traffic. Transportation need not be provided if adequate public transportation is available.

There is a procedure whereby a parent may petition the school board to conduct a study and make findings regarding alleged safety hazards. The initial determination of what constitutes a serious hazard is made by the school board with review by the Illinois Department of Transportation (IDOT) in consultation with the State Superintendent of Education. IDOT's decision may be appealed to circuit court under the provisions of the Administrative Review Act.

105 ILCS 5/29-3
735 ILCS 5/3-101 et seq.

11:390 Is a school district required to provide transportation to and from summer school classes?

A school district is not required to provide summer school transportation except for special education students. If the school district chooses to provide transportation, it may charge participating students a transportation fee not to exceed cost.

105 ILCS 5/29-3.2a

11:394 Must a school district provide transportation to and from extracurricular activities?

The school district may elect to provide transportation, but is not required to do so. The school district may charge for the transportation in an amount not to exceed its cost (which can include a reasonable allowance for depreciation of the vehicles used). If the school board elects not to provide transportation it should carefully consider the practical aspects and risks associated with having students drive themselves and other students to and from such events and should weigh those risks against the value of the program offered and the cost of providing transportation.

105 ILCS 5/29-3.1

ACADEMIC CLUBS AND EXTRACURRICULAR ACTIVITIES

11:400 Do students have a right to fairness in the selection process for student clubs?

A student does not have a property interest in membership in a particular student club or activity. Therefore, a suit based solely on the fairness of the selection process for membership in the club or activity without the allegation of some other constitutional deprivation will fail.

Dangler v. Yorktown Central Schools, 771 F. Supp. 625 (S.D. N.Y. 1991)

Price v. Young, 580 F. Supp. 1 (E.D. Ark. 1983)

Karnstein v. Pewaukee School Board, 557 F. Supp. 565 (E.D. Wisc. 1983)

Dallam v. Cumberland Valley School District, 391 F. Supp. 358 (M.D. Pa. 1975)

11:403 May a school prevent a student from participating in extracurricular activities because of pregnancy or because the student has had a child out of wedlock?

Cases wherein the school officials have health or safety concerns about the student's participation should be distinguished from cases wherein the desire to exclude is based on moral or character considerations. When a student's health or safety might be endangered by participation, school officials may prevent the student's participation on the same grounds for which they would exclude any other student with any other medical condition. Generally, school officials should seek advice from a physician before making the exclusion decision.

Students may not be denied admission or otherwise excluded from activities (e.g., National Honor Society) because of character or moral concerns relating to pregnancy or giving birth out of wedlock, because to do so would likely violate both Title IX and the Pregnancy Discrimination Act. Character or moral considerations generally have as their basis the school's disapproval of premarital sex, but such policies target pregnant students and female students who have given birth out of wedlock, without affecting male students or female students who have had premarital sex without having become pregnant.

Christian Legal Society v. Martinez, et al., 130 S.Ct. 2971, 561 U.S. 661, 177 L. Ed. 2d 838 (2010)

Chipman v. Grant County School District, 30 F. Supp. 2d 975 (E.D. Ky. 1998)

11:404 May a school district prevent the formation of clubs promoting gay rights?

If a high school's practice or policy has created a limited open forum, preventing the formation of a club because of its views constitutes viewpoint discrimination and is impermissible. When a high school allows some non-curricular student groups, it cannot deny others on the basis of religion, political, philosophical, or other content of speech at the student meetings. A school board may not foreclose access to a limited open forum merely by labeling a group "curriculum related."

It is likely that a school board could require approved student groups to comply with the school's non-discrimination policies, thereby preventing clubs from excluding students who disagree with the club's philosophy or mission.

Badger Catholic v. Walsh, et al., 620 F. 3d 775 (7th Cir. 2010)

Christian Legal Society v. Martinez, et al., 130 S.Ct. 2971, 561 U.S. 661, 177 L. Ed. 2d 838 (2010)

Boyd County High School Gay-Straight Alliance v. Board of Education of Boyd County, 258 F. Supp. 2d 667 (E.D. Ky. 2003)

Colin v. Orange Unified School District, 83 F. Supp. 2d 1135 (C.D. Cal. 2000)

East High School Prism Club v. Seidel, 95 F. Supp. 2d 1239 (D. Utah 2000)

East High Gay/Straight Alliance v. Board of Education of Salt Lake City School District, 81 F. Supp. 2d 1166 (D. Utah 1999)

11:405 What grade-point average must a student maintain to be eligible for extracurricular activities?

Beginning with the 1998-1999 school year, school districts that maintain a high school must have a "no-pass, no-play" policy. The relevant statute does not mandate a specific minimum average, but it does require the school board to "establish, implement and enforce a uniform and consistent policy" under which a student in grades 9-12 who fails to maintain a specified minimum grade point average or a specified minimum grade in each course in which the student is enrolled, or both, is suspended from further participation in any school-sponsored or school-supported athletic or extracurricular activities for a specified period or until a specified minimum grade point average or minimum grade or both are earned by the student.

105 ILCS 5/10-20.30

11:407 May school officials ban same-sex couples from prom?

While this matter has not been tested in Illinois, nor is there a decision to provide guidance from a relevant federal court, it is unlikely that a rule preventing same-sex couples from attending prom would withstand judicial scrutiny.

775 ILCS 5/1-102

McMillen v. Itawamba County School District, 702 F. Supp. 2d. 699 (N.D. Miss. 2010)

Fricke v. Lynch, 491 F. Supp. 381 (D.R.I. 1980)

SEXUAL HARASSMENT OF STUDENTS

11:410 What is Title IX?

Title IX is a federal statute that prohibits discrimination on the basis of sex. Title IX provides in part:

"No person in the United States shall, on the basis of sex, be excluded from participation in, be denied the benefits of, or be subjected to discrimination under any education program or activity receiving Federal financial assistance."

20 U.S.C. 1681

11:413 May a student bring a suit under Title IX for sexual harassment by a teacher?

Sexual harassment of a student by a teacher is prohibited by Title IX and provisions of the Illinois Human Rights Act. There are two kinds of sexual harassment: sexual harassment that occurs when the teacher conditions the grant of a benefit on the receipt of a sexual favor (or punishes the student for rejecting the favor) and hostile environment harassment that occurs when there is a sexually intimidating, hostile, or offensive environment. An individual's personal liability is broad. An educational employer's liability is relatively narrow.

34 C.F.R. 106.31 et seq.

Hansen v. Board of Trustees of Hamilton Southeastern School Corporation, 551 F. 3d 599 (7th Cir. 2008)

Doe By and Through Doe v. Petaluma City School District, 54 F. 3d 1447 (9th Cir. 1996) reversing 830 F. Supp. 1560 (N.D. Cal. 1993)

Franklin v. Gwinnett County Public Schools, 112 S. Ct. 1028, 503 U.S. 60, 117 L. Ed. 2d 208 (1992)

11:416 Does a policy or rule prohibiting harassment of students abridge the harasser's free speech rights?

A school may categorically prohibit lewd, vulgar, or profane language; and a school may regulate school-sponsored speech (that is, speech that a reasonable observer would view as the school's own speech) on the basis of any legitimate pedagogical concern. Speech falling outside of these categories may be regulated only if it would substantially disrupt school operations or interfere with the right of others to equal access to educational programs.

Unpopular speech, when it does not pose a realistic threat of substantial disruption or when it does not interfere with a victim's ability to equally access the educational program, is protected. The mere fact that someone might take offense at the content of speech is not sufficient justification for prohibiting it. A school may not prohibit speech based on the "mere desire to avoid the discomfort and unpleasantness that always accompany an unpopular viewpoint."

Saxe, et al. v. State College Area School District, 240 F. 3d 200 (3rd Cir. 2001)

11:418 Under what circumstances may school district officials be held liable for the sexual abuse of a student by a school employee?

School officials may be held liable if they:

1) Had notice of unconstitutional conduct;

2) Demonstrated deliberate indifference or tacitly authorized known acts of discrimination or harassment;

3) Failed to take remedial steps; and

4) The failure resulted in damage to the child.

The supervisors of harassers can be liable themselves if they know about the conduct and facilitate it, approve it, condone it, or turn a blind eye for fear of what they might see.

T.E., et. al v. Grindle, 599 F. 3d 583 (7th Cir. 2010)

Hansen v. Board of Trustees of Hamilton Southeastern School Corporation, 551 F. 3d 599 (7th Cir. 2008)

Bell v. Board of Education of County of Fayette, 290 F. Supp. 2d 701 (S.D. W.Va. 2003), motion for new trial 2006 WL 516773 (S.D. W.Va., March 1, 2006)

Gebser et al. v. Lago Vista Independent School District, 118 S. Ct. 1989, 524 U.S. 274, 141 L. Ed. 2d 277 (1998)

Canutillo Independent School District v. Leija, 101 F. 3d 393 (5th Cir. 1997) reh. and sugg. for reh. den. 106 F. 3d 399, cert. den. 117 S. Ct. 2434, 520 U.S. 1265, 138 L. Ed. 2d 195

Smith v. Metropolitan School District, Perry Township, 128 F. 3d 1014 (7th Cir. 1997)

Rosa H. v. San Elizario Independent School District, 106 F. 3d 648 (5th Cir. 1997)

Jojola v. Chavez, 55 F. 3d 488 (10th Cir. 1995)

Doe v. Taylor Independent School District, 15 F. 3d 443 (5th Cir. 1994)

11:420 Must a student harassment plaintiff prove that sexual advances from a school employee were unwelcome?

In a Title IX suit for damages, the age of the student will determine whether or not such a proof is necessary. A student under age 17 cannot consent to sexual advances. In other possible related causes of action (a teacher dismissal case, for example) age and consent may be irrelevant.

720 ILCS 5/11-1.50

720 ILCS 5/11-1.60

Mary M. v. North Lawrence Community School Corp., 951 F. Supp. 820 (S.D. Ind. 1997) rev. 31 F. 3d 1220 (7th Cir. 1997) reh. den., cert. den. 118 S. Ct. 2369, 524 U.S. 952, 141 L. Ed. 2d 737 (1998)

11:423 May a student who has been sexually harassed by a school employee sue for money damages?

Money damages are available under Title IX of the Education Amendments of 1972, under Section 1983, or by filing a state tort claim. Under Title IX, a plaintiff may not recover using principles of agency (the school is responsible for its employee's actions whether it knows about them or not) or constructive notice (the school was responsible because it should have known what its employee was doing), nor can a plaintiff recover alleging the school had a duty to protect the student from harm.

Damages are available if the school district acts with deliberate indifference, but school officials must first have actual knowledge of the harassment and must have substantial control over both the harasser and the context in which the known harassment occurs.

Doe ex rel. Doe v. Lawrence Hall Youth Services, 2012 IL App (1st) 103758, 966 N.E. 2d 52, 358 Ill. Dec. 867

Doe v. White, 409 Ill.App.3d 1087, 951 N.E.2d 216, 351 Ill.Dec. 396 (4th Dist. 2011), 2012 Il 112479, 973 N.E. 2d 880, 362 Ill. Dec. 484, on rem. 2014 IL App. (4th) 131004

Doe-2 v. McLean County Unit District No. 5, 593 F. 3d 507 (7th Cir. 2010)

Fitzgerald v. Barnstable School Committee, 129 S. Ct. 788, 555 U.S. 246, 172 L. Ed. 2d 582 (2009)

Gebser et al. v. Lago Vista Independent School District, 118 S. Ct. 1989, 524 U.S. 274, 141 L. Ed. 2d 277 (1998)

Gates v. Unified School District No. 449 of Leavenworth County, 996 F. 2d 36 (10th Cir. 1993)

Franklin v. Gwinnett County Public Schools, 112 S. Ct. 1028, 503 U.S. 60, 117 L. Ed. 2d 208 (1992)

Doe v. Taylor Independent School District, 975 F. 2d 137 (5th Cir. 1992)

11:425 Must a school district take action to prevent student-to-student sexual harassment?

A school must take action to stop student-to-student sexual harassment that occurs when students are involved in school activities or otherwise under the supervision of school authorities and when such harassment is known to school officials. To prevail in a student-to-student case, the plaintiff must show:

1) The victim was subjected to unwelcome harassment based on gender;

2) The harassment was sufficiently severe or pervasive and objectively offensive that it can be said to deprive the victim of access to educational opportunities or benefits provided by the school (hostile environment); and

3) The school knew of the harassment and failed to take appropriate remedial action.

School officials have Title IX liability only when they are "deliberately indifferent" to acts of student-on-student sexual harassment and only when their response is "clearly unreasonable in light of the known circumstances."

P.H. v. School District of Kansas City, Missouri, 265 F. 3d 653 (8th Cir. 2001)

Vance v. Spencer County Public School District, 231 F. 3d 253 (6th Cir. 2000)

Adusumilli v. Illinois Institute of Technology, 191 F. 3d 455 (7th Cir. 1999)

Davis v. Monroe County Board of Education, 119 S. Ct. 1661, 526 U.S. 629, 143 L. Ed. 2d 839 (1999)

Doe v. University of Illinois, 138 F. 3d 653 (7th Cir. 1998)

Seamons v. Snow, 84 F. 3d 1226 (10th Cir. 1996)

Doe By and Through Doe v. Petaluma City School District, 54 F. 3d 1447 (9th Cir. 1996) reversing 830 F. Supp. 1560 (N.D. Cal. 1993)

D.R. v. Middle Bucks Area Vocational Technical School, 972 F. 2d 1364 (3rd Cir. 1992) cert. den. 113 S. Ct. 1045, 506 U.S. 1079, 122 L. Ed. 2d 354 (1993)

Franklin v. Gwinnett County Public Schools, 112 S. Ct. 1028, 503 U.S. 60, 117 L. Ed. 2d 208 (1992)

11:427 Which factors will the courts consider in determining whether there is a student-to-student hostile environment?

To determine whether an environment is hostile because of student-to-student sexual harassment, the court considers:

1) The frequency of the conduct;

2) The severity of the conduct;

3) Whether the conduct is physically threatening or humiliating rather than merely offensive; and

4) Whether the conduct unreasonably interfered with the victim's performance.

Gabrielle M. v. Park Forest-Chicago Heights School District No. 163, 315 F. 3d 817 (7th Cir. 2003)

Davis v. Monroe County Board of Education, 119 S. Ct. 1661, 526 U.S. 629, 143 L. Ed. 2d 839 (1999)

11:430 Does a school district have a duty to protect a student from harassment based on the victim's homosexuality?

Discrimination on the basis of sexual orientation is protected in the Illinois Human Rights Act and the courts are issuing decisions that suggest the trend is to provide protection under federal law for homosexuals, often through Title IX claims. A school district's duties and potential liabilities are no greater than those applicable in the instance of gender-based sexual harassment allegations that require actual notice to school officials and deliberate indifference or tacit endorsement of the harassment.

775 ILCS 5/1-102

Lawrence v. Texas, 123 S. Ct. 2472, 539 U.S. 538, 156 L. Ed. 2d 508 (2003)

Ray v. Antioch Unified School District, 107 F. Supp. 2d 1165 (N.D. Cal. 2000)

Doe v. Dallas Independent School District, 153 F. 3d 211 (5th Cir. 1998)

Nabozny v. Podlesny, et al., 92 F. 3d 446 (7th Cir. 1996)

Kinman v. Omaha Public School District, 94 F. 3d 463 (8th Cir. 1996)

11:432 What accommodations must be made for transgendered students?

This an emerging and controversial area of the law. On February 22, 2017, the U.S. Department of Education Office of Civil Rights (OCR) issued a "Dear Colleague" letter withdrawing 2016 guidance on transgender students. OCR had taken the position that Title IX requires that when requested, transgendered students must have access to the restrooms and locker rooms of the gender with which they identify. OCR also allowed gender-neutral, individual user facilities for any student who does not want to share sex-segregated facilities. While OCR's position on these issues has changed, school officials should be cautious because the Illinois Human Rights Act may provide protections for transgendered students in Illinois that are not available elsewhere. The Seventh Circuit Court of Appeals has issued an opinion on the subject. Transgender accommodations have been controversial and sometimes unpopular with other students and community members but the Seventh Circuit has considered and rejected related arguments in at least one fact situation, holding: "A transgender student's presence in the restroom provides no more of a risk to other student's privacy rights than the presence of an overly curious student of the same biological sex who decides to sneak glances at his or her classmates."

775 ILCS 5/1-102 (A)

34 C.F.R. 106.31(b)

Whitaker by Whitaker v. Kenosha Unified School District No. 1 Board of Education, 858 F. 3d 1034 (7th Cir. 2017)

G.G. ex rel. Grimm v. Gloucester County School Board, 822 F. 3d 709 (4th Cir. 2016)

11:435 Does a school district have a constitutional duty to protect a student from harm?

Unless particular facts exist that establish that the school district has a custodial relationship with respect to the student, a school district has no affirmative duty to protect the student from harm. The state has a duty to protect when the student is in the involuntary custody of the state, or when the state creates a dangerous situation or renders the student more vulnerable to danger. The student's mandatory attendance at school is not sufficient to create such a custodial relationship. To create constitutional duty, affirmative action by a state actor to harm a student or to subject the student to danger is necessary.

Doe v. White, 409 Ill.App.3d 1087, 951 N.E.2d 216, 351 Ill.Dec. 396 (4th Dist. 2011), 2012 Il 112479, 973 N.E. 2d 880, 362 Ill. Dec. 484, on rem. 2014 IL App. (4th) 131004

Martin v. Shawano-Gresham School District, 295 F. 3d 701 (7th Cir. 2002) cert. den. 123 S. Ct. 601, 537 U.S. 1047, 154 L. Ed. 2d 520 (2002)

Stevens v. Umsted, 131 F. 3d 697 (7th Cir. 1997)

Becerra v. Asher, 105 F. 3d 1042 (5th Cir. 1997) supp. on den. of reh., reh. and sugg. for reh. den. 111 F. 3d 894 (1997)

Seamons v. Snow, 84 F. 3d 1226 (10th Cir. 1996)

Wilson v. Webb, 869 F. Supp. 496 (W.D. Ky. 1994)

Doe v. Board of Education of Hononegah School District No. 207, 833 F. Supp. 1366 (N.D. Ill. 1993)

DeShaney v. Winnebago County Department of Social Services, 109 S. Ct. 998, 489 U.S. 189, 103 L. Ed. 2d 249 (1989)

11:440 Must a school district defend an employee charged by a student or staff member with sexual misconduct?

A school board's duty to indemnify and defend employees against civil rights damages and claims is triggered when scope of employment allegations are made in the lawsuit.

However, if other facts alleged in the complaint make it impossible to conclude that the employee's improper actions were within the scope of employment, the employer will be relieved of its duty to indemnify and defend. If the lawsuit alleges sexual misconduct and that misconduct as alleged serves no conceivable public purpose and advances completely personal objectives, the employer has no duty to indemnify and defend.

105 ILCS 5/10-20.20

Deloney v. Board of Education of Thornton Township School District No. 205, Cook County, Illinois, 281 Ill. App. 3d 775, 666 N.E. 2d 792, 217 Ill. Dec. 123 (1st Dist. 1996)

11:442 When are an employee's actions deemed to be within his or her "scope of employment"?

When an employee commits an act of misconduct within the scope of his or her employment, his or her employer under certain circumstances may be held liable for the act.

The courts find that an act is within the scope of employment if the act is of the kind the employee is employed to perform; occurs substantially within authorized time and space limits; and is actuated, at least in part, by a purpose to serve the employer.

The courts distinguish a "detour" where the employee's deviation for personal reasons is still sufficiently related to employment so the employer can be held liable from "frolic" where the employee's personal business is unrelated to employment.

Doe ex rel. Doe v. Lawrence Hall Youth Services, 2012 IL App (1st) 103758, 966 N.E. 2d 52, 358 Ill. Dec. 867

Deloney v. Board of Education of Thornton Township School District No. 205, Cook County, Illinois, 281 Ill. App. 3d 775, 666 N.E. 2d 792, 217 Ill. Dec. 123 (1st Dist. 1996)

11:445 How long after the occurrence of an alleged incident of abuse may a student wait to bring a claim against a school or a school official before the claim is barred?

A 2013 change in the limitations period allows claims not time-barred on January 25, 2013 to be brought at any time.

Before this change in the law, statutes of limitations prevented the award of damages for certain stale claims, but the limitations period in abuse cases was long. In cases in which the plaintiff was an adult at the time of the injury, the limitations period usually began running at the moment of the injury. In the instance of claims involving underage plaintiffs, the limitations period did not begin to run until the minor reached majority — 18 years of age in Illinois.

Generally, in repressed memory cases, the limitation period began when the victim knew or reasonably should have known of the injury. In 2010, the General Assembly significantly lengthened the limitations period which had been 10 years (five years in repressed memory cases). The limitations period for sexual abuse cases in Illinois is now 20 years.

735 ILCS 5/13-202.2

Doe v. Hinsdale Township High School District 86, et al., 388 Ill. App. 3d 995, 905 N.E. 2d 343, 328 Ill. Dec. 809 (2nd Dist. 2009)

M.H.D. v. Westminster School, 172 F. 3d 797 (11th Cir. 1999)

W.J.L. v. Bugge, 573 N.W. 2d 677 (Minn. Sup. Ct. 1998)

Ernstes v. Warner, 860 F. Supp. 1338 (S.D. Ind. 1994)

11:450 Does the exposure of a student to sexually explicit curriculum material constitute sexual harassment?

Probably not. While opt-out opportunities should be offered to parents and students who may be offended by sexually explicit material, absent a showing of actions by school officials that would shock the conscience, no cause of action for exposure to such material would survive.

Brown v. Hot, Sexy and Safer Productions, Inc. 68 F. 3d 525 (1st Cir. 1995) cert. den., 116 S. Ct. 1044, 516 U.S. 1159, 134 L. Ed. 2d 191 (1996)

11:455 May a school district retaliate against a person who reports gender discrimination but does not suffer discrimination?

Title IX implies a cause of action for retaliation by individuals who are not victims of gender discrimination but are victims of retaliation because they complained about gender discrimination suffered by others.

Jackson v. Birmingham Board. of Education, 125 S. Ct. 1497, 544 U.S. 167, 161 L. Ed. 2d 361 (2005)

HOME SCHOOLING

11:460 May a school district or the State Board of Education adopt rules regulating home schools?

Courts in other states have upheld state regulation of home schooling, including certification requirements for home-school teachers and minimum curriculum requirements, finding that the state has a compelling interest in the education of children. In Illinois, however, the General Assembly has opted to not interfere with home schooling and has not enacted legislation.

Local school districts have the authority to regulate their own programs, which has the indirect effect of regulating certain aspects of home schooling to the extent home-schooled students avail themselves of various aspects of the public school program.

State v. Schmidt, 505 N.E. 2d 627 (Ohio 1987)
State v. Patzer, 382 N.W. 2d 631 (North Dakota 1986)
State v. Rivinius, 328 N.W. 2d 220 (North Dakota 1982)
People v. Levisen, 404 Ill. 574, 90 N.E. 2d 213, (1950)

11:465 Must a school district accept a home-schooled student for enrollment in some, but not all, public school classes?

This is an unsettled area of the law. There is a School Code provision that governs part-time attendance and that permits a school board to limit enrollment to situations where space permits and to applications submitted before May 1 of any year. If a school district has a policy that limits the enrollment of part-time students, the policy must be uniformly applied and must serve a legitimate state interest. The policy must limit enrollment prohibitions to situations wherein the school district lacks space or other resources to properly educate the child.

Until the courts resolve this issue, the safer approach is to admit home-schooled students on a part-time basis except when it can be shown the school district would suffer real hardship and has a policy prohibiting such enrollment.

105 ILCS 5/10-20.24
Swanson v. Guthrie Independent School District No. I-1, 942 F. Supp. 511 (W.D. Okla. 1996)

11:470 May a school district limit a home schooler's access to participation in extracurricular activities?

It is not clear whether the School Code provision governing part-time attendance has application to extra-curricular activities. A school district can probably establish a policy that requires students to be in attendance before they are eligible to participate in extracurricular activities.

105 ILCS 5/10-20.24
IHSA By-law 3.020 et seq.
Swanson v. Guthrie Independent School District No. I-1, 942 F. Supp. 511 (W.D. Okla. 1996)
Kaptien v. Conrad School District, 931 P. 2d 1311 (Mont. 1997)
Bradstreet v. Sobol, 650 N.Y.S. 2d 402 (1996)

11:475 May a school district discriminate against a parent or a student because the student is home schooled?

Many home schoolers have elected home schooling because of their underlying religious beliefs. School attempts to retaliate against home schoolers for the election of a non-public education implicate First Amendment issues.

Peterson v. Minidoka County School District No. 331, 118 F. 3d 1351 (9th Cir. 1997)

OTHER STUDENT ISSUES

11:500 May a school district regulate a student's self-administration of asthma medication?

A school must permit the self-administration of medication by a pupil with asthma, provided that:

1) The parents or guardians of the pupil provide to the school written authorization from the parents or guardians for the self-administration of medication or use of an epinephrine auto-injector, written

authorization from the pupil's physician, physician assistant, or advanced practice registered nurse.

2) The parents or guardians of the pupil provide to the school the prescription label which must contain the name of the medication, the prescribed dosage, and the time at which or circumstances under which medication is to be administered; or for the use of an epinephrine auto-injector a written statement from the pupil's physician, physician assistant, or advanced practice registered nurse containing the name and purpose of the use of an epinephrine auto-injector, the prescribed dosage, and the time or times at which or the special circumstances under which the medication or use of an epinephrine auto-injector is to be administered. The information provided shall be kept on file in the office of the school nurse or, in the absence of a school nurse, the school's administrator.

A school district or nonpublic school may authorize the provision of an epinephrine auto-injector to a student or any personnel authorized under a student's Individual Health Care Action Plan, Illinois Food Allergy Emergency Action Plan and Treatment Authorization Form, or plan pursuant to Section 504 of the federal Rehabilitation Act of 1973 to administer an epinephrine auto-injector to the student, that meets the prescription on file.

The school district may authorize a school nurse to do the following:

1) Provide an epinephrine auto-injector to a student or any personnel authorized under a student's Individual Health Care Action Plan, Illinois Food Allergy Emergency Action Plan and Treatment Authorization Form, or 504 plan to administer an epinephrine auto-injector to the student, that meets the prescription on file;

2) Administer an epinephrine auto-injector that meets the prescription on file to any student who has an Individual Health Care Action Plan, Illinois Food Allergy Emergency Action Plan and Treatment Authorization Form, or 504 plan that authorizes the use of an epinephrine auto-injector; and

3) Administer an epinephrine auto-injector to any student that the school nurse in good faith professionally believes is having an anaphylactic reaction.

The school district must inform the parents or guardians of the pupil, in writing, that the school district and its employees and agents including a physician providing standing protocol or prescription for school epinephrine auto-injectors are to incur no liability, except for willful and wanton conduct, as a result of any injury arising from the self-administration of medication or use of an epinephrine auto-injector regardless of whether authorization was given by the pupil's parents or guardians or by the pupil's physician, physician assistant, or advanced practice registered nurse. The parents or guardians of the pupil must sign a statement acknowledging that the school district and its employees and agents incur no liability, except for willful and wanton conduct, as a result of any injury arising from the self-administration of medication or use of an epinephrine auto-injector regardless of whether authorization was given by the pupil's parents or guardians or by the pupil's physician, physician assistant, or advanced practice registered nurse.

When a school nurse or trained personnel administers an epinephrine auto-injector to a student whom the school nurse or trained personnel in good faith professionally believes is having an anaphylactic reaction, notwithstanding the lack of notice to the parents or guardians of the pupil or the absence of the parents or guardians signed statement acknowledging no liability, except for willful and wanton conduct, the school district or nonpublic school and its employees and agents, including a physician, physician assistant, or advanced practice nurse providing standing protocol or prescription for school epinephrine auto-injectors, are to incur no liability, except for willful and wanton conduct, as a result of any injury arising from the use of an epinephrine auto-injector regardless of whether authorization was given by the pupil's parents or guardians or by the pupil's physician, physician's assistant, or advanced practice registered nurse.

The permission for self-administration of medication or use of an epinephrine auto-injector is effective for the school year for which it is granted and must be renewed each subsequent school year.

Provided that the requirements in the law are fulfilled, a pupil with asthma may possess and use his or her medication, or a pupil may possess and use an epinephrine auto-injector, while in school, while at a school-sponsored activity, while under the supervision of school personnel, or before or after normal school activities, such as while in before-school or after-school care on school-operated property or while being transported on a school bus.

The school district may maintain at a school in a secure location that is accessible before, during, and after school a supply of epinephrine auto-injectors. A physician, certain trained physician's assistants, and/or certain trained advanced practice nurses may prescribe epinephrine auto-injectors in the name of the school district school to be maintained for use when necessary. The school district supply of epinephrine auto-injectors may be provided to and utilized by any student authorized to self-administer that meets the prescription on file or by any personnel authorized under a student's Individual Health Care Action Plan, Illinois Food Allergy Emergency Action Plan and Treatment Authorization Form, or 504 plan to administer an epinephrine auto-injector to the student, that meets the prescription on file. When a student does not have an epinephrine auto-injector or a prescription for an epinephrine auto-injector on file, the school nurse may utilize the school district school supply of epinephrine auto-injectors to respond to anaphylactic reaction, under a standing protocol from a physician licensed to practice medicine in all its branches and the requirements in the law.

In 2016, the relevant statute was amended to require that school districts annually request an asthma action plan from the parents or guardians of students with asthma. The change also requires a biennial training requirement for school personnel.

105 ILCS 5/22-30

In re Estate of Jeffrey Stewart, 2016 IL App (2d) 151117, 60 N.E. 3d 896, 406 Ill. Dec. 345

11:502 What must a student be permitted to do to manage his or her diabetes?

Provided that the student is authorized according to his or her diabetes care plan, a student must be permitted to check blood glucose when and wherever needed; administer insulin with the insulin delivery system used by the student; treat hypoglycemia and hyperglycemia and otherwise attend to the care and management of his or her diabetes in the classroom, in any area of the school or school grounds, and at any school-related activity or event in accordance with the diabetes care plan; and possess on his or her person, at all times, the supplies and equipment necessary to monitor and treat diabetes, including, but not limited to, glucometers, lancets, test strips, insulin, syringes, insulin pens and needle tips, insulin pumps, infusion sets, alcohol swabs, a glucagon injection kit, glucose tablets, and food and drink, in accordance with the diabetes care plan.

105 ILCS 145/30

11:503 May a student be restricted in his or her participation in school activities because of diabetes?

A school district may not restrict the assignment of a student with diabetes to a particular school on the basis that the school does not have a full-time school nurse, nor may a school deny a student access to any school or school-related activities on the basis that a student has diabetes.

105 ILCS 145/35

11:504 What duties may be performed by a diabetes care aide?

Delegated care aides perform the duties necessary to assist a student with diabetes in accordance with his or her diabetes care plan. Such an aide must be trained to perform his or her duties. (The relevant law defines the training.)

In accordance with the student's diabetes care plan or when an unexpected snack or meal requires a dose of insulin not anticipated by a student's diabetes care plan, the delegated care aide must consult with the parent or guardian, school nurse where available, or health care provider to confirm that the insulin dosage is appropriate given the number of carbohydrates to be taken and the student's blood glucose level as determined by a glucometer reading.

The principal must facilitate compliance with the provisions of a diabetes care plan. Delegated care aides are authorized to provide assistance by a student's parents or guardian and the school district.

A school or a school employee is not liable for civil or other damages as a result of conduct, other than willful or wanton misconduct, related to the care of a student with diabetes. A school employee shall not be subject to any disciplinary proceeding resulting from an action taken in compliance with this Act, unless the action constitutes willful or wanton misconduct.

105 ILCS 145/20
105 ILCS 145/25
105 ILCS 145/45

11:520 May school personnel insist that a student be medicated to maximize the student's educational opportunities?

Each school board is required to adopt and implement a policy prohibiting any disciplinary action against a student based totally or in part on the refusal of a student's parent or guardian to administer or consent to the administration of psychotropic or psycho-stimulant medication to a student.

The policy must require that, at least once every two years, the in-service training of certified school personnel and administrators include training on current best practices regarding the identification and treatment of attention deficit disorder and attention deficit hyperactivity disorder, the application of non-aversive behavioral interventions in the school environment, and the use of psychotropic or psycho-stimulant medication for school-age children. School medical staff, an Individualized Education Program team, or a professional worker as defined in Section 14-1.10 of the School Code may recommend that a student be evaluated by an appropriate medical practitioner and school personnel may consult with the practitioner with the consent of the student's parents or guardian.

105 ILCS 5/10-20.36

11:540 What rules govern the care of students with food allergies?

Beginning in 2010 the State Board of Education (ISBE) and the Department of Public Health (DPH), and an ad hoc committee established by ISBE and DPH developed guidelines for the management of students with life-threatening food allergies. The committee includes experts in the field of food allergens, representatives on behalf of students with food allergies, representatives from the several public school management organizations, including school administrators, principals, and school board members, and representatives from the Illinois Education Association and the Illinois Federation of Teachers. The guidelines include, but are not limited to

1) Education and training for school personnel who interact with students with life-threatening food allergies, such as school and school district administrators, teachers, school advisors and counselors, school health personnel, and school nurses, on the management of students with life-threatening food allergies, including training related to the administration of medication with an auto-injector;

2) Procedures for responding to life-threatening allergic reactions to food;

3) A process for the implementation of individualized health care and food allergy action plans for every student with a life-threatening food allergy; and

4) Protocols to prevent exposure to food allergens.

Each school board must have a policy based on the guidelines developed by the committee for the management of students with life-threatening food allergies enrolled in its schools.

105 ILCS 5/2-3.149

11:600 May a school district distribute condoms to students?

It is likely that a school distribution program would survive parental objections and court challenges. Parents have a liberty interest to be free from unnecessary governmental intrusion in the rearing of their children, but mere exposure to a program offered at school does not amount to unconstitutional interference without some compulsory aspect to the program. Plaintiffs have also failed to convince the courts that a voluntary distribution program violates parental or student rights to free exercise of religion.

Curtis v. School Committee of Falmouth, 652 N.E. 2d 580 (Ma. 1995)

Carey v. Population Services International, 97 S. Ct. 2010, 431 U.S. 678, 52 L. Ed. 2d 675 (1977)

11:630 Must school officials notify the student's parents when they learn the student is contemplating an abortion?

Illinois has a law requiring notification of an adult family member by the physician or his or her agent at least 48 hours before an abortion is performed on an unemancipated minor. The law does not require that school officials provide the notice. Historically, the law has not been enforced with respect to the physicians to whom it applies because the courts have enjoined its enforcement. (As a practical matter, no parental notice has been provided in Illinois.)

School officials may voluntarily disclose such information to parents. In fact, however, there is substantial risk no matter whether school officials decide to disclose or to withhold information. School officials should, therefore, proceed with extreme caution in advising a child and in considering whether to notify the child's parents. In a situation where the child's safety is not a concern, the child should be encouraged to notify her parents or to seek counsel from a trusted family member, adult friend of the family, member of the clergy, or other outside counselor.

750 ILCS 70/1 et seq.

Zbaraz v. Madigan, 572 F. 3d 370 (7th Cir. 2009); 2008 WL 589028, N.D. Ill., February 28, 2008 (No. 84 C 771)

11:650 May a school district collect student fingerprints or use voice, eye, or facial scans of students?

Biometric information is any information that is collected through an identification process for individuals based on their unique behavioral or physiological characteristics, including fingerprint, hand geometry, voice, or facial recognition or iris or retinal scans.

School districts that collect biometric information from students must adopt policies that require written permission from the individual who has legal custody of the student, as defined in Section 10-20.12b of the School Code, or from the student if he or she has reached the age of 18. The school district must discontinue of use of a student's biometric information when the student graduates or withdraws from the school district, or when the school district receives a written request for discontinuation by the individual having legal custody of the student, or by the student if he or she has reached the age of 18. The school district must destroy all of a student's biometric information within 30 days after the biometric information is discontinued.

Biometric information may be used solely for identification or fraud prevention and may not be sold, leased, or disclosed of to another person or entity, unless the individual who has legal custody of the student or the student, if he or she has reached the age of 18, consents to the disclosure or the disclosure is required by court order.

The school district must protect biometric information by safely storing it and preventing its transmission and/or disclosure.

A failure to provide written consent by the individual who has legal custody of the student or by the student, if he or she has reached the age of 18, must not be the basis for refusal of any services otherwise available to the student.

105 ILCS 5/10-20.40

12: STUDENT DISCIPLINE

DISCIPLINARY AUTHORITY

12:10 Who is responsible for maintaining student discipline in the public schools?

Teachers, other certificated employees, and any other person whether or not a certificated employee who provides a related service for or with respect to a student have a statutory duty to maintain discipline in school, on school grounds, at extracurricular events, and with respect to all school programs. Each school board must establish a policy on student discipline.

105 ILCS 5/24-24

Prest by Prest v. Sparta Community Unit School District No. 140, 157 Ill. App. 3d 569, 510 N.E. 2d 595, 109 Ill. Dec. 727 (5th Dist. 1987)

12:20 What is "in loco parentis"?

"In loco parentis" means in place of parent. The phrase is used in education to describe the relationship of certificated school officials to students. While certain school officials have in loco parentis authority by statute, the power of school officials to exercise control over students is not as broad as that of a parent.

The doctrine of in loco parentis protects certain school district employees from liability for employment related acts of ordinary negligence. Such employees may create liability for the school district resulting from certain employment related acts that constitute willful and wanton misconduct.

105 ILCS 5/24-24

Ausmus by Ausmus v. Board of Education of City of Chicago, 155 Ill. App. 3d 705, 508 N.E. 2d 298, 108 Ill. Dec. 137 (1st Dist. 1987)

Montag v. Board of Education, School District No. 40, Rock Island County, 112 Ill. App. 3d 1039, 446 N.E. 2d 299, 68 Ill. Dec. 565 (3rd Dist. 1983)

People v. Davis, 88 Ill. App. 3d 728, 410 N.E. 2d 673, 43 Ill. Dec. 673 (2nd Dist. 1980)

Thomas v. Chicago Board of Education, 60 Ill. App. 3d 729, 377 N.E. 2d 355 (1st Dist. 1978), rev. on other grounds 77 Ill. 2d 165, 395 N.E. 2d 538, 32 Ill. Dec. 308 (1979)

Kobylanski v. Chicago Board of Education, 63 Ill. 2d 165, 347 N.E. 2d 705 (1976)

12:30 May a school district extend its disciplinary control of students to instances of misbehavior that occur off school grounds?

A school district's authority to regulate student conduct on or off school grounds is limited to that conduct that relates to the administration of the school's educational process. Frequently, school officials will want to discipline because the student's misconduct is serious, or is very unpopular in the community and school officials fail to consider whether or not the behavior was school related.

If school officials determine to proceed with a disciplinary response, it is imperative they have appropriate evidence and witnesses. In some circumstances, it is impossible to provide a student offender with appropriate due process because a criminal prosecution is pending and law enforcement officials control the witnesses and the evidence necessary to conduct a hearing. An arrest, a ticket, and/or a charge are allegations of misconduct, not proofs of misconduct. Police reports and other written evidence (except a written confession used against its author) are arguably hearsay and are potentially suspect in disciplinary hearings without the testimony of the officers who prepared them.

The Illinois Human Rights Act prohibits the use of the fact of an arrest to discipline an individual. It does not prohibit the knowledge of the arrest to obtain other information to establish that the person actually engaged in the conduct for which he or she was arrested.

775 ILCS 5/2-103(B)

Decatur Police Benevolent and Protective Association Labor Committee v. City of Decatur, 2012 IL App (4th) 110764, 968 N.E. 2d 749, 360 Ill. Dec. 256

Morse et al. v. Frederick, 127 S. Ct. 2618, 551 U.S. 393, 168 L. Ed. 2d 290 (2007)

Klein v. Smith, 635 F. Supp. 1440 (Me. 1986)

Board of Education of Rogers, Arkansas v. McCluskey, 102 S. Ct. 3469, 458 U.S. 966, 73 L. Ed. 2d 1273 (1982) on rem. 688 F. 2d 596, reh. den. 103 S. Ct. 16 103 S. Ct. 16, __ U.S. __, 73 L. Ed. 2d 1402 (1982)

McNaughton v. Circleville Board of Education, 46 Ohio Misc. 12, 345 N.E. 2d 649 (1974)

12:35 May school officials adopt a student "no loitering" policy?

A "no loitering" policy will not present constitutional concerns with respect to speech or assembly so long as school officials can show a justifiable governmental reason for the policy, such as the avoidance of damage to property or the prevention of traffic hazards posed by students.

Wiemerslage v. Maine Township High School District 207, 29 F. 3d 1147 (7th Cir. 1994)

12:40 May a school board establish rules of conduct governing spectators at extracurricular activities?

A school board may make and enforce reasonable rules of conduct and sportsmanship for all athletic and extracurricular school events. Any person who violates the rules, whether adult or student, may be denied admission to school events for not more than one year, provided a written 10-day notice of the violation is given and a school board hearing is held on the violation. There is no provision of the Open Meetings Act that permits the hearing to be held in closed session; it must be a public hearing.

The administration of any school may sign a complaint as agent of the school against any person committing any offense at a school event.

105 ILCS 5/24-24

12:45 May students be disciplined by assignment of Saturday detentions?

A school district may assign students to serve Saturday detentions. However, teachers may not be required to teach on Saturdays. Provided the school district has complied with its bargaining obligations, it may seek teacher volunteers to supervise a Saturday detention class.

105 ILCS 5/24-2

12:46 Must a school district provide transportation for students required to attend after-school detention?

If the student is required to attend the detention, the school district must provide advance notice to the parents and must provide transportation for those students for whom the district provides transportation to and from school (no transportation is required for walkers). The common method of avoiding the requirement is to offer a disciplinary alternative to the student and his or her parents.

105 ILCS 5/29-3

105 ILCS 5/29-3.1

12:50 May school officials demand a public apology from a student who has misbehaved and withhold participation in some activity if the student refuses?

The First Amendment rights of the student are implicated in cases that arise from something inappropriate the student has said or written. The courts have permitted school officials to require a public apology from a student (as a condition for participation) if the offending speech was "school sponsored" rather than private and provided the motivation of school officials is "pedagogical."

Student speech cases tend to be fact driven and school officials contemplating requiring an apology should carefully consider the seriousness of the offending speech, the context in which it occurred and how the apology might be enforced (the nature of what school officials propose to withhold).

Seamons v. Snow, 206 F. 3d 1021 (10th Cir. 2000)

Hysaw v. Washburn University of Topeka, 690 F. Supp. 940 (D. Kan. 1987)

12:60 What input on student discipline policies must a school board allow members of the public?

Every school board is required to establish a parent-teacher advisory committee on student discipline and school bus safety. The committee maintains a reciprocal reporting system between local law enforcement officials and the school district regarding criminal offenses committed by students. Schools are required to provide parents with a copy of the student discipline policy within 15 days of the start of school each year or within 15 days after a student who transfers into the district starts classes and must inform students of the contents of the student discipline policy.

105 ILCS 5/10-20.14

23 Ill. Admin. Code 1.280

12:65 Are the rules contained in student handbooks enforceable as contracts?

In order for a student handbook to rise to the level of a contract, the handbook must do something more than restate existing law or legal obligation. The handbook must contain a clear promise to act in a certain way under a specific set of circumstances and those actions promised must be more than school officials are required to do under the law.

Mulvey v. Carl Sandburg High School, 2016 IL App (1st) 151615, 66 N.E. 3d 507, 408 Ill. Dec. 715

Harris v. Adler School of Professional Psychology, 309 Ill. App. 3d 856, 723 N.E. 2d 717, 243 Ill. Dec. 414 (1st Dist. 1999)

PARENT AND STUDENT PROTECTIONS

12:70 What is due process?

There are two types of due process, substantive and procedural. Both relate to the fairness of rules regulating conduct. Substantive due process requires rules be reasonably defined, fairly administered, and related to a valid purpose. In general, to make a substantive due process claim the plaintiff must prove the exercise of governmental power was without reasonable justification and shocks the conscience. Procedural due process refers to the procedures employed to guarantee substantive due process.

To determine what process is constitutionally due, the courts balance three factors:

1) The private interest that will be affected by the official action;

2) The risk of an erroneous deprivation of the interest through the procedures used and the probable value, if any, of additional or substitute procedural safeguards; and

3) The government's interest.

Tun v. Whitticker, 398 F. 3d 899 (7th Cir. 2005)

Gilbert v. Homar, 117 S. Ct. 1807, 520 U.S. 924, 138 L. Ed. 2d 120 (1997) on rem. 149 F. 3d 1164 (3rd Cir.1998)

Cleveland Board of Education v. Loudermill, 105 S. Ct. 1487, 470 U.S. 532, 84 L. Ed. 2d 494 (1985) on rem. 763 F. 2d 202 (6th Cir. 1985)

Goss v. Lopez, 95 S. Ct. 729, 419 U.S. 565, 42 L. Ed. 2d 725 (1975)

Wood v. Strickland, 95 S. Ct. 992, 420 U.S. 308, 43 L. Ed. 2d 214 (1975), reh. den. 95 S. Ct. 1589, 42 U.S. 921, 43 L. Ed. 2d 790 (1975)

12:75 Must school rules be specific to be enforceable?

School officials must take care in writing student disciplinary rules so that the rules are not overly broad. However, because school officials need to be able to impose disciplinary sanctions for a wide range of unanticipated conduct disruptive of the educational process, school disciplinary rules need not be as detailed as the Criminal Code. To show a rule is constitutionally infirm, a student must show the rule is impermissibly vague in all of its applications.

Fuller, et al. v. Decatur Public School Board of Education School District No. 61, 251 F. 3d 662 (7th Cir. 2001)

Bethel School District No. 403, et al. v. Fraser, 106 S. Ct. 3159, 478 U.S. 675, 92 L. Ed. 2d 549 (1986)

In Village of Hoffman Estates v. Flipside, 102 S. Ct. 2023, 456 U.S. 950, 72 L. Ed. 2d 476 (1982)

12:80 In what instances is a student entitled to a hearing before discipline can be invoked by school authorities?

Some form of hearing is required in each instance when, as a result of the discipline, the student will be deprived of access to educational services.

105 ILCS 5/10-22.6

Goss v. Lopez, 95 S. Ct. 729, 419 U.S. 565, 42 L. Ed. 2d 725 (1975)

Wood v. Strickland, 95 S. Ct. 992, 420 U.S. 308, 43 L. Ed. 2d 214 (1975), reh. den. 95 S. Ct. 1589, 42 U.S. 921, 43 L. Ed. 2d 790 (1975)

Linwood v. Board of Education of Peoria School District 150, 463 F. 2d 763 (7th Cir. 1972)

12:90 Must a student be given a "Miranda warning" before being questioned about a matter that may lead to his or her discipline?

A Miranda warning advises the person being interrogated that he or she need not self-incriminate and that he or she has a right to counsel. School officials are not required to give Miranda warnings before interrogations of students. Miranda warnings are necessary if the student is taken into custody by police officials.

The concept of self-incrimination, however, transcends Miranda. School officials should be careful not to create a self-incrimination issue by their use of procedures that coerce confessions. This caution is especially pertinent in cases where a serious deprivation is contemplated (when expulsion is sought or when criminal charges may result).

Providing a child less due process may have the benefit of allowing school officials to obtain more information, but sometimes presents issues at hearing. The better procedure is to provide the student with more due process than is required. There is generally no harm (and probably benefit) in giving Miranda warnings in situations where they are not required.

People v. Pankhurst, 365 Ill. App. 3d 248, 848 N.E. 2d 628, 302 Ill. Dec. 329 (2nd Dist. 2006)

Yarborough v. Alvarado, 124 S. Ct. 2140, 541 U.S. 652, 158 L. Ed. 2d 938 (2004)

12:100 Are communications between a student and an administrator, school psychologist, or school social worker considered privileged?

There is no privilege with respect to communications between school officials and students. School officials, including most classes of school employees who receive information that they are asked to hold in confidence, may be required to testify as to the content of conversations they have with students. The Illinois School Student Records Act (ISSRA) contains a confidentiality statement that may, under some circumstances, protect from disclosure confidential communications by parents or students to school personnel or by parents or students to law enforcement personnel working in schools. The ISSRA names physician, psychologist or other psychotherapist, school social worker, school counselor, school psychologist, or school social worker, school counselor, or school psychologist intern who works under the direct supervision of a school social worker, school counselor, or school psychologist as school employees who may have privilege under some circumstances. Whether or not a privilege exists in any particular case will be fact driven.

In 2009, the School Student Records Act was amended to bar school officials from subjecting a school employee to adverse employment action, the threat of adverse employment action, or any manner of discrimination because the employee is acting or acted to protect communications as privileged or confidential pursuant to applicable provisions of state or federal law, rule, or regulation.

105 ILCS 10/5(f)

Cook County Federal Savings and Loan Association v. Griffin, 73 Ill. App. 3d 210, 391 N.E. 2d 473, 29 Ill. Dec. 210 (1st Dist. 1979)

12:110 May a parent bring a suit for damages against a drug dealer who sells drugs to the parent's child?

The Parental Right of Recovery Act provides any person who (1) sells or transfers an illegal drug to a minor, or (2) supplies to a seller or to any other person an illegal drug that is ultimately sold or transferred to a minor under circumstances where it is reasonably foreseeable the drug may eventually be sold or transferred to a minor is liable to the parent or legal guardian of the minor to whom such illegal drug is sold or transferred for any damages proximately caused by the sale or transfer.

The parent or legal guardian may recover actual damages suffered by the parent or legal guardian resulting from the sale or transfer of the illegal drug to the minor, including pain and suffering. A parent or legal guardian who is awarded damages under the Act may be entitled to punitive damages and/or attorney fees.

740 ILCS 120/3

STUDENT EXPRESSION AND DRESS

12:120 Does the First Amendment protect student political expression?

The First Amendment protects student speech. A school board may not regulate a student's individual political expression unless it can show the expression is obscene or that without regulation there would be material and substantial disorder or invasion of the rights of others or that the speech would interfere with the school's educational mission. The outcome of speech cases is often fact driven and school officials seeking to regulate student speech should be mindful that the degree to which the regulated speech is offensive is significant to the outcome of a legal challenge if such a challenge ensues. Maturity is also a factor. The younger the students, the more latitude school officials have in limiting expression.

It is enough if there are facts that might reasonably lead school officials to forecast substantial disruption. If school officials can show that the speech will lead to a "decline in students' test scores, an upsurge in truancy or other symptoms of a sick school — symptoms therefore of substantial disruption — the school can forbid the speech."

When the speech might reasonably be perceived to bear the imprimatur of the school, school officials are entitled to greater control over student expression. School officials have the discretion to disassociate the school from an entire range of speech, including speech that is ungrammatical, poorly written, inadequately researched, biased or prejudiced, vulgar or profane, or unsuitable for immature audiences.

One court has recognized a distinction between the government regulating the citizenry in its sovereign capacity, and managing programs that citizens participate in voluntarily (such as extracurricular activities). The court held that governmental actions are subject to a lower level of First Amendment scrutiny when the governmental function operating is not the power to regulate or license, as lawmaker, but, rather, as proprietor, to manage its internal operations.

K.J. et al. v. Sauk Prairie School District et al, __ F. Supp. __ (W. Dist. Wis. 2012)

Zamecnik v. Indian Prairie School District No. 204, 636 F. 3d 874 (7th Cir. 2011)

Lowery v. Euverard, 497 F. 3d 584 (6th Cir.) 2007.

Wisniewski v. Board of Education of Weedsport Central School District, 494 F. 3d 34 (2nd Cir. 2007)

Guiles v. Marineau et al., 461 F. 3d 320 (2nd Cir. 2006)

Wilson ex rel. Geiger v. Hinsdale Elementary School District 181, 349 Ill. App. 3d 243, 810 N.E. 2d 637, 284 Ill. Dec. 847 (2nd Dist. 2004)

Fleming v. Jefferson County School District R-1, 298 F. 3d 918 (10th Cir. 2002) cert. den. 123 S. Ct. 893, 537 U.S. 1110, 154 L. Ed. 2d 783 (2002)

Barrett v. University of Mississippi, 232 F. 3d 208 (5th Cir. 2000)

West v. Derby Unified School District, 206 F. 3d 1358 (10th Cir. 2000)

Denno v. School Board of Volusia County, Florida, 193 F. 3d 1178 (11th Cir. 1999)

Chandler v. McMinnville School District, 978 F. 2d 524 (9th Cir. 1992)

Tinker v. Des Moines Independent School District, 89 S. Ct. 733, 393 U.S. 503, 21 L. Ed. 2d 731 (1969)

12:121 May school officials restrict student speech that is derogatory of another student's race, religion, or sexual orientation?

A line of cases is emerging that would allow school officials to regulate student speech that is derogatory if the speech injures "public school students by verbal assaults on the basis of a core identifying characteristic such as race, religion, or sexual orientation." The courts have reasoned that students have a right, while at school, to be "secure and to be let alone" and that schools have an "interest, if not duty, to protect minority groups from harassing conduct."

The outcome of speech cases is often fact driven, and school officials seeking to regulate student speech should be mindful that the degree to which the regulated speech is offensive is significant to the outcome of a legal challenge if a plaintiff emerges.

Zamecnik v. Indian Prairie School District No. 204, 636 F. 3d 874 (7th Cir. 2011)

Harper v. Poway Unified School District, 445 F. 3d 1166 (9th Cir. 2006), vacated as moot, 127 S. Ct. 1484, 549 U.S. 1262, 167 L. Ed. 2d 225 (2007)

Nixon v. Northern Local School District Board of Education, 383 F. Supp. 2d 965 (S.D. Ohio 2005)

Muller by Muller v. Jefferson Lighthouse School, 98 F. 3d 1530 (7th Cir. 1996)

12:122 May school officials regulate speech that promotes the use of illegal drugs?

Deterring drug use by schoolchildren is an "important — indeed, perhaps compelling" interest. School officials may, consistent with the First Amendment, restrict student speech at a school event when that speech is reasonably viewed as promoting drug use. While such speech might be protected outside of school, the nature of student rights "is what is appropriate for children in school."

School officials should be very careful not to overreach. It is a message that advocates drug use that can restricted. Speech that is political (such as a message advocating the legalization of marijuana) or religious has First Amendment protection.

Morse et al. v. Frederick, 127 S. Ct. 2618, 551 U.S. 393, 168 L. Ed. 2d 290 (2007)

12:123 May a school district prohibit student political buttons?

A school district may not restrict student political speech absent a showing of substantial disruption or material interference with school activities. Therefore, absent such a showing, "scab buttons" during a teacher strike, candidate buttons during a political campaign, or other political speech that is neither offensive nor vulgar may not be regulated.

Chandler v. McMinnville School District, 978 F. 2d 524 (9th Cir. 1992)

12:125 May a school board or school administration establish a student dress code?

Courts recognize a student's right to freedom of expression. While there is not absolute uniformity of judicial interpretation, caution is advisable in the adoption of student dress codes or hair-length regulations. To safely regulate, a school board must demonstrate disruption of the orderly process of a school function, or endangerment to health or safety. Definitions for unacceptable dress are difficult to write and a school official charged with writing definitions should be mindful not to discriminate on the basis of gender.

105 ILCS 5/10-22.25b

Phoenix Elementary School District No. 1 v. Green, 943 P. 2d 836 (1997)

Alabama and Coushatta Tribes of Texas v. Trustees of Big Sandy, 817 F. Supp. 1319 (E.D. Tex. 1993)

Olesen v. Board of Education of School District 228, 676 F. Supp. 820 (N.D. Ill. 1987)

Harper v. Edgewood Board of Education, 655 F. Supp. 1353 (S.D. Ohio 1987)

Copeland v. Hawkins, 352 F. Supp. 1022 (N.D. Ill. 1973)

Arnold v. Carpenter, 459 F. 2d 939 (7th Cir. 1972).

Laine v. Dittman, 125 Ill. App. 2d 136, 259 N.E. 2d 824 (2nd Dist. 1970)

Breen v. Kahl, 419 F. 2d 1034 (7th Cir. 1969)

12:126 May a school board adopt a mandatory dress code that requires students to wear uniforms to school?

Illinois statutes permit a school board to "adopt a school uniform or dress code policy that governs all or certain individual attendance centers that is necessary to maintain the orderly process of a school function or prevent the endangerment of student health or safety."

A school board contemplating a mandatory uniform or dress code policy should carefully examine court decisions cited here and elsewhere in this section to determine the legality of any specific limitation contemplated. Mandatory uniform policies are constitutionally suspect, as are many common dress code limitations.

105 ILCS 5/10-22.25b

Phoenix Elementary School District No. 1 v. Green, 943 P. 2d 836 (1997)

12:127 May a school board ban student tattoos or non-ear piercings?

The courts have given student tattoos and body piercings First Amendment protections when a school district has been unable to demonstrate health or safety concerns. School officials should be mindful not to create gender discrimination issues in instances when regulation would be otherwise appropriate (if boys are required to remove piercings during physical education, the rule must apply to girls as well).

Stephenson v. Davenport Community School District, 110 F. 3d 1303 (8th Cir. 1997)

Olesen v. Board of Education of School District 228, 676 F. Supp. 820 (N.D. Ill. 1987)

12:128 May a school board ban student T-shirts that contain offensive sayings or which depict offensive or obscene material?

The courts are divided as to the breadth of school's authority to regulate student speech in this context. To safely regulate, the school should have a clear policy prohibiting the item to be banned and must show that the speech would undermine the authority of school administrators or disrupt school operations. Speculation as to the potential for subversion of authority or disruption will likely be insufficient to support regulation.

Many of the court cases in this area are fact driven. The more excessive the conduct being regulated, the more likely the courts are to uphold the school's right to establish limitations.

105 ILCS 5/10-22.25b

Guiles v. Marineau et al., 461 F. 3d 320 (2nd Cir. 2006)

Sypniewski v. Warren Hills Regional Board of Education, 307 F. 3d 243 (3rd Cir. 2002) cert. den. 123 S. Ct. 207, 538 U.S. 1033, 155 L. Ed. 2d 1062 (2003)

Boroff v. Van Wert City Board of Education, 220 F. 3d 465 (6th Cir. 2000) cert. den. 121 S. Ct. 1355, 532 U.S. 920, 149 L. Ed. 2d 286 (2001)

Pyle v. Hadley School Committee, 861 F. Supp. 157 (D. Mass. 1994)

McIntire v. Bethel Independent School District No. 3, 804 F. Supp. 1415 (W.D. Okla. 1992)

Broussard v. School Board of the City of Norfolk, 801 F. Supp. 1526 (E.D. Va. 1992)

Poling v. Murphy, 872 F. 2d 757 (6th Cir. 1989)

Gano v. School District 411, 674 F. Supp. 796 (D.C. Ida. 1987)

STUDENT PUBLICATIONS

12:130 May school officials regulate student publications?

In 2016, the General Assembly enacted the Speech Rights of Student Journalists Act which provides that a student journalist has the right to exercise freedom of speech and of the press in school-sponsored media, regardless of whether the media is supported financially by the school district or by use of school facilities or produced in conjunction with a class in which the student is enrolled. Under the terms of the Act the student is responsible for determining the news, opinion, feature, and advertising content of school-sponsored media. Prior restraint of material prepared for official school publications is prohibited under the Act. The Act does not authorize or protect expression by a student journalist that is libelous, slanderous, or obscene; constitutes an unwarranted invasion of privacy; violates federal or state law; or incites students to commit an unlawful act, to violate policies of the school district, or to materially and substantially disrupt the orderly operation of the school.

Student personal expression is not subject to the same limitations and is broadly protected by the First Amendment. Thus, publications not sponsored by the school are not subject to regulation by the school, other than through reasonable rules regulating distribution on school premises.

105 ILCS 80/10

105 ILCS 80/15

Rosenberger v. Rector and Visitors of the University of Virginia, 115 S. Ct. 2510, 515 U.S. 819, 132 L. Ed. 2d 700 (1995)

Hazelwood v. Kuhlmeier, 108 S. Ct. 562, 484 U.S. 260, 98 L. Ed. 2d 592 (1988), on rem. 840 F. 2d 596 (8th Cir. 1988)

Scoville v. Board of Education of Joliet Township High School District 204, 425 F. 2d 10 (7th Cir. 1972)

Fujishama v. Board of Education, 460 F. 2d 1355 (7th Cir. 1972)

12:133 What are a public forum, a limited public forum, and a non-public forum?

A public forum is a forum that has, by tradition, been held open for free expression. In these places, the state must show a narrowly tailored compelling state interest to limit debate. The compelling state interest standard is very difficult to meet.

A non-public forum is one that has been traditionally restricted by the state so that expression has been limited to comport with the purpose of the property. To regulate debate in a non-public forum, the state need only avoid the suppression of speech based solely on its content and demonstrate a rational reason to regulate.

A limited public forum is an otherwise non-public forum that the state has intentionally opened for expressive use by the public. In a limited public forum, the state must show a compelling state interest to limit debate and the regulation must be narrowly tailored to meet that objective.

In forum analysis, the difficult determination is whether a forum has remained non-public or, because certain uses have been permitted, the forum has become a limited public forum.

In forum analysis the plaintiff is seeking access to a place. Forum analysis is not appropriate when the plaintiff is seeking access to an intended (sometimes captive) audience. A classroom, for example, does not become a public forum because a guest lecturer from outside is invited to talk to the class.

Milwaukee Deputy Sheriff's Association. v. Clarke, 574 F. 3d 370 (7th Cir. 2009)

Planned Parenthood of Southern Nevada v. Clark County School District, 941 F. 2d 817 (9th Cir. 1991)

Perry Education Association v. Perry Local Educators' Association, 103 S. Ct. 948, 460 U.S. 37, 74 L. Ed. 2d 794 (1983)

12:135 May school officials regulate the content of advertising in school publications?

In most circumstances, school publications are not public forums and schools have a right to impose reasonable restrictions on the advertisements that may appear in them. Schools may adopt reasonable policies for the acceptance and rejection of advertisements in school publications, such as the school yearbook, newspaper, and athletic programs.

DiLoreto v. Board of Education of Downey Unified School District, 196 F. 3d 958 (9th Cir. 1999)

Yeo v. Town of Lexington, 131 F. 3d 241 (1st Cir. 1997) cert. den. 118 S. Ct. 2060, 524 U.S. 904, 141 L. Ed. 2d 138 (1998)

Planned Parenthood of Southern Nevada v. Clark County School District, 941 F. 2d 817 (9th Cir. 1991)

Hazelwood v. Kuhlmeier, 108 S. Ct. 562, 484 U.S. 260, 98 L. Ed. 2d 592 (1988), on rem. 840 F. 2d 596 (8th Cir. 1988)

12:137 May school officials regulate the content of advertising sold to be displayed on school grounds?

School officials can, by policy, regulate advertising displayed on school grounds. Advertising messages are common in school athletic facilities and in school cafeterias. In most cases, school officials seek to limit the content of the message to make it conform to the school's educational mission. For example, a school would likely prevent a sign promoting a bar, but allow a sign promoting a local sporting goods store. A school might seek to limit the size, shape, or color of a sign or tone down its message.

In most cases, schools exercise substantial control over the messages conveyed in advertising that is permitted and, in general, the school's regulation of the message or manner of delivery converts private speech into government speech. The courts have held that such advertising bears the imprimatur of the school and is generally perceived by the viewer as a school message.

Mech v. School Board of Palm Beach County, 806 F. 3d 1070 (11th Cir. 2015)

12:140 May a school board adopt rules regulating the distribution of student publications?

A school board may establish reasonable regulations setting forth the time, manner, and place at which distribution of student written material may occur.

Fujishama v. Board of Education, 460 F. 2d 1355 (7th Cir. 1972)

12:145 May a school district regulate personal student internet sites, messages, or webpages?

Unless school officials can show that the message, page, or site and its contents would materially interfere with or disrupt the educational process, or substantially interfere with school discipline, a student's private (non-school computer) message, page, or site is protected by the First Amendment. Even if the messages posted are unpopular or critical of the school or school officials, and even if the messages are obnoxious or insulting, school officials may not limit them, because to do so would be an impermissible attempt to regulate speech based solely on its content. If the posted material is obscene or specifically threatens a person or incites others to violence, school officials may have criminal or school disciplinary options.

Under appropriate circumstances school officials may regulate what material or data may be accessed, keyboarded, saved, or loaded on school-owned computers.

Layshock ex rel. Layshock v. Hermitage School District 593 F. 3d 249 (3rd Cir. 2010)

J.S. ex rel. Snyder v. Blue Mountain School District; 593 F. 3d 286 (3rd Cir. 2010)

Doninger v. Niehoff, 527 F. 3d 41 (2nd Cir. 2008)

Beidler v. North Thurston School District, Docket No. 99-2-00236-6, Wash. Super. Ct. 2000

J.S. v. Bethlehem Area School District, 757 A. 2d 412 (Pa. Commw. Ct. 2000)

Emmett v. Kent School District No. 415, 92 F. Supp. 2d 1088 (W.D. Wash. 2000)

Urofsky v. Gilmore, 161 F. 3d 191 (4th Cir 1999)

Beussink v. Woodland R-IV School District, 30 F. Supp. 2d 1175 (E.D. Mo. 1998)

12:146 Are schools required to have filtering software on their computers that prevent students from accessing inappropriate material on the internet?

A school may not receive benefits under certain federal laws, including service discounts under the Telecommunications Act or the Elementary and Secondary Education Act, unless the school has filters that block student access to certain inappropriate internet sites and adopts a safety policy requiring the filters. The filtering device must block entry to visual depictions that are obscene or child pornography and must protect against material that is harmful to minors. The filter may be disabled by an administrator, supervisor or other authorized person for bona fide research or another lawful purpose.

Schools are required to enforce the use of the filters. Under the Telecommunications Act, a school must have a safety policy that addresses access by minors to inappropriate materials on the internet; the safety and security of minors when using electronic mail or chat rooms; unauthorized access to sites or other unlawful activities by minors online; unauthorized disclosure, use, or dissemination of personal identification information regarding minors; and measures designed to restrict minors' access to material harmful to minors. Schools are required to hold a public hearing before the adoption of the required policy.

20 U.S.C. 6777 et seq.

47 U.S.C. 254(h)

12:147 What is the Student Online Personal Protection Act?

In 2017, the General Assembly enacted the Student Online Personal Protection Act, the purpose of which is to ensure that student data will be protected when it is collected by educational technology companies. The statute targets personally identifiable information or information that is linked to personally identifiable information. The Act prohibits "operators" (internet websites, certain services, and applications) from various activities, including targeted advertising, sale, and use of protected information.

105 ILCS 85/1 et seq.

12:148 May a student be suspended or expelled for making internet threats?

A 2011 amendment to Section 10-22.6 of the School Code limits the ability of school officials to discipline students for having made internet threats. It provides that a student may be suspended or expelled from school in accordance with state law, "as determined on a case by case basis, if (i) the student has been determined to have made an explicit threat on an internet website against a school employee, a student, or any school-related personnel, (ii) the internet website through which the threat was made is a site that was accessible within the school at the time the threat was made or was available to third parties who worked or studied within the school grounds at the time the threat was made, and (iii) the threat could be reasonably interpreted as threatening to the safety and security of the threatened individual because of his or her duties or employment status or status as a student inside the school."

The language of the statute may make it more difficult to discipline students for school-related threats made from home computers.

105 ILCS 5/10-22.6

12:149 May school officials ask for or require a student or his or her parent to provide a password or account information to gain access to the student's social networking account or profile on a social networking website?

A new law in 2013 requires that school officials must provide notification to the a student and his or her parent or guardian that the school may request or require a student to provide a password or other related account information in order to gain access to the student's account or profile on a social networking website if the school has reasonable cause to believe that the student's account on a social networking website contains evidence that the student has violated a school disciplinary rule or policy. The notification must be published in the elementary or secondary school's disciplinary rules, policies, or handbook or communicated by similar means.

105 ILCS 75/15

PROHIBITED BEHAVIORS

12:150 Are there criminal penalties for the unlawful use of weapons on school grounds?

There are criminal penalties ranging from Class A misdemeanor to Class X felony for unlawful use of weapons on school grounds. The statutory definition of what constitutes a weapon is broad.

720 ILCS 5/24-1

12:152 How does the concealed carry law affect the regulation of weapons at school?

Schools are prohibited zones for concealed carry. Students are generally too young to have concealed carry licenses (21 is the minimum age). Schools are required to post signage regarding concealed carry prohibitions. Licensees can carry weapons into parking lots and store licensed firearms in their vehicles by law (a school district cannot prohibit firearms in it parking lots).

430 ILCS 66/25
430 ILCS 66/65
www.isp.state.il.us/media/pressdetails.cfm?ID=762

12:155 What is the penalty for a student who is found to have brought a weapon to school?

Illinois law provides that "a student who is determined to have brought a weapon to school, any school sponsored activity or event which bears a reasonable relationship to school shall be expelled for a period of not less than two calendar years, except that the expulsion period may be modified by the superintendent and the superintendent's determination may be modified by the board on a case by case basis." The Illinois concealed carry law provides that "a licensee under this Act shall not knowingly carry a firearm on or into: Any building, real property, and parking area under the control of a public or private elementary or secondary school."

20 U.S.C. 7961
105 ILCS 5/10-22.6 (d)
430 ILCS 66/65
United States v. Lopez, 115 S. Ct. 1624, 514 U.S. 549, 131 L. Ed. 2d 626 (1995)
Honig v. Doe, 108 S. Ct. 592, 484 U.S. 305, 98 L. Ed. 2d 686 (1988)

12:156 Must school officials report gun or drug incidents at school to law enforcement authorities?

Upon receipt of any written, electronic, or verbal report from any school personnel regarding a verified incident involving a firearm or drugs at school or on any school owned or leased property (including vehicles), the superintendent or his or her designee must immediately report the incident to local law enforcement authorities and to the State Police in a form, manner, and frequency prescribed by the State Police. For the purposes of this law, firearm has the meaning set forth in the Firearm Owners Identification Card Act, and drugs means cannabis as defined in the Cannabis Control Act or narcotic drug as defined in the Controlled Substances Act.

It is the duty of the principal of a public elementary or secondary school, or his or her designee, to report to the municipal police department or office of the county sheriff of the municipality or county where the school is located, violations of Section 5.2 of the Cannabis Control Act, violations of Section 401 and subsection (b) of Section 407 of the Illinois Controlled Substances Act, and violations of the Methamphetamine Control and Community Protection Act occurring in a school, on the real property comprising any school, on a public way within 1,000 feet of a school, or in any conveyance owned, leased, or contracted by a school to transport students to or from school or a school related activity within 48 hours of becoming aware of the incident.

105 ILCS 5/10-27.1A
105 ILCS 5/10-27.1B
105 ILCS 127/2
430 ILCS 65/1.1
720 ILCS 550/3
720 ILCS 570/102

12:157 What is a weapon for school disciplinary purposes?

The term "weapon" means possession, use, control, or transfer of any gun, rifle, shotgun, a weapon as defined by Section 921 of Title 18 of United States Code, firearm as defined in Section 1.1 of the Firearm Owners Identification Act, or use of a weapon as defined in Section 24-1 of the Criminal Code or any other object if used or attempted to be used to cause bodily harm including but not limited to knives, brass knuckles, billy clubs, or look-a-likes of any weapon as defined in this section. Such items as baseball bats, pipes, bottles, locks, sticks, pencils, and pens may be considered weapons if used or attempted to be used to cause bodily harm.

105 ILCS 5/10-22.6(d)

12:160 What is the penalty for unlawful sale or delivery of firearms on school property?

Any person 18 years of age or older who knowingly sells, gives, or delivers any firearm of a size which may be concealed upon the person to any person under 18 years of age or a firearm of any size to a person under 18 who does not possess a valid Firearm Owner's Identification Card commits a Class 1 felony if the offense takes place in any school, on the real property comprising a school, within 1,000 feet of the real property comprising a school, at a related activity, or on or within 1,000 feet of any conveyance owned leased or contracted by a school or school district to transport students to or from school or a school related activity, regardless of the day or time of year at which the offense was committed. The penalty for conviction of a Class 1 felony is four to 15 years in prison and a fine of up to $25,000.

A person 18 years of age or older convicted of unlawful sale of firearms, when the firearm that was sold or given to another person under 18 years of age was used in the commission of or attempt to commit a forcible felony, is fined or imprisoned, or both, not to exceed the maximum provided for the most serious forcible felony so committed or attempted by the person under 18 years of age who was sold or given the firearm.

720 ILCS 5/24-3

730 ILCS 5/5-4.5-30

12:163 Is there a criminal penalty for possession of alcohol on school grounds?

Any person who has alcoholic liquor in his or her possession on public school property on school days or at events on public school property when children are present is guilty of a petty offense, unless the alcoholic liquor (i) is in the original container with the seal unbroken and is in the possession of a person who is not otherwise legally prohibited from possessing the alcoholic liquor, or (ii) is in the possession of a person in or for the performance of a religious service or ceremony authorized by the school board.

235 ILCS 5/6-16(e)

12:165 May a student possess an electronic paging device or a cellular telephone in school?

Before 2002, a statute prohibited possession of cellular phones and pagers by students in schools without the special permission of an administrator and the school board. In 2002, the legislature amended the statute to allow school boards the authority to establish rules and disciplinary procedures regarding the use or possession of cellular radio telecommunication devices by a student while in a school or on school property, during regular school hours or at any other time.

105 ILCS 5/10-20.28

105 ILCS 5/10-21.10

12:170 Are fraternities, sororities, or secret organizations permitted in public schools?

A school board must suspend or expel any pupil who is a member or who becomes or promises to become a member, or who becomes pledged to become a member, or who solicits any other person to promise to join or be pledged to become a member, of any public school fraternity, sorority, or secret society.

105 ILCS 5/31-3 et seq.

12:175 Under what circumstances may a student be disciplined for having made a threat?

The law is unsettled with respect to the outer edges of a school district's authority to aggressively discipline students for having made threats. The courts consider threats in the context of the totality of the circumstances surrounding the threat and the reasonableness of a school official's forecast of substantial disruption or material interference with school activities. A school official investigating a threat should determine:

1) Is the threat immediate or remote? Did the threat constitute a prediction or promise of harm to persons or property, or was it vague and difficult to particularize?

2) Did the person making the threat understand his or her actions to be threatening?

3) How plausible is the threat?

4) How did the person who was the object of the threat react to the threat? Did he or she react to the threat as if it was a plausible promise that harm would be done?

5) What factors in the threat maker's personal profile make the threat more or less credible?

LaVine v. Blaine School District, 257 F. 3d 981 (9th Cir. 2001)

Lovell v. Poway Unified School District, 90 F. 3d 367 (9th Cir. 1996)

Tinker v. Des Moines Independent School District, 89 S. Ct. 733, 393 U.S. 503, 21 L. Ed. 2d 731 (1969)

12:180 Are there criminal penalties for using threats to recruit students into street gangs?

A person who knowingly, expressly, or impliedly threatens to do bodily harm or does bodily harm to an individual or to that individual's family or uses any other criminally unlawful means to solicit or cause any person to join, or deter any person from leaving any organization or association, regardless of the nature of such organization or association, is guilty of a Class 3 felony.

The matter becomes a Class 2 felony when a person older than 18 years threatens a person younger than 18 years. A person convicted of violation of this statute cannot be sentenced to probation, conditional discharge, or periodic imprisonment.

720 ILCS 5/12-6.5 et seq.

In Interest of V.W., 112 Ill. App. 3d 587, 445 N.E. 2d 445, 67 Ill. Dec. 965 (1st. Dist. 1983)

CORPORAL PUNISHMENT

12:190 Does state law authorize the use of corporal punishment in Illinois schools?

State law prohibits corporal punishment. The School Code requires each school district to adopt a policy that prohibits intentional infliction of bodily harm, slapping, paddling, or prolonged maintenance of students in physically painful positions.

The School Code permits teachers, other certificated employees, and any other person who provides a related service for or with respect to a student to use reasonable force "to maintain safety for the other students, school personnel, or persons or for the purpose of self-defense or for the defense of property...."

105 ILCS 5/24-24

Wallace v. The Batavia School District 101, 68 F. 3d 1010 (7th Cir. 1995)

Thrasher v. General Casualty Co. of Wisconsin, 732 F. Supp. 966 (W.D. Wisc. 1990)

Metzger by and through Metzger v. Osbeck, 841 F. 2d 518 (3rd Cir. 1988)

Wisconsin v. Pea Ridge School District, 855 F. 2d 560 (8th Cir. 1988)

Hall v. Tawney, 621 F. 2d 607 (4th Cir. 1980)

Carter v. State Board of Education, 90 Ill. App. 3d 1042, 414 N.E. 2d 153, 46 Ill. Dec. 431 (1st Dist. 1980)

Ingraham v. Wright, 97 S. Ct. 1401, 430 U.S. 651, 51 L. Ed. 2d 711 (1977)

Baker v. Owen, 395 F. Supp. 294 (M.D.N.C. 1975), aff'd. 96 S. Ct. 210, 423 U.S. 907, 46 L. Ed. 2d 137 (1975)

City of Macomb v. Gould, 104 Ill. App. 2d 361, 244 N.E. 2d 634 (3rd Dist. 1969)

12:195 May a student be punished by being physically restrained?

The State Board of Education has adopted rules governing use of "time out" and the physical restraint of students. The following forms of punishment are prohibited:

1) Use of a locked room other than one with a locking mechanism that engages only when a key or handle is being held by a person;

2) Use of a confining space such as a closet or box;

3) Use of a room where the student cannot be continually observed; or

4) Use of any other room or enclosure or time-out procedure that is contrary to State Board of Education guidelines.

The use of physical restraints is prohibited except when (i) the student poses a physical risk to himself, herself, or others; (ii) there is no medical contraindication to its use; and (iii) the staff applying the restraint have been trained in its safe application.

"Restraint" does not include momentary periods of physical restriction by direct person-to-person contact, without the aid of material or mechanical devices, accomplished with limited force and that are designed (i) to prevent a student from completing an act that would result in potential physical harm to self or another or damage to property, or (ii) to remove a disruptive student who is unwilling to voluntarily leave the area.

The use of physical restraints that are consistent with the law may be included in a student's Individualized Education Program where deemed appropriate by the student's Individualized Education Program team. Whenever physical restraints are used, school personnel must fully document the incident, including the events leading up to the incident, the type of restraint used, the length of time the student is restrained, and the staff involved. The parents or guardian of a student must be informed whenever physical restraints are used.

105 ILCS 5/2-3.130

105 ILCS 5/10-20.33

23 Ill. Admin. Code 1.280

23 Ill. Admin. Code 1.285

STUDENT SEARCHES

12:230 What is permissible in conducting student searches?

The Fourth Amendment's prohibition of unreasonable searches and seizures applies to searches conducted by public school officials. The balance between a student's legitimate expectations of privacy and a school's legitimate need to maintain an appropriate environment for learning requires some easing of the restrictions to which searches by public authorities are ordinarily subject.

School officials need not obtain a warrant before searching a student. A search is justified at its inception when there are reasonable grounds for suspecting the search of a particular child will turn up evidence the student has violated or is violating either the law or the rules of the school.

A search is permissible in its scope when the measures adopted are reasonably related to the objectives of the search and not excessively intrusive in light of the age and sex of the student and the nature of the infraction. If the scope of a search is too aggressive or if the search otherwise violates the Fourth Amendment, the school district may have liability for the constitutional violation and whatever is found during the search may not be used in any disciplinary context.

105 ILCS 5/10-22.6(e)

Howlett by and through Howlett v. Rose, 110 S. Ct. 2430, 496 U.S. 356, 110 L. Ed. 2d 332 (1990) on rem. 571 So. 2d 29 (1990)

New Jersey v. T.L.O., 105 S. Ct. 733, 469 U.S. 325, 83 L. Ed. 2d 720 (1985)

12:231 May school officials strip search a student?

The Fourth Amendment does not prohibit invasive searches, but rather, limits the circumstances under which such searches are constitutional. A school district should exercise extraordinary care that constitutional requirements are met before an invasive search is attempted. Unless school officials have reasonable particularized suspicion with respect to the suspect and the item school officials are looking for presents an immediate threat to the safety of school personnel or students, a strip search is unconstitutionally invasive.

105 ILCS 5/10-22.6(e)

Safford Unified School District No. 1 v. Redding, 129 S. Ct. 2633, 557 U.S. 364, 174 L. Ed. 2d 354 (2009)

Bell v. Marseilles Elementary School, 160 F. Supp. 2d 883 (N.D. Ill. 2001)

Thomas v. Roberts, 261 F. 3d 1160 (11th Cir. 2001)

Jenkins v. Talladega City Board of Education, 95 F. 3d 1036 (11th Cir. 1996)

Cornfield By Lewis v. School District No. 230, 991 F. 2d 1316 (7th Cir. 1993)

12:232 May school officials require a student to take a pregnancy test?

The conduct of a pregnancy test is a search within the meaning of the Fourth Amendment. Unless school officials have legitimate health concerns, requiring such a test even for student-athletes is an unreasonable search.

Gruenke v. Seip, 225 F. 3d 290 (3rd Cir. 2000)

12:234 May school officials conduct random drug testing of student-athletes?

The procedures used to conduct random drug testing of student-athletes are searches within the meaning of the Fourth Amendment. However, under certain narrowly defined circumstances, random drug testing of student-athletes is permissible.

In determining the reasonableness of a search, the courts examine whether the school has a legitimate governmental interest in testing which outweighs the athlete's Fourth Amendment right to be free from such a search.

The manner in which drug testing is performed is critical; the privacy interests of the students from whom urine is to be collected must be protected. The urine tests must look for standard drugs only, not medical conditions, and the test results must be released to a limited number of school officials.

A 2009 law required the Illinois High School Association to implement a random drug-testing program. The law was repealed in July 2011.

105 ILCS 25/2

Board of Education of Independent School District No. 92 of Pottawatomie County v. Earls, 122 S. Ct. 2559, 536 U.S. 822, 153 L. Ed. 2d 735 (2002)

Todd, et al. v. Rush County Schools, et al., 133 F. 3d 984 (7th Cir. 1998) reh. and sugg. for reh. den. 139 F. 3d 571, cert. den. 119 S. Ct. 68, 525 U.S. 824, 142 L. Ed. 2d 53 (1998)

Vernonia School District 47J, v. Wayne Acton, et ux., etc., 115 S. Ct. 2386, 515 U.S. 646, 132 L. Ed. 3d 564 (1995)

Moule v. Paradise Valley Unified School District No. 69, 863 F. Supp. 1098 (D.C. Ariz. 1994)

12:235 May school officials conduct random drug testing of students in other extracurricular activities or as a condition precedent to the privilege of driving to school?

A school district contemplating random testing should proceed with caution. In 2002, a divided United States Supreme Court approved of suspicionless drug testing of students involved in extracurricular activities. The court held that such testing is a reasonable means of furthering a school district's important interest in preventing and deterring drug use among schoolchildren and it does not violate the Fourth Amendment. With a carefully crafted policy, a school district may conduct such tests as a condition of participation in extracurricular activities or as a condition of the privilege of driving to school, provided the test results are not used for the discipline of a student testing positive. The student and his or her family must be given an opportunity to explain a positive test result and must be given an opportunity for re-testing. The school's response to a positive test must be limited to removal from the activity.

Board of Education of Independent School District No. 92 of Pottawatomie County v. Earls, 122 S. Ct. 2559, 536 U.S. 822, 153 L. Ed. 2d 735 (2002)

Tannahill v. Lockney Independent School District, 133 F. Supp. 2d 919 (N.D. Tex. 2001)

Joy v. Penn-Harris-Madison School Corporation, 212 F. 3d 1052 (7th Cir. 2000)

Linke v. Northwestern School Corp., __ Ind. App. __, 734 N.E. 2d 252 (Ind. App. 2000)

Miller v. Wilkes, 172 F. 3d 574 (8th Cir. 1999)

Todd, et al. v. Rush County Schools, et al., 133 F. 3d 984 (7th Cir. 1998) reh. and sugg. for reh. den. 139 F. 3d 571, cert. den. 119 S. Ct. 68, 525 U.S. 824, 142 L. Ed. 2d 53 (1998)

Willis v. Anderson Community School Corporation, 158 F. 3d 415 (7th Cir. 1998), cert. den. 119 S. Ct. 1254, 526 U.S. 1019, 143 L. Ed. 2d 351 (1999)

12:236 May school officials use a breathalyzer to test each student before the students enter an extracurricular activity, such as a prom?

The use of a breathalyzer is a search within the meaning of the Fourth Amendment. A search of all students entering an activity is random because school officials cannot claim they have reasonable suspicion as to any particular student. This is so whether or not school officials give prior warning of the test and it is so even if students consent to the test as a condition of entry into the event.

Whether a random search of students under these conditions is legal or not is fact specific. School officials contemplating such a search should exercise extreme caution in meeting the prerequisites specified in case law. School officials must be able to show less intrusive methods would not suffice to meet their objectives.

Board of Education of Independent School District No. 92 of Pottawatomie County v. Earls, 122 S. Ct. 2559, 536 U.S. 822, 153 L. Ed. 2d 735 (2002)

Tannahill v. Lockney Independent School District, 133 F. Supp. 2d 919 (N.D. Tex. 2001)

Joy v. Penn-Harris-Madison School Corporation, 212 F. 3d 1052 (7th Cir. 2000)

Linke v. Northwestern School Corp., __ Ind. App. __, 734 N.E. 2d 252 (Ind. App. 2000)

Knox County Education Association v. Knox County Board of Education, 158 F. 3d 361 (6th Cir. 1998), cert. den. 120 S. Ct. 46, 528 U.S. 812, 145 L. Ed. 2d 41 (1999)

Miller v. Wilkes, 172 F. 3d 574 (8th Cir. 1999)

Todd, et al. v. Rush County Schools, et al., 133 F. 3d 984 (7th Cir. 1998) reh. and sugg. for reh. den. 139 F. 3d 571, cert. den. 119 S. Ct. 68, 525 U.S. 824, 142 L. Ed. 2d 53 (1998)

Willis v. Anderson Community School Corporation, 158 F. 3d 415 (7th Cir. 1998), cert. den. 119 S. Ct. 1254, 526 U.S. 1019, 143 L. Ed. 2d 351 (1999)

12:238 What is "reasonable suspicion"?

There is reasonable suspicion to search when school officials reasonably infer from all the circumstances that the student is committing, is about to commit, or has committed an offense. School officials must identify specific articulated facts which, when taken with their natural inferences, make the intrusion reasonable.

The facts need not rise to the level of probable cause, but they must be more than a hunch. A school official's search may be as thorough as required by the circumstances.

Bridgman v. New Trier High School District No. 203, 128 F. 3d 1146 (7th Cir. 1997)

People v. Taylor, 253 Ill. App. 3d 768, 625 N.E. 2d 785, 192 Ill. Dec. 630 (4th Dist. 1993)

New Jersey v. T.L.O., 105 S. Ct. 733, 469 U.S. 325, 83 L. Ed. 2d 720 (1985)

Terry v. Ohio, 88 S. Ct. 1868, 392 U.S. 1, 20 L. Ed. 2d 889 (1968)

12:240 May school officials search school lockers used by students?

School officials should inform students that school lockers are school district property made available to students for their convenience. Lockers may be searched randomly and without meeting any cause standard.

The nature of locker use and locker construction create evidentiary problems that make it difficult to discipline students solely on the basis of the fruits of a locker search.

105 ILCS 5/10-22.6 (e)

Chicago Firefighters Local 2 v. Chicago, 717 F. Supp. 134 (N.D. Ill. 1989)

O'Connor v. Ortega, 107 S. Ct. 1492, 480 U.S. 709, 94 L. Ed. 2d 714 (1987)

New Jersey v. T.L.O., 105 S. Ct. 733, 469 U.S. 325, 83 L. Ed. 2d 720 (1985)

Picha v. Wieglos, 410 F. Supp. 1214 (N.D. Ill. 1976)

12:242 May school officials search other places on school grounds?

An Illinois statute permits searches of "lockers, desks, parking lots, and other school property owned or controlled by the school as well as personal effects left in those places and areas by students without notice or the consent of the student and without a search warrant." However, the statute does not restrict the Fourth Amendment rights of students, and school officials should be very cautious when conducting searches that infringe the privacy rights of students. The Illinois statute does not universally permit the warrantless search of student automobiles or student personal effects in which the student has an expectation of privacy.

If a search is conducted in a place where a student has no expectation of privacy, proving what is found in that place belongs to any particular student is problematic. Therefore, a student disciplinary case based on such evidence is often difficult.

105 ILCS 5/10-22.6(e)

12:250 Does the Fourth Amendment protect students from physical seizure by school officials?

Seizures of students by school officials are subject to constraints of the Fourth Amendment. However, the reasonableness of a Fourth Amendment seizure must be evaluated in the context of the school environment, where restricting the liberty of students is a necessary component of the educational process.

A teacher or administrator who seizes a student violates the Fourth Amendment only when the restriction of liberty is "unreasonable under the circumstances then existing and apparent." A person is seized within the meaning of the Fourth Amendment when, by a show of authority or use of physical force, his or her freedom of movement is restrained. If the person subject to questioning is free to disregard the questions and walk away, there is no intrusion on the person's liberty or privacy such that the Fourth Amendment requires a particularized and objective justification.

Stockton v. City of Freeport, Texas, 147 F. Supp. 2d 642 (S.D. Tex. 2001)

Milligan v. City of Slidell, 226 F. 3d 653 (5th Cir. 2000)

People v. Parker, 284 Ill. App. 3d 860, 672 N.E. 2d 813, 219 Ill. Dec. 960 (1st Dist. 1996)

Wallace v. The Batavia School District 101, 68 F. 3d 1010 (7th Cir. 1995)

POLICE SEARCHES AND ARRESTS

12:300 What standard applies to student searches when law enforcement officers are involved?

When school officials involve police officers in searches of students conducted in schools, the search standard may increase from "reasonable suspicion" to "probable cause." What standard applies to any particular search depends upon whether the search is one in which

1) School officials initiate the search and where police involvement is minimal;

2) School police or liaison police officers are acting on their own authority; or

3) Outside police officers initiate a search where the involvement of school officials is limited.

Probable cause exists if the facts and circumstances are sufficient to warrant a prudent person, or one of reasonable caution, to believe in the circumstances shown the suspect has committed an offense. A court evaluates probable cause not with the benefit of hindsight, and not on the facts as perceived by an omniscient observer, but on the facts as they appeared to a reasonable person in the defendant's position, even if that reasonable belief turned out to be incorrect.

An increase in the search standard from reasonable suspicion to probable cause is significant, because if officials have not met the appropriate search standard at the initiation of the search, the fruits of the search may not be used to discipline the offender. This principle is known as the exclusionary rule.

There is at least one federal court of appeals that has held the exclusionary rule does not apply to school administrative searches. The exclusionary rule applies to administrative searches conducted in Illinois.

Generally, searches by school officials where police involvement is minimal or searches by school police or liaison officers are held to the reasonable suspicion standard, and school searches by outside officers acting on their own authority require probable cause. A search warrant may be required under certain circumstances when police officials are involved with school officials in the conduct of a search.

Stokes v. Board of Education of the City of Chicago, 599 F. 3d 617 (7th Cir. 2010)

Shade v. City of Farmington, 309 F. 3d 1054 (8th Cir. 2002)

In re Randy G., 28 P. 3d 239 (Cal. 2001)

Thompson v. Carthage, 87 F. 3d 979 (8th Cir. 1996)

People v. Dilworth, 169 Ill. 2d 195, 661 N.E. 2d 310,214 Ill. Dec. 456 (1996), cert. den. 116 S. Ct. 1692, 517 U.S. 1197, 134 L. Ed. 2d 793 (1996)

In re S.F., 607 A. 2d 793 (Pa. Super. 1992)

Skinner v. Railway Labor Executives' Association, 109 S. Ct. 1402, 489 U.S. 602, 103 L. Ed. 2d 639 (1989)

Treasury Employees' Union v. Van Raab, 109 S. Ct. 1384, 489 U.S. 656, 103 L. Ed. 2d 685 (1989)

New Jersey v. T.L.O., 105 S. Ct. 733, 469 U.S. 325, 83 L. Ed. 2d 720 (1985)

Martens v. District No. 220 Board of Education, 620 F. Supp. 29 (N.D. Ill. 1985)

Picha v. Wieglos, 410 F. Supp. 1214 (N.D. Ill. 1976)

12:310 Are police dog searches of school grounds legal?

Police dogs may not be used to conduct generalized searches of students or places where students have a reasonable expectation of privacy. Police dogs may be used to conduct searches of public places on school grounds, including school parking lots (but not necessarily the automobiles located on the parking lots).

Whether or not additional cause or a warrant may be necessary before a more intrusive search is conducted after a police dog alerts is a matter that depends on the facts surrounding the particular search.

The fruits of searches of public places are often useless to discipline student offenders because the discovered contraband cannot be certainly connected to any particular student.

105 ILCS 5/10-22.6(e)

Jennings v. Joshua Independent School District, 948 F. 2d 194 (5th Cir. 1991) reh. den. 952 F. 2d 402, cert. den. 112 S. Ct. 2303, 504 U.S. 956, 119 L. Ed. 2d 226 (1992)

Horton v. Goose Creek, 690 F. 2d 470, reh. den. 693 F. 2d 524 (5th Cir. 1982) cert. den. 103 S. Ct. 3536, 363 U.S. 1207, 77 L. Ed. 2d 1387 (1982)

Zamora v. Pomeroy, 639 F. 2d 662 (10th Cir. 1981)

Doe v. Renfrow, 475 F. Supp. 1012, aff'd in part, rem. in part, 631 F. 2d 582 (7th Cir. 1980) cert. den. 101 S. Ct. 3015, 451 U.S. 1022, 69 L. Ed. 2d 395 (1981)

Camara v. Municipal Court of City and County of San Francisco, 87 S. Ct. 1727, 387 U.S. 523, 18 L. Ed. 2d 930 (1967)

12:315 May school officials use metal detectors to randomly search students?

The use of a metal detector is a search within the meaning of the Fourth Amendment. Provided the search is justified at its inception by the reality of violence in the schools and the search as conducted is reasonably related in scope to the circumstances that justified the interference in the first place, a metal detector search may be legal. School officials should exercise caution to be sure any such search meets the guidelines required by the courts.

Bourgeois v. Peters, 387 F. 3d 1303 (11th Cir. 2004)

People v. Pruitt et al., 278 Ill. App. 3d 194, 662 N.E. 2d 540, 214 Ill. Dec. 974 (1st Dist. 1996)

United States v. Epperson, 454 F. 2d 769 (4th Cir. 1972)

12:317 May school officials require that a student whom they suspect has committed an act of misconduct be searched by a metal detector?

A metal detector search is a warrantless search. In order for a warrantless search to be permissible under the Fourth Amendment, there must be reasonable grounds for suspecting that the search will turn up evidence the student has violated or is violating either the law or the rules of the school.

A school official contemplating a metal detector search should be aware that a distinction must be drawn between a student who voluntarily and without any coercion submits to a metal detector search and a student who is detained and required to submit to a search. The former search requires no cause, while the latter requires either reasonable suspicion or probable cause depending on the circumstances. A student may not be detained for a search against his or her will or required to submit to a search unless the appropriate search standard has been met.

People v. Parker, 284 Ill. App. 3d 860, 672 N.E. 2d 813, 219 Ill. Dec. 960 (1st Dist. 1996)

12:320 If a police dog alerts on a student's locked car in the school parking lot, may school officials or the police open the car and search it?

If the student is 18 years of age or over and gives consent for the search, the car may be searched. If the student is under 18, the student's parents must give consent or a warrant must be obtained in order to conduct a completely safe search.

105 ILCS 5/10-22.6(e)

12:330 Under what circumstances may law enforcement authorities enter school buildings?

Law enforcement authorities may enter school buildings when they have reason to believe a crime has been committed, when they possess a warrant, or when they have been invited into the school by school officials. A school district may regulate by policy access to students by law enforcement authorities who do not possess warrants.

42 U.S.C. 1983

New Jersey v. T.L.O., 105 S. Ct. 733, 469 U.S. 325, 83 L. Ed. 2d 720 (1985)

Zamora v. Pomeroy, 639 F. 2d 662 (10th Cir. 1981)

Doe v. Renfrow, 475 F. Supp. 1012, aff'd in part, rem. in part, 631 F. 2d 582 (7th Cir. 1980) cert. den. 101 S. Ct. 3015, 451 U.S. 1022, 69 L. Ed. 2d 395 (1981)

Picha v. Wieglos, 410 F. Supp. 1214 (N.D. Ill. 1976)

12:340 Must a school district allow police officials to question or arrest students during the school day?

A police officer must be permitted to arrest a student on school property during the school day when the officer possesses a warrant or when the officer is in hot pursuit of a suspect. A school district may regulate by policy warrantless police interrogations.

U.S. v. Hollingsworth, 495 F. 3d 795 (7th Cir. 2007)

Doe v. Renfrow, 475 F. Supp. 1012, aff'd in part, rem. in part, 631 F. 2d 582 (7th Cir. 1980) cert. den. 101 S. Ct. 3015, 451 U.S. 1022, 69 L. Ed. 2d 395 (1981)

Picha v. Wieglos, 410 F. Supp. 1214 (N.D. Ill. 1976)

12:345 Can parents require prior notification of — or participation in — the questioning of students by law enforcement or school officials?

School officials should be mindful of local school policies or rules that govern parental notification or participation. The Fourth Circuit has held, "The Constitution does not impose a duty of parental notification before the pupil's disciplinary detainment while such school guardianship persists." The court reasoned that school officials "must have the leeway to maintain order on school premises and secure a safe environment."

Wofford v. Evans, 390 F. 3d 318 (4th Cir. 2004)

12:350 What notice does a school district receive if one of its students is involved in juvenile proceedings?

All courts and law enforcement agencies of the state and its political subdivisions must report to the principal of any public school whenever an enrolled child is detained for proceedings under the Juvenile Court Act or for any criminal offense, including gang activity, or any violation of a municipal or county ordinance. The report must include the basis for detaining the child, the circumstances surrounding the events that led to the child's detention, and the status of proceedings. The report must be updated as appropriate to notify the principal of developments and the disposition of the matter.

The information derived from this report must be kept separate from and must not become a part of the official school record of the child and is not a public record. Such information must be used solely by the principal, counselors, and teachers of the school to aid in the rehabilitation of the child.

105 ILCS 5/10-20.14
105 ILCS 5/22-20
705 ILCS 405/1-1

12:355 How must a school district respond to reports of bullying?

A school board is required to have a student discipline policy that includes provisions to address students who have demonstrated behaviors that put them at risk for aggressive behavior, "including without limitation, bullying as defined in the policy." The policy defines bullying as "any severe or pervasive physical or verbal act or conduct, including communications made in writing or electronically directed toward a student or students that has or can be reasonably predicted to have the effect of" placing a student in reasonable fear of harm, having a detrimental effect on the student's physical or mental health or substantially interfering with a student's academic performance or the student's ability to participate in school activities.

The policy must include procedures for notifying parents or legal guardians and early intervention procedures based on available community and district resources.

School officials will have protection from liability when they take bullying reports seriously and respond to such reports in an attempt to end the bullying, even if the response is ultimately ineffective. The courts treat such decisions by administrators as discretionary acts and school officials have immunity from liability for discretionary acts under the Tort Immunity Act.

105 ILCS 5/10-20.14
105 ILCS 5/27-23.7
745 ILCS 10/2-201 et seq.
Mulvey v. Carl Sandburg High School, 2016 IL App (1st) 151615, 66 N.E. 3d 507, 408 Ill. Dec. 715
Hascall v. Williams, 2013 IL App (4th) 121131, 996 N.E. 2d 1168, 375 Ill. Dec. 112

12:360 Must law enforcement officials cooperate with school officials in the prosecution of juveniles charged with school-related criminal offenses?

The Juvenile Justice Reform Act of 1998 permits law enforcement agencies to disclose certain student juvenile criminal records to school officials. The provision of such information is limited to records transmitted to the appropriate school official by a local law enforcement agency under a reciprocal reporting system established and maintained between the school district and the local law enforcement agency concerning a minor enrolled in the school district who has been arrested for a felony or a Class A or B misdemeanor.

Juvenile court records are not available to school officials. The Juvenile Court act provides that a juvenile adjudication is never to be considered a conviction, nor may an adjudicated individual be considered a criminal. Unless expressly allowed by law, a juvenile adjudication does not operate to impose upon the individual any of the civil disabilities ordinarily imposed by or resulting from conviction. Unless expressly allowed by law, adjudications do not prejudice or disqualify the individual in any civil service application or appointment, from holding public office, or from receiving any license granted by public authority. All juvenile records that have not been expunged are sealed and may never be disclosed to the general public or otherwise made widely available. Sealed records may be obtained only under specific statutorily defined circumstances and when their use is needed for good cause and with an order from the juvenile court.

105 ILCS 5/22-20
705 ILCS 405/1-8
705 ILCS 405/5-905

SUSPENSION AND EXPULSION

12:380 What is a student disciplinary suspension?

A student disciplinary suspension is a temporary removal from school or from riding a school bus for a maximum of 10 days per suspension. Except under some circumstances involving some students classified as in need of special education, a suspension is permitted for gross disobedience or misconduct. A suspension from riding a school bus may exceed 10 days for safety reasons. A 2016 amendment to the relevant law commonly known as Senate Bill 100 requires that "school officials limit the number and duration of expulsions and suspensions to the greatest extent practicable," use expulsion and suspension only for legitimate educational purposes, and that school officials consider forms of non-exclusionary discipline prior to using out-of-school suspensions or expulsions.

105 ILCS 5/10-22.6(b)

Goss v. Lopez, 95 S. Ct. 729, 419 U.S. 565, 42 L. Ed. 2d 725 (1975)

Linwood v. Board of Education of Peoria School District 150, 463 F. 2d 763 (7th Cir. 1972)

12:390 Which school officials may suspend a student from school?

A school board may authorize the superintendent, principal, assistant principal, or dean of students to suspend a student for gross disobedience or misconduct if the student has been provided the requisite due process and proper notice has been given. A 2011 amendment to the School Code provides:

"A pupil who is suspended in excess of 20 school days may be immediately transferred to an alternative program.... A pupil must not be denied transfer because of the suspension, except in cases in which such transfer is deemed to cause a threat to the safety of students or staff in the alternative program."

105 ILCS 5/10-22.6(b)

105 ILCS 5/13B-20.25

12:400 What procedures must be followed to notify a student's parents of his or her suspension from school?

Any suspension must be immediately reported to the parents or guardian of a student along with a full statement of the reasons for the suspension and a notice of right to a review. The school board must be given a summary of the notice, including the reason for the suspension and its duration.

Upon request of the parents or guardian, the school board or a hearing officer appointed by it must review the action of the suspending school official. At the review, the parents or guardian of the student may appear and discuss the suspension with the school board or its hearing officer.

If a hearing officer is appointed by the board, he or she must report to the board a written summary of the evidence heard at the meeting. After its hearing, or upon receipt of the written report of its hearing officer, the board may take such action as it finds appropriate. A 2016 amendment to the relevant statute requires that if a student is suspended, the board must, in a written suspension decision, detail the specific act of gross disobedience or misconduct resulting in the decision to suspend. The suspension decision must also include a rationale as to the specific duration of the suspension. The statute provides that a pupil who is suspended in excess of 20 school days may be immediately transferred to an alternative program. "A pupil must not be denied transfer because of the suspension, except in cases in which such transfer is deemed to cause a threat to the safety of students or staff in the alternative program."

105 ILCS 5/10-22.6(b)

Coronado v. Valleyview Public School District 365-U, 537 F. 3d 791 (7th Cir. 2008)

12:405 May school officials refuse to register a new student who is serving a suspension in another school district?

A school district may adopt a policy providing that if a student is suspended or expelled for any reason from any public or private school in this or any other state, the student must complete the entire term of the suspension or expulsion before being admitted into the school district. The policy must provide for placement of the student in an alternative school program for the remainder of the suspension or expulsion unless the child is a threat to the safety of students or staff in the alternative school program.

105 ILCS 5/2-3.13a

105 ILCS 5/10-22.6(g)

12:410 What due process is required with respect to a student suspension from school?

A student must be provided with the following due process in connection with any suspension from school:

1) Oral or written notice of the charges and evidence supporting the charges;

2) If the charges are denied, a student must be given an opportunity to explain his or her version of the events to the suspending school official;

3) The suspension (except from riding a bus for safety reasons) may not exceed 10 days, although additional requirements apply to suspensions after the

enactment of P.A. 99-456 (commonly known as Senate Bill 100);

4) To have his or her parents or guardian immediately receive a report of the suspension along with a full statement of the reasons for it and a notice of right to review;

5) If a hearing is requested, the parents or guardian may appear and may discuss the suspension with the board or its hearing officer;

6) Any decision rendered must be in writing and based upon the evidence; and

7) With respect to any suspension invoked, the student has a right to be informed of its beginning and ending dates and the rationale for the duration of the suspension, and in the case of a suspension of longer than four school days whether there are any appropriate and available support services.

The rules regulating the suspension of a student identified as in need of special education are different, and disposition will depend upon the facts presented in each case.

105 ILCS 5/10-22.6(b)

Sieck v. Oak Park-River Forest High School District No. 200, 807 F. Supp. 73 (N.D. Ill. 1992)

Carey v. Piphus, 97 S. Ct. 1642, 435 U.S. 247, 52 L. Ed. 2d 355 (1978)

Goss v. Lopez, 95 S. Ct. 729, 419 U.S. 565, 42 L. Ed. 2d 725 (1975)

12:415 What limitations are there on the length of a suspension or expulsion?

In 2016, P.A. 99-456, commonly known as Senate Bill 100, established limitations on school officials' ability to suspend and/or expel students from school. It provides that out-of-school suspensions of three days or less may be used only if the student's continuing presence in school would pose a threat to school safety or a disruption to other students' learning opportunities. Threat to school safety or a disruption to other students' learning opportunities is determined on a case-by-case basis by the school board or its designee. School officials are required to make all reasonable efforts to resolve threats, address disruptions, and minimize the length of suspensions to the greatest extent practicable. Out-of-school suspensions of longer than three days, expulsions, and disciplinary removals to alternative schools may be used only if other appropriate and available behavioral and disciplinary interventions have been exhausted and the student's continuing presence in school would either pose a threat to the safety of other students, staff, or members of the school community or substantially disrupt, impede, or interfere with the operation of the school. The determination of whether appropriate and available behavioral and disciplinary interventions have been exhausted is made by school officials. School officials are required to make all reasonable efforts to resolve such threats, address such disruptions, and minimize the length of student exclusions to the greatest extent practicable. In the case of either suspension or expulsion, school officials are required to document whether other interventions were attempted or whether it was determined that there were no other appropriate and available interventions.

105 ILCS 5/10-22.6 (b-5)

105 ILCS 5/10-22.6 (b-15)

105 ILCS 5/10-22.6 (b-20)

12:417 Must suspended or expelled students be provided support services?

P.A. 99-456 (Senate Bill 100) requires that students who are suspended out-of-school for longer than four school days must be provided appropriate and available support services during the period of their suspension. Appropriate and available support services are determined by school authorities. In the decision it must be documented whether such services are to be provided or whether it was determined that there are no appropriate and available services.

105 ILCS 5/10-22.6 (b-25)

12:419 Must suspended students be allowed to make up missed work?

Suspended students, including those who are suspended from the school bus who do not have alternate transportation to school, must have the opportunity to make up work for equivalent academic credit. It is the responsibility of a student's parent or guardian to notify school officials that a pupil suspended from the school bus does not have alternate transportation to school.

105 ILCS 5/10-22.6 (b-30)

12:440 What is a student disciplinary expulsion?

A student disciplinary expulsion is the removal of a student from school for gross disobedience or misconduct for a period of time ranging from in excess of 10 days to a definite period of time not to exceed two school years.

Prior to a 2011 change in the statute, it was possible to expel a student without provision of regular educational services. Now, this is a possible outcome only if the student threatens the safety of students or staff in the alternative program. Enrollment in a charter alternative learning opportunities program is open to any pupil who has been expelled or suspended for more than 20 days.

A 2016 amendment to the relevant law (the amendment is commonly known as Senate Bill 100) requires that "school officials limit the number and duration of expulsions and suspensions to the greatest extent practicable," use expulsion and suspension only for legitimate educational purposes, and that school officials consider forms of non-exclusionary discipline prior to using out-of-school suspensions or expulsions.

105 ILCS 5/10-22.6(a)

105 ILCS 5/13B-20.25

Robinson v. Oak Park and River Forest High School, Board of Education District 200, 213 Ill. App. 3d 77, 571 N.E. 2d 931, 156 Ill. Dec. 951 (1st Dist. 1991)

Betts v. Board of Education of City of Chicago, 466 F. 2d 629 (7th Cir. 1972)

12:445 May a school district expel a preschool student?

A 2017 change in the law prohibits the expulsion of preschool students. The law contains a list of required interventions and includes protocols in the event a child presents a "serious safety threat."

105 ILCS 5/2-3.71

12:450 Which school officials have authority to expel a student from school?

Only a school board may expel a student. Its authority to expel may not be delegated. A school board may consider recommendations from the administration and may appoint a hearing officer to conduct an expulsion hearing, but must retain authority to render the final decision.

105 ILCS 5/10-22.6(a)

12:460 May a school board expel a student for an indefinite period?

A student, other than a student identified as in need of special education (or for whom a special education needs issue exists), may be expelled for a definite period of time not to exceed two school years.

A 2011 amendment to the relevant statute provides "An expelled pupil may be immediately transferred to an alternative program. A pupil must not be denied transfer because of the expulsion, except in cases in which such transfer is deemed to cause a threat to the safety of students or staff in the alternative program." Enrollment in a charter alternative learning opportunities program is open to any pupil who has been expelled or suspended for more than 20 days.

105 ILCS 5/10-22.6(a)

105 ILCS 5/10-22.6(d)

105 ILSC 5/13B-20.25

Linwood v. Board of Education of Peoria School District 150, 463 F. 2d 763 (7th Cir. 1972)

12:465 May a student be fined as a disciplinary consequence?

A student may not be issued a monetary fine or fee as a disciplinary consequence, though this does not preclude requiring a student to provide restitution for lost, stolen, or damaged property.

105 ILCS 5/10-22.6(i)

12:470 What procedures must a school board follow in expelling a student from school?

When a student is accused of gross disobedience or misconduct sufficiently severe to warrant expulsion, the expulsion may not take place until after the parents have been requested to appear at a meeting of the school board, or with a hearing officer appointed by it, to discuss the student's behavior. Notice of hearing must be made by registered or certified mail and must state the time, place, and purpose of the meeting. If the board expels a student it must issue a written decision detailing the specific reasons why removing the student from the learning environment is in the best interest of the school and a rationale as to the duration of the expulsion. If a hearing officer is appointed by the board, he or she must report to the board a written summary of the evidence heard at the meeting and the board may take such action thereon as it finds appropriate.

The rules regulating the expulsion of students identified as in need of special education are different from the above.

5 ILCS 120/2

105 ILCS 5/10-22.6(a)

Coronado v. Valleyview Public School District 365-U, 537 F. 3d 791 (7th Cir. 2008)

Robinson v. Oak Park and River Forest High School, Board of Education District 200, 213 Ill. App. 3d 77, 571 N.E. 2d 931, 156 Ill. Dec. 951 (1st Dist. 1991)

Linwood v. Board of Education of Peoria School District 150, 463 F. 2d 763 (7th Cir. 1972)

Betts v. Board of Education of City of Chicago, 466 F. 2d 629 (7th Cir. 1972)

Whitfield v. Simpson, 312 F. Supp. 889 (N.D. Ill. 1970)

12:475 What due process is required with respect to a student expulsion from school?

A student must be provided with the following due process with respect to any expulsion from school:

1) The expulsion shall take place only after a student's parents or guardian have been requested to appear at a meeting of the school board, or with a hearing officer appointed by it, to discuss the student's behavior. A student may be suspended from school pending this meeting but must be provided the due process required to support a suspension;

2) A notice of hearing must be sent to the parents or guardian by registered or certified mail stating the time, place, and purpose of the hearing;

3) The school board or its appointed hearing officer must provide a full statement of the reasons for the proposed expulsion at the hearing and must provide notice of the date on which the proposed expulsion is to become effective;

4) The student is entitled to consult with counsel at the student's expense (this right is to be distinguished from the right to be represented by counsel at the hearing);

5) Adequate time must be given to prepare a defense;

6) The student must be given an opportunity to call and examine witnesses, to cross-examine opposing witnesses, and to introduce evidence;

7) The decision to expel or not to expel must be made by the school board, must be in writing, and must be based upon the evidence presented. The student has a right to be informed of the expulsion's beginning and ending dates, the rationale for the duration of the expulsion, and whether there are any appropriate and available support services.

105 ILCS 5/10-22.6(a)

Coronado v. Valleyview Public School District 365-U, 537 F. 3d 791 (7th Cir. 2008)

Camlin v. Beecher Community School District, et al. 339 Ill. App. 3d 1013, 791 N.E. 2d 1097, 274 Ill. Dec. 331 (3rd Dist. 2003)

Colquitt v. Rich Township High School District No. 227, 298 Ill. App. 3d 856, 699 N.E. 2d 1109, 232 Ill. Dec. 924 (1st Dist. 1998)

Osteen v. Henley, 13 F. 3d 221 (7th Cir. 1993)

Newsome v. Batavia Local School District, 842 F. 2d 920 (6th Cir. 1988)

Carey v. Piphus, 97 S. Ct. 1642, 435 U.S. 247, 52 L. Ed. 2d 355 (1978)

Wood v. Strickland, 95 S. Ct. 992, 420 U.S. 308, 43 L. Ed. 2d 214 (1975), reh. den. 95 S. Ct. 1589, 42 U.S. 921, 43 L. Ed. 2d 790 (1975)

Linwood v. Board of Education of Peoria School District 150, 463 F. 2d 763 (7th Cir. 1972)

12:476 In possession cases involving drugs, weapons, or alcohol, is it necessary to prove the student knew he or she possessed the banned item?

Often, when school officials seek to discipline a student for a possession offense, the student will assert that the items found in his or her possession are not his or hers or that he or she "did not know they were there." This defense is common when, for example, a weapon is found in a backpack, or drug paraphernalia is found in a student's car. Frequently, school officials will seek to discipline not just for what the student knew he or she had in his or her possession, but what the student should have known he or she possessed.

When a student asserts the "it's not mine" defense, school officials should be careful to establish a link between the student and the illicit item and should be careful to prove "what the student should have known." In these cases, school officials should be especially careful to read the policies that prohibit the behavior narrowly.

Butler v. Rio Rancho Public Schools Board of Education, 341 F. 3d 1197 (10th Cir. 2003)

Seal v. Morgan, 229 F. 3d 567 (6th Cir. 2000)

12:477 May an expulsion hearing witness be protected by introducing a written statement rather than requiring that the witness appear?

A student accused of wrongdoing and facing expulsion has the constitutional right to confront and cross examine his or her accusers. The admission of statements rather than the production of the witness denies the accused his or her right to test the evidence against him or her. Courts will consider the substitution of written statements for live testimony only when there is a real and demonstrated threat of retaliation against the witness or when a written statement is available but the witness is unavailable.

A school district seeking to protect a child witness would be wise to have evidence that such protection is necessary to protect the welfare of the child witness or that the witness would be traumatized by the presence of the "defendant." The trauma must be significant and not merely excitement, nervousness, or reluctance to testify.

Coronado v. Valleyview Public School District 365-U, 537 F. 3d 791 (7th Cir. 2008)

Colquitt v. Rich Township High School District No. 227, 298 Ill. App. 3d 856, 699 N.E. 2d 1109, 232 Ill. Dec. 924 (1st Dist. 1998)

Maryland v. Craig, 110 S. Ct. 3157, 497 U.S. 836, 111 L. Ed. 2d 666 (1990)

12:478 Is a verbatim transcript required in an expulsion hearing?

The absence of a court reporter, in and of itself, is neither a denial of due process nor a denial of equal protection. There is no requirement to provide a stenographer's transcript in every case so long as there is some other means to allow for adequate and effective review.

Colquitt v. Rich Township High School District No. 227, 298 Ill. App. 3d 856, 699 N.E. 2d 1109, 232 Ill. Dec. 924 (1st Dist. 1998)

12:480 What factors will a court consider in reviewing a school board's decision to expel a student?

In reviewing a school board's decision to expel, the court will consider:

1) The egregiousness of the student's conduct;

2) The history or record of the student's past conduct;

3) The likelihood that such conduct will affect the delivery of educational services to other students;

4) The severity of the punishment; and

5) The interest of the child.

After the enactment of P.A. 99-456 (Senate Bill 100) the court will also consider whether or not school officials limited expulsions "to the greatest extent practicable," whether there were other appropriate and available interventions (and whether they were exhausted), whether school officials considered other forms of non-exclusionary discipline prior to using expulsion, and other limitations the statute imposes.

A 2017 change in the law adds additional factors that must be considered in cases when the expulsion is from a program that is funded by a block grant.

Wilson ex rel. Geiger v. Hinsdale Elementary School District 181, 349 Ill. App. 3d 243, 810 N.E. 2d 637, 284 Ill. Dec. 847 (2nd Dist. 2004)

Robinson v. Oak Park and River Forest High School, Board of Education District 200, 213 Ill. App. 3d 77, 571 N.E. 2d 931, 156 Ill. Dec. 951 (1st Dist. 1991)

12:485 As part of an expulsion motion, may a school board ban a student from being on school grounds or attending a school event?

Expulsion transforms a person's status from student to general member of the public. A member of the public does not have a protected liberty interest in accessing school grounds (or any other constitutional right of access) and therefore a school board need not provide due process in connection with its imposition of a ban from school grounds.

Hannemann v. Southern Door County School District, 673 F. 3d 746 (7th Cir. 2012)

12:490 May a student who has been suspended or expelled from one school district enroll and attend classes in another school district during the term of the suspension or expulsion?

The School Code provides that if a student has been suspended or expelled for knowingly possessing in a school building or on school grounds a weapon as defined in the Gun Free Schools Act, for knowingly possessing, selling, or delivering in a school building or on school grounds a controlled substance or cannabis, or for battering a staff member of the school, and if the period of suspension or expulsion has not expired at the time the student attempts to transfer into another public school in the same or any other school district:

1) Any school student records required to be transferred must include the date and duration of the period or suspension or expulsion; and

2) The student must not be permitted to attend class in the public school into which he or she is transferring until the student has served the entire period of the suspension or expulsion imposed by the school from which the student is transferring except that the school board must approve placement of the student in an alternative school.

No school district is required to admit a new student who is transferring from an out-of-state public school unless the parent or guardian of the student certified in writing that the student is not currently serving a suspension or expulsion.

A school district that anticipates denying a student enrollment by reason of this statute should carefully consider

1) Whether the school district that suspended or expelled the student complied with all School Code requirements and procedural and substantive due process requirements in imposing the suspension or expulsion; and

2) Whether or not the student is properly a resident of the school district in which he or she seeks to enroll.

A school district may adopt a policy providing that if a student is suspended or expelled for any reason from any public or private school in Illinois or any other state, the student must complete the entire term of the suspension or expulsion before being admitted into the school district. The policy must allow placement of the student in an alternative school program if available for the remainder of the suspension or expulsion. Enrollment in a charter alternative learning opportunities program is open to any pupil who has been expelled or suspended for more than 20 days.

105 ILCS 5/2-3.13a

105 ILCS 5/13B-20.25

12:495 What process is due a student whom the school district contemplates suspending or expelling from athletics or other extracurricular activity?

Many athletic suspensions and expulsions and some extracurricular exclusions have high community visibility and often result in media coverage. Disciplinary outcomes are often challenged by parents.

School officials should take great care to examine all the facets of a proposed suspension or expulsion before proceeding to any disciplinary conclusion. They should be certain there is sufficient connection between the events and school or educational interests so as to give the school district, rather than the student's parents or the criminal or juvenile justice system, authority to invoke discipline.

School districts or school officials may adopt team rules, athletic codes, student handbook provisions, and/or policies governing athletic or extracurricular conduct and eligibility. Having done so, however, a school district will be required to follow its own policies and procedures to the letter. School officials should take care to insure that relevant provisions agree from source to source.

One Illinois appellate court case suggests no due process is necessary in the case of an athletic or extracurricular exclusion unless a school's rules, regulations, or policies entitle the student to due process. However, the case warns that "school officials cannot impose student punishment in a completely arbitrary and capricious manner." The case suggests that, "in order to establish a violation of a student's substantive, rather than procedural due process rights, the student must show arbitrary and capricious conduct on the part of school officials."

Better Government Association v. Illinois High School Association, 2017 IL 121124, __ N.E. __, __ Ill. Dec. __

Jordan by Edwards v. O'Fallon Township High School District No. 203 Board of Education, 302 Ill. App. 3d 1070, 706 N.E. 2d 137, 235 Ill. Dec. 877 (5th Dist. 1999)

Peterson v. Independent School District No. 811, 999 F. Supp. 665 (D. Minn. 1998)

Robinson v. Illinois High School Association, 45 Ill. App. 2d 277, 195 N.E. 2d 38 (2nd Dist. 1963) cert. den. 85 S. Ct. 647, 379 U.S. 960, 13 L. Ed. 2d 555 (1965)

ALTERNATIVE SCHOOLS

12:500 What is an alternative school?

An alternative school created under the Safe Schools Law is a school intended to educate disruptive students who would otherwise be subject to suspension or expulsion. Such students may be administratively transferred to the alternative school, but the transferring school may lose some options in the event the student misbehaves in the alternative school setting.

105 ILCS 5/13A-4

12:510 How is an alternative school established under the Safe Schools Law?

The regional superintendent, after consultation with each local superintendent of schools in the regional superintendent's region and the regional board, determines the location and need of the alternative school within the region. The regional superintendent must consider

1) The possible utilization of existing buildings, including but not limited to governmental buildings that are, or could reasonably be made, usable;

2) Which option would be least costly; and

3) Distances that administratively transferred students would need to travel and the costs of that travel.

Upon the determination of the need for establishment of an alternative school, each school district located within the region shall provide the regional superintendent with a copy of the district's discipline policies and procedure for effecting suspension or expulsion. Thereafter, the regional superintendent in cooperation with a representative from each school district in the region shall establish an alternative school program and each school district in the region shall adopt policies and procedures for the identification and placement of students in the program.

105 ILCS 5/13A-3

12:520 May an educational service region have more than one alternative school?

Upon recommendation of the regional superintendent and with the approval of the State Board of Education, an educational service region may add one or more alternative schools to the region. In determining whether an additional school is necessary and appropriate, the State Board considers

1) The geographic size of the educational service region and distances that students within that region must travel in order to attend the existing alternative school;

2) The student population of schools comprising the educational service region and the likely student population of all alternative school programs within that region if the petition is granted;

3) Any other logistical considerations; and

4) The cost necessitated by establishing an additional alternative school in that educational service region.

105 ILCS 5/13A-3(f)

12:530 Who is a "disruptive student" within the meaning of the Safe Schools Law?

A disruptive student includes students in grades 6-12 who have been found eligible for suspension or expulsion through the discipline process established by the school district. School officials may not administratively transfer a student to an alternative school without first providing the student with due process as provided in the law and by reason of the school district's discipline policies.

105 ILCS 5/13A-2.5

12:540 May a school district avoid special education implications by transferring a behavior disordered student to an alternative school?

No.

105 ILCS 5/13A-1 (k)
105 ILCS 5/13A-1 (l)

12:550 What is an alternative education plan?

At the earliest time following an administrative transfer to an alternative school, appropriate personnel from the sending school district and appropriate personnel of the alternative program shall meet to develop an alternative education plan for the student. The student's parent or guardian shall be invited to the meeting. The student may be invited. The alternative educational plan must include

1) The duration of the plan, including a date after which the student may be returned to the regular educational program in the transferring district;

2) The specific academic and behavioral components of the plan; and

3) The method and time frame for reviewing the student's progress.

105 ILCS 5/13A-4

12:560 What happens if the parents of a student placed in an alternative school object to the child's return to the regular school program?

If the parent or guardian of a student who is scheduled to be returned to the regular educational program in the public schools of the district files a written objection to the return with the principal of the alternative school, the matter shall be referred by the principal to the regional superintendent of the educational service region in which the alternative school is located for a hearing. Notice of the hearing must be given by the regional superintendent to the student's parent or guardian. After the hearing, the regional superintendent may take such action as he or she finds appropriate and in the best interest of the student. The determination of the regional superintendent is final.

105 ILCS 5/13A-4

13: CHILDREN WITH DISABILITIES AND SPECIAL EDUCATION

SPECIAL EDUCATION DEFINED

13:10 What is "special education"?

"Special education" is instruction provided at no cost to parents or guardians specifically designed to provide a child with certain educational disabilities a "free and appropriate public education" as directed by the federal Individuals with Disabilities Education Act (IDEA) and state law.

Special education may be conducted in the classroom, in the home, in hospitals or institutions, and/or in other settings and must, when appropriate, include the provision of non-educational services necessary to support education. Special education includes instruction in physical education.

20 U.S.C. 1401(29)

105 ILCS 5/14-8.02

Irving Independent School District v. Tatro, 104 S. Ct. 3371, 468 U.S. 883, 82 L. Ed. 2d 664 (1984), on rem. 741 F. 2d 82 (1984)

13:15 What is the difference between IDEA and Section 504?

Section 504 refers to a civil rights law (Section 504 of the Rehabilitation Act of 1973) that protects the rights of persons with disabilities. It is primarily distinguished from the Individuals with Disabilities Education Act (IDEA) in that it covers children with disabilities when those disabilities do not adversely affect the child's educational performance (children with disabilities who do not qualify for special education).

Section 504 covers individuals who meet the definition of qualified "handicapped" persons — children who have a physical or mental impairment that substantially limits a major life activity or who are regarded as handicapped by others. Section 504 compliance does not require the formalized procedures required by IDEA. But a child who qualifies must have a 504 plan and the school district must provide impartial hearings for parents who disagree with the identification, evaluation, or placement of the student. No parental consent is required and there are no "stay-put" provisions.

29 U.S.C. 701 et seq.

www2.ed.gov/about/offices/list/ocr/504faq.html

13:20 What are the elements of a "free and appropriate public education"?

A free and appropriate public education for children with disabilities includes special education and related services that (1) are provided at public expense, under public supervision and direction, and without charge; (2) meet the standards of the State Board of Education and federal rules and regulations; (3) include preschool, elementary, or secondary school education; and (4) are provided in conformity with the Individualized Education Program as required by state and federal law.

20 U.S.C. 1401(9)

34 C.F.R. 300.101

34 C.F.R. 300.102

23 Ill. Admin. Code 226.50

Ross ex rel. Ross v. Board of Education of Township High School Dist. 211, 486 F. 3d 279 (7th Cir. 2007)

13:25 Is a school district required to maximize a student's educational benefit to meet the free and appropriate standard?

No. In meeting the free and appropriate standard a school district must provide the student with some educational benefit, but need not provide the optimum educational placement or deliver optimum educational services. The child's Individualized Education Program (IEP) must be reasonably calculated to enable the child to make progress in light of the child's circumstances. The "fact-intensive" process of reasonably calculating appropriateness requires the expertise of school officials with input of the child's parents or guardians. A child's IEP need not aim for grade-level advancement if that is not a reasonable prospect.

There is no requirement in the Individuals with Disabilities Education Act that a child be provided with religious or cultural instruction.

Endrew F. ex rel. Joseph F. v. Douglas County School District R.E. 1, 137 S. Ct. 988, __ U.S. __, 197 L. Ed 2d 335 (2017)

M.L. v. Smith, __ F. 3d __ (4th Cir. 2017)

M.B. ex rel. Berns v. Hamilton Southeastern Schools, 668 F. 3d 851 (7th Cir. 2011)

J.S.K. v. Hendry County School Board, 941 F. 2d 1563 (11th Cir. 1991)

Board of Education of Hendrick Hudson Central School District, Board of Education Westchester County v. Rowley, 102 S. Ct. 3034, 458 U.S. 176, 73 L. Ed. 2d 690 (1982)

13:30 Must school buildings and/or programs be accessible to handicapped persons?

The Rehabilitation Act requires program accessibility for handicapped persons. It mandates:

1) All new facilities must be constructed so as to be readily accessible and usable by handicapped persons.

2) Although every existing facility need not be totally physically accessible, programs must be accessible.

3) While flexibility is allowed in choosing methods that make programs in existing facilities accessible, structural changes in facilities must be undertaken if no other means of assuring program accessibility is available.

The Americans with Disabilities Act also contains requirements that apply to schools.

29 U.S.C. 701 et seq.

42 U.S.C. 12101 et seq.

71 Ill. Admin. Code 400.110 et seq.

71 Ill. Admin. Code 400.310

13:40 What is "mainstreaming"?

"Mainstreaming" is educational jargon for an application of the principle of "least restrictive environment." Mainstreaming is the placement of children with disabilities to the maximum extent appropriate, with children who do not have disabilities. Placement in special classes, separate schools, or other removal of children with disabilities from the regular educational environment may occur only when the nature or the severity of the disability is such that education in a regular class with the use of supplementary aids and services cannot be achieved satisfactorily.

20 U.S.C. 1412(a)(5)

34 C.F.R. 300.114 et seq.

105 ILCS 5/14-8.02

23 Ill. Admin. Code 226.75

Beth B. v. Clay, 282 F. 3d 493 (7th Cir. 2002) cert. den. 123 S. Ct. 412, 537 U.S. 948, 154 L. Ed. 2d 292 (2002)

Board of Education of Sacramento City School District v. Holland, 786 F. Supp. 874 (E.D. Cal. 1992)

Evans v. District No. 17 of Douglas County, 841 F. 2d 824 (8th Cir. 1988)

Martin v. School Board of Prince Georges County, 3 Va. App. 197, 348 S.E. 2d 857 (1986)

Community High School District No. 155 v. Denzby Veronico, 124 Ill. App. 3d 129, 463 N.E. 2d 998, 79 Ill. Dec. 444 (2nd Dist. 1984)

13:45 Under what conditions should a student with a disability be educated in a regular classroom?

A student with a disability must be educated in a regular classroom if the child can receive a satisfactory education in the class with the help of support services, even if the regular class is not the best academic setting for the child. The education of the child in a regular classroom is sometimes called "full inclusion." Four factors are considered in the placement analysis: academic benefits to the child, nonacademic benefits to the child, possible negative effects on other students, and cost to the school district.

34 C.F.R. 300.114 et seq.

Board of Education of Sacramento City School District v. Holland, 786 F. Supp. 874 (E.D. Cal. 1992)

Greer v. Rome City School District, 950 F. 2d 688 (11th Cir. 1991)

13:47 How are speech students counted in the computation of special education students in a regular education classroom?

With respect to any state statute or administrative rule that defines a general education classroom to be composed of a certain percentage of students with Individualized Education Programs (IEPs), that term excludes students receiving speech-only services outside of the general education classroom if the instruction the students receive in the general education classroom does not require modification.

105 ILCS 5/14-2

INDIVIDUALIZED EDUCATION PROGRAM

13:50 What is an Individualized Education Program (IEP)?

The term Individualized Education Program (IEP), means a written statement for each child with a disability that is developed, reviewed, and revised in accordance with special education law. The IEP statement must include the following:

1) A statement of the child's present levels of educational and functional performance, including how the child's disability affects the child's involvement and progress in the general curriculum; or for a preschool child, how the disability affects the child's participation in appropriate activities; or for children with disabilities who take alternate assessments aligned to alternate achievement standards, a description of benchmarks or short-term objectives.

2) A statement of measurable annual goals, including academic and functional goals, that reflect consideration of the State Goals for Learning and the Illinois Learning Standards, as well as benchmarks or short-term objectives developed in accordance with the child's present levels of educational performance, related to meeting the child's needs that result from the child's disability, to enable the child to be involved in and progress in the general curriculum or, for preschool children, to participate in activities appropriate to the child's age and meeting each of the child's other educational needs that result from the child's disability.

3) A description of how the child's progress toward his or her annual goals will be measured and when periodic progress reports toward meeting annual goals will be provided.

4) A statement of the special education and related services and supplementary aids and services, based on peer-reviewed research to the extent practicable, to be provided to the child, or on behalf of the child, in a statement of program modifications or supports for school personnel that will be provided for the child to advance appropriately toward attaining the annual goals; to be involved in and make progress in the general education curriculum and to participate in extracurricular and other non-academic activities; and to be educated and participate with other children with disabilities and non-disabled children in activities.

5) An explanation of the extent, if any, to which the child will not participate with non-disabled children in the regular class and in activities.

6) A statement of any individual appropriate accommodations that are necessary to measure the academic achievement and functional performance of the child on state and district wide assessments and if the IEP team determines that the child will take an alternative assessment on a particular state or district=wide assessment of student achievement, a statement of why the child cannot participate in regular assessment and the particular alternative assessment selected is appropriate for the child.

7) The projected date for the beginning of the services and modifications and the anticipated frequency, location, and duration of those services and modifications.

8) Beginning not later than the first IEP to be in effect when the child is 16, and updated annually thereafter, appropriate measurable post-secondary goals based upon age-appropriate transition assessments related to training, education, employment, and, where appropriate, independent living skills.

9) The transition services (including courses of study) needed to assist the child in reaching those post-secondary goals.

10) Beginning not later than one year before the child reaches the age of majority under state law, a statement that the child has been informed of the child's rights that will transfer to the child on reaching age 18, unless the child lacks capacity.

The IEP of a student who may, after reaching age 18, become eligible to participate in the home-based support services program for mentally disabled adults authorized by the Developmental Disability and Mental Disability Services Act [405 ILCS 80/2-1 et seq.] must set forth specific plans related to that program that conform to the requirements of Section 14-8.02 of the School Code.

An IEP commits the school district to its terms.

20 U.S.C. 1401(14)
20 U.S.C. 1414(d) et seq.
34 C.F.R. 300.22
34 C.F.R. 300.320 et seq.
105 ILCS 5/14-8.02
405 ILCS 80/0.01 et seq.
23 Ill. Admin. Code 226.230 et seq.

13:51 Do procedural flaws in an IEP require a finding that the IEP denied the child a free and appropriate education?

Procedural flaws will not require such finding unless the procedural inadequacies result in the loss of educational opportunity for the child.

Ross ex rel. Ross v. Board of Education of Township. High School Dist. 211, 486 F. 3d 279 (7th Cir. 2007)

13:52 What must be included in the IEP of a student who requires a behavioral intervention plan?

The IEP of a student who requires a behavioral intervention plan must summarize the findings of the functional behavioral assessment; summarize prior intervention(s) implemented; describe any behavioral intervention(s) to be used, including those aimed at developing or strengthening alternative or more appropriate behaviors; identify the measurable behavioral changes expected and method(s) of evaluation; identify a schedule for a review of the intervention's effectiveness; and identify provisions for communicating with the parents about their child's behavior and coordinating school-based and home-based interventions.

23 Ill. Admin. Code 226.230 b)

13:53 What must be considered in the development of an IEP for a student with autism?

In the development of the Individualized Education Program for a student who has a disability on the autism spectrum (which includes autistic disorder, Asperger's disorder, pervasive developmental disorder not otherwise specified, childhood disintegrative disorder, and Rett Syndrome, as defined in the Diagnostic and Statistical Manual of Mental Disorders, fourth edition (DSM-IV, 2000)), the IEP team must consider all of the following factors:

1) The verbal and nonverbal communication needs of the child;

2) The need to develop social interaction skills and proficiencies;

3) The needs resulting from the child's unusual responses to sensory experiences;

4) The needs resulting from resistance to environmental change or change in daily routines;

5) The needs resulting from engagement in repetitive activities and stereotyped movements;

6) The need for any positive behavioral interventions, strategies, and supports to address any behavioral difficulties resulting from autism spectrum disorder; and

7) Other needs resulting from the child's disability that impact progress in the general curriculum, including social and emotional development.

Hjortness ex rel. Hjortness v. Neenah Joint School Dist., 507 F. 3d 1060 (7th Cir. 2007)

13:54 What is an IEP team?

The term "Individualized Education Program team" means a group of individuals composed of

1) The parents of a child with a disability;

2) Not less than one regular education teacher of such child (if the child is, or may be, participating in the regular education environment);

3) Not less than one special education teacher, or where appropriate, not less than one special education provider of such child;

4) A representative of the local educational agency who is qualified to provide, or supervise the provision of, specially designed instruction to meet the unique needs of children with disabilities and is knowledgeable about the general education curriculum; and is knowledgeable about the availability of resources of the local educational agency;

5) An individual who can interpret the instructional implications of evaluation results, who may be a member of the team described in 2) through 4) above;

6) At the discretion of the parent or the agency, other individuals who have knowledge or special expertise regarding the child, including related services personnel as appropriate; and

7) Whenever appropriate, the child with a disability.

20 U.S.C. 1414(d)(1)(B)
34 C.F.R. 300.23

13:56 When may a member of the IEP team be absent from an IEP meeting?

A member of the IEP team is not required to attend an IEP meeting, in whole or in part, if the parent of a child with a disability and the local educational agency agree that the attendance of the member is not necessary because the member's area of the curriculum or related services is not being modified or discussed in the meeting

A member of the IEP team may be excused from attending an IEP meeting, in whole or in part, when the meeting involves a modification to or discussion of the member's area of the curriculum or related services, if the parent and the local educational agency consent to the excusal; and the member submits, in writing to the parent and the IEP team, input into the development of the IEP prior to the meeting.

A parent's agreement to the foregoing must be in writing.

20 U.S.C. 1414(d)(1) c)

Hjortness ex rel. Hjortness v. Neenah Joint School District, 507 F. 3d 1060 (7th Cir. 2007)

13:58 What must an IEP team consider in the development of an IEP?

In the development of the IEP, the team must consider

1) The strengths of the child;

2) The concerns of the parents for enhancing the education of their child;

3) The results of the initial evaluation or most recent evaluation of the child;

4) The academic, developmental, and functional needs of the child;

5) In the case of a child whose behavior impedes the child's learning or that of others, consider the use of positive behavioral interventions, and supports and other strategies to address that behavior;

6) In the case of a child with limited English proficiency, consider the language needs of the child as such needs relate to the child's IEP;

7) In the case of a child who is blind or visually impaired, provide for instruction in Braille and the use of Braille unless the IEP team determines, after an evaluation of the child's reading and writing skills, needs, and appropriate reading and writing media (including an evaluation of the child's future needs for instruction in Braille or the use of Braille), that instruction in Braille or the use of Braille is not appropriate for the child;

8) Consider the communication needs of the child, and in the case of a child who is deaf or hard of hearing, consider the child's language and communication needs, opportunities for direct communications with peers and professional personnel in the child's language and communication mode, academic level, and full range of

needs, including opportunities for direct instruction in the child's language and communication mode; and

9) Consider whether the child needs assistive technology devices and services.

To be substantively appropriate, the IEP must be formulated so that the child would receive the basic floor of opportunity consisting of access to specialized instruction and related services which are individually designed to provide educational benefit to the child.

When a child has been educated in another school district or private placement, it is appropriate for the new IEP to contain substantially similar goals and objectives as were contained in the preceding IEP.

20 U.S.C. 1414(d)(3)

Marshall Joint School District No. 2 v. C.D. ex rel. Brian D., 618 F. 3d 632 (7th Cir. 2010)

Hjortness ex rel. Hjortness v. Neenah Joint School Dist., 507 F. 3d 1060 (7th Cir. 2007)

13:60 May a school district excuse a child from physical education if the student is eligible for special education?

If a student is between grades 3-12, is eligible for special education, and the student's parent or guardian agrees that the student must utilize the time set aside for physical education to receive special education support and services, then the student may be excused from physical education.

If there is no agreement between the parent or guardian and the IEP team, but the Individualized Education Program team determines that the student must utilize the time set aside for physical education for special education support and services, then the finding (or agreement) must be made a part of the student's Individualized Education Program.

A student requiring adapted physical education must receive that service in accordance with the IEP developed for the pupil.

105 ILCS 5/27-6(b)

Marshall Joint School District No. 2 v. C.D., et. al, 618 F. 3d 632 (7th Cir. 2010)

ELIGIBILITY FOR SPECIAL EDUCATION

13:64 When does a school district's obligation to provide special education to a disabled child end?

The protections of "stay put" and all other special education entitlements (except remedial orders for compensatory education) cease when a child reaches the age of 21 under federal law. In 2007, Illinois extended the educational obligation of Illinois school districts for an additional year (through the age of 21, which means the day before the student's 22nd birthday).

Board of Education of Oak Park and River Forest High School District v. Illinois State Board of Education, 79 F. 3d 654 (7th Cir. 1996)

13:70 For which children must a public school district provide special education?

Every public school district must provide special education facilities and programs to all children between the ages of 3-21 (the day before the student's 22nd birthday) who are enrolled in schools geographically located in the district or who are residents of the school district who are found to require special education services and including students who have been suspended or expelled from school.

Under most circumstances a school district is responsible for the delivery of special education to children enrolled in schools geographically located in the district, including those who are enrolled in nonpublic schools or are wards of the state, and children who are living in orphanages, foster homes, children's homes, and state housing units.

20 U.S.C. 1412(a)(1)(A)

34 C.F.R. 300.8

34 C.F.R. 300.111

105 ILCS 5/14-1.02

105 ILCS 5/14-7.03

23 Ill. Admin. Code 226.50

Nickerson v. Thompson, 504 F. 2d 813 (7th Cir. 1974)

13:71 How is the resident district determined when there is a question where the parents of the special education student reside?

Resident district determinations had broader significance under the law before the most recent reauthorization of the Individuals with Disabilities Education Act. The resident district is the one in which the parent or guardian, or both parent and guardian of the student reside when

1) The parent has legal guardianship of the student and resides within Illinois; or

2) An individual guardian who resides in Illinois has been appointed by the courts; or

3) An Illinois public agency has legal guardianship and the student resides either in the home of the parent or within the same district as the parent; or

4) An Illinois court orders residential placement but the parents retain any legal rights or guardianship and have not been subject to a termination of parental rights order.

In cases of divorced or separated parents, when only one parent has legal guardianship or custody, the district in which the parent having legal guardianship or custody resides is the resident district. When both parents retain legal guardianship or custody, the resident district is the district of the parent who claims the child as a dependent on his or her federal income tax return.

When the parent or individual who has legal guardianship lives outside Illinois, the parent, legal guardian, or placing agent must make arrangements to provide reimbursement to the Illinois school district.

105 ILCS 5/14-1.11

13:72 When is the school district in which the student resides the resident district?

Resident district determinations had broader significance under the law before the most recent reauthorization of the Individuals with Disabilities Education Act. Under state law, the resident district is the school district in which the student resides when

1) The parent has legal guardianship but the location of the parent is unknown;

2) An individual guardian has been appointed but the location of the guardian is unknown;

3) The student is 18 years of age or older and no legal guardian has been appointed;

4) The student is legally an emancipated minor; or

5) An Illinois public agency has legal guardianship and such agency or any court in the state has placed the student residentially outside the school district in which the parent lives.

In cases where an Illinois public agency has legal guardianship and has placed the student residentially outside of Illinois, the last school district that provided at least 45 days of educational service to the student continues to be the district of residence until the student is no longer under guardianship of an Illinois public agency or until the student is returned to Illinois.

The residence of a homeless student is the Illinois district in which the student enrolls for educational services.

105 ILCS 5/14-1.11a

13:80 How is a child's eligibility for special education programs and services determined?

A free and appropriate public education must be available to all children with disabilities. Children are eligible for special education if a determination of eligibility results from a case study reviewed by professional personnel in a multidisciplinary staff conference and after recommendation of qualified specialists.

20 U.S.C. 1400 et seq.
34 C.F.R. 300.101
105 ILCS 5/14-8.02
23 Ill. Admin. Code 226.50
Max M. v. Illinois State Board of Education, 585 F. Supp. 317, on reconsideration 629 F. Supp. 1504 (N.D. Ill. 1984)
Max M. v. Thompson, 585 F. Supp. 317, on reconsideration 592 F. Supp. 1437 (N.D. Ill. 1984)

13:85 When must special education services be provided?

Special education and related services must be provided in accordance with the student's IEP no later than 10 school attendance days after notice is provided to the parents.

34 C.F.R. 300.503
105 ILCS 5/14-8.02(b)

13:90 Who are "children with specific learning disabilities?"

"Children with specific learning disabilities" means children between the ages of 3 and 21 years who have a disorder in one or more of the basic psychological processes involved in understanding or in using language, spoken or written, that may manifest itself in imperfect ability to listen, think, speak, read, write, spell, or do mathematical calculations. Such disorders include conditions such as perceptual disabilities, brain injury, minimal brain dysfunction, dyslexia, and developmental aphasia.

An eligible student who requires continued public school educational experience to facilitate his or her successful transition and integration into adult life is eligible for such services through age 21, inclusive, which means the day before the student's 22nd birthday. The term does not include children who have learning problems that are primarily the result of visual, hearing, or motor disabilities; of an intellectual disability; emotional disturbance; or environmental, cultural, or economic disadvantage.

20 U.S.C. 1401(30)
105 ILCS 5/2-3.161
105 ILCS 5/14-1.03a
105 ILCS 5/14-1.02
23 Ill. Admin. Code 226.75

13:95 What is meant by "children with disabilities" as defined by The Individuals with Disabilities Education Act?

"Children with disabilities" is defined as children with intellectual disabilities; hearing impairments (including deafness); speech or language impairments; visual impairments (including blindness); serious emotional disturbance; orthopedic impairments; autism; traumatic brain injury; other health impairments or specific learning disabilities; and who by reason thereof need special education and related services.

20 U.S.C. 1401(3)
105 ILCS 5/14-1.02
23 Ill. Admin. Code 226.75

13:96 What is meant by "children with disabilities" for children aged 3 to 9 years as defined by The Individuals with Disabilities Education Act?

"Children with disabilities" for children aged 3 to 9 may include, at the discretion of the state and the local school district, children with developmental delays as defined by the state and as measured by appropriate diagnostic instruments and procedures in one or more of the following areas: physical development, cognitive development, communication development, social or emotional development, or adaptive development; and who by reason thereof need special education and related services.

20 U.S.C. 1401 (3)(B)

13:100 Do children with Acquired Immune Deficiency Syndrome (AIDS) or other serious illnesses qualify for special education?

The Individuals with Disabilities Education Act applies to AIDS victims or to other children with serious medical conditions only if their physical condition is such that it adversely affects their educational performance.

Robertson by Robertson v. Granite City Community Unit School District No. 9, 684 F. Supp. 1002 (S.D. Ill. 1988)

Doe by Doe v. Belleville Public School District No. 118, 672 F. Supp. 342 (S.D. Ill. 1987)

13:110 Are school districts required to provide special education services to eligible students who reside in the school district but who attend nonpublic schools?

The school district has the obligation to identify and provide services to all students who are in need of special education and related services, including students who are homeless, wards of the state, or attend private, parochial, or home schools.

A school board is required to accept for part-time attendance eligible children with disabilities who are enrolled in nonpublic schools located geographically within the district. Transportation for students in part-time attendance must be provided only if required in the child's Individualized Education Program on the basis of the child's disabling condition or as the location of the special education program may require.

20 U.S.C. 1412(3)
20 U.S.C. 1412(10)
34 C.F.R. 300.130 et seq.
105 ILCS 5/14-6.01
23 Ill. Admin. Code 226.100

13:114 May a school district provide special education services on site at a parochial school?

Yes. However:

1) Only public employees can deliver the services;

2) Assignment of public employees should be made without regard to the religious affiliation of the employee;

3) All religious symbols should be removed from the private school classroom where services are to be delivered;

4) Consultations between the public school teacher and the private school teacher should be limited to mutual concerns regarding the students' public education; and

5) There should be monitoring of the program for separation of religious and secular purposes.

Helms v. Picard, 151 F. 3d 347 (5th Cir. 1999)

Agostini v. Felton, 117 S. Ct. 1997, 521 U.S. 203, 138 L. Ed. 2d 391 (1997)

SPECIAL PROGRAMS AND SERVICES

13:120 What special education facilities and services must school districts provide for qualified students with disabilities?

Special educational facilities and services include special schools; special classes; special housing, including residential facilities; special instruction; special reader service; braillists and typists for visually disabled children; sign language interpreters; transportation; maintenance; instructional material; physical and/or occupational therapy; professional consultant services; medical services only for diagnostic and evaluation purposes provided by a physician licensed to practice medicine in all its branches to determine a child's need for special education and related services; psychological services; school social worker services; special administrative services; salaries of all required special personnel; and other special educational services, including special equipment for use in the classroom required by the child because of his or her disability if such services or special equipment are approved by the State Superintendent of Education and the child is eligible under the regulations of the State Board of Education.

105 ILCS 5/14-1.08

105 ILCS 5/10-20.60

13:140 What are "related services" in the context of special education?

"Related services" means transportation and such developmental, corrective, and other supportive services (including speech-language pathology and audiology services, interpreting services, psychological services, physical and occupational therapy, recreation, including therapeutic recreation, social work services, school nurse services designed to enable a child with a disability to receive a free appropriate public education as described in the child's IEP, counseling services, including rehabilitation counseling, orientation and mobility services, and medical services, except that such medical services shall be for diagnostic and evaluation purposes only, as may be required to assist a child with a disability to benefit from special education and includes the early identification and assessment of handicapping conditions in children.

It is unsettled law, but it may be possible for a school district to argue undue burden in an attempt to avoid providing certain related medical services.

20 U.S.C. 1401(26)

34 C.F.R. 300.34

23 Ill. Admin. Code 226.310

Jenna R.P. v. City of Chicago School District No. 299, 2013 IL App (1st) 112247, 3 N.E. 3d 927, 378 Ill. Dec. 362

Stratham School District v. Beth P., 2003 WL 260728 (D. N.H., Feb 05, 2003)

Cedar Rapids Community School District v. Garret F ex rel. Charlene F, 119 S. Ct. 992, 526 U.S. 66, 143 L. Ed. 2d 154 (1999)

Morton Community Unit School District No. 709 v. J.M., 152 F. 3d 583 (7th Cir. 1998) cert. den. 119 S. Ct. 1140, 526 U.S. 1004, 143 L. Ed. 2d 208 (1999)

Irving Independent School District v. Tatro, 104 S. Ct. 3371, 468 U.S. 883, 82 L. Ed. 2d 664 (1984), on rem. 741 F. 2d 82 (1984)

13:143 What is a service animal?

Service animals, such as guide dogs, signal dogs, or any other animal individually trained to perform tasks for the benefit of a student with a disability, must be permitted to accompany that student at all school functions whether in or outside the classroom.

In 2012, perhaps because of a legislative error, Illinois repealed the Service Animal Access Act. It is unlikely the outcome of a service animal case will be affected by the repeal.

105 ILCS 5/14-6.02

720 ILCS 5/48-8

K.D. ex rel. Nichelle D. v. Villa Grove Community Unit School District No. 302, 403 Ill. App. 3d 1082, 936 N.E. 690, 344 Ill. Dec. 161 (4th Dist. 2010)

Kalbfleisch v. Columbia Community Unit School District No. 4, 396 Ill. App. 3d 1105, 920 N.E. 2d 651, 336 Ill. Dec.442 (5th Dist. 2009)

13:145 What are supplementary aids and services?

Supplementary aids and services are aids, services, and other supports that are provided in regular education classes or other education-related settings to enable children with disabilities to be educated with non-disabled children to the maximum extent appropriate under special education law.

20 U.S.C. 1401(33)

34 C.F.R. 300.42

13:150 Under what circumstances must a school district provide a child with a disability with medical services?

A school district is not required to provide special education students with medical services except for purposes of diagnosis or evaluation. Related services do not include those performed by licensed physicians or dentists (except for diagnostic or evaluative services or consultation to staff), registered or licensed practical nurses (except when functioning as school nurses), or other medical personnel involved in the provision of ongoing medical care.

Medically related services that could be provided by a nurse or a trained layperson that are necessary to permit a student to benefit from special education must be provided.

Beginning in 2013 a nurse who conducts a medical review of a student must have a school service personnel license endorsed for school nursing, a license endorsed to practice medicine in all its branches or a bachelor's degree or higher and a license issued under the Nurse Practice Act. Only a school nurse who holds a school service personnel license endorsed for school nursing (a licensed school nurse) can make recommendations regarding educational interventions, accommodations, or modifications to a student's IEP based on the findings of the student's medical review.

34 C.F.R. 300.34

105 ILCS 5/10-22.21b

225 ILCS 60/1 et seq.

225 ILCS 65/50-1 et seq.

23 Ill. Admin. Code 25.245

23 Ill. Admin. Code 226.840

Morton Community Unit School District No. 709 v. J.M., 152 F. 3d 583 (7th Cir. 1998) cert. den. 119 S. Ct. 1140, 526 U.S. 1004, 143 L. Ed. 2d 208 (1999)

Cedar Rapids Community School District v. Garret F ex rel. Charlene F, 119 S. Ct. 992, 526 U.S. 66, 143 L. Ed. 2d 154 (1999)

Bevin H. by Michael H. v. Wright, 666 F. Supp. 71 (W.D. Pa. 1987)

Irving Independent School District v. Tatro, 104 S. Ct. 3371, 468 U.S. 883, 82 L. Ed. 2d 664 (1984), on rem. 741 F. 2d 82 (1984)

Max M. v. Illinois State Board of Education, 585 F. Supp. 317, on reconsideration 629 F. Supp. 1504 (N.D. Ill. 1984)

Max M. v. Thompson, 585 F. Supp. 317, on reconsideration 592 F. Supp. 1437 (N.D. Ill. 1984)

Darlene L. v. Illinois State Board of Education, 568 F. Supp. 1340 (N.D. Ill. 1983)

T.G. on Behalf of D.G. v. Board of Education of Piscataway, New Jersey, 576 F. Supp. 420 (D.C. N.J. 1983) aff'd. 738 F. 2d 420, cert. den. 105 S. Ct. 592, 469 U.S. 1086, 83 L. Ed. 2d 701 (1984)

13:153 What is a medical review?

A medical review is the ongoing assessment of a student's medical and health status that determines whether the student's health is adversely affecting educational performance. A student who is being evaluated or re-evaluated must be provided assessment in all areas related to the student's suspected disability including, if appropriate, health, vision, and hearing. The assessment must also be sufficiently comprehensive to identify all the child's needs for special education and related services.

34 C.F.R. 300.34

34 C.F.R. 300.304

13:155 When must a school district provide home or hospital instruction?

A child qualifies for home or hospital instruction if it is anticipated that, due to a medical condition, the child will be unable to attend school, and instead must be taught at home or in the hospital for a period of two or more consecutive weeks or on an ongoing intermittent basis. "Ongoing intermittent basis" means that the child's medical condition is of such a nature or severity that it is anticipated that the child will be absent from school due to the medical condition for periods of at least two days at a time, multiple times during the school year totaling at least 10 days or more of absences.

There must be no requirement that a child be absent from school a minimum number of days before the child qualifies for home or hospital instruction. In order to establish eligibility for home or hospital services, a student's parent or guardian must submit to the child's school district of residence a written statement from a physician licensed to practice medicine in all of its branches, licensed physician assistant, or licensed advanced practice nurse stating the existence of such medical condition, the impact on the child's ability to participate in education, and the anticipated duration or nature of the child's absence from school. Home or hospital instruction may begin upon receipt of a written physician's statement, but instruction must begin not later than five school days after the school district receives the physician's statement.

Special education and related services required by the child's IEP or services and accommodations required by the child's federal Section 504 plan must be implemented as part of the child's home or hospital instruction, unless the IEP team or federal Section 504 plan team determines that modifications are necessary during the home or hospital instruction due to the child's condition

105 ILCS 5/10-22.6a

105 ILCS 5/14-13.01

13:160 Must a school district provide an interpreter for a deaf student?

If the child's Individualized Education Program (IEP) requires an interpreter, an interpreter must be provided at school district expense.

23 Ill. Admin. Code 226.310

Zobrest v. Catalina Foothills School District, 113 S. Ct. 2462, 506 U.S. 813, 125 L. Ed. 2d 1 (1993)

Board of Education of Hendrick Hudson Central School District, Board of Education Westchester County v. Rowley, 102 S. Ct. 3034, 458 U.S. 176, 73 L. Ed. 2d 690 (1982)

13:161 Must a school district provide an on-site interpreter, teaching aide, or consultant teacher on private school grounds?

No. Provided the school district provides an opportunity for the student to receive a free appropriate public education, it has met its obligation. A school district must expend an "amount equal to a proportionate amount of federal funds" to educate such students.

20 U.S.C. 1412(a)(10)(A) et seq.

105 ILCS 5/14-6.01

23 Ill. Admin. Code 226.300 et seq.

Celafu on Behalf of Celafu v. East Baton Rouge Parish School Board, 907 F. Supp. 966, vac. 103 F. 3d 393, opinion withdrawn and superseded on reh. 117 F. 3d 231, rev. 117 F. 3d 231 (5th Cir. 1997)

Board of Education of Enlarged City School District of the City of Watervliet v. Russman, 117 S. Ct. 2502, 521 U.S. 111, 138 L. Ed. 2d 1008 (1997)

Unified School District No. 259 v. Fowler and Fowler v. Unified School District No. 259, 117 S. Ct. 2503, 521 U.S. 1115, 138 L. Ed. 2d 1008 (1997)

13:165 What are transition services?

"Transition services" means a coordinated set of activities for a child with a disability that (i) is designed to be within a results-oriented process that is focused on improving the academic and functional achievement of the child with a disability to facilitate the child's movement from school to post-school activities, including post-secondary education, vocational education, integrated employment (including supported employment), continuing and adult education, adult services, independent living, or community participation; (ii) is based on the individual child's needs, taking into account the child's strengths, preferences, and interests; and (iii) includes instruction, related services, community experiences, the development of employment and other post-school adult living objectives, and, if appropriate, acquisition of daily living skills, benefits planning, work incentives education, and the provision of a functional vocational evaluation.

Transition services for a child with a disability may be special education if provided as specially designed instruction or a related service if required to assist a child with a disability to benefit from special education.

20 U.S.C. 1401(34)

34 C.F.R. 300.34

105 ILCS 5/10-20.31

105 ILCS 5/14-8.03

23 Ill. Admin. Code 226.75

13:167 When must transition services begin?

Transition services must begin no later than the first Individualized Education Program (IEP) in effect when the student turns age 14 1/2 (or younger if determined appropriate by the IEP team) and must be updated annually thereafter. The IEP must include (i) measurable post-secondary goals based upon age-appropriate transition assessments and other information available regarding the student that are related to training, education, employment, and, where appropriate, independent living skills and (ii) the transition services needed to assist the student in reaching those goals, including courses of study.

Transition services end when the student leaves school or when the student's eligibility for services ends due to age.

105 ILCS 5/14-8.03

13:170 What special training is required of persons employed to work in special education programs?

No person may be employed to teach any class or program in special education who does not hold a valid teaching certificate as provided by law and unless he or she has had special training as the State Board of Education may require. All other professional personnel employed in any class, service, or program authorized by law must hold the certificate and shall have received such training as the State Board of Education may require.

A school board may employ necessary workers to assist properly certified teachers with the special education facilities, but such workers must have training prescribed by the State Board of Education.

105 ILCS 5/14-9.01

EVALUATION AND PLACEMENT

13:190 What is the definition of "evaluation" in the context of special education?

"Evaluation" means procedures used in accordance with federal and state regulations to determine whether a child has a disability and the nature and extent of the special education and related services the child needs.

20 U.S.C. 1414 (a)(1) et seq.

34 C.F.R. 300.15

34 C.F.R. 300.301

105 ILCS 5/14-8.02(b)

23 Ill. Admin. Code 226.75

23 Ill. Admin. Code 226.130

Jamie S. v. Milwaukee Public Schools, 668 F. 3d 481 (7th Cir. 2012)

13:200 Who may refer a child for a special education evaluation?

A referral may be made by any concerned person, including but not limited to school district personnel, the parent of a child, an employee of a community service agency, another professional having knowledge of a child's problems, a child, or an employee of the State Board of Education.

23 Ill. Admin. Code 226.110 b)

13:210 How often must a special education student be reevaluated?

A school district must reevaluate an eligible child when the local educational agency determines that the educational or related service needs, including improved academic achievement and functional performance, of the child warrant a reevaluation or if the child's parents or teacher request a reevaluation.

A reevaluation must not occur more frequently than once a year, unless the parent and the local educational agency agree otherwise and at least once every three years unless the parent and the local educational agency agree that a reevaluation is unnecessary.

The district must reevaluate an eligible child before determining that the child is no longer eligible for special education services. A reevaluation is not required for a student who graduates from high school with a regular high school diploma or its equivalent or attains the age of 21. The educational status and continued special education placement of each child must be reviewed at least annually in a conference attended by those professionals working with the student, the parents, the child when appropriate, the special education director or designee who is qualified to supervise the provision of special education, and others at the discretion of the parent or school district.

20 U.S.C. 1414(a)(2)
34 C.F.R. 300.303
23 Ill. Admin Code 226.120

13:213 How are mid-year changes made in an IEP?

Changes to an IEP may be made either by the entire IEP team, or by the local education agency and the parent by written agreement. In either case, upon request, the parent must be provided with a revised copy of the IEP with the changes incorporated.

20 U.S.C. 1414(d)(3)(D)
20 U.S.C. 1414(d)(3)(F)
34 C.F.R. 300.324
34 C.F.R. 300.328

13:215 Does a special education student's Individualized Education Program (IEP) necessarily follow him or her from elementary school to high school?

When a special education student reaches 14 1/2 years old, the elementary district in which the student resides must notify the high school district in which the student resides of the student's special education eligibility, program, and evaluation data. The high school district may accept the current placement or may elect to conduct its own evaluation and multidisciplinary conference and formulate its own IEP.

105 ILCS 5/14-6.01

13:216 What happens to the IEP of a child who transfers from one school district to another?

When a child transfers within the same academic year, who enrolls in a new school, and who had an IEP that was in effect in the same state, the local educational agency shall provide the child with a free appropriate public education, including services comparable to those described in the previously held IEP, in consultation with the parents until such time as the local educational agency adopts the previously held IEP or develops, adopts, and implements a new IEP that is consistent with federal and state law. When a child transfers school districts within the same academic year, who enrolls in a new school, and who had an IEP that was in effect in another state, the local educational agency in addition to doing everything that is required in the case of an in-state transfer may, if necessary, conduct an evaluation.

The new school in which the child enrolls must take reasonable steps to promptly obtain the child's records, including the IEP and supporting documents and any other records relating to the provision of special education or related services to the child, from the previous school in which the child was enrolled and the previous school in which the child was enrolled must take reasonable steps to promptly respond to such request from the new school.

20 U.S.C. 1414(d)(2)(C)
23 Ill. Admin. Code 226.50 a)

13:220 When is a special education student eligible for placement in a residential facility?

When a residential placement for educational purposes is considered, the necessity for the placement must be individually based upon evidence the student's needs are so profound or unusual that his or her educational needs cannot be met in a less restrictive placement. The evidence from recent diagnostic assessments and other pertinent information must indicate that, while the student can benefit from instructional services, he or she is so severely disabled his or her educational needs cannot be met in a less restrictive environment.

If there is evidence of a condition that presents a danger to the physical well-being of the student or to other students, the evidence may be considered a factor in making a residential placement.

23 Ill. Admin. Code 226.330

Jenna R..P. v. City of Chicago School District No. 299, 2013 IL App (1st) 112247, 3 N.E. 3d 927, 378 Ill. Dec. 362

Vander Malle v. Ambach, 667 F. Supp. 1015 (S.D. N.Y. 1987)

Cochran v. District of Columbia, 660 F. Supp. 314, (D.C. D.C. 1987)

Christopher T. by Brogna v. San Francisco Unified School District, 553 F. Supp. 1107 (N.D. Cal. 1982)

RIGHTS OF CHILDREN AND PARENTS

13:230 What notice must a school board publish concerning the education of children with disabilities residing in the district?

A school board must publish a public notice regarding the right of all children with disabilities to a free and appropriate public education. The notice must be published in a school district newsletter of general circulation or in the newsletter of another governmental entity of general circulation in the district or, if neither is available in the district, in a newspaper of general circulation in the district.

The notice must identify the location and phone number of the office or agent of the school district to whom inquiries should be directed regarding the identification, assessment, and placement of such children. A school board must provide, upon request, written materials and other information that indicates the specific policies, procedures, rules, and regulations regarding the identification, evaluation, or educational placement of children with disabilities. Such information shall include all rights and entitlements of such children and of the opportunity to present complaints with respect to any matter relating to educational placement of the student, or the provision of a free and appropriate public education, and to have an impartial due process hearing on the complaint. The notice must inform the parents or guardian in the parents' or guardian's native language, unless it is clearly not feasible to do so, of their rights and all procedures available.

The notice shall also inform the parents or guardian of the availability upon request of a list of free or low-cost legal and other relevant services available locally to assist parents or guardians in exercising their entitlements under the School Code.

105 ILCS 5/14-6.01

13:235 Do the parents of a special education student have rights under IDEA?

Parents of special education children have rights that are independent of those of their children, and those rights are enforceable under the Individuals with Disabilities Education Act. Parents have the right to participate not only in the implementation of IDEA's procedures, but also in the substantive formation of their child's educational program. Because parents enjoy rights under IDEA, they are entitled to prosecute IDEA claims on their own behalf.

Winkelman ex rel. Winkelman v. Parma City School District, 127 S. Ct. 1994, 550 U.S. 516 , 167 L. Ed. 2d 904 (2007)

13:240 Must a school district obtain parental consent before conducting a special education evaluation of a student?

A school district proposing to conduct an initial evaluation to determine if a child qualifies for special education must obtain informed parental consent before conducting the evaluation. Parental consent for evaluation is not consent for placement for receipt of special education or related services.

If the parent does not provide consent for an initial evaluation or the parent fails to respond to a request to provide the consent, the local educational agency may pursue the initial evaluation of the child by using due process procedures. If the parent refuses to consent, the local educational agency is barred from providing special education and related services to the child (no due process is available).

20 U.S.C. 1414(a)(1)(D)
20 U.S.C. 1415
34 C.F.R. 300.9
34 C.F.R. 300.300
105 ILCS 5/14-8.02
23 Ill. Admin. Code 226.110 d)
23 Ill. Admin. Code 226.570

13:250 If the school district has obtained a proper parental consent for a special education evaluation, must the school district obtain another parental consent for any reevaluation?

Yes.

20 U.S.C. 1414(a)(1)(D)(2)
105 ILCS 5/14-8.02(b)
23 Ill. Admin. Code 226.540

13:255 Under what circumstances must experts or parents be permitted to observe special education students or programs?

A qualified professional is an individual who holds credentials to evaluate the child in the domain or domains for which an evaluation is sought or an intern working under the direct supervision of a qualified professional, including a master's or doctoral degree candidate.

To ensure that a parent can participate fully and effectively with school personnel in the development of appropriate educational and related services for his or her child, the parent, an independent educational evaluator, or a qualified professional retained by or on behalf of a parent or child must be afforded reasonable access to educational facilities, personnel, classrooms, and buildings and to the child. These requirements apply to any public school facility, building, or program and to any facility, building, or program supported in whole or in part by public funds.

Prior to visiting a school, school building, or school facility, the parent, independent educational evaluator, or qualified professional may be required by the school district to inform the building principal or supervisor in writing of the proposed visit, the purpose of the visit, and the approximate duration of the visit. The visitor and the school district must arrange the visit or visits at times that are mutually agreeable.

Visitors must comply with school safety, security, and visitation policies at all times. Visitors must be required to comply with the requirements of applicable privacy laws, including those laws protecting the confidentiality of education records. The visitor must not disrupt the educational process.

A parent must be afforded reasonable access of sufficient duration and scope for the purpose of observing his or her child in the child's current educational placement, services, or program or for the purpose of visiting an educational placement or program proposed for the child.

An independent educational evaluator or a qualified professional retained by or on behalf of a parent or child must be afforded reasonable access of sufficient duration and scope for the purpose of conducting an evaluation of the child; the child's performance; the child's current educational program, placement, services, or environment; or any educational program, placement, services, or environment proposed for the child, including interviews of educational personnel; child observations; assessments; tests or assessments of the child's educational program, services, or placement; or of any proposed educational program, services, or placement.

If one or more interviews of school personnel are part of the evaluation, the interviews must be conducted at a mutually agreed-upon time, date, and place that do not interfere with the school employee's school duties. The school district may limit interviews to personnel having information relevant to the child's current educational services, program, or placement or to a proposed educational service, program, or placement.

105 ILCS 5/14-8.02(g-5)

13:260 May parents challenge the conclusions and recommendations of a multidisciplinary staff conference?

Yes. At the conclusion of the multidisciplinary staff conference, the parent or guardian of the child must be given a copy of the multidisciplinary conference summary report and recommendations, including options considered, and must be informed of their right to obtain an independent educational evaluation if they disagree with the findings. If the school district's evaluation is shown to be inappropriate, the school district must reimburse the parent for the cost of the independent evaluation.

The State Board of Education supplies school districts with a list of suggested independent evaluators and must make the list available to parents at their request. A school district must make the list available to parents at the time they are informed of their right to obtain an independent educational evaluation. However, a school district may initiate an impartial due process hearing within five days of any written parent or guardian request for an independent educational evaluation to show that its evaluation is appropriate. If the final decision is the evaluation is appropriate, the parent retains the right to an independent educational evaluation, but not at public expense.

An independent educational evaluation at public expense must be completed within 30 days of a parent or guardian's written request unless the school district initiates an impartial due process hearing or the parent or guardian or school district offers reasonable grounds to show that the 30-day time period should be extended. If the due process hearing decision indicates the parent or guardian is entitled to an independent educational evaluation, it must be completed within 30 days of the decision unless the parent or guardian or the school district offers reasonable grounds to show the 30-day period should be extended.

If a parent disagrees with the summary report or recommendations of the multidisciplinary conference or the findings of any educational evaluation that results therefrom, the school district cannot proceed with a placement based upon the evaluation and the child must remain in his or her regular classroom setting or other current placement.

34 C.F.R. 300.502
105 ILCS 5/14-8.02
23 Ill. Admin. Code 226.180

13:264 May a non-custodial parent have input on a special education decision?

The Individuals with Disabilities Education Act grants rights to "parents," and the regulatory definition of "parent" includes all biological parents, which implies that a divorced parent may retain some statutory rights. In the instance of a divorce, the order granting the divorce and defining the rights of the parties regarding custody (and later modifications) will serve to define the rights of the custodial and non-custodial biological parents.

In joint custody, joint decision-making situations, the parents have rights with respect to special education decision-making similar to those of married couples. In the instance of non-joint custody situations, usually one parent has final decision-making authority and the other has specified lesser rights.

Even a non-custodial parent probably retains some authority that must be respected as conditions precedent to any decision requiring parental consent. Ultimately, however, if the divorced parents without joint custody disagree about educational decisions, then the view of the parent with educational decision-making authority prevails as the parental position.

Navin v. Park Ridge School District No. 64, 270 F. 3d 1147 (7th Cir. 2001)

13:270 What right of review exists if the parents and the school district fail to agree on an appropriate special education placement for a particular child?

A parent, a school district, or a student may request an impartial due process hearing for any reason connected to the identification, evaluation, or placement of, or the provision of services to, a student who is or may be eligible for services. No other party has standing.

20 U.S.C. 1414(f)

34 C.F.R. 300.500 et seq.

105 ILCS 5/14-8.02(h)

105 ILCS 5/14-8.02a

13:275 Is parental hostility to a school district's proposed educational placement an appropriate factor to consider when analyzing the placement's expected educational benefits?

Yes, although hostility is a fact question that may be rebutted with evidence to the contrary at hearing.

Board of Education of Community Consolidated School District 21 v. Brozer, 938 F. 2d 712 (7th Cir. 1991)

13:278 May parents insist on a date and time for IEP meetings?

IEP meetings must be scheduled at a mutually agreeable time and place. Mutual agreement does not allow one party to dictate that a meeting be held at a particular time or place.

34 C.F.R. 300.322(a)(2)

B.H. by her mother and next friend, S.H. v. Joliet School District No. 86, No. 08 C 4974 (March 19, 2010)

13:280 Is a school district required to permit parental involvement in formulating and implementing an Individualized Education Program (IEP)?

Parents must be given, on an ongoing basis, reasonable opportunity for comment on and input into their child's educational program.

23 Ill. Admin. Code 226.210

Dellmuth v. Muth, 109 S. Ct. 2397, 491 U.S. 223, 105 L. Ed. 2d 181 (1989) on rem. sub nom.

Muth v. Central Bucks School District, 884 F. 2d 1384 (3rd Cir. 1989)

Muth v. Central Bucks School District, 839 F. 2d 113 (3rd Cir. 1988) cert. den. 109 S. Ct. 103, cert. granted 109 S. Ct. 52, rev. sub nom. on other grounds

13:285 How does a special education student who attains majority obtain the right to makes his or her own educational decisions?

When a student who is eligible for special education (including those who are incarcerated in a state or local correctional institution) reaches the age of 18 years, all rights accorded to the student's parents transfer to the student except as otherwise detailed below. Nothing in the law prevents a student with a disability who has reached majority age the right to have an adult of his or her choice, including, but not limited to, the student's parent, assist the student in making decisions regarding the student's Individualized Education Program.

Each school district must notify the student and the student's parents of the transfer of rights in writing at a meeting convened to review the student's Individualized Education Program during the school year in which the student turns 17 years of age. At that time, the school district must provide the student with a copy of the Delegation of Rights form described in Section 14-6.10 of the School Code. The school district must mail the notice and a copy of the Delegation of Rights form to the student and to the student's parents, addressed to their last known address, if they do not attend the meeting.

Rights shall not transfer from the parents to the student if either of the following apply:

1) The student with a disability who has reached the age of majority has been adjudged incompetent under state law; or

2) The student has not been adjudged incompetent under state law, but the student has executed a delegation of rights to make educational decisions in a form set forth in the law for the purpose of appointing the student's parent or other adult to represent the educational interests of the student.

A student may terminate the delegation of rights at any time and assume the right to make decisions regarding his or her education. The delegation of rights must meet all of the following requirements:

1) It shall remain in effect for one year after the date of execution, but may be renewed annually with the

written or other formal authorization of the student and the person the student delegates to represent the educational interests of the student;

2) It shall be signed by the student or verified by other means, such as audio or video or other alternative format compatible with the student's disability showing that the student has agreed to the terms of the delegation.

3) It shall be signed or otherwise manifest verification that the designee accepts the delegation.

4) It shall include declarations that the student is 18 years of age or older, intends to delegate his or her educational rights under federal and state law to a specified individual who is at least 18 years of age, has not been adjudged incompetent under state law, is entitled to be present during the development of the student's Individualized Education Program and to raise issues or concerns about the student's Individualized Education Program, will be permitted to terminate the delegation of rights at any time, and will notify the school district immediately if the student terminates the delegation of rights.

105 ILCS 5/14-6.10

13:290 Do the course requirements for receiving a high school diploma apply to special education or students with disabilities whose education is governed by an Individualized Education Program?

No.

105 ILCS 5/27-22

13:295 Must a special education student be permitted to participate in graduation ceremonies?

Beginning in 2005, each school district that operates a high school must have a policy and procedures that allow a child with a disability who will have completed four years of high school at the end of a school year to participate in the graduation ceremony of the student's high school graduating class and receive a certificate of completion if the student's Individualized Education Program prescribes special education, transition planning, transition services, or related services beyond the student's four years of high school.

The policy and procedures must require timely and meaningful written notice to children with disabilities and their parents or guardians.

105 ILCS 5/14-16

13:300 May a student with a disability be retained in grade level or prevented from graduating for failure to pass a minimal competency test?

No student with a qualifying disability may be denied promotion, graduation, or a general diploma on the basis of failing a minimal competency test when the failure can be directly related to the student's disability.

105 ILCS 5/2-3.64
105 ILCS 5/14-6.01

13:310 What special provisions exist for special education students affected by a teachers strike?

If a strike by educational employees results in the closing of schools, and the district is party to a joint agreement for special education, any resident students who are enrolled in special education programs of the joint agreement district must be permitted to attend special education programs in any other district that is a party to the same joint agreement and whose schools are not closed as a result of the strike.

105 ILCS 5/10-22.31

FINANCIAL OBLIGATIONS

13:320 If a school district accepts a properly placed non-resident child with a disability, which school district bears the cost of the child's education?

If a school district accepts a non-resident child with a disability for admission into any of its special education programs pursuant to the child's Individualized Education Program (IEP), the school district in which the child resides bears the cost of educational services provided the child.

Doe v. Sanders, 189 Ill. App. 3d 572, 545 N.E. 2d 454, 136 Ill. Dec. 930 (1st Dist. 1989)

William C. v. Board of Education of the City of Chicago, 71 Ill. App. 3d 793, 390 N.E. 2d 479, 28 Ill. Dec. 312 (1st Dist. 1979)

13:325 Which school district must pay for a child's special education costs if the child is placed in an out-of-district residential facility?

A child in need of special education who is properly placed in a residential facility is presumed to be a resident of the school district in which his or her parents reside. Unless a contrary residence is proven (usually by showing that the parents no longer have custody and control of the child) the school district in which the parents reside is responsible for the costs of the residential placement.

105 ILCS 5/14-7.05

William C. v. Board of Education, City of Chicago, 71 Ill. App. 3d 793, 390 N.E. 2d 479, 28 Ill. Dec. 312 (1st Dist. 1979)

School District No. 153, Cook County v. School District 154 1/2, Cook County, 54 Ill. App. 3d 587, 370 N.E. 2d 22, 12 Ill. Dec. 399 (1st Dist. 1977)

13:327 Who must pay for a child's special education costs if the child is placed in an out-of-district residential facility as a result of a court order?

Under the provisions of the Juvenile Court Act, a court has the authority to make a placement decision regarding a delinquent minor including committing him or her to an agency for placement or to an institution appropriate for delinquent minors. A 2008 amendment to the Juvenile Court Act provides that "in instances in which educational services are to be provided to a minor in a residential facility where the minor has been placed by the court, costs incurred in the provision of those educational services must be allocated based on the requirements of the School Code."

705 ILCS 405/5-710 (6)

705 ILCS 405/5-740

People v. D.D. and Oak Park River Forest High School District 200, 337 Ill. App. 3d 998, 778 N.E. 2d 10, 272 Ill. Dec. 706 (1st Dist. 2002)

13:328 Which school district pays the educational costs associated with a student's residential placement?

For any student with a disability in a residential facility placement made or paid for by an Illinois public state agency or made by any court in this state, the school district of residence as provided in Article 14 of the School Code is responsible for the costs of educating the child and is reimbursed for those costs as provided in the School Code. Subject to this section and relevant state appropriation, the resident district's financial responsibility and reimbursement is calculated in accordance with the provisions of Section 14-7.02 of the School Code.

In those instances in which a district receives a block grant pursuant to Article 1D of the School Code, the district's financial responsibility is limited to the actual educational costs of the placement, which must be paid by the district from its block grant appropriation. Resident district financial responsibility and reimbursement applies for both residential facilities that are approved by the State Board of Education and non-approved facilities, subject to the requirements of this section.

The Illinois placing agency or court remains responsible for funding the residential portion of the placement and for notifying the resident district prior to the placement, except in emergency situations. The residential facility in which the student is placed must notify the resident district of the student's enrollment as soon as practicable after the placement. Failure of the placing agency or court to notify the resident district prior to the placement does not absolve the resident district of financial responsibility for the educational costs of the placement; however, the resident district is not financially responsible unless and until it receives written notice of the placement by either the placing agency, court, or residential facility.

The placing agency or parent must request an Individualized Education Program (IEP) meeting from the resident district if the placement would entail additional educational services beyond the student's current IEP. The district of residence retains control of the IEP process, and any changes to the IEP are done in compliance with the federal Individuals with Disabilities Education Act.

Payments are made by the resident district to the entity providing the educational services, whether the entity is the residential facility or the school district wherein the facility is located, no less than once per quarter unless otherwise agreed to in writing by the parties.

A residential facility providing educational services within the facility, but not approved by the State Board of Education, is required to demonstrate proof to the State Board of (i) appropriate certification of teachers for the student population, (ii) age-appropriate curriculum, (iii) enrollment and attendance data, and (iv) the ability to implement the child's IEP. A school district is under no obligation to pay such a residential facility unless and until such proof is provided to the State Board's satisfaction.

When a dispute arises over the determination of the district of residence, any person or entity, including without limitation a school district or residential facility, may make a written request for a residency decision to the State Superintendent of Education, who, upon review of materials submitted and any other items of information he or she may request for submission, shall issue his or her decision in writing. The decision of the State Superintendent of Education is final.

105 ILCS 5/14-7.03

105 ILCS 5/14-7.05

13:330 May a school district pass on to parents any portion of the tuition charge for a student with a disability who is appropriately placed in a nonpublic school?

The education of children with disabilities is the responsibility of the school district and no part of the tuition charged by a nonpublic facility may be passed on to the parents of the child with a disability if the child is appropriately placed in the nonpublic facility.

Elliot v. Board of Education of the City of Chicago, 64 Ill. App. 3d 229, 380 N.E. 2d 1137, 20 Ill. Dec. 928 (1st Dist. 1978)

13:340 What is the effect of unilateral residential placement of special education students by their parents?

If a child with a disability has available a free and appropriate public education, the school district has otherwise complied with special education laws and the parents choose to place the child in a private school or facility, the school board is not required to pay for the child's education at the private school or facility. Disagreements between a parent and a school regarding the availability of a program appropriate for the child and the question of financial responsibility are subject to due process procedures.

When parents fail to cooperate with a school district by depriving school officials of a reasonable opportunity to evaluate a student, the parents are barred from raising a claim for reimbursement for a unilateral placement, even if the placement is appropriate.

20 U.S.C. 1412(a)(10)(C)

20 U.S.C. 1415

34 C.F.R. 300.130 et seq.

23 Ill. Admin. Code 226.340

Jenna R.P. v. City of Chicago School District No. 299, 2013 IL App (1st) 112247, 3 N.E. 3d 927, 378 Ill. Dec. 362

Forest Grove School District v. T.A., 129 S. Ct. 2484, 557 U.S. 230, 174 L. Ed. 2d 168 (2009)

Board of Education of City School District of City of New York v. Tom F. ex rel. Gilbert F., not reported in F. Supp. 2d, 2005 WL 22866 (S.D. N.Y., 2005), (2nd Cir. 2006) (not selected for publication in the Federal Reporter, NO. 05-0566), 128 S. Ct. 17, 551 U.S. 1180, 168 L. Ed. 2d 794 (2007)

Dale M. ex rel. Alice M. v. Board of Education of Bradley Bourbonnais High School District No. 307, 237 F. 3d 813 (7th Cir. 2001), cert. den. 122 S. Ct. 546, 534 U.S. 1020, 151 L. Ed. 2d 423, (2001)

Patricia P. v. Board of Education of Oak Park, 203 F. 3d 462 (7th Cir. 2000)

Florence County School District Four v. Carter, 112 S. Ct. 1932, 504 U.S. 906, 118 L. Ed. 2d 540 (1993)

Burlington School Committee of the Town of Burlington, Massachusetts v. Department of Education of Massachusetts, 105 S. Ct 1996, 471 U.S. 359, 85 L. Ed. 2d 385 (1985)

13:350 Are there circumstances under which a school district may be held liable for the costs associated with the parent of a child with a qualifying disability removing the child from a public school program and unilaterally placing the child in a private facility?

A school district may be liable for the costs of such a placement if the child's physical health would be endangered if an alternative placement were not made, or if the school district has acted in bad faith by failing to comply with statutory provisions for resolving the dispute over the child's educational placement, or if the school district has not otherwise provided the child with an appropriate educational placement.

Forest Grove School District v. T.A., 129 S. Ct. 2484, 557 U.S. 230, 174 L. Ed. 2d 168 (2009)

Florence County School District Four v. Carter, 112 S. Ct. 1932, 504 U.S. 906, 118 L. Ed. 2d 540 (1993)

Anderson v. Thompson, 658 F. 2d 1205 (7th Cir. 1981)

DISCIPLINE OF STUDENTS WITH DISABILITIES

13:360 May a school district suspend a special education student for disciplinary reasons?

A suspension in this context is defined as a removal from the child's current educational setting for not more than 10 consecutive school days for each disciplinary event. A child may be suspended for disciplinary reasons for up to 10 cumulative days (not necessarily consecutive) during a school year without the requirement that the school district provide services to the child. After 10 cumulative days, the school district must provide services to the child during the term of the suspension or expulsion, whether or not the removal constitutes a change in placement.

In-school suspensions that isolate the child or deny him or her access to mainstreaming or aspects of his or her Individualized Education Program count as suspension days in the above calculations. A school district may suspend a child for a cumulative number of days in a school year in excess of 10 if the suspensions taken together do not constitute a change in placement.

To suspend a special education student for more than 10 days in a school year, the school district must have procedures in place that allow the members of the student's Individualized Education Program (IEP) team to determine whether each suspension event constitutes a change in placement. The IEP team must consider such factors as the total amount of time the student is excluded from school, the proximity of the suspensions to one another and the length of each suspension.

While there appears to be legislative intent to permit broader use of disciplinary suspensions (in excess of 10 cumulative days in a school term) in the reauthorized special education law, until there is clear judicial interpretation of certain conflicts in the statute and the rules, the safer approach for school officials is to limit cumulative suspensions to not more than 10 days per school year.

20 U.S.C. 1415

34 C.F.R. 300.530 et seq.

105 ILCS 5/14-8.05

23 Ill. Admin. Code 226.400

Parents of Student W. v. Payallup School District No. 3, 31 F. 3d 1489 (9th Cir. 1994)

Honig v. Doe, 108 S. Ct. 592, 484 U.S. 305, 98 L. Ed. 2d 686 (1988)

Board of Education City of Peoria v. Illinois State Board of Education, 531 F. Supp. 148 (C.D. Ill. 1982)

13:370 May a school district expel a special education student from school?

Unlike a short-term disciplinary suspension, an expulsion is a change in placement. If the behavior giving rise to the expulsion is found to be related to the child's disability, expulsion may not be invoked. The law is unsettled as to whether a special education student may be expelled from school when the behavior giving rise to the discipline is not related to the child's disability. It is clear, however, that after "expulsion" the school district must continue to provide services to the child.

A formal special education staffing must be held prior to any disciplinary hearing to determine the relatedness of the student's alleged misbehavior to his or her disability. This hearing is commonly called "a manifestation hearing."

A school district may seek injunctive relief to bar a dangerous student from school pending disposition of change in placement proceedings.

2016 changes in the law resulting from the enactment of P.A. 99-456 (commonly known as Senate Bill 100) add additional procedures and limitations on school officials' ability to suspend and expel. The reader is directed to the series of questions and answers beginning at 12:380 for an overview of the changes resulting from Senate Bill 100.

105 ILCS 5/14-8.01

105 ILCS 5/14-8.05

23 Ill. Admin. Code 226.400

Doe v. Board of Education of Oak Park and River Forest High School District 200, 115 F. 3d 1273 (7th Cir. 1997)

Commonwealth of Virginia v. Riley, 86 F. 3d 1337 (4th Cir. 1996)

Metropolitan School District of Wayne Township, Marion County Indiana v. Davila, 969 F. 2d 485 (7th Cir. 1992) cert. den. 113 S. Ct. 1360, 507 U.S. 949, 122 L. Ed. 2d 740 (1993)

Honig v. Doe, 108 S. Ct. 592, 484 U.S. 305, 98 L. Ed. 2d 686 (1988)

S-1 v. Turlington, 635 F. 2d 342 (5th Cir. 1981)

13:371 Under what circumstances may a special education child be placed in an alternative educational setting for disciplinary reasons?

In general, a special education student may be removed from a current educational setting for more than 10 school days if his or her Individualized Education Program (IEP) is amended to allow for the change in placement or the behavior is determined not to be a manifestation of the child's disability.

School personnel may remove a student to an interim alternative educational setting for not more than 45 school days without regard to whether the behavior is determined to be a manifestation of the child's disability, in cases where a child carries or possesses a weapon to or at school, on school premises, or to or at a school function under the jurisdiction of a state or local educational agency; or knowingly possesses or uses illegal drugs, or sells or solicits the sale of a controlled substance, while at school, on school premises, or at a school function under the jurisdiction of a state or local educational agency; or has inflicted serious bodily injury upon another person while at school, on school premises, or at a school function under the jurisdiction of a state or local educational agency.

Not later than the date on which the decision to take disciplinary action is made, the local educational agency must notify the parents of that decision and of all procedural safeguards. The interim alternative educational setting is determined by the IEP team.

In this context, illegal drug means controlled substance but does not include a substance that is legally possessed or used under the supervision of a licensed health care professional or that is legally possessed or used under any other authority under any provision of federal law. In this context, the term "dangerous weapon" means a weapon, device, instrument, material, or substance, animate or inanimate, that is used for, or is readily capable of, causing death or serious bodily injury, except that such term does not include a pocket knife with a blade of less than 2 1/2 inches in length.

18 U.S.C. 930(g)(2)
18 U.S.C. 1365(h)(3)
20 U.S.C. 1415(k)
34 C.F.R. 300.530 et seq.
105 ILCS 5/14-8.02b(ii)
23 Ill. Admin. Code 226.400

13:372 What is a manifestation hearing?

Within 10 school days of any decision to change the placement of a child with a disability because of a violation of a code of student conduct, the local educational agency, the parent, and relevant members of the IEP team (as determined by the parent and the local educational agency) must review all relevant information in the student's file, including the child's IEP, any teacher observations, and any relevant information provided by the parents to determine if the conduct in question was caused by, or had a direct and substantial relationship to, the child's disability; or if the conduct in question was the direct result of the local educational agency's failure to implement the IEP.

If the local educational agency, the parent, and relevant members of the IEP team determine the conduct in question was caused by, or had a direct and substantial relationship to, the child's disability; or if the conduct in question was the direct result of the local educational agency's failure to implement the IEP; the conduct shall be determined to be a manifestation of the child's disability.

If the local educational agency, the parent, and relevant members of the IEP team make the determination that the conduct was a manifestation of the child's disability, the IEP team must conduct a functional behavioral assessment and implement a behavioral intervention plan for the child, provided that the local educational agency had not conducted such assessment prior to such determination before the behavior that resulted in a change in placement. When a behavioral intervention plan has been developed, school officials generally review the plan and modify it, as necessary, to address the behavior and return the child to the placement from which the child was removed, unless the parent and the local educational agency agree to a change of placement as part of the plan modification.

20 U.S.C. 1415(k)(E)
34 C.F.R. 300.530 et seq.

13:373 Under what circumstances may an expedited hearing occur?

The parent of a child with a disability who disagrees with any decision regarding disciplinary placement, or a manifestation determination, or a local educational agency that believes that maintaining the current placement of the child is substantially likely to result in injury to the child or to others, may request a hearing in which case a hearing officer hears and makes a determination regarding the appeal.

In making the determination, the hearing officer may order a change in placement of a child. In such situations, the hearing officer may return a child with a disability to the placement from which the child was removed, or order a change in placement of a child with a disability to an appropriate interim alternative educational setting for not more than 45 school days if the hearing officer determines that maintaining the current placement of the child is substantially likely to result in injury to the child or to others.

When an appeal has been requested by either the parent or the local educational agency the child must remain in the interim alternative educational setting pending the decision of the hearing officer or until the expiration of the time period provided, whichever occurs first, unless the parent and the state or local educational agency agree otherwise; and the state or local educational agency must arrange for an expedited hearing, which must occur within 20 school days of the date the hearing is requested and must result in a determination within 10 school days after the hearing.

20 U.S.C. 1415(k)
105 ILCS 5/14-8.02b

13:375 What factors must a school district consider in the discipline of a student with disabilities?

When behavioral interventions are used, they must take into consideration the pupil's physical freedom and social interaction, and must be administered in a manner that respects human dignity and personal privacy and that ensures a pupil's right to placement in the least restrictive environment. Behavioral management plans must be developed and used, to the extent possible, in a consistent manner when a local educational agency has placed a student in a day or residential setting for education purposes.

105 ILCS 5/14-8.05

13:380 Under what circumstances may a child avoid discipline by asserting eligibility for special education?

If school officials knew the child had a disability and needed special education services before the misconduct occurred but failed to act, the child may be able to avoid or postpone the imposition of discipline. If school officials failed to identify or ignored a request for services the child may request an evaluation and has the right to remain in his or her then-current placement until the evaluation is completed.

School officials may be vulnerable to such a demand when the parent of the child has expressed concern in writing to supervisory or administrative personnel of the appropriate educational agency, or a teacher of the child, that the child is in need of special education and related services or the parent has requested an evaluation of the child or the teacher of the child or other personnel of the local educational agency has expressed specific concerns about a pattern of behavior demonstrated by the child, directly to the director of special education or to other supervisory personnel of the agency.

A local educational agency does not have knowledge that the child is a child with a disability if the parent of the child has not allowed an evaluation of the child or has refused services or the child has been evaluated and it was determined that the child was not a child with a disability.

20 U.S.C. 1415(k)(5)(B)

S.W. v. Holbrook Public Schools, 221 F. Supp. 2d 222 (D. Mass., 2002)

SPECIAL EDUCATION FACILITIES

13:410 May a school board use its special education tax levy to construct buildings?

Yes. By proper resolution, the school board may accumulate funds in the special education fund for up to eight years for building purposes.

105 ILCS 5/17-2.2a

13:420 What may school districts do with special education facilities no longer needed for special education purposes?

If it is no longer feasible or economical to utilize classroom facilities constructed with revenues raised and accumulated by the tax for special education building purposes, the district may use such facilities for regular school purposes with the approval of the regional superintendent of schools and the State Superintendent of Education. The district must make comparable facilities available for special education purposes at another attendance center that is in a more practical location due to the proximity of the students served.

By unanimous consent of participating school districts, a cooperative special education district may exercise the same discretion.

105 ILCS 5/17-2.2a

SPECIAL EDUCATION JOINT AGREEMENTS

13:430 Must each school district maintain special education facilities?

Each school district must establish and maintain such special educational facilities as may be needed for children with disabilities who are residents of the school district. School districts need not provide special education facilities independently, however. School districts are empowered to enter into joint agreements as a means for providing such required facilities.

105 ILCS 5/14-4.01

13:440 What governs the formation of a special education school district?

The School Code permits school districts to enter into joint agreements to provide special education services and facilities for the education of students. A copy of any joint agreement or amendment to a joint agreement entered into on or after January 1, 1989 must be filed with the State Board of Education.

105 ILCS 5/10-22.31

13:450 How may a joint agreement be amended?

A joint agreement may be amended at any time as provided in the joint agreement, or if the joint agreement does not provide a procedure for amendment, it may be amended at any time by adoption of concurring resolutions by the school boards of all the member districts.

105 ILCS 5/10-22.31

13:460 Under what circumstances may a school district withdraw from a special education joint agreement?

A school district desiring to withdraw from a joint agreement may petition the regional board or boards of school trustees exercising oversight or governance over any of the districts in the joint agreement. Upon receipt of a petition for withdrawal, the regional boards of school trustees having jurisdiction over the cooperating districts must publish notice and conduct a joint hearing on the issue. The notice and hearing procedures are conducted as provided in detachment cases. Approval of a withdrawal petition requires "a two-thirds vote of all trustees of those regional boards, at a joint meeting." A withdrawal takes effect as provided in Section 7-9 of the School Code.

In instances in which more than one regional board of school trustees exercises oversight or governance over any of the districts in the joint agreement, a joint hearing, in accordance with rules adopted by the State Board of Education. In instances in which a single regional board of school trustees holds the hearing, approval of the petition must be by a two-thirds majority vote of the school trustees. In instances in which a joint hearing of two or more regional boards of school trustees is required, approval of the petition must be by a two-thirds majority of all those school trustees present and voting.

Notwithstanding the provisions of Article 6 of the School Code, in instances in which the competent regional board or boards of school trustees has been abolished, petitions for withdrawal shall be made to the school boards of those districts that fall under the oversight or governance of the abolished regional board of school trustees in accordance with rules adopted by the State Board of Education on the issue as provided in Section 7-6 of the School Code. No such petition may be considered, however, unless in compliance with Section 7-8 of the School Code. If any petition is approved by a two-thirds vote of all trustees of those regional boards, at a joint meeting, the withdrawal takes effect as provided in Section 7-9 of the School Code.

A joint agreement may be amended at any time upon the adoption of concurring resolutions by the school boards of all member districts. Such an amendment may include the removal of a school district from or the addition of a school district to the joint agreement without a petition if all member districts adopt concurring resolutions to that effect.

105 ILCS 5/7-6
105 ILCS 5/7-8
105 ILCS 5/7-9
105 ILCS 5/10-22.31

SPECIAL EDUCATION DUE PROCESS HEARINGS

13:500 Who may request a special education due process hearing?

A hearing may be requested by a parent or guardian, student of at least 18 years of age, an emancipated student, or a school district.

20 U.S.C. 1415 et seq.
34 C.F.R. 300.507 et seq.
105 ILCS 5/14-8.02
105 ILCS 5/14-8.02a(f)

13:505 What must be included in a due process complaint?

A complaint notice is confidential. It must be provided to the other party, with respect to any matter relating to the identification, evaluation, or educational placement of the child; or the provision of a free appropriate public education to such child; and must set forth an alleged violation that occurred not more than two years before the date the parent or public agency knew or should have known about the alleged action that forms the basis of the complaint except that the time line shall not apply to a parent if the parent was prevented from requesting a due process hearing due to specific misrepresentations by the local educational agency that it had resolved the problem forming the basis of the complaint; or the local educational agency's withholding of information from the parent that was required to be provided to the parent.

The complaint notice must be sent to the state educational agency; and it must include the name of the child, the address of the residence of the child (or available contact information in the case of a homeless child), and the name of the school the child is attending, a description of the nature of the problem of the child relating to such proposed initiation or change, including facts relating to the problem; and a proposed resolution of the problem to the extent known and available to the party at the time.

20 U.S.C. 1415 (b)(6)
20 U.S.C. 1415 (b)(7)
20 U.S.C. 1415 (f)(3)(d)
34 C.F.R. 300.508 et seq.

13:510 Under what circumstances may parents of a handicapped child bring suit in court to determine the child's appropriate placement before they have exhausted administrative remedies?

Normally an IDEA plaintiff must exhaust remedies available under IDEA before bringing suit. There are limited exceptions to this rule. If the remedy sought under another statute is not denial of a free and appropriate education, then exhaustion of remedies under IDEA is not required. A suit may also be brought before administrative remedies are exhausted in an emergency situation when exhaustion would cause the child to suffer serious and irreversible mental or physical damage.

20 U.S.C. 1415 (l)

Fry v. Napoleon Community Schools, 137 S. Ct. 743, __ U.S. __, 197 L. Ed. 2d 46 (2016)

Jamie S. v. Milwaukee Public Schools, 668 F. 3d 481 (7th Cir. 2012)

Komninos v. Upper Saddle River Board of Education, 13 F. 3d 775 (3rd Cir. 1994)

13:515 What change in placement is possible for a child with a qualifying disability from the time a local level due process hearing is requested until all appeals have been exhausted?

During the pendency of any special education proceeding, unless the school district and the parents or guardian otherwise agree, the student must remain in the then-current educational placement, or if applying for initial admission to the school district, must, with the consent of the parents or guardian, be placed in the school district program until all such proceedings have been completed.

Generally, the terms of the last IEP should be enforced without exception as the stay-put relief. If a school has provided a particular service in the past, it need not be provided in a stay-put situation if it was not within the governing IEP. If the parties dispute what the IEP requires, the court evaluates the IEP as a whole and determines whether the disputed matter is required under the terms of the IEP.

Under usual circumstances, the court will not go beyond the four corners of the IEP to make that determination. However, if the instrument is vague as to how goals are to be achieved, then the court can turn to extrinsic evidence to determine the intent of those who formulated the plan.

20 U.S.C. 1415(j)

34 C.F.R. 300.518

105 ILCS 5/14-8.02(k)

John M. v. Board of Education of Evanston Township High School District 202, 502 F. 3d 708 (7th Cir. 2007)

Florence County School District Four v. Carter, 112 S. Ct. 1932, 504 U.S. 906, 118 L. Ed. 2d 540 (1993)

Honig v. Doe, 108 S. Ct. 592, 484 U.S. 305, 98 L. Ed. 2d 686 (1988)

Walker v. Cronin, 107 Ill. App. 3d 1053, 438 N.E. 2d 582, 63 Ill. Dec. 651 (1st Dist. 1982)

13:520 What is a child's current educational placement if a child has not yet acquired an Individualized Education Program (IEP)?

Stay-put provisions of the Individuals with Disabilities Education Act require that a child's educational program not be changed during the pendency of a dispute over the placement. If a child does not yet have an IEP when a dispute over the child's appropriate placement arises, the child must remain in the last placement in which the child was receiving an education until the dispute is resolved or until the parents otherwise agree.

If the dispute arises when the school district has expulsion proceedings pending, stay-put provisions effectively block the expulsion if the school district knew or reasonably should have known of the student's disability.

20 U.S.C. 1415(j)

105 ILCS 5/14-8.02a(j)

Rodiriecus L. By Betty H. v. Waukegan School District No. 60, 90 F. 3d 249 (7th Cir. 1996)

Thomas v. Cincinnati Board of Education, 918 F. 2d 618 (6th Cir. 1990)

13:525 What notice obligations does a school district have when a due process request has been made?

If a school district is requesting the hearing, the school district makes its request in writing to the State Board of Education and must thereafter promptly mail a copy of the request to the parents or guardian of the student at their last known address. A parent, guardian, or student request is made in writing to the superintendent of schools who must forward the request to the State Board of Education within five days of receipt.

105 ILCS 5/14-8.02a(f)

23 Ill. Admin. Code 226.610

34 C.F.R. 300.503 et seq.

13:526 What must be included in a change of placement (or refusal to change placement) notice?

A prior written notice must include

1) A description of the action proposed or refused by the agency;

2) An explanation of why the agency proposes or refuses to take the action and a description of each evaluation procedure, assessment, record, or report the agency used as a basis for the proposed or refused action;

3) A statement that the parents of a child with a disability have protection under the procedural safeguards of this subchapter and, if this notice is not an initial referral for evaluation, the means by which a copy of a description of the procedural safeguards can be obtained;

4) Sources for parents to contact to obtain assistance in understanding the provisions of this subchapter;

5) A description of other options considered by the IEP team and the reason why those options were rejected; and

6) A description of the factors that are relevant to the agency's proposal or refusal.

20 U.S.C. 1415(c)(1)

13:527 How must a school district respond to a complaint?

If the local educational agency has not sent a prior written notice to the parent regarding the subject matter of the parent's due process complaint notice, the local educational agency must, within 10 days of receiving the complaint, send to the parent a response that must include an explanation of why the agency proposed or refused to take the action raised in the complaint; a description of other options that the IEP team considered and the reasons why those options were rejected; a description of each evaluation procedure, assessment, record, or report the agency used as the basis for the proposed or refused action; and a description of the factors that are relevant to the agency's proposal or refusal.

A response filed by a local educational agency does not preclude the local educational agency from asserting that the parent's due process complaint notice was insufficient where appropriate.

20 U.S.C. 1415(c)(2)(B)

13:528 When may a due process complaint be amended?

A party may amend its due process complaint notice only if the other party consents in writing to the amendment and is given the opportunity to resolve the complaint through a meeting as provided in the statute or the hearing officer grants permission, except that the hearing officer may only grant such permission at any time not later than five days before a due process hearing occurs.

20 U.S.C. 1415(c)(2)(E)

13:530 Do parents of students with qualifying disabilities have a right to counsel at special education due process hearings?

Parents and guardians of students with qualifying disabilities have the right to be represented by counsel at their own expense. After certain findings, the school district may be required to reimburse the parents and guardians of such students for their attorney fees.

Doe v. Baltimore County, Maryland Board of Education, 165 F. 3d 260 (4th Cir. 1999)

John T. v. Marion Independent School District, 173 F. 3d 684 (9th Cir. 1999)

Warner v. Independent School District No. 625, 134 F. 3d 1333 (8th Cir 1998), cert. den. 119 S. Ct. 67, 525 U.S. 823, 142 L. Ed. 2d 53 (1998)

Fenneman v. Town of Gorham, 802 F. Supp. 542 (D.C. Me. 1992)

McSomebodies v. Burlingame Elementary School, 897 F. 2d 974 (9th Cir. 1989)

Moore v. District of Columbia, 886 F. 2d 335 (D.C. Cir. 1989)

Mitten by and through Mitten v. Muscogee County School District, 877 F. 2d 932 (11th Cir. 1989) cert. den. 110 S. Ct. 1117, 493 U.S. 1072, 107 L. Ed. 2d 1024 (1990)

Duane M. v. Orleans Parish School Board, 861 F. 2d 115 (5th Cir. 1988)

Eggers v. Bullit County School District, 854 F. 2d 892 (6th Cir. 1988)

Daniel B. v. Wisconsin Dept. of Public Instruction, 581 F. Supp. 585 (D.C. Wisc.), 776 F. 2d 1051 (7th Cir. 1984) cert. den. 106 S. Ct. 1462, 475 U.S. 1083, 89 L. Ed. 2d 719 (1984)

New York Gaslight Club, Inc. v. Carey, 100 S. Ct. 204, 444 U.S. 897, 62 L. Ed. 2d 132 (1980)

13:535 How are due process hearing officers selected?

Due process hearing officers are qualified by the State Board of Education and selected by the parties from lists of five names each provided by the State Board of Education using an alternate strike system. The State Board of Education provides panels by use of a rotating selection system.

105 ILCS 5/14-8.02a(b)
105 ILCS 5/14-8.02a(f)

13:538 Are special education due process hearings open or closed to the public?

A special education due process hearing is closed to the public unless the parents or guardian request that it be open to the public.

105 ILCS 5/14-8.02a(g)

13:540 When and where are due process hearings held?

The hearing must be held at a time and place that are reasonably convenient to the parties. At the request of a party, the hearing officer must hold the hearing at a no-cost neutral site.

105 ILCS 5/14-8.02a(g)

13:541 What is special education mediation?

Mediation is voluntary and may not be used to deny or delay a parent's right to a due process hearing or to deny any other rights provided in the law. Mediation is conducted by a qualified and impartial mediator who is trained in effective mediation techniques.

20 U.S.C. 1415(e)
34 C.F.R. 300.506

13:542 What is a preliminary meeting?

A preliminary meeting is required under the law, whereas mediation is voluntary. Unless the parents and the local educational agency agree in writing to waive the meeting, or agree to use the mediation process, prior to the opportunity for an impartial due process hearing the local educational agency must convene a meeting with the parents and the relevant member or members of the IEP team who have specific knowledge of the facts identified in the complaint within 15 days of receiving notice of the parents' complaint.

The meeting must include a representative of the agency who has decision-making authority on behalf of the agency. The meeting cannot include an attorney of the local educational agency unless the parent is accompanied by an attorney. At the meeting, the parents of the child must have an opportunity to discuss their complaint and the facts that form the basis of the complaint, and the local educational agency must be provided the opportunity to resolve the complaint.

20 U.S.C. 1415(f)(B)(I)
34 C.F.R. 300.510

13:543 What is a special education pre-hearing conference?

A hearing officer must convene a pre-hearing conference no later than 14 days before the scheduled date for the due process hearing. The parties receive 10 days advance notice of the pre-hearing conference that may be conducted in person or by telephone.

105 ILCS 5/14-8.02a(f)

13:545 What disclosures are required at a pre-hearing conference?

Each party must disclose

1) Whether it is represented by legal counsel or intends to retain legal counsel;

2) The matters it believes to be in dispute and the specific relief to be sought;

3) Whether there are any additional evaluations for the student that it intends to introduce into the hearing record that have not been previously disclosed;

4) A list of all documents it intends to introduce into the hearing record;

5) The names of all witnesses it intends to call.

105 ILCS 5/14-8.02a(g)

13:547 What happens if a party fails to timely disclose evidence to the other party?

Any party to a due process hearing has the right to prohibit the introduction of evidence at the hearing that has not been disclosed to that party at least five business days before the hearing.

20 U.S.C. 1415(f)(2)
34 C.F.R. 300.512 et seq.
105 ILCS 5/14-8.02a(g)

13:550 What evidence must a school district present at a due process hearing?

The school district must present evidence that the special education needs of the child have been appropriately identified and that the special education program and related services proposed to meet the needs of the child are adequate, appropriate, and available. If at issue, the school district must present evidence that it has properly identified and evaluated the nature and severity of the student's suspected or identified disability; and that, if the student has been or should have been determined eligible for special education and related services, that it is providing or has offered a free appropriate public education to the student in the least restrictive environment, consistent with procedural safeguards and in accordance with the students Individualized Education Program.

34 C.F.R. 300.512 et seq.
105 ILCS 5/14-8.02a(g)

13:552 What rights do the parties have at a due process hearing or on appeal?

Any party has the right to

1) Be accompanied and advised by counsel and by individuals with special knowledge or training with respect to the problems of children with disabilities;

2) Present evidence and confront, cross-examine, and compel the attendance of witnesses;

3) A written, or, at the option of the parents, electronic verbatim record of such hearing; and

4) Written, or, at the option of the parents, electronic findings of fact and decisions, which findings and decisions shall be made available to the public consistent with the requirements of special education law relating to the confidentiality of data, information, and records and shall be transmitted to the advisory panel established under special education law.

20 U.S.C. 1415(h)
20 U.S.C. 1417(b)
34 C.F.R. 300.512 et seq.
105 ILCS 5/14-8.02a(g)
23 Ill. Admin. Code 226.625

13:553 Which party has the burden of proof in a due process hearing?

In the relevant U.S. Supreme Court case, the court distinguished burden of persuasion from burden of production. The court concluded that the party seeking relief has the burden of persuasion in a special education due process case.

Schaffer ex rel. Schaffer v. Weast, 126 S. Ct. 528, 546 U.S. 49, 126 S. Ct. 528, 163 L. Ed. 2d 387 (2005)

13:557 What elements must a due process decision contain?

In addition to being in writing and containing findings of fact and conclusions of law, the decision must specify the educational and related services that must be provided to the student in accordance with the student's needs.

34 C.F.R. 300.513
105 ILCS 5/14-8.02a(h)

13:560 May a party seek clarification of a hearing officer's decision?

A party may request clarification of a hearing officer's decision by submitting a request in writing to the hearing officer within five days of the party's receipt of the decision. The request for clarification must specify the portions of the decision for which clarification is sought and must be mailed to all the parties and to the State Board of Education.

The hearing officer must issue a clarification of the specified portion of the decision or issue a partial or full denial of the request in writing within 10 days of receipt of the request and mail copies to all parties to whom the decision was mailed. The parties may not request reconsideration of the decision itself.

105 ILCS 5/14-8.02a(h)

13:562 How may a due process hearing result be appealed?

Any party aggrieved by the decision has the right to begin a civil action with respect to the issues presented in the impartial due process hearing. The action must be brought in a court of competent jurisdiction within 90 days from the date of the decision of the hearing officer.

The limitations period for seeking review of the decision is tolled from the date a request for clarification is submitted until the date the hearing officer acts upon the request.

20 U.S.C. 1415(h)(2)(B)
34 C.F.R. 300.514
105 ILCS 5/14-8.02a(h)
105 ILCS 5/14-8.02a(i)

13:565 Can a successful special education parent recover attorney fees?

A court, in its discretion, may award reasonable attorneys' fees as part of the costs to a prevailing party who is the parent of a child with a disability or to a prevailing party who is a state educational agency or local educational agency against the attorney of a parent who files a complaint or subsequent cause of action that is frivolous, unreasonable, or without foundation, or against the attorney of a parent who continued to litigate after the litigation clearly became frivolous, unreasonable, or without foundation; or to a prevailing state educational agency or local educational agency against the attorney of a parent, or against the parent, if the parent's complaint or subsequent cause of action was presented for any improper purpose, such as to harass, to cause unnecessary delay, or to needlessly increase the cost of litigation.

A court may award attorney fees only in those cases where the plaintiff has prevailed by securing a material alteration of the legal relationship between the parties, either, for example, by court ordered consent decree or an enforceable judgment.

Fees awarded must be based on rates prevailing in the community in which the action or proceeding arose for the kind and quality of services furnished. No bonus or multiplier may be used in calculating the fees.

Attorneys' fees may not be awarded and related costs may not be reimbursed for services performed subsequent to the time of a written offer of settlement to a parent if the offer is made within the time prescribed by Rule 68 of the Federal Rules of Civil Procedure or, in the case of an administrative proceeding, at any time more than 10 days before the proceeding begins if the offer is not accepted within 10 days; and the court or administrative hearing officer finds that the relief finally obtained by the parents is not more favorable to the parents than the offer of settlement.

Attorneys' fees may not be awarded relating to any meeting of the IEP team unless the meeting is convened as a result of an administrative proceeding or judicial action, or, at the discretion of the state, for a mediation.

Notwithstanding a Rule 68 tender, an award of attorneys' fees and related costs may be made to a parent who is the prevailing party and who was substantially justified in rejecting the settlement offer.

Except in any action or proceeding if the court finds that the state or local educational agency unreasonably protracted the final resolution of the action or proceeding or there was a violation of this section, whenever the court finds

1) The parent, or the parent's attorney, during the course of the action or proceeding, unreasonably protracted the final resolution of the controversy;

2) The amount of the attorneys' fees otherwise authorized to be awarded unreasonably exceeds the hourly rate prevailing in the community for similar services by attorneys of reasonably comparable skill, reputation, and experience;

3) The time spent and legal services furnished were excessive considering the nature of the action or proceeding; or

4) The attorney representing the parent did not provide to the local educational agency the appropriate information in the notice of the complaint, the court shall reduce, accordingly, the amount of the attorneys' fees awarded

20 U.S.C. 1415(h)(3)

Bingham v. New Berlin School District, 550 F. 3d 601 (7th Cir. 2008)

T.D. v. LaGrange School District No. 102, 222 F. Supp. 2d 1062 (N.D. Ill. 2002), rev'd, 349 F. 3d 469 (7th Cir. 2003)

Buckhannon Board & Care Home, Inc. v. West Virginia Department of Health and Human Resources, 121 S. Ct. 1835, 532 U.S. 598, 149 L. Ed. 2d 855 (2001)

G.M. ex rel. R.F. v. New Britain Board of Education, 173 F. 3d 77 (2nd Cir. 1999)

McCartney C. By Sara S. v. Herrin Community Unit School District No. 4, 21 F. 3d 173 (7th Cir. 1994)

13:570 Can a successful special education plaintiff recover expert witness fees after a civil trial?

A school district is not required to reimburse parents who prevail in a special education case for the cost of their expert witnesses.

20 U.S.C. 1415(i)(C) et seq.

Fed.R.Civ.P. 54(d)(1)

Arlington Central School District v. Murphy, 126 S. Ct. 2455, 548 U.S. 291, 165 L. Ed. 2d 526 (2006)

Cynthia K. v. Board of Education of Lincoln-Way High School District No. 210, No. 95 C 7172, 1996 U.S. Dist. LEXIS 4054, 1996 WL 164381

Hunger v. Leininger, 15 F. 3d 664 (7th Cir. 1994) cert. den. 115 S. Ct. 123, 513 U.S. 839, 130 L. Ed. 2d 67

DAS v. McHenry School District No. 15, 41 F. 3d 1510 (7th Cir. 1994)

West Virginia Hospitals v. Casey, 111 S. Ct. 1138, 499 U.S. 83, 113 L. Ed. 2d 68 (1991)

13:580 What weight is given to the testimony of doctors or psychologist witnesses in due process hearings?

The Seventh Circuit has held that it is inappropriate to defer to the opinion of a single psychologist, particularly when that opinion is in conflict with the opinions of teachers and other professionals. The deference is to trained educators, not necessarily psychologists.

While psychologists have a role to play and contribute meaningful insight to the evaluation of a student, the school district is required to bring a variety of persons familiar with a child's needs to an IEP meeting, including specifically teachers.

A doctor's diagnosis and input on a child's medical condition is important and bears on the team's informed decision on a student's needs but a physician cannot simply prescribe special education.

M.B. ex rel. Berns v. Hamilton Southeastern Schools, 668 F. 3d 851 (7th Cir. 2011)

13:590 How do procedural defects affect the outcome of a due process hearing?

If the defects result in the loss of educational opportunity for the child, they deny the child a free and appropriate public education. If the defects are procedural and do not result in loss of educational opportunity, they are not likely to affect outcome.

M.B. ex rel. Berns v. Hamilton Southeastern Schools, 668 F. 3d 851 (7th Cir. 2011)

14: RELIGION AND RACE AND THE PUBLIC SCHOOLS

A. RELIGIOUS ISSUES

CONSTITUTIONAL PRINCIPLES

14:10 What constitutional principle underlies all legal questions regarding separation of church and state?

The First Amendment to the United States Constitution provides in part:

"Congress shall make no law respecting the establishment of religion, or prohibiting the free exercise thereof."

The first part is known as the "establishment" clause and the second part is known as the "free exercise" clause. It is balancing the establishment clause against the free exercise clause that makes the analysis of religious freedom questions difficult. Often a situation that seems clearly consistent with the establishment clause is not so clearly consistent with the free exercise clause, and vice versa.

14:20 What test do the courts apply to determine whether a government action is constitutional under the establishment clause?

The test, commonly called the "Lemon Test," requires that the government action must have a secular purpose, its primary effect must neither advance nor inhibit religion, and the action must not cause excessive government entanglement with religion.

The second prong of the Lemon Test requires no inquiry into the government's intent. The appearance of endorsement of religion alone can send a message to non-adherents that they are outsiders and an accompanying message to adherents that they are insiders. A government practice can violate the establishment clause if a reasonable person, apprised of the circumstances surrounding the challenged government act, would conclude that it amounted to an endorsement of religion. The objective reasonable person in this test is presumed to be informed and familiar with the history of the government practice at issue.

In a 2011 case wherein the plaintiffs alleged coercion, the Seventh Circuit Court of Appeals described a three-point coercion test: Has the state acted, does the action amount to coercion, and is the object of the coercion religious or secular?

There is some sentiment on the court for the principle that religious expression cannot violate the establishment clause when it is purely private and occurs in a traditional or designated public forum that is publicly announced and open to all on equal terms.

Doe ex rel. Doe v. Elmbrook School District, 658 F. 3d. 710 (7th Cir. 2011)

Milwaukee Deputy Sheriff's Association. v. Clarke, 574 F. 3d 370 (7th Cir. 2009)

Capitol Square Review and Advisory Board v. Pinette, 114 S. Ct. 626, 510 U.S. 1307, 126 L. Ed. 2d 636 (1995)

Lemon v. Kurtzman, 91 S. Ct. 2105, 403 U.S. 602, 29 L. Ed. 2d 745 (1971), reh. den. 92 S. Ct. 24, 404 U.S. 876, 30 L. Ed. 2d 123, on rem. 348 F. Supp. 300, aff'd. 93 S. Ct. 1463, 411 U.S. 192, 36 L. Ed. 2d 151 (1971)

14:25 What is the Religious Freedom Restoration Act?

In 1998, the State of Illinois enacted a Religious Freedom Restoration Act that provides that the government may not "substantially burden a person's exercise of religion, even if the burden results from a rule of general applicability, unless it demonstrates that application of the burden to the person is in furtherance of a compelling government interest and is the least restrictive means of furthering that compelling governmental interest."

The constitutionality of the Religious Freedom Restoration Act is uncertain.

775 ILCS 35/1 et seq.

City of Boerne v. P.F. Flores, 117 S. Ct. 2157, 521 U.S. 507, 138 L. Ed. 2d 624 (1997)

14:30 May the state compel students to attend public schools?

The free exercise clause of the First Amendment has been read by the courts to prevent the state from compelling public school attendance. The state may require all students, public and parochial, to receive a minimum number of hours of instruction from qualified teachers in a prescribed secular curriculum.

105 ILCS 5/26-1 et seq.

Wisconsin v. Yoder, 92 S. Ct. 1526, 406 U.S. 205, 32 L. Ed. 2d 15 (1972)

Board of Education of Central School District No. 1 v. Allen, 88 S. Ct. 1923, 392 U.S. 236, 20 L. Ed. 2d 1060 (1968)

Pierce v. Society of Sisters of the Holy Names of Jesus and Mary, 45 S. Ct. 571, 268 U.S. 510, 69 L. Ed 1070 (1925)

Meyer v. State of Nebraska, 43 S. Ct. 625, 262 U.S. 390, 67 L. Ed. 1042 (1923)

14:35 May a school district release students during the school day for religious instruction?

A school district must allow any child over 12 and less than 14 years of age release time to attend confirmation classes. Whether release time is permissible for other kinds of religious instruction depends upon the underlying facts. The more the facts suggest public school endorsement of, or entanglement with, religion, the less likely the courts will approve any particular practice. Release time for religious classes held within the public schools or the expenditure of public funds for religious education are, in most cases, prohibited.

105 ILCS 5/26-1

Zorach v. Clauson, 92 S. Ct. 679, 343 U.S. 306, 96 L. Ed. 954 (1952)

Illinois ex rel. McCollum v. Board of Education of School District No. 71, Champaign County, Illinois, 68 S. Ct. 461, 333 U.S. 203, 92 L. Ed. 649 (1948)

People ex rel. Latimer v. Board of Education of the City of Chicago, 394 Ill. 228, 68 N.E. 2d 305 (1946)

14:37 May a school district directly or indirectly penalize a student who is absent from school for religious reasons?

A school district must permit students to freely exercise their religions. A policy limiting the number of excused student absences or exacting an academic penalty for absences resulting from the celebration of religious holidays or participation in other religious activities would violate the free exercise clause.

105 ILCS 5/26-1

Church of God v. Amarillo Independent School District, 511 F. Supp. 613 (N.D. Tex. 1981)

PRAYER

14:40 May students pray in school?

Yes. So long as the students respect school rules, regulations, and policy regarding disruption of the educational process, students may pray in school. This means students may read their Bibles during study hall or other non-structured time, may say grace, and may discuss religion with their peers during non-directed free time, such as time spent on the playground, on a school bus, in the hallways or in the cafeteria.

105 ILCS 20/5

Chandler v. James, 180 F. 3d 1254 (11th Cir. 1999)

Bown v. Gwinnett County School District, 112 F. 3d 1464 (11th Cir. 1997)

Clark v. Dallas Independent School District, 806 F. Supp. 116 (N.D. Tex. 1992)

Wallace v. Jaffree, 105 S. Ct. 2479, 472 U.S. 38, 86 L. Ed. 2d 29 (1985)

14:50 Is a moment of silence for voluntary student prayer permissible?

The recitation of any state composed or endorsed prayer in school is constitutionally prohibited. This is true even if students are not required to participate in the prayer, and even if the prayer is facially neutral as to religious denomination.

Illinois has a statute, known as the Silent Reflection and Student Prayer Act. The Act was amended in 2007 to make a moment of silence mandatory (before the 2007 amendment, the moment of silence was permissive). The statute's constitutionality was challenged by a Chicago-area atheist and his or her daughter. After lengthy litigation, the statute was found constitutional because the court found it serves the secular purpose of having a uniform moment of quiet reflection to calm school children before they start the day, it does not have the principal or primary effect of promoting religion, nor is the statute unconstitutionally vague.

105 ILCS 20/1

Sherman ex rel. Sherman v. Koch, 623 F. 3d 501(7th Cir. 2010)

Bown v. Gwinnet County School District, 112 F. 3d 1464 (11th Cir. 1997)

Wallace v. Jaffree, 105 S. Ct. 2479, 472 U.S. 38, 86 L. Ed. 2d 29 (1985)

School District of Abington Township v. Schempp, 83 S. Ct. 1560, 374 U.S. 203, 10 L. Ed. 2d 844 (1963)

Engel v. Vitale, 82 S. Ct. 1261, 370 U.S. 421, 8 L. Ed. 2d 601 (1962)

14:53 Does the recitation of the Pledge of Allegiance in school violate the First Amendment?

Ceremonial references to a deity are distinguished by the courts from prayer, benedictions, or invocations. The Pledge of Allegiance in school is permissible so long as students who object are not compelled to participate. An Illinois law requires the recitation of the Pledge of Allegiance "by pupils" in Illinois public elementary and secondary schools each day.

The language of the law might lead the reader to conclude students who object to the recitation of the pledge may be compelled to participate. A message from the Governor to the General Assembly at the time of a 2002 amendment to the statute suggests otherwise.

105 ILCS 5/27-3

Elk Grove Unified School District v. Newdow, 124 S. Ct. 2301, 542 U.S. 1, 159 L. Ed. 2d 98 (2004), reh. den. 125 S. Ct. 21, 542 U.S. 961, 159 L. Ed. 2d 851 (2004)

Sherman v. Community Consolidated School District No. 21 of Wheeling Township, 980 F. 2d 437 (7th Cir. 1992) cert. den. 113 S. Ct. 2439, 508 U.S. 950, 124 L. Ed. 2d 658 (1993)

14:55 May a school coach lead his or her players in voluntary prayer at an athletic contest?

No. Such a prayer would violate the establishment clause of the Constitution. A coach is a mentor and a role model for student athletes and a representative of the employing school. While at school and at work the coach is not just an ordinary citizen and a coach must be careful not to press his or her particular views on "the impressionable and captive minds before him."

Kennedy v. Bremerton School District, 869 F. 3d 816 (9th Cir. 2017)

Santa Fe Independent School District v. Doe, 120 S. Ct. 2266, 530 U.S. 290, 147 L. Ed. 2d 295 (2000)

Doe v. Duncanville Independent School District, 986 F. 2d 953 (5th Cir. 1993)

14:60 Is a non-sectarian graduation ceremony benediction, invoking the deity and delivered by a member of the clergy, permissible?

No. A non-sectarian benediction, invoking the deity and delivered by a member of the clergy, at a public school graduation ceremony violates the First Amendment's establishment clause. A school district may not avoid establishment clause implications by making the graduation ceremony or the prayer voluntary.

Lee v. Weisman, 112 S. Ct. 2649, 505 U.S. 577, 120 L. Ed. 2d 467 (1992)

Stein v. Plainwell Community Schools, 610 F. Supp. 43, rev. 822 F. 2d 1406 (6th Cir. 1987)

Marsh v. Chambers, 103 S. Ct. 3330, 463 U.S. 783, 77 L. Ed. 2d 1019 (1983)

14:61 May a student volunteer write and deliver a non-sectarian invocation or benediction at graduation?

The answer to this question depends upon the facts surrounding the composition and delivery of the prayer. Prayers composed and delivered by students and that do not carry the endorsement of the school district or from which the school district disassociates itself are more likely to be constitutionally permissible than those that seem to carry the endorsement of the school district.

A democratically conducted student vote to pray does not render the prayer permissible, and delegation of the decision to pray to students is not in and of itself sufficient to disentangle the state from the impermissible aspects of prayer in the context of a graduation exercise otherwise controlled by school officials.

Does 1-7 v. Round Rock Independent School District, 540 F. Supp. 2d 735 (W. D. Tex. 2008)

Doe v. The School District of the City of Norfolk, 340 F. 3d 605 (8th Cir. 2003)

Niemeyer v. Oroville Union School District, 228 F. 3d 1092 (9th Dist. 2000), cert. den. 121 S. Ct. 1228, 532 U.S.905, 149 L. Ed. 2d 2138 (2001)

Santa Fe Independent School District v. Doe, 120 S. Ct. 2266, 530 U.S. 290, 147 L. Ed. 2d 295 (2000)

Adler v. Duval County, 851 F. Supp. 446, aff'd. 112 F. 3d 1475 (11th Cir. 1999), reh. and sugg. for reh. den. 120 F. 3d 276 (2000) pet. for writ of cert. den. 122 S. Ct. 664. 534 U.S. 1065, 151 L. Ed. 2d 579

Ingebretsen on Behalf of Ingebretsen v. Jackson Public School District, 88 F. 3d 274 (5th Cir. 1996), reh. and reh. den., cert. den. Moore v. Ingebretsen 117 S. Ct. 388, 519 U.S. 965, 136 L. Ed. 2d 304 (1997)

Goluba v. School District of Ripon, 45 F. 3d 1035 (7th Cir. 1995)

Harris v. Joint School District No. 241, 821 F. Supp. 638 (D.C. Ida. 1993) 41 F. 3d 447 (9th Cir. 1994) vac. 115 S. Ct. 2604, 515 U.S. 1104, 132 L. Ed. 2d 849 (1995) on rem. 62 F. 3d 1233, cert. granted, vacating *Citizen's Preserving America's Heritage, Inc. v. Harris*, 115 S. Ct. 2604, 515 U.S. 1104, 132 L. Ed. 2d 849, op. vac. 62 F. 3d 1233 (9th Cir. 1996)

American Civil Liberties Union of New Jersey v. Blackhorse-Pike Regional Board of Education, 84 F. 3d 1431 (3rd Cir. 1996)

Lee v. Weisman, 112 S. Ct. 2649, 505 U.S. 577, 120 L. Ed. 2d 467 (1992)

Jones v. Clear Creek Independent School District, 930 F. 2d 416 (5th Cir. 1991) vac. and rem. 112 S. Ct. 3020, 505 U.S. 1215, 120 L. Ed. 2d 892 (1992) on rem. 977 F. 2d 963 (5th Cir. 1993)

14:62 May a school district sponsor a baccalaureate ceremony?

Under the U.S. Supreme Court decision in *Lee v. Weisman*, a baccalaureate ceremony is unconstitutional if the school district or its agents sponsor, direct, or participate. As is the case in the analysis of school prayer questions, whether or not the ceremony is voluntary for the students is not relevant to its constitutionality.

Under circumstances wherein it may appear that the state is endorsing a privately organized baccalaureate ceremony it may be necessary for school officials to affirmatively disclaim official endorsement.

Lee v. Weisman, 112 S. Ct. 2649, 505 U.S. 577, 120 L. Ed. 2d 467 (1992)

Lemon v. Kurtzman, 91 S. Ct. 2105, 403 U.S. 602, 29 L. Ed. 2d 745 (1971), reh. den. 92 S. Ct. 24, 404 U.S. 876, 30 L. Ed. 2d 123, on rem. 348 F. Supp. 300, aff'd. 93 S. Ct. 1463, 411 U.S. 192, 36 L. Ed. 2d 151 (1971)

14:64 May a school district use a church sanctuary for graduation ceremonies?

The answer will be specific to the facts of the situation. If the sanctuary is the only group meeting place available in a very small community ravaged by a disaster or if religious symbols are removed, the sanctuary might not raise constitutional issues.

Displaying religious iconography and distributing religious literature in a classroom is likely unconstitutional because the practice may do more than provide public school students with the knowledge of religious tenets; the concern is that the displays tend to promote religious beliefs and students might feel pressure to adopt them. The same problem exists with "pervasive displays of iconography and proselytizing material at a public secondary school graduation."

To be constitutional, the site must not have the effect of communicating a message of government endorsement or disapproval of religion. To determine whether it does or doesn't, the courts assess the totality of the circumstances surrounding the display to determine whether a reasonable person would believe the display amounts to an endorsement of religion. The key question is whether a given practice sends a message to non-adherents that they are outsiders, not full members of the political community.

A student or community vote on the location of graduation does nothing to lessen constitutional concerns if they are otherwise present.

Doe ex rel. Doe v. Elmbrook School District, 687 F. 3d 840 (7th Cir. 2012)

14:70 May a school board open its meetings with a prayer?

Probably not. At least one federal circuit court has determined that prayer at a school board meeting (that is open to the public and at which students are sometimes present) violates the establishment clause. The court considered and rejected the argument that the "deliberative body" exception should apply. That exception permits, for example, prayer at the beginning of sessions of the General Assembly.

Coles v. Cleveland Board of Education, 950 F. Supp. 1337, rev. 171 F. 3d 369 (6th Cir. 1999)

PAROCHIAL SCHOOL SERVICES

14:80 Is it constitutionally permissible for a public school district to provide transportation for parochial school students?

A public school district must provide transportation for parochial school students under certain circumstances and subject to certain limitations. If a school district provides a school bus or other conveyance to transport students to and from school, it must transport, without charge, certain parochial school students who live along the public school district's regular bus routes.

A public school is required to provide such transportation to non-public school students only on the same basis on which transportation is provided to public school students. If a parochial school holds classes on a day public school students are not being transported, the public school is not obligated to transport them.

105 ILCS 5/29-4 et seq.

C.E. v. Board of Education of East St. Louis School District, 2012 IL App (5th) 110390, 970 N.E. 2d 1287, 361 Ill. Dec. 341

People ex rel. Board of Education of School District 142, Cook County v. Illinois Board of Education, 62 Ill. 2d 517, 344 N.E. 2d 5 (1976)

Board of Education School District 142 v. Bakalis, 54 Ill. 2d 448, 299 N.E. 2d 737 (1973)

Everson v. Board of Education of Ewing Township, 67 S. Ct. 504, 330 U.S. 1, 91 L. Ed. 711 (1947) reh. den. 67 S. Ct. 962, 330 U.S. 855, 91 L. Ed. 1297 (1947)

14:90 May a public school board assign public school teachers to perform secular teaching duties in a parochial school?

A public school district may permit public school teachers (including Title I teachers), guidance counselors, psychologists, teacher aides, consulting teachers, or social workers to teach secular subjects on site in parochial schools. A public school must assign a sign language interpreter for a child with a disability enrolled in a parochial school.

Agostini v. Felton, 117 0S. Ct. 1997, 521 U.S. 203, 138 L. Ed. 2d 391 (1997)

Zobrest v. Catalina Foothills School District, 113 S. Ct. 2462, 506 U.S. 813, 125 L. Ed. 2d 1 (1993)

14:95 May parochial school teachers instruct students on public school grounds during the public school day?

No. Public schools may not allow religious instruction by anyone during the school day.

Doe v. Shenandoah County School Board, 737 F. Supp. 913 (W.D. Va. 1990)

Doe v. Human, 725 F. Supp. 1499 (W.D. Ark. 1989) aff'd. without opinion 923 F. 2d 857 (8th Cir. 1990) cert. den. 111 S. Ct. 1315, 499 U.S. 922, 113 L. Ed. 2d 248 (1991)

14:100 May a school board provide free diagnostic services, such as speech, hearing, and psychological services, for nonpublic school students on public school property?

Yes.

Wolman v. Walter, 97 S. Ct. 2593, 433 U.S. 229, 53 L. Ed. 2d 714 (1977)

14:110 Are school voucher laws constitutional?

The constitutionality of voucher programs remains uncertain. In 2002, the United States Supreme Court in a 5-4 vote approved of Cleveland, Ohio's voucher program, but it is not at all certain what the Court would do with a program based on a slightly different set of facts.

Voucher programs allow the expenditure of specified public funds for private and sometimes sectarian education, usually at the discretion of individual taxpayers. Advocates of public education generally oppose voucher laws. Those who are critical of public education or who support religious education generally favor such laws.

In the Cleveland case the Court held that, "When a government aid program is neutral with respect to religion and provides assistance directly to a broad class of citizens, who, in turn, direct government aid to religious schools wholly as a result of their own genuine and independent private choice, the program is not readily subject to challenge under the establishment clause."

Zelman v. Simmons-Harris, 122 S. Ct. 2460, 536 U.S. 639, 153 L. Ed. 2d 604 (2002)

Mitchell v. Helms, 120 S. Ct 2530, 530 U.S. 793, 147 L. Ed. 2d 660 (2000) pet. for reh. den. 121 S. Ct. 15, 530 U.S. 1296, 147 L. Ed. 2d 1039 (2000)

Holmes v. Bush, 767 So. 2d 668 (Fla. Cir. Ct. 2000)

Mueller v. Allen, 103 S. Ct. 3062, 463 U.S. 388, 77 L. Ed. 2d 721 (1983)

SCHOOL FACILITIES

14:120 May a school board regulate or prohibit the distribution of religious literature on school grounds?

Students and members of the public are not agents of the state. However, the interplay between the school and persons seeking to use the school as a conduit to distribute a religious message may have the effect of having a religious purpose, advancing religion or entangling the state with religion, any of which violates the establishment clause of the U.S. Constitution. Whether any particular distribution of material violates the establishment clause or not is a fact question that requires an analysis of the time, place, means, and circumstances of the distribution.

If a student seeks to distribute material in a nonpublic forum (e.g., a K-8 grade building), prior restraint is constitutional if the prior restraint is reasonable. To be reasonable, the restraint must be narrowly drawn, reasonable, and must contain definite standards for school officials to follow.

While being cautious not to violate the establishment clause, a school district must also be mindful not to abridge the free speech rights of private persons, including students. A school district may adopt reasonable rules regarding the time, place, and manner of distribution of religious materials by private persons.

20 U.S.C. 4071

Bourgeois v. Peters, 387 F. 3d 1303 (11th Cir. 2004)

Peck et al. v. Upshur County Board of Education, 155 F. 3d 274 (4th Cir. 1998)

Muller v. Jefferson Lighthouse School, 98 F. 3d 1530 (7th Cir. 1996)

Berger by Berger v. Rensselaer Central School Corporation, 982 F. 2d 1160 (7th Cir. 1993) reh. den., 113 S. Ct. 2344, 508 U.S. 911, 124 L. Ed. 2d 254 (1993)

Hedges by and through Hedges v. Wauconda Community Unit School District No. 118 et al., 807 F. Supp. 444, 9 F. 3d 1295 (7th Cir. 1993)

Board of Education of Westside Community Schools v. Mergens, 110 S. Ct. 2356, 496 U.S. 226, 110 L. Ed. 2d 191 (1990)

Garnett v. Renton School District, 865 F. 2d 608 (9th Cir. 1989)

Widmar v. Vincent, 102 S. Ct. 269, 454 U.S. 263, 70 L. Ed. 2d 440 (1981)

14:123 May a school district erect a Christmas tree or display religious symbols?

How a particular display is analyzed for its constitutionality is dependent on the nature of the display; whether it is intended to be permanent, how it is paid for and its intended purpose. Christmas decorations are usually temporary and whether any particular religious symbol or display violates the establishment clause depends upon the underlying facts. If the court determines the display has the primary effect of advancing or inhibiting religion, it is found unconstitutional.

The same symbol may be found proper or improper depending upon the context in which it is displayed. A display accompanied by a religious message might, for example, make an otherwise permissible display unconstitutional.

Symbols can be used to proselytize and in appropriate circumstances coerced engagement with religious iconography and messages might take on the nature of religious exercise or forced inculcation of religion. But the establishment clause does not shield citizens from encountering the beliefs or symbols of any faith to which they do not subscribe and the court will look to the purpose, design, context, and implementation of the encounter with a religious symbol to determine whether or not it is constitutional. People take offense at all manner of religious and nonreligious messages, but offense alone is not enough to establish a constitutional violation

Where religious symbols are encountered is important to determining whether or not they are constitutional. A religious symbol on school property might convey a strong belief that the government endorses the beliefs expressed in the symbol. But when a school makes temporary use of a private facility (such as a church building) for a short time, an observer would not understand the message to have been made by or approved of by the state.

Any religious display must have a valid educational purpose.

Freedom from Religion Foundation v. Concord Community Schools, __ F. 3d __ (7th Cir. 2017)

Doe ex rel. Doe. v. Elmbrook School District, 658 F. 3d. 710 (7th Cir. 2011)

Pleasant Grove City, Utah, et al. v. Summum, 129 S. Ct. 1125, 555 U.S. 460, 172 L. Ed. 2d 856, (2009)

Sechler v. State College Area School District, 121 F. Supp. 2d 439 (M.D. Pa. 2000)

Capitol Square Review and Advisory Board v. Pinette, 114 S. Ct. 626, 510 U.S. 1307, 126 L. Ed. 2d 636 (1995)

Bloomingdale Public Schools v. Washgesic, 33 F. 3d 679 (6th Cir. 1994)

Clever v. Cherry Hill Township Board of Education, 838 F. Supp. 929 (D.C. N.J. 1993)

Lee v. Weisman, 112 S. Ct. 2649, 505 U.S. 577, 120 L. Ed. 2d 467 (1992)

Allegheny County v. American Civil Liberties Union, Greater Pittsburgh Chapter, 109 S. Ct. 3086, 492 U.S. 573, 106 L. Ed. 2d 472 (1989) on rem. 887 F. 2d 260 (3rd Cir. 1989)

Lemon v. Kurtzman, 91 S. Ct. 2105, 403 U.S. 602, 29 L. Ed. 2d 745 (1971), reh. den. 92 S. Ct. 24, 404 U.S. 876, 30 L. Ed. 2d 123 (1971), on rem. 348 F. Supp. 300, aff'd. 93 S. Ct. 1463, 411 U.S. 192, 36 L. Ed. 2d 151 (1971)

14:125 Do student-initiated religious displays violate the establishment clause?

Temporary displays (such as student artwork displayed in a hall) may be individual speech and therefore probably do not implicate establishment clause issues. But more permanent displays (such as a mural painted on a wall or a construction) are more likely to be seen as state-sponsored speech. Even speech that in another context might be considered private, once made permanent in the form of a mural or a construction, may raise entanglement of church and state questions. The analysis of any display issue is fact specific.

Doe ex rel. Doe. v. Elmbrook School District, 658 F. 3d. 710 (7th Cir. 2011)

Seidman v. Paradise Valley Unified School District No. 69, 327 F. Supp. 1098 (D. Ariz. 2004)

Fleming v. Jefferson County School District R-1, 298 F. 3d 918 (10th Cir. 2002), cert. den. 123 S. Ct. 893, 537 U.S. 1110, 154 L. Ed. 2d 783 (2002)

Gernetzke v. Kenosha Unified School District No. 1, 274 F. 3d 464 (7th Cir. 2001), cert. den. 122 S. Ct. 1606, 535 U.S. 1017, 152 L. Ed. 2d 620 (2002)

14:126 May a school district post The Ten Commandments in school board offices or in classrooms?

No. The posting of The Ten Commandments in a public school violates the establishment clause.

McCreary County, Kentucky v. American Civil Liberties Union of Kentucky, 125 S. Ct. 2722, 545 U.S.844, 162 L. Ed. 2d 729 (2005)

Van Orden v. Perry, 125 S. Ct. 2854, 545 U.S. 126, 162 L. Ed. 2d. 607 (2005)

Stone v. Graham, 101 S. Ct. 192, 449 U.S. 39, 66 L. Ed. 2d 199 (1980) reh. den. 101 S. Ct. 904, 449 U.S. 1104, 66 L. Ed. 2d 832 (1981) on rem. 612 S.W. 2d 133 (S. Ct. of Ky. 1981)

14:130 May a school board deny an adult, non-curriculum related religious organization the use of school facilities?

Requests by churches or other adult, non-curriculum related organizations for the after-hours use of school facilities must be handled in a non-discriminatory manner. An organization may not be denied access purely on the basis of its religious convictions. If the school district has allowed non-religious groups open access to school facilities, it has probably created an open public forum.

The existence of a limited open forum may not prevent the school board from adopting a policy prohibiting the holding of religious services or religious instruction on school grounds. In situations when school districts have created a limited open forum, school officials should be careful that if they have determined to restrict speech on the basis of a type of speech that they do not discriminate on the basis of viewpoint.

The Bronx Household of Faith v. Community School District No. 10, 127 F. 3d 207 (2nd Cir. 1997)

Fairfax Covenant Church v. Fairfax County School Board, 17 F. 3d 703 (4th Cir. 1994)

Grace Bible Fellowship v. School Administration, District 5, 941 F. 2d 45 (1st Cir. 1991)

Youth Opportunities Unlimited v. Board of Public Education, 769 F. Supp. 1346 (W.D. Pa. 1991)

Lemon v. Kurtzman, 91 S. Ct. 2105, 403 U.S. 602, 29 L. Ed. 2d 745 (1971), reh. den. 92 S. Ct. 24, 404 U.S. 876, 30 L. Ed. 2d 123 (1971), on rem. 348 F. Supp. 300, aff'd. 93 S. Ct. 1463, 411 U.S. 192, 36 L. Ed. 2d 151 (1971)

14:140 Must school boards permit student religious groups to use school property when not in use by the district for other school purposes?

The federal Equal Access Act provides that student religious organizations must be given the same access to secondary school facilities as any other student organization unless the school board limits access to those organizations that are curriculum related.

For a group to be curriculum related:

1) The subject matter of the group must be actually taught, or will soon be taught in a regularly offered course;

2) The subject matter of the group concerns the body of courses as a whole;

3) Participation in the group is required for a particular course; or

4) Participation in the group results in academic credit.

For almost all school districts, limitation is an unacceptable alternative because it would result in the elimination of access for many popular groups.

The Act applies to secondary schools, although the definition of secondary school may be ambiguous and under certain circumstances may include middle or junior high schools. To avoid establishment clause concerns schools should limit an outside group's access to facilities to non-instructional time. Non-instructional time is not necessarily limited to before or after school times.

The Equal Access Act contains a "safe harbor" provision that requires schools to offer a fair opportunity to meet. Schools must provide that (1) the meeting is voluntary and student initiated; (2) the school does not sponsor the meeting; (3) school officials do not participate in any religious meetings; (4) the meeting does not substantially and materially interfere with educational activities; and (5) non-school persons may not direct, conduct, control, or regularly attend activities of students groups.

The Boy Scouts of America Equal Access Act (BSEA), however, applies to any school district that receives federal funds. The BSEA provides that if a school allows youth or community groups to meet in its facilities before or after school, it may not deny similar access to, or discriminate against the Boy Scouts or any other group listed in the BSEA. The application of the BSEA is not limited to secondary schools nor is it limited to student-initiated meetings. The BSEA merely permits meetings and use of facilities. It does not require nor authorize school sponsorship of any group that is authorized to meet.

The U.S. Supreme Court has suggested that an elementary school may create a limited open forum for speech. If so, any restriction on speech school officials seek to impose must not discriminate on the basis of viewpoint, and the restriction must be reasonable in light of the purpose served by the forum.

School employees may be passive supervisors but may not be active participants in student religious organizations without raising establishment clause issues for the school district.

A 2004 Eighth Circuit case suggests an elementary school teacher's participation in after-school student religious club activities at his or her own school where children have parental permission to participate in the club is permissible. This decision conflicts directly with a provision in the Equal Access Act (which applies to secondary schools only). It is uncertain how the courts will resolve the apparent conflict.

20 U.S.C. 4071

20 U.S.C. 7905

Wigg v. Sioux Falls School District 49-5, 382 F. 3d 807 (8th Cir. 2004)

Donovan v. Punxsutawney Area School Board, 336 F. 3d 211(3rd Cir.2003)

Good News v. Milford Central School, 121 S. Ct. 2093, 533 U.S. 98, 150 L. Ed. 2d 151 (2001)

Rosenberger et al. v. Rector and Visitors of the University of Virginia, 115 S. Ct. 2510, 515 U.S. 819, 132 L. Ed. 2d 700 (1995)

Pope v. East Brunswick Board of Education, 12 F. 3d 1244 (3rd Cir. 1993)

Board of Education of Westside Community Schools v. Mergens, 110 S. Ct. 2365, 496 U.S. 226, 110 L. Ed. 2d 191 (1990)

Garnett v. Benton School District, 865 F. 2d 1211 (9th Cir. 1989)

Widmar v. Vincent, 102 S. Ct. 269, 454 U.S. 263, 70 L. Ed. 2d 440 (1981)

14:145 Must a school district permit local clergy to use school facilities for a privately organized baccalaureate?

If the school permits use of its facilities by other non-school groups, it must make its facilities available on the same bases to the non-school organizers of a high school baccalaureate ceremony. If it appears by reason of the location of the services that the school is endorsing the baccalaureate, school officials should disclaim such endorsement.

Good News/Good Sports Club v. School District of City of LaDue, 859 F. Supp. 1239, (D.C. 1993) 28 F. 3d 1501 (8th Cir. 1994) cert. den., reh. and sugg. for reh. den., 115 S. Ct. 2640, 515 U.S. 1173, 132 L. Ed. 2d 878 (1995)

Lamb's Chapel v. Center Moriches Union Free School District, 113 S. Ct. 2141, 508 U.S. 384, 124 L. Ed. 2d 352 (1993)

14:150 May teachers hold prayer meetings with students in school facilities before or after school?

No. Teachers are bound by the prohibitions of the First Amendment that bar a teacher from advancing religion when the teacher is acting in his or her official capacity.

May v. Evansville-Vanderburg School Corporation, 787 F. 2d 1005 (7th Cir. 1986)

CURRICULAR ISSUES

14:200 May a school district include religious instruction in its curriculum?

A school district may include instruction in comparative religions and Bible history, and may educate students about religion in general, but may not sponsor or advocate the teaching of a particular religion or group of religions (such as Christianity, Judaism, or Islam), religious practice, or religious belief.

Gibson v. Lee County School Board, 1 F. Supp. 2d 1426 (M.D. Fla. 1998)

Edwards v. Aguillard, 107 S. Ct. 2573, 482 U.S. 578, 96 L. Ed. 2d 510 (1987)

Stone v. Graham, 101 S. Ct. 192, 449 U.S. 39, 66 L. Ed. 2d 199 (1980) reh. den. 101 S. Ct. 904, 449 U.S. 1104, 66 L. Ed. 2d 832 on rem. 612 S.W. 2d 133 (S. Ct. of Ky. 1981)

School District of Abington Township v. Schempp, 83 S. Ct. 1560, 374 U.S. 203, 10 L. Ed. 2d 844 (1963)

14:205 May a school district include a Bible literacy course in its curriculum?

It is almost certainly possible to construct a Bible literacy curriculum and teach a course that passes constitutional muster. But a school district contemplating the creation of a course curriculum should be wary that the impetus to add such a curriculum usually comes from religious individuals or groups that seek to advocate a particular religious agenda and if the adopted curriculum is not facially neutral, school officials will, at a minimum, create controversy and possibly invite an expensive and divisive constitutional challenge.

If school officials determine to add such a course, seeking input from diverse viewpoints in the community would be wise and choosing a teacher or teachers who can refrain from advocating for one religion or another would be wiser. Teachers selected to teach such a curriculum should have academic credentials to support their competency.

Gibson v. Lee County School Board, 1 F. Supp. 2d 1426 (M.D. Fla. 1998)

Herdahl v. Pontotoc County School District, 933 F. Supp. 582 (N.D. Miss. 1996)

Hall v. Board of Commissioners of Conecuh County, 656 F. 2d 999 (5th Cir. 1981)

School District of Abington Township v. Schempp, 83 S. Ct. 1560, 374 U.S. 203, 10 L. Ed. 2d 844 (1963)

Illinois ex rel. McCollum v. Board of Education of School District No. 71, Champaign County, Illinois, 68 S. Ct. 461, 333 U.S. 203, 92 L. Ed. 649 (1948)

14:210 May parents object to curriculum content on the grounds that a student's participation violates the child's free exercise of religion?

Parental objections of this type are common. Usually a school can defend by allowing the objecting child to opt out of the objectionable portion of the curriculum (by curriculum substitution or removal to home or private school).

Leebaert v. Harrington, 332 F. 3d 134 (2nd Cir. 2003)

Mozert v. Hawkins County, 827 F. 2d 1058 (6th Cir. 1987)

Thomas v. Review Board, 101 S. Ct. 1425, 450 U.S. 707, 67 L. Ed. 2d 624 (1981)

Sherbert v. Verner, 83 S. Ct. 1790, 374 U.S. 398, 10 L. Ed. 2d 965 (1963)

14:220 May a teacher prevent a student from preparing a school paper on a religious theme?

A student's right to freedom of expression may be limited to achieve an educational goal. For example, free speech rights or the right to religious expression may be limited when either interferes with the educational process.

A teacher may prevent a student from writing a research paper on a religious theme if the topic interferes with the goals of the assignment, even if the topic otherwise would constitute exercise of religious freedom and otherwise would be permissible in an educational setting.

Settle v. Dickson County School Board, 53 F. 3d 152 (6th Cir. 1995)

14:225 Does a school musical group performing religious songs violate the establishment clause?

Whether or not there is an establishment clause violation will depend upon the facts surrounding the performance. Most school Christmas programs or holiday-time choir performances do not violate the establishment clause because they would not lead a reasonable observer to conclude the activity was promoting religion or advancing a particular religious belief.

Freedom from Religion Foundation v. Concord Community Schools, __ F. 3d __ (7th Cir. 2017)

Bauchman by and through Bauchman v. West High School, 900 F. Supp. 254 aff'd. *Bauchman for Bauchman v. West High School*, 132 F. 3d 542 (10th Cir. 1997) cert. den. 118 S. Ct. 2370, 524 U.S. 953, 141 L. Ed. 2d 738 (1998)

R.J.J. v. Shineman, 658 S.W. 2d 910 (Mo. App. 1983)

14:230 May a school district require a teacher to teach evolution if the teacher has religious objections to doing so?

Such a teacher may be required to teach evolution and should be directed not to discuss the Biblical view of the subject with his or her students.

Helland v. South Bend Community School Corporation, 93 F. 3d 327 (7th Cir. 1996)

Peloza v. Capistrano Unified School District, 37 F. 3d 517 (9th Cir. 1994)

14:231 May a school district curriculum include alternatives to evolution such as creation science or intelligent design?

Curriculum materials that attempt to inject the Biblical view of the origins of man or to attack the scientific underpinnings of evolution have been given many creative names. To the extent a curriculum attempts to offer the Biblical view of the origin of man or challenges a scientific theory with a religious theory it will not likely survive a challenge in court.

Neither creation science nor intelligent design (or any other attempt to undermine evolution science with the Biblical view of the origins of man or the universe) is likely to survive a First Amendment challenge. Attempts to undermine evolutionary science by requiring disclaimers, or by suggestion of alternative explanations for the origins of life are not likely to survive a challenge either.

Kitzmiller v. Dover Area School District, 400 F. Supp.2d 707 (M.D. Pa. 2005)

Selman v. Cobb County School District, 390 F. Supp. 2d 1286 (N.D. Ga. 2005)

Freiler v. Tangipahoa Parish Board of Education, 185 F. 3d 337 (5th Cir. 1999)

Edwards v. Aguillard, 107 S. Ct. 2573, 482 U.S. 578, 96 L. Ed. 2d 510 (1987)

B. RACIAL ISSUES

SCHOOL DESEGREGATION

14:400 What constitutional principle underlies school desegregation?

School segregation by race deprives minority students of equal protection, which is guaranteed by the 14th Amendment to the U.S. Constitution.

Brown v. Board of Education of Topeka, Shawnee County, Kansas, 74 S. Ct. 686, 347 U.S. 483, 98 L. Ed. 873, 38 ALR 2d 1180, supp. 75 S. Ct. 753, 349 U.S. 294, 99 L. Ed. 1083 (1954)

14:410 What is the role of the Illinois State Board of Education in preventing school segregation?

When the State Board of Education receives a complaint signed by at least 50 residents of a school district or 10 percent of the residents of a district, whichever is less, charging either students have been segregated on the basis of race, nationality, or religion, or school employees or applicants for employment have been discriminated against on the same bases, the State Board must notify the district of the complaint and, within 30 days, set a hearing on the charges. If, after hearing, it is determined the charges are valid, the State Board must send its findings to the Illinois Attorney General for prosecution.

105 ILCS 5/18-12

Aurora East School District No. 131 v. Cronin, 92 Ill. 2d 305, 442 N.E. 2d 511, 66 Ill. Dec. 85 (1982)

14:420 May school officials admit students to school programs under a system intended to take into account the race of the students?

Racial or ethnic classifications of any sort are inherently suspect and call for strict judicial scrutiny. The goal of racial diversity will support the consideration of race in affirmative action programs intended to encourage minority participation. However, such programs may not preclude applicants solely on the basis of race.

Gratz v. Bollinger, 123 S. Ct. 2411, 539 U.S. 244, 156 L. Ed. 2d 257 (2003)

Green v. County School Board of New Kent County, 88 S. Ct. 1689, 391 U.S. 430, 2d 257 (2003)

Regents of the University of California v. Bakke, 98 S. Ct. 2733, 438 U.S. 265, 57 L. Ed. 2d 750 (1978)

SEGREGATION REMEDIES

14:440 If a school system is found to be segregated, how quickly must the district act to rectify the problem?

A school district's obligation is to end segregation at once and to operate now and hereafter only integrated schools.

Alexander v. Holmes County Board of Education, 90 S. Ct. 21, 396 U.S. 19, 24 L. Ed. 2d 19 (1969)

14:450 What must a school district do to comply with a desegregation order?

A school district subject to a desegregation order must remedy the racial imbalance that resulted in the constitutional violation. A school district may not be required to fully integrate its schools to accomplish this. Once racial imbalance due to the constitutional violation has been remedied, the school district is under no duty to remedy imbalance that is caused by demographic factors.

Freeman v. Pitts, 112 S. Ct. 1430, 503 U.S. 467, 118 L. Ed. 2d 108 (1992)

14:460 Is the purpose of a plan significant in determining whether or not it advances desegregation objectives?

The purpose of a plan is significant in that it must comport with the requirements of the law. More important from the standpoint of judicial scrutiny is whether or not the effect of the plan ends segregation.

Wright v. Council of the City of Emporia, 92 S. Ct. 2196, 407 U.S. 451, 33 L. Ed. 2d 51 (1972)

14:470 If a school system is found to be segregated, will an "open enrollment" plan suffice to desegregate it?

Open enrollment or free transfer plans are not sufficient to alone serve to desegregate a school system that has been found to be segregated. A school board must take affirmative steps to assure that racial discrimination is eliminated. Open enrollment plans are not inherently suspect, they simply may not be enough to achieve desegregation.

Green v. County School Board of New Kent County, 88 S. Ct. 1689, 391 U.S. 430, 20 L. Ed. 2d 716 (1968)

Monroe v. Board of Commissioners of City of Jackson, Tennessee, 88 S. Ct. 1700, 391 U.S. 450, 20 L. Ed. 2d 733 (1968)

Raney v. Board of Education of Gould School District, 88 S. Ct. 1697, 391 U.S. 443, 20 L. Ed. 2d 727 (1968)

14:472 May a school district that is not subject to a desegregation order use race as a factor in assigning its students to schools?

Even if the school district's motive is to "balance" schools by race or to "prevent" segregation, enrollment plans that consider race only will fail as unconstitutional. The U.S. Supreme Court has held that "racial balance is not to be achieved for its own sake" and that "outright racial balancing" is "patently unconstitutional." It is possible that a school assignment plan that considered a broad array of diversity factors in the assignment of students to schools would be constitutional.

The court has observed that racial balancing is not a compelling state interest unless it is used as a remedy for the effects of past intentional discrimination. The court has also recognized student body diversity in higher education as a compelling state interest.

Parents Involved in Community Schools v. Seattle School District No. 1, 127 S. Ct. 2738, 551 U.S. 701, 168 L. Ed. 2d 508 (2007)

Grutter v. Bollinger, 123 S. Ct. 2325, 539 U.S. 306,156 L. Ed. 2d 304 (2003)

14:480 Is a law constitutional when it prohibits assignment of students to an attendance center on the basis of race but forbids busing such students?

Laws that forbid busing for purposes of integration are unconstitutional because they deprive school officials of a tool necessary to eliminate segregation.

20 U.S.C. 1701 et seq.

North Carolina State Board of Education v. Swann, 91 S. Ct. 1284, 402 U.S. 43, 28 L. Ed. 2d 586 (1971)

14:490 Does a court have the power to order a multi-district remedy when one school district produces a segregative effect in one or more other school districts?

The court has such power if it can be shown that the discriminatory acts of the state or one or more school districts have been a substantial cause of inter-district segregation. An inter-district desegregation order is, however, an extreme remedy that would be ordered only very reluctantly by a court. To justify an inter-district remedy, it must be shown that the state or the outlying districts engaged in activity that had a cross-district discriminatory effect.

20 U.S.C. 1715

Milliken v. Bradley, 94 S. Ct. 3112, 418 U.S. 717, 41 L. Ed. 2d 1069, on rem. 402 F. Supp. 1096, on rem. 411 F. Supp. 943, aff'd. cause rem. 540 F. 2d 229, aff'd. 97 S. Ct. 2749, 433 U.S. 267, 53 L. Ed. 2d 745 (1977) on rem. 620 F. 2d 1143, cert. den. 101 S. Ct. 2017, 449 U.S. 870, 66 L. Ed. 2d 89 (1980)

14:500 What criteria are considered when a court is petitioned for relief from a desegregation order?

The court considers:

1) Compliance with the desegregation decree in areas where relief is sought;

2) The necessity or practicality of retaining judicial supervision in other areas; and

3) Good faith efforts by the school district towards the students and parents in the disfavored race in complying with the desegregation decree.

Missouri v. Jenkins, 115 S. Ct. 2573, 515 U.S. 1139, 132 L. Ed. 2d 824 (1995)

EMPLOYMENT

14:510 In determining whether an employer has discriminated, with what is the racial composition of employees compared?

In determining whether there is a pattern or practice of racial discrimination, a comparison is made between the percentage of minority employees and the percentage of minorities in the relevant labor pool. Once discrimination has been established by statistical work force disparities, the employer is given an opportunity to show that the claimed discriminatory pattern is a product of hiring that occurred before the enactment of title VII of the 1964 Civil Rights Act rather than unlawful post-Act discrimination.

Hazelwood School District v. U.S., 97 S. Ct. 2736, 433 U.S. 299, 53 L. Ed. 2d 768 (1977)

International Brotherhood of Teamsters v. U.S., 97 S. Ct. 1843, 431 U.S. 324, 52 L. Ed. 2d 396 (1977)

14:520 Is a testing program that has a racially disproportionate impact unconstitutional?

If the test is otherwise non-discriminatory and there is a rational relationship between the test and its constitutional purpose, the test is not unconstitutional simply because it has a racially disproportionate impact. However, an employer may not require a test where there is no showing that test criteria are significantly related to job performance and the test has a disparate impact on blacks.

National Education Association v. South Carolina, 98 S. Ct. 756, 434 U.S. 1026, 54 L. Ed. 2d 775 (1978) affirming *U.S. v. State of South Carolina*, 445 F. Supp. 1094 (D.C. S.C. 1978)

Washington v. Davis, 96 S. Ct. 2040, 426 U.S. 229, 48 L. Ed. 2d 597 (1976)

Griggs v. Duke Power Company, 91 S. Ct. 849, 401 U.S. 424, 28 L. Ed. 2d 158 (1971)

14:530 May a school board adopt a plan to hire minorities in specified numbers in order to remedy past discrimination?

If the plan is justified by a compelling state interest in eliminating the discriminatory exclusion of minorities and is narrowly tailored to serve that purpose, an affirmative action plan is constitutional. Quota relief is a temporary remedy that is used to create as quickly as possible a climate in which neutral employment criteria can successfully operate to select public employees solely on the basis of job-related merit.

Messer v. Meno, 936 F. Supp. 1280 (W.D. Tex. 1996) aff'd. in part rev. in part 130 F. 3d 130 (5th Cir. 1997)

United States v. Paradise, 107 S. Ct. 706, 480 U.S. 149, 102 L. Ed. 2d 854 (1987)

Wygant v. Jackson Board of Education, 106 S. Ct. 1842, 476 U.S. 267 (1986) reh. den. 106 S. Ct. 3320, 478 U.S. 1014, 92 L. Ed. 2d 728 (1986)

Local 28 of the Sheet Metal Workers International Association v. Equal Employment Opportunities Commission, 106 S. Ct. 3019, 478 U.S. 421, 92 L. Ed. 2d 344 (1986)

14:540 May a school board require that a certain percentage of bids be let to minority contractors?

To do so, the school board must demonstrate a compelling state interest justifying the plan. The school board must have a proven history of discrimination that the plan is narrowly tailored to remedy.

To determine whether there is a history of discrimination, the appropriate test is to compare the percentage of minority business enterprises in the relevant market that are qualified to undertake the work to be let with the percentage of total relevant dollars that are awarded to minority business enterprises.

City of Richmond v. J.A. Croson Co., 109 S. Ct. 706, 488 U.S. 469, 102 L. Ed. 2d 854 (1989)

Fullilove v. Klutznick, 100 S. Ct. 2758, 448 U.S. 448, 65 L. Ed. 2d 902 (1980)

14:550 What is the meaning of the word "race" in the context of civil rights statutes?

When enacting federal civil rights law, Congress intended to protect from discrimination identifiable classes of persons who are subjected to intentional discrimination solely because of their ancestry or ethnic characteristics. Such discrimination is racial discrimination that Congress intended civil rights law to forbid, whether or not it would be classified as racial in terms of modern scientific theory. A distinctive physiognomy is not essential to qualify for civil rights anti-discrimination protection.

42 U.S.C. 1981

Abdullahi v. Prada, 520 F. 3d 710 (7th Cir. 2008)

St. Francis College v. Al-Khazraji, 107 S. Ct. 2022, 481 U.S. 604, 95 L. Ed. 2d 582 (1987)

14:600 What constitutes race-based "hostile environment" discrimination?

Title VII of the Civil Rights Act prohibits employers from discriminating against a person with respect to compensation, terms, conditions, or privileges of employment because of the individual's race. To prove "hostile environment" the plaintiff must prove that the work environment was both objectively and subjectively offensive, that the harassment was based on race, that the conduct was either severe or pervasive, and that there was a basis for employer liability.

Employers are strictly liable for harassment inflicted by supervisors, but they can assert an affirmative defense when the harassment does not result in tangible employment action. A supervisor is someone with power to directly affect the terms and conditions of a person's employment.

If only co-workers are responsible for making a work environment hostile, the plaintiff must show that the employer has been negligent either in discovering or remedying the harassment. An employer's liability for co-worker harassment is not triggered unless the employee notifies the employer about an instance of racial harassment.

An employer can avoid liability for its employee's harassment if it takes prompt and appropriate corrective action reasonably likely to prevent harassment from recurring. Title VII does not require an employer's response to successfully prevent subsequent harassment, though it should be reasonably calculated to do so.

Vance v. Ball State, 646 F. 3d 461 (7th Cir. 2011)

14:610 How does an employee prove racial discrimination?

The plaintiff can provide either direct or circumstantial evidence of discrimination. Under the direct method, the evidence points directly to a discriminatory reason for the employer's actions.

Under the circumstantial method, the plaintiff must show evidence that if taken together would allow a reasonable fact-finder to infer discriminatory intent. The courts use what is commonly referred to as the "McDonnell Douglas" test to establish circumstantial discrimination. Under McDonnell Douglas, the plaintiff must show he or she is a member of a protected class, he or she performed his or her job to the employer's expectations, he or she suffered an adverse employment action, and one or more similarly situated individuals outside the protected class were treated better. If the plaintiff makes a prima facie case then the employer must prove a legitimate, nondiscriminatory reason for the challenged action. If the employer is able to do that, the plaintiff has the burden to prove the employer's reason was pretext.

The courts will consider:

- Suspicious timing;
- Evidence that employees outside the plaintiff's protected group, but who are otherwise similarly situated, received systematically better treatment; and
- Evidence that a qualified plaintiff was replaced by or was passed over for a position in favor of a person who was not in the protected group and the employer's reason for not choosing the plaintiff was pretextual.

Ferrill v. Oak Creek-Franklin School District, _ F. 3d 7th Cir. 2017)

Abuelyaman v. Illinois State University, 667 F. 3d 800 (7th Cir. 2011)

McDonnell Douglas Corp. v. Green, 93 S. Ct. 1817, 411 U.S. 792, 36 L.Ed. 2d 668 (1973)

14:620 How does an employee prove that a failure to promote was racially motivated?

Failure to promote claims are only actionable if not receiving the position is a materially adverse employment action. Generally this means the position for which the employee was rejected offered markedly greater compensation, responsibility, or title. The elements of a failure to promote claim require the employee to show he or she was a member of the protected class, he or she was qualified for the position, he or she was rejected for the position, and the employer promoted someone outside the protected class who was better qualified.

Riley v. Elkhart Community Schools, 829 F. 3d 886 (7th Cir. 2016)

15: TERMS AND CONDITIONS OF TEACHER EMPLOYMENT

STATE CERTIFICATION (LICENSURE)

15:10 Who is a teacher?

A teacher, for most purposes under Illinois law, is any school district employee whose job requires teacher licensure/certification. The term "teacher" usually includes superintendents, principals, other licensed administrators, guidance counselors, deans, and classroom teachers and may include other job titles.

105 ILCS 5/24-11(a)

105 ILCS 5/10-23.8

105 ILCS 5/10-23.8a

Lester v. Board of Education of School District No. 119, Jo Daviess County, 87 Ill. App. 2d 269, 230 N.E. 2d 893 (2nd Dist. 1967)

15:20 Must all teachers be licensed?

The licensure system in Illinois changed in 2013. Previously, the laws referred to teacher certification (and there are still some remaining references in the law during the transition period). Persons employed in school districts who are required to be licensed must have one of the following licenses: a professional educator license; a professional educator license with stipulations; or a substitute teaching license.

References in law regarding individuals certified or certificated or required to be certified or certificated under Article 21 of the School Code also include individuals licensed or required to be licensed. The first year of all licenses ends on June 30 following one full year of the license being issued.

No one may be licensed to teach or supervise or be otherwise employed in the public schools who is not of good character and at least 20 years of age. In determining good character, the State Superintendent of Education must take into consideration the disciplinary actions of other states or national entities against certificates or licenses issued by those states and held by individuals from those states.

Any felony conviction may be taken into consideration; however, no one may be licensed to teach or supervise who has been convicted of an offense listed in Section 21B-80 of the School Code. Unless the conviction is for an offense in Section 21B-80, an applicant must be permitted to submit character references or other written material before such a conviction or other information regarding the applicant's character may be used by the State Superintendent of Education as a basis for denying the application.

No person otherwise qualified may be denied the right to be licensed or to receive training for the purpose of becoming an educator because of a physical disability, including, but not limited to, visual and hearing disabilities; nor can a school district refuse to employ a teacher on those grounds, provided that the person is able to carry out the duties of the position for which he or she applies. No person may be granted or continue to hold an educator license who has knowingly altered or misrepresented his or her qualifications, in Illinois or any other state, in order to acquire or renew the license. Any other license issued held by the person may be suspended or revoked by the State Educator Preparation and Licensure Board, depending upon the severity of the alteration or misrepresentation.

No one may teach or supervise in the public schools nor receive for teaching or supervising any part of any public school fund who does not hold an educator license granted by the State Superintendent of Education except a member of the armed forces who is employed as a teacher of subjects in the Reserve Officers' Training Corps of any school, nor to an individual teaching a dual credit course as provided for in the Dual Credit Quality Act.

105 ILCS 5/21B-5 et seq.

110 ILCS 27-1 et seq.

Frazier v. Garrison Independent School District, 980 F. 2d 1514 (5th Cir. 1993)

15:26 What is a new teacher induction and mentoring program?

A 2003 statute requires school districts to establish in conjunction with their exclusive bargaining representatives new teacher induction and mentoring programs.

Each new teacher induction and mentoring program must be based on a plan that does all of the following:

1) Assigns a mentor teacher to each new teacher for a period of at least two school years;

2) Aligns with the Illinois Professional Teaching Standards content area standards applicable to local school improvement and professional development plans, if any;

3) Addresses all of the following elements and how they will be provided;

a) Mentoring and support of the new teacher;

b) Professional development specifically designed to ensure the growth of the new teacher's knowledge and skills;

c) Formative assessment designed to ensure feedback and reflection, which must not be used in any evaluation of the new teacher; and

4) Describes the role of mentor teachers, the criteria and process for their selection, and how they will be trained, provided that each mentor teacher shall demonstrate the best practices in teaching his or her respective field of practice. A mentor teacher may not directly or indirectly participate in the evaluation of a new teacher pursuant to Article 24A of the School Code or the evaluation procedure of the public school.

105 ILCS 5/21A-10
105 ILCS 5/21A-15
105 ILCS 5/21A-20

15:27 May a person who does not have conventional training in education acquire a teaching license?

Beginning on January 1, 2013 a new alternative licensure program was created and an old program phased out. The new program is comprised of four phases including two years of supervised residency with a co-teacher and teacher mentor. The alternate certification requires that the candidate have a college degree, a minimum grade point average, requires completion of certain course content and successful completion of a test of basic skills and content area and compliance with other requirements contained in the relevant statute.

105 ILCS 5/21B-50

15:28 How may a retiring teacher maintain his or her license?

For any renewal cycle in which a licensee retires during the renewal cycle, the licensee must complete professional development activities on a prorated basis depending on the number of years during the renewal cycle the educator held an active license. If a licensee retires during a renewal cycle, the licensee must notify the State Board of Education using ELIS (Educator Licensure Information System) that the licensee wishes to maintain the license in retired status and must show proof of completion of professional development activities on a prorated basis for all years of that renewal cycle for which the license was active.

105 ILCS 5/21B-45 (e) (6)

15:30 Are there different certification (licensure) requirements for teachers at different grade levels and for teaching different subject matters?

Yes.

105 ILCS 5/21-1a et seq.
23 Ill. Admin. Code 1.710
23 Ill. Admin. Code 1.720
23 Ill. Admin. Code 1.730
23 Ill. Admin. Code 1.737
23 Ill. Admin. Code 1.745 et seq.
23 Ill. Admin. Code Appendix A

15:32 Can special education teachers receive categorical certification?

Beginning with the 2002-2003 school term, the State Teacher Certification Board (now called the State Educator Preparation and Licensure Board) began certifying special education teachers in specialized categories of disability. Certification is possible in one or more categories if the special education teacher applies and qualifies for such certification. The categories are

1) Learning behavior specialist I;

2) Learning behavior specialist II;

3) Teacher of students who are blind or visually impaired;

4) Teacher of students who are deaf or hard of hearing;

5) Speech-language pathologist; and

6) Early childhood special education teacher.

105 ILCS 5/21-28

15:34 Who is a qualified worker?

"Qualified worker" means a trained specialist and includes a behavior analyst, licensed school nurse, professional consultant, registered therapist, school nurse intern, school counselor, school counselor intern, school psychologist, school psychologist intern, school social worker, school social worker intern, special administrator or supervisor giving full time to special education, speech language pathologist, speech language pathologist intern, and teacher of students with IEPs who meets the requirements of Article 14 of the School Code, who has the required special training in the understandings, techniques, and special instructional strategies for children with disabilities and who delivers services to students with IEPs, and any other trained specialist set forth by the State Board of Education in rules.

Before 2009, the School Code referred to the persons described in the relevant statute as "professional workers."

105 ILCS 5/14-1.10

15:40 Does a teaching license indicate the subject areas the teacher may teach?

New licenses are "endorsed with specific areas and grade levels in which the individual is eligible to practice." Until June 30, 2013, teaching licenses issued after June 30, 1986, were endorsed by the State Board of Education for each subject the holder of the license was certified to teach. Licenses that were issued prior to July 1, 1986, may have been endorsed on the date of issue (depending on the date of issue) or may, on application to the State Board of Education, be endorsed for each subject the holder is certified to teach.

105 ILCS 5/21B-20

Zink v. Board of Education of Chrisman, 146 Ill. App. 3d 1016, 497 N.E. 2d 835, 100 Ill. Dec. 657 (4th Dist. 1986)

15:42 What are the certification requirements for school counselors?

A school counselor must have a School Service Personnel license endorsed in school counseling and who either holds or is qualified for an elementary, secondary, special K-12, or special preschool-age 21 license or in lieu of holding or qualifying for a teaching license, has fulfilled such other requirements as the State Board of Education and the State Educator Preparation and Licensure Board have established.

An individual who has completed an approved program in another state may apply for a School Service Personnel license endorsed in school counseling and will receive a license if a review of credentials indicates that he or she meets the additional requirements of the referenced rules.

105 ILCS 5/10-22.24a

15:45 What are the licensure requirements for school nurses?

A school board may employ a registered professional nurse and may define the duties of the nurse consistent with the rules established by the State Board of Education. Beginning in 2013, only licensed school nurses may make medical review recommendations in the construct of student IEPs.

Nurses first employed on or after July 1, 1976, whose duties require teaching or the exercise of instructional judgment or educational evaluation of pupils must have a school service personnel license. To obtain a school service personnel license, the applicant must have a bachelor's degree.

A school district may employ a nonlicensed registered nurse to narrowly perform some nursing (no instruction-related) services.

105 ILCS 5/10-22.23

23 Ill. Admin. Code 1.760

23 Ill. Admin. Code 25.245

225 ILCS 60/1 et seq.

225 ILCS 65/1 et seq.

Winters v. Board of Education of Piasa Community Unit School District No. 9 of Macoupin County, 66 Ill. App. 3d 918, 384 N.E. 2d 519, 23 Ill. Dec. 725 (4th Dist. 1978)

15:50 Must a school board help a teacher secure a teaching license?

It is the sole responsibility of a teacher to apply for and secure teaching certification/licensure.

Hagopian v. Board of Education of Tampico Community Unit School District No. 4 of Whiteside and Bureau Counties, 56 Ill. App. 3d 940, 372 N.E. 2d 990, 14 Ill. Dec. 711 (3rd Dist. 1978), app. after rem. 83 Ill. App. 3d 1097, 404 N.E. 2d 899, 39 Ill. Dec. 308, (3rd Dist. 1980), rev. on other grounds 84 Ill. 2d 436, 420 N.E. 2d 147, 50 Ill. Dec. 830 (1981)

Relph v. Board of Education of Depue Unit School District No. 103 of Bureau County, 84 Ill. 2d 436, 420 N.E. 2d 147, 50 Ill. Dec. 830 (1978)

15:60 Under what conditions may a teacher's certificate/license be suspended or revoked?

The State Superintendent of Education has the exclusive authority to initiate the suspension for up to five calendar years or revocation of any license, including any administrative license or endorsement, for abuse or neglect of a child; immorality; a condition of health detrimental to the welfare of pupils; incompetency;, unprofessional conduct (which includes the failure to disclose on an employment application any previous conviction for a sex offense as defined in Section 21B 80 of the School Code or any other offense committed in any other state or against the laws of the United States that, if committed in Illinois, would be punishable as a sex offense (as defined in section 21B-80; the neglect of any professional duty; willful failure to report an instance of suspected child abuse or neglect as required by the Abused and Neglected Child Reporting Act; failure to establish satisfactory repayment on an educational loan guaranteed by the Illinois Student Assistance Commission; or just cause.

Before a 2009 change in the law, a regional superintendent of schools had authority to suspend a license for one year.

Incompetency means two or more school terms of service for which the license holder has received an unsatisfactory rating on a performance evaluation conducted pursuant to Article 24A of the School Code within a period of seven school terms of service. In determining whether to initiate action against one or more licenses based on incompetency and the recommended sanction for such action, the State Superintendent must consider factors that include without limitation all of the following:

1) Whether the unsatisfactory evaluation ratings occurred prior to June 13, 2011.

2) Whether the unsatisfactory evaluation ratings occurred prior to or after the PERA (Performance Evaluation Reform Act, P.A. 96-861) implementation date (2015 for some districts and 2016 for most districts) defined in Section 24A-2.5 of the School Code, of an evaluation system for teachers in a school district.

3) Whether the evaluator or evaluators who performed an unsatisfactory evaluation met the pre-certification and training requirements in Section 24A-3 of the School Code.

4) The time between the unsatisfactory evaluation ratings.

5) The quality of the remediation plans associated with the unsatisfactory evaluation ratings and whether the license holder successfully completed the remediation plans.

6) Whether the unsatisfactory evaluation ratings were related to the same or different assignments performed by the license holder.

7) Whether one or more of the unsatisfactory evaluation ratings occurred in the first year of a teaching or administrative assignment.

When initiating an action against one or more licenses, the State Superintendent may seek required professional development as a sanction in lieu of or in addition to suspension or revocation. Any such required professional development must be at the expense of the license holder, who may use, if available and applicable to the requirements established by administrative or court order, training, coursework, or other professional development funds in accordance with the terms of an applicable collective bargaining agreement entered into after June 13, 2011, unless that agreement specifically precludes use of funds for that purpose.

Before 2011, the license revocation process had rarely been employed and then only in the most extreme fact situations. The number of cases brought has increased after Senate Bill 7 in 2011 but it remains uncertain how many of the cases will end in revocation.

105 ILCS 5/2-3.9

105 ILCS 5/21B-1 et seq.

105 ILCS 5/21B-75

105 ILCS 5/24A-1 et seq.

Board of Education of Park Forest Heights School District No. 163 v. The State Teacher Certification Board, et al., 363 Ill. App. 3d 433, 842 N.E. 2d 1230, 299 Ill. Dec. 878, (1st Dist. 2006) cert. den. 219 Ill. 2d 561, 852 N.E. 2d 238, 303 Ill. Dec. 831 (2006)

15:62 What is unprofessional conduct?

Unprofessional conduct includes neglect or unnecessary delay in making of statistical and other reports required by school officers, refusal to attend or participate in institutes, teachers' meetings, professional readings, or to meet other reasonable requirements of the regional superintendent or State Superintendent of Education.

Unprofessional conduct also includes conduct that violates the standards, ethics, or rules applicable to the security, administration, monitoring, or scoring of, or the reporting of scores from, any assessment test -administered under Section 2-3.64 or that is known or intended to produce or report manipulated or artificial, rather than actual, assessment or achievement results or gains from the administration of those tests or examinations

105 ILCS 21B-75

15:66 How are suspension and revocation hearings conducted?

The State Superintendent of Education must, upon receipt of evidence of abuse or neglect of a child, immorality, a condition of health detrimental to the welfare of pupils, incompetency, unprofessional conduct, the neglect of any professional duty, or other just cause, further investigate and, if and as appropriate, serve written notice to the individual and afford the individual opportunity for a hearing prior to suspension or revocation; but the State Superintendent is under no obligation to initiate such an investigation if the Department of Children and Family Services is investigating the same or substantially similar allegations and its child protective service unit has not made its determination, as required under Section 7.12 of the Abused and Neglected Child Reporting Act.

If the State Superintendent of Education does not receive from an individual a request for a hearing within 10 days after the individual receives notice, the suspension or revocation immediately takes effect in accordance with the notice. If a hearing is requested within 10 days after notice of an opportunity for hearing, it acts as a stay of proceedings until the State Educator Preparation and Licensure Board issues a decision. Any hearing takes place in the educational service region where the educator is or was last employed and in accordance with rules adopted by the State Board of Education (ISBE), in consultation with the State Educator Preparation and Licensure Board, and the rules must include without limitation provisions for discovery and the sharing of information between parties prior to the hearing. The standard of proof is by the preponderance of the evidence. The decision of the State Educator Preparation and Licensure Board is a final administrative decision and is subject to judicial review by appeal of either party.

ISBE may refuse to issue or may suspend the license of any person who fails to file a return or to pay the tax, penalty, or interest shown in a filed return or to pay any final assessment of tax, penalty, or interest, as required by any tax act administered by the Department of Revenue, until such time as the requirements of any such tax act are satisfied.

The State Superintendent of Education or designee may initiate and conduct such investigations as may be reasonably necessary to establish the existence of any alleged misconduct. At any stage of the investigation, the State Superintendent may issue a subpoena requiring the attendance and testimony of a witness, including the license holder, and the production of any evidence, including files, records, correspondence, or documents, relating to any matter in question in the investigation. The subpoena may require a witness to appear at ISBE at a specified date and time and shall specify any evidence to be produced. The license holder is not entitled to be present, but the State Superintendent must provide the license holder with a copy of any recorded testimony prior to a hearing. Such recorded testimony must not be used as evidence at a hearing, unless the license holder has adequate notice of the testimony and the opportunity to cross-examine the witness. Failure of a license holder to comply with a duly issued, investigatory subpoena may be grounds for revocation, suspension, or denial of a license.

All correspondence, documentation, and other information received by the regional superintendent of schools, the State Superintendent of Education, ISBE, or the State Educator Preparation and Licensure Board are confidential and must not be disclosed to third parties, except as necessary for the State Superintendent of Education or designee to investigate and prosecute, pursuant to a court order, for disclosure to the license holder or his or her representative, or as otherwise required and provided that any such information admitted into evidence in a hearing is exempt from this confidentiality and non-disclosure requirement.

The State Superintendent of Education or designee has the power to administer oaths to witnesses at any hearing conducted before the State Educator Preparation and Licensure Board. The State Superintendent of Education or designee is authorized to subpoena and bring before the State Educator Preparation and Licensure Board any person in Illinois and to take testimony either orally or by deposition or by exhibit, with the same fees and mileage and in the same manner as prescribed by law in judicial proceedings in civil cases in circuit courts of this State.

Any circuit court, upon the application of the State Superintendent of Education or the license holder, may, by order duly entered, require the attendance of witnesses and the production of relevant books and papers as part of any investigation or at any hearing the State Educator Preparation and Licensure Board is authorized to conduct and the court may compel obedience to its orders by proceedings for contempt.

105 ILCS 5/21B-75

15:68 Must a school board make a report to the State Board of Education when one of its teachers is convicted of a felony?

Whenever the holder of any teaching license who is employed by a school district is convicted after trial or by a plea of guilty of any offense for which a sentence of death "or a term of imprisonment in a penitentiary for one year or more is provided," the school board must promptly notify the State Board of Education in writing of the name of the license holder and location of the court in which the conviction occurred.

105 ILCS 5/21B-85

15:70 What protection does a school district have that a teacher or other licensed employee will not lie about his or her qualifications on a job application?

An applicant for a teacher, principal, superintendent, or other licensed position who willfully makes a false statement that is material to his or her qualifications for employment on a job application is guilty of a Class A misdemeanor. There also are penalties for failure to include important job application information and the applicant risks licensure penalties.

In considering discipline, school officials should be careful to distinguish falsification from omission and carefully consider whether they can prove intent. An employment application should include inquiries about all the information the employer can legally obtain that the employer deems relevant to the job.

105 ILCS 5/21B-75

105 ILCS 5/22-6.5

Jackson v. Board of Education of the City of Chicago, 2016 IL App (1st) 141388, 53 N.E. 3d 381, 403 Ill. Dec. 327

15:75 What recourse is available to a school board if a teacher signs an initial employment contract but refuses to perform?

There is no mechanism whereby a school board can compel a teacher to specifically perform teaching duties pursuant to contract. A school board might sue the teacher for breach of contract, but damages would likely be limited to the cost of finding a suitable replacement. A school district might seek a license suspension for unprofessional conduct, but it is doubtful that a suspension would result except when the underlying facts suggest extreme conduct.

105 ILCS 5/21B-75

105 ILCS 5/24-14

LICENSE RENEWAL

15:80 What is the procedure for renewal of a teaching license?

Licenses to teach are issued in five-year cycles and there are professional development requirements that must be completed by the license renewal applicant. If a person holds a license endorsed in more than one area that has different renewal requirements, the person must follow the renewal requirements for the position for which he or she spends the majority of his or her time working. Any Professional Educator Licenses not renewed lapse on September 1 of that year. If the license holder has an email address on file, an email notice is sent. Lapsed licenses may be reinstated. The procedures generally require the licensee to make up missed professional development hours, pay a cash penalty (or completion of nine hours of course work), pay back fees, and complete professional development.

An unregistered license is invalid after September 1 for employment and "performance of services in an Illinois public or state operated school or cooperative and in a charter school." Any license or endorsement may be voluntarily surrendered by the license holder. A voluntarily surrendered license, except a substitute teaching license, is treated as a revoked license.

105 ILCS 5/21B-45

15:82 May a teacher be dismissed for allowing his or her license to lapse?

There is a statutory procedure that allows lapsed teaching licenses to be renewed. At some point, presumably, a teacher's having allowed his or her license to lapse and failing to renew it after being directed to do so becomes an irremediable failure to act, but under normal circumstances a lapsed license will not support dismissal.

105 ILCS 5/21B-45(b)

Moore v. Board of Education of the City of Chicago, 2016 IL App (1st) 133148, 56 N.E. 3d 457, 404 Ill. Dec. 473

ADDITIONAL TEACHER QUALIFICATIONS

15:100 May a school board require a teacher to undergo a psychiatric examination to determine mental fitness to teach?

Yes. A psychiatric exam may be required in appropriate circumstances. A fitness for duty exam does not implicate the Mental Health and Developmental Disabilities Confidentiality Act because the Act only applies to situations in which the patient is seeking treatment for a mental health condition. The scope of the required release to school officials in a fitness for duty evaluation may be an issue and school officials should carefully consider the scope of the release before the exam is required.

105 ILCS 5/24-5

740 ILCS 110/1 et seq.

Goral v. Illinois State Board of Education, 2013 IL App (1st) 130752, 3 N.E. 3d 365, 378 Ill. Dec. 85

Dusanek v. Hannon, 677 F. 2d 538 (7th Cir. 1982)

Tetmeir v. Board of Education of School District No. 149, Cook County, 5 Ill. App. 3d 982, 284 N.E. 2d 380 (1st Dist. 1972)

15:110 May a school board require teachers to demonstrate continued professional growth?

A school board may require teachers to demonstrate continued professional growth provided, however, that the requirements are not contrary to the teacher certification/licensure statutes.

Before the teacher registration and renewal law was amended in 1998, 1999, and 2013, some collective bargaining agreements and some school board policy manuals contained continuing education requirements. Most of these provisions are likely to be deleted or altered significantly because the professional development plans previously required by local policy or bargaining agreement are now required by statute.

105 ILCS 5/24-5

Heifner v. Board of Education of Morris Community Unit School District No. 101, Grundy County, 32 Ill. App. 3d 83, 335 N.E. 2d 600 (3rd Dist. 1975)

Last v. Board of Education of Community Unit School District No. 321, Winnebago and Stephenson Counties, 37 Ill. App. 2d 159, 185 N.E. 2d 282 (2nd Dist. 1962)

Richards v. Board of Education of Township High School District No. 201, 21 Ill. 2d 104, 171 N.E. 2d 37 (1960)

TEACHING ASSIGNMENTS AND WORKLOADS

15:160 May a school board assign or transfer teachers to and from positions for which they are qualified at will?

School boards should be mindful of constitutional restrictions (such as a civil rights implications), or a limitation contained in a collective bargaining agreement when considering assignment or transfer. A school board may not use transfer to defeat the tenure rights of teachers and should consider the bargaining implications of any transfer decision before implementation of the transfer.

A 2011 amendment to the School Code codified the transfer process. It provides that a school district's selection of a candidate for a new or vacant teaching position being filled for reasons other than recall must be based upon the consideration of factors that include without limitation certifications, qualifications, merit and ability (including performance evaluations, if available), and relevant experience, provided that the length of continuing service with the school district must not be considered as a factor, unless all other factors are determined by the school district to be equal.

A school district's decision to select a particular candidate to fill a new or vacant position is not subject to review under grievance resolution procedures adopted pursuant to subsection (c) of Section 10 of the Illinois Educational Labor Relations Act, provided that, in making such a decision, the district does not fail to adhere to procedural requirements in a collective bargaining agreement relating to the filling of new or vacant teaching positions. Provisions regarding the filling of new and vacant positions in a collective bargaining agreement between a school district and the exclusive bargaining representative of its teachers in existence on June 13, 2011 must remain in full force and effect for the term of the agreement, unless terminated by mutual agreement.

The law provides that nothing in it (i) limits or otherwise impacts school districts' management right to hire new employees, (ii) affects what currently is or may be a mandatory subject of bargaining under the Illinois Educational Labor Relations Act, or (iii) creates a statutory cause of action for a candidate or a candidate's representative to challenge a school district's selection decision based on the school district's failure to adhere to the requirements of Section 24-1.5 of the School Code.

The change in the law does not substantively change the employer's authority to transfer or fill vacancies, but it probably does provide a means to question the decision if the relevant collective bargaining agreement has a provision that allows access to the grievance process.

105 ILCS 5/24-1.5

105 ILCS 5/24-12

115 ILCS 5/10(c)

Stamper v. Board of Education of Elementary School District No. 143, 141 Ill. App. 3d 884, 491 N.E. 2d 36, 96 Ill. Dec. 222 (1st Dist. 1986)

Peters v. Board of Education of Rantoul Township High School District No. 193 of Champaign County, 97 Ill. 2d 166, 454 N.E. 2d 310, 73 Ill. Dec. 450 (1983)

15:162 Can the transfer of a teacher from one class to another or one grade level to another constitute adverse action under civil rights law?

An adverse employment action must materially alter the terms and conditions of employment and to be adverse it must be more than an inconvenience or an alteration of job responsibilities. The Seventh Circuit Court of Appeals has held, ". . . not everything that makes an employee unhappy is an actionable adverse action."

There are three general categories of adverse employment actions:

1) Those where employee compensation, fringe benefits, or other financial terms of employment are diminished (including termination);

2) Lateral transfers with no change in financial terms where an employee's career prospects are reduced by preventing use of skills and experience so that the skills are likely to atrophy and the career stunted;

3) Where the employee is not moved to a different job or the skill requirements of his or her present job are altered but the work conditions in which the employee works are changed in a way that subjects the employee to a humiliating, degrading, unsafe, unhealthful, or otherwise significantly negative alteration in workplace environment.

Courts are loath to recognize grade level "demotions" (third grade to first grade) or in subject level "demotions" (honors English to remedial English) as adverse.

Dass v. Chicago Board of Education, 675 F. 3d 1060 (7th Cir. 2012)

15:170 Does a teacher's tenured status restrict the authority of a school board to assign the teacher?

Tenure does not limit the power of a school board to transfer or assign a teacher to a position for which the teacher is certified and qualified. The provisions of a collective bargaining agreement or duty to bargain obligations may limit the school board, however, as may a section of the School Code added by legislation enacted in 2011.

105 ILCS 5/24-1.5

Stamper v. Board of Education of Elementary School District No. 143, 141 Ill. App. 3d 884, 491 N.E. 2d 36, 96 Ill. Dec. 222 (1st Dist. 1986)

15:180 Is there a statutory limit on the work load that may be assigned a school teacher?

There is no statutory provision or State Board of Education rule or regulation governing teacher workload. Workload is to be distinguished from "preparations." Workload is the number of class periods in a specified time period for which any teacher is responsible. Preparations is the number of different lesson plans for different subjects or grade levels that a teacher must prepare in a specified time period. A maximum workload may exist by reason of a provision in a collective bargaining agreement.

15:190 Is there a maximum number of preparations a high school teacher may be assigned?

At one time the State Board of Education had adopted a rule that provided: "No (high school) teacher should have more than five different preparations." The rule did not prevent the assignment of a high school teacher to more than five preparations, but in any event, the rule no longer exists. There are differences in the meanings of teaching load, preparations, and class assignments.

23 Ill. Admin. Code 1.410 et seq.

15:200 Is a teacher entitled to a duty-free lunch?

Every teacher whose duties require attendance at school for four or more clock hours in any school day must be allowed a duty-free lunch period equal to the regular school lunch period but not less than 30 minutes during each school day.

105 ILCS 5/24-9

Board of Education of Community Unit School District No. 4, Champaign County v. Champaign Education Association, 15 Ill. App. 3d 335, 304 N.E. 2d 138 (4th Dist. 1973)

15:210 Do statutes fix the length of a teacher's workday?

The School Code does not fix the length of a teacher's workday. Statutes set forth the minimum number of pupil attendance hours required in order to receive state financial aid. Absent a recognized bargaining unit, a school board may unilaterally establish length of workday. In school districts with recognized bargaining units, workday must be bargained at prescribed times on demand.

15:220 May a school board require a teacher to teach on Saturday?

A school board may not require its teachers to teach on Saturdays or to work on legal school holidays. School boards are also prohibited from making any deduction from the time or compensation of a teacher on account of any legal or special holiday.

105 ILCS 5/24-2

District 300 Education Association v. Board of Education of Dundee Community Unit School District No. 300 of Kane et al. Counties, 31 Ill. App. 3d 550, 334 N.E. 2d 165 (2nd Dist. 1975)

15:230 May a school board assign its teachers to perform extracurricular duties?

A teacher may be assigned to extracurricular duties that are reasonably related to the educational program and that are not onerous, unreasonably time consuming, demeaning to the professional stature of the teacher, or assigned in a discriminatory manner. The performance of extra duties and the salary therefor must be bargained at appropriate times on demand by a recognized bargaining representative.

Where a collective bargaining contract includes an extra duty salary schedule and no limitations on the assignment of extra duties, the union has effectively conceded that the school board has the authority to make extra duty assignments.

Lewis v. North Clay Community Unit School District No. 25, 181 Ill. App. 3d 689, 537 N.E. 2d 435, 130 Ill. Dec. 368 (5th Dist. 1989)

Board of Education of Berwyn School District No. 100 v. Metskas, 106 Ill. App. 3d 943, 436 N.E. 2d 587, 62 Ill. Dec. 561 (1st Dist. 1982)

Littrell v. Board of Education of Cave in Rock Community Unit School District No. 2, 45 Ill. App. 3d 690, 360 N.E. 2d 102, 4 Ill. Dec. 355 (5th Dist. 1977)

District 300 Education Association v. Board of Education of Dundee Community Unit School District No. 300 of Kane et al. Counties, 31 Ill. App. 3d 550, 334 N.E. 2d 165 (2nd Dist. 1975)

Simcox v. Board of Education of Lockport Township High School District No. 205, 443 F. 2d 40 (7th Cir. 1970)

15:235 May a teacher use a "just cause" provision in a collective bargaining agreement to challenge his or her discipline or dismissal from an extra duty assignment?

A "just cause" provision is one that requires that an employee's discipline be "fair" or for "just cause." A "just cause" provision in a collective bargaining agreement is fully enforceable to the extent it is used to challenge the discipline or dismissal of a teacher from an extra duty assignment. Moreover, a teacher assigned to an extra duty job may have an expectation of continued employment by reason of the facts surrounding his or her employment and retention from year to year in the extra duty job.

Griggsville-Perry Community Unit District No. 4 v. Illinois Educational Labor Relations Board, 2013 IL 113721, 984 N.E. 2d 440, 368 Ill. Dec. 494

Princeville Community Unit School District No. 326, 13 PERI 1017 (IELRB Opinion and Award, Dec. 6, 1996)

Board of Education of Rockford School District No. 205, v. The Illinois Educational Labor Relations Board, 165 Ill. 2d 80, 649 N.E. 2d 369, 208 Ill. Dec. 313 (1995)

PROBATIONARY EMPLOYMENT

15:250 What is the maximum length of time a school board may require a teacher to serve as a probationary employee?

Section 24-11 of the School Code was completely re-written when the General Assembly passed Senate Bill 7 (P.A. 97-08) in 2011. The new statute changed the probationary period, but did not necessarily clarify ambiguities in the old statute and created a number of new unanswered questions.

Perhaps more important, the change in the statute calls into question how useful decades of court decisions interpreting the old statute may be in providing guidance for interpretation of the new statute. The new statute considers (for the first time) performance ratings of teachers in probationary service to determine the length of the probationary period.

The new statute provides that for any teacher who is first employed as a full-time teacher in a school district or program on or after the PERA (Performance Evaluation Reform Act; P.A. 96-861) implementation date (2015 for some school districts and 2016 for most school districts), the probationary period is one of the following periods, based upon the teacher's school terms of service and performance, before the teacher enters upon contractual continued service in the district or in all of the programs that the teacher is legally qualified to hold. The probationary period for teachers first employed before the PERA implementation date is defined by the terms of the old statute (four years for most teachers). Under the new statute, the probationary period is

1) Four consecutive school terms of service in which the teacher receives overall annual evaluation ratings of at least "Proficient" in the last school term and at least "Proficient" in either the second or third school term. If, at the conclusion of four consecutive school terms of service that count toward attainment of contractual continued service, the teacher's performance does not qualify the teacher for contractual continued service, then the teacher shall not enter upon contractual continued service and must be dismissed. The written notice of dismissal must contain specific reasons;

2) Three consecutive school terms of service in which the teacher receives three overall annual evaluations of "Excellent" (the written notice of dismissal must contain specific reasons); or

3) Two consecutive school terms of service in which the teacher receives two overall annual evaluations of "Excellent," but only if the teacher (i) previously attained contractual continued service in a different school district or program in the state; (ii) voluntarily departed or was honorably dismissed from that school district or program in the school term immediately prior to the teacher's first school term of service applicable to the attainment of contractual continued service under this subdivision; and (iii) received, in his or her two most recent overall annual or biannual evaluations from the prior school district or program, ratings of at least "Proficient," with both such ratings occurring after the school district's or program's PERA implementation date.

If a performance evaluation is not conducted for any school term when such evaluation is required to be conducted under Section 24A-5 of the School Code, then the teacher's performance evaluation rating for such school term for purposes of determining the attainment of contractual continued service is deemed "Proficient."

For the purposes of determining contractual continued service, a school term is counted only toward attainment of contractual continued service if the teacher actually teaches or is otherwise present and participating in the district's or program's educational program for 120 days or more, provided that the days of leave under the federal Family and Medical Leave Act that the teacher is required to take until the end of the school term are considered days of teaching or participation in the district's or program's educational program. A school term that is not counted toward attainment of contractual continued service is not be considered a break in service for purposes of determining whether a teacher has been employed for four consecutive school terms, provided the teacher actually teaches or is otherwise present and participating in the district's or program's educational program in the following school term.

Any full-time teacher who does not receive written notice from the employing board at least 45 days before the end of any school term and whose performance does not require dismissal after the fourth probationary year must be re-employed for the following school term.

105 ILCS 5/24-11

15:260 Does a leave of absence interrupt the running of the four-year probationary period?

Under "old" Section 24-11, the probationary period runs continuously for four years of employment and is not interrupted by ordinary paid leaves of absence for illness (even if the leave is for an extended period of time). Agreed-upon unpaid leaves or unpaid leaves taken pursuant to the Family and Medical Leave Act or authorized in a collective bargaining agreement also may not interrupt the probationary period. The courts have not specifically addressed the matter of unpaid leaves and the outcome of a case on the subject may depend on the underlying facts, but to be safe, an employer should assume that the probationary period runs for four consecutive years.

This question most frequently arises when an employee is about to acquire tenure and the employer seeks additional time to evaluate the employee or seeks to prevent the acquisition of tenure without having done appropriate documentation to support a dismissal. Doing careful evaluations and making decisions about retention or dismissal of non-tenured employees early in the probationary period prevent the issue from arising.

The General Assembly re-wrote Section 24-11 of the School Code in 2011 when it enacted Senate Bill 7 (P.A. 97-08). Most provisions of the "new" 24-11 did not take effect until a district's PERA (Performance Evaluation Reform Act; P.A. 96-861) implementation date (for some school districts 2015 and for most school districts, 2016). It is unclear whether the pertinent section of the new law applies or does not apply before the district's PERA implementation date.

Under the new law, for the purposes of determining contractual continued service, a school term is counted only toward attainment of contractual continued service if the teacher actually teaches or is otherwise present and participating in the district's or program's educational program for 120 days or more, provided that the days of leave under the federal Family and Medical Leave Act that the teacher is required to take until the end of the school term are considered days of teaching or participation in the district's or program's educational program.

A school term that is not counted toward attainment of contractual continued service is not considered a break in service for purposes of determining whether a teacher has been employed for four consecutive school terms, provided the teacher actually teaches or is otherwise present and participating in the district's or program's educational program in the following school term.

105 ILCS 5/24-11

Wood v. North Wamac School District No. 186, 386 Ill. App. 3d 874, 899 N.E. 2d 578, 326 Ill.Dec.361 (5th Dist. 2008)

SUBSTITUTE TEACHERS

15:300 Who may be employed as a substitute teacher?

A fully licensed teacher may be employed as a substitute teacher. A teacher not fully licensed to teach the subject or grade level for which a substitute is sought may be employed, provided that the teacher holds a substitute teacher's license.

A substitute teacher's license may be issued upon request of the regional superintendent of schools in any region in which the teacher is to teach. To qualify, an applicant must either hold a valid teaching license, or hold a bachelor's degree, or have had two years of teaching experience and meet other State Board of Education rules and regulations. Substitute teacher licenses are not endorsed and are valid for five years.

105 ILCS 5/21B-20
105 ILCS 5/21B-40

15:304 How does a person become a substitute teacher?

A person holding a valid substitute teacher's license, early childhood license, elementary license, high school license, or a special license can register as a substitute teacher with the regional superintendent of schools in each educational service region where the person will be employed.

A person who registers as a substitute teacher with the regional superintendent of schools is responsible for

1) The payment of fees to apply for and register the license for its period of validity, although 2017 legislation makes it possible for a substitute teacher who has substituted for at least 10 days within one year of issuance of the license to recover the fees;

2) Authorization of a criminal history records check and checks of the Statewide Sex Offender Database and Statewide Child Murderer and Violent Offender Against Youth Database, as provided in Section 10-21.9 of the School Code;

3) Payment of the cost of the criminal history records check and checks of the Statewide Sex Offender Database and Statewide Child Murderer and Violent Offender Against Youth Database;

4) Providing evidence of physical fitness and freedom from communicable disease as required by Section 24-5 of the School Code.

The regional superintendent of schools maintains a file for each registered substitute teacher in the educational service region that includes a copy of the person's license, the results from the criminal history records check and checks of the Statewide Sex Offender Database and Statewide Child Murderer and Violent Offender Against Youth Database, a copy of the physical examination, and a copy of the tuberculin skin test. The regional superintendent of schools issues a signed and sealed certificate of authorization to the substitute teacher that verifies that the substitute teacher has completed the registration process and is thereby approved to substitute teach in the public schools of the educational service region. This license must be presented to all prospective employing school districts in the educational service region, who must photocopy the license and keep a copy of the license with employment records for the substitute teacher.

Persons wishing to substitute teach in more than one educational service region shall register as a substitute teacher with the appropriate regional superintendents of schools. The registration process shall include all items listed above with the exception of the authorization of a criminal history records check and checks of the Statewide Sex Offender Database and Statewide Child Murderer and Violent Offender Against Youth Database and the accompanying payment of associated fees. If the substitute teacher has been issued a signed and sealed license of authorization from another regional superintendent of schools, the registering entity may photocopy the license for its files and verify the substitute teacher's registration status.

105 ILCS 5/21B-20
105 ILCS 5/21B-40
105 ILCS 5/24-5

15:310 How many days a year may an individual be employed as a substitute teacher?

A substitute teacher's license is issued for teaching in all grades upon request of the regional superintendent of schools of any region in which the teacher is to teach. A substitute teacher's license is valid for teaching in any county. The license may be issued to persons who either hold a license valid for teaching in the common schools as shown on the face of the license, hold a bachelor's degree or higher from an institution of higher learning accredited by the North Central Association or other comparable regional accrediting association, or have been graduated from a recognized institution of higher learning with a bachelor's degree or higher. The license expires on June 30 in the fourth year from date of issue. Substitute teacher's licenses are not subject to endorsement.

A teacher holding a substitute teacher's license may teach only in the place of a certified teacher who is under contract with the employing board and may teach only when no appropriate fully certified teacher is available to teach in a substitute capacity. If, however, there is no certified teacher under contract because of an emergency situation, then a school district may employ a substitute teacher for no longer than 30 calendar days per each vacant position in the district if the district notifies the appropriate regional office of education within five business days after the employment of the substitute teacher in the emergency situation. An emergency situation is one in which an unforeseen vacancy has occurred and a teacher is unable to fulfill his or her contractual duties or teacher capacity needs of the district exceed previous indications, and the district is actively engaged in advertising to hire a fully certified teacher for the vacant position.

There is no limit on the number of days that a substitute teacher may teach in a single school district, provided that no substitute teacher may teach for longer than 90 school days for any one certified teacher under contract in the same school year.

A teacher holding an early childhood license, an elementary license, a high school license, or a special license may also substitute teach in grades K-12, but only in the place of a certified teacher who is under contract with the employing board, and may not teach for longer than 120 days for any one certified teacher under contract in the same school

At some point, a long-term substitute may no longer be a short-term employee within the meaning of the Illinois Educational Labor Relations Act (and thereby be entitled to bargaining unit representation and placement on the salary schedule).

When substitute teaching is partly on a daily and partly on an hourly basis, a school day is considered to be five hours.

115 ILCS 5/2(q)
105 ILCS 5/21B-20
Woods v. East St. Louis School District No. 189, 147 Ill. App. 3d 776, 498 N.E. 2d 801, 101 Ill. Dec. 477 (5th Dist. 1986)

15:320 Do minimum salary laws apply to a substitute teacher?

There is no minimum or maximum salary law that applies to a teacher serving as a day-to-day substitute. However, if a substitute teacher is employed for an extended period in the same position, his or her status may be changed from substitute teacher to full-time temporary teacher, in which case minimum salary laws or collectively bargained provisions applicable to full-time licensed employees may apply.

105 ILCS 5/24-8

115 ILCS 5/2 (q)

Woods v. East St. Louis School District No. 189, 147 Ill. App. 3d 776, 498 N.E. 2d 801, 101 Ill. Dec. 477 (5th Dist. 1986)

EVALUATING TEACHERS

15:340 Who must a school district evaluate?

A school district must evaluate each of its tenured teachers at least once in the course of any two years, a principal and assistant principal on a single year contract by March 1 of each year, and a principal and assistant principal on a multi-year contract by March 1 of the contract's final year. A school district must evaluate its non-tenured teachers once each school year. After September 1, 2012, any tenured teacher whose performance is rated as either "needs improvement" or "unsatisfactory" must be evaluated at least once in the school year following the receipt of the rating.

105 ILCS 5/24A-5

105 ILCS 5/24A-8

105 ILCS 5/24A-15

15:345 Are schools required to have a formal evaluation plan?

Each school district must establish, in cooperation with its teachers or, when applicable, with the official bargaining representative of its teachers, a plan for evaluating its teachers. Beginning with the 2006-2007 school term, school boards were required to have an evaluation plan for principals and evaluations for assistant principals were required beginning in 2011.

105 ILCS 5/24A-4

105 ILCS 5/24A-15

Board of Education of Leroy Community Unit School District No. 2 v. Illinois Educational Labor Relations Board, 199 Ill. App. 3d 347, 556 N.E. 2d 857, 145 Ill. Dec. 239 (4th Dist. 1990) 149 Ill. 2d 496, 599 N.E. 2d 892, 174 Ill. Dec. 808 (1992)

15:350 What must be included in an evaluation plan?

Legislation passed in January 2010 (P.A. 96-861) requires that as of September 1, 2012, evaluation plans include a description of each teacher's duties and responsibilities and of the standards to which that teacher is expected to conform.

The plan may provide for evaluation of personnel whose positions require administrative certification by independent evaluators not employed by or affiliated with the school district. The results of the school district administrators' evaluations must be reported to the employing school board, together with such recommendations for remediation as the evaluator or evaluators may deem appropriate.

Evaluation of teachers whose positions do not require administrative certification must be conducted by an administrator qualified under Section 24A-3 of the School Code and must include at least the following components:

1) Personal observation of the teacher in the classroom by the evaluator or by a district administrator qualified under Section 24A-3 unless the teacher has no classroom duties;

2) Consideration of the teacher's attendance, planning, and instructional methods; classroom management, where relevant; and competency in the subject matter taught, where relevant;

3) By no later than the applicable implementation date, consideration of student growth as a significant factor in the rating of the teacher's performance;

4) Prior to September 1, 2012, rating of the teacher's performance as "excellent," "satisfactory," or "unsatisfactory;" or "excellent," "proficient," "needs improvement," or "unsatisfactory";

5) On and after September 1, 2012, rating of the performance of tenured teachers as "excellent," "proficient," "needs improvement," or "unsatisfactory";

6) Specification as to the teacher's strengths and weaknesses, with supporting reasons for the comments made; and

7) Inclusion of a copy of the evaluation in the teacher's personnel file and provision of a copy to the teacher.

105 ILCS 5/24A-5

Buchna v. Illinois State Board of Education, 342 Ill. App. 3d 934, 795 N.E. 2d 1045, 277 Ill. Dec. 377, (3rd Dist. 2003)

15:355 How must existing evaluation plans be changed after passage of Race to the Top legislation?

Race to the Top legislation passed in January 2010 requires each school district to develop, in cooperation with its teachers or, where applicable, the exclusive bargaining representatives of its teachers, an evaluation plan for all teachers. Teacher means any and all school district employees regularly required to be certified under the laws relating to the certification of teachers.

By no later than the applicable implementation date, each school district must, in good faith cooperation with its teachers or, where applicable, the exclusive bargaining representatives of its teachers, incorporate the use of data and indicators on student growth as a significant factor in rating teaching performance, into its evaluation plan for all teachers, both tenured and non-tenured. The plan must at least meet the standards and requirements for student growth and teacher evaluation established under Section 24A-7 of the School Code, and specifically describe how student growth data and indicators will be used as part of the evaluation process; how this information will relate to evaluation standards, the assessments, or other indicators of student performance that will be used in measuring student growth and the weight that each will have; the methodology that will be used to measure student growth; and the criteria other than student growth that will be used in evaluating the teacher and the weight that each will have.

To incorporate the use of data and indicators of student growth as a significant factor in rating teacher performance into the evaluation plan, the district must use a joint committee composed of equal representation selected by the district and its teachers or, where applicable, the exclusive bargaining representative of its teachers. If, within 180 calendar days of the committee's first meeting, the committee does not reach agreement on the plan, then the district must implement the model evaluation plan established under Section 24A-7 with respect to the use of data and indicators on student growth as a significant factor in rating teacher performance.

105 ILCS 5/24A-4

15:360 What are the implementation dates for changes in evaluation plans resulting from Race to the Top legislation?

For school districts having less than 500,000 inhabitants and receiving a Race to the Top Grant or School Improvement Grant, the date specified in those grants for implementing an evaluation system for teachers and principals incorporating student growth as a significant factor is the implementation date.

For the lowest performing 20 percent of remaining school districts having less than 500,000 inhabitants (with the measure of and school year or years used for school district performance to be determined by the State Superintendent of Education at a time determined by the State Superintendent), the implementation date was September 1, 2015.

For all other school districts having less than 500,000 inhabitants, the implementation date was September 1, 2016.

A school district and the exclusive bargaining representative of its teachers could jointly agree in writing to an earlier implementation date, provided that the date must not be earlier than September 1, 2013. The written agreement of the district and the exclusive bargaining representative must have been transmitted to the State Board of Education.

105 ILCS 5/24A-2.5

15:365 Who is authorized to evaluate teachers?

Race to the Top legislation passed in January 2010 (P.A. 96-861) defines evaluator as an administrator qualified under Section 24A-3 of the School Code; or other individuals qualified under Section 24A-3, provided that, if the other individuals are in the bargaining unit of a district's teachers, the district and the exclusive bargaining representative of that unit must agree to those individuals evaluating other bargaining unit members.

A school district would be very unwise to permit bargaining unit members to evaluate other bargaining unit members in any situation where the resulting evaluation might be used as evidence or when the content of the resulting evaluation might be disputed (dismissal for cause or when grouping placement is questioned in a reduction in force).

Section 24A-3 requires the school board to require its evaluators to participate in an in-service training on the evaluation of licensed personnel provided or approved by the State Board of Education prior to undertaking any evaluation and at least once during each license renewal cycle. Any evaluator undertaking an evaluation after September 1, 2012 must first successfully complete a pre-qualification program provided or approved by the State Board of Education.

105 ILCS 5/24A-2.5
105 ILCS 5/24A-3
23 Ill. Admin. Code 50.400

15:370 What rating system must be used to evaluate a teacher?

If the employer intends to use its teacher evaluation plan to discipline or dismiss a teacher, the district's plan must comply with the relevant statute that contains baseline components that must be included in the plan.

Until September 1, 2012 the rating system used could include at least the following three ratings: "excellent," "satisfactory," and "unsatisfactory." After September 1, 2012 evaluation plans that are used to evaluate teachers, principals, and assistant principals must use the four categories "excellent," "proficient," "needs improvement," and "unsatisfactory."

The amendment of an evaluation plan is a mandatory subject of bargaining.

105 ILCS 5/24A-5

Buchna v. Illinois State Board of Education, 342 Ill. App. 3d 934, 795 N.E. 2d 1045, 277 Ill. Dec. 377, (3rd Dist. 2003)

15:375 How is student growth measured for purposes of performance evaluation?

The State Board of Education has rules relating to the methods for measuring student growth including, but not limited to, limitations on the age of useable data; the amount of data needed to reliably and validly measure growth for the purpose of teacher and principal evaluations; and whether and at what time annual state assessments may be used as one of multiple measures of student growth.

The State Board also has rules defining the term "significant factor" for purposes of including consideration of student growth in performance ratings and controlling for such factors as student characteristics (including, but not limited to, students receiving special education and English Language Learner services), student attendance, and student mobility so as to best measure the impact that a teacher, principal, school, and school district have on students' academic achievement; establishing minimum requirements for district teacher and principal evaluation instruments and procedures, and establishing a model evaluation plan for use by school districts in which student growth shall comprise 50 percent of the performance rating.

105 ILCS 5/24A-7

15:380 What procedures are required when a tenured teacher receives a rating of "needs improvement" or "unsatisfactory?"

If a tenured teacher receives an unsatisfactory evaluation rating the following procedures are required:

1) Within 30 school days after the completion of an evaluation rating a tenured teacher as "needs improvement," development by the evaluator, in consultation with the teacher and taking into account the teacher's ongoing professional responsibilities including his or her regular teaching assignments, of a professional development plan directed to the areas that need improvement and any supports that the district will provide to address the areas identified as needing improvement.

2) Within 30 school days after completion of an evaluation rating a tenured teacher as "unsatisfactory," development and commencement by the district, or administrator qualified under Section 24A-3, of a remediation plan designed to correct deficiencies cited, provided the deficiencies are deemed remediable. The remediation plan for unsatisfactory tenured teachers must provide for 90 school days of remediation within the classroom, unless an applicable collective bargaining agreement provides for a shorter duration. Evaluations must be issued within 10 days after the conclusion of the respective remediation plan. However, the school board does not lose jurisdiction to discharge a teacher in the event the evaluation is not issued within 10 days after the conclusion of the respective remediation plan.

3) Participation in the remediation plan by a tenured teacher rated "unsatisfactory," an evaluator and a district administrator qualified under Section 24A-3, and a consulting teacher selected by the evaluator by the participating administrator or by the principal of the teacher who was rated "unsatisfactory," which consulting teacher is an educational employee as defined in the Educational Labor Relations Act, has at least five years' teaching experience, and a reasonable familiarity with the assignment of the teacher being evaluated, and who received an "excellent" rating on his or her most recent evaluation. Where no teachers who meet these criteria are available within the district, the district must request and the applicable regional office of education must supply, to participate in the remediation process, an individual who meets these criteria.

In a district having a population of less than 500,000 with an exclusive bargaining agent, the bargaining agent may, if it so chooses, supply a roster of qualified teachers from whom the consulting teacher is selected. That roster must, however, contain the names of at least five teachers, each of whom meets the criteria for consulting teacher with regard to the teacher being evaluated, or the names of all teachers so qualified if that number is less than five. In the event of a dispute as to qualification, the State Board determines qualification.

4) A mid-point and final evaluation by an evaluator during and at the end of the remediation period, immediately following receipt of a remediation plan. Each evaluation must assess the teacher's performance during the time period since the prior evaluation; provided the last evaluation must also include an overall evaluation of the teacher's performance during the remediation period. A written copy of the evaluations

and ratings, in which any deficiencies in performance and recommendations for correction are identified, must be provided to and discussed with the teacher within 10 school days after the date of the evaluation, unless an applicable collective bargaining agreement provides to the contrary.

5) Evaluations and ratings once every 30 school days for the 90 school-day remediation period immediately following receipt of a remediation plan. These subsequent evaluations must be conducted by an evaluator qualified under Section 24A-3. The consulting teacher must provide advice to the teacher rated "unsatisfactory" on how to improve teaching skills and to successfully complete the remediation plan. The consulting teacher must participate in developing the remediation plan, but the final decision as to the evaluation must be done solely by the evaluator administrator, unless an applicable collective bargaining agreement provides to the contrary. Evaluations at the conclusion of the remediation process are separate and distinct from the required annual evaluations of teachers and are not subject to the guidelines and procedures relating to those annual evaluations. The evaluator may but is not required to use the forms provided for the annual evaluation of teachers in the district's evaluation plan.

6) In school districts having a population of less than 500,000, reinstatement to the evaluation schedule set forth in the district's evaluation plan a schedule of biennial evaluation for any tenured teacher who achieves a rating equal to or better than "satisfactory" or "proficient" in the school year following a rating of "needs improvement" or "unsatisfactory" completes the 90 school day remediation plan with a "satisfactory" or better rating, unless the district's plan regularly requires more frequent evaluations.

7) Dismissal in accordance with Section 24-12 of any teacher who fails to complete any applicable remediation plan with a rating equal to or better than a "satisfactory" or "proficient" better rating. Districts and teachers subject to dismissal hearings are precluded from compelling the testimony of consulting teachers at such hearings under Section 24-12, either as to the rating process or for opinions of performances by teachers under remediation. Nothing in this Section or Section 24A-4 or 24A-5 of the School Code prevents immediate dismissal of a teacher for deficiencies that are irremediable or for actions which are injurious to or endanger the health or person of students in the classroom or school, or preventing the dismissal or non-renewal of non-tenured teachers for any reason not prohibited by applicable employment, labor, and civil rights laws.

Failure to strictly comply with the time requirements contained in Section 24A-5 does not invalidate the results of the remediation plan. But employers should beware; most teacher dismissal challenges are based on procedural defects in the remediation or dismissal process and substantial failures to comply with statutory directives may result in an unfavorable outcome for the employer.

105 ILCS 5/24A-5

Board of Education of Valley View Community Unit School District 365-U v. Illinois State Board of Education, 2013 IL App (3d) 120373, 1 N.E. 3d 905, 377 Ill. Dec. 804

MacDonald v. State Board of Education, 2012 IL App (4th) 110599, 966 N.E. 2d 322, 359 Ill. Dec. 1

15:381 Under what circumstances may a teacher be dismissed for failure to successfully complete a remediation plan?

Dismissal challenges are almost always focused on procedural defects in the performance of the evaluator, rather than on the substantive performance of the teacher. The evaluator must meet every required timeline and must follow every procedural component contained in the evaluation plan in order to be successful if challenged.

Board of Education of Waukegan Community Unit School District No. 60 v. Orbach, 2013 IL App (2d) 120504, 991 N.E. 2d 951, 372 Ill. Dec. 361

15:385 What period of time is required for remediation of a tenured teacher?

A school district must provide for 90 school days of remediation within the classroom.

105 ILCS 5/24A-5

15:387 How are days counted in teacher evaluation, remediation or discharge?

The day count in the evaluation, remediation, and discharge statutes should be read carefully. If the statute in question lacks specific reference to school days, the count should be made by using calendar days.

105 ILCS 5/24-11

105 ILCS 5/24-12

105 ILCS 5/24A-1 et seq.

MacDonald v. State Board of Education, 2012 IL App (4th) 110599, 966 N.E. 2d 322, 359 Ill. Dec. 1

15:390 May a school district seek a waiver for evaluation plan components?

After the implementation date specified in 2010 legislation modifying evaluation requirements in the School Code, a school district may not seek a waiver or seek a modification of a mandate regarding the requirements for student performance data to be a significant factor in teacher or principal evaluations or for teachers and principals to be rated using the four categories of "excellent," "proficient," "needs improvement," or "unsatisfactory." On the applicable implementation date, any previously authorized waiver or modification from such requirements terminated.

105 ILCS 24A-2.5

TEACHER COMPENSATION

15:400 Is there a statutory minimum teacher salary?

Yes. Before the Illinois Educational Labor Relations Act was enacted, the General Assembly legislated a teacher salary floor similar to a minimum wage. The minimum teacher salary provision has long been obsolete because of inflation and collective bargaining. A school board must pay minimum annual salaries of $10,000 for a teacher holding a bachelor's degree and $11,000 for a teacher holding a master's degree. The following minimum increases must be paid:

- $750 after five years of experience for a teacher with less than a bachelor's degree;
- $1,000 after five years and $1,600 after eight years for a teacher with a bachelor's degree;
- $1,250 after five years and $2,000 after eight years for a teacher with a master's degree.

The minimum salary statute is ambiguous as to what constitutes "years of experience" both for purposes of prior experience credit and for purposes of salary schedule advancement after initial employment.

105 ILCS 5/24-8

Winters v. Board of Education of Piasa Community Unit School District No. 9 of Macoupin County, 66 Ill. App. 3d 918, 384 N.E. 2d 519, 23 Ill. Dec. 725 (4th Dist. 1978)

Hardway v. Board of Education of Lawrenceville Township High School District No. 71, 1 Ill. App. 3d 298, 274 N.E. 2d 213 (5th Dist. 1971)

15:410 Is there a minimum salary provision that applies to summer school employment?

No. Summer school salaries may be established by a school board subject only to minimum hourly wage provisions and collective bargaining requirements.

29 U.S.C. 201 et seq.

15:420 Must a school board recognize all prior teaching experience of a new employee on its salary schedule?

Illinois appellate courts are divided on this issue. The safer approach is to recognize full prior experience credit. A school board that fully recognizes prior experience must be cautious that it does not commit age discrimination by screening out all older and more experienced job applicants in the hiring process.

105 ILCS 5/24-8

Equal Employment Opportunity Commission v. Francis W. Parker School, Memorandum Opinion 1993 U.S. Dist. Lexis 3600, 91 C 4674, 61 F.E.P. 967 (BNA) (N.D. Ill. 1993)

Winters v. Board of Education of Piasa Community Unit School District No. 9 of Macoupin County, 66 Ill. App. 3d 918, 384 N.E. 2d 519, 23 Ill. Dec. 725 (4th Dist. 1978)

Hardway v. Board of Education of Lawrenceville Township High School District No. 71, 1 Ill. App. 3d 298, 274 N.E. 2d 213 (5th Dist. 1971)

15:430 When must a teacher submit evidence of additional education in order to advance on the salary schedule?

Unless a collective bargaining agreement provides otherwise, a teacher who submits a certificate of completion to the school office prior to the first day of the school term must be considered to have the degree stated on the certificate.

105 ILCS 5/24-8

Board of Education of Valley View Community Unit School District No. 365U v. Schmidt, 64 Ill. App. 3d 513, 381 N.E. 2d 400, 21 Ill. Dec. 291 (1st Dist. 1978)

15:432 May a school board "freeze" teacher salaries?

A teacher salary "freeze" is a denial of teacher access to a salary schedule step increase and no increase in base salary. Increases in the base salary are generally within the control of the school board provided the board meets its bargaining obligations. Absent contract language to the contrary or specific bargaining history, a school board may "freeze" base salary by simply refusing to offer an increase in the base.

"Freezing" teachers on step (denying a step increase) is more complicated. "Status quo" rules may require that the school board grant a step increase to teachers until a contrary result is bargained. Bargaining such a result would likely be difficult, if not impossible. Whether or not a school board must grant step increases for years of experience depends, in large measure, upon its previous bargaining history.

In general a "hard freeze" refers to holding an employee's salary to the same amount paid the previous year. A "soft freeze" keeps the schedule the same but allows step and lane movement.

Vienna School District No. 55 v. Illinois Educational Labor Relations Board, 162 Ill. App. 3d 503, 515 N.E. 2d 476, 113 Ill. Dec. 667 (4th Dist. 1987)

15:440 Is a school board required to pay its teachers "vacation time?"

No statute requires a school board to pay teachers vacation pay.

15:450 If a teacher is honorably dismissed as a result of a reduction in force, when must the teacher be paid all accrued earnings?

Any teacher honorably dismissed as a result of a decrease in the total number of teachers or the discontinuance of some educational service must be paid all earned compensation on or before the third business day following the last day of pupil attendance in the regular school term.

105 ILCS 5/24-12

15:460 How may teachers be held to account for school property in their possession?

Each teacher has a statutory duty to protect school district property. No teacher may be paid unless the teacher has satisfactorily accounted for books, apparatus, and other property belonging to the school district.

105 ILCS 5/24-17

15:470 What options are available to a school district that is financially unable to pay its teachers?

A school district may choose either of two procedures when unable to pay teachers' wages for lack of funds. The school district may establish a voucher system of expenditures, or may require the district treasurer to pay funds of the school district upon an order of the school board signed by the president.

When an order issued for the wages of a teacher is presented to the treasurer and is not paid for want of funds, the treasurer is required to endorse over his or her signature "not paid for want of funds" with the date of presentation and shall keep a record of that endorsement. The order, thereafter, bears interest at a rate not exceeding the maximum rate authorized by the Bond Authorization Act until the maturity date established by the school board or, in the absence of such maturity date, until the treasurer notifies the clerk or secretary in writing that he or she has funds to pay the order.

When the treasurer obtains sufficient funds to pay any such order, he or she must set them aside for such purpose and shall not use them to pay any other order until the order previously presented and not paid is paid or otherwise discharged.

30 ILCS 305/0.01
105 ILCS 5/8-16

15:480 Must a school district post the salaries of its certified employees on the internet?

Each school board must report to the State Board of Education, on or before October 1 of each year, the base salary and benefits of the superintendent and all its administrators and teachers. Prior to this annual report, the information must be presented at a regular school board meeting, subject to applicable notice requirements, and then posted on the website of the school district, if any.

105 ILCS 5/10-20.47

LEAVES

15:540 May a school board allow sabbatical leave?

A school board may, by statutory authority, grant a sabbatical leave of absence to a teacher, principal, or superintendent performing contractual continued service, for a period of at least four school months but not in excess of one school term, for resident study, research, travel, or other purposes designed to improve the school system.

The statute that sets forth the conditions under which a sabbatical leave may be granted contains numerous and complicated procedural conditions for the leave. A school board may provide additional leave, provide leave for other classes of employees, or add procedural requirements not contained in statute in a collectively bargained agreement or, absent a recognized bargaining representative, by the adoption of a policy.

105 ILCS 5/24-6.1

Thrash v. Board of Education School District No. 189, 106 Ill. App. 3d 182, 435 N.E. 2d 866, 62 Ill. Dec. 68 (5th Dist. 1982)

15:550 Is personal leave or professional leave required by law?

Personal leave is paid leave of absence, with or without procedural or use restrictions, and is commonly provided to teachers in amounts ranging from one to three days per year. Professional leave is paid or partially paid leave to attend meetings relating to the improvement of teaching. Neither leave is required by law. A school board may bargain either leave, or in the absence of a timely demand to bargain from a recognized bargaining representative, may regulate such leave by adoption of policy.

15:560 How much sick leave is provided a teacher by law?

Unless a collective bargaining agreement, or board policy in the absence of a recognized bargaining representative, provides more, each full-time teacher is entitled by statute to a minimum of 10 sick leave days at full pay in each school year. Unused sick leave must be allowed to accumulate to a minimum available leave of 180 days at full pay, including the leave of the current year.

105 ILCS 5/24-6

15:565 Must a school board allow bereavement leave?

For a death in the immediate family, a teacher can use paid sick leave to the extent he or she has such leave available. Another possible paid leave option is personal leave. Access to and use of personal leave is generally limited by contract or by policy, but the limitations do not usually require that the death be in the immediate family. Sometimes, collective bargaining agreements contain a paid or unpaid bereavement leave option. Employees who qualify for the Family and Medical Leave Act can access up to 10 work days of unpaid leave for the death of a child.

30 ILCS 105/5.875
105 ILCS 5/24-6

15:570 Must a school board provide part-time teachers sick leave benefits?

There is no statutory requirement that part-time teachers be provided with sick leave benefits. Sick leave is a mandatory subject of bargaining. If part-time teachers are included in a recognized bargaining unit, their sick leave benefits will be stated in a collective bargaining agreement. If part-time teachers are not represented, a school board may unilaterally establish their sick leave benefits.

105 ILCS 5/24-6

15:580 May a teacher be disciplined for excessive use of sick leave?

A teacher may not be disciplined for appropriate use of accumulated sick leave. When a teacher claims to be sick (or claims to be caring for an immediate family member who is "seriously ill"), it is very difficult for the employer to prove, if challenged, otherwise. Once a teacher has exhausted accumulated sick leave, the teacher may not be discharged if the disability giving rise to the use of sick leave is caused by a temporary incapacity.

A school board may collectively bargain a provision in its contract or, in the absence of a recognized bargaining representative or in the absence of demand to bargain by a bargaining representative, adopt a policy defining permanent incapacity and listing it as cause for dismissal.

105 ILCS 5/10-22.4
105 ILCS 5/24-6
105 ILCS 5/24-13

Board of Education, School District No. 151, Cook County v. Illinois State Board of Education, 154 Ill. App. 3d 175, 507 N.E. 2d 134, 107 Ill. Dec. 470 (1st Dist. 1987)

deOliveira v. State Board of Education, 158 Ill. App. 3d 111, 511 N.E. 2d 172, 110 Ill. Dec. 337 (2nd Dist. 1987)

Elder v. Board of Education of School District No. 127 1/2, Cook County, 60 Ill. App. 2d 56, 508 N.E. 2d 423 (1st Dist. 1965)

15:590 Does a teacher lose accumulated sick leave by reason of school district combination?

If by reason of any change in the boundaries of a school district, or by reason of the creation of a new school district, the employment of a teacher is transferred to a new or different school board, the accumulated sick leave of the teacher is not lost but is transferred to the new or different school district.

105 ILCS 5/24-6

TEACHER RESIGNATIONS

15:600 When may a tenured teacher resign without penalty?

A tenured teacher may resign at any time by agreement of the school board or by serving at least 30-days written notice upon the secretary of the board. However, no teacher may resign during the school year to accept another teaching assignment without the concurrence of the school board. A teacher who resigns on terms inconsistent with the above risks suspension of his or her teaching license for a period not to exceed one year.

105 ILCS 5/21B-75
105 ILCS 5/24-14

Board of Education of Park Forest Heights School District No. 163 v. The State Teacher Certification Board, et al., 363 Ill. App. 3d 433, 842 N.E. 2d 1230, 299 Ill. Dec. 878, (1st Dist. 2006) cert. den. 219 Ill. 2d 561, 852 N.E. 2d 238, 303 Ill. Dec. 831 (2006)

Braught v. Board of Education of Mount Prospect School District No. 57, 136 Ill. App. 3d 486, 483 N.E. 2d 623, 91 Ill. Dec. 277 (1st Dist. 1985)

15:610 When is a teacher's resignation effective?

In the sense that an unwilling teacher cannot be compelled to perform teaching duties, a teacher resignation is effective when the teacher determines to resign. Whether or not a school board can penalize the teacher for having resigned without the consent of the school board is determined by the facts of each resignation. When a particular resignation is perfected depends upon the timing of the intended resignation and the facts surrounding its delivery.

Braught v. Board of Education of Mount Prospect School District No. 57, 136 Ill. App. 3d 486, 483 N.E. 2d 623, 91 Ill. Dec. 277 (1st Dist. 1985)

Arduini v. Board of Education of Pontiac Township High School District 90, Livingston County, 92 Ill. 2d 197, 441 N.E. 2d 73, 65 Ill. Dec. 281 (1982)

Gras v. Clark, 46 Ill. App. 3d 803, 361 N.E. 2d 316, 5 Ill. Dec. 177 (2nd Dist. 1977)

TEACHERS RETIREMENT SYSTEM

15:700 Are teachers covered by Social Security?

No deduction or employer contribution is made from teacher pay for Social Security. Teachers may make Social Security payments by having non-teaching jobs for which such contributions are made. Before the summer of 2003, Teacher Retirement System (TRS) contributions were paid only on summer teaching jobs for which the teacher had an extended contract and summer teaching jobs for which there was no extended contract were not subject to TRS payments. Beginning with the summer of 2003 the extended contract requirement was dropped.

Teachers are required to participate in the Teacher Retirement System. Teachers and other school employees hired after March 31, 1986, are subject to a 1.45 percent Medicare tax.

26 U.S.C. 3121(b)(10)

40 ILCS 5/21-101 et seq.

40 ILCS 5/21-102.12 et seq.

15:710 What contribution to the Teacher Retirement System on behalf of each teacher is required?

A school board is required to contribute 9 percent of each teacher's gross pay to the Teacher Retirement System (TRS). Gross pay includes sums paid the teacher for extra duties and certain fringe benefits provided under a cafeteria plan. TRS has gross income treatments that differ from Internal Revenue Service treatments, and a school board should be wary to examine both effects when considering any new fringe benefit program.

Beginning July 1, 1998 school districts were required to pay an employer contribution to TRS on behalf of each teacher. The rate is .58 percent of each teacher's salary.

40 ILCS 5/16-152

40 ILCS 5/16-158

15:715 What was the pension reform bill?

In 2013, the General Assembly passed P.A. 98-599, a comprehensive pension reform bill that had an effective date of June 1, 2014. The bill was declared unconstitutional.

P.A. 98-599

40 ILCS 5/16-101 et seq.

In re Pension Reform Litigation, 2015 IL 118585

15:720 What is the significance of the multiplier .098901 for Teacher Retirement System contribution purposes?

If a teacher's gross pay including Teacher Retirement System (TRS) contribution equals X, then the amount of the TRS contribution is calculated by multiplying X(.09). If the amount of X(.09) is subtracted from the teacher's gross pay, the result is the teacher's taxable pay. To get from the teacher's taxable pay to the teacher's gross pay, one must multiply taxable pay by 1.098901. To determine the amount of TRS contribution due knowing only the amount of a teacher's taxable pay, one must multiply taxable pay by .098901. The multiplier .098901 is unnecessary and burdensome if the teacher's gross pay is known. At various times when the pension contribution has been at different statutory rates, the multiplier has been a different number.

40 ILCS 5/16-152 et seq.

15:725 How many days in a school year must a teacher work to receive a full year of TRS service credit?

A teacher must work and be paid for 170 days (out of the 180 workdays that are routinely scheduled in a teacher's un-extended work year). That means that paid sick leave never results in a service credit reduction, nor do pay docks of 10 days or less during a school term.

80 Ill. Admin. Code 1650.320

15:730 What is the Teacher Health Insurance Security Fund?

This fund finances the cost of health benefits for retired teachers. On July 1, 1995, all active contributors to the Teacher Retirement System were required to begin making contributions toward the cost of annuitant and survivor health benefits. On July 1, 2005, the rate was .80 percent of salary. Beginning July 1, 2007 the rate increases annually to a percentage of salary to be determined by the Department of Central Management Services that in each fiscal year shall not exceed 105 percent of the percentage of salary actually required to be paid in the previous fiscal year.

5 ILCS 375/6.6

15:740 What is the amount of the employer contribution for retired teacher health benefits?

Beginning January 1, 2002, school boards were required to make employer contributions toward the cost of annuitant and survivor health benefits. The employer contribution began at 0.4 percent of each teacher's salary. Beginning July 1, 2005, the employer contribution rose to 0.6 percent of each teacher's salary and beginning July 1, 2007, the rate increased to a percentage of salary to be determined by the Department of Central Management Services that in each fiscal year must not exceed 105 percent of the percentage of salary actually required to be paid in the previous fiscal year.

5 ILCS 375/6.6

RETIREMENT INCENTIVES

15:760 What is the 6 percent cap?

Prior to 2005, there was no penalty to the employer for any increase in wages or benefits paid to a teacher prior to retirement. For a number of years before the 2005 change in the relevant statute, the Teacher Retirement System (TRS) had what was commonly called "the 20 percent rule." Under that rule, TRS recognized an increase in earnings of 20 percent or less in pension computable years for purposes of making pension calculations, but there was no employer penalty for payments to employees that exceeded 20 percent.

The new relevant pension provision provides: "If the amount of a participant's earnings for any academic year used to determine the final rate of earnings exceeds the amount of his or her earnings with the same employer for the previous academic year by more than 6 percent, the participant's employer must pay to the System [TRS], in addition to all other payments required under this Section and in accordance with guidelines established by the System, the present value of the increase in benefits resulting from the portion of the increase in earnings that is in excess of 6 percent."

The present value is computed by TRS on the basis of the actuarial assumptions and tables. Employer contributions required under this provision are paid in the form of a lump sum within 90 days after receipt of the bill. There is a statutory procedure that allows the dispute of a TRS bill within 30 days of its receipt.

40 ILCS 5/16-158(f)
80 Ill. Admin Code 1650.481
80 Ill. Admin Code 1650.482
80 Ill. Admin Code 1650.483

15:761 Which service credit years are included in the 6 percent cap calculation?

The cap applies to creditable earnings received by a teacher (or other Teacher Retirement System member) during the best four consecutive years in the last 10 before the employee retires. Generally, the best four consecutive years are the last four before retirement.

80 Ill. Admin. Code 1650.460 b

15:762 What is excluded from the 6 percent cap calculations?

The penalty provisions do not apply to:

1) Earnings increases paid to participants under contracts or collective bargaining agreements entered into, amended, or renewed before June 1, 2005;

2) Salary increases given to a teacher who is 10 or more years from retirement eligibility (pursuant to 40 ILCS 5/16-132 or 16-133.2)

3) Overload work, including summer school, when the school district has certified to TRS (and TRS has approved) that the work is for the sole purpose of classroom instruction in excess of the standard number of classes for a full-time teacher in a school district during the school year and the salary increases are equal to or less than the rate of pay for classroom instruction computed on the teacher's current salary and work schedule;

4) Promotion for which the employee is required to hold a license or supervisory endorsement issued by the State Educator Preparation and Licensure Board that is a different certification or supervisory endorsement than is required for the teacher's previous position and to a position that has existed and been

filled by a member for no less than one complete academic year and the salary increase from the promotion is an increase that results in an amount no greater than the lesser of the average salary paid for other similar positions in the district requiring the same certification or the amount stipulated in the collective bargaining agreement for a similar position requiring the same certification.

5) Any payment to the teacher from the State of Illinois or the State Board of Education over which the employer does not have discretion, notwithstanding that the payment is included in the computation of final average salary.

6) Any salary increase described in 40 ILCS 5/16-158(g) given on or after July 1, 2011 but before July 1, 2014 under a contract or collective bargaining agreement entered into, amended, or renewed on or after June 1, 2005 but before July 1, 2011. Notwithstanding any other provision of the relevant law, any payments made or salary increases given after June 30, 2014 are used in assessing payment for any amount due under 40 ILCS 5/16-158 (f).

40 ILCS 5/16-132
40 ILCS 5/16-133.2
40 ILCS 5/16-158

15:766 What is salary (creditable earnings) for teacher pension purposes?

Salary means any form of creditable compensation received by a teacher in consideration of services rendered as a teacher, subject to all applicable limits and restrictions imposed on qualified plans under the Internal Revenue Code. The term "teacher" in this context includes administrators and other licensed employees who are Teacher Retirement System (TRS) members. "Salary" directly related to specific work performed during a school year is recognized on an accrual basis. Other creditable compensation is recognized on a cash basis. TRS has, by rule, the right to determine the year of salary recognition. TRS recognizes as salary:

1) The gross amount of compensation earned or accruing to a teacher during the school year in a function requiring certification as a teacher.

2) Additional compensation earned during the school year for the performance of extra duties, not requiring teacher certification, but which involve the supervision of students or are related to the academic program, provided the teacher is employed as a full-time or part-time contractual teacher and establishes active service credit in that position during the school year.

3) The amount of back salary awarded to a teacher as a result of a settlement or judgment obtained due to a disputed dismissal, suspension, or demotion. Court costs, attorney's fees, other compensatory damages, and punitive damages are not reportable as salary. The back salary amount reported to TRS is equal to the amount the teacher would have earned had the dispute not occurred, regardless of the actual amount paid.

4) Lump-sum payments (e.g., retirement incentives, bonuses, payments for unused vacation and sick days) received by the teacher or becoming due and payable to the teacher prior to or concurrent with receipt of final paycheck for regular earnings.

5) Contributions made by or on behalf of the member to qualified deferred compensation plans (sections 401(a) and 457(b) of the Internal Revenue Code), salary reduction plans or tax sheltered annuities under section 403(b) of the Internal Revenue Code.

6) Amounts that would otherwise qualify as salary under all the above but are not received directly by the teacher because they are used to finance benefit options in a flexible benefit plan; provided, however, that to be reportable, a flexible benefit plan cannot include non-qualifying deferred compensation. For the System's purposes, a flexible benefit plan is an option offered by an employer to its employees covered under TRS to receive an alternative form of creditable compensation in lieu of employer-provided insurance.

TRS does not recognize as salary:

1) Lump-sum payments (e.g., retirement incentives, bonuses, payments for unused vacation and sick days) becoming due and payable to the member subsequent to receipt of final paycheck for regular earnings.

2) Any lump sum payment made after the death of the member.

3) Expense reimbursements, expense allowances, or fringe benefits unless included in a reportable flexible benefit plan.

4) Any moneys received by the member under the Workers' Compensation Act or the Workers' Occupational Diseases Act.

5) Compensation for extra duties not requiring teacher certification performed by substitute and part-time non-contractual teachers.

6) Any amount paid in lieu of discontinued or decreased non-reportable benefits, or reported in lieu of previously non-reported compensation, where the conversion occurs in the teacher's final seven years of service. If any form of non-creditable or non-reported compensation in any of the teacher's last seven creditable school years of employment exceeds that of any other subsequent year, TRS will presume the difference to have been converted into salary in the subsequent year. To overcome the presumption, the member must submit documentary evidence to TRS that clearly and convincingly proves that the change in compensation structure was due to a change in a collectively bargained agreement applicable to all individuals covered by the agreement, a change in employer policies

affecting a group of similarly situated members some of whom are not within seven years of retirement eligibility, or a change in family status, and not to increase final average salary.

7) Any amount paid by an employer as the employer's onetime contribution (or on behalf of the employee as the employee's one-time contribution) required by the TRS as part of the statutory early retirement option in Section 16-133.2 of the TRS pension law.

8) Options to take salary in lieu of employment-related expense allowances or reimbursements.

9) Employer payment of the member's Teachers Health Insurance Security Fund contribution.

10) Commissions (i.e., payments to a member based upon a percentage formula).

11) Contributions to and distributions from nonqualified deferred compensation arrangements.

12) Employer contributions to and distributions from medical spending accounts.

80 Ill. Admin. Code 1650.450

Sartwell v. Board of Trustees of the Teachers' Retirement System of the State of Illinois, 403 Ill. App. 3d 719, 936 N.E. 2d 610, 344 Ill. Dec. 81 (4th Dist. 2010)

15:770 May the employer 6 percent cap payments be passed along to employees if the parties agree to do so in a collective bargaining agreement?

No.

40 ILCS 5/15-155(g)

Teacher Retirement System Employer Bulletin 06-03

15:780 What is a sick leave balloon?

A sick leave balloon is an extraordinary grant of sick leave intended to provide a teacher with service credit for retirement purposes. Prior to a 2005 change in pension law, it was common for employers to provide teachers nearing retirement with additional sick leave beyond the normal contractual annual allotment.

Because extraordinary grants of sick leave (more than 20 days in a school year including personal leave days) awarded in the last four years prior to retirement now result in a Teacher Retirement System (TRS) cash penalty imposed on the employer, what was a once common benefit has become very expensive and most employers will seek to end balloon benefits wherever they exist.

The pension reform legislation passed in 2013 precludes payment for unused sick leave or vacation time (administrators) for employees who become members of TRS after June 1, 2014.

40 ILCS 5/15-155

40 ILCS 5/16-121

80 Ill. Admin. Code 1650.350

15:790 What was ERO?

In 2016 the General Assembly allowed the program known as Early Retirement Option (ERO) to sunset. From 2005 to 2016 ERO had allowed certain employees to retire before full retirement age provided certain employer and employee penalties were paid. There is no longer an ERO option for teachers. Surviving references to ERO in collective bargaining agreements are no longer valid nor enforceable. The contributions employees made to ERO (.004 of creditable earnings) were returned to the employees in late 2016. The effect of the ERO sunset slightly reduced the creditable earnings of each active employee, thereby slightly decreasing their retirement annuity.

16: TEACHER TENURE AND SENIORITY RIGHTS

TEACHER TENURE

16:10 Do all teachers enjoy the same employment rights under Illinois law?

Illinois teachers fall into three broad categories for purposes of statutory employment rights:

Probationary teachers who are not in their last year of probationary service have the fewest rights. All part-time teachers who have not achieved and maintained tenured status have rights similar to such probationary teachers.

Probationary teachers in their final year of probationary service comprise the second category, and have slightly greater rights than other probationary teachers.

The third category is comprised of tenured teachers, who have dramatically more rights than either of the other two categories of teachers.

105 ILCS 5/24-11
105 ILCS 5/24-12

16:20 What is tenure?

Tenure is the common name for contractual continued service, which is the status conferred by law upon certificated employees who have satisfactorily completed a term of probationary employment. The employee in contractual continued service is

1) Deemed to be continuously employed from year to year unless given proper notice of honorable dismissal (layoff) or dismissal for cause;

2) Granted seniority rights. Before a 2011 change in the law, tenured teachers were entitled to seniority rights granted by law or a collective bargaining agreement in the event a school board reduced its staff or discontinued a program; after the change, both seniority and performance evaluations factor in when layoffs are contemplated; and

3) Entitled to substantial rights of due process in the event of dismissal for cause.

105 ILCS 5/24-12

16:30 What is the difference between contractual continued service and tenure?

There is no difference between the terms. Tenure is the common name for contractual continued service.

105 ILCS 5/24-11
105 ILCS 5/24-12

16:40 What is the difference between a probationary teacher and a non-tenured teacher?

The terms have the same meaning, as does the phrase "teacher who has not entered into contractual continued service."

16:50 Must a tenured teacher be issued an annual employment contract?

Tenured teachers have a continuing employment relationship that does not require the issuance of an annual contract. Assuming there is no collectively bargained provision that prevents the issuance of an annual contract and no demand to bargain, a school board may issue individual teacher contracts. The terms of the contract must be consistent with the terms of applicable collectively bargained provisions.

A tenured teacher cannot be compelled to sign such a contract, but may voluntarily enter into a contract providing for additional obligations in exchange for additional benefits.

Bond v. Board of Education of Mascoutah Community Unit School District No. 19, 81 Ill. 2d 242, 408 N.E. 2d 714, 42 Ill. Dec. 136 (1980)

Bagley v. Board of Education of Seneca Community Consolidated School District No. 170, LaSalle County, 83 Ill. App. 3d 247, 403 N.E. 2d 1285, 38 Ill. Dec. 681 (3rd Dist. 1980) aff'd. 81 Ill. 2d 477, 419 N.E. 2d 1165, 50 Ill. Dec. 716 (1980)

Littrell v. Board of Education of Cave in Rock Community Unit School District No. 2, 45 Ill. App. 3d 690, 360 N.E. 2d 102, 4 Ill. Dec. 355 (5th Dist. 1977)

Davis v. Board of Education of Aurora Public School District No. 131 of Kane County, 19 Ill. App. 3d 644, 312 N.E. 2d 335 (2nd Dist. 1974)

16:55 Does tenure protect a teacher's right to a particular job assignment?

The safeguards of tenure do not assure employment in a particular job assignment, grade level, or attendance center, but rather protect the individual's job as a teacher.

Caviness v. Board of Education of Ludlow Community Consolidated School District No. 142 of Champaign County, 59 Ill. App. 3d 28, 375 N.E. 2d 157, 16 Ill. Dec. 526 (4th Dist. 1978)

Danno v. Peterson, 421 F. Supp. 950 (N.D. Ill. 1976)

Van Dyke v. Board of Education of School District No. 57, Cook County, 115 Ill. App. 2d 10, 254 N.E. 2d 76 (1st Dist. 1969)

ACQUISITION OF TENURE

16:60 Which employees may acquire tenure?

A teacher may acquire tenure. The term "teacher" in this context includes all school district employees whose jobs require teacher certification. Superintendents, principals, other administrators, deans, department heads, and counselors may acquire teacher tenure if such employees meet statutory requirements.

Tenure does not attach to a particular job, but rather to teaching employment in the school district generally. For example, a principal cannot earn tenure as a principal, but earns tenure as a teaching employee.

105 ILCS 5/10-23.8 et seq.

105 ILCS 5/24-12

Davis v. Board of Education of Farmer City-Mansfield Community Unit School District No. 17, 63 Ill. App. 3d 495, 380 N.E. 2d 58, 20 Ill. Dec. 381 (4th Dist. 1978)

Lester v. Board of Education of School District No. 119, Jo Daviess County, 87 Ill. App. 2d 269, 230 N.E. 2d 893 (2nd Dist. 1967)

16:70 When does a teacher acquire tenure?

Senate Bill 7 (P.A. 97-08), enacted in 2011, changed the system by which teachers acquire tenure.

Before 1998, for a teacher employed in a particular school district, tenure was achieved after service of a probationary period of two full-time consecutive school terms unless the teacher was given written notice of dismissal by the school board. The notice had to state the specific reason for the dismissal, be delivered by certified mail, return receipt requested, at least 45 days before the end of the school term.

Under the law as it existed beginning January 1, 1998 (which was in effect for some districts until 2016), for a teacher first employed by a school district on or after January 1, 1998 but before the new law took effect, and who had not before that date already achieved tenure in that district, the probationary period is four consecutive school terms. The relevant old statute does not provide guidance as to the meaning of the term "first employed." A collective bargaining agreement may require notice in excess of 45 days.

The new statute provides that for any teacher who is first employed as a full-time teacher in a school district or program on or after the PERA (Performance Evaluation Reform Act; P.A. 96-861) implementation date (2015 for some school districts and 2016 for most school districts), the probationary period is one of the following periods, based upon the teacher's school terms of service and performance, before the teacher enters upon contractual continued service in the district or in all of the programs that the teacher is legally qualified to hold. Under the new statute, the probationary period is:

1) Four consecutive school terms of service in which the teacher receives overall annual evaluation ratings of at least "proficient" in the last school term and at least "proficient" in either the second or third school term. If, at the conclusion of four consecutive school terms of service that count toward attainment of contractual continued service, the teacher's performance does not qualify the teacher for contractual continued service, then the teacher shall not enter upon contractual continued service and must be dismissed. The written notice of dismissal must contain specific reasons

2) Three consecutive school terms of service in which the teacher receives three overall annual evaluations of "excellent" (the written notice of dismissal must contain specific reasons); or

3) Two consecutive school terms of service in which the teacher receives two overall annual evaluations of "excellent," but only if the teacher (i) previously attained contractual continued service in a different Illinois school district or program; (ii) voluntarily departed or was honorably dismissed from that school district or program in the school term immediately prior to the teacher's first school term of service applicable to the attainment of contractual continued service under this paragraph; and (iii) received, in his or her two most recent overall annual or biennial evaluations from the prior school district or program, ratings of at least "proficient," with both such ratings occurring after the school district's or program's PERA implementation date. The teacher must provide official copies of his or her two most recent overall annual or biennial evaluations from the prior school district or program to the new school district or program within 60 days from the teacher's first day of service with the new school district or program. The prior school district or program must provide the teacher with official copies of his or her two most recent overall annual or biennial evaluations within 14 days after the teacher's request. If a teacher has requested official copies prior to 45 days after the teacher's first day of service with the new school district or program and the teacher's prior school district or program fails to provide the teacher with the official copies, then the time period for the teacher to submit the official copies to his or her new school district or program must be extended until 14 days after receipt of such copies from the prior school district or program. If the prior school district

or program fails to provide the teacher with the official copies required within 90 days from the teacher's first day of service with the new school district or program, then the new school district or program must rely upon the teacher's own copies of his or her evaluations.

If a performance evaluation is not conducted for any school term when evaluation is required to be conducted under Section 24A-5 of the School Code, then the teacher's performance evaluation rating for such school term for purposes of determining the attainment of contractual continued service is deemed "proficient."

For the purposes of determining contractual continued service, a school term is counted only toward attainment of contractual continued service if the teacher actually teaches or is otherwise present and participating in the district's or program's educational program for 120 days or more, provided that the days of leave under the federal Family and Medical Leave Act that the teacher is required to take until the end of the school term are considered days of teaching or participation in the district's or program's educational program. A school term that is not counted toward attainment of contractual continued service is not be considered a break in service for purposes of determining whether a teacher has been employed for four consecutive school terms, provided the teacher actually teaches or is otherwise present and participating in the district's or program's educational program in the following school term.

Any full-time teacher who does not receive written notice from the employing board at least 45 days before the end of any school term and whose performance does not require dismissal after the fourth probationary year must be re-employed for the following school term.

For the purpose of determining contractual continued service, the first probationary year is any full-time employment from a date before November 1 through the end of the school year.

A school board may not award tenure sooner than the statute allows.

105 ILCS 5/24-11

Dunlop v. Colgan, 687 F. Supp. 406 (N.D. Ill. 1988)

Williams v. Board of Education of Hardin County Community Unit School District No. 1, 166 Ill. App. 3d 765, 520 N.E. 2d 954, 117 Ill. Dec. 603 (5th Dist. 1988) app. den. 121 Ill. 2d 587, 526 N.E. 2d 841, 122 Ill. Dec. 448 (1988)

Bessler v. Board of Education of Charter School District No. 150 of Peoria County, 43 Ill. App. 3d 322, 356 N.E. 2d 1253, 1 Ill. Dec. 920 (3rd Dist. 1977), aff'd. in part, rev. in part 69 Ill. 2d 191, 370 N.E. 2d 1050, 13 Ill. Dec. 23 (1978)

16:80 Does a teacher hired to replace a teacher on an approved leave of absence acquire tenure?

Tenure is not acquired by a person while employed to replace a teacher who is in the military service of the United States, one who is serving in the General Assembly, or one who by agreement of a school board is on leave to teach in a Department of Defense dependents' school. In any other circumstance, whether or not a teacher replacing a teacher on an approved leave of absence acquires tenure or not is a fact-specific question.

105 ILCS 5/24-13

105 ILCS 5/24-13.1

Fisher v. Board of Education of West Washington County Community Unit District No. 10, Washington County, 181 Ill. App. 3d 653, 537 N.E. 2d 354, 130 Ill. Dec. 287 (5th Dist. 1989)

16:90 If a certified teacher is employed in a special education district or cooperative, in which school district or districts does such a teacher acquire tenure?

Senate Bill 7 (P.A. 97-08) changed the language of the super-tenure paragraphs of Section 24-11 of the School Code. The super-tenure changes have an effective date beginning with the start of the 2011-2012 school term.

Tenure in all participating school districts is commonly called super-tenure. Teachers employed in a special education cooperative after 1987 cannot acquire super-tenure but do have bumping rights into member districts on the occasion of the dissolution of the special education district.

Employment in a special educational joint agreement is deemed a continuation of all previous certificated employment of the teacher in the joint agreement whether the employer of the teacher was the joint agreement, the regional superintendent, or one of the participating districts in the joint agreement.

For any teacher employed after July 1, 1987 as a full-time teacher in a program of a special education joint agreement, whether the program is operated by the joint agreement or a member district on behalf of the joint agreement, in the event of a reduction in the number of programs or positions in the joint agreement in which the notice of dismissal is provided on or before the end of the 2010-2011 school term, the teacher in contractual continued service is eligible for employment in the joint agreement programs for which the teacher is legally qualified in order of greater length of continuing service in the joint agreement, unless an alternative method of determining the sequence of dismissal is established in a collective bargaining agreement.

For any teacher employed after July 1, 1987 as a full-time teacher in a program of a special education joint agreement, whether the program is operated by the joint agreement or a member district on behalf of the joint agreement:

1) In the event of a reduction in the number of programs or positions in the joint agreement in which the notice of dismissal is provided during the 2011-2012 school term or a subsequent school term, the teacher must be included on the honorable dismissal lists of all joint agreement programs for positions for which the teacher is qualified and is eligible for employment in those programs in accordance with subsections (b) and (c) of Section 24-12 of the School Code and the applicable honorable dismissal policies of the joint agreement;

2) In the event of the dissolution of the joint agreement, in which the notice to teachers of the dissolution is provided during the 2010-2011 school term, the teacher in contractual continued service who is legally qualified must be assigned to any comparable position in a member district currently held by a teacher who has not entered upon contractual continued service or held by a teacher who has entered upon contractual continued service with a shorter length of contractual continued service;

3) In the event of the dissolution of the joint agreement in which the notice to teachers of the dissolution is provided during the 2011-2012 school term or a subsequent school term, the teacher who is qualified must be included on the order of honorable dismissal lists of each member district and must be assigned to any comparable position in any such district in accordance with subsections (b) and (c) of Section 24-12 of the School Code and the applicable honorable dismissal policies of each member district.

105 ILCS 5/14-9.01

105 ILCS 5/24-11

Seim v. Board of Education of Community Unit School District No. 87 of McLean County, 21 Ill. App. 3d 386, 315 N.E. 2d 282 (4th Dist. 1974)

16:100 Do teachers employed in a joint agreement vocational area center have super-tenure?

No.

Aken v. Board of Control of Lake County Area Vocational Center, 237 Ill. App. 3d 97, 604 N.E. 2d 524, 178 Ill. Dec. 268 (2nd Dist. 1992)

Koppi v. Board of Control of Whiteside Area Vocational Center, 133 Ill. App. 3d 591, 479 N.E. 2d 36, 88 Ill. Dec. 701 (3rd Dist. 1985)

16:105 Can a teacher employed by an alternative school achieve tenure?

If the teacher is employed by the regional superintendent of schools, then the teacher may achieve tenure as an employee of the regional superintendent in the alternative school. The law is unclear as to the status of the teacher with respect to alternative school tenure if the teacher is employed by the regional superintendent while on leave from a school district served by the regional superintendent.

105 ILCS 5/13A-1(l)

16:110 Does service as a teacher's aide or a paraprofessional count toward earning tenure if the person so employed has teacher certification?

No.

Strejcek v. Board of Education of Berwyn School District No. 100, 78 Ill. App. 3d 400, 397 N.E. 2d 448, 33 Ill. Dec. 942 (1st Dist. 1979)

16:115 Is substitute teaching counted as probationary service?

Substitute teachers — even those employed on a fulltime equivalent basis — are not probationary tenure track teachers.

Harbaugh v. Board of Education of the City of Chicago, 716 F. 3d 983 (7th Cir. 2013)

Booker v. Hutsonville, 107 Ill. App. 3d, 437 N.E. 2d 937, 63 Ill. Dec. 288 (5th Dist. 1982)

16:120 Is a teacher employed in a program that is wholly federally funded accruing time toward the acquisition of tenure?

Probably not. Courts have found teachers employed in programs that are wholly federally funded are not "full-time teachers" within the meaning of teacher tenure laws.

Kuykendall v. Board of Education of Evanston Township High School District No. 202, 111 Ill. App. 3d 809, 444 N.E. 2d 766, 67 Ill. Dec. 530 (1st Dist. 1982)

16:130 Can a teacher earn tenure in an extra-duty assignment?

No. Tenure is not acquired in-position, but as a generic teaching employee of the school district. A coach cannot acquire tenure as a coach. A collective bargaining agreement may, however, extend contractual rights to such employees and it is safer when contemplating dismissal for cause to provide some due process.

Smith v. Board of Education of Urbana School District No. 116, 708 F. 2d 258 (7th Cir. 1983)

Brunstrom v. Board of Education of Riverdale Community Unit School District 100 of Rock Island County, 52 Ill. App. 3d 653, 367 N.E. 2d 1065, 10 Ill. Dec. 456 (3rd Dist. 1977)

16:150 If two or more school districts combine, do the tenured teachers from the predecessor school districts lose tenure?

No. If by reason of any change in the boundaries of school districts, or by reason of the creation of a new school district, the position held by any teacher having tenured status is transferred from one school board to the control of a new or different board, the tenure of the teacher is not lost. The new or different school board is subject to the tenure laws with respect to the teacher in the same manner as if the teacher were its employee and had been its employee during the time the teacher was actually employed by the board from whose control the position was transferred.

105 ILCS 5/24-11

PART-TIME TEACHERS

16:160 Can a part-time teacher acquire tenure?

No. To acquire tenure, an employee must complete the statutory period of full-time service. However, a part-time teacher can have tenure if the tenure was acquired while the teacher was in full-time service (and the teacher was later reduced to part-time status).

105 ILCS 5/24-11

Kuykendall v. Board of Education of Evanston Township High School District No. 202, 111 Ill. App. 3d 809, 444 N.E. 2d 766, 67 Ill. Dec. 530 (1st Dist. 1982).

Johnson v. Board of Education of Decatur School District No. 61 of Macon County, 87 Ill. App. 3d 441, 409 N.E. 2d 139, 42 Ill. Dec. 644 (4th Dist. 1980) aff'd. 85 Ill. 2d 338, 423 N.E. 2d 903, 53 Ill. Dec. 234 (1981)

16:170 May a school board confer tenure on a part-time teacher or on a teacher who has served less than the requisite probationary period?

No. Tenure attaches by operation of law, not by any action taken by a school board. A school board cannot "confer" tenure. The requisite probationary period must be served. However, a school board that makes a promise to a teacher may be held to its bargain if the promise has the requisite elements to elevate it to a contract. The promise of tenure may confer upon a teacher rights other than tenure.

Faculty Association of District 205, IEA-NEA v. Illinois Educational Labor Relations Board, 175 Ill. App. 3d 880, 530 N.E. 2d 548 (4th Dist. 1988) app. den. 124 Ill. 2d 554 (1989)

Evans v. Benjamin School District No. 25, 134 Ill. App. 3d 875, 480 N.E. 2d 1380, 89 Ill. Dec. 637 (2nd Dist. 1985)

Kuykendall v. Board of Education of Evanston Township High School District No. 202, 111 Ill. App. 3d 809, 444 N.E. 2d 766, 67 Ill. Dec. 530 (1st Dist. 1982)

SENIORITY AND REDUCTION IN FORCE

16:190 Do probationary or part-time teachers accrue seniority rights?

Prior to the enactment of Senate Bill 7 (P.A. 97-08), probationary and part-time teachers had no seniority rights recognized by statute. Such employees sometimes had seniority rights conferred by a collective bargaining agreement. After enactment of SB 7 and beginning with the 2011-2012 school term for every district except those that are grandfathered, probationary and part-time teachers have seniority rights in the event of a reduction in force subject to the complicated limitations of the grouping requirements in Section 24-12.

105 ILCS 5/24-12

16:200 What is RIF?

RIF is an acronym for "reduction in force," which is the decision of a school board to decrease the number of teachers employed or to discontinue some particular type of teaching service.

105 ILCS 5/24-12

16:210 What is the difference between the terms "layoff" and "reduction in force?"

An employee is laid off when an employer conducts a reduction in force.

16:220 What seniority rights may tenured teachers assert against less senior teachers in the event of a reduction in force?

Senate Bill 7 (P.A. 97-08) made major changes to the application of seniority in instances of layoff and recall. Seniority rights are only pertinent as between teachers in grouping two with the same performance rating and as between teachers within groupings three and four.

Before SB 7, a school board contemplating a reduction in teaching force (RIF) was first compelled to remove or dismiss all non-tenured teachers in a particular position before removing or dismissing any tenured teacher who was legally qualified to hold the position. As between tenured teachers, the teacher or teachers with the shorter length of continuing service to the district had to be dismissed first unless an alternate method of determining the sequence of dismissal was established in a collective bargaining agreement.

A school board must comply with all procedures required by its collective bargaining agreement in conducting a RIF.

Illinois is in the Seventh Circuit Court of Appeals, as is Indiana. A 2017 Seventh Circuit decision in an Indiana case creates some uncertainty about the constitutionality of SB 7 in that it may impair the contractual rights of tenured teachers who are dismissed before similarly qualified non-tenured teachers.

105 ILCS 5/24-12

Elliott v. Board of School Trustees of Madison Consolidated Schools, __ F. 3d __ (7th Cir. 2017)

Schaefer v. Board of Education of Arlington Heights School District No. 25, 157 Ill. App. 3d 884, 510 N.E. 2d 1186, 110 Ill. Dec. 155 (1st Dist. 1987) app. den. 116 Ill. 2d 576, 515 N.E. 2d 126, 113 Ill. Dec. 317 (1987)

Catron v. Board of Education of Kansas Community Unit School District No. 3 of Edgar County, 126 Ill. App. 3d 693, 467 N.E. 2d 621, 81 Ill. Dec. 750 (4th Dist. 1984)

Birk v. Board of Education of Flora Community Unit School District No. 35, Clay County, 104 Ill. 2d 252, 472 N.E. 2d 407, 84 Ill. Dec. 447 (1984)

Wilson v. Board of Education Limestone Walters School District No. 316, 127 Ill. App. 3d 433, 468 N.E. 2d 995, 82 Ill. Dec. 341 (3rd Dist. 1984)

Caviness v. Board of Education of Ludlow Community Consolidated School District No. 142 of Champaign County, 59 Ill. App. 3d 28, 375 N.E. 2d 157, 16 Ill. Dec. 526 (4th Dist. 1978)

16:230 Is the reduction of a tenured teacher from 10-month employment to 9-month employment a reduction in force?

Yes. The reduction of a tenured teacher's employment from a 10-month extended contract to a 9-month regular contract is a reduction in force and is subject to the grouping requirements of Section 24-12. Absent agreement from the teacher, the reduction of a tenured teacher from full-time to part-time may only be accomplished at the beginning of a new school term following legally sufficient notice to the teacher at least 45 days before the end of the preceding school term. The notification procedure is the same as that required for notice of dismissal or layoff.

105 ILCS 5/24-12

Duncan v. Board of Education of United Township High School District No. 30, 177 Ill. App. 3d 806, 532 N.E. 2d 927, 127 Ill. Dec. 98 (3rd Dist. 1988)

Pennell v. Board of Education of Equality Community Unit School District 4, Gallatin County, 137 Ill. App. 3d 139, 484 N.E. 2d 445, 91 Ill. Dec. 886 (5th Dist. 1986)

Birk v. Board of Education of Flora Community Unit School District No. 35, Clay County, 104 Ill. 2d 252, 472 N.E. 2d 407, 84 Ill. Dec. 447 (1984)

Wilson v. Board of Education Limestone Walters School District No. 316, 127 Ill. App. 3d 433, 468 N.E. 2d 995, 82 Ill. Dec. 341 (3rd Dist. 1984)

16:235 Can a tenured teacher who accepts a part-time position and later requests return to full-time teaching assert bumping rights against a new non-tenured teacher?

Under most circumstances, bumping rights can be asserted only when a reduction in force triggers the bumps. When, however, a tenured teacher has retained tenure after a reduction to part-time status, the tenured teacher may later return to full-time status by asserting bumping rights against a new non-tenured teacher who has been hired to teach in a position that the tenured teacher is qualified to fill.

Deem v. Board of Education of Triad Community Unit School District No. 2, Madison County, 200 Ill. App. 3d 903, 558 N.E. 2d 291, 146 Ill. Dec. 328 (5th Dist. 1990)

16:240 What is required to reduce a tenured teacher from full-time to part-time employment?

Pursuant to Senate Bill 7 (P.A. 97-08), enacted in 2011, the notice period is 45 days before the end of the school term before which the reduction is to take place and the layoff order is governed by the grouping requirements of Section 24-12 of the School Code. A teacher can agree to the reduction at any time.

Under the law as it existed before changes made by SB 7, without the agreement of the teacher, the reduction of a tenured teacher from full-time to part-time employment could only be accomplished at the beginning of a new school term following legally sufficient notice to the teacher at least 60 days before the end of the preceding school term. The notification procedure is the same as that required for notice of dismissal or layoff. The seniority rights of tenured teachers must be respected in any such reduction and all collectively bargained procedures must be followed.

105 ILCS 5/24-12

Pennell v. Board of Education of Equality Community Unit School District 4, Gallatin County, 137 Ill. App. 3d 139, 484 N.E. 2d 445, 91 Ill. Dec. 886 (5th Dist. 1986)

Board of Education of Bremen Community High School District No. 228, Cook County v. Bremen District No. 228 Joint Faculty Association, 114 Ill. App. 3d 1051, 449 N.E. 2d 960, 70 Ill. Dec. 613 (1st Dist. 1983) aff'd. in part, rev. in part on other grounds 101 Ill. 2d 115, 461 N.E. 2d 406, 77 Ill. Dec. 783 (1983)

Hagopian v. Board of Education of Tampico Community Unit School District No. 4 of Whiteside and Bureau Counties, 56 Ill. App. 3d 940, 372 N.E. 2d 990, 14 Ill. Dec. 711 (3rd Dist. 1978) app. after rem. 83 Ill. App. 3d 1097, 404 N.E. 2d 899, 39 Ill. Dec. 308 (3rd Dist. 1980), rev. on other grounds 84 Ill. 2d 436, 420 N.E. 2d 147, 50 Ill. Dec. 830 (1981)

16:250 If a teacher has earned tenure and later is reduced to part time without a break in service, does the teacher lose tenure?

No.

Wilson v. Board of Education Limestone Walters School District No. 316, 127 Ill. App. 3d 433, 468 N.E. 2d 995, 82 Ill. Dec. 341 (3rd Dist. 1984)

Caviness v. Board of Education of Ludlow Community Consolidated School District No. 142 of Champaign County, 59 Ill. App. 3d 28, 375 N.E. 2d 157, 16 Ill. Dec. 526 (4th Dist. 1978)

Brown v. Board of Education, Galatia Community Unit School Dist. No. 1, 38 Ill. App. 3d 403, 347 N.E. 2d 791 (5th Dist. 1976) app. after rem., People ex rel. Brown v. Board of Education, Galatia Community Unit School Dist. No. 1, Galatia, 66 Ill. App. 3d 169, 383 N.E. 2d 711, 22 Ill. Dec. 903 (5th Dist. 1978)

16:260 In a reduction in force, must all non-tenured teachers be dismissed before the first tenured teacher is dismissed?

Under the law as it existed before enactment of Senate Bill 7 (P.A. 97-08), a non-tenured teacher had to be reduced first only if he or she held a position that was targeted for reduction or if he or she was bumped by a teacher with greater seniority.

Under SB 7, no distinction is made between tenured and probationary employees and the order of layoff is governed initially by groupings — teachers in grouping one are dismissed before teachers in grouping two, teachers in grouping two are dismissed before teachers in grouping three, and so forth. The new law contains complicated procedures to distinguish the layoff order of teachers in each grouping.

105 ILCS 5/24-12

Piquard v. Board of Education of Pekin Community High School District No. 303, 242 Ill. App. 3d 477, 610 N.E. 2d 757, 182 Ill. Dec. 888 (3rd Dist. 1993)

16:270 In what manner must a school board notify a teacher of honorable dismissal by reason of reduction in teaching force or discontinuance of teaching service?

Senate Bill 7 (P.A. 97-08) changed the notice requirements. For dismissals and recalls in which the notice of dismissal occurred during the 2011-2012 school term or thereafter, when any teacher, whether or not in contractual continued service, is removed or dismissed as a result of a decision of the school board to decrease the number of teachers employed by the board, a decision of a school board to discontinue some particular type of teaching service, or a reduction in the number of programs or positions in a special education joint agreement, then written notice must be mailed to the teacher and also given to the teacher either by certified mail, return receipt requested, or personal delivery with receipt at least 45 days before the end of the school term, together with a statement of honorable dismissal and the reason therefore.

The sequence of dismissal may not impair the operation of any affirmative action program in the school district, regardless of whether it exists by operation of law or is conducted on a voluntary basis by the board.

For dismissals and recalls in which the notice and of dismissal occurred on or before the end of the 2010-2011 school term, if a teacher on tenure is removed or dismissed as a result of the decision of the school board to decrease the number of teachers employed by the board or to discontinue some particular type of teaching service, a written notice must be mailed to the teacher and also given the teacher either by certified mail, return receipt requested, or personal delivery with receipt at least 60 days before the end of the school term, together with a statement of honorable dismissal and the reason therefor. Probationary teachers, except those in their final probationary year, need not be provided reasons for their terminations. The relevant statute requires that these employees be properly notified of termination not later than 45 days before the end of the school term. However, in the case of a reduction in force, the exercise of bumping rights by tenured teachers over non-tenured teachers may create issues unless the reduction in force decisions are made by the employing school board in advance of the notice requirements for tenured teachers and the termination notices are sent at essentially the same time to both tenured and non-tenured teachers who are being bumped and such notices are received by the tenured teachers at least 60 days before the end of the school term.

The notice requirements of the old statutes were amended in 1998. A school district contemplating the non-renewal or layoff of an employee should make sure its local policies, evaluation plans, and contracts do not require notification timelines that are different from those required by statute.

105 ILCS 5/24-12

Koerner v. Joppa Community High School District No. 21, 143 Ill. App. 3d 162, 492 N.E. 2d 1017, 97 Ill. Dec. 358 (5th Dist. 1986)

16:280 When must a school board hold a public hearing before conducting a reduction in force?

Whenever the number of honorable dismissal notices based upon economic necessity exceeds five or 150 percent of the average number of teachers honorably dismissed in the preceding three years, whichever is greater, then the school board must hold a hearing on the question of the dismissals. Following the hearing and board review, the action to approve any such reduction in staff requires a majority vote of the school board.

105 ILCS 5/24-12

Wheatley v. Board of Education of Township High School District No. 205, Cook County, 113 Ill. App. 3d 129, 446 N.E. 2d 1257, 68 Ill. Dec. 860 (1st Dist. 1983)

SENIORITY AND BUMPING

16:290 At what date are teacher qualifications fixed for purposes of a school board decision to reduce force?

A school board must base its decision to reduce force on the qualifications held by a teacher at the time the decision to reduce force is made and on the groupings as they existed in the sequence of honorable dismissal list distributed to the exclusive representative 75 days before the end of the school term, except that teachers in grouping one may be moved to another grouping until as late as 45 days before the end of the school term.

105 ILCS 5/24-12

Hagopian v. Board of Education of Tampico Community Unit School District No. 4 of Whiteside and Bureau Counties, 56 Ill. App. 3d 940, 372 N.E. 2d 990, 14 Ill. Dec. 711 (3rd Dist. 1978) app. after rem. 83 Ill. App. 3d 1097, 404 N.E. 2d 899, 39 Ill. Dec. 308 (3rd Dist. 1980), rev. on other grounds 84 Ill. 2d 436, 420 N.E. 2d 147, 50 Ill. Dec. 830 (1981)

16:300 Are the terms "legally qualified" and "certified" synonymous?

No. "Certified" refers to State Board of Education teacher certification. "Legally qualified" has a wider meaning. A teacher may be certified to hold a position, but not legally qualified to hold it.

Zink v. Board of Education of Chrisman, 146 Ill. App. 3d 1016, 497 N.E. 2d 835, 100 Ill. Dec. 657 (4th Dist. 1986)

Lenard v. Board of Education of Fairfield School District No. 112 of Wayne County, 57 Ill. App. 3d 853, 373 N.E. 2d 477, 15 Ill. Dec. 131 (5th Dist. 1978), app. after rem. 74 Ill. 2d 260, 384 N.E. 2d 1321, 24 Ill. Dec. 163 (1978)

16:310 Must a school board develop a teacher seniority list?

Before the enactment of Senate Bill 7 (P.A. 97-08) in 2011, a school district was required each year, in consultation with any exclusive bargaining representatives, to establish a list categorized by positions, showing the length of continuing service of each teacher in the district who is qualified to hold any position. Copies of this list were distributed to the exclusive bargaining representative on or before February 1 of each year. Briefly after the passage of Senate Bill 7 there was no requirement that a seniority list (as distinguished from a sequence of honorable dismissal list categorized by positions and groupings) be maintained or circulated.

In 2013, a paragraph was added to Section 24-12 of the School Code requiring that each year each school board, in consultation with its exclusive representative, establish a list showing the length of continuing service of each teacher (seniority list) who is qualified to hold "any such positions," unless an alternate method of determining sequence of dismissal is established, in which case the list must be made in accordance with the alternate method. Copies of the list must be distributed to the exclusive representative at least 75 days before the end of the school term. The seniority list presumably is distributed to teachers as contrasted with the honorable dismissal list (below) which is given to the exclusive representative.

SB 7 (P.A. 97-08) also requires that each school board, including the governing board of a joint agreement, in consultation with any exclusive employee representative, each year establish a sequence of honorable dismissal list categorized by positions and the groupings defined in Section 24-12 of the School Code. Copies of the list must be distributed to the exclusive bargaining representative at least 75 days before the end of the school term, except the school district or joint agreement may, with notice to any exclusive employee representatives move teachers from grouping one into another grouping during the period of time from 75 days until 45 days before the end of the school term.

105 ILCS 5/24-12

16:315 Is the definition of seniority a mandatory subject of bargaining?

Yes. If questions arise that have not been fully bargained with respect to computation of seniority affecting a recognized bargaining unit, the school board may unilaterally define seniority only after notice to the union and in the absence of a union demand to bargain thereafter.

115 ILCS 5/10

16:320 What are bumping rights?

When a more senior teacher "bumps" a less senior teacher from his or her job in the event of a reduction in force, he or she exercises "bumping rights." Prior to the enactment of Senate Bill 7 (P.A. 97-08), bumping rights derived from statutory seniority applied only to tenured teachers unless a collective bargaining agreement extended such rights to other classes of teachers. After the enactment of SB 7, bumping rights are probably exercised within groupings.

105 ILCS 5/24-12

Caviness v. Board of Education of Ludlow Community Consolidated School District No. 142 of Champaign County, 59 Ill. App. 3d 28, 375 N.E. 2d 157, 16 Ill. Dec. 526 (4th Dist. 1978)

16:330 Is a school board required to realign teaching assignments in a reduction in force to protect the jobs of senior tenured teachers?

Assuming the case law prior to the 2011 enactment of Senate Bill 7 (P.A. 97-08) is adopted by the courts and applies after the enactment of SB 7, a school board is not required to combine parts of existing teaching assignments in a reduction in force (RIF) to protect the jobs of senior teachers. Absent a collectively bargained provision to the contrary, bumping rights may be exercised by teachers to claim "whole positions."

A school board may not realign teaching assignments in a RIF to defeat the rights of a senior teacher.

105 ILCS 5/24-12

Peters v. Board of Education of Rantoul High School District No. 193 of Champaign County, 97 Ill. 2d 166, 454 N.E. 2d 310, 73 Ill. Dec. 450 (1983)

16:340 For how long after layoff does a teacher have recall rights?

For layoffs and recalls for which the notice of dismissal occurred on or before the end of the 2010-11 school term, unless a collective bargaining agreement provides otherwise, only tenured teachers have recall rights. Recall rights extend for one calendar year from the beginning of the school term following the layoff, unless the original layoff exceeded 15 percent of the number of full-time equivalent positions filled by certified employees (excluding principals and administrative personnel) during the preceding school year, in which case the recall rights extend for two calendar years from the beginning of the school term following the layoff.

For layoffs and recalls for which notice is provided during the 2011-12 school term or thereafter, if the board or joint agreement has any vacancies for the following school term or within one calendar year from the beginning of the following school term, the positions thereby becoming available must be tendered to the teachers so removed or dismissed who were in groupings three or four of the sequence of dismissal and are qualified to hold the positions, based upon legal qualifications and any other qualifications established in a district or joint agreement job description, on or before the May 10 prior to the date of the positions becoming available, provided that if the number of honorable dismissal notices based on economic necessity exceeds 15 percent of the number of full-time equivalent positions filled by certified employees (excluding principals and administrative personnel) during the preceding school year, then the recall period is for the following school term or within two calendar years from the beginning of the following school term. Among teachers eligible for recall pursuant to the preceding sentence, the order of recall must be in inverse order of dismissal, unless an alternative order of recall is established in a collective bargaining agreement or contract between the board and a "professional faculty members' organization."

105 ILCS 5/24-12

Walter v. Board of Education of Quincy School District No. 172, 93 Ill. 2d 101, 442 N.E. 2d 870, 66 Ill. Dec. 309 (1982)

Huetteman v. Board of Education of Community Unit School District 3A, 56 Ill. App. 3d 933, 372, N.E. 2d 716, 14 Ill. Dec. 520 (4th Dist. 1978)

16:350 Do probationary employees have recall rights after layoff?

Not if they were laid off on or before the end of the 2010-2011 school term unless they were granted recall rights in a collective bargaining agreement. Before Senate Bill 7 (P.A. 97-08), statutory preferential right of recall applied to tenured teachers and support staff only. Beginning with the 2011-2012 school term, probationary employees have recall rights equal to those of tenured teachers subject to the grouping restrictions of Section 24-12 .

105 ILCS 5/10-23.5
105 ILCS 5/24-11
105 ILCS 5/24-12

DETERMINING THE SEQUENCE OF HONORABLE DISMISSALS

16:400 How is the sequence of teacher dismissals determined when a school board decides to eliminate teaching positions or programs?

Each teacher must be categorized into one or more positions which the teacher is qualified to hold, based upon legal qualifications and any other qualifications established in a district or joint agreement job description, on or before the May 10 prior to the school year during which the sequence of dismissal is determined. Within each position and subject to agreements made by the joint committee on honorable dismissals, the school district or joint agreement must establish four groupings of teachers qualified to hold the position as follows:

Grouping one consists of each teacher not in contractual continued service who has not received a performance evaluation rating, is employed for one school term or less to replace a teacher on leave or is employed on a part-time basis. Part-time basis means a teacher who is employed to teach less than a full-day teacher workload or less than five days of the normal student attendance week, unless otherwise provided for in a collective bargaining agreement.

A teacher who is employed as a full-time teacher but who actually teaches or is otherwise present and participating in the district's educational program for less than a school term, or who, in the immediately previous school term, was employed on a full-time basis and actually taught or was otherwise present and participated in the district's educational program for 120 days or more, is not considered employed on a part-time basis.

Grouping two consists of each teacher with a needs improvement or unsatisfactory performance evaluation rating on either of the teacher's last two performance evaluation ratings.

Grouping three consists of each teacher with a performance evaluation rating of at least satisfactory or proficient on both of the teacher's last two performance evaluation ratings, if two ratings are available, or on the teacher's last performance evaluation rating, if only one rating is available, unless the teacher qualifies for placement into grouping four.

Grouping four consists of each teacher whose last two performance evaluation ratings are excellent and each teacher with two excellent performance evaluation ratings out of the teacher's last three performance evaluation ratings with a third rating of satisfactory or proficient.

105 ILCS 5/24-12

16:410 How is the sequence of teacher dismissals determined within a grouping?

Among teachers qualified to hold a position, teachers must be dismissed in the order of their groupings, with teachers in grouping one dismissed first and teachers in grouping four dismissed last.

Within grouping one, the sequence of dismissal is at the discretion of the school district or joint agreement.

Within grouping two, the sequence of dismissal is based upon average performance evaluation ratings, with the teacher or teachers with the lowest average performance evaluation rating dismissed first. A teacher's average performance evaluation rating is calculated using the average of the teacher's last two performance evaluation ratings, if two ratings are available, or the teacher's last performance evaluation rating, if only one rating is available, using the following numerical values: 4 for excellent; 3 for proficient or satisfactory; 2 for needs improvement; and 1 for unsatisfactory.

As between or among teachers in grouping two with the same average performance evaluation rating and within each of groupings three and four, the teacher or teachers with the shorter length of continuing service with the school district or joint agreement must be dismissed first unless an alternative method of determining the sequence of dismissal is established in a collective bargaining agreement or contract between the board and a professional faculty members' organization.

105 ILCS 5/24-12

16:420 Under what circumstances is a district grandfathered with respect to the requirements of Senate Bill 7?

Any provisions regarding the sequence of honorable dismissals and recall of honorably dismissed teachers in a collective bargaining agreement entered into on or before January 1, 2011 and in effect on June 13, 2011 that may conflict with the changes in Section 24-11 mandated by Senate Bill 7 (P.A. 97-08) remain in effect through the expiration of the agreement or June 30, 2013, whichever is earlier.

105 ILCS 5/24-12

16:430 What is a joint committee as called for by amendments to Section 24-12 of the School Code?

Each school district and special education joint agreement must use a joint committee composed of equal representation selected by the school board and its teachers or, if applicable, the exclusive bargaining representative of its teachers, to address the matters described in paragraphs (b) and (c) of Section 24-12 of the School Code, as follows:

1) The joint committee must consider and may agree to criteria for excluding from grouping two and placing into grouping three a teacher whose last two performance evaluations include a needs improvement and either a proficient or excellent.

2) The joint committee must consider and may agree to an alternative definition for grouping four, which definition must take into account prior performance evaluation ratings and may take into account other factors that relate to the school district's or program's educational objectives. An alternative definition for grouping four may not permit the inclusion of a teacher in the grouping with a needs improvement or unsatisfactory performance evaluation rating on either of the teacher's last two performance evaluation ratings.

3) The joint committee may agree to including within the definition of a performance evaluation rating a performance evaluation rating administered by a school district or joint agreement other than the school district or joint agreement determining the sequence of dismissal.

4) For each school district or joint agreement that administers performance evaluation ratings that are inconsistent with either of the rating category systems specified in subsection (d) of Section 24A-5 of the School Code, the school district or joint agreement must consult with the joint committee on the basis for assigning a rating that complies with subsection (d) of Section 24A-5 of the School Code to each performance evaluation rating that will be used in a sequence of dismissal.

5) Upon request by a joint committee member submitted to the employing board by no later than 10 days after the distribution of the sequence of honorable dismissal list, a representative of the employing board shall, within five days after the request, provide to members of the joint committee a list showing the most recent and prior performance evaluation ratings of each teacher identified only by length of continuing service in the district or joint agreement and not by name. If, after review of this list, a member of the joint committee has a good faith belief that a disproportionate number of teachers with greater length of continuing service with the district or joint agreement have received a recent performance evaluation rating lower than the prior rating, the member may request that the joint committee review the list to assess whether such a trend may exist. Following the joint committee's review, but by no later than the end of the applicable school term, the joint committee or any member or members of the joint committee may submit a report of the review to the employing board and exclusive bargaining representative, if any.

Nothing in 5) above impacts the order of honorable dismissal or a school district's or joint agreement's authority to carry out a dismissal in accordance with the relevant provisions of Section 24-12.

The joint committee must be established and the first meeting of the joint committee must have occurred on or before December 1 in each school year.

105 ILCS 5/24-12

16:440 What limitations are there to the authority of the joint committee?

Agreement by the joint committee as to a matter requires the majority vote of all committee members, and if the joint committee does not reach agreement on a matter, then the otherwise applicable requirements of Section 24-12 (b) apply. Except as explicitly set forth in Section 24-12 (c), a joint committee has no authority to agree to any further modifications to the requirements for honorable dismissals set forth in Section 24-12 (a).

105 ILCS 5/24-12

16:450 Does the joint committee's agreement on a matter end at the beginning of the next school year?

No. The agreement of a joint committee on a matter applies to the sequence of dismissal until the agreement is amended or terminated by the joint committee. It is unclear how a contrary agreement bargained by the parties after the joint committee reaches agreement should be interpreted. It also is unclear whether or not a joint committee agreement can have a sunset provision to avoid the effects of status quo on the bargaining process.

105 ILCS 5/24-12

17: SCHOOL EMPLOYMENT IN GENERAL

EMPLOYMENT STANDARDS

17:10 May a school board require employees to show evidence of freedom from communicable diseases?

A school board must require a new employee to present evidence of physical fitness to perform the duties assigned and freedom from communicable disease. Evidence must consist of a physical examination by a physician licensed in Illinois or any other state to practice medicine and surgery in all its branches or an advanced practice nurse who has a written collaborative agreement with a collaborating physician that authorizes the advanced practice nurse to perform health examinations or a physician assistant who has been delegated the authority to perform health examinations by his or her supervising physician, not more than 90 days preceding the time of presentation to the school board. The cost of the examination is paid by the employee. A new or existing employee may be subject to additional health examinations, including screening for tuberculosis, as required by rules adopted by the Department of Public Health or by order of a local public health official.

A school board may from time to time require an examination of any employee by a physician licensed in Illinois to practice medicine and surgery in all of its branches and must pay the expenses of this examination from school funds.

105 ILCS 5/24-5

17:20 Must a school board conduct criminal history records checks on applicants for employment?

A school board may not knowingly employ a person for whom a fingerprint based criminal history records check and check of the Statewide Sex Offender Database and Statewide Murderer and Violent Offender Against Youth Database has not been begun. Applicants for employment with a school district are required as a condition of employment to authorize an investigation to determine if they have been convicted of any of a specified list of criminal and drug offenses. A school board may not knowingly employ a person who has been convicted of any of a list of offenses specified.

Beginning in 2010, student teachers were required to authorize criminal history records checks before participation in any field experience in a public school.

105 ILCS 5/10-21.9
105 ILCS 5/21B-80

17:25 Which offenses prohibit employment by an Illinois school district?

An individual may not be employed by an Illinois school district if the applicant's employment requires a criminal history records check and the applicant has been convicted of indecent solicitation of a child, public indecency (if punished as a Class 4 felony), sexual exploitation of a child, permitting sexual abuse of a child, failure to report sexual abuse of a child, custodial sexual misconduct, presence within a school zone by a child sex offender, sexual predator and child sex offender, sexual misconduct with a person with a disability, solicitation for a sexual act, promoting prostitution, promoting juvenile prostitution, patronizing a prostitute, patronizing a juvenile prostitute, obscenity, child pornography, duty of commercial film and photographic print processor or computer technician to report sexual depiction of children, harmful material, posting of identifying or graphic information on a pornographic Internet site or possessing graphic information with pornographic material (if punished as a Class 3 felony), child pornography by a sex offender, grooming, traveling to meet a minor, drug induced infliction of aggravated battery to a child athlete, criminal sexual assault, aggravated criminal sexual assault, predatory criminal sexual assault of a child, criminal sexual abuse, aggravated criminal sexual abuse, ritual mutilation or ritualized abuse of a child, drug induced infliction of harm to a child athlete, unauthorized video recording under certain circumstances or any attempt to commit any of the foregoing and any offense committed or attempted in any other state which, if committed or attempted in this state, would have been punishable as one or more of the foregoing offenses.

In 2009, the General Assembly made major changes to the list of disqualifying offenses. The relevant law contains this statement: "The changes made by Public Act 96-431 to this definition are declaratory of existing law." Drug offenses are defined as:

1) Any offense defined in the Cannabis Control Act except possession offenses involving less than 10 grams and/or manufacture, delivery, or possession with intent to deliver offenses involving less than 2.5 grams and any offense for which the holder of any certificate is placed on probation under the provisions of Section 10 of that Act, provided that

if the terms and conditions of probation required by the court are not fulfilled, the offense is not eligible for this exception;

2) Any offense defined in the Illinois Controlled Substances Act, except any offense for which the holder of any certificate is placed on probation under the provisions of Section 410 of that Act, provided that if the terms and conditions of probation required by the court are not fulfilled, the offense is not eligible for this exception;

3) Any offense defined in the Methamphetamine Control and Community Protection Act, except any offense for which the holder of any certificate is placed on probation under the provision of Section 70 of that Act, provided that if the terms and conditions of probation required by the court are not fulfilled, the offense is not eligible for this exception;

4) Any attempt to commit any of the foregoing offenses; and

5) Any offense committed or attempted in any other state or against the laws of the United States which, if committed or attempted in this state, would have been punishable as one or more of the foregoing offenses.

Sentence within the meaning of the statute includes any period of supervision or probation that was imposed either alone or in combination with a period of incarceration.

The law also provides that an individual may not be employed by an Illinois school district if the applicant's employment requires a criminal history records check and the applicant or license applicant has been convicted of attempting to commit, conspiring to commit, soliciting or committing any sex offense, first degree murder, attempted first degree murder, conspiracy to commit first degree murder, attempted conspiracy to commit first degree murder, or a Class X felony or any offense committed or attempted in any other state or against the laws of the United States that, if committed or attempted in this state, would have been punishable as one or more of the foregoing offenses, the State Superintendent of Education shall forthwith suspend the certificate.

The records check statute requires license suspension or denial of license application for anyone convicted of a drug offense (as defined in the statute) until seven years following the end of the sentence for the criminal offense. A school board cannot knowingly employ a person who has been found under the Juvenile Court Act to be a perpetrator of sexual or physical abuse of any minor under 18 years of age.

A felony conviction of an applicant for a license may be taken into consideration by the state with regard to the issuance of a license, and a felony conviction that has occurred in the last seven years can be taken in to account when an employer contemplates employment.

The state's attorney is required to notify the superintendent of a school district by sending a letter by first class mail when an employee with a teaching certificate is convicted of a felony.

55 ILCS 5/3-9005
105 ILCS 5/10-21.9
105 ILCS 5/21B-80

17:30 Are criminal history records checks required for employees of an independent contractor doing business with a school district?

If the employees of the independent contractor have direct, daily contact with students, a criminal history records check is required. Charter bus service contracts for the "transportation of pupils to interscholastic athletic of interscholastic or school sponsored activities" must contain a criminal history records check notification clause.

105 ILCS 5/10-21.9
105 ILCS 5/21B-80

17:31 When must a superintendent of schools report employee abuse or neglect to the State Superintendent of Education?

A 2009 addition to the criminal records check statute requires the superintendent of an employing school board to notify in writing the State Superintendent of Education and the applicable regional superintendent of schools of any certificate holder whom he or she has reasonable cause to believe has committed an intentional act of abuse or neglect with the result of making a child an abused child or a neglected child, as defined in Section 3 of the Abused and Neglected Child Reporting Act, and that act resulted in the certificate holder's dismissal or resignation from the school district. This notification must be submitted within 30 days after the dismissal or resignation.

The certificate holder must also be contemporaneously sent a copy of the notice by the superintendent. All correspondence, documentation, and other information so received by the regional superintendent of schools, the State Superintendent of Education, the State Board of Education, or the State Teacher Certification Board is confidential and must not be disclosed to third parties, except (i) as necessary for the State Superintendent of Education or his or her designee to investigate and prosecute pursuant to Article 21 (certificate suspension and revocation); (ii) pursuant to a court order; (iii) for disclosure to the certificate holder or his or her representative; or (iv) as otherwise provided in this Article and provided that any such information admitted into evidence in a hearing is exempt from this confidentiality and non-disclosure requirement.

Except for an act of willful or wanton misconduct, any superintendent who provides notification as required in this subsection has immunity from any liability, whether civil or criminal or that otherwise might result by reason of such action.

105 ILCS 5/10-21.9

17:33 May an employer be liable for failing to investigate an employee's criminal history at the time of hiring?

Yes; mere reliance on a criminal history records check is not sufficient to protect the employer from the potential for liability. If the employer fails to adequately investigate the background of the employee before the employee is hired and the employee later harms a third party, the employer may be liable for negligently hiring or retaining the employee if the employer knew or should have known the employee was unfit for the job to which he or she was assigned.

How much diligence an employer must exercise to investigate the background of a job candidate is proportionate to the nature of the job to which the employee will be assigned.

Doe v. White, 409 Ill.App.3d 1087, 951 N.E.2d 216, 351 Ill.Dec. 396 (4th Dist. 2011), 2012 Il 112479, 973 N.E. 2d 880, 362 Ill. Dec. 484, on rem. 2014 IL App. (4th) 131004

Doe-2 v. McLean County Unit District No. 5, 593 F. 3d 507 (7th Cir. 2010)

Hansen v. Board of Trustees of Hamilton Southeastern School Corporation, 551 F. 3d 599 (7th Cir. 2008)

Geise v. Phoenix Company of Chicago, Inc., 159 Ill. 2d 507, 639 N.E. 2d 1273, 203 Ill. Dec. 454 (1994)

Fallon v. Indian Trail School, 148 Ill. App. 3d 931, 500 N.E. 2d 101, 102 Ill. Dec. 479 (2nd Dist. 1986)

Bates v. Doria, 150 Ill. App. 3d 1025, 502 N.E. 2d 454, 104 Ill. Dec. 191 (2nd Dist. 1986)

17:34 Must school officials disclose the outcome of a Department of Children and Family Services (DCFS) report to a prospective employer?

A 2008 amendment to the Abused and Neglected Child Reporting Act requires that, if an employee of a school district has made a report or caused a report to be made to DCFS involving the conduct of a current or former employee of the school district and a request is made by another school district for information concerning the job performance or qualifications of the current or former employee because he or she is an applicant for employment with the requesting school district, the superintendent of the school district to which the request is being made must disclose to the requesting school district the fact that an employee of the school district has made a report involving the conduct of the applicant or caused a report to be made to DCFS.

Only the fact that an employee of the school district has made a report involving the conduct of the applicant or caused a report to be made to DCFS may be disclosed by the superintendent of the school district to which the request for information concerning the applicant is made, and this fact may be disclosed only in cases where the employee and the superintendent have not been informed by the Department that the allegations were unfounded.

An employee of a school district who is or has been the subject of a report during his or her employment with the school district must be informed by that school district that if he or she applies for employment with another school district, the superintendent of the former school district, upon the request of the school district to which the employee applies, will notify the requesting school district that the employee is or was the subject of such a report.

325 ILCS 5/4

17:35 May an employer be liable for obscuring a work history of criminal misconduct of a former employee?

A school district that attempts to obscure the criminal misconduct of a former employee risks liability if the employee commits a subsequent similar criminal act during employment by a later employer. The victim will likely be unable to recover, but the subsequent employer may have a cause of action if the employer has a special or fiduciary relationship with the plaintiff that raises a duty to speak. A school district should notify all relevant state agencies of criminal misconduct committed by its employees.

Doe v. White, 409 Ill.App.3d 1087, 951 N.E.2d 216, 351 Ill.Dec. 396 (4th Dist. 2011), 2012 Il 112479, 973 N.E. 2d 880, 362 Ill. Dec. 484, on rem. 2014 IL App. (4th) 131004

Doe-2 v. McLean County Unit District No. 5, 593 F. 3d 507 (7th Cir. 2010)

Doe v. Methacton School District, 880 F. Supp. 380 (E.D. Pa. 1995)

17:38 May an employer ask an employee for his or her social media passwords?

The relevant law underwent a major rewrite in 2016. It contains specific directions as to what an employer can and cannot do with respect to the online accounts of employees. In general, it is unlawful for an employer to request, require, or coerce any employee or prospective employee to provide a user name or password or other related account information in order to gain access to the employee's or prospective employee's personal online account or to demand access in any manner to an employee's or prospective employee's personal online account.

An employer has a right to create and maintain lawful workplace policies governing the use of the employer's electronic equipment, including policies regarding internet use, social networking site use, and electronic mail use; and monitor usage of the employer's electronic equipment and the employer's electronic mail without requesting or requiring any employee or prospective employee to provide any password or other related account information in order to gain access to the employee's or prospective employee's account or profile on a social networking website.

An employer may obtain prospective employee or current employee information that is in the public domain or otherwise in compliance with the relevant statute.

820 ILCS 55/10

17:40 May a school district give employment preference to veterans?

If all bargaining obligations are met, a school district may give preferential treatment in employment to veterans of any branch of United States military service.

775 ILCS 5/2-104(2)

17:44 May a school board require its employees to be residents of the school district?

Residency may not be used as a factor in filling any teaching or support staff position or in the determination of compensation, retention, promotion, assignment, or transfer. A superintendent of schools may be required to reside in the school district.

105 ILCS 5/10-23.5

105 ILCS 5/24-4.1

17:46 What is an I-9 form?

School officials must complete and retain an I-9 form that documents the citizenship status of each individual hired. The form is required for both citizens and non-citizens. On the form, the employer must verify the employment eligibility and identity documents presented by the employee and record the document information on the Form I-9.

The U.S. Citizenship and Immigration Service website dealing with Form I-9 can be found at *www.uscis.gov/i-9*.

17:47 May a school district have an anti-nepotism rule that forbids or restricts the employment of spouses of school board members or staff supervisors?

Yes, anti-nepotism rules are legally permissible generally. Although Illinois law prevents discrimination by reason of marital status, the term "marital status" means a person's state of being married, single, separated, divorced, or widowed. The definition does not include the identity of a person's spouse.

105 ILCS 5/10-22.4

775 ILCS 5/1-103(J)

Ellis v. United Parcel Service, 523 F. 3d 823 (7th Cir. 2008)

Boaden v. State Department of Law Enforcement, 171 Ill. 2d 230, 664 N.E. 2d 61, 215 Ill. Dec. 664 (1996)

River Bend Community Unit School District No. 2 v. Illinois Human Rights Commission et al., 232 Ill. App. 3d 838, 597 N.E. 2d 842, 173 Ill. Dec. 868 (3rd Dist. 1992) app. den. 147 Ill. 2d 637, 606 N.E. 2d 1235, 180 Ill. Dec. 158 (1993)

Kraft, Inc. v. State of Minnesota, 284 N.W. 2d 386 (Minn. Sup. Ct. 1979)

Hollister v. North, 50 Ill. App. 3d 56, 365 N.E. 2d 258, 8 Ill. Dec. 20 (4th Dist. 1977)

17:50 If a school board elects not to hire a qualified job applicant, must it give reasons for the rejection?

Provided there is no policy or contract provision to the contrary and provided there are no constitutional implications to the rejection, a school board may decide not to hire any job applicant without giving reasons, notwithstanding the applicant is qualified to meet the needs of the school district as specified in the job announcement.

Halfacre v. Board of Education of School District No. 167, 331 Ill. App. 404, 73 N.E. 2d 124 (1947)

COMPENSATION

17:60 Does the Federal Fair Labor Standards Act apply to public schools?

Yes. A public school board is subject to the requirements of the Act, including its minimum wage and overtime provisions. Teachers are not subject to the provisions of the Act; support staff members are.

29 U.S.C. 201 et seq.

Garcia v. San Antonio Metropolitan Transit Authority, 105 S. Ct. 1005, 469 U.S. 528, 83 L. Ed. 2d 1016 (1985)

17:65 What is the Illinois minimum wage?

The minimum wage applies to workers who are 18 years of age or older. On and after July 1, 2010 the minimum wage is $8.25 per hour. During the first 90 consecutive calendar days after the employee is initially employed by the employer, the employee may be paid a wage that is 50 cents per hour less than the then current minimum wage. An employee who is less than 18 may be paid a wage that is 50 cents per hour less than the then current minimum wage. There are other exceptions to the minimum wage law.

820 ILCS 105/4

17:70 What is the federal Equal Pay Act?

The federal Equal Pay Act is a non-discrimination law. It provides in part:

"No employer ... shall discriminate, within any establishment in which such employees are employed, between employees on the basis of sex by paying wages to employees in such establishment at a rate less than the rate at which he or she pays wages to employees of the opposite sex in such establishment for equal work on jobs the performance of which requires equal skill, effort, and responsibility, and that are performed under similar working conditions, except where such payment is made pursuant to (i) a seniority system; (ii) a merit system; (iii) a system that measures earnings by quantity or quality of production; or (iv) a differential based on any other factor other than sex."

An employer who is paying a wage rate differential in violation of the above is prohibited from reducing the wage rate of any employee in order to comply.

The State of Illinois has a parallel provision in the Equal Pay Act of 2003 and a civil rights law that prevents discrimination by reason of gender by any unit of state, county, or local government.

29 U.S.C. 206(d)(1)

740 ILCS 23/5

820 ILCS 112/1 et seq.

17:80 May an employer offer retirement incentives that diminish as an employee ages?

This is an unsettled area of the law, but one where employers often do not recognize the risks. Incentive or benefit programs that provide greater incentives or better benefits to younger employees present age discrimination issues, even if the reason for the incentive or benefit structure is not connected to age.

Age discrimination concerns are present when the employer provides better insurance benefits for retired employees who are not eligible for Medicare than for retirees who are eligible, or when retirement incentives treat younger employees more favorably than older employees.

Before an employer considers such a program, fact specific counsel should be sought.

AARP v. E.E.O.C., 383 F. Supp. 2d 705 (E.D. Pa. 2005)

Erie County Retirees Association v. County of Erie, Pennsylvania, 220 F. 3d 193 (3rd Cir. 2000) on rem. 140 F. Supp. 2d 466 (W.D. Pa. 2001)

17:85 May retirees sue the school district for benefits granted under previous collective bargaining agreements?

Because retirees are no longer school employees nor members of a bargaining unit, a question arises as to their standing to sue. Unions need not bargain on behalf of retirees, but retirees are not without protection because vested retirement rights may not be altered without the retiree's consent.

Federal courts have regularly permitted retirees to sue to enforce rights to retirement benefits allegedly contained in collective bargaining agreements. A promise in a collective bargaining agreement to pay certain benefits to a class of employees makes those employees third-party beneficiaries of the agreement.

29 U.S.C. 185

Haake, et al. v. The Board of Education for Township High School Glenbard District 87, 399 Ill. App. 3d 121, 925 N.E. 2d 297, 338 Ill. Dec. 800 (2nd Dist. 2010)

17:90 Must an employer pay for earned vacation time at termination?

No statute requires an employer to grant employees paid vacation. No statute requires that an employer allow employees to accumulate earned vacation ("use it or lose it" provisions are permissible).

However, unless otherwise provided in a collective bargaining agreement, whenever a contract of employment or employment policy provides for paid vacations and an employee resigns or is terminated without having taken all vacation time earned in accordance with such contract of employment or employment policy, the monetary equivalent of all earned vacation shall be paid to the employee as part of his or her final compensation at his or her final rate of pay and no employment contract or employment policy may provide for forfeiture of earned vacation time upon separation.

820 ILCS 115/5

SALARY DEDUCTIONS

17:100 Is a school board required to withhold union dues from salary?

A school board must, upon the written request of an employee, withhold from the compensation of that employee any dues, payments, or contributions payable by such employee to any employee labor organization as defined in the Illinois Educational Labor Relations Act. Under such arrangement, an amount must be withheld from each regular payroll period that is equal to the pro rata share of the annual dues plus any payments or contributions.

The school board must transmit such withholdings to the specified labor organization within 10 working days from the time of the withholding. Dues deduction procedures are usually contained in collective bargaining agreements.

105 ILCS 5/24-21.1

115 ILCS 5/1 et seq.

17:110 What is "fair share?"

If included in a collective bargaining agreement, a fair share clause requires a school board to deduct from each employee's salary a sum equal to the union's cost of representing the employee in the bargaining process and for grievance representation. Usually the fair share fee is a percentage of union dues in excess of 75 percent and often approaching 100 percent. The specific percentage is established by a union showing of the actual cost of representation.

A fair share provision is a common union bargaining demand. A school board may, but need not, agree to fair share.

115 ILCS 5/11

Ysursa, Secretary of State of Idaho, et al. v. Pocatello Education Association, et al., 129 S. Ct. 1093, 555 U.S. 353, 172 L. Ed.2d 770 (2009)

Chicago Teachers Union Local 1, AFT, AFL-CIO v. Hudson, 106 S. Ct. 1066, 475 U.S. 292, 89 L. Ed. 2d 232 (1986)

Abood v. Detroit Board of Education, 97 S. Ct. 1782, 431 U.S. 209, 52 L. Ed. 261, reh. den. 97 S. Ct. 2989, 433 U.S. 915, 53 L. Ed. 2d 1102 (1977)

17:120 Must a school board withhold delinquent child or family service payments from an employee's salary?

A school district may receive a certified Order for Support and an Income Withholding Notice directing the district to deduct child or family support payments from the salary of an employee. In addition to the required support payment, a school district may deduct a $5 fee per month from the income of the employee in order to meet the requirements of this law.

305 ILCS 5/10-16.2

750 ILCS 22/605 et seq.

HOLIDAYS, LEAVES, AND VACATION

17:140 Which holidays are school holidays?

A teacher cannot be required to teach on Saturdays nor on legal school holidays, which are January 1, New Year's Day; the third Monday in January, the birthday of Dr. Martin Luther King, Jr.; February 12, the birthday of President Abraham Lincoln; the first Monday in March, Casimir Pulaski's birthday; Good Friday; the day designated as Memorial Day by federal law; July 4, Independence Day; the first Monday in September, Labor Day; the second Monday in October, Columbus Day; November 11, Veteran's Day; the Thursday in November commonly called Thanksgiving Day; and December 25, Christmas Day.

Other school employees cannot be required to work on legal school holidays, other than those educational support school employees whose presence is necessary because of an emergency or for the continued operation of school facilities or property.

A school board may grant a special holiday whenever in its judgment it is advisable, except that no special holiday may be declared on an election day when members of the Illinois General Assembly are elected. No deduction may be made from the time or compensation of a school employee on account of any legal or special holiday.

Treatment of holidays may have collective bargaining implications with respect to recognized bargaining units.

105 ILCS 5/24-2

District 300 Education Association v. Board of Education of Dundee Community Unit School District No. 300 of Kane County, et al., 31 Ill. App. 3d 550, 334 N.E. 2d 165 (2nd Dist. 1975)

17:142 Must hourly employees be paid for hours not worked on legal school holidays?

There is no law that requires that employees be paid for work not done on a holiday if the holiday falls on a day when they were not scheduled to work. For example, a 10-month employee (August-June) need not be paid for July 4th.

On the other hand, an hourly employee must be paid for a holiday that occurs during his or her regular work schedule. Collective bargaining agreements and employer policy manuals usually define holiday pay.

105 ILCS 5/24-2

17:146 Must a school district grant employees time off with pay for religious holidays?

No. School districts must reasonably accommodate the religious practices of their employees but no statute or case law requires that such employees be paid for time off to celebrate religious holidays. Time off must be provided unless the employer can show that such time off would cause undue hardship with respect to school operations.

Reasonable accommodation might include use of personal days or compensatory time (weekend work, special assignments, or curriculum work, for example). The manner in which a school district determines to accommodate the religious practices of its employees is a mandatory subject of bargaining.

42 U.S.C. 2000e et seq.

Ansonia Board of Education v. Philbrook, 107 S. Ct. 367, 479 U.S. 60, 93 L. Ed. 2d 305 (1986)

Hunterdon Central High School Board of Education v. Hunterdon Central High School Teachers Association, 174 N.J. Super. 468, 416 A. 2d 980 (App Div. 1980) aff'd. 86 N.J. 43, 429 A. 2d 354 (1981)

17:150 What is sick leave?

By law, sick leave may be used for personal illness, quarantine at home, serious illness or death in the immediate family or household, or birth, adoption, or placement for adoption. The use provision was broadened by the General Assembly in 2007 by the addition of the phrase "birth, adoption, or placement for adoption." The phrase probably allows both males and females to access sick leave for the specified events.

Before the 2007 amendment, sick leave was only available (by law) to females who were disabled by reason of maternity or childbirth; however many employers had practices that were more generous than the minimum required by law.

The definition of sick leave is largely academic in any case, because when an employee claims personal or family illness, even when the employer suspects that the employee or family member is not ill, proving sick leave abuse is very difficult.

Immediate family as defined in the law means parents, spouse, brothers, sisters, children, grandparents, grandchildren, parents-in-law, brothers-in-law, sisters-in-law, and legal guardians although most collective bargaining agreements have much broader definitions of immediate family.

105 ILCS 5/24-6

17:160 When may a school board require an employee to provide a physician's certificate documenting the employee's illness?

Unless a collective bargaining agreement or board policy provides otherwise, a school board may require a certificate from a physician licensed in Illinois to practice medicine and surgery in all its branches, an advanced practice nurse who has a written collaborative agreement with a collaborating physician that authorizes the advanced practice nurse to perform health examinations, physician assistant who has been delegated the authority to perform health examinations by his or her supervising physician, or if the treatment is by prayer or spiritual means, a spiritual adviser or practitioner of the teacher's or employee's faith as a basis for pay during sick leave after an absence of three days for personal illness or 30 days for birth, or as the school board may deem necessary in other cases.

If a school board requires a certificate as a basis for pay during leave of less than three days for personal illness, the school board must pay the expenses incurred by the employee in obtaining the certificate.

For paid leave for adoption or placement for adoption, the school board may require that the teacher or other employee provide evidence that the formal adoption process is underway, and such leave is limited to 30 days unless a longer leave has been negotiated with the exclusive bargaining representative

105 ILCS 5/24-5

Deizman v. Board of Education District 201, Cook County, 53 Ill. App. 3d 1050, 369 N.E. 2d 257 (1st Dist. 1977)

Lippincott v. Board of Education of Community Unit School District No. 5 of Coles County, 342 Ill. App. 642, 97 N.E. 2d 566 (3rd Dist. 1951)

17:165 What is the Victim's Economic Security and Safety Act?

In 2003, the Illinois General Assembly established a statutory domestic or sexual violence leave, the provisions of which are similar to the provisions of the federal Family and Medical Leave Act. The relevant statute provides that an employee who is a victim of domestic or sexual violence or has a family or household member who is a victim of domestic or sexual violence "whose interests are not adverse to the employee as it relates to the domestic or sexual violence" may take unpaid leave from work to address domestic or sexual violence by

1) Seeking medical attention for, or recovering from, physical or psychological injuries caused by domestic or sexual violence to the employee or the employee's family or household member;

2) Obtaining services from a victim services organization for the employee or the employee's family or household member;

3) Obtaining psychological or other counseling for the employee or the employee's family or household member;

4) Participating in safety planning, temporarily or permanently relocating, or taking other actions to increase the safety of the employee or the employee's family or household member from future domestic or sexual violence or ensure economic security; or

5) Seeking legal assistance or remedies to ensure the health and safety of the employee or the employee's family or household member, including preparing for or participating in any civil or criminal legal proceeding related to or derived from domestic or sexual violence.

The employee is entitled to a total of 12 workweeks of unpaid leave during any 12-month period. The Act does not create a right for an employee to take unpaid leave that exceeds the unpaid leave time allowed under, or is in addition to the unpaid leave time permitted by, the Family and Medical Leave Act. The leave may be taken intermittently or on a reduced work schedule.

During any period that an employee takes domestic or sexual violence leave, the employer must maintain coverage for the employee and any family or household member under any group health plan for the duration of such leave at the level and under the conditions coverage would have been provided if the employee had continued in employment continuously for the duration of the leave.

29 U.S.C. 2601 et seq.

820 ILCS 180/1 et seq.

17:170 Must a pregnant employee be permitted to use sick leave for pregnancy?

A school board must allow use of sick leave for employees who are disabled because of pregnancy. However, unless a collective bargaining agreement so provides, a school board need not permit the use of sick leave for pregnancy without disability.

Where no bargaining agreement provides to the contrary, a school board may require a certificate to establish a pregnant woman's inability to work. Under certain circumstances specified in Section 24-6 of the School Code, the employer may be required to pay for the certificate. When a pregnant employee uses accumulated sick leave for pregnancy based disability, she must return to work when her disabling condition no longer exists.

42 U.S.C. 2000e et seq.

105 ILCS 5/24-6

Maganuco v. Leyden Community High School District No. 212, 867 F. 2d 974 (7th Cir. 1989)

Scherr v. Woodland Consolidated School District No. 50, 867 F. 2d 974 (7th Cir. 1989)

Winks v. Board of Education of Normal Community Unit School District No. 5 of McLean County, 78 Ill. 2d 128, 398 N.E. 2d 823, 34 Ill. Dec. 832 (1979)

17:180 Is a school board required by law to grant maternity leave?

Maternity, paternity, and parental leave are permissive under the law, but no such leave is required. However, a school board may not discriminate against pregnant employees with respect to the grant or denial of unpaid leaves of absence.

A school board may bargain leaves, or in the absence of a recognized bargaining representative or if a bargaining representative fails to make timely demand to bargain, may regulate leaves by adoption of policy.

42 U.S.C. 2000e et seq.

Schafer v. Board of Public Education of School District of Pittsburgh, 732 F. Supp. 565 (W.D. Pa. 1990)

Winks v. Board of Education of Normal Community Unit School District No. 5 of McLean County, 78 Ill. 2d 128, 398 N.E. 2d 823, 34 Ill. Dec. 832 (1979)

17:190 May a school board require an employee to take a maternity leave?

A school board may not require an employee to take maternity leave if the employee is physically able to work.

42 U.S.C. 2000e et seq.

Cleveland Board of Education v. LaFleur, 94 S. Ct. 791, 414 U.S. 632, 39 L. Ed. 2d 52 (1974)

17:200 May a collective bargaining agreement require a pregnant employee to choose between paid disability leave or unpaid leave of absence so as to prevent the employee from combining the two leaves?

Yes, provided employees who are not pregnant are also prohibited from combining a disability leave with unpaid leave of absence.

Equal Employment Opportunity Commission v. Elgin Teachers Association, 780 F. Supp. 1195 (N.D. Ill. 1991)

Maganuco v. Leyden Community High School District 212, 939 F. 2d 440 (7th Cir. 1991)

17:210 What procedures may an employer use to determine whether a pregnant employee is able to work?

An employer may not single out pregnancy-related conditions for special procedures for determining an employee's ability to work. An employer may use any procedure used to determine the ability of any other employee to work and apply that procedure to pregnancy-related conditions.

If an employer requires employees to submit a medical certificate before granting leave or paying sick leave benefits, the employer may require employees affected by pregnancy related conditions to submit such certification.

42 U.S.C. 2000e et seq.

Cleveland Board of Education v. LaFleur, 94 S. Ct. 791, 414 U.S. 632, 39 L. Ed. 2d 52 (1974)

17:220 Must a school district include maternity coverage in a health insurance program that it provides for its employees?

An employer must include maternity coverage in any health insurance program that the employer provides for its employees.

42 U.S.C. 2000e(k)

29 C.F.R. 1604.10

17:225 Must a school board pay an employee who is called to active military service?

Any certificated or non-certificated employee who is a member of any reserve component of the United States armed services who is mobilized to active military duty on or after August 1, 1990 must receive the "same regular compensation" and health insurance or other benefits the employee was receiving at the time of the call-up minus the amount of the employee's base pay for military service for the duration of the active military service.

Any full-time employee of a school district, other than an independent contractor, who is a member of any reserve component of the United States Armed Forces or of any reserve component of the Illinois State Militia, must be granted leave from his or her public employment for any period actively spent in military service, including

1) Basic training;

2) Special or advanced training, whether or not within the state, and whether or not voluntary; and

3) Annual training.

During these leaves, the employee's seniority and other benefits must continue to accrue.

During leaves for annual training, the employee must continue to receive his or her regular compensation as a public employee. During leaves for basic training and up to 60 days of special or advanced training, if the employee's compensation for military activities is less than his or her compensation as a public employee, he or she shall receive his or her regular compensation as a public employee minus the amount of his or her base pay for military activities.

There is no statutory obligation to pay employees who are called to active service under other circumstances. Such employees may avail themselves of paid or unpaid leave provisions in a relevant collective bargaining agreement or policy. Wages and leave provisions applicable to persons called to active service are mandatory subjects of bargaining and if the provisions of a relevant collective bargaining agreement are more generous, the collective bargaining agreement controls.

An employer must provide unpaid leave to a member of the civil air patrol under circumstances defined in the law.

38 U.S.C. 4312

20 C.F. R. 1002.181 et seq.

5 ILCS 325/1

105 ILCS 5/10-20.7b

820 ILCS 148/1 et seq.

WORK DAY

17:230 Must non-certificated employees be provided a break during the workday?

There is no statutory provision that requires an employer to provide employees with break time during the workday other than for a meal. Employers are required to permit employees who are to work for seven and a half continuous hours or longer at least 20 minutes for a meal period beginning no later than five hours after the start of the work period unless a collectively bargained agreement provides a more generous meal schedule. The meal break requirement does not apply to employees who monitor individuals with developmental disabilities or mental illness, or both, and who, in the course of those duties, are required to be on call during an entire eight-hour work period; however, those employees must be allowed to eat a meal during the eight-hour work period while continuing to monitor those individuals.

Teachers are entitled to a duty-free lunch period equal to the regular school lunch period but no less than 30 minutes.

105 ILCS 5/24-9
820 ILCS 140/3

17:235 Must an employer permit time off for breast-feeding at work?

An employer must provide reasonable unpaid break time each day to an employee who needs to express breast milk for her infant child. The break time must, if possible, run concurrently with any break time already provided to the employee. An employer is not required to provide break time if to do so would unduly disrupt the employer's operations.

The employer is also required to make reasonable efforts to provide a room or other location in close proximity to the work area, other than a toilet stall, where the employee can express her milk in privacy.

820 ILCS 260/10
820 ILCS 260/15

17:240 Must an employer provide an employee time off to donate blood?

The law provides that an employee who has been employed as a full-time employee for at least six months may be entitled to blood donation leave with pay after obtaining approval of the employer. An employee may use up to one hour to donate blood every 56 days in accordance with appropriate medical standards established by the American Red Cross, America's Blood Centers, the American Association of Blood Banks, or other nationally recognized standards.

A more generous time off provision may exist in a collective bargaining agreement.

820 ILCS 149/10

17:245 Must an employer provide time off for a parent to attend school conferences?

An Illinois employer who employs 50 or more employees must grant an employee leave of up to a total of eight hours during any school year, no more than four hours of which may be taken on any given day, to attend school conferences or classroom activities related to the employee's child if the conference or classroom activities cannot be scheduled during non-work hours. No leave may be taken unless the employee has exhausted all accrued vacation leave, personal leave, compensatory leave, and any other leave except sick leave and disability leave.

Before arranging attendance at the conference or activity, the employee must provide the employer with a written request for leave at least seven days in advance of the time the employee is required to utilize the visitation right. In emergency situations, no more than 24 hours' notice is required. The employee must consult with the employer to schedule the leave so as not to disrupt unduly the operations of the employer. The leave may be paid or unpaid at the discretion of the employer.

For regularly scheduled, non-emergency visitations, schools must make time available for visitation during both regular school hours and evening hours. An employee may choose the opportunity to make up the time taken on a different day or shift as directed by the employer. An employee cannot be required to make up the time taken, but if an employee does not make up the time, the employee cannot be compensated for the time taken. An employee who does make up the time must be paid at the same rate as paid for normal working time.

Employers must make a good faith effort to permit an employee to make up the time taken. If no reasonable opportunity exists for the employee to make up the time, the employee must not be paid for the time. A reasonable opportunity to make up the time taken does not include the scheduling of make-up time in a manner that would require the payment of overtime.

If unpaid leave conflicts with the unreduced compensation requirement for exempt employees under the federal Fair Labor Standards Act, an employer may require an employee to make up the leave hours within the same pay period. Each public and private school is required to notify parents or guardians of the school's students of their school visitation rights.

Upon completion of school visitation rights by a parent or guardian, the school administrator must provide the parent or guardian documentation of the school visitation. The parent or guardian is required to submit the verification to the employer. The standard form of documentation shall include, but not be limited to, the exact time and date the visitation occurred and ended. Failure of a parent or guardian to submit the verification statement from the school to his or her employer within two working days of the school visitation subjects the employee to the standard disciplinary procedures imposed by the employer for unexcused absences from work.

No employee may lose any employee benefits, except as otherwise provided in the instant law, for exercising rights under this law. Employer must comply with any collective bargaining agreement or employee benefit plan except that the rights afforded by the law may not be diminished by any collective bargaining agreement or employee benefit plan.

820 ILCS 147/10 et seq.

WORKERS' COMPENSATION

17:250 Do the Workers' Compensation Act and the Occupational Disease Act apply to school employees?

The Workers' Compensation Act and the Occupational Disease Act provide benefits, on a no-fault basis, to which school employees may be entitled in the event of job-related injury, illness, or death. An employee may qualify for medical expense reimbursement, compensation for lost earnings, and/or permanent disability payments for work-related injury, illness, or death.

820 ILCS 305/1(a)1 et seq.

820 ILCS 310/1 et seq.

17:260 What is a work-related injury?

To be eligible for worker compensation benefits, an employee must have sustained a work-related injury. When the employee has a pre-existing condition, the employee must show that a work-related accidental injury aggravated or accelerated the pre-existing disease such that the employee's current condition of ill-being is causally connected to the work-related injury. The accidental injury need neither be the sole causative nor the primary causative factor, as long as it was a causative factor in the resulting condition of ill-being.

Elgin Board of Education School District U-46 v. Illinois Workers' Compensation Commission, 409 Ill. App. 3d 943, 949 N.E. 2d 198, 350 Ill. Dec. 710 (1st Dist. 2011)

17:265 Are worker compensation benefits available to workers paid by outside organizations, such as the PTA?

A school district may be treated as an employer for worker compensation purposes whether or not the school district pays direct compensation to a worker if the work performed by the worker is primarily for the benefit of the school district and a school district supervisor controls the employee and supervises his or her work.

Board of Education of the City of Chicago v. Industrial Commission, 57 Ill. 2d 330, 312 N.E. 2d 244 (1974)

17:270 Are volunteer workers eligible for worker compensation benefits?

No.

Board of Education of the City of Chicago v. Industrial Commission, 53 Ill. 2d 167, 290 N.E. 2d 247 (1972)

17:275 May an employee recover both sick leave and worker compensation benefits at the same time?

Absent a collectively bargained agreement to the contrary, an employee is entitled to an election of benefits — either sick leave at full pay (to the extent the employee has such benefits available) or worker compensation benefits (to the extent of eligibility).

Chicago Board of Education v. Chicago Teachers Union, 86 Ill. 2d 469, 427 N.E. 2d 1199, 56 Ill. Dec. 653 (1981)

17:278 Does the employer receive credit for salary paid to an employee eligible for worker compensation?

Employee benefits under worker compensation law in Illinois are computed on the basis of average weekly wage. The statute provides four methods of making the wage calculation. The employer is entitled to compensation payments made pursuant to the worker compensation law. When an employer pays money other than compensation payments required by the worker compensation law to an eligible employee, the employer receives credit for each such payment to the extent of its temporary total disability liability. Employers may not receive credit to which they might otherwise have entitlement if a collective bargaining agreement or policy provide employees entitlement to benefits that exceed those required by law.

820 ILCS 305/8

820 ILCS 305/10

Elgin Board of Education School District U-46 v. Illinois Workers' Compensation Commission, 409 Ill. App. 3d 943, 949 N.E. 2d 198, 350 Ill. Dec. 710 (1st Dist. 2011)

UNEMPLOYMENT INSURANCE

17:280 Are school employees eligible for unemployment compensation benefits?

School employees may be eligible for unemployment compensation if the conditions of the former employee's severance are qualifying. Employees discharged for cause or who leave work voluntarily are usually ineligible for unemployment compensation. Persons otherwise eligible for unemployment compensation may be disqualified if they are not able, available for, and actively seeking work.

820 ILCS 405/100 et seq.

17:290 Is an employee eligible for unemployment compensation benefits after resignation?

An employee may be eligible for unemployment compensation after a voluntary resignation if the resignation was for "good cause."

Davis v. Board of Review of the Department of Labor, 125 Ill. App. 3d 67, 465 N.E. 2d 576, 80 Ill. Dec. 464 (1st Dist. 1984)

17:300 Are school employees eligible for unemployment compensation between school terms?

A person is ineligible for benefits, on the basis of wages for service in employment in an instructional, research, or principal administrative capacity performed for an educational institution, during a period between two successive academic years, or during a period of paid sabbatical leave provided for in the person's contract, if the person performed such service in the first of such academic years [or terms] and if there is a contract or a reasonable assurance the person will perform service in any capacity for any educational institution in the second of such academic years [or terms].

820 ILCS 405/612

Doran v. Department of Labor, 116 Ill. App. 3d 471, 452 N.E. 2d 118, 72 Ill. Dec. 186 (1st Dist. 1983)

17:310 May an employee receiving worker compensation benefits be concurrently eligible for unemployment compensation?

No.

820 ILCS 405/606

AMERICANS WITH DISABILITIES ACT

17:350 What is the Americans with Disabilities Act?

The Americans with Disabilities Act (ADA) is a federal law that prohibits discrimination against persons with disabilities. The ADA requires that the employer make reasonable accommodation for a qualified individual with a disability unless accommodation would cause an undue hardship.

42 U.S.C. 12111 et seq.

17:355 What is the meaning of "disability" under the ADA?

In 2008 Congress amended the ADA to overrule the Supreme Court's decisions in Toyota and Sutton cited below and to reinstate the court's findings in School Board of Nassau County v. Arline (also cited below) and to clarify the intent of Congress regarding the Act's coverage.

A disability is a physical or mental impairment that substantially limits one or more of the major life activities of an individual. The Act requires that there be a record of the impairment and requires that the individual be regarded as having such an impairment. Congress intended that the term "disability" under the Act provide individuals with broad coverage "to the maximum extent permitted under the terms of the Act."

Congress specifically rejected the Supreme Court's finding in Toyota that the term "substantially limits" as it is used in the ADA means "an individual must have an impairment that prevents or severely restricts the individual from doing activities that are of central importance to most people's daily lives."

The determination of whether an impairment substantially limits a major life activity is made without regard to the ameliorative effects of mitigating measures. Such measures include the following:

1) Medication, medical supplies, equipment, or appliances, low-vision devices (which do not include ordinary eyeglasses or contact lenses), prosthetics including limbs and devices, hearing aids and cochlear implants or other implantable hearing devices, mobility devices, or oxygen therapy equipment and supplies;

2) Use of assistive technology;

3) Reasonable accommodations or auxiliary aids or services; or

4) Learned behavioral or adaptive neurological modifications.

Major life activities include, but are not limited to, caring for oneself, performing manual tasks, seeing, hearing, eating, sleeping, walking, standing, lifting, bending, speaking, breathing, learning, reading, concentrating, thinking, communicating, and working. A major life activity also includes the operation of a major bodily function, including but not limited to, functions of the immune system, normal cell growth, digestive, bowel, bladder, neurological, brain, respiratory, circulatory, endocrine, and reproductive functions.

The inability to perform a particular job for a particular employer is not sufficient to establish a substantial limitation on the ability to work; rather, the impairment must substantially limit employment generally. To be substantially limited in the major life activity of working, the person must be significantly restricted in the ability to perform either a class of jobs or a broad range of jobs in various classes as compared to the average person having comparable training, skills, and abilities.

An individual meets the requirement of being regarded as having an impairment if the individual establishes that he or she has been subjected to an action prohibited under the ADA because of an actual or perceived physical or mental impairment whether or not the impairment limits or is perceived to limit a major life activity. Impairments with an actual or expected duration of six months or less are transitory and not covered. An impairment that is episodic or in remission is a disability if it would substantially limit a major life activity when active.

42 U.S.C. 12102(2)

29 C.F.R. 1630.2(j)(3)(i)

Hanson v. Caterpillar, 688 F. 3d 816 (7th Cir. 2012)

Powers v. USF Holland, 667 F. 3d 815 (7th Cir. 2011)

Toyota Motor Manufacturing, Inc. v. Williams, 122 S. Ct. 681, 534 U.S. 184, 151 L. Ed. 2d 615 (2002)

Sutton v. United Airlines, 119 S. Ct. 2139, 527 U.S. 483, 144 L. Ed. 2d 450 (1999)

Bragdon v. Abbott, 118 S. Ct. 2196, 524 U.S. 624, 141 L. Ed. 2d 540 (1998)

Swain v. Hillsborough County School Board, 146 F. 3d 855 (11th Cir. 1998)

Olson v. Dubuque Community School District, 137 F. 3d 609 (8th Cir. 1998)

School Board of Nassau County v. Arline, 107 S. Ct. 1123, 480 U.S. 273, 94 L. Ed. 2d 307 (1987)

17:358 What is an adverse employment action under the ADA?

An employment action must be a materially adverse change to implicate a right under the Americans with Disabilities Act (ADA).

Mere lateral transfers, room or school changes, or simple assignment changes are not likely materially adverse. To be materially adverse, a change must be more than mere inconvenience, such as a loss of salary or benefits.

Galabya v. New York City Board of Education, 202 F. 3d 636 (2nd Cir. 2000)

17:360 Who is a qualified individual with a disability under the ADA?

A qualified individual with a disability is an individual who, with or without reasonable accommodation, can perform the essential functions of the job. A qualified individual must satisfy the requisite skill, experience, education, and other job-related requirements of the employment position he or she holds or desires and establish that he or she can perform the essential functions of the position with or without accommodation. An employer who denies reasonable accommodation to a qualified person with a disability who, with reasonable accommodation, could perform the essential functions of the job has committed a discriminatory act under the ADA.

42 U.S.C. 12111(8)

Kotwica v. Rose Packing Co. 637 F. 3d 744 (7th Cir. 2011)

Dargis v. Sheehan, 526 F. 3d 981 (7th Cir. 2008)

Harton v. City of Chicago Department of Public Works and Department of Transportation, 301 Ill. App. 3d 378, 703 N.E. 2d 493, 234 Ill. Dec. 632 (1st Dist. 1998) app. den. 182 Ill. 2d 549, 707 N.E. 2d 239, 236 Ill. Dec. 669 (1999)

Nowak v. St. Rita High School, 142 F. 3d 999 (7th Cir. 1998)

Brickers v. Cleveland Board of Education, 145 F. 3d 846 (6th Cir. 1998)

17:361 What is reasonable accommodation?

An employer violates the ADA by not making reasonable accommodation to the known physical or mental limitations of an otherwise qualified individual with a disability unless the employer can show that the accommodation would impose an undue hardship on the operation of its business. The failure to engage in the interactive process required by the ADA is not an independent basis for liability under the statute and that failure is actionable only if it prevents identification of an appropriate accommodation for a qualified individual.

42 U.S.C. 12112(b)(5)(A)

Basden v. Professional Transportation, Inc. __ F. 3d __ (7th Cir. 2013)

Equal Employment Opportunity Commission v. Autozone, 630 F. 3d 635 (7th Cir. 2010)

17:362 Is a medical condition that can be treated (a mental disorder, for example) a disability within the meaning of the ADA?

The determination as to whether a particular condition constitutes a disability within the meaning of the Americans with Disabilities Act is based on the employee's unmedicated or untreated state.

Cassimy v. Board of Education of Rockford District 205, 461 F. 3d 932 (7th Cir. 2006)

Taylor v. Phoenixville School District, 174 F. 3d 142 (3rd Cir. 1999)

17:366 What is "associational discrimination" under the ADA?

The Americans with Disabilities Act prohibits an employer from discriminating against an employee because of the known disability of a person with whom the employee is known to have a relationship or association. "Associational discrimination" claims are unlike other ADA claims because the employer is not required to provide reasonable accommodation for workers who are not themselves disabled.

To prevail, a plaintiff must prove he or she was qualified for the job at the time of the adverse employment action, was subjected to an adverse employment action, was known by his or her employer at the time to have a relative or associate with a disability, and his or her case must fall into one of the three relevant categories of expense, distraction, or association.

Although an employer need not accommodate an employee because of the employee's association with a disabled person, the employer cannot discriminate against the employee for unfounded assumptions about the need to care for a disabled person. For example, an employer cannot refuse to hire on the basis of speculation about absences that might occur in the future to care for a disabled spouse. Once hired, an employee who has to care for a disabled spouse can be fired without violation of the ADA if the employee's absences violate a neutral employer policy regarding absenteeism or tardiness because there is no requirement to accommodate.

School officials should be careful to examine all relevant state statutes, rules and regulations and their district collective bargaining agreements before reaching disciplinary conclusions.

42 U.S.C. 12112 (b)(4)

29 C.F.R. 1630.8

Magnus v. St. Mark United Methodist Church, 688 F. 3d 331 (7th Cir. 2012)

17:370 What is "undue hardship" under the ADA?

The employer need not provide a reasonable accommodation if to do so would create significant difficulty or expense, or if to do so would create a direct threat to health and safety.

42 U.S.C. 12111(3)

42 U.S.C. 12111(10)

Vande Zande v. Wisconsin Department of Administration, 44 F. 3d 538 (7th Cir. 1995)

17:374 Must an employer provide accommodation if the requested accommodation conflicts with an established seniority system?

When the accommodation requested by an employee conflicts with an employer's established seniority rules, the accommodation is ordinarily, as a matter of law, not reasonable. The principle applies equally to collectively bargained seniority systems and those imposed unilaterally by the employer.

Once the employer has established that the requested accommodation would violate an existing seniority system, the employee has the burden to show special circumstances that make an exception to the system reasonable under a particular set of facts.

E.E.O.C. v. United Airlines, 693 F. 3d 760 (7th Cir. 2012)

U.S. Airways v. Barnett, 122 S. Ct. 1516, 535 U.S. 391, 152 L. Ed. 2d 589 (2002)

17:375 Must an employer give transfer preference to reasonably accommodate a disabled employee if there is a more qualified candidate?

An employer does not violate the Americans with Disabilities Act by giving a position to a better-qualified candidate rather than to an employee needing assignment.

E.E.O.C. v. United Airlines, 693 F. 3d 760 (7th Cir. 2012)

E.E.O.C. v. Humiston-Keeling, 227 F. 3d 1024 (7th Cir. 2000)

17:380 Is an employer required to reassign an employee to reasonably accommodate him or her?

In most cases, the employer is not required to reassign an employee to reasonably accommodate him or her, nor to create a new job. The employer's obligation is limited to the duty to find reasonable accommodation to allow the employee to perform the essential functions of the job in his or her current assignment.

Dargis v. Sheehan, 526 F. 3d 981 (7th Cir. 2008)

Willis v. Conopco, Inc. 108 F. 3d. 282 (11th Cir. 1997)

Hartlein v. Illinois Power Co., 151 Ill. 2d 142, 601 N.E. 2d 720, 176 Ill. Dec. 22 (1992)

Illinois Bell Telephone Company v. Human Rights Commission, 190 Ill. App. 3d 1036, 547 N.E. 2d 499, 138 Ill. Dec. 332 (1st Dist. 1989) app. den. 129 Ill. 2d 563, 550 N.E. 2d 556, 140 Ill. Dec. 671 (1990)

17:384 Does an employer assume liability if it tries to accommodate an employee and the employee is subsequently injured in the process of performing his or her accommodated job?

Probably not. The employer does not assume a duty of care to the employee by trying to accommodate the employee's disability. When an employee continues to work and does not follow doctor's orders, the employer will not have Americans with Disabilities Act exposure if the employee is injured on the job.

One Illinois appellate court has reasoned that to hold that an employer has a duty would deter employers from attempting to accommodate employees with temporary work restrictions.

Brown v. Walker Nursing Home, Inc. 307 Ill. App. 3d 721, 718 N.E. 2d 373, 240 L. Ed. 2d 892 (4th Dist. 1999)

17:390 Must an employee provide the employer with information about his or her disability so that the employer can make reasonable accommodation decisions?

To trigger the employer duty to reasonably accommodate, the employer must have knowledge of the disability or the employee must inform the employer of the disability. Thereafter, the employer must make a reasonable effort to determine a reasonable accommodation. The employee and the employer are then required to work together to determine a reasonable accommodation.

42 U.S.C. 12112(b)(5)

56 Ill. Admin. Code 2500.40

Dargis v. Sheehan, 526 F. 3d 981 (7th Cir. 2008)

Beck v. University of Wisconsin Board of Regents, 75 F. 3d 1130 (7th Cir. 1996)

17:400 What is the effect of a rejection by an employee of an employer's offer of reasonable accommodation?

If an employee rejects an offer by his or her employer of a reasonable accommodation necessary to perform the essential functions of his or her position, the employee loses his or her protection under the ADA because he or she is no longer a qualified individual with a disability.

Kerno v. Sandoz Pharmaceuticals Corp., No. 93 C 20012, 1994 U.S. Dist. Lexis 13265, 1994 WL 511289

17:410 May a school board dismiss or otherwise discipline an employee who cannot perform his or her job because he or she has a disability?

An employee with a disability may be dismissed or disciplined if he or she cannot do the work his or her job requires and the employee cannot be otherwise accommodated by the employer. A plaintiff claiming discrimination must show that he or she is an individual with a disability within the meaning of the law; is otherwise qualified for the job; has been excluded from programs solely because of the disability; and the school receives federal funds.

An employer is permitted to treat regular attendance as an essential job requirement and need not accommodate erratic or unreliable attendance. An employee whose disability prevents him or her from coming to work regularly cannot perform the essential functions of the job and, as a result, cannot be a qualified individual for ADA purposes.

Basden v. Professional Transportation, Inc. 714 F. 3d 1034 (7th Cir. 2013)

Byrne v. Board of Education, School of West Allis-West Milwaukee, 979 F. 2d 560 (7th Cir. 1992)

School Board of Nassau County v. Arline, 107 S. Ct. 1123, 480 U.S. 273, 94 L. Ed. 2d 307 (1987)

17:415 Does an employee's eligibility for temporary total disability benefits end when the employee is dismissed for cause?

The test for determining whether an employee is entitled to continued benefits is whether the employee remains temporarily totally disabled as a result of a work-related injury, and whether the employee is capable of returning to the work force. Benefits may be terminated if the employee refuses to undergo or refuses to cooperate with treatment essential to recovery, but whether or not the employee left the workforce as a result of misconduct unrelated to the disability is irrelevant to receipt of continued benefits.

Interstate Scaffolding, Inc. v. Illinois Workers' Compensation Commission, 236 Ill. 2d 132, 923 N.E. 2d 266, 337 Ill. Dec. 707 (2010)

17:420 How does an employer distinguish temporary disability from permanent disability (permanent inability to perform the job)?

Section 24-13 of the School Code provides that a teacher's contractual continued service (tenure) shall not be affected by temporary illness or disability. Other state and federal statutes (the Americans with Disability Act or the Illinois Human Rights Act, for example) might be used to challenge a disability determination for other classes of school employees.

In order to distinguish temporary from permanent disability, the employer must first adopt a policy or work rule defining the distinction. The employer must be very careful to adopt a policy that is explicit in defining when a temporary disability has become permanent.

An Illinois court has implicitly approved of a policy that defined permanent disability as having occurred when an employee missed 90 consecutive workdays in the same school term after having exhausted available sick leave. It seems likely that a court would disapprove of a permanent disability determination while the employee had any form of approved leave available.

105 ILCS 5/24-13

Board of Education, School District No. 151, Cook County v. Illinois State Board of Education, 154 Ill. App. 3d 175, 507 N.E. 2d 134, 107 Ill. Dec. 470 (1st Dist. 1987)

Elder v. Board of Education of School District 127 1/2 of Cook County, 60 Ill. App. 2d 56, 208 N.E. 2d 423 (1st Dist. 1965)

EMPLOYEE SPEECH

17:450 Is private employee speech protected by the First Amendment?

When school employees speak, write, or act on their own time on topics unrelated to their employment, such speech can have First Amendment protection, absent some governmental justification far stronger than mere speculation in regulating it. Courts examine the "content, form, and context of a given statement, as revealed by the whole record," in assessing whether an employee's speech addresses a matter of public concern.

The standard for determining whether expression is of public concern is the same standard used to determine whether a common-law action for invasion of privacy is present. That standard is something that is a subject of legitimate news interest; that is, a subject of general interest and of value and concern to the public at the time of publication. It does not require that speech relate to an issue of exceptional significance. The inappropriateness or controversial character of a statement is irrelevant to the question of whether it deals with a matter of public concern.

Assuming the matter is of public concern, a court evaluating restraints on a public employee's speech under the First Amendment must balance interests of the employee as a citizen in commenting upon matters of public concern against the interests of the state as the employer in promoting efficiency of public services it performs through its employees.

Craig v. Rich Township High School District, 736 F. 3d 1110 (7th Cir. 2013

Garcetti v. Ceballos, 126 S.Ct. 1951, 547 U.S. 410, 164 L. Ed. 2d 689 (2006)

City of San Diego, California v. Roe, 125 S. Ct. 521, 543 U.S. 77, 160 L. Ed. 2d 410 (2004)

Melzer v. Board of Education of City School District of City of New York, 336 F. 3d 185 (2nd Cir. 2003)

Connick v. Myers, 103 S. Ct. 1684, 461 U.S. 138, 75 L. Ed. 2d 708 (1983)

Pickering v. Board of Education of Township High School District No. 205, Will County, Illinois, 88 S. Ct. 1731, 391 U.S. 563, 20 L. Ed. 2d 811 (1968)

17:451 May an employee be dismissed for publicly criticizing school board decisions?

The First Amendment right to freedom of speech applies to employees. Employees may speak out publicly on issues of public concern without fear of reprisal.

Freedom of speech is not absolute, however. There are circumstances under which an employee may be disciplined by reason of something he or she has said. Only speech on matters of public concern is protected. Courts have tended to interpret public concern to mean broad social or policy issues.

Teachers who speak on self-serving issues risk discipline. The three steps the courts apply when deciding these cases are as follows:

1) Would the employee's speech be protected by the First Amendment were it spoken by someone who was not a public employee?

2) Is the speech a matter of public concern or a personal grievance?

3) Does the employer have a convincing reason to forbid the speech?

In mixed-issue cases (when the speech contains some matters of public concern but is also self-serving), the courts will frequently balance the importance of the speech against the employer's interest in maintaining order and its interest in effective operation.

In the age of social media and personal blogs, school employees must be mindful of their roles as government employees. In order for employee speech to be protected, the employee must speak as a citizen and not as an employee. Speech that relates solely to mundane employment grievances does not implicate a matter of public concern and is therefore not protected by the First Amendment. In order for the government to establish its interest in regulating the speech, it need not show actual disruption if it is able to show the disruption is likely to occur because of the speech.

Munroe v. Central Bucks School District, 805 F. 3d 454 (3rd 2015)

Garcetti v. Ceballos, 126 S.Ct. 1951, 547 U.S. 410, 164 L. Ed. 2d 689 (2006)

Colleen M. Wales v. Board of Education of Community Unit School District 300, et al., 120 F. 3d 82 (7th Cir. 1997)

Khuans v. School District 110, 123 F. 3d 1010 (7th Cir. 1997)

Dishnow v. School District of Rib Lake, 77 F. 3d 194 (7th Cir. 1996)

Waters v. Churchill, 114 S. Ct. 1878, 511 U.S. 661, 128 L. Ed. 2d 686 (1994)

Sanguigni v. Pittsburgh Board of Public Education, 968 F. 2d 393 (3rd Cir. 1992)

Stroman v. Colleton County School District, 981 F. 2d 152 (4th Cir. 1992)

Vukadinovich v. Board of School Trustees of the Michigan City Area Schools, 978 F. 2d 403 (7th Cir. 1992)

Rankin v. McPherson, 107 S. Ct. 2891, 483 U.S. 378, 97 L. Ed. 2d 315 (1987)

Knapp v. Whitaker, 757 F. 2d 827 (7th Cir. 1985)

Connick v. Myers, 103 S. Ct. 1684, 461 U.S. 138, 75 L. Ed. 2d 708 (1983)

Mt. Healthy City School District Board of Education v. Doyle, 97 S. Ct. 568, 429 U.S. 274, 50 L. Ed. 2d 471 (1977) app. after rem. 670 F. 2d 59 (6th Cir. 1982) (1977)

Brubaker v. Board of Education of School District No. 149, Cook County, 502 F. 2d 973 (7th Cir. 1974)

Pickering v. Board of Education of Township High School District No. 205, Will County, Illinois, 88 S. Ct. 1731, 391 U.S. 563, 20 L. Ed. 2d 811 (1968)

17:452 Do employees in policy-making positions have less free speech protection than other school employees?

As a rule, a school board cannot retaliate against its employees for engaging in constitutionally protected speech. To prevail, an employee must show that he or she engaged in speech protected by the First Amendment and that his or her speech was "a substantial or motivating factor" in the employer's challenged actions.

For purpose of determining First Amendment free speech rights of a school employee, a "policy-making employee" is one whose position authorizes, either directly or indirectly, meaningful input into decision-making on issues where there is room for principled disagreement on goals or their implementation. It is necessary to go beyond labels to consider the nature of the responsibilities in question. An individual's job title will not decide his or her fate as a policy-making employee, but rather the actual duties of the position are examined and evaluated.

The First Amendment does not prohibit the discharge of a policy-making employee who engages in speech that implicates his or her political viewpoints. In determining whether a school employee's speech is protected, the courts apply a fact-specific balancing test to determine whether the interests of the employee, as a citizen, in commenting upon matters of public concern, outweigh the interest of the employer in promoting the efficiency of the public services it performs through its employees. The test considers:

1) Whether the statement would create problems in maintaining discipline by immediate supervisors or harmony among co-workers;

2) Whether the employment relationship is one in which personal loyalty and confidence are necessary;

3) Whether the speech impeded the employee's ability to perform her daily responsibilities;

4) The time, place, and manner of the speech;

5) The context in which the underlying dispute arose;

6) Whether the matter was one on which debate was vital to informed decision making; and

7) Whether the speaker should be regarded as a member of the general public.

Demers v. Austin, 729 F. 3d. 1011 (9th Cir. 2012)

Vargas-Harrison v. Racine Unified School District, 272 F. 3d 964 (7th Cir. 2001) cert. den. 123 S. Ct. 120, 537 U.S. 826, 154 L. Ed. 2d 38 (2002)

Horwitz v. Board of Education of Avoca School District No. 37, 260 F. 3d 602, 618 (7th Cir.2001)

Myers v. Hasara, 226 F. 3d 821 (7th Cir. 2000)

Pickering v. Board of Education of Township High School District No. 205, Will County, Illinois, 88 S. Ct. 1731, 391 U.S. 563, 20 L. Ed. 2d 811 (1968)

17:455 May a school board adopt an employee dress code?

Yes, although there are a number of hazards in the drafting of a policy that a school board should be careful to avoid.

First, the implementation of a dress code is a mandatory subject of bargaining and requires the school board to meet its bargaining obligations in the event of a demand to bargain by an employee bargaining agent.

Second, the drafting of a dress code that passes constitutional muster is tricky. The code cannot infringe on the rights of employees that are otherwise protected (sex, religion or speech discrimination, for example) without the demonstration of a compelling government interest (which is a very high standard and difficult to meet).

A dress code must be reasonably related to the school's educational mission and must employ the least restrictive means to obtain the desired end. The purpose for the dress code should be clearly stated in the policy.

Jespersen v. Harrah's Operating Co., Inc., 444 F. 3d 1104 (9th Cir. 2006)

Mississippi Employment Security Commission v. McGlothin, 556 So. 2d 324 (Miss. 1990)

East Hartford Education Association v. Board of Education, 562 F. 2d 83 (2nd Cir. 1977)

Ball v. Kerrville Independent School District, 529 S.W. 2d 792 (Tex. 1975)

Blanchet v. Vermillion Parish School Board, 220 So. 2d 534 (La. 1969)

17:460 May a school district discriminate against employees on the basis of political preference?

No. A school district may not discriminate as to promotion, recall, transfer, or hiring based on party affiliation.

Rutan v. Republican Party of Illinois, 110 S. Ct. 2729, 497 U.S. 62, 111 L. Ed. 2d 52, reh. den. 111 S. Ct. 13, 111 L. Ed. 2d 828 (1990)

Branti v. Finkel, 100 S. Ct. 1287, 445 U.S. 507, 63 L. Ed. 2d 574 (1980)

Elrod v. Burns, 96 S. Ct. 2673, 427 U.S. 347, 49 L. Ed. 2d 547 (1976)

17:465 What factors do the courts consider when an employee alleges direct evidence of discrimination?

To make a case of direct discrimination requires either an outright admission by the decision-maker that the challenged action was undertaken because of the plaintiff's age, sex, national origin, etc., or a "convincing mosaic of circumstantial evidence that points directly to a discriminatory reason for the employer's action."

The Seventh Circuit Court of Appeals has recognized three different types of circumstantial evidence of intentional discrimination:

1) Suspicious timing, ambiguous oral or written statements, behavior toward or directed at other employees in the protected group, and other bits and pieces from which an inference of discriminatory intent might be drawn;

2) Evidence of similarly situated employees outside the protected class receiving systematically better treatment; and

3) Evidence that the plaintiff was qualified for the job in question but was passed over in favor of a person outside the protected class and the employer's stated reason was a pretext for discrimination.

To be useful in proving discrimination, isolated comments must be contemporaneous with the adverse action or causally related to it.

Dass v. Chicago Board of Education, 675 F. 3d 1060 (7th Cir. 2012)

17:470 May employees engage in political campaigning or other political activities?

Employees may engage in political campaigning or other political activities. But the Local Governmental Employees Political Rights Act prevents employees from exercising such rights or "engaging in political activities while at work or on duty." Political rights are defined by the Act to include the right to petition, make public speeches, to campaign for or against political candidates, to speak out on questions of public policy, to distribute political literature, to make campaign contributions, and to seek public office. The right to engage in political activities away from work extends not only to conventional political causes, but also to political organizations that hold unpopular or controversial views.

A school board may regulate the espousal of political views in the classroom by establishment of curriculum.

50 ILCS 135/1

Castle v. Colonial School District, 933 F. Supp. 458 (E.D. Pa. 1996)

McLaughlin v. Tilendis, 398 F. 2d 287 (7th Cir. 1968)

17:475 May a school district limit what employees may keystroke, access, or download into school owned computers?

School districts may place reasonable limits on what employees may do with school-owned computers and networks. Where collective bargaining agreements cover employees affected by a school district computer use policy, school districts should take care that all bargaining obligations are considered and met.

Urofsky v. Gilmore, 167 F. 3d 191 (4th Cir 1999)

17:480 May a school board discipline a teacher for inappropriate classroom speech?

The First Amendment rights of teachers to free speech are limited while they are in the classroom because the classroom is not a public forum and public school employers may limit classroom speech to promote educational goals. A school board may make reasonable rules regarding appropriate speech in the classroom and may discipline those who break those rules.

Teachers have a right to notice as to what speech is prohibited, but the school need not expressly prohibit every imaginable inappropriate conduct by teachers. The relevant inquiry is whether, given school policies, rules and regulations. and other communication from the school to the teacher, it was reasonable to expect the teacher would know the conduct was prohibited.

Grossman v. South Shore Public School District, 507 F. 3d 1097 (7th Cir. 2007)

Mayer v. Monroe County Community School Organization, 474 F. 3d 477 (7th Cir. 2007) pet. for cert. den. 128 S. Ct. 160, 552 U.S. 823, 169 L. Ed. 2d 32 (2007)

Lacks v. Ferguson-Florissant Reorganized School District, R-2, 147 F. 3d 718 (8th Cir. 1998) sugg. for reh. den. 154 F. 3d 904, cert. den. 119 S. Ct. 1158, 526 U.S. 1012, 143 L. Ed. 2d 233

Ward v. Hickey, 996 F. 2d 448 (1st Cir. 1993)

Miles v. Denver Public Schools, 944 F. 2d 773 (10th Cir. 1991)

Krizek v. Board of Education, 713 F. Supp. 1131 (N.D. Ill. 1989)

Hazelwood v. Kuhlmeier, 108 S. Ct. 562, 484 U.S. 260, 98 L. Ed. 2d 592 (1988), on rem. 840 F. 2d 596 (8th Cir. 1988)

Zykan v. Warsaw Community School Corporation, 631 F. 2d 1300 (7th Cir. 1980)

17:481 May a teacher be disciplined for refusal to participate in the Pledge of Allegiance?

A public school teacher may not disregard the prescribed curriculum, even when the curriculum conflicts with his or her religious principles. Cases will likely be fact-based and dependent on how clearly the curriculum requires participation in the act or teaching of the subject. Employee refusal to participate in the Pledge of Allegiance is based on a different legal principle than is student refusal to participate.

Palmer v. Board of Education of City of Chicago, 603 F. 2d 1271 (7th Cir. 1979)

17:482 May a school board discipline a teacher for the teacher's selection of controversial instructional material?

A school board may discipline a teacher for the teacher's failure to follow clear and established curriculum. In this context a school board could, for example, ban classroom profanity of any kind or limit the exposure of students to graphic sex or violence in movies shown in class.

A school board should be careful in considering discipline that the speech rights of the teacher have been considered and that the school district has legitimate pedagogical concerns.

Boring v. Buncombe County Board of Education, 98 F. 3d 1474 (4th Cir. 1998)

Lacks v. Ferguson-Florissant Reorganized School District, R-2, 147 F. 3d 718 (8th Cir. 1998) sugg. for reh. den. 154 F. 3d 904, cert. den. 119 S. Ct. 1158, 526 U.S. 1012, 143 L. Ed. 2d 233 (1999)

17:486 May an employee successfully defend against employer discipline for religious proselytizing by using a religious freedom defense?

Persons with strongly held religious views sometimes seek to impose their views on others. Such conduct occurs in the workplace when employees seek to influence the views of other employees, students, or the employer. The proselytizing may involve posting signs, wearing buttons, distributing printed material, or speech.

To establish religious discrimination on the basis of a failure-to-accommodate theory under Title VII of the Civil Rights Act of 1964, an employee must first set forth a prima facie case that

1) He or she had a bona fide religious belief, the practice of which conflicts with an employment duty;

2) He or she informed the employer of the belief and conflict; and

3) The employer discharged, threatened, or otherwise subjected him or her to an adverse employment action because of his or her inability to fulfill the job requirement.

If an employee makes out a prima facie failure-to-accommodate case, the burden then shifts to the employer to show that it initiated good faith efforts to accommodate reasonably the employee's religious practices or that it could not reasonably accommodate the employee without undue hardship.

An employer need not accommodate an employee's religious beliefs if doing so would result in discrimination against his or her co-workers or deprive them of contractual or other statutory rights. Title VII does not require an employer to accommodate an employee's desire to impose his or her religious beliefs upon co-workers.

42 U.S.C. 2000e

Powell v. Yellow Book U.S.A., Inc., 445 F. 3d 1074 (8th Cir. 2006)

Peterson v. Hewlett-Packard Co., 358 F. 3d 599 (9th Cir. 2004)

Buonanno v. AT&T Broadband LLC, 313 F. Supp. 2d 1069 (D. Colo. 2004)

Anderson v. USF Logistics, Inc., 274 F. 3d 470 (7th Cir. 2001)

Chalmers v. Tulon Co. of Richmond, 101 F. 3d 1012 (4th Cir. 1996) cert. den. 118 S. Ct. 58, 522 U.S. 813, 139 L. Ed. 2d 21 (1997)

17:488 If a school employer directs a teacher to stop proselytizing to students, may the teacher defend by asserting his or her First Amendment right to "free speech"?

Forum analysis does not apply (public forum, limited public forum, non-public forum). A school district may impose certain restraints on the speech of its employees that would be unconstitutional if applied to the general public. The courts apply a test that considers an employee's right to engage in speech and balance it against the employer's right to protect its own legitimate interests in performing its mission.

A federal appeals court (9th Circuit) has distilled the test as follows: whether the employee spoke on a matter of public concern; whether he or she spoke as a private citizen; whether his or her speech was a substantial or motivating factor in the adverse employment action; whether the school had an adequate justification for treating him or her differently from other members of the general public; and whether the school employer would have taken the adverse employment action absent the protected speech. The test is sequential and if the employee fails to satisfy any of the steps, the inquiry ends (and the employee loses).

The courts reason that when a citizen enters government service, the citizen by necessity must accept certain limitations on his or her freedom or else there would be little chance for the efficient provision of government services. If the teacher's speech owes its existence to his or her position as a teacher then he or she is speaking as an employee, not as a private citizen, and the teacher is unable to meet the second prong of the test. Several courts have reasoned that "when a teacher speaks as a government employee, the school board that hires that speech can regulate what is or is not expressed." The Poway court held: "The Constitution does not entitle teachers to present personal views to captive audiences against the instructions of elected officials ... teachers do not cease acting as teachers each time the bell rings or the conversation moves beyond the narrow topic of curricular instruction. Rather, because of the position of trust and authority they hold and the impressionable minds with which they interact, teachers necessarily act as teachers ... when at school or a school function, in the general presence of students [or] in a capacity one might reasonably view as official."

Johnson v. Poway Unified School District, 658 F. 3d 954 (9th Cir, 2011)

Mayer v. Monroe County Community School Organization, 474 F. 3d 477 (7th Cir. 2007) pet. for cert. den. 128 S. Ct. 160, 552 U.S. 823, 169 L. Ed. 2d 32 (2007)

Pickering v. Board of Education of Township High School District No. 205, Will County, Illinois, 88 S. Ct. 1731, 391 U.S. 563, 20 L. Ed. 2d 811 (1968)

17:490 May school officials audio tape a teacher's classroom instruction without the teacher's consent?

The Illinois eavesdropping statute provides in part that a person commits eavesdropping when he or she knowingly and intentionally uses an eavesdropping device for the purpose of hearing or recording all or any part of any conversation or intercepts, retains, or transcribes electronic communication unless he or she does so with the consent of all the parties to the conversation or electronic communication.

Conversation under the law is any oral communication between two or more persons regardless of whether one or more of the parties intended the communication to be of a private nature under circumstances justifying that exception.

An Illinois appellate court has held that "because Illinois citizens are entitled to be safeguarded from unnecessary governmental surveillance and other unreasonable intrusions into their privacy, the statutory restraints on eavesdropping must be strictly construed with respect to all requests and consents to the use of an eavesdropping device."

Before classroom instruction can be audio recorded, school officials must obtain the consent of anyone whose speech would be recorded by the audio device.

720 ILCS 5/14-1

720 ILCS 5/14-2

Plock, et al. v. Board of Education of Freeport School District No. 145, 396 Ill. App. 960, 920 N.E. 1087, 336 Ill. Dec. 497 (2nd Dist. 2009)

SEXUAL HARASSMENT

17:500 What is sexual harassment?

Sexual harassment is any unwelcome sexual advances or requests for sexual favors or any conduct of a sexual nature when:

1) Submission to such conduct is made either explicitly or implicitly a term or condition of an individual's employment;

2) Submission to or rejection of such conduct by an individual is used as the basis for employment decisions affecting such individual; or

3) Such conduct has the purpose or effect of substantially interfering with an individual's work performance or creating an intimidating, hostile, or offensive working environment.

42 U.S.C. 2000e et seq.

29 C.F.R. 1604.11

775 ILCS 5/1-101 et seq.

Henson v. City of Dundee, 682 F. 2d 897 (11th Cir. 1982)

Bundy v. Jackson, 641 F. 2d 934 (D.C. Cir. 1981)

Tomkins v. Public Service Electric and Gas Company, 568 F. 2d 1044 (3rd Cir. 1977)

17:502 What is the limitations period for Title VII claims?

The Title VII statute of limitations is 180 days after the alleged unlawful employment practice occurred, except that if the victim has initially instituted proceedings with a state or local agency (the Department of Human Rights, for example) the charge must be filed within 300 days. For a claim based on a discrete act, the limitations period precludes recovery if the act happened outside the limitations period. But in a hostile environment case the court may consider the entire scope of the hostile work environment, including behavior that occurred outside the statutory time period, so long as an act contributing to the hostile environment takes place within the statutory time period.

Jones v. Res-Care, Inc., 613 F.3d 665 (7th Cir. 2010)

Turner v. The Saloon, Ltd., et al., 595 F. 3d 679 (7th Cir. 2010)

National Railroad Passenger Corp. v. Morgan, 122 S. Ct. 2061, 536 U.S. 101, 153 L. Ed. 2d 106 (2002)

17:504 May a plaintiff recover under Title VII alleging agency principles?

Unlike Title IX, which governs employee-student harassment, Title VII, which governs employer-employee cases, permits causes of action premised on principles of agency (the school is responsible for its employee's actions) or constructive notice (the school was responsible because it knew or should have known what its employee was doing and failed to stop it). A school is liable for the actions of its employees when the employer was negligent or reckless, or when the employee purported to speak or act on behalf of the employer and there was reliance on the authority, or when the employee was aided in accomplishing the act by the existence of his or her agency relationship with the employer.

In order to be actionable under Title VII a sexually objectionable environment must be both objectively and subjectively offensive, one that a reasonable person would find hostile or abusive and one that the victim in fact did perceive to be so.

Constructive discharge Title VI claims require the plaintiff to prove the employer's discriminatory conduct forced the plaintiff to resign because his or her working conditions from the standpoint of a reasonable employee had become unbearable.

42 U.S.C. 2000e(b)

Patterson v. Indiana Newspapers, Inc., 589 F. 3d 357 (7th Cir. 2009)

Mosher v. Dollar Tree Stores, 240 F. 3d 662 (7th Cir. 2001) cert. den. 122 S. Ct. 617, 534 U.S. 104, 151 L. Ed. 2d 539 (2001)

Burlington Industries, Inc. v. Kimberly B. Ellerth, 118 S. Ct. 2257, 524 U.S. 742, 141 L. Ed. 2d 633 (1998)

Faragher v. City of Boca Raton, 118 S. Ct. 2275, 524 U.S. 775, 141 L. Ed. 2d 662 (1998) on rem. 166 F. 3d 1152 (11th Cir. 1999)

Gebser et al. v. Lago Vista Independent School District, 118 S. Ct. 1989, 524 U.S. 274, 141 L. Ed. 2d 277 (1998)

Meritor Savings Bank v. Vinson, 106 S. Ct. 2399, 477 U.S. 57, 91 L. Ed. 2d 49 (1986) on rem. Vinson v. Taylor 801 F. 2d 1436 (D.C. Cir. 1986)

17:505 What is the standard of liability for the employer when a supervisor sexually harasses an employee?

In 2009, the Illinois Supreme Court found that Illinois employers are "strictly liable for the sexual harassment of an employee by a supervisory employee" even when "the supervisor has no authority to affect the terms and conditions of the complainant's employment."

Sangamon County Sheriff's Department v. Illinois Human Rights Commission, 233 Ill. 2d 125, 908 N.E. 2d 125, 908 N.E. 2d 39, 330 Ill. Dec. 187 (2009)

17:508 What defense does an employer have to a charge of agency-based sexual harassment?

To assert a defense, the employer must be able to demonstrate that it exercised reasonable care to prevent and correct promptly any sexually harassing behavior and that the employee unreasonably failed to take advantage of any preventive or corrective opportunities provided by the employer or to avoid harm otherwise. The defense is not available when a supervisor's harassment culminates in a tangible employment action that produces a significant change in employment status, such as hiring, firing, failing to promote, demotion, or undesirable reassignment, or a significant change in benefits.

2017 legislation requires that a school employer have a sexual harassment policy that prohibits sexual harassment and includes details on how an individual can report an allegation of sexual harassment, including options for making a confidential report to a supervisor, ethics officer, Inspector General, or the Department of Human Rights. The policy must prohibit retaliation for reporting sexual harassment allegations, including availability of whistleblower protections and the consequences of a violation of the prohibition on sexual harassment and the consequences for knowingly making a false report.

The Seventh Circuit has held that "the adoption of a sexual harassment policy alone will not shield a school district from its responsibility to actively prevent sexual harassment in the workplace. The complaint mechanism must be reasonable and what is reasonable depends on, among other things, the capabilities of the class of employees in question. Moreover, the policy must not only be reasonably effective on paper, but also reasonably effective in practice."

5 ILCS 430/70-5

E. E. O. C. v. Management Hospitality of Racine, 666 F. 3d 422 (7th Cir. 2012)

Mosher v. Dollar Tree Stores, 240 F. 3d 662 (7th Cir. 2001) cert. den. 122 S. Ct. 617, 534 U.S. 104, 151 L. Ed. 2d 539 (2001)

Faragher v. City of Boca Raton, 118 S. Ct. 2275, 524 U.S. 775, 141 L. Ed. 2d 662 (1998) on rem. 166 F. 3d 1152 (11th Cir. 1999)

17:510 What is a hostile environment for purposes of establishing sexual harassment?

A hostile environment exists when the workplace is permeated with discriminatory behavior that is sufficiently severe or pervasive to create an environment a reasonable person would find hostile or abusive. The harassing conduct need not be both severe and pervasive. One instance of conduct that is sufficiently severe may be enough. The courts may also consider the victim's subjective perception of abusiveness. The victim must subjectively believe that the harassment is sufficiently severe or pervasive to have altered the work environment and the harassment must also be sufficiently severe or pervasive from the standpoint of a reasonable person to create a hostile work environment. The harassment must be gender based.

Whether an environment is abusive is determined by examination of all the circumstances; which includes the frequency of the conduct, its severity, whether it is physically threatening or humiliating or merely offensive, and whether it unreasonably interferes with work performance. Offhand comments, isolated incidents, and simple teasing do not rise to the level of conduct that alters terms and conditions of employment. The fact that the conduct involves touching as opposed to verbal behavior increases the severity of the situation, especially when the touching is of an intimate body part.

The harassment need not be based on unwelcome sexual advances, requests for sexual favors, or other verbal or physical conduct of a sexual nature. Conduct demonstrating anti-female animus can support a hostile work environment claim, but the environment must be both subjectively and objectively offensive.

Turner v. The Saloon, Ltd., et al., 595 F. 3d 679 (7th Cir. 2010)

Scruggs v. Garst Seed Company, 587 F. 3d 832 (7th Cir. 2009)

Coolidge v. Consolidated City of Indianapolis, 505 F. 3d 731 (7th Cir. 2007)

Clark County School District v. Breeden, 121 S. Ct. 1508, 532 U.S. 268, 149 L. Ed. 2d 509 (2001), pet. for reh. den. 121 S. Ct. 2264, 533 U.S. 912, 150 L. Ed. 2d 248 (2001)

Butler v. Ysleta Independent School District, 161 F. 3d 263 (5th Cir. 1998)

Harris v. Forklift Systems, Inc., 114 S. Ct. 367, 510 U.S. 17, 126 L. Ed. 2d 295 (1993)

Meritor Savings Bank v. Vinson, 106 S. Ct. 2399, 477 U.S. 57, 91 L. Ed. 2d 49 (1986) on rem. Vinson v. Taylor 801 F. 2d 1436 (D.C. Cir. 1986)

17:520 Must a person prove injury to prove sexual harassment?

To prove hostile environment, the offensive conduct need not seriously affect the person psychologically, nor need the conduct lead to injury.

Harris v. Forklift Systems, Inc., 114 S. Ct. 367, 510 U.S. 17, 126 L. Ed. 2d 295 (1993)

17:530 May a sexual harassment victim bring a tort claim against an employer in court?

Tort remedies (bringing a lawsuit for damages) are probably not available unless the victim first exhausts remedies available under the Illinois Human Rights Act.

Geise v. Phoenix Co. of Chicago, 159 Ill. 2d 507, 639 N.E. 2d 1273, 203 Ill. Dec. 454 (1994)

17:540 What constitutes retaliation under Title VII?

To prove retaliation, a plaintiff must show a statutorily protected activity, a materially adverse action taken by the employer, and a causal connection between the two. A plaintiff must show that a reasonable employee would have found the employer's action materially adverse and such an employee would have been dissuaded from filing or supporting a charge of discrimination. Suspicious timing alone is insufficient to support a retaliation claim, although the closer two events are in time, the more likely it is that the first caused the second.

An empty threat that quickly dissipates before the employee becomes aware of it does not constitute materially adverse action, nor generally do stand-alone written warnings.

Thompson v. North American Stainless, LP, 131 S. Ct. 863, 562 U.S.170, 178 L. Ed. 2d 694 (2011)

Benuzzi v. Board of Education of the City of Chicago, 647 F. 3d 652 (7th Cir. 2011)

Turner v. The Saloon, Ltd., et al., 595 F. 3d 679 (7th Cir. 2010)

Burlington Northern and Santa Fe Railway Co. v. White, 126 S. Ct. 2405, 548 U.S. 53, 165 L. Ed. 2d 345 (2006)

17:570 May an employer discipline or dismiss an employee because of the employee's sexual orientation?

A plaintiff has a number ways to attack such an allegation of discrimination. Title VII of the Civil Rights Act of 1964 prohibits an employer from discriminating against an individual because of the person's sex with respect to his or her compensation, terms, conditions, or privileges of employment. Nothing in Title VII bars a claim of discrimination because of sex merely because the plaintiff and defendant are of the same sex.

The successful Title VII plaintiff must show that members of one sex are exposed to disadvantageous terms or conditions of employment to which members of the other sex are not exposed and that the conduct at issue was not merely tinged with offensive sexual connotations, but actually constituted discrimination because of sex. The behavior complained of must be so objectively offensive as to alter the conditions of the victim's employment. The objective severity of the harassment is judged from the perspective of a reasonable person in plaintiff's position considering all the circumstances.

In order to establish an equal protection violation, a plaintiff must show that the defendants intentionally treated him or her differently because of his or her membership in the class to which he or she belonged (i.e., homosexuals), and because homosexuals do not enjoy any heightened protection under the Constitution, that the discriminatory intent was not rationally related to a legitimate state interest. A showing that the defendants were negligent will not suffice. The plaintiff must show the defendants "acted either intentionally or with deliberate indifference" to complaints of harassment because of homosexuality.

Discrimination based on the basis of sexual orientation is sex discrimination under federal law. The Seventh Circuit has held that discrimination based on gender identity, change of sex, and/or transgender status violates Title VII.

The Illinois Civil Rights Act was amended in 2008 to prohibit gender-based discrimination. It is unclear whether this change will be interpreted to include claims based on sexual orientation.

42 U.S.C. 2000e-2(a)(1)

740 ILCS 23/5

Hively v. Ivy Tech, __ F. 3d. __

Macy v. Holder, No.012012082, 2012 WL 1435995 (E.E.O.C. Apr. 20, 2012)

Lawrence v. Texas, 123 S. Ct. 2472, 539 U.S. 538, 156 L. Ed. 2d 508 (2003)

Schroeder v. Hamilton School District, 282 F. 3d 946 (7th Cir. 2002), cert. den. 123 S. Ct. 435, 537 U.S. 974, 154 L. Ed. 2d 330 (2002)

Oncale v. Sundowner Offshore Services, Incorporated, et al., 83 F. 3d 118 (5th Cir. 1995) reh. and sugg. for reh. den. 95 F. 3d 56, cert. granted 117 S. Ct. 2430, 520 U.S. 1263, 138 L. Ed. 2d 192, rev. 118 S. Ct. 998, 523 U.S. 75, 140 L. Ed. 2d 201, on rem. 140 F. 3d 595 (1998)

Romer v. Evans, 116 S. Ct. 1620, 517 U.S. 620, 134 L. Ed. 2d 855 (1996)

17:571 May a school district restrict a teacher's assignment because of the teacher's sexual orientation?

No. To remove a teacher or refuse to assign a teacher to a duty because the teacher is gay or lesbian violates the teacher's right to equal protection. Moreover, a school district may not limit the speech of gay or lesbian teachers (even with respect to their sexual orientation) absent a showing of a compelling state interest, and then only when the restriction is narrowly tailored to meet the desired end.

740 ILCS 23/5

Weaver v. Nebo School District, 29 F. Supp. 2d 1279 (D. Utah 1998)

AGE DISCRIMINATION

17:590 Is discrimination on the basis of age prohibited?

The Illinois Human Rights Act prohibits discrimination on the basis of age, as does the federal Age Discrimination in Employment Act (ADEA), which makes it unlawful "to fail or refuse to hire or to discharge any individual or otherwise discriminate against any individual ... because of such individual's age." An ADEA violation occurs when a plaintiff presents evidence that an employee's discharge was "because of his or her age." Age must have played a role in the employer's decision-making process and had a determinative influence on the outcome.

A plaintiff pursuing an ADEA claim has two ways to make a prima facie case. Either he or she can present direct evidence that the discharge was because of age, or can present indirect evidence to demonstrate that the employment decision "was motivated by the employer's discriminatory animus." To establish a prima facie case by the indirect method, a plaintiff must prove that:

- He or she is a member of a protected group;
- His or her performance met the employer's expectations;
- Despite his or her performance, he or she was subject to an adverse employment action, and

• The employer treated similarly situated employees under age 40 more favorably.

The plaintiff has the ultimate burden of persuading the trier of fact that the employer intentionally discriminated against him or her based upon age.

29 U.S.C. 623(a)(1)

775 ILCS 5/1-101, et seq.

Gross v. FBL Financial Services, Inc., 129 S. Ct. 2343, 557 U.S. 167, 174 L. Ed.2d 119 (2009)

Van Antwerp v. City of Peoria, 627 F. 3d 295 (7th Cir. 2010)

Michas v. Health Cost Controls of Illinois, 209 F. 3d 687 (7th Cir. 2000)

17:600 May a school district use age as a qualification for employment or promotion?

Federal law prohibits age-related discrimination in the hiring, promotion, and other conditions of employment for employees age 40 and over. A school board may attach age requirements to a job if it can show age is a bona fide occupational qualification.

29 U.S.C. 621 et seq.

29 C.F.R. 1625.1 et seq.

775 ILCS 5/1-101 et seq.

Cline v. General Dynamics Land Systems, Inc., 124 S. Ct. 1236, 540 U.S. 581, 157 L. Ed. 2d 1094 (2004)

17:610 May a school board adopt a mandatory employee retirement policy for employees who reach a specified age?

No. A mandatory retirement policy for any class of employees without demonstration of bona fide occupational qualification violates the federal Age Discrimination Act.

29 U.S.C. 623(f)(2)

29 C.F.R. 1625.1 et seq.

775 ILCS 5/1-101 et seq.

17:620 What is required to obtain a release to prevent an age discrimination claim?

If an employer attempts to resolve an age discrimination claim in return for a release from liability, the Older Workers Benefit Protection Act requires the employer give the employee a reasonable amount of time in which to consider his or her options and seven days after the signing of a release to reconsider.

29 U.S.C. 626 (f)(1)

Oubre v. Entergy Operations, Inc. 118 S. Ct. 838, 522 U.S. 422, 139 L. Ed. 2d 849 (1998) on rem. 136 F. 3d 1342 (5th Cir. 1999)

Kimel v. Florida Board of Regents, 120 S.Ct. 631, 528 U.S. 62, 145 L.Ed.2d 522, (2000)

17:625 May a collective bargaining agreement require that age discrimination claims be arbitrated?

The United States Supreme Court has held that the Age Discrimination in Employment Act (ADEA) does not preclude an employer and union from requiring the arbitration (rather than the litigation in a court of law) of ADEA claims. The court held that, as in any contractual negotiation, a union may agree to the inclusion of an arbitration provision in a collective bargaining agreement in return for other concessions from the employer. Courts generally may not interfere in this bargained-for exchange.

14 Penn Plaza LLC v. Pyett, 129 S. Ct. 24, 566 U.S. 247, 171 L. Ed. 2d 927 (2009)

DISCIPLINE AND DISMISSAL

17:630 Is an employee entitled to union representation of his or her choosing during an employer interview when the employer is considering disciplining the employee or investigating an incident that might reasonably lead to discipline of the employee?

An employee is entitled to knowledgeable representation, not necessarily the representation of his or her choosing. A representative with basic factual familiarity with the matter under investigation will suffice; the employer need not delay proceedings to wait for a union representative with training or prior experience representing employees in disciplinary matters.

Unless a collective bargaining agreement provides otherwise, the employee must request representation. An employee is not entitled to Miranda-like warnings. Generally, it is in the best interest of the employer to provide representation for the employee, whether or not the employee asks for it.

Speed District 802 v. Warning, 242 Ill. 2d 1292, 95 N.E. 2d 1069, 35 Ill. Dec. 241 (2011)

Hubbard v. Illinois State Labor Relations Board and Village of Streamwood, 293 Ill. App. 3d 1122, 718 N.E. 2d 1083, 241 Ill. Dec. 229 (1st Dist. 1997)

17:640 Are "last chance agreements" permissible?

In a last chance agreement, the employer agrees to withdraw the threat of discipline in exchange for the employee's agreement to refrain from future infractions and to give up the right to review in the event of future discipline, including the right to arbitration under a collectively bargained grievance procedure.

The presumption in favor of arbitrability is overcome only if the last chance agreement expressly excludes a particular grievance from arbitration. The last chance agreement must expressly exclude grievances based on the employee's guilt or innocence of the subsequent infraction and must expressly exclude grievances on the nature of the discipline to be effective to bar last chance grievances.

United Steelworkers of America v. Lukens Steel Co., 969 F. 2d 1468 (3rd Cir. 1992)

17:643 When are employees "similarly situated" for purposes of showing that an employee performed his or her job according to expectations, but experienced discrimination?

Similarly situated employees must be directly comparable in all material respects. The plaintiff must identify a comparison employee who held the same job, engaged in the same or comparable misconduct, did not have the characteristics the plaintiff claims as the reason for the discrimination, and was treated more favorably. Ordinarily a plaintiff cannot be similarly situated to an employee to whom he or she is subordinate.

Abuelyaman v. Illinois State University, 667 F. 3d 800 (7th Cir. 2011)

Patterson v. Indiana Newspapers, Inc., 589 F. 3d 357 (7th Cir. 2009)

17:645 What is an adverse employment action that results from discrimination?

The federal Seventh Circuit Court of Appeals has observed that such cases fall into three groups:

1) Those that involve the employee's current wealth such as compensation, fringe benefits, and financial terms of employment including termination;

2) The employee's career prospects, thus impacting the employee's future wealth; and

3) Changes to the employee's work conditions, including subjecting the employee to humiliating, degrading, unsafe, unhealthy, or otherwise significant negative alteration in the workplace environment.

Lucero v. Nettle Creek School Corporation, 566 F. 3d 720 (7th Cir. 2009)

17:647 When is an employer's reason for taking an employment action "pretextual"?

Pretext includes more than just faulty reasoning or mistaken judgment on the part of an employer; it is a lie; specifically a phony reason for some action. If the employer honestly believed the reason it proffers for its employment decision, the reason is not pretextual.

Scruggs v. Garst Seed Company, 587 F. 3d 832 (7th Cir. 2009)

17:650 May an employee be discharged for insubordination?

Insubordination can be grounds for dismissal of an employee. Insubordination is a willful or intentional disregard of the lawful and reasonable rules or instructions of the employer.

To determine whether a rule is reasonable, the courts will consider the rule's relationship to workplace efficiency, safety, or discipline; its clarity or precision; and the extent to which it infringes upon an employee's legally protected behavior. There must be some connection between the rule and employment, and a rule is not reasonable unless it provides guidelines that are or should be known by the employee.

Warnings or disciplinary measures contemplated for violations of the rule must be both explicit and specific to the conduct for which an employee would be reprimanded.

Board of Education of Round Lake Area Schools, Community Unit School District No. 116 v. The State Board of Education, John F. Rozner and Barbara Cohn, 292 Ill. App. 3d 101, 685 N.E. 2d 412, 226 Ill. Dec. 309 (2nd Dist. 1997)

Caterpillar, Inc. v. Fehrenbacher, 286 Ill. App. 3d 614, 676 N.E. 2d 710, 221 Ill. Dec. 907 (2nd Dist. 1997)

17:660 Can an employer discharge, refuse to hire, or otherwise discriminate against a woman because she has had or is contemplating having an abortion?

No.

42 U.S.C. 2000e et seq.

17:670 May a school board dismiss an employee who has been charged with a felony?

Persons charged with crimes are presumed to be innocent until proven guilty. Investigation, arrest, and/or indictment do not establish guilt. In order to dismiss a contractual employee for commission of a crime, the employer must provide the employee with requisite procedural and substantive due process.

The employer has the burden of proving the crime was committed and must show that the crime had a connection to the employee's employment sufficient to warrant dismissal.

Decatur Police Benevolent and Protective Association Labor Committee v. City of Decatur, 2012 IL App (4th) 110764, 968 N.E. 2d 749, 360 Ill. Dec. 256

McBroom v. Board of Education District No. 205, 144 Ill. App. 3d 463, 494 N.E. 2d 1191, 98 Ill. Dec. 864 (2nd Dist. 1986)

17:680 Must an employee charged with a felony be provided a pre-suspension hearing before he or she is suspended without pay?

When a school board must act quickly, or when it is impractical to provide pre-deprivation due process, post-deprivation due process is sufficient. If an important government interest is present and that interest is accompanied by a substantial assurance that the deprivation is not baseless or unwarranted, in limited cases demanding prompt action there is justification for postponing the opportunity to be heard until after the initial deprivation.

Gilbert v. Homar, 117 S. Ct. 1807, 520 U.S. 924, 138 L. Ed. 2d 120 (1997) on rem. 149 F. 3d 1164 (3rd Cir. 1998)

17:685 May a school board recover the salary it pays to an employee placed on paid administrative leave pending a criminal conviction?

In 2008, the General Assembly added a statute that theoretically allows a government employer to recover compensation and benefits paid to an employee during the time he or she is on voluntary or involuntary administrative leave pending a criminal conviction. Because the employer often has limited evidence of the employee's wrongdoing in such situations, it is common for the employer to place an accused employee on administrative leave pending the outcome of criminal proceedings.

Criminal proceedings can be protracted. A year or more from charge to sentencing is not uncommon, even in simple matters.

When the employer has evidence of wrongdoing sufficient to proceed to hearing, the better approach is to schedule a hearing and dismiss the employee before the criminal outcome. When the employer lacks evidence sufficient to conduct a hearing, a paid leave or allowing the employee to continue to work during the pendency of the criminal matter are the only appropriate choices.

The recovery of compensation and benefits is speculative because a former employee may not have the financial resources to repay compensation and benefits received during the leave, even if the employer obtains a judgment. Moreover, a dismissal of the employee must precede recovery and the costs associated with conduct of a dismissal hearing (particularly in the case of a tenured teacher) can be substantial. The change in the statute will, however, probably provide the employer with leverage to encourage resignation and settlement in most such cases.

5 ILCS 430/5-60

17:690 May a school board dismiss an employee who has been convicted of a crime?

The employer must demonstrate the crime had a connection to the employee's employment and was sufficiently serious to warrant dismissal. The employer must provide the employee with requisite substantive and procedural due process prior to dismissal. The employer should be mindful that the criminal records check statute specifies a list of offenses that disqualify employees from employment. School officials should be cautious when attempting to dismiss an employee for conviction of an offense other than a listed offense.

105 ILCS 5/21B-80

Reinhardt v. Board of Education of Alton Community Unit School District No. 11, Madison and Jersey Counties, 19 Ill. App. 3d 481, 311 N.E. 2d 710 (5th Dist. 1974) vac. on other grounds 61 Ill. 2d 101, 329 N.E. 2d 218 (1975)

17:700 May a school district discipline or dismiss an employee for actions for which the employee was criminally charged but acquitted?

The same set of facts may support both a criminal acquittal and defensible school discipline. The charges underlying a criminal case and those inherent in a disciplinary case, the elements of each case, and the burdens of proof for each are generally different.

Hall v. Board of Education of the City of Chicago, 227 Ill. App. 3d 560, 592 N.E. 2d 245, 169 Ill. Dec. 758 (1st Dist. 1992)

17:703 What is the limitations period for bringing a cause of action to challenge a dismissal?

A delay of longer than six months from the date of termination, or the date the plaintiff acquires knowledge of his or her right (whichever is later) to the filing of suit, is per se unreasonable and justifies dismissal on the ground of laches if the dismissed employee can show no reasonable excuse for the delay and the employer would suffer prejudice by having to pay both a replacement worker's salary and a successful plaintiff's back wages during the period of delay.

Usually, prejudice is demonstrated by an employer showing that a replacement worker has been hired. The limitation period appears to apply whether the employee seeks reinstatement or monetary damages or both and appears to apply to tenured teachers, non-tenured teachers, and in cases involving the dismissal of non-certified employees.

In cases where laches does not apply, the limitations period is five years.

735 ILCS 5/13-205

Bill v. Board of Education of Cicero School District 99, 351 Ill. App. 3d 47, 285 Ill. Dec. 784, 812 N.E. 2d 604 (1st Dist. 2004), pet. for leave to app. den. 211 Ill. 2d 571, 823 N.E. 2d 962, 291 Ill. Dec. 376 (2004)

17:707 What is the consequence for the school district if documents important to a discrimination case are missing?

An employer's destruction of or inability to produce a document, standing alone, does not warrant an inference that the document, if produced, would have contained information adverse to the employer's case. In order to draw an inference that missing documents contain information adverse to the employer, the plaintiff must show the employer intentionally destroyed the documents in bad faith. The crucial element in a spoliation claim is not the fact that the documents were destroyed, but that they were destroyed for the purpose of hiding adverse information.

Some courts have found that a spoliation sanction is appropriate only where a party has a duty to preserve evidence because it knew or should have known litigation was imminent. Before any document that may be significant to litigation is destroyed, school officials should investigate whether a records retention statute applies (Local Records Act or the School Student Records Act, for example).

Norman-Nunnery v. Madison Area Technical College, 625 F. 3d 422 (7th Cir. 2010)

17:710 What is attorney-client privilege?

Attorney-client privilege protects communications made in confidence by school officials to an attorney acting as an attorney for the purpose of obtaining legal advice. The privilege belongs to the client, although an attorney may assert the privilege on the client's behalf. To determine whether a communication falls within the protection of attorney-client privilege, the court decides whether legal advice of any kind was sought from a professional legal adviser acting as such and whether the communication was related to that purpose and made in confidence by the client.

Privilege is an especially important consideration when school officials seek advice fearing or concerned about a possible consequence during investigations and/or when preparing for trial or hearing.

Sandra T.E., et al. v. South Berwyn School District 100 and Sidley Austin LLP., 600 F. 3d. 612 (7th Cir. 2010)

OTHER EMPLOYMENT ISSUES

17:715 What is the difference between an independent contractor and an employee?

Knowing whether a person is an employee or an independent contractor is important because an employer must withhold income taxes, withhold and pay retirement system payments and Medicare taxes, and pay unemployment tax on wages paid to an employee. Withholdings are generally not required if the relationship is between an employer and an independent contractor.

The Internal Revenue Service uses no bright line test to determine whether a person is one or the other. But it does consider several easy to understand factors.

A person is an employee if the employer controls the work to be performed and how it will be performed, even if the employee has considerable freedom of action. If the employer controls such things as when and where to do the work, what tools or equipment to use, what workers to hire or to assist with the work, where to purchase supplies and services, what work must be performed by a specified individual, what order or sequence to follow when performing the work, the worker is an employee and not an independent contractor. The more detailed the employer's instructions are to the worker, the more likely he or she is an employee and not an independent contractor.

A written contract indicating that someone is an independent contractor will not be sufficient to establish that it is so. The relationship between the parties will be the determining factor.

www.irs.gov / Businesses / Small-Businesses-&-Self-employed / Independent-Contractor-Self-Employed-or-Employee

17:720 May a school board policy give employees a right to continuing employment or create employee-enforceable property rights?

A school board policy can give rise to constitutionally protected property rights. If, for example, the school board adopts a clearly worded "just cause" dismissal policy that contains a promise, and if the school board disseminates that policy to non-certified employees, and if the employees implicitly accept the policy, the policy is enforceable by the employee against the school district as if the policy were a contract between the employee and employer.

Hohmeier v. Leyden Community High Schools District 212, 954 F. 2d 461 (7th Cir. 1992)

Mitchell v. Jewel Food Stores, 142 Ill. 2d 152, 568 N.E. 2d 827, 136 Ill. Dec. 813 (1990)

Fumarolo v. Chicago Board of Education, 142 Ill. 2d 54, 566 N.E. 2d 1283, 153 Ill. Dec. 177 (1990)

Duldulao v. St. Mary of Nazareth Hospital Center, 115 Ill. 2d 482, 505 N.E. 2d 314, 106 Ill. Dec. 8 (1986)

17:725 Can a school board's policies create contracts that may be relied upon by employees and enforced against the school board?

A school board's rules, regulations, or policies when reasonably relied upon by employees may bind the school board. To rise to the level of a contract, the policy, rule, or regulation must contain a promise that is clear enough for an employee to believe it is an offer. The offer must be disseminated to the employee so the employee is aware of its contents and believes it is an offer. And the employee must accept the offer by beginning or continuing to work after learning of the offer.

Doyle v. Holy Cross Hospital, 186 Ill. 2d 104, 708 N.E. 2d 1140, 237 Ill. Dec. 100 (1999)

Condon v. American Telephone and Telegraph Company, Inc., 210 Ill. App. 3d 701, 569 N.E. 2d 518, 155 Ill. Dec. 337 (2nd Dist 1991) app. den. 141 Ill. 2d 537, 580 N.E. 2d 110, 162 Ill. Dec. 484 (1992)

Duldulao v. Saint Mary of Nazareth Hospital Center, 115 Ill. 2d 482, 505 N.E. 2d 314, 106 Ill. Dec. 8 (1987)

17:730 What control may a school board exercise with respect to employee "moonlighting?"

Unless a school board can demonstrate the employee's second job is negatively affecting his or her performance at school, the school board may not regulate or restrict the employee's outside activities.

Cook County College Teachers Union Local 1600 IFT, AFT, AFL-CIO v. Board of Trustees Community College District No. 505, Cook County, 134 Ill. App. 3d 489, 481 N.E. 2d 40, 89 Ill. Dec. 688 (1st Dist. 1985)

Kaufmann v. Board of Trustees Community Consolidated District 508, 522 F. Supp. 90 (N.D. Ill. 1981)

Meridith v. Board of Education of Community Unit School District No. 7, 7 Ill. App. 2d 477, 130 N.E. 2d 5 (3rd Dist. 1955)

Yuhas v. Libbey-Owens-Ford Company, 562 F. 2d 496 (7th Cir. 1976) cert. den. 98 S. Ct. 1510, 435 U.S. 934, 55 L. Ed. 2d 531 (1978)

17:740 Do statutes require report of attacks on school personnel?

Upon receipt of a written complaint from any school personnel, a superintendent must report any incident of battery committed against a teacher, teacher personnel, or administrative personnel to local law enforcement authorities immediately after the occurrence of the attack and to the Department of State Police's Illinois Uniform Crime Reporting Program no later than three days after the occurrence of the attack.

105 ILCS 5/10-21.7

17:750 May a school district require its employees to administer medication to students?

Neither teachers nor other non-administrative school employees, except certified school nurses and non-certificated registered professional nurses, can be required to administer medication to students. This prohibition includes uncertified school nurses. Volunteers may be sought, and certified school nurses may be required, to administer medication, but potential bargaining obligations should be considered in each case.

105 ILCS 5/10-22.21b

17:760 May a nurse refuse to administer prescribed medication if he or she believes the medication would be harmful to the child?

If the school district has a policy that allows the nurse to refuse to administer medication in excess of Physician's Desk Reference (PDR) recommendations, the nurse may refuse to administer medication that violates the terms of the policy.

Davis v. Francis Howell School District, 104 F. 3d 204 (8th Cir. 1998)

17:770 May schools conduct suspicionless searches of school employees?

The Fourth Amendment to the Constitution prohibits unreasonable searches and seizures.

The Sixth Circuit federal court of appeals has found that the need to assure drug-free teachers outweighs the teachers' privacy expectations because teachers serve in safety sensitive positions. The court permitted urinalysis drug testing for certain employees who were candidates for and attempting to transfer to a select group of positions. Random testing was not involved. The court's decision was narrow and any school district contemplating such searches should limit the tests to safety-sensitive positions. Such positions might include administrators, teachers, aides, secretaries, and bus drivers.

The Fifth Circuit has approved a policy requiring suspicionless random testing of custodial personnel.

A school district contemplating an employee search policy should consider bargaining implications and the possibility that while another federal appeals court may have approved such searches, the Seventh Circuit (which has jurisdiction over Illinois school districts) has not offered an opinion on the matter and may have a contrary view.

Hearn v. Savannah, Georgia Board of Public Education, 191 F. 3d 1329 (11th Cir. 1999)

Knox County Education Association v. Knox County Board of Education, 158 F. 3d 361 (6th Cir. 1998), cert. den. 120 S. Ct. 46, 528 U.S. 812, 145 L. Ed. 2d 41 (1999)

Aubrey v. School Board of Lafayette Parish, 92 F. 3d 316 (5th Cir. 1996) app. after rem. 148 F. 3d 559 (5th Cir. 1998)

17:775 Under what circumstances may an employer conduct a search of an employee's office, work area, or computer?

The Fourth Amendment prohibition of unreasonable search and seizure protects employees from unreasonable searches by employers or their agents. The search standard with respect to such searches is lower, however, than the criminal standard (probable cause).

An employee may plausibly claim a privacy right when the employee subjectively believed that the area searched was private and the employee's belief was reasonable in light of what a reasonable person would conclude about the privacy determination. A search is appropriate if the employer has reasonable suspicion that a rule, policy, or regulation was violated and the search that results is reasonable in scope.

A policy or rule announcing that an employee has no expectation of privacy on a work issued electronic device will not protect the employer from searches that are too broad, The safer approach is for the employer to identify and provide notice to employees as to where, when and under what circumstances employees should not have a reasonable expectation of privacy (as school officials often do when notices are placed in the student handbook that students should not have an expectation of privacy in their lockers) and to exercise extreme caution in the execution of such searches.

City of Ontario, California v. Quon, 130 S. Ct. 2619, 560 U.S.746, 177 L. Ed. 2d 216 (2010)

Biby v. Board of Regents, University of Nebraska at Lincoln, 419 F. 3d 845 (8th Cir. 2005)

United States v. Slanina, 283 F. 3d 670 (5th Cir. 2002), rem. on other grounds 123 S. Ct. 69, 537 U.S. 802, 154 L. Ed. 2d 3 (2001), aff'd on rem. 359 F. 3d 356 (5th Cir. 2004) cert. den.125 S. Ct. 288, 160 L. Ed. 2d 73 (2004)

United States v. Angevine, 281 F. 3d 1130 (10th Cir. 2002) cert. den. 123 S. Ct. 182, 537 U.S. 845, 154 L. Ed. 2d 71 (2002)

United States v. Simons, 206 F.3d 392 (4th Cir. 2000) cert. den., 122 S. Ct. 292, 534 U.S. 930 151 L. Ed. 2d 216 (2001)

O'Connor v. Ortega, 107 S. Ct. 1492, 480 U.S. 709, 94 L. Ed. 2d 714 (1987)

17:780 Are school employees subject to the State Gift Ban Act?

Yes. All school employees, both certificated and non-certificated, are subject to the gift ban provisions of the State Officials and Employees Ethics Act.

5 ILCS 430/10-10

17:790 Are school employees protected by the Illinois Civil Union law?

In 2011, Illinois enacted a civil union law that allows same-sex couples (and others) to apply for, certify, and register civil unions. The civil union law was not repealed when, in 2013, Illinois amended it Marriage and Dissolution of Marriage Act to legalize same-sex marriages effective June 1, 2014. Both a marriage between persons of the same sex, or a civil union, or a substantially similar legal relationship other than common law marriage, legally entered into in another jurisdiction, is recognized in Illinois.

750 ILCS 5/201 et. seq.

750 ILCS 75/1 et seq.

FAMILY AND MEDICAL LEAVE ACT

17:900 Who is eligible for Family and Medical Leave Act leave?

An eligible employee is one who has been employed for at least 12 months by the employer with respect to whom leave is properly requested under law and who has been employed for at least 1,250 hours of service with the employer during the previous 12-month period. It does not include any employee of an employer who is employed at a worksite at which the employer employs less than 50 employees if the total number of employees employed by that employer within 75 miles of that worksite is less than 50.

29 U.S.C. 2611(2)

Bailey v. Pregis Innovative Packaging, Inc., 800 F. 3d 748 (7th Cir. 2010)

Townsend-Taylor v. Ameritech Services, Inc., 523 F. 3d 815 (7th Cir. 2008)

Touvell v. Ohio Department of Mental Retardation and Developmental Disabilities, 422 F. 3d 392 (6th Cir. 2005)

Laro v. New Hampshire, 259 F. 3d 1 (1st Cir. 2001)

Sims v. University of Cincinnati, 219 F. 3d 559 (6th Cir. 2000)

17:903 What family situations entitle an eligible employee to access Family and Medical Leave Act leave?

An eligible employee is entitled to a total of 12 workweeks of leave during any 12-month period for one or more of the following:

1) The birth of a son or daughter of the employee and in order to care for such son or daughter;

2) The placement of a son or daughter with the employee for adoption or foster care;

3) In order to care for the spouse, or a son, daughter, or parent, of the employee, if such spouse, son, daughter, or parent has a serious health condition;

4) Because of a serious health condition that makes the employee unable to perform the functions of the position of such employee; or

5) Because of any qualifying exigency as determined by Department of Labor regulation arising out of the fact that the spouse, or a son, daughter, or parent of the employee is on active duty (or has been notified of an impending call or order to active duty) in the Armed Forces in support of a contingency operation. An eligible employee who is the spouse, son, daughter, parent, or next of kin of a covered service member is entitled to a total of 26 workweeks of leave during a 12-month period to care for the service member.

The leave described in 5) is only available during a single 12-month period. During the single 12-month period, an eligible employee shall be entitled to a combined total of 26 workweeks of leave under 1) and 3). Nothing in this paragraph limits the availability of leave under 1) during any other 12-month period. Leave for birth or adoption is available only during the first 12 months after the birth or adoption.

29 U.S.C. 2612(a)

820 ILCS 151/10

Touvell v. Ohio Department of Mental Retardation and Developmental Disabilities, 422 F. 3d 392 (6th Cir. 2005)

Laro v. New Hampshire, 259 F. 3d 1 (1st Cir. 2001)

Sims v. University of Cincinnati, 219 F. 3d 559 (6th Cir. 2000)

17:905 What must an employee prove to show his or her employer has interfered with the employee's right to access Family and Medical Leave Act (FMLA) leave?

To prove interference with FMLA entitlement, the employee must prove he or she was eligible for FMLA protections, his or her employer was covered by FMLA, the employee was entitled to FMLA leave, the employee provided sufficient notice to take the leave, and the employer denied the FMLA benefits to which the employee was entitled. An employee need not expressly assert rights under FMLA or even mention the FMLA; the employee need merely note that the leave is requested for a reason covered by FMLA.

29 C.F.R. 825.303(b)

Righi v. SMC Corp., 632 F. 3d 404 (7th Cir. 2011)

17:908 Under what circumstances may Family and Medical Leave Act leave be taken on an intermittent basis?

Family and Medical Leave Act (FMLA) leave may not be taken intermittently for childbirth or adoption or on a reduced leave schedule unless the employee and the employer otherwise agree. FMLA for a medical reason (care of another person with a serious health condition or personal serious health condition) may be taken intermittently or on a reduced leave schedule when medically necessary. The taking of leave intermittently or on a reduced leave schedule does not result in a reduction in the total amount of leave to which the employee is entitled under FMLA beyond the amount of leave actually taken

In any case in which an eligible employee employed principally in an instructional capacity by any such educational agency or school requests leave for a medical reason (care of another person with a serious health condition or personal serious health condition) that is foreseeable based on planned medical treatment and the employee would be on leave for greater than 20 percent of the total number of working days in the period during which the leave would extend, the school district may require the employee elect either to take leave for periods of a particular duration, not to exceed the duration of the planned medical treatment; or to transfer temporarily to an available alternative position offered by the employer for which the employee is qualified, and that has equivalent pay and benefits and better accommodates recurring periods of leave than the regular employment position of the employee.

29 U.S.C. 2612 (b)

29 U.S.C. 2618 (c)

Touvell v. Ohio Department of Mental Retardation and Developmental Disabilities, 422 F. 3d 392 (6th Cir. 2005)

Laro v. New Hampshire, 259 F. 3d 1 (1st Cir. 2001)

Sims v. University of Cincinnati, 219 F. 3d 559 (6th Cir. 2000)

17:910 May the employer transfer an employee who requests a Family and Medical Leave Act leave?

If an employee requests intermittent leave, or leave on a reduced leave schedule that is foreseeable based on planned medical treatment, the employer may require the employee to transfer temporarily to an available alternative position offered by the employer for which the employee is qualified and that has equivalent pay and benefits; and better accommodates recurring periods of leave than the regular employment position of the employee.

29 U.S.C. 2612(b)(2)

Touvell v. Ohio Department of Mental Retardation and Developmental Disabilities, 422 F. 3d 392 (6th Cir. 2005)

Laro v. New Hampshire, 259 F. 3d 1 (1st Cir. 2001)

Sims v. University of Cincinnati, 219 F. 3d 559 (6th Cir. 2000)

17:915 May an employer require an employee to substitute other available leave for Family and Medical Leave Act leave?

An eligible employee may elect, or an employer may require the employee, to substitute any of the accrued paid vacation leave, personal leave, or family leave of the employee for leave provided in any case except in the instance of serious personal health condition for any part of the 12-week period of such leave under such subsection.

An eligible employee may elect, or an employer may require the employee, to substitute any of the accrued paid vacation leave, personal leave, or medical or sick leave of the employee for leave for a medical reason (care of another person with a serious health condition or personal serious health condition) for any part of the 12-week period of such leave under such subsection.

29 U.S.C. 2612(d)(2)

Touvell v. Ohio Department of Mental Retardation and Developmental Disabilities, 422 F. 3d 392 (6th Cir. 2005)

Laro v. New Hampshire, 259 F. 3d 1 (1st Cir. 2001)

Sims v. University of Cincinnati, 219 F. 3d 559 (6th Cir. 2000)

17:920 What benefits is an employee entitled to on return from a Family and Medical Leave Act leave?

An employee is entitled to be restored to the position of employment held by the employee when the leave commenced; or to be restored to an equivalent position with equivalent employment benefits, pay, and other terms and conditions of employment. The taking of leave must not result in the loss of any employment benefit accrued prior to the date on which the leave commenced.

The law does not entitle an employee to the accrual of any seniority or employment benefits during any period of leave or any right, benefit, or position of employment other than any right, benefit, or position to which the employee would have been entitled had the employee not taken the leave.

29 U.S.C. 2614(a)

Daugherty v. Wabash Center, Inc., 577 F. 3d 747 (7th Cir. 2009)

Touvell v. Ohio Department of Mental Retardation and Developmental Disabilities, 422 F. 3d 392 (6th Cir. 2005)

Laro v. New Hampshire, 259 F. 3d 1 (1st Cir. 2001)

Sims v. University of Cincinnati, 219 F. 3d 559 (6th Cir. 2000)

17:925 Must an employer continue to pay health insurance premiums during Family and Medical Leave Act (FMLA) leave?

During any period that an eligible employee takes leave under the FMLA, the employer must maintain coverage under any "group health plan" for the duration of such leave at the level and under the conditions coverage would have been provided if the employee had continued in employment continuously for the duration of such leave.

The employer may recover the premium that the employer paid for maintaining coverage for the employee under such group health plan during any period of unpaid leave under FMLA if the employee fails to return from FMLA leave after the period of leave to which the employee is entitled has expired; and the employee fails to return to work for a reason other than the continuation, recurrence, or onset of a serious health condition that entitles the employee to leave for a medical reason (care of another person with a serious health condition or personal serious health condition); or other circumstances beyond the control of the employee.

29 U.S.C. 2614(c)

Touvell v. Ohio Department of Mental Retardation and Developmental Disabilities, 422 F. 3d 392 (6th Cir. 2005)

Laro v. New Hampshire, 259 F. 3d 1 (1st Cir. 2001)

Sims v. University of Cincinnati, 219 F. 3d 559 (6th Cir. 2000)

17:930 What special rules apply to Family and Medical Leave Act (FMLA) leave requests that are made near the end of a school term?

In the case of any eligible employee employed principally in an instructional capacity by any educational agency or school, if the eligible employee begins FMLA leave more than five weeks prior to the end of the academic term, the agency or school may require the employee to continue taking leave until the end of the term, if the leave is of at least three-weeks duration and the return to employment would occur during the three-week period before the end of the term.

If the eligible employee begins FMLA leave for any reason under the law except personal serious health condition during the period that commences five weeks prior to the end of the academic term, the agency or school may require the employee to continue taking leave until the end of the term, if the leave is of greater than two-weeks duration and the return to employment would occur during the two-week period before the end of the term.

If the eligible employee begins FMLA leave for any reason under the law except personal serious health condition during the period that commences three weeks prior to the end of the academic term and the duration of the leave is greater than five working days, the agency or school may require the employee to continue to take leave until the end of the term.

29 U.S.C. 2618(d)

Touvell v. Ohio Department of Mental Retardation and Developmental Disabilities, 422 F. 3d 392 (6th Cir. 2005)

Laro v. New Hampshire, 259 F. 3d 1 (1st Cir. 2001)

Sims v. University of Cincinnati, 219 F. 3d 559 (6th Cir. 2000)

17:935 What are the elements of retaliation under the Family and Medical Leave Act (FMLA)?

A plaintiff must have direct or circumstantial evidence of the employer's discriminatory motive or establish that after taking FMLA leave he or she was treated less favorably than other similarly situated employees who did not take FMLA leave, even though he or she was performing his or her job in a satisfactory manner. A plaintiff need not prove that retaliation was the only reason for the alleged discriminatory conduct, but may establish an FMLA retaliation claim by showing the protected conduct was a substantial or motivating factor in the employer's decision. A motivating factor does not amount to a but-for factor or the only factor, but is rather a factor that motivated the defendant's actions.

Direct evidence of retaliation generally involves an admission or statement by the decision-maker regarding his or her discriminatory intent. Circumstantial evidence allows the tier or fact to infer intentional discrimination by the decision maker.

Long v. Teachers' Retirement System of Illinois, 585 F. 3d 344 (7th Cir. 2009)

Lewis v. School District #70, 523 F. 3d 730 (7th Cir. 2008)

17:940 May an employee be dismissed for excessive absence after having taken or while eligible for leave under the Family and Medical Leave Act (FMLA)?

An employer is entitled to evaluate employee performance irrespective of leave use or entitlement. An employer may not dismiss or discipline an employee who has legitimate entitlement to leave by reason of use or entitlement to leave.

If an employee's performance is called into question at a time when the employee is suffering some FMLA use qualifying event, the employer should take great care that the school official who is evaluating performance is actually focused on failure to perform, not the employee's absences.

The employer should go to great lengths to attempt to accommodate absences by use of temporary transfer of the employee if feasible (particularly in the case of intermittent leave usage) or by hiring a temporary replacement for the employee during the period of absence (to take up workload.)

Daugherty v. Wabash Center, Inc., 577 F. 3d 747 (7th Cir. 2009)

Lewis v. School District #70, 523 F. 3d 730 (7th Cir. 2008)

17:945 Is an employee who is abusing drugs or alcohol entitled to FMLA leave?

Substance abuse can qualify as a serious health condition within the meaning of the Family and Medical Leave Act (FMLA) if treatment for substance abuse involves in-patient care or continuing treatment by a health care provider. Under the Americans with Disabilities Act, an employer may hold an employee who is an alcoholic to the same qualification standards for employment or job performance and behavior that the employer holds other employees, even if any unsatisfactory performance or behavior is related to the alcoholism of the employee.

42 U.S.C. 1214(c)(4)

29 C.F.R. 825.114(a)

29 C.F.R. 825.114(d)

Ames v. Home Depot, 629 F. 3d 665 (7th Cir. 2011)

17:950 When an employee returns to work after an FMLA leave, must he or she be returned to the same position held when the leave began?

An employee on Family and Medical Leave Act (FMLA) leave has the right to be restored to the same or an equivalent position that the employee had before he or she took the leave. An equivalent position is one with equivalent "benefits, pay and other terms and conditions of employment." If the employee cannot perform an essential function of his or her original position because of a physical or mental condition, the employee has no right to restoration to a different position under FMLA. There is no such thing as FMLA "light duty."

29 U.S.C. 2614(a)(1)

29 C.F.R. 825.214(b)

James v. Hyatt Regency Chicago, 707 F. 3d 775 (7th Cir. 2013)

17:960 May an employee be dismissed while using FMLA leave?

The Family and Medical Leave Act (FMLA) does not prohibit an employer from dismissing an employee when reasons, apart from FMLA leave, support that action. But because of the combination of issues (FMLA and independent reasons for discharge), school officials should be especially careful in documenting the facts supporting dismissal.

Weaver v. Board of Education of the City of Chicago, 2017 IL App. (1st) 161764, 76 N.E. 3d 811, 412 Ill. Dec. 745

18: TEACHER DISMISSAL FOR CAUSE

DISMISSAL OF THE PROBATIONARY TEACHER

18:10 What steps must be taken when a school district intends not to renew the contract of probationary teacher not in his or her final year of probation?

The probationary period changed with a 1998 amendment to the School Code that increased the probationary period from two to four years and again in 2011 with the enactment of Senate Bill 7 (P.A. 97-08). The probationary period remained four years for all teachers in all school districts until the Performance Evaluation Reform Act (PERA, P.A. 96-861) implementation date (2015 for some school districts and 2016 for most school districts).

After the PERA implementation date, the probationary period is either two, three, or four years, depending upon the probationary teacher's evaluation outcomes and after consideration of certain other factors contained in the statute.

Under any of the applicable variations of the statute to dismiss a teacher who is not in his or her final year of probationary employment, the school district must (a) fully comply with its evaluation plan and collectively bargained evaluation procedure, if applicable, and (b) give written notice of dismissal by certified mail, return receipt requested. The notice must be received by the teacher at least 45 days before the end of the school term. If a school board fails to give such notice, the teacher is re-employed for the following school term.

Often, collective bargaining agreements, policies, and/or evaluation plans have different notice requirements from that provided in the statute. The employer should be careful to meet all relevant notice requirements.

While no case law or statute requires that a non-tenured teacher's evaluation must evidence the defects that underlie the dismissal notice, to avoid litigation (and cost of defense), the employer should be sure the teacher has ample warning that the teacher's job is in jeopardy.

Litigation often occurs because the teacher or the union views the dismissal as "unfair." Administrators should not assume that there will be no consequence if a non-tenured teacher is dismissed without supporting evidence and warning to the teacher of his or her deficiencies. The further the teacher is into the probationary period, the greater such concerns become. Warning ideally will be evidenced in evaluations or written warnings delivered to the teacher sufficiently early in the school year that the teacher has a reasonable opportunity to correct the noted deficiencies.

105 ILCS 5/24-11

Wood v. North Wamac School District No. 186, 386 Ill. App. 3d 874, 899 N.E. 2d 578, 326 Ill. Dec. 361 (5th Dist. 2008)

Bill v. Board of Education of Cicero School District 99, 351 Ill. App. 3d 47, 285 Ill. Dec. 784, 812 N.E. 2d 604 (1st Dist. 2004), pet. for leave to app. den. 211 Ill. 2d 571, 823 N.E. 2d 962, 291 Ill. Dec. 376 (2004)

Cler v. Akers, et al., No. 02-2071 (C.D. Ill. 2002)

Hoyleton Education Association and Hoyleton Community Consolidated School District No. 29, 6 PERI 1027 (IELRB Hearing Officer, February 8, 1990)

Board of Education of Community Unit School District No. 1 v. Compton, 123 Ill. 2d 216, 526 N.E. 2d 149, 122 Ill. Dec. 9 (1988)

18:20 What steps must be taken when a school district intends not to renew the contract of a final-year probationary teacher?

The Performance Evaluation Reform Act (PERA, P.A. 96-861) changed the length of probationary service. But until a school district's PERA implementation date (2015 for some school districts and 2016 for most school districts), probationary service remained four years. After the PERA implementation date, the probationary period is either two, three, or four years depending upon the probationary teacher's evaluation outcomes and after consideration of certain other factors contained in the statute.

To dismiss a teacher in his or her final probationary year at the end of a school term, the school district must have fully complied with its evaluation plan and collectively bargained evaluation procedure, if applicable.

No later than 45 days before the end of the final probationary school term, the final year probationary teacher must receive written notice of dismissal from the school board. Often, collective bargaining agreements, policies, and/or evaluation plans have different notice requirements from that provided in the statute. The employer should be careful to meet all relevant notice requirements. The notice must state the specific reason for the dismissal, and it must be delivered by certified mail, return receipt requested. If a school board fails to give such notice, the teacher is re-employed for the following school term.

105 ILCS 5/24-11

Wood v. North Wamac School District No. 186, 386 Ill. App. 3d 874, 899 N.E. 2d 578, 326 Ill. Dec.361 (5th Dist. 2008)

People ex rel. Head v. Board of Education of Thornton Fractional South High School District No. 215, 95 Ill. App. 3d 78, 419 N.E. 2d 505, 50 Ill. Dec. 397 (1st Dist. 1981)

Wade v. Granite City Community Unit School District No. 9, Madison County, 71 Ill. App. 2d 34, 218 N.E. 2d 19 (5th Dist. 1966)

18:25 May a non-tenured teacher file a grievance alleging violation of a "just cause" provision in the collective bargaining agreement to challenge his or her dismissal?

A "just cause" provision is one that requires that an employee's discipline be "fair" or for "just cause." When a provision of a collective bargaining agreement is in violation of, inconsistent with, or in conflict with an Illinois statute, it may not be "implemented in an arbitration award." A just cause provision in a collective bargaining agreement is inconsistent with and conflicts with the Illinois statutes that govern the dismissal of tenured and non-tenured teachers.

Non-tenured teachers have no specific right to retention. The Cobden court held: "Requiring [a school district] to fully document the reasons for not renewing employment of a probationary teacher would infringe on the [school district's] duty to ensure that only the most qualified teachers are selected for continued employment after a probationary 'try out.'"

Defending a non-tenure teacher dismissal challenge is time-consuming and expensive, and such challenges are not uncommon. School officials should be careful to document teacher deficiencies prior to discharge to reduce the risk of having to defend.

105 ILCS 5/10-22.4

105 ILCS 5/24-11

115 ILCS 5/10(b)

Cobden Unit School District No. 17 v. Illinois Educational Labor Relations Board, 2012 IL App (1st) 10716, 966 N.E. 2d 503, 359 Ill. Dec. 182

Niles Township High School District No. 219 v. Illinois Educational Labor Relations Board, 379 Ill. App. 3d 22, 883 N.E. 2d. 29, 318 Ill. Dec. 195 (1st Dist. 2007)

Board of Education of Rockford School District No. 205, v. The Illinois Educational Labor Relations Board, 165 Ill. 2d 80, 649 N.E. 2d 369, 208 Ill. Dec. 313 (1995)

Midwest Central Education Association v. Illinois Educational Labor Relations Board, et al., 277 Ill. App. 3d 440, 660 N.E. 2d 151, 213 Ill. Dec. 984 (1st Dist. 1995)

18:30 Must a notice to remedy deficiencies be issued or a remediation plan be instituted before a probationary employee is dismissed?

The remediation plan requirements of Section 24A of the School Code apply to tenured employees only. If a school board seeks to dismiss a probationary employee at the end of a school term, no notice to remedy is necessary unless otherwise required by school board policy or as collectively bargained.

A notice to remedy may be necessary under certain circumstances if dismissal is sought during a school term.

105 ILCS 5/24-11

105 ILCS 5/24A-1 et seq.

Cobden Unit School District No. 17 v. Illinois Educational Labor Relations Board, 2012 IL App (1st) 10716, 966 N.E. 2d 503, 359 Ill. Dec. 182

18:40 May a school board dismiss a non-tenured (probationary) teacher during a school term?

A school board may dismiss a non-tenured teacher during the school year. However, such teachers are contractual employees of the school district and have a "property right" to employment for the term of their contracts. To dismiss such an employee the school board has the burden to prove breach of contract and must accord the employee substantive and procedural due process.

Board of Regents of State Colleges v. Roth, 92 S. Ct. 2701, 408 U.S. 564, 33 L. Ed. 2d 548 (1972)

18:50 Is a probationary teacher entitled to a hearing on the reasons for dismissal if his or her contract is not being renewed for the following year?

The School Code does not require a hearing for a probationary teacher to examine the reasons for dismissal. When a school board has fully complied with statutory and local contract requirements, rules, and regulations, no hearing is required unless the reasons for the dismissal raise constitutional issues with respect to the teacher's dismissal.

Cobden Unit School District No. 17 v. Illinois Educational Labor Relations Board, 2012 IL App (1st) 10716, 966 N.E. 2d 503, 359 Ill. Dec. 182

Howard v. Board of Education of Freeport School District No. 145, 160 Ill. App. 3d 309, 513 N.E. 2d 545, 112 Ill. Dec. 131 (2nd Dist. 1987)

Newborn v. Morrison, 440 F. Supp. 623 (N.D. Ill. 1977)

Mt. Healthy City School District Board of Education v. Doyle, 97 S. Ct. 568, 429 U.S. 274, 50 L. Ed. 2d 471 (1977) app. after rem. 670 F. 2d 59 (6th Cir. 1982)

Bishop v. Wood, 96 S. Ct. 2074, 426 U.S. 341, 48 L. Ed. 2d 864 (1976)

Board of Regents of State Colleges v. Roth, 92 S. Ct. 2701, 408 U.S. 564, 33 L. Ed. 2d 548 (1972)

18:60 Under what circumstances does a school board infringe on a teacher's constitutionally protected liberty interests so as to give rise to due process?

A teacher's constitutionally protected liberty interests may be infringed when (a) the cause for dismissal does serious damage to the person's standing and associations in the community, or (b) the cause for dismissal creates a stigma or inability to take advantage of future employment opportunities.

If a school board infringes on a teacher's constitutionally protected liberty interests in dismissal proceedings, the teacher will be entitled to certain due process guarantees including, upon demand by the teacher, a name-clearing hearing.

Zellner v. Herrick, 639 F. 3d 371 (7th Cir. 2011)

Batagiannis v. West Lafayette Community School Corporation, 454 F. 3d 738 (7th Cir. 2006)

Strasburger v. Board of Education Hardin County Community Unit School District No. 1, et al., 143 F. 3d 351 (7th Cir. 1998)

Austin v. Board of Education of Georgetown Community Unit School District No. 3 of Vermilion County, Illinois, 562 F. 2d 446 (7th Cir. 1977)

Bishop v. Wood, 96 S. Ct. 2074, 426 U.S. 341, 48 L. Ed. 2d 864 (1976)

Miller v. School District No. 167, Cook County, Illinois, 354 F. Supp. 922 (N.D. Ill. 1973), aff'd. on other grounds 495 F. 2d 658, reh. den. 500 F. 2d 711 (7th Cir. 1974)

Hostrop v. Board of Junior College District 515, Cook and Will Counties and State of Illinois, 471 F. 2d 488 (7th Cir. 1972) cert. den. 93 S. Ct. 2150, 411 U.S. 967, 36 L. Ed. 2d 688 (1973) on rem. 399 F. Supp. 609, aff'd. in part, rev. in part 523 F. 2d 569, cert. den. 96 S. Ct. 1748, 425 U.S. 963, 48 L. Ed. 2d 208 (1974)

Board of Regents of State Colleges v. Roth, 92 S. Ct. 2701, 408 U.S. 564, 33 L. Ed. 2d 548 (1972)

Perry v. Sindermann, 92 S. Ct. 2694, 408 U.S. 593, 33 L. Ed. 2d 570 (1972)

DISMISSAL OF THE TENURED TEACHER

18:70 May a tenured teacher be fired?

A tenured teacher may be dismissed for commission of a dismissible offense as defined by statute, provided however the school board first must comply with the procedural requirements of its collective bargaining agreement and must provide the requisite statutory substantive and procedural due process.

105 ILCS 5/10-22.4

105 ILCS 5/24-12

Board of Trustees of Community College District No. 508 v. Cook County College Teachers Union Local 1600, AFT, IFT, AFL-CIO, 167 Ill. App. 3d 998, 522 N.E. 2d 93, 118 Ill. Dec. 638 (1st Dist. 1987)

Chicago Board of Education v. Payne, 102 Ill. App. 3d 741, 430 N.E. 2d 310, 58 Ill. Dec. 368 (1st Dist. 1981)

Lowe v. Board of Education of City of Chicago, 76 Ill. App. 3d 348, 395 N.E. 2d 59, 32 Ill. Dec. 122 (1st Dist. 1979)

Fender v. School District No. 25, Arlington Heights, Cook County, 37 Ill. App. 3d 736, 347 N.E. 2d 270 (1st Dist. 1976)

Gould v. Board of Education of Ashley Community Consolidated School District No. 15 of Washington County, 32 Ill. App. 3d 808, 336 N.E. 2d 69 (5th Dist. 1975)

18:72 What is the likelihood of the repeal of the tenure law?

In addition to being politically improbable, a repeal of the tenure law would probably affect only teachers who had not yet acquired tenure and would not serve to remove tenure protections from teachers who already have them. The practical effect would be that unions would attempt to bargain the equivalent of tenure contract by contract.

Indiana ex rel. Anderson v. Brant, 58 S. Ct. 443, 303 U.S. 95, 82 L. Ed. 685 (1938)

18:80 How many school board votes are required to dismiss a tenured teacher?

A motion to dismiss a tenured teacher for cause requires a majority vote of all the members of the school board to carry.

105 ILCS 5/24-12

18:90 To what kind of notice of causes for dismissal is a tenured teacher entitled?

A tenured teacher is entitled to a dismissal notice, or bill of particulars, that states both the cause or causes for the dismissal and the charge or charges supporting the dismissal action. The notice must be sufficiently precise in order that the teacher is fully informed of the causes and charges and is able to prepare a defense.

105 ILCS 5/10-22.4

105 ILCS 5/24-12

Carrao v. Board of Education, City of Chicago, 46 Ill. App. 3d 33, 360 N.E. 2d 536, 4 Ill. Dec. 600 (1st Dist. 1977)

Reinhardt v. Board of Education of Alton Community Unit School District No. 11, 61 Ill. 2d 101, 329 N.E. 2d 218 (1975)

Wade v. Granite City Community Unit School District No. 9, Madison County, 71 Ill. App. 2d 34, 218 N.E. 2d 19 (5th Dist. 1966)

Donahoo v. Board of Education of School District No. 303 Moultrie County, 346 Ill. App. 241, 104 N.E. 2d 833 (3rd Dist. 1952), rev. 413 Ill. 422, 109 N.E. 2d 787 (1952)

CAUSES FOR DISMISSAL

18:100 What causes will support the dismissal of a tenured teacher?

A school board may dismiss a tenured teacher for incompetency, cruelty, negligence, immorality, or other sufficient cause. A teacher may also be dismissed on the basis of performance, and may be dismissed whenever, in the school board's opinion, he or she is not qualified to teach or whenever the interests of the schools require it.

Temporary mental or physical incapacity to perform teaching duties, as found by a medical examination, is not a cause for dismissal.

To support a tenured teacher dismissal, a school board must prove a serious infraction or series of infractions; must comply with all of its own internal rules, regulations, and policies regarding dismissal, including relevant contract provisions and its evaluation plan; must comply with all relevant statutory requirements; and must provide the teacher with requisite substantive and procedural due process.

105 ILCS 5/10-22.4

105 ILCS 5/24-12

Wells v. Board of Education of Community Consolidated School District No. 64, Cook County, 85 Ill. App. 2d 312, 230 N.E. 2d 6 (1st Dist. 1967)

18:110 What is required to dismiss a tenured teacher for incompetency?

Incompetency is a remediable offense. A school board is required to attempt to cure incompetency by evaluation and the adoption of a remediation plan prior to dismissal.

105 ILCS 5/10-22.4

105 ILCS 5/24-12

105 ILCS 5/24A-1 et seq.

18:120 What is cruelty?

Cruelty is the intentional or malicious infliction of physical or mental suffering upon other persons. Cruelty as a cause of tenured teacher dismissal may be either remediable or irremediable depending upon its seriousness.

Lowe v. Board of Education, City of Chicago, 76 Ill. App. 3d 148, 395 N.E. 2d 59, 32 Ill. Dec. 112 (1st Dist. 1979)

Welch v. Board of Education of Bement Community Unit School District No. 5 of Piatt County, 45 Ill. App. 3d 35, 358 N.E. 2d 354, 3 Ill. Dec. 679 (4th Dist. 1977)

Rolando v. School Directors of District No. 125, 44 Ill. App. 3d 658, 358 N.E. 2d 945, 3 Ill. Dec. 402 (3rd Dist. 1976)

18:130 What is negligence?

Negligence is failing to do something a reasonable person would ordinarily do under a particular set of circumstances or doing something that a reasonable and prudent person would ordinarily not do under a given set of circumstances and conditions. Negligence as a cause for dismissal of a tenured teacher may be either remediable or irremediable depending on the circumstances and degree of negligence.

105 ILCS 5/10-22.4

105 ILCS 5/24-12

Board of Education of Niles Township High School District No. 219 Cook County v. Epstein, 72 Ill. App. 3d 723, 391 N.E. 2d 114, 28 Ill. Dec. 915 (1st Dist. 1979)

18:140 What is immorality?

Immorality is behavior that is inimical to the public welfare according to the standards of society. It is "shameless conduct showing moral indifference to the opinions of the good and respectable members of the community." A dismissal for immorality will not be sustained unless the school board can prove the conduct of the teacher has had some serious negative impact on the teacher's relationship with students, effectiveness in the classroom, relationship with teacher's superiors, or the operation of a school district. Dismissals for immorality often raise constitutional questions.

105 ILCS 5/10-22.4

105 ILCS 5/24-12

Jackson v. Board of Education of the City of Chicago, 2016 IL App (1st) 141388, 53 N.E. 3d 381, 403 Ill. Dec. 327

Board of Education of Tonica Community Unit School District No. 360, LaSalle County v. Sickley, 133 Ill. App. 3d 921, 479 N.E. 2d 1142, 89 Ill. Dec. 136 (3rd Dist. 1985)

Reinhardt v. Board of Education of Alton Community Unit School District No. 11, 61 Ill. 2d 101, 329 N.E. 2d 218 (1975)

Lombardo v. Board of Education School District No. 27, Cook County, 100 Ill. App. 2d 108, 241 N.E. 2d 495 (1st Dist. 1968)

18:150 What is insubordination?

Insubordination is willful disregard of implied or specific legitimate directives or an attitude so defiant as to be equivalent. Insubordination is usually a remediable offense and requires legally sufficient warning prior to dismissal.

Christopherson v. Spring Valley Elementary School District, 90 Ill. App. 3d 460, 413 N.E. 2d 199, 45 Ill. Dec. 866 (3rd Dist. 1980)

Allione v. Board of Education, South Fork Community High School District No. 310, Christian County, 29 Ill. App. 2d 261, 173 N.E. 2d 13 (3rd Dist. 1961)

Beilan v. Board of Public Education of Philadelphia, 78 S. Ct. 1317, 357 U.S. 399, 2 L. Ed. 2d 1414 (1958)

18:160 May a tenured teacher be dismissed for conduct that occurs away from school and during non-school hours?

To dismiss a tenured teacher for behavior that occurs away from school and during non-school hours, the school board must be able to demonstrate that the conduct had a sufficiently serious negative impact on a legitimate school-related objective to warrant dismissal of the teacher.

A teacher has constitutional rights that protect the teacher from school board interference in private non-school-related conduct. The private deportment of a teacher is properly of concern to a school board only when the behavior of the teacher interferes with the effectiveness of the teacher as a teacher in the school district or with the overall operation of the school district.

Carrao v. Board of Education, City of Chicago, 46 Ill. App. 3d 33, 360 N.E. 2d 536, 4 Ill. Dec. 600 (1st Dist. 1977)

Reinhardt v. Board of Education of Alton Community Unit School District No. 11, 61 Ill. 2d 101, 329 N.E. 2d 218 (1975)

18:170 May a school board dismiss a tenured teacher for conduct that occurred during the teacher's supervision of extracurricular activities?

The teacher may be dismissed if the conduct is sufficiently serious to support dismissal and is either irremediable or repeated after legally sufficient warning. Dismissal requires full procedural compliance with applicable statutes and collectively bargained provisions.

105 ILCS 5/10-22.4

18:175 May a tenured teacher be dismissed for conduct that prevents him or her from functioning as a role model to students?

A teacher's actions are subject to much greater scrutiny than those of the average person. A tenured teacher may be dismissed without a prior warning when it can be shown that the teacher's conduct:

1) Has significantly harmed his or her reputation and credibility;

2) Has sufficiently damaged the respect and esteem in which the teacher is held by his or her co-workers and other members of the school community;

3) When the teacher can no longer serve as a credible role model for students; and

4) When the conduct giving rise to the dismissal could not have been corrected had the teacher been warned.

McCullough v. Illinois State Board of Education, 204 Ill. App. 3d 1082, 562 N.E. 2d 1233, 150 Ill. Dec. 430 (5th Dist. 1990)

McBroom v. Board of Education District No. 205, 144 Ill. App. 3d 463, 494 N.E. 2d 1191, 98 Ill. Dec. 864 (2nd Dist. 1986)

Chicago Board of Education v. Payne, 102 Ill. App. 3d 741, 430 N.E. 2d 310, 58 Ill. Dec. 368 (1st Dist. 1981)

Scott v. Board of Education, 20 Ill. App. 2d 292, 156 N.E. 2d 1 (4th Dist. 1959)

REMEDIABILITY

18:180 What is irremediable conduct?

Conduct is irremediable when the damage that has been done to students, faculty, or the school is irreparable. Consideration is also given to whether or not the conduct could have been corrected had the employee been warned.

Board of Education of City of Chicago v. Harris, 218 Ill. App. 3d 1017, 578 N.E. 2d 1244, 161 Ill. Dec. 598 (1st Dist. 1991)

McCutcheon v. Board of Education, City of Chicago, 94 Ill. App. 3d 993, 419 N.E. 2d 451, 50 Ill. Dec. 343 (1st Dist. 1981)

Board of Education of School District No. 131 v. Illinois State Board of Education, 82 Ill. App. 3d 820, 403 N.E. 2d 277, 38 Ill. Dec. 189 (2nd Dist. 1980)

Waller v. Board of Education Century School District No. 100, 13 Ill. App. 3d 1056, 302 N.E. 2d 190 (5th Dist. 1973)

18:190 Who determines whether a conduct giving rise to discipline is remediable or irremediable?

A school board is empowered to make an initial determination of the remediability or irremediability of conduct. The school board's decision is subject to review by a hearing officer in a dismissal case and in some cases reviewable in other tribunals with respect to other forms of discipline.

The determination of the remediability of any particular conduct is important in deciding whether the employee requires legally sufficient warning before dismissal. If conduct is determined to be irremediable, no such warning is necessary before dismissal.

105 ILCS 5/24-12

105 ILCS 5/24-16.5

105 ILCS 5/24A-1 et seq.

Beggs v. The Board of Education of Murphysboro Community Unit School District No. 186, 2016 IL 120236, 45 N.E. 3d 722, 399 Ill. Dec. 51

Gilliland v. Board of Education of Pleasant View Consolidated School District No. 622 of Tazewell County, 67 Ill. 2d 143, 365 N.E. 2d 322, 8 Ill. Dec. 84 (1977)

Welch v. Board of Education of Bement Community Unit School District No. 5 of Piatt County, 45 Ill. App. 3d 35, 358 N.E. 2d 354, 3 Ill. Dec. 679 (4th Dist. 1977)

Fender v. School District No. 25, Arlington Heights, 37 Ill. App. 3d 736 (1st Dist. 1976)

Everett v. Board of Education of District 201, Cook County, 22 Ill. App. 3d 594, 317 N.E. 2d 753 (1st Dist. 1974)

Waller v. Board of Education Century School District No. 100, 13 Ill. App. 3d 1056, 302 N.E. 2d 190 (5th Dist. 1973)

Miller v. Board of Education, School District No. 132, Cook County, 51 Ill. App. 2d 20, 240 N.E. 2d 471 (1st Dist. 1964)

18:195 Can conduct that is remediable become irremediable if warning would not cure the defect?

Whether a cause for dismissal is irremediable is a question of fact. When an employee proclaims that he or she will not abide by and openly challenges an appropriate direction from the school board and when the employee is told that he or she risks dismissal if he or she defies the board and when the employee does what he or she threatened anyway, the employee makes remediable conduct irremediable. Courts have held that an open challenge to the authority of a school board is behavior that cannot be changed by warning.

Open defiance is to be distinguished from an allegation that the employee knew or should have known that some conduct was inappropriate.

Board of Education of Joliet Township High School District No. 204 v. Betts, 331 Ill. App. 3d 131, 770 N.E. 2d 711, 264 Ill. Dec. 406 (3rd Dist. 2002)

Christopherson v. Spring Valley Elementary School District, 90 Ill. App. 3d 460, 413 N.E. 2d 199, 45 Ill. Dec. 866 (3rd Dist. 1980)

Yuen v. Board of Education of Community Unit School District No. 46, Kane County, 77 Ill. App. 2d 353, 222 N.E. 2d 570 (3rd Dist. 1966)

18:200 Which party has the burden of proving irremediability?

The school board has the burden of proving that conduct leading to dismissal is not remediable.

Gilliland v. Board of Education of Pleasant View Consolidated School District No. 622 of Tazewell County, 67 Ill. 2d 143, 365 N.E. 2d 322, 8 Ill. Dec. 84 (1977)

18:210 If a tenured teacher's conduct is properly determined to be irremediable, must a school board issue a warning (notice to remedy) before dismissal?

No. A notice to remedy is essential only where the teacher's conduct is determined to be remediable.

Lowe v. Board of Education, City of Chicago, 76 Ill. App. 3d 348, 395 N.E. 2d 59, 32 Ill. Dec. 112 (1st Dist. 1979)

Welch v. Board of Education of Bement Community Unit School District No. 5 of Piatt County, 45 Ill. App. 3d 35, 358 N.E. 2d 354, 3 Ill. Dec. 679 (4th Dist. 1977)

Wells v. Board of Education of Community Consolidated School District No. 64, Cook County, 85 Ill. App. 2d 312, 230 N.E. 2d 6 (1st Dist. 1967)

18:220 If a school board determines a teacher's behavior is improper and remediable but not related to classroom competence, what warning is required prior to dismissal?

If a school board has determined a tenured teacher's improper but remediable behavior is related to classroom competence, the remediation requirements of Section 24A of the School Code apply. If the behavior is not related to classroom competence, or is related to the classroom competence of a non-tenured teacher whom the school board is seeking to dismiss before the end of the school term, the school board must invoke the following procedures prior to dismissal:

1) The teacher must be provided with a notice to remedy the behavior in question;

2) The notice must specifically identify the objectionable behavior and state that if not remedied the teacher may be subject to dismissal;

3) The notice must provide the teacher with reasonably specific corrective action the school board requires the teacher to undertake if appropriate; and

4) The notice must identify a reasonable period of time in which the school board expects the corrective action to be successfully completed if appropriate.

105 ILCS 5/24-12

Grissom v. Board of Education of Buckley Loda Community School District No. 8, 75 Ill. App. 2d 314, 388 N.E. 2d 398, 26 Ill. Dec. 683 (4th Dist. 1979)

Gilliland v. Board of Education of Pleasant View Consolidated School District No. 622 of Tazewell County, 67 Ill. 2d 143, 365 N.E. 2d 322, 8 Ill. Dec. 84 (1977)

Paprocki v. Board of Education of McHenry Community High School District No. 156, 31 Ill. App. 3d 112, 334 N.E. 2d 841 (2nd Dist. 1975)

Everett v. Board of Education of District 201, Cook County, 22 Ill. App. 3d 594, 317 N.E. 2d 753 (1st Dist. 1974)

Waller v. Board of Education Century School District No. 100, 13 Ill. App. 3d 1056, 302 N.E. 2d 190 (5th Dist. 1973)

Wells v. Board of Education of Community Consolidated School District No. 64, Cook County, 85 Ill. App. 2d 312, 230 N.E. 2d 6 (1st Dist. 1967)

Werner v. Community Unit School District No. 4, Marshall County, 40 Ill. App. 491, 190 N.E. 2d 184 (2nd Dist. 1963)

18:230 What is a notice to remedy?

A notice to remedy is a legally sufficient written warning issued by a school board and properly delivered to an employee that warns the employee of improper conduct and the consequences thereof.

105 ILCS 5/24-12

Paprocki v. Board of Education of McHenry Community High School District No. 156, 31 Ill. App. 3d 112, 334 N.E. 2d 841 (2nd Dist. 1975)

18:235 May a teacher file a grievance challenging a notice to remedy?

When a provision of a collective bargaining agreement is in violation of, inconsistent with, or in conflict with an Illinois statute it may not be "implemented in an arbitration award." The procedural requirements in the law for dismissal of a teacher incorporate the school board's duty to make the initial determination of whether a teacher's conduct is remediable. Therefore, a teacher may not challenge the employer's determination to issue a notice to remedy by use of the grievance procedure.

105 ILCS 5/10-22.4

105 ILCS 5/24-12

115 ILCS 5/10(b)

Board of Education of Rockford School District No. 205, v. The Illinois Educational Labor Relations Board, 165 Ill. 2d 80, 649 N.E. 2d 369, 208 Ill. Dec. 313 (1995)

18:240 How much time must teachers be given to correct remediable deficiencies?

A school board must give a teacher a reasonable amount of time to remedy. The amount of time that is necessary depends upon the deficiencies to be remedied.

105 ILCS 5/24-12

Board of Education of School District No. 131 v. Illinois State Board of Education, 82 Ill. App. 3d 820, 403 N.E. 2d 277, 38 Ill. Dec. 189 (2nd Dist. 1980)

Litin v. Board of Education of City of Chicago, 72 Ill. App. 3d 889, 391 N.E. 2d 62, 28 Ill. Dec. 863 (1st Dist. 1979)

Aulwurm v. Board of Education of Murphysboro Community Unit School District of Jackson County, 67 Ill. 2d 434, 317 N.E. 2d 1337 (1977)

DUE PROCESS AND TEACHER DISMISSAL

18:250 What pre-hearing procedures apply to the dismissal of a tenured teacher?

A "Loudermill-type" pre-termination hearing may be required before the school board votes on the dismissal of a teacher. Under limited circumstances that are fact-driven, post-deprivation due process may be sufficient. The school board must approve a motion containing specific charges by a majority vote of all its members. Written notice of the charges must be mailed to the teacher and also given to the teacher either by certified mail, return receipt requested, or personal delivery with receipt within five days of the adoption of the motion.

The notice must contain a bill of particulars and the teacher must be given notice of his or her right to request a hearing. No hearing on the charges is required unless the teacher, within 17 days of receiving the notice, requests in writing of the school board a hearing be scheduled before a mutually selected hearing officer or a hearing officer selected by the board. Any written notice sent on or after July 1, 2012 must inform the teacher of the right to request a hearing before a mutually selected hearing officer, with the cost of the hearing officer split equally between the teacher and the board, or a hearing before a board-selected hearing officer, with the cost of the hearing officer paid by the board.

105 ILCS 5/24-12

Baird v. Board of Education for Warren Community School District No. 205, 389 F. 3d 685 (7th Cir. 2004)

Gilbert v. Homar, 117 S. Ct. 1807, 520 U.S. 924, 138 L. Ed. 2d 120 (1997) on rem. 149 F. 3d 1164 (3rd Cir. 1998)

Massie v. East St. Louis School District No. 189, 203 Ill. App. 3d 965, 561 N.E. 2d 246, 148 Ill. Dec. 940 (5th Dist. 1990)

Cleveland Board of Education v. Loudermill, 105 S. Ct. 1487, 470 U.S. 532, 84 L. Ed. 2d 494 (1985) on rem. 763 F. 2d 202 (6th Cir. 1985)

Morelli v. Board of Education of District 303, Tazewell County, 42 Ill. App. 3d 722, 356 N.E. 2d 438, 1 Ill. Dec. 312 (3rd Dist. 1976)

18:255 What act sets in motion a teacher dismissal?

A teacher dismissal case begins when a school board adopts a resolution calling for the teacher's dismissal.

Goral v. Illinois State Board of Education, 2013 IL App (1st) 130752, 3 N.E. 3d 365, 378 Ill. Dec. 85

18:260 Is pre-hearing discovery permitted in a tenured teacher dismissal?

The hearing officer must allow for interrogatories and requests for production of documents, and may allow for other discovery, subject to reasonable limitations set by him, in the order reflecting the pre-hearing conference or any future order. Discovery depositions are prohibited. Application for discovery must be made by written motion to the hearing officer, with copies to the other party. The motion must state the specific nature of the discovery and the circumstances necessitating the discovery. If interrogatories are sought, a copy of the interrogatories must be attached to the motion. The hearing officer must rule on the motion within five days after receipt of the motion, sending copies of the decision to both parties. The ruling must set a date by which discovery must be completed. In the case of interrogatories, receipt of the hearing officer's ruling generally is service of the interrogatories.

In ruling on the motion, the hearing officer may not permit discovery that will unnecessarily delay the proceedings or harass a party, and must allow only that discovery that will further the resolution of the dispute, avoid surprise to a party, or aid in doing substantial justice. Each party providing answers to discovery requests must sign his or her responses under oath, and each attorney making objections shall sign his or her objections under oath. Other pretrial motions may be filed and resolved prior to the hearing at the discretion of the hearing officer, provided that no motion may be resolved prior to the hearing that would result in a default judgment against the tenured teacher.

Any party who proceeds to hearing after knowledge that any provision of the rules has not been complied with prior to the hearing, and who fails to state the objection in writing to the hearing officer, waives his or her right to object.

105 ILCS 5/24-12

23 Ill. Admin. Code 51.55

18:270 How is a tenured teacher dismissal hearing conducted?

The hearing officer must exclude witnesses during the testimony of other witnesses upon the motion of either party, except that, at any time, one representative of each party in addition to counsel (or other authorized representative) must be allowed to be present, even if that representative is also a witness. In open hearings, individuals who are not witnesses are not affected by exclusion.

The parties may be present and represented by counsel and by other authorized representatives. The order of proceeding is as follows:

1) The hearing is opened by the recording of the place, time, and date of the hearing; the presence of the hearing officer and the parties and counsel, if any; and any stipulations as to facts. Prehearing motions submitted in accordance with State Board rules and not previously disposed of are heard.

2) Upon the opening of the hearing, the hearing officer must allow the parties to make opening statements.

3) The board must proceed first to present its evidence and has the burden of proof. The parties may agree to take witnesses out of order and if they do, the hearing officer may vary the procedure under which the board presents its case first;

4) Either party may offer evidence and witnesses, cross examine the witnesses, offer evidence, and present a defense or rebuttal.

5) All testimony must be taken under oath or affirmation administered by the hearing officer.

6) The hearing officer may issue subpoenas requiring the attendance of witnesses and subpoenas duces tecum, and, at the request of either of the parties, must issue the requested subpoenas but may limit the number of witnesses to be subpoenaed on behalf of either party to not more than seven.

7) The hearing officer must cause a record of the proceedings to be kept and must employ a competent reporter to take the testimony. The parties pay for the attendance and services of the court reporter as well as for the transcript, if any, ordered by the hearing officer for the purpose of making the decision.

8) Exhibits, when offered by either party, may be received in evidence by the hearing officer. The names and addresses of all witnesses and exhibits, in order received, must be made a part of the record. The hearing officer must make rulings on the admissibility of exhibits.

9) The hearing officer, for good cause shown, may continue the hearing upon the request of the teacher or the board or upon his or her own initiative.

10) The hearing may proceed in the absence of either party, who, after due notice, fails to be present or fails to obtain a continuance.

11) The hearing must begin within 75 days and conclude within 120 days after the appointment of the hearing officer, barring modification of these timelines by the hearing officer upon a showing of good cause or mutual agreement of the parties. "Good cause" means the illness or otherwise unavoidable emergency of the teacher, district representative, their legal representatives, the hearing officer, or an essential witness as indicated in each party's pre-hearing submission.

12) When the hearing officer determines that neither party has further proof to offer or witnesses to be heard, he or she must declare the hearing concluded and so note in the record.

13) At the close of the hearing, the hearing officer must direct the parties to submit post-hearing briefs no later than 21 days after receipt of the transcript, unless extended by the hearing officer for good cause or by mutual agreement of the parties. Post-hearing briefs may not exceed 50 pages in length, unless the hearing officer determines in a written order that the circumstances of a particular matter warrant a limitation shorter or longer than 50 pages. Either party may waive submission of a brief. If written briefs are to be submitted subsequently, the hearing officer must so note in the record.

14) At the conclusion of the hearing, each party may make an oral closing statement incorporating arguments of fact and law.

15) The hearing is not closed until all evidence has been submitted and briefs have been timely received by the hearing officer. The hearing officer must notify the parties, in writing, of the closing date of the record. A copy of the notice shall be forwarded to the State Board of Education.

23 Ill. Admin. Code 51.60

18:280 Who may serve as a hearing officer for a tenured teacher dismissal?

The hearing officer in a tenured teacher dismissal case must be selected through a statutory procedure from a list supplied by the State Board of Education. Hearing officers must possess the following minimum qualifications:

1) He or she must be accredited by a national arbitration association.

2) Except with respect to hearings involving the Chicago Public Schools, he or she must be a nonresident of the school district involved in the hearing at the time of the hearing.

3) He or she must be disinterested and impartial.

4) He or she must have no financial or personal interest in the result of the hearing.

105 ILCS 5/24-12

23 Ill. Admin. Code 51.40

18:290 Is a tenured teacher dismissal hearing open to the public?

The hearing is closed to the public unless one of the parties requests that it be open and the hearing officer orders it open. In practice, such hearings are routinely closed.

105 ILCS 5/24-12

23 Ill. Admin. Code 51.60

18:300 Who pays the hearing officer in a tenured teacher dismissal case?

The per diem allowance for the hearing officer is generally paid by the State Board of Education. For dismissal cases after July 1, 2012, there is a complicated alternative procedure that may be elected by the parties.

105 ILCS 5/24-12

23 Ill. Admin. Code 51.40(f)

18:305 How is the hearing officer in a tenured teacher dismissal case selected?

Within five business days after receiving a notice of hearing in which either notice to the teacher was sent before July 1, 2012 or, if the notice was sent on or after July 1, 2012, the teacher has requested a hearing before a mutually selected hearing officer, the State Board of Education (ISBE) must provide a list of five prospective, impartial hearing officers from the master list of qualified, impartial hearing officers maintained by ISBE. Each person on the master list must be accredited by a national arbitration organization and have had a minimum of five years of experience directly related to labor and employment relations matters between educational employers and educational employees or their exclusive bargaining representatives and, beginning September 1, 2012, must have participated in training provided or approved by ISBE for teacher dismissal hearing officers so that he or she is familiar with issues generally involved in evaluative and non-evaluative dismissals.

If notice to the teacher was sent before July 1, 2012 or, if the notice was sent on or after July 1, 2012, the board and the teacher or their legal representatives within three business days must alternately strike one name from the list provided by ISBE until only one name remains. Unless waived by the teacher, the teacher has the right to proceed first with the striking. Within three business days of receipt of the first list provided by ISBE, the board and the teacher or their legal representatives must each have the right to reject all prospective hearing officers named on the first list and notify ISBE of such rejection to require ISBE to provide a second list of five prospective, impartial hearing officers, none of whom were named on the first list. Within three business days after receiving this notification request for a second list, ISBE must appoint a qualified person from the master list who did not appear on the list sent to the parties to serve as the hearing officer, unless the parties notify it that they have chosen to alternatively select a hearing officer.

If the teacher has requested a hearing before a hearing officer selected by the board, the board must select one name from the master list of qualified impartial hearing officers maintained by ISBE within three business days after receipt and must notify ISBE of its selection.

A hearing officer mutually selected by the parties, selected by the board, or selected through an alternative selection process cannot be a resident of the school district, must be available to commence the hearing within 75 days and conclude the hearing within 120 days after being selected as the hearing officer, and must issue a decision as to whether the teacher must be dismissed and give a copy of that decision to both the teacher and the board within 30 days from the conclusion of the hearing or closure of the record, whichever is later.

In the alternative to selecting a hearing officer from the first or second list received from ISBE, accepting the appointment of a hearing officer by ISBE or if the ISBE cannot provide a list or appoint a hearing officer that meets the foregoing requirements, the board and the teacher or their legal representatives may mutually agree to select an impartial hearing officer who is not on the master a list received from ISBE either by direct appointment by the parties or by using procedures for the appointment of an arbitrator established by the Federal Mediation and Conciliation Service or the American Arbitration Association. The parties must notify ISBE of their intent to select a hearing officer using an alternative procedure within three business days of receipt of a list of prospective hearing officers provided by ISBE, notice of appointment of a hearing officer by ISBE, or receipt of notice from ISBE that it cannot provide a list that meets the foregoing requirements, whichever is later.

105 ILCS 5/24-12

23 Ill. Admin. Code 51.40(b)

18:310 What procedures are followed in appointing a hearing officer to a tenured teacher dismissal case?

Major revisions to the hearing officer appointment procedures were made in 2012. Both the School Code and the Administrative Code contain complicated revised procedures for the appointment of hearing officers.

105 ILCS 5/24-12

23 Ill. Admin. Code 51.40

18:320 How does a hearing officer render a decision in a tenured teacher dismissal case?

Generally, the hearing officer must, within 30 days after the hearing is concluded or the record is closed, whichever is later, render a final decision as to whether the tenured teacher is dismissed. A 2012 change in the statute and rules governing teacher dismissals made the procedures substantially more complicated than they were previously.

105 ILCS 5/24-12

105 ILCS 5/24-16

23 Ill. Admin. Code 51.70

18:325 What is the role of the hearing officer in the dismissal process?

When a school board adopts charges to dismiss a teacher, it sets the dismissal process in motion. Administrators investigate and gather evidence and the school board charges the teacher. The hearing officer's authority is not limited to rendering a decision as to whether or not the school board has proven its case by a preponderance of the evidence. The hearing officer has authority to evaluate all issues, weigh the evidence, and determine whether or not the charges were sufficiently grave to justify dismissal. No dismissal occurs until the hearing officer renders a decision.

Board of Education of Community Consolidated School District No. 54 v. Spangler, 328 Ill. App. 3d 747, 762 N.E. 2d 452, 263 Ill. Dec. 1 (1st Dist. 2002)

Board of Education of Round Lake Area Schools, Community Unit School District No. 116 v. The State Board of Education, John F. Rozner and Barbara Cohn, 292 Ill. App. 3d 101, 685 N.E. 2d 412, 226 Ill. Dec. 309 (2nd Dist. 1997)

18:330 What rules of evidence apply to tenured teacher dismissal hearings?

The parties may offer any evidence as they desire, and each party must produce any additional evidence as the hearing officer may deem necessary to an understanding and determination of the dispute. The hearing officer is the judge of the relevancy and materiality of the evidence offered and strict conformity to legal rules of evidence is not necessary. Objections to evidentiary offers may be made and are noted in the record.

The hearing officer has the power to make rulings, including the power to exclude evidence. "Offers of Proof" are permitted. Any witness designated as hostile by the hearing officer may be examined as if under cross-examination. If the hearing officer grants a party's request to submit a document after the evidentiary portion of the hearing is closed, the party must file that document with the hearing officer and with the other party within the time designated by the hearing officer.

105 ILCS 5/24-12

23 Ill. Admin. Code 51.60

18:340 What burden of proof does a school board have in a teacher dismissal case?

A school board must prove its case by a preponderance of the evidence.

Board of Education of Minooka Community Consolidated School District No. 201 v. Ingels, 75 Ill. App. 3d 334, 394 N.E. 2d 69, 31 Ill. Dec. 153 (3rd Dist. 1979)

18:350 May a school board raise charges not included in the bill of particulars for the first time at a dismissal hearing?

New charges or proofs unrelated to the bill of particulars are not permitted.

105 ILCS 5/24-12

Aulwurm v. Board of Education of Murphysboro Community Unit School District of Jackson County, 67 Ill. 2d 434, 317 N.E. 2d 1337 (1977)

18:360 What is the time limit for appealing a hearing officer's decision in a teacher dismissal case?

Appeal must be perfected within 35 days of the date the hearing officer's decision was served on the party affected by the decision.

735 ILCS 5/3-103

Board of Education of St. Charles Community Unit School District No. 303 v. Adelman, 137 Ill. App. 3d 965, 485 N.E. 2d 584, 92 Ill. Dec. 773 (2nd Dist. 1985)

18:365 For purposes of administrative review is the hearing officer's opinion reviewable?

The decision of the school board is the final decision for purposes of administrative review. The board must consider the record of the proceedings in rendering a decision. The relevant statute vests the board with final decision-making authority after the hearing officer's recommendation is reported to the board. The board is obligated to consider the decision of the hearing officer in reaching a decision.

School officials should be mindful that most disputed dismissal cases turn on questions of procedural compliance with the statute and with evaluation plan components and not with the substantive conclusions of school officials.

Beggs v. The Board of Education of Murphysboro Community Unit School District No. 186, 2016 IL 120236, 45 N.E. 3d 722, 399 Ill. Dec. 51

OPTIONAL ALTERNATIVE DISMISSAL

18:370 What is the optional alternative evaluative dismissal process for PERA evaluations?

The optional alternative evaluative dismissal process for PERA (Performance Evaluation Reform Act, P.A. 96-861, implemented in 2015 for some school districts and 2016 for most school districts) applies to school districts and special education joint agreements and is an alternative to use of Section 24-12 hearing procedures.

A board may dismiss a teacher who has entered upon contractual continued service under the optional evaluative dismissal process if the following are met:

1) The cause of dismissal is that the teacher has failed to complete a remediation plan with a rating equal to or better than a "proficient" rating;

2) The "unsatisfactory" performance evaluation rating that preceded remediation resulted from a PERA evaluation; and

3) The school district has complied with the pre-remediation and remediation activities required in the law.

Each school district electing to use the optional alternative evaluative dismissal must comply with the pre-remediation and remediation activities and requirements in the relevant law:

Before a school district's first remediation relating to a dismissal, the school district must create and establish a list of at least two evaluators who will be available to serve as second evaluators. The school district must provide its teacher representatives with an opportunity to submit additional names of teacher evaluators who will be available to serve as second evaluators and who will be added to the list created and established by the school district, provided that, unless otherwise agreed to by the school district, the teacher representatives may not submit more teacher evaluators for inclusion on the list than the number of evaluators submitted by the school district. Each teacher evaluator must either have National Board of Professional Teaching Standards certification, with no "unsatisfactory" or "needs improvement" performance evaluating ratings in his or her two most recent performance evaluation ratings; or "excellent" performance evaluation ratings in two of his or her three most recent performance evaluations, with no "needs improvement" or "unsatisfactory" performance evaluation ratings in his or her last three ratings. If the teacher representatives do not submit a list of teacher evaluators within 21 days after the school district's request, the school district may proceed with a remediation using a list that includes only the school district's selections.

Either the school district or the teacher representatives may revise or add to their selections for the list at any time with notice to the other party, subject to the limitations above. Before a school district's first remediation relating to a dismissal, the school district must, in good faith cooperation with its teacher representatives, establish a process for the selection of a second evaluator from the list created above. Such process may be amended at any time in good faith cooperation with the teacher representatives. If the teacher representatives are given an opportunity to cooperate with the school district and elect not to do so, the school district may, at its discretion, establish or amend the process for selection. Before the hearing officer and as part of any judicial review of a dismissal under this section, a teacher may not challenge a remediation or dismissal on the grounds that the process used by the school district to select a second evaluator was not established in good faith cooperation with its teacher representatives.

For each remediation preceding a dismissal the school district shall select a second evaluator from the list of second evaluators created above using the selection process. The selected second evaluator may not be the same person who determined the teacher's "unsatisfactory" performance evaluation rating preceding remediation, and, if the second evaluator is an administrator, may not directly report to the person who determined the teacher's "unsatisfactory" performance evaluation rating preceding remediation. The school district's authority to select a second evaluator from the list of second evaluators must not be delegated or limited through any agreement with the teacher representatives, provided that nothing prohibits a school district and its teacher representatives from agreeing to a formal peer evaluation process as permitted under Article 24A of the School Code that could be used to meet the requirements for the selection of second evaluators.

The second evaluator selected must either conduct the mid-point and final evaluation during remediation or conduct an independent assessment of whether the teacher completed the remediation plan with a rating equal to or better than a "proficient" rating. The independent assessment must include, but is not limited to, personal or video-recorded observations of the teacher that relate to the teacher practice components of the remediation plan. The evaluator who rated a teacher as "unsatisfactory" may participate in the remediation.

105 ILCS 5/24-16.5

18:380 How does a school district initiate dismissal proceedings under optional alternative evaluative dismissal?

The school board must first provide written notice to the teacher within 30 days after the completion of the final remediation evaluation. The notice must comply with the applicable hearing requirements and, in addition, must specify that dismissal is sought under optional alternative evaluative dismissal and include a copy of each performance evaluation relating to the scope of the hearing.

The applicable hearing requirements apply to the teacher's request for a hearing, the selection and qualifications of the hearing officer, and pre-hearing and hearing procedures, except that all of the following must be met:

1) The hearing officer must, in addition to meeting the qualifications set forth in the applicable hearing requirements, have successfully completed the pre-qualification program described in Section 24A-3 (b) of the School Code, unless the State Board of Education waives this requirement to provide an adequate pool of hearing officers for consideration.

2) The school district must demonstrate that the "unsatisfactory" performance evaluation rating that preceded remediation applied the teacher practice components and student growth components and determined an overall evaluation rating of "unsatisfactory" in accordance with the standards and requirements of the school district's evaluation plan; that the remediation plan complied with the requirements of Section 24A-5 of the School Code; that the teacher failed to complete the remediation plan with a performance evaluation rating equal to or better than a "proficient" rating, based upon a final remediation evaluation meeting the applicable standards and requirements of the school district's evaluation plan; and that if the second evaluator selected does not conduct the mid-point and final evaluation and makes an independent assessment that the teacher completed the remediation plan with a rating equal to or better than a "proficient" rating, the school district must demonstrate that the final remediation evaluation is a more valid assessment of the teacher's performance than the assessment made by the second evaluator.

The teacher may only challenge the substantive and procedural aspects of the "unsatisfactory" performance evaluation rating that led to the remediation, the remediation plan, and the final remediation evaluation. To the extent the teacher challenges procedural aspects, including any in applicable collective bargaining agreement provisions, of a relevant performance evaluation rating or the remediation plan, the teacher must demonstrate how an alleged procedural defect materially affected the teacher's ability to demonstrate a level of performance necessary to avoid remediation or dismissal or successfully complete the remediation plan. Without any such material effect, a procedural defect must not impact the assessment by the hearing officer, board, or reviewing court of the validity of a performance evaluation or a remediation plan.

The hearing officer must only consider and give weight to performance evaluations relevant to the scope of the hearing.

Each party is given two days to present evidence and testimony relating to the scope of the hearing, unless a longer period is mutually agreed to by the parties or deemed necessary by the hearing officer to enable a party to present adequate evidence and testimony to address the scope of the hearing, including due to the other party's cross-examination of the party's witnesses.

The provisions of Section 24-12 of the School Code pertaining to the decision or recommendation of the hearing officer do not apply to optional alternative evaluative dismissal proceedings. For any dismissal proceedings under optional alternative evaluative dismissal, the hearing officer does not issue a decision, and issues instead, findings of fact and a recommendation, including the reasons therefor, to the board to either retain or dismiss the teacher and gives a copy of the report to both the teacher and the superintendent of the school district. The hearing officer's findings of fact and recommendation must be issued within 30 days from the close of the record of the hearing.

The State Board of Education will adopt rules regarding the length of the hearing officer's findings of fact and recommendation. If a hearing officer fails without good cause, specifically provided in writing to both parties and the State Board of Education, to render a recommendation within 30 days after the hearing is concluded or the record is closed, whichever is later, the parties may mutually agree to select a hearing officer pursuant to the alternative procedure, as provided in Section 24-12, to rehear the charges heard by the hearing officer who failed to render a recommendation or to review the record and render a recommendation.

The local board, within 45 days after receipt of the hearing officer's findings of fact and recommendation, must decide, through adoption of a written order, whether the teacher must be dismissed from its employ or retained, provided that only PERA-trained board members may participate in the vote with respect to the decision.

If the board dismisses the teacher notwithstanding the hearing officer's recommendation of retention, the board shall make a conclusion, giving its reasons therefor, and such conclusion and reasons must be included in its written order. The failure of the board to strictly adhere to the timelines contained in this section does not render it without jurisdiction to dismiss the teacher. The board does not lose jurisdiction to discharge the teacher if the hearing officer fails to render a recommendation within the time specified. The decision of the board is final, unless the teacher elects judicial review.

If the board retains the teacher, the board shall enter a written order stating the amount of back pay and lost benefits, less mitigation, to be paid to the teacher, within 45 days of its retention order.

105 ILCS 5/24-16.5

18:385 What appeal is available after an optional alternative evaluative dismissal?

A teacher dismissed under optional alternative evaluative dismissal may apply for and obtain judicial review of a decision of the board in accordance with the provisions of the Administrative Review Law, except as follows: For a teacher dismissed by a school district having less than 500,000 inhabitants after the hearing officer recommended dismissal, judicial review must be taken directly to the appellate court of the judicial district in which the board maintains its primary administrative office, and any direct appeal to the appellate court must be filed within 35 days from the date that a copy of the decision sought to be reviewed was served upon the teacher; and for all school districts, if the hearing officer recommended dismissal, the decision of the board may be reversed only if it is found to be arbitrary, capricious, an abuse of discretion, or not in accordance with law.

In the event judicial review is instituted by a teacher, any costs of preparing and filing the record of proceedings must be paid by the teacher. If a decision of the board is adjudicated upon judicial review in favor of the teacher, then the court shall remand the matter to the board with direction for entry of an order setting the amount of back pay, lost benefits, and costs, less mitigation. The teacher may challenge the board's order setting the amount of back pay, lost benefits, and costs, less mitigation, through an expedited arbitration procedure with the costs of the arbitrator borne by the board.

105 ILCS 5/24-16.5

Beggs v. The Board of Education of Murphysboro Community Unit School District No. 186, 2016 IL 120236, 45 N.E. 3d 722, 399 Ill. Dec. 51

18:390 May a collective bargaining agreement waive the district's right to access optional alternative evaluative dismissal?

A school district may not, through agreement with a teacher or its teacher representatives, waive its right to dismiss a teacher under optional alternative evaluative dismissal.

105 ILCS 5/24-16.5

TEACHER SUSPENSION

18:400 May a school board suspend a tenured teacher without pay pending the outcome of a dismissal hearing?

If, in the opinion of a school board, the interests of the school require it, the board may suspend a teacher without pay pending a dismissal hearing. However, if reinstated, the teacher must have lost salary restored.

105 ILCS 5/24-12

Gilbert v. Homar, 117 S. Ct. 1807, 520 U.S. 924, 138 L. Ed. 2d 120 (1997) on rem. 149 F. 3d 1164 (3rd Cir. 1998)

Spinelli v. Immanuel Evangelical Lutheran Congregation, Inc., 144 Ill. App. 3d 325, 494 N.E. 2d 196, 98 Ill. Dec. 269 (2nd Dist. 1986) aff'd. in part, rev. in part 118 Ill. 2d 389, 515 N.E. 2d 1222, 113 Ill. Dec. 915 (1987)

Yuen v. Board of Education of Community Unit School District No. 46, Kane County, 77 Ill. App. 2d 353, 222 N.E. 2d 570 (3rd Dist. 1966)

Pearson v. Board of Education of Community Unit School District No. 5 of Macoupin County, 27 Ill. App. 2d 12, 169 N.E. 2d 7 (3rd Dist. 1960)

18:410 Must a school board provide a teacher a hearing on a suspension without pay pending dismissal?

It is likely that no hearing beyond that required to review the dismissal need be provided because the relevant statute specifies all necessary procedures. However, there is some case law that suggests a separate hearing must be held before the suspension without pay is invoked.

105 ILCS 5/24-12

Baird v. Board of Education for Warren Community School District No. 205, 389 F. 3d 685 (7th Cir. 2004)

Massie v. East St. Louis School District No. 189, 203 Ill. App. 3d 965, 561 N.E. 2d 246, 148 Ill. Dec. 940 (5th Dist. 1990)

Spinelli v. Immanuel Evangelical Lutheran Congregation, Inc., 144 Ill. App. 3d 325, 494 N.E. 2d 196, 98 Ill. Dec. 269 (2nd Dist. 1986) aff'd. in part, rev. in part 118 Ill. 2d 389, 515 N.E. 2d 1222, 113 Ill. Dec. 915 (1987)

Cleveland Board of Education v. Loudermill, 105 S. Ct. 1487, 470 U.S. 532, 84 L. Ed. 2d 494 (1985) on rem. 763 F. 2d 202 (6th Cir. 1985)

Barszcz v. Board of Trustees of Community College District No. 504, Cook County, 400 F. Supp. 675 (N.D. Ill. 1975)

18:420 May a school board suspend a teacher without pay for disciplinary reasons without a dismissal pending?

A school board may invoke a disciplinary suspension without pay provided it has an underlying collectively bargained contract provision allowing such a suspension or, in the absence of a demand to bargain it by a recognized bargaining unit, a policy allowing such a suspension. The teacher must be provided with due process (a formal hearing before the board) before the suspension takes effect.

Spinelli v. Immanuel Evangelical Lutheran Congregation, Inc., 144 Ill. App. 3d 325, 494 N.E. 2d 196, 98 Ill. Dec. 269 (2nd Dist. 1986) aff'd. in part, rev. in part 118 Ill. 2d 389, 515 N.E. 2d 1222, 113 Ill. Dec. 915 (1987)

18:430 May a teacher challenge a temporary disciplinary suspension through the collective bargaining agreement grievance procedure?

Yes, provided there is a clause in the agreement supporting the challenge and provided the suspension is not in conjunction with pending dismissal proceedings. The arbitration of a grievance arising from the temporary disciplinary suspension of a teacher is not inconsistent with or in conflict with the implied power of the district to suspend nor, is it in violation of, inconsistent with, or in conflict with any statute.

115 ILCS 5/10(b)

Granite City Community Unit School District No. 9 v. Illinois Educational Labor Relations Board, 279 Ill. App. 3d 439, 664 N.E. 2d 1060, 216 Ill. Dec. 132 (4th Dist. 1996)

Spinelli v. Immanuel Evangelical Lutheran Congregation, Inc., 144 Ill. App. 3d 325, 494 N.E. 2d 196, 98 Ill. Dec. 269 (2nd Dist. 1986) aff'd. in part, rev. in part 118 Ill. 2d 389, 515 N.E. 2d 1222, 113 Ill. Dec. 915 (1987)

19: SCHOOL ADMINISTRATORS

DUTIES OF ADMINISTRATORS

19:10 What are the duties of a superintendent?

A superintendent has charge of the administration of the schools under the direction of the school board. In addition to administrative duties, a superintendent is required to make recommendations to the board concerning the budget; building plans; the locations of sites; the selection, retention, and dismissal of teachers and all other employees; and the selection of textbooks, instructional material, and courses of study.

The superintendent has reporting responsibilities under the Abused and Neglected Child Reporting Act. The superintendent must keep or cause to be kept the records and accounts as directed and required by the board, aid in making reports required by the board, and perform such other duties as the board may delegate to him.

105 ILCS 5/10-21.4

19:15 What are the duties of a chief school business official?

The school board has authority to establish the duties of a chief school business official. In school districts large enough to employ a business official, such a person generally is assigned financial responsibilities such as budget preparation, collection and oversight of state aid data, and expenditure responsibilities that would otherwise be performed by the superintendent.

105 ILCS 5/10-22.23a

19:20 What are the duties of a principal?

A principal must hold a valid supervisory or administrative certificate. He or she supervises the operation of one or more attendance centers. The principal administers duties under the supervision of the superintendent, and in accordance with reasonable rules and regulations of the school board, for the planning, operation, and evaluation of the educational program of the attendance area to which he or she is assigned.

A principal's job description must specify his or her primary responsibility is the improvement of instruction. A majority of the principal's time must be spent on curriculum and staff development through both formal and informal activities, establishing clear lines of communication regarding school goals, accomplishments, practices, and policies with parents and teachers.

A principal is required to submit recommendations to the superintendent concerning the appointment, retention, promotion, and assignment of all personnel assigned to the attendance center.

105 ILCS 5/10-21.4a

19:25 May an administrator issue a teacher a notice to remedy?

A notice to remedy is an official warning to a teacher that the teacher's behavior, if not remedied, may lead to dismissal. Only a school board may issue a notice to remedy. Therefore no disciplinary letter signed by a superintendent or principal is a notice to remedy and such a letter from an administrator has a less serious disciplinary effect.

105 ILCS 5/24-12

Board of Education of School District No. 131 v. Illinois State Board of Education, 82 Ill. App. 3d 820, 404 N.E. 2d 277, 38 Ill. Dec. 189 (2nd Dist. 1980)

19:30 May a school district employ one administrator as both superintendent and principal?

Yes, provided the full-time equivalency of the combination results in a maximum of one full-time position.

23 Ill. Admin. Code 1.310 c)

19:40 May a school board assign one principal to supervise more than one attendance center?

Yes.

23 Ill. Admin. Code 1.310

Kenny v. Interim General Superintendent of Schools, 112 Ill. App. 3d 342, 445 N.E. 2d 356, 67 Ill. Dec. 876 (1st Dist. 1983)

Dolnick v. General Superintendent of Schools of Chicago, 67 Ill. App. 3d 8, 384 N.E. 2d 408, 23 Ill. Dec. 614 (1st Dist. 1978)

19:50 Who may serve as principal in the absence of the principal?

If a principal is absent due to extended illness or leave of absence, an assistant principal may be assigned as acting principal. At one time, the State Board of Education imposed a time limit for such service and at one time there was a statutory limit.

105 ILCS 5/10-21.4a

23 Ill. Admin. Code 1.310

ADMINISTRATOR QUALIFICATIONS

19:60 What is required to be a superintendent of schools?

A superintendent endorsement requires completion of a program approved by the State Board of Education for the preparation of superintendents of schools, at least two years of experience employed as a full-time principal, director of special education, or chief school business official in a public school or in a state-recognized nonpublic school in which the chief administrator is required to have the licensure necessary to be a principal in a public school in Illinois and where a majority of the teachers are required to have the licensure necessary to be instructors in a public school in Illinois, and has passed the required state tests; or of any holder who has completed a program from out-of-state that has a program with recognition standards comparable to those approved by the State Superintendent of Education and holds the general administrative, principal, or chief school business official endorsement and who has had two years of experience as a principal, director of special education, or chief school business official while holding a valid educator license or certificate comparable in validity and educational and experience requirements and has passed the appropriate state tests, as provided in Section 21B-30 of the School Code. The superintendent endorsement allows service only as a superintendent or assistant superintendent.

Prior to 2013, a superintendent of schools was required to have a master's degree and hold a state certificate with a superintendent endorsement. An endorsement required the successful completion of at least 30 semester hours of graduate credit beyond the master's degree in a program for the preparation of superintendents of schools, including 16 semester hours of graduate credit in professional education. Endorsement also required at least two years' experience as an administrator or supervisor in public schools, the State Board of Education, educational service regions, or in certain approved non-public schools, or two years of experience as a supervisor or administrator while holding an all-grade supervisory certificate or a certificate comparable in validity and educational and experience requirements.

105 ILCS 5/21B-25 (D)

19:63 What is required to be a chief school business official?

A chief school business official endorsement requires a professional educator license, a master's degree or higher, two years of full-time administrative experience in school business management or two years of university-approved practical experience, and a minimum of 24 semester hours of graduate credit in a program approved by the State Board of Education for the preparation of school business administrators and by passage of the applicable State tests.

The endorsement may also be affixed to the professional educator license of any holder who qualifies by having a master's degree in business administration, finance, public administration, or accounting and who completes an additional six semester hours of internship in school business management from a regionally accredited institution of higher education and passes the applicable state tests. The endorsement is required for any individual employed as a chief school business official.

105 ILCS 5/21B-25 (C)

19:65 What is required to be a principal?

A principal, assistant principal, assistant superintendent, and related or similar positions as determined by the State Superintendent of Education must have a general administrative endorsement. The endorsement requires at least 20 semester hours of graduate credit in educational administration and supervision.

Endorsement for a principal license also requires at least four years of full-time teaching experience or until June 30, 2020, school service personnel experience in an Illinois public school or certain non-public schools. Fewer than four years' experience is allowed by the State Board of Education and the State Educator and Licensure Board under certain limited circumstances.

105 ILCS 5/21B-25

105 ILCS 5/21B-60

19:70 Are there continuing education requirements for administrators who evaluate certified personnel?

Administrators who evaluate certified personnel must participate in a State Board of Education training program on evaluation of certified personnel at least once every two years.

105 ILCS 5/24A-3

19:75 Are department chairpersons required to have administrative or supervisory teaching certificates?

Department chairpersons are required to have administrative or supervisory endorsements if first assigned to their jobs after September 1, 1978 and if their jobs require supervision or evaluation of teachers.

105 ILCS 5/21B-25 (E)

23 Ill. Admin. Code 1.310 b)

19:78 Is there an alternative route to administrator certification?

The alternative licensure program that existed before 2013 has been phased out. No one may be admitted to the old alternative certification program after September 1, 2012 and candidates admitted on or before September 1, 2012 were required to complete the old program before September 1, 2013.

Beginning on January 1, 2013 a new alternative licensure program is in place. It is comprised of three phases: a course of study, assignment to a full-time position for one year, and comprehensive assessment. The alternate certification requires that the candidate have a master's degree, a minimum of five years in a management position other than education, successful completion of a test of basic skills and content area, and compliance with other requirements contained in the relevant statute.

105 ILCS 5/21-5e

105 ILCS 5/21B-15

105 ILCS 21B-55

ADMINISTRATOR RECERTIFICATION

19:80 For what period of time is an administrative license valid?

Administrative licenses are issued on a five-year renewal cycle. There are professional development requirements for different classes of administrators (those actively working in administrative positions; those working, but not in administrative positions; and those who are retired, for example).

A licensee who has not fulfilled professional development renewal requirements at the end of any five-year cycle is ineligible to register his or her license and may submit an appeal to the State Superintendent. There are procedures set forth in the statute which allow licensees to reinstate lapsed licenses. The procedures generally require the licensee to make up missed professional development hours, pay a cash penalty (or complete course work), pay back fees, and complete professional development.

An unregistered license is invalid after September 1 for employment and "performance of services in an Illinois public or state operated school or cooperative and in a charter school." Any license or endorsement may be voluntarily surrendered by the license holder. A voluntarily surrendered license, except a substitute teaching license, is treated as a revoked license.

105 ILCS 5/21B-45

EMPLOYMENT CONTRACTS

19:100 May a school board issue multi-year employment contracts to its administrators?

For new contracts issued after December 31, 1997 and after the expiration of contracts in effect on January 1, 1998, school districts may only employ administrators under a one-year contract or a performance-based multi-year contract for a period not exceeding five years. Beginning in 2011, assistant principals were explicitly covered by the relevant section of the School Code. Contracts in effect at the time of the amendment were grandfathered until their expiration.

Before January 1, 1998, superintendents or principals could be issued multi-year contracts without performance provisions, and rollover clauses were permissible.

105 ILCS 5/10-23.8

105 ILCS 5/10-23.8a

Board of Education of Schaumburg Community Consolidated School District No. 54 v. Teachers' Retirement System of the State of Illinois, 2013 IL App (4th) 120419, 985 N.E. 2d 305, 368 Ill. Dec. 732

19:110 What is a performance-based contract?

The School Code requires that multi-year administrator contracts be linked to student performance and academic improvement within the district. Performance-based contracts must include goals and indicators of student performance and academic improvement as determined by the local school board to measure the performance and effectiveness of the administrator and such other information as the local school board may determine.

105 ILCS 5/10-23.8

105 ILCS 5/10-23.8a

Wynn v. Board of Education of School District No. 159, 815 F. Supp. 2d 1007 (N.D. Ill. 2011) 2011 WL 1882454 (May 17, 2011)

19:120 Which administrators may be issued performance contracts?

Before January 1, 1998, the School Code explicitly authorized multi-year contracts only for superintendents and principals. In 2011 assistant principals were added.

The statute requires that if any class of administrator is issued a multi-year contract after December 31, 1997, it must be a performance-based contract.

105 ILCS 5/10-23.8

105 ILCS 5/10-23.8a

19:130 For what term may administrator contracts be issued?

Before January 1, 1998, the School Code permitted a one-year contract for any class of administrator, a two-year contract for a first time superintendent or principal, or a three-year contract for an experienced superintendent or principal.

For administrator contracts of all types executed after December 31, 1997, the School Code authorizes either a contract for a period not to exceed one year or a performance-based contract for a period not exceeding five years.

105 ILCS 5/10-23.8

105 ILCS 5/10-23.8a

19:135 What happens if an administrator has no written contract?

An administrator who does not have a written contract with his or her employer has a constructive contract of one year's duration.

105 ILCS 5/10-23.8

105 ILCS 5/10-23.8a

Board of Education of Schaumburg Community Consolidated School District No. 54 v. Teachers' Retirement System of the State of Illinois, 2013 IL App (4th) 120419, 985 N.E. 2d 305, 368 Ill. Dec. 732

19:140 May an administrator rely on an oral multi-year agreement?

A multi-year agreement that lacks all the elements necessary to form a contract violates the Illinois statute of frauds. The statute of frauds requires that multi-year contracts be reduced to writing to be enforceable. Oral multi-year extensions of written contracts also violate the statute of frauds.

For multiple documents to satisfy the statute of frauds, all essential terms of the contract must be in writing, there must be a connection between the documents, physical or otherwise, so as to demonstrate that they relate to the same contract.

The statute of frauds may be overcome by misrepresentation by word or conduct about material facts or concealment of material facts. The statute of frauds does not bar enforcement of an oral contract if there has been part performance by one party in reliance on the promise of the other party.

740 ILCS 80/1

McInerney v. Charter Golf, Inc., 176 Ill. 2d 482, 680 N.E. 2d 1347, 223 Ill. Dec. 911 (1997)

Dickens v. Quincy College Corporation, 245 Ill. App. 3d 1055, 615 N.E. 2d 381, 185 Ill. Dec. 822 (4th Dist. 1993)

Johnson v. George J. Ball, Inc., 248 Ill. App. 3d 859, 617 N.E. 2d 1355, 187 Ill. Dec. 634 (2nd Dist. 1993)

19:150 May a school board write residency requirements into a principal, assistant principal, or superintendent's contract?

Residency requirements may be included and are enforceable in a superintendent's contract. Unless residency was made an express condition of the principal's or assistant principal's employment or continued employment as a principal or an assistant principal at the time of the person's initial employment as a principal or assistant principal, residency within the school district may not at any time thereafter be made a condition of that person's employment or continued employment as a principal or assistant principal.

The residency within a school district of a principal or assistant principal may not be considered in determining the compensation, assignment, or transfer of a principal or assistant principal to an attendance center.

105 ILCS 5/10-21.4a

105 ILCS 5/24-4.1

19:160 What is a rollover provision in an administrator's employment contract?

Before January 1, 1998, the School Code permitted the extension of a principal's or superintendent's multi-year contract for an additional three years at the end of any year. Some principal and superintendent contracts written before January 1, 1998 automatically extended for an additional three years at the end of each year if the school board did not give notice of non-renewal.

The contract clause that provides for automatic contract extension is commonly called a "rollover" or "evergreen" clause. Rollover clauses may not be included in administrator contracts executed after December 31, 1997.

105 ILCS 5/10-23.8

105 ILCS 5/10-23.8a

19:170 Does an administrator's multi-year contract survive the dissolution or consolidation of the school district that employs him?

The liabilities of dissolved school districts, including the remaining obligations under any multi-year administrator contracts, become the responsibility of the annexing or newly consolidated district.

105 ILCS 5/7-12
105 ILCS 5/11E-105
105 ILCS 5/11E-110

ADMINISTRATOR COMPENSATION

19:190 Is there a maximum amount of compensation that can be paid to school administrators?

No. Administrator compensation is established by the local school board based on the market and what the board feels the district can afford. There is, however, a cap on the amount of increase each year in expenditures for administrative purposes, which includes compensation among other things.

105 ILCS 5/17-1.5

TENURE

19:200 May an administrator acquire tenure?

Any administrator who has teacher certification, and if first employed by his or her employer before January 1, 1998, acquires tenure after employment for two full-time consecutive school terms unless the administrator is employed under the terms of a multi-year contract.

Any administrator who has teacher certification and who was employed after December 31, 1997 but before the district's Performance Evaluation Reform Act (PERA, P.A. 96-186 and Senate Bill 7, P.A. 97-08) implementation date (2015 for some districts and 2016 for most districts), acquires tenure after employment for four full-time consecutive school terms unless the administrator is employed under the terms of a multi-year contract.

After the PERA implementation date, the probationary period will be two, three, or four years depending on the underlying facts and subject to complex conditions contained in the relevant statute.

However, the tenured administrator is not necessarily entitled to any particular position. Rather, tenure entitles the administrator to continued employment in the district so long as there is a position available for which he or she is qualified.

105 ILCS 5/10-23.8
105 ILCS 5/10-23.8a
105 ILCS 5/24-11 et seq.

Davis v. Board of Education of Farmer City-Mansfield Community Unit School District, 63 Ill. App. 3d 495, 380 N.E. 2d 58, 20 Ill. Dec. 381 (4th Dist. 1978)

Lane v. Board of Education of Fairbury Cropsey Community Unit School District No. 3, 38 Ill. App. 3d 742, 348 N.E. 2d 470 (4th Dist. 1976)

Danno v. Peterson, 421 F. Supp. 950 (N.D. Ill. 1976)

Lester v. Board of Education of School District No. 119 of Jo Daviess County, 87 Ill. App. 2d 269, 230 N.E. 2d 893 (2nd Dist. 1967)

McNely v. Board of Education of Community Unit School District No. 7, 9 Ill. 2d 143, 137 N.E. 2d 63 (1956)

19:210 If an administrator has acquired tenure and is subsequently removed from an administrative position, does he or she have "bumping rights?"

Yes. Although after Senate Bill 7 (P.A. 97-08) school districts should be careful to include administrators on their May 10 and 75-day lists.

105 ILCS 5/24-12

Brubaker v. Community Unit School District No. 16, Sangamon and Morgan Counties, 46 Ill. App. 3d 588, 360 N.E. 2d 1228, 4 Ill. Dec. 853 (4th Dist. 1977).

19:220 Does an administrative employee waive any rights by accepting a multi-year employment contract?

By accepting the terms of a multi-year contract, an administrator waives all rights otherwise granted him or her under Sections 24-11 through 24-16 of the School Code, which includes tenure rights, for the duration of the contract but does not lose previously acquired tenure rights.

105 ILCS 5/10-23.8
105 ILCS 5/10-23.8a

RECLASSIFICATION OF PRINCIPALS

19:300 What rights are due principals or assistant principals on demotion or reclassification to a lower-paying position?

A 2011 amendment to the School Code requires that reclassification procedures apply to all principals (previously it had applied only to principals with two or more years of administrative service in the school district) and for the first time to assistant principals.

A 2006 addition and 2010 amendment to the School Code requires that school districts have a principal evaluation plan and complete the evaluation of a principal not later than March 1 in the last year of the principal's contract. Those requirements were extended to include assistant principals in 2011.

No principal or assistant principal may be reclassified by demotion or reduction in rank from one position in a school district to another for which a lower salary is paid without written notice from the board of the proposed reclassification by April 1 of the year in which the principal's or assistant principal's contract expires. Within 10 days of the principal's or assistant principal's receipt of this notice, the school board must provide the principal or assistant principal with a written statement of facts regarding the reclassification, and the principal or assistant principal must be granted, upon request, a private hearing with the board to discuss the reclassification.

If the principal or assistant principal is not satisfied with the results of the private hearing, he or she may within five days thereafter request a public hearing on the reclassification. The principal or assistant principal may be represented by counsel at either hearing.

If the school board decides to proceed with the reclassification, it must give the principal or assistant principal written notice of its decision within 15 days of the private hearing, or 15 days of the public hearing, whichever is later. The decision of the school board thereupon becomes final. Nothing in the law prohibits a school board from ordering lateral transfers of principals or assistant principals to positions of similar rank and equal salary.

105 ILCS 5/10-23.8b

105 ILCS 5/24A-15

Meadows v. School District U-46, 141 Ill. App. 3d 335, 490 N.E. 2d 140, 95 Ill. Dec. 667 (2nd Dist. 1986)

Swanson v. Board of Education of Foreman Community Unit School District No. 124, Mason County, 135 Ill. App. 3d 466, 481 N.E. 2d 1248, 90 Ill. Dec. 337 (4th Dist. 1985)

Lyznicki v. Board of Education, School District No. 167, Cook County, 707 F. 2d 949 (7th Cir. 1983)

19:310 Is an administrator entitled to hearing officer review of a school board decision to reclassify, demote, or reassign?

No. However, under certain circumstances and when the administrator had been employed under a one-year contract, a reclassification, demotion, or reassignment may be a reduction-in-force within the meaning of Sections 24-11 or 24-12 of the School Code.

105 ILCS 5/10-23.8b

NON-RENEWAL AND DISMISSAL

19:400 May a school board dismiss an administrator during the term of his or her contract?

A school board may not dismiss an administrator during the term of his or her contract without providing both substantive and procedural due process. The type of due process necessary varies according to the kind of contract the administrator has. Under certain circumstances the due process protections of the teacher tenure laws apply.

A school board seeking to dismiss an administrator during the term of his or her contract must be able to prove substantial breach of contract by the administrator.

If the administrator has a present entitlement, and when the only available post-termination remedy is the opportunity to bring a state breach of contract suit, a pre-termination hearing is required. The pre-termination hearing must fully satisfy the due process requirements of notice, opportunity to be heard, confrontation, and cross-examination.

105 ILCS 5/24-12

Board of Education of Bremen High School District No. 228 v. Mitchell, 387 Ill.App.3d 117, 899 N.E.2d 1160, 326 Ill. Dec. 509 (1st Dist. 2008)

Baird v. Board of Education for Warren Community School District No. 205, 389 F. 3d 685 (7th Cir. 2004)

Bakalis v. Golembeski, 35 F. 3d 318 (7th Cir. 1994)

19:410 What rights are due an administrator on dismissal?

A school board seeking to dismiss a superintendent at the end of his or her contract must abide by the express terms of the contract and comply with notice and seniority provisions of School Code Section 24-12 if the administrator has achieved tenure in the school district and is not serving under a multi-year contract. If the superintendent is serving under a multi-year contract, he or she must be given notice not later than the date specified in the contract or April 1, whichever is earlier.

School Code Section 10-21.4 requires that notice and the specific reason therefor be given to the superintendent not later than April 1 of the year the superintendent's contract expires, but this date is often misleading because the superintendent's contract may require earlier notification.

A school board seeking to dismiss a principal or assistant principal at the end of the principal's or assistant principal's contract term must abide by the express terms of the employee's contract and comply with notice and seniority provisions of School Code Section 24-12 if the principal or assistant principal has achieved tenure in the school district and is not serving under a multi-year contract. In addition, the school district must have adopted a principal or assistant principal evaluation plan (as may be applicable), complied with the terms of the plan and completed the evaluation of the principal or assistant principal by March 1 of the year during which it seeks termination.

Before a 2011 change in the statute, a principal or assistant principal who was serving under a one-year contract and who had not achieved tenure was only entitled to notice required under his or her contract or the notice required by Section 24-11 of the School Code, whichever was earlier. Beginning in 2012 principals and assistant principals whom the school district seeks to remove may only be removed after compliance with reclassification procedures. In addition, the school district must have adopted a principal or assistant principal evaluation plan (as may be relevant), complied with the terms of the plan, and completed the evaluation of the principal or assistant principal by March 1 of the year during which it seeks termination.

The reclassification procedures require that a principal or assistant principal may be reclassified if notified of the proposed reclassification before April 1 of the year t contract expires and provided the required reclassification procedures are followed. In addition, the school district must have adopted a principal or assistant principal (as may be relevant) evaluation plan, complied with the terms of the plan, and completed the evaluation of the principal or assistant principal by March 1 of the year during which it seeks termination.

An administrator other than a principal or a superintendent serving under a one-year contract and who has not achieved tenure must be given the notice required under his or her contract or the notice required by Section 24-11 of the School Code, whichever is earlier. An administrator other than a principal or a superintendent serving under a multi-year contract must be given notice as provided for in the contract.

Any administrator who has teacher certification and who was employed after December 31, 1997 but before the district's Performance Evaluation Reform Act (PERA, P.A. 96-186 and Senate Bill 7, P.A. 97-08) implementation date (2015 for some districts and 2016 for most districts) acquires tenure after employment for four full-time consecutive school terms unless the administrator is employed under the terms of a multi-year contract.

After the PERA implementation date, the probationary period will be two, three, or four years depending on the underlying facts and subject to complex conditions contained in the relevant statute.

An administrator with teaching tenure may be relieved of administrative duties, but is entitled to bump into a teaching job for which he or she is qualified. For superintendents first employed by their school boards before January 1, 1998, tenure is or was achieved after two consecutive full-time years of service.

105 ILCS 5/10-21.4
105 ILCS 5/10-21.4a
105 ILCS 5/10-23.8
105 ILCS 5/10-23.8b
105 ILCS 5/24-11
105 ILCS 5/24-12
105 ILCS 5/24A-15

Baird v. Board of Education for Warren Community School District No. 205, 389 F. 3d 685 (7th Cir. 2004)

19:420 Is a terminated administrator entitled to reinstatement if the dismissal is challenged and the employee prevails?

Probably not. The employee is not entitled to the office. The office may be withdrawn if the agreed compensation is paid.

Batagiannis v. West Lafayette Community School Corporation, 454 F. 3d 738 (7th Cir. 2006)

20: EDUCATIONAL SUPPORT EMPLOYEES

DUTIES OF EDUCATIONAL SUPPORT EMPLOYEES

20:10 Who are the educational support employees of a school district?

The School Code uses the terms "educational support personnel," to include all employees whose positions do not require state teacher licensure. Before the change in teacher licensure provisions, educational support personnel were referred to as non-certificated employees. Both terms encompass secretarial and clerical employees, maintenance and janitorial staff, bookkeepers, bus drivers, security staff, and food service employees, among others.

20:20 May a school board employ educational support personnel to assist in academically-related activities?

A school board may employ nonteaching personnel or use volunteer personnel for nonteaching duties not requiring instructional judgment or evaluation of pupils. A school board may utilize volunteer personnel or employ educational support personnel as paraprofessionals (or "teacher aides") to assist in the instruction of pupils, so long as each individual is under the immediate supervision of a teacher who holds a valid certificate and is directly engaged in teaching subject matter or conducting activities.

To "assist in the instruction of pupils," i.e., to serve as a paraprofessional, means to support teachers through interactions with students that will help them master curricular content, such as by tutoring; or to assist with classroom management, such as by organizing instructional materials.

Each paraprofessional must be under the direct supervision and control of a fully certificated teacher when assisting with instruction, whether this occurs in classrooms, laboratories, shops, playgrounds, libraries, or other educational settings where instructional judgment requires the supervision of a fully certificated teacher. The certificated teacher must be responsible for planning the activities to be conducted by the paraprofessional and for evaluating the pupils with whom the paraprofessional works. The certificated teacher must be continuously aware of the paraprofessional's activities. The teacher must be responsible for controlling the paraprofessional's activities and must be able to modify them at any time.

Paraprofessionals cannot be utilized as substitutes for or replacement of certificated teachers, and they must not have equivalent responsibilities. Certificated teachers must exercise professional judgment when assigning duties to paraprofessionals and must retain the responsibility for determining students' scholastic activities.

Each school district must:

1) Submit a list of all paraprofessionals it employs to the State Superintendent of Education with its annual application for recognition;

2) Maintain a file for each paraprofessional that describes his or her functions and includes a statement of approval and evidence that he or she has met the rules requirements of 23 Ill. Admin. Code 25.510; and

3) Be responsible for ensuring that no individual is employed as a paraprofessional without a statement of approval, except as otherwise permitted and that paraprofessionals are assigned only to tasks for which their approval is valid.

A school board may designate persons of good character to serve as supervisors, chaperones, or sponsors, either on a voluntary or on a compensated basis, for school activities not connected with the academic program of the schools. A school board may utilize educational support employees, under the direction of a certified teacher, for providing specialized instruction related to a course assigned to the licensed teacher on a regular basis, not otherwise readily available in the immediate school environment, in the fields for which they are particularly qualified or skilled.

Educational support personnel in special education programs under contract to the local board of education, other than paraprofessionals, are governed by 23 Ill. Admin. Code 226.10 et seq. (Special Education). Beginning July 1, 2006, educational interpreters for persons who are deaf or hard of hearing must be approved pursuant to 23 Ill. Admin. Code 25.550 (Approval of Educational Interpreters).

A school board may also utilize persons who are completing clinical experiences or student teaching subject to rules contained in 23 Ill. Admin. Code 1.630 f) and may, with the prior approval of the regional superintendent of schools and consistent with rules contained at 23 Ill. Admin. Code 1.630 g), utilize noncertified persons to provide specialized instruction not otherwise readily available in the immediate school environment in the fields for which they are particularly qualified by reason of specialized knowledge or skill.

105 ILCS 5/10-22.34 et seq.

23 Ill. Admin. Code 1.630

23 Ill. Admin. Code 25.510

23 Ill. Admin. Code 25.550

23 Ill. Admin. Code 226.10 et seq.

20:30 What licensure requirements apply to playground supervisors, cafeteria supervisors, or study hall monitors?

Playground and cafeteria supervisors do not require licensure. Neither position involves instruction or instructional judgment. A 1993 amendment to the School Code allows educational support personnel to supervise study halls. There are bargaining implications involved in assigning such duties to either licensed or non-licensed staff.

105 ILCS 5/10-22.34 et seq.

23 Ill. Admin. Code 1.630

20:40 May a school board assign a teacher aide to substitute teach when the aide's supervising teacher is absent?

A teacher aide cannot legally substitute teach unless he or she holds certification (licensure) as a teacher or substitute teacher.

105 ILCS 5/10-22.34

105 ILCS 5/21B-1 et seq.

23 Ill. Admin. Code 1.630

20:50 May a school board hire extra-duty supervisors or chaperons?

A school board may designate persons of good character to serve as supervisors, chaperons, or sponsors, either on a voluntary or on a compensated basis, for school activities not connected with the academic programs of the schools.

105 ILCS 5/10-22.34a

23 Ill. Admin. Code 1.630

20:60 Do educational support personnel enjoy the same defenses against tort liability that are accorded teachers under the principles of "in loco parentis?"

No. Illinois law accords licensed employees special protections against liability for student injuries. Whereas the negligence standard that applies to teachers in the supervision of students is "willful and wanton misconduct," the standard for an educational support employee is ordinary negligence.

In the area of liability for student injuries, the protections of "in loco parentis" represent an important distinction between licensed and other staff.

People v. Davis, 88 Ill. App. 3d 728, 410 N.E. 2d 673, 43 Ill. Dec. 473 (2nd Dist. 1980)

Edmunson v. Chicago Board of Education, 62 Ill. App. 3d 211, 379 N.E. 2d 27, 19 Ill. Dec. 512 (1st Dist. 1978)

Possekel v. O'Donnell, 51 Ill. App. 3d 313, 366 N.E. 2d 589, 9 Ill. Dec. 332 (1st Dist. 1977)

WAGES AND HOURS

20:70 What are the maximum hour limits of the Fair Labor Standards Act?

A school board is required to abide by the provisions of the federal Fair Labor Standards Act (FLSA). The FLSA requires that employees be paid overtime at the rate of not less than 1.5 times the regular hourly rate for time worked over 40 hours in any workweek.

School administrators and teachers are usually exempt from the provisions of the FLSA. The FLSA wage and hour limits almost always apply to educational support personnel. The FLSA contains many technical provisions that define inclusions and exclusions.

29 U.S.C. 201 et seq.

29 U.S.C. 207

29 U.S.C. 213

20:72 What is the test to determine whether an employee is exempt from overtime because he or she is employed in an administrative capacity?

In order for a worker to be deemed employed in a bona fide administrative capacity, the performance of his or her primary duty must demand the exercise of discretion and judgment on matters of significance.

29 C.F.R. 541.200(a)(3)

29 U.S.C. 202(a)

Urnikis-Negro v. American Family Property Services, 616 F. 3d. 665 (7th Cir. 2010)

20:74 Can a worker who is subject to the wage and hour provisions of the Fair Labor Standards Act be paid in some manner other than an hourly wage?

The pay of workers subject to the wage and hour provisions of the Fair Labor Standards Act may be paid by piece rate, salary, commission, or other basis. However, any overtime compensation due must be computed from the hourly rate that is derived from the payment method used. It is necessary to compute the regular hourly rate of such employees during each workweek.

29 C.F.R. 778.109

Urnikis-Negro v. American Family Property Services, 616 F. 3d. 665 (7th Cir. 2010)

Overnight Motor Transportation Co. v. Missel, 62 S. Ct. 1216, 316 U.S. 572, 86 L. Ed. 1682 (1942)

20:75 When does an employee workday begin and when does it end under the Fair Labor Standards Act?

An employee's compensable workday begins when he or she starts his or her principal work activity and ends when that activity ends. The employee must be compensated for the period between the commencement and the completion on the same workday of the employee's principal activity or activities.

Work is physical or mental exertion (whether burdensome or not) controlled or required by the employer and pursued necessarily and primarily for the benefit of the employer and his or her business. Under the Fair Labor Standards Act, employers are not required to pay employees for the time spent performing preliminary or postliminary activities that occur either prior to the time on a particular workday at which such employee commences, or subsequent to the time on any particular work day at which he or she ceases such principal activity or activities.

Ordinarily, showering or dressing for work (the most common such activities) are considered preliminary or postliminary. However, an employee can be compensated for activities, such as washing or changing clothes, if these activities are integral and indispensable to that employee's employment.

29 USC 254(a)

Kellar v. Summit Seating, Inc., 664 F. 3d 169 (7th Cir. 2011)

Spoerle, et al. v. Kraft Foods Global, Inc., 614 F. 3d 427 (7th Cir. 2010)

Musch v. Domtar Industries, 587 F. 3d 857 (7th Cir. 2009)

IBP v. Alvarez, 546 U.S. 21, 126 S. Ct. 514, 163 L. Ed. 2d 288 (2006)

20:80 Can the overtime provisions of the Fair Labor Standards Act be avoided by providing employees with compensatory time off?

In most cases, the obligation to pay overtime cannot be satisfied by giving the employee compensatory time off unless the compensatory time off is given in the week in which the overtime occurred. There are very limited exceptions to this rule. The most common exceptions are those memorialized in a collective bargaining agreement or in a written agreement entered into with the employee (such an agreement must be with the union for a represented employee) before the overtime was accrued.

Employees may accrue up to 160 straight time hours (240 overtime hours) of compensatory time. Time above 160 straight time hours must be paid at the overtime rate. An employee must be allowed to use compensatory time within a reasonable period after the request is made provided the time off does not unduly disrupt the operation of the school.

29 U.S.C. 201 et seq.

Christensen v. Harris County, 120 S. Ct. 1665, 529 U.S. 576, 146 L. Ed. 2d 621 (2000)

20:90 Can an employer avoid the hour and overtime provisions of the Fair Labor Standards Act by employing the same employee in two different jobs?

The overtime pay provisions of the Fair Labor Standards Act apply to employees who are employed by a single employer in two different jobs. In most cases, a school district must pay overtime to an employee who exceeds 40 hours in a workweek even if the excess results from the employee working more than one job for the same employer.

29 U.S.C. 207 (f)

20:100 Is an employer obligated to pay overtime to an employee who voluntarily works overtime?

The employer may be required to pay overtime for such work if the work is known to, and tacitly approved by, the employee's supervisors. The employee bears the burden of proving that he or she performed the overtime work. The employer has an obligation to exercise control and see that work is not performed if the employer does not want it to be performed. The employer cannot sit back and accept the benefits of work without compensating its employees for the work. The duty arises even when the employer has not requested the overtime be performed or does not want the employee to work or where the employee fails to report overtime hours.

The mere creation of a rule against overtime is not enough. However, an employer is not obligated to pay for work it did not know about and had no reason to know about. The court need only be satisfied that the employer did not have opportunity to know through exercise of reasonable diligence.

29 U.S.C. 207

Kellar v. Summit Seating, Inc., 664 F. 3d 169 (7th Cir. 2011)

20:101 Is an employer obligated to pay an educational support employee overtime if the employee also has an extra duty and, as a result of work performed in fulfilling extra duty responsibilities, works more than 40 hours in a work week?

Teachers are exempt from the overtime provisions of the Fair Labor Standards Act (FLSA), so this issue does not commonly arise when teachers perform extra duties. The issue does arise, however, when full-time educational support employees for the same employer also coach or perform other extra duties.

Both the U.S. Department of Labor and a U.S. Court of Appeals have held that under certain circumstances extra duties are voluntary and therefore exempt from the overtime provisions of the FLSA if the individual receives no compensation or is paid expenses, reasonable benefits, or a nominal fee to perform the services for which the individual volunteered and the services are not the same type of services which the individual is employed to perform for the school district. It is critical that the individual offers services freely and without pressure or coercion, direct or implied, from the employer for the exemption to apply.

A nominal fee must not be a substitute for compensation, must not be tied to productivity and is examined by the total amount of payments made in the context of the economic realities of the particular situation.

Usually, extra duty stipends do not compensate for services rendered (coaches put in many voluntary hours) and they are not tied to productivity (the coach does not receive more pay if he or she is more successful) and are therefore exempt from the overtime provisions of the FLSA.

29 U.S.C. 203(e)(4)(A)

29 C.F.R. 553.101

U.S. Department of Labor Opinion Letter FLSA 2018-6

Purdham, et al. v. Fairfax County School Board and Fairfax County Schools, 637 F. 3d 421 (4th Cir. 2011)

20:102 Do paid leaves count as hours for purposes of computing overtime?

The Fair Labor Standards Act requires that an employer pay overtime at the rate of 1.5 times straight time salary after an employee has worked 40 hours in a workweek. Payments that are made for occasional periods when the employee is not at work due to vacation, holiday, illness, failure of the employer to provide sufficient work, or other similar cause are not treated as hours worked for purposes of computing overtime. Neither are such hours credited toward overtime.

An employer policy, rule, regulation, or collectively bargained agreement to the contrary may produce a different result.

29 C.F.R. 778.218 et seq.

20:110 Can the wage and hour provisions of the Fair Labor Standards Act be avoided by bargaining a contrary result?

Compliance with the Fair Labor Standards Act cannot normally be avoided by collectively bargaining a contrary lesser result. There are very limited exceptions that involve guaranteed hour agreements.

29 U.S.C. 201 et seq.

RETIREMENT PROGRAM

20:120 What state retirement program serves educational support employees and how are employee contributions to the program treated?

Educational support employees of the school district are covered by the Illinois Municipal Retirement Fund (IMRF). Each school district must pay employee contributions to the IMRF for all compensation earned. Such contributions are treated as employer contributions in determining tax treatment under the Internal Revenue Code and are thereby treated as non-taxable income for IRS purposes.

40 ILCS 5/7-132

40 ILCS 5/7-171

20:124 Are IMRF employees subject to the six percent pension earnings cap?

A new law in 2011 provides that if an Illinois Municipal Retirement Fund (IMRF) employee's reported earnings for any of the 12-month periods used to determine the final rate of earnings exceeds the employee's 12-month reported earnings with the same employer for the previous year by the greater of six percent or 1.5 times the annual increase in the Consumer

Price Index-U for the preceding September, the school board that paid those earnings must pay to IMRF, in addition to any other required contributions, the present value of the increase in the pension resulting from the portion of the increase in salary that is in excess of the greater of 6 percent or 1.5 times the annual increase in the Consumer Price Index-U as determined by IMRF. Present value is computed on the basis of the actuarial assumptions and tables used in the most recent actuarial valuation of IMRF that is available at the time of the computation.

Whenever it determines that a payment is or may be required, IMRF calculates the amount of the payment and bills the employer for that amount. The bill specifies the calculations used to determine the amount due. If the employer disputes the amount of the bill, it may, within 30 days after receipt of the bill, apply to IMRF in writing for a recalculation. The application must specify in detail the grounds for the dispute.

40 ILCS 5/7-172

20:125 What is excluded from the IMRF pension earnings cap?

When assessing payment for any amount due, IMRF excludes earnings increases resulting from overload or overtime earnings and earnings increases attributable to standard employment promotions resulting in increased responsibility and workload. The cap does not apply to earnings increases paid to individuals under contracts or collective bargaining agreements entered into, amended, or renewed before January 1, 2012, earnings increases paid to members who are 10 years or more from retirement eligibility, or earnings increases resulting from an increase in the number of hours required to be worked. IMRF also excludes earnings attributable to personnel policies adopted before January 1, 2012 as long as those policies are not applicable to employees who begin service on or after January 1, 2012.

40 ILCS 5/7-172

20:126 What disclosure requirements apply to pay increases after an employee has announced his or her retirement?

In 2016, the General Assembly enacted the Government Wage Transparency Act which requires certain procedures and disclosures if a pay increase or a lump-sum payment is made by an employer to an employee after the employee has expressed his or her intent to retire or withdraw from service and would have the effect of increasing the employee's reportable monthly earnings from that employer by more than 6 percent compared to the previous month; and is be made between 12 months and 90 days prior to the employee's expected termination of service. Disclosable payment does not include a refund of contributions or any payment required to be paid by state or federal law.

The payment is prohibited unless the school board has first discussed the specific payment to be made at an open meeting. At the meeting, the governing body shall disclose (1) the identity of the employee, (2) the purpose and amount of the increase or payment, (3) the proposed retirement date, (4) the effect of the payment upon the expected retirement annuity of the employee, and (5) the effect of the payment upon the liability of the employer to IMRF.

50 ILCS 155/5

20:127 What is the IMRF 600-hour rule?

To be eligible to participate in the Illinois Municipal Retirement Fund (IMRF), an employee must be "expected to work" at least 600 hours in the next 12-month period. To determine expectation, the job description and the history of the position are considered. Eligibility is based on expectation, not the number of hours the employee actually works.

If an employee is hired in the middle of a calendar year, the 600-hour computation is made for the next 12 months, not for the remainder of the current calendar year.

If an employee works multiple jobs for the same employer, all his or her positions are combined to determine whether or not he or she meets the 600-hour standard. The requirements of a position must be evaluated annually to determine eligibility. An employee who is expected to work for less than 600 hours in the next 12-month period is not eligible to participate in IMRF.

Other governmental entities have the option to change the hours worked standard from 600 to 1,000. School districts and special education cooperatives do not have this option.

40 ILCS 5/7-137

www.imrf.org/pubs/forms/form_series_misc/ENROLLED.pdf

www.imrf.org/pubs/er_pubs/aamanual/online_aa_manual/3.20_a.htm

20:129 What is the IMRF "return-to-work" rule?

Generally, an Illinois Municipal Retirement Fund (IMRF) pension is suspended if a retiree returns to work for any IMRF employer in a position that qualifies for IMRF coverage (meets the 600-hour rule). The employee's pension payments stop and the retiree is reenrolled as an active IMRF member (who must make contributions). Once the member retires again, the pension is reinstated (service credit is recomputed).

If the retiree is elected to a public office, the pension is suspended even if the elected position qualifies for IMRF coverage. The pension is suspended only if the pension is based on any service credit earned while participating in IMRF in that elected office or the retiree elects to participate in IMRF while holding that elected office.

Social Security return-to-work rules are different from IMRF rules. There is no relationship between the Social Security retirement test on earnings and IMRF coverage rules. The Social Security retirement test is based on dollar earnings, whereas the IMRF test is based solely on the 600-hour rule. If the position qualifies for IMRF coverage, IMRF benefits are suspended even though Social Security may continue to pay its benefits.

Most retirees continue to receive the IMRF pension if the position to which they return to work does not qualify for IMRF coverage.

40 ILCS 5/7-141.1(g)

Prazen v. Shoop, 2012 IL App (4th) 120048, 974 N.E. 2d 1006, 363 Ill. Dec. 209

SICK LEAVE

20:130 Are educational support employees entitled to minimum sick leave by law?

If an educational support employee is eligible to participate in the Illinois Municipal Retirement Fund under the 600-hour standard or under any other eligibility participation standard allowed by Section 7-198 of the Illinois Pension Code, the employee is entitled to a minimum statutory grant of 10 sick leave days per year cumulative to a minimum of 180 days. The minimums set forth above may be increased by contract when a bargaining unit is involved or by school board policy in other instances.

105 ILCS 5/24-6

20:134 Are educational support employees entitled to bereavement leave?

If the employee qualifies for sick leave under the Illinois Municipal Retirement Fund 600-hour standard, or if the employee has accumulated sick leave, the employee may use paid sick leave for a death in the immediate family. The employee may use paid personal leave pursuant to the terms set forth in policy or a collective bargaining agreement usually without the immediate family restriction. If the employee qualifies, the employee may access unpaid leave under the Family and Medical Leave Act (FMLA). A statute new in 2016 allows FMLA qualified employees to access 10 work days of unpaid leave for the death of a child.

30 ILCS 105/5.874

105 ILCS 5/24-6

DISMISSAL

20:140 Is an educational support employee entitled to due process prior to dismissal for cause?

When dismissal for cause is contemplated in the middle of a school year, such employees frequently have an expectation of employment beyond mere notice, because of the actions of their employers. An employer guarantee to an employee of re-employment to avoid the employee's summer unemployment compensation claim might, for example, create a property right in continued employment and require the employer to provide substantive and procedural due process before the employee can be dismissed.

Likewise, the existence of a "just cause" provision or a procedural due process clause in a collective bargaining agreement might provide the employee with rights beyond those contained in the law.

The statute governing the notice that must be given non-certified employees before termination was amended in 1997. Employers should be certain their policies conform to the changes before implementing the presumably less stringent notice requirements of the amended statute.

To dismiss an educational support employee for cause during the term of his or her employment expectation requires a pre-termination hearing that allows the employee a fair opportunity to refute the alleged causes for dismissal. The employee must be given enough facts to prepare a defense. Usually, that means names, dates, and the circumstances of the allegations. In cases of disciplinary suspension based on criminal charges, a pre-disciplinary hearing may not be required if due process is promptly provided.

105 ILCS 5/10-23.5

Griggsville-Perry Community Unit District No. 4 v. Illinois Educational Labor Relations Board, 2013 IL 113721, 984 N.E. 2d 440, 368 Ill. Dec. 494

Baird v. Board of Education for Warren Community School District No. 205, 389 F. 3d 685 (7th Cir. 2004)

Gilbert v. Homar, 117 S. Ct. 1807, 520 U.S. 924, 138 L. Ed. 2d 120 (1997) on rem. 149 F. 3d 1164 (3rd Cir. 1998)

Cleveland Board of Education v. Loudermill, 105 S. Ct. 1487, 470 U.S. 532, 84 L. Ed. 2d 494 (1985) on rem. 763 F. 2d 202 (6th Cir. 1985)

20:142 May a school board create an at-will employment relationship with its educational support employees?

Whether or not an at-will relationship exists is a fact question that requires an examination of the employment relationship between the employer and employee. Employer policies, rules and regulations, employment documents, and other evidence of the relationship between the parties will define whether educational support employees are at-will or contractual and whether or not any particular employee has an expectation of continued employment.

An employer wanting to rely on an at-will relationship should be certain its policy manual and employee handbook do not contain just cause dismissal language or promises of continuing employment. The safer approach for most employers is to assume its non-certificated employees are year-to-year contractual employees.

Haag, et al v. The Board of Education of Streator Elementary District 44, 2017 IL App (3d) 150643, 79 N.E. 3d 722, 414 Ill. Dec. 87

Griggsville-Perry Community Unit District No. 4 v. Illinois Educational Labor Relations Board, 2013 IL 113721, 984 N.E. 2d 440, 368 Ill. Dec. 494

Ross v. May Company, 377 Ill. App. 3d 387, 880 N.E. 2d 210, 316 Ill. Dec. 232 (1st Dist. 2007)

Doyle v. Holy Cross Hospital, 186 Ill. 2d 104, 708 N.E. 2d 1140, 237 Ill. Dec. 100 (1999)

Spear v. North Shore School District No. 112, 291 Ill. App. 3d 117, 683 N.E. 2d 218, 225 Ill. Dec. 274 (2nd Dist. 1997) app. den. 175 Ill. 2d 555, 689 N.E. 2d 147, 228 Ill. Dec. 726 (1997)

Rojicek v. Community Consolidated School District No. 15, 888 F. Supp. 878 (N.D. Ill. 1995)

20:143 May an educational support employee use a "just cause" provision in a collective bargaining agreement to challenge his or her discipline or dismissal?

A "just cause" provision is one that requires that an employee's discipline be "fair" or for "just cause." A "just cause" provision in a collective bargaining agreement covering educational support employees is probably enforceable.

105 ILCS 5/10-23.5

Board of Education of Rockford School District No. 205, v. The Illinois Educational Labor Relations Board, 165 Ill. 2d 80, 649 N.E. 2d 369, 208 Ill. Dec. 313 (1995)

Midwest Central Education Association v. Illinois Educational Labor Relations Board, et al., 277 Ill. App. 3d 440, 660 N.E. 2d 151, 213 Ill. Dec. 894 (1st Dist. 1995)

20:150 Do educational support personnel have seniority rights?

Unless a collective bargaining agreement provides otherwise, educational support personnel acquire seniority within the respective category of position in which they are employed from the first day of continuous service to the school district.

105 ILCS 5/10-23.5

20:160 Are part-time educational support personnel entitled to seniority rights?

Yes. Unlike teachers whose seniority is affected by evaluation, both full- and part-time educational support personnel are entitled to seniority by law and without any performance component.

105 ILCS 5/10-23.5

20:170 Do educational support personnel serve a probationary period before earning seniority rights?

No. Seniority accrues to educational support personnel employees from their first day of employment, rather than after a probationary period.

105 ILCS 5/10-23.5

20:180 What is the procedure for reducing the number of educational support staff employed by the district?

Except in instances of layoff when a subcontract of the work is contemplated and unless a collective bargaining agreement provides otherwise, or in the instance of a reduction due to an unforeseen reduction in the student population (which requires written notice five days in advance hand-delivered and mailed), when the school board decides to decrease the number of educational support staff employed or to discontinue some particular type of educational support service, written notice must be mailed to the employee and also given to the employee either by certified mail, return receipt requested or personal delivery with receipt, at least 30 days before the employee is removed or dismissed, together with a statement of honorable dismissal and the reason therefor.

The employee(s) with the shorter length of continuing service with the district, within the respective category of position, must be dismissed first unless an alternative method of determining the sequence of dismissal is lawfully established in a collective bargaining agreement.

A collectively bargained alternative provision for determining the sequence of dismissal must not impair the operation of any affirmative action program in the district, regardless of whether it exists by operation of law or is conducted on a voluntary basis by the board.

105 ILCS 5/10-23.5

Haag, et al v. The Board of Education of Streator Elementary District 44, 2017 IL App (3d) 150643, 79 N.E. 3d 722, 414 Ill. Dec. 87

Buckellew v. Board of Education of Georgetown-Ridge Farm Community Unit School District No. 4, 214 Ill. App. 3d 506, 575 N.E. 2d 556, 159 Ill. Dec. 58 (4th Dist. 1991)

20:182 Is a reduction in support staff work hours a reduction in force within the meaning of the law?

Prior to August 23, 2007, case law limited the application of the statute that governs the procedures for reduction in force of support staff to the removal or dismissal of support employees and not to the reduction of their hours. A 2007 change in the statute makes the statutory reduction procedures applicable to work hour reductions as well as layoffs.

The statute also provides "... if the reduction in hours is due to an unforeseen reduction in the student population, then the written notice must be mailed and given to the employee at least five days before the hours are reduced."

Georgetown-Ridge Farm Community Unit School District No. 4, 10 PERI 1045 (IELRB Opinion and Order, March 1, 1994)

Buckellew v. Board of Education of Georgetown-Ridge Farm Community Unit School District No. 4, 214 Ill. App. 3d 506, 575 N.E. 2d 556, 159 Ill. Dec. 58 (4th Dist. 1991)

20:183 Must a school district follow the notice provisions of the reduction-in-force laws with respect to the reduction of temporary or substitute support employees?

No.

Buckellew v. Board of Education of Georgetown-Ridge Farm Community Unit School District No. 4, 214 Ill. App. 3d 506, 575 N.E. 2d 556, 159 Ill. Dec. 58 (4th Dist. 1991)

20:186 Are support staff employees protected in the case of a school deactivation?

Before a 2007 change in the law, such employees had no protection. Beginning August 17, 2007, when the deactivation of school facilities becomes effective, the transfer of educational support personnel employees shall apply — as governed by 105 ILCS 10-23.5(b) — and the positions at the school facilities being deactivated that are held by educational support personnel employees at the time of the deactivation are transferred to the control of the board or boards that will be receiving the district's students on the following basis:

1) Positions of such educational support personnel employees that were full-time positions are transferred to the control of whichever of the boards the employees request, with the educational support personnel employees making these requests proceeding in the order of those with the greatest length of continuing service with the board to those with the shortest length of continuing service with the board, provided that the number selecting one board over another board or other boards must not exceed that proportion of students going to such board or boards; and

2) Positions of such educational support personnel employees that were full-time positions and as to which there is no selection left under the above are transferred to the appropriate board.

The length of continuing service of any educational support personnel employee thereby transferred to another district is not lost and the receiving board is subject to the provisions of the School Code with respect to that transferred educational support personnel employee in the same manner as if the educational support personnel employee was the district's employee during the time the educational support personnel employee was actually employed by the board of the deactivating district from which the position was transferred.

105 ILCS 5/10-22.22b

20:188 When a new school district is formed, what happens to the non-certified employees of the old district or districts?

In the case of a new school district or districts formed in accordance with Article 11E of the School Code, a school district (or districts) that annexes all of the territory of one or more entire other school districts in accordance with Article 7 of the School Code, or a school district receiving students from a deactivated school facility in accordance with Section 10-22.22b of this Code, the employment of educational support personnel in the new, annexing, or receiving school district immediately following the reorganization is governed by Section 10-23.5b of the School Code.

Lists of the educational support personnel employed in the individual districts for the school year immediately prior to the effective date of the new district or districts, annexation, or deactivation are combined for the districts forming the new district or districts, for the annexed and annexing districts, or for the deactivating and receiving districts, as the case may be. The combined list must be categorized by positions, showing the length of continuing service of each full-time educational support personnel employee who is qualified to hold any such position. If there are more full-time educational support personnel employees on the combined list than there are available positions in the new, annexing, or receiving school district, then the employing school board must first remove or dismiss those educational support personnel employees with the shorter length of continuing service within the respective category of position, following the reduction in force procedures in Section 10-23.5 of the School Code.

The employment and position of each educational support personnel employee on the combined list not so removed or dismissed is transferred to the new, annexing, or receiving school board, and the new, annexing, or receiving school board is subject to the School Code with respect to any educational support personnel employee so transferred as if the educational support personnel employee had been the new, annexing, or receiving board's employee during the time the educational support personnel employee was actually employed by the school board of the district from which the employment and position were transferred.

The 2007 changes do not apply to the formation of a new district or districts in accordance with Article 11E of the School Code, the annexation of one or more entire districts in accordance with Article 7 of the School Code, or the deactivation of a school facility in accordance with Section 10-22.22b of the School Code if those events occurred on or before July 1, 2007.

105 ILCS 5/7-1 et seq.
105 ILCS 5/10-22.22b
105 ILCS 5/10-23.5
105 ILCS 5/11E-1 et seq.

20:190 Do educational support personnel have recall rights after layoff?

Yes. After a layoff, any vacancies occurring for the following school term or within one year from the beginning of that school term must be tendered to the employees removed from that specific category of position or any other category if the employees are qualified to hold such positions. A 2007 statutory change in Section 10-23.5 of the School Code requires that the board consider the qualifications of employees in the recall pool who were removed from positions other than the vacant position.

105 ILCS 5/10-23.5

Haag, et al v. The Board of Education of Streator Elementary District 44, 2017 IL App (3d) 150643, 79 N.E. 3d 722, 414 Ill. Dec. 87

20:200 Must a school board recall educational support personnel from a layoff pool in seniority order?

Employees need not be recalled from the recall pool in seniority order unless a collective bargaining agreement requires it.

105 ILCS 5/10-23.5

SCHOOL BUS DRIVERS

20:210 What are the qualifications for employment as a school bus driver?

A school bus driver must hold a valid school bus driver permit. To obtain a permit; an applicant must submit the results of a medical examination showing physical fitness to operate a school bus; submit to and pass a fingerprint-based criminal records check; have a safe driving record pursuant to statutory definition; demonstrate he or she has never been convicted of any of a list of specified criminal offenses; be at least 21 years of age; has not within the last five years been adjudged to be afflicted with or suffering from any mental disability or disease; and holds a valid and properly classified driver's license that has not been revoked, suspended, or canceled during the previous three years, or has not has his or her commercial motor vehicle driving privileges disqualified during the previous three years.

There are numerous other requirements contained in the relevant statute, including many that define offenses that disqualify a person, upon conviction, from holding a bus driver permit.

49 C.F.R. 382.301
625 ILCS 5/6-106.1

20:214 What must an employer do before employing a school bus driver?

The employer is responsible for conducting pre-employment interviews, distributing school bus driver applications and medical forms to be completed by the applicant, and submitting the applicant's fingerprint cards to the State Police. The employer must certify in writing to the Secretary of State that all pre-employment conditions have been met including completion of the criminal background check.

625 ILCS 5/6-106.1

20:220 May a school board suspend or revoke an employee's school bus driver permit?

No. The Secretary of State may suspend or revoke a school bus driver permit for specific causes provided in Illinois motor vehicle laws. A school board does not have this authority.

625 ILCS 5/6-106.1 (g)

20:230 What happens if a school bus driver fails the drug and alcohol test required by statute?

If an applicant fails to obtain a negative result on the mandatory drug and alcohol test necessary to obtain a school bus driver permit, the Secretary of State must refuse the applicant a permit for a period of three years.

625 ILCS 5/6-106.1 (g)

20:240 May a school bus driver who has an accident while driving a school bus refuse a drug or alcohol test?

No. The driver is subject to the implied consent requirements for commercial motor vehicle drivers.

49 C.F.R. 382.211
49 C.F.R. 382.303
625 ILCS 5/6-516(c)
625 ILCS 5/11-501.2

21: COLLECTIVE BARGAINING

ILLINOIS EDUCATIONAL LABOR RELATIONS ACT

21:10 What is the Illinois Educational Labor Relations Act?

The Illinois Educational Labor Relations Act is a state law that regulates the recognition of exclusive bargaining representatives and the collective bargaining relationships and procedures for all public school employers and all public school employees in the state.

Under terms of the Act, covered employees may organize, form, join, or assist in employee organizations, or engage in lawful concerted activities for the purpose of collective bargaining or other mutual aid and protection, or bargain collectively through representatives of their own free choice. Except as limited by the Act, employees also have the right to refrain from any or all such activities.

115 ILCS 5/1 et seq.
115 ILCS 5/3

21:20 Does the National Labor Relations Board have any jurisdiction with respect to Illinois educational labor relations?

No.

21:30 How is the Illinois Educational Labor Relations Act implemented and enforced?

The Illinois Educational Labor Relations Board (IELRB) promulgates and enforces rules necessary to carry out the purposes of the Act.

115 ILCS 5/1 et seq.

21:40 What is the Illinois Educational Labor Relations Board?

The Illinois Educational Labor Relations Board (IELRB) is a seven-member board appointed by the Governor with the advice and consent of the Senate. No more than four IELRB members may be from the same political party. Members must have a minimum of five years' experience directly related to labor and employment relations in representing educational employers or educational employees in collective bargaining matters.

Members of the IELRB generally serve six-year terms of office. However, the number of members making up the Board was increased in 1998 from three to five and during the transition, one member will serve a four-year term. The two new members appointed as a result of legislation passed in 2000 will each serve initial terms of six years. Members of the IELRB may be removed only by the Governor upon notice and only for neglect of duty or malfeasance in office and for no other cause.

115 ILCS 5/5

Board of Education of Mundelein Elementary School District No. 75 v. Illinois Educational Labor Relations Board, 179 Ill. App. 3d 696, 534 N.E. 2d 1022, 128 Ill. Dec. 577 (4th Dist. 1989)

21:50 Do rulings of the Illinois Educational Labor Relations Board have the effect of law?

Yes. But any party aggrieved by a final order of the Illinois Educational Labor Relations Board may appeal to either the First or Fourth District Appellate Courts at the option of the appellant.

115 ILCS 5/16

21:60 Does the Open Meetings Act apply to collective bargaining negotiations and grievance arbitrations?

No. Bargaining meetings at which collective bargaining will occur and arbitration hearings are not subject to the Open Meetings Act. The notice requirements and the closed meeting exceptions of the Open Meetings Act are not applicable.

School board meetings held solely to develop strategy, at which no bargaining actually occurs, and board meetings to plan arbitration strategy are subject to the Open Meetings Act.

115 ILCS 5/18

COVERED EMPLOYERS AND EMPLOYEES

21:70 Which employers are covered by the Illinois Educational Labor Relations Act?

Employers covered by the Act are the governing body of a public school district, including the governing body of a charter school; a contract school or contract turnaround school; combination of public school districts including the governing body of joint agreements of any type formed by two or more school districts; a subcontractor of instructional services of a school district (other than Chicago Public Schools), combination of school districts, charter school, contract school or contract turnaround school; and any State agency whose major function is providing educational services.

"Educational employer" or "employer" does not include a Financial Oversight Panel created pursuant to Section 1A-8 of the School Code due to a district violating a financial plan or an approved nonpublic special education facility that contracts with a school district or combination of school districts to provide special education services pursuant to Section 14-7.02 of the School Code, but does include a School Finance Authority created under Article 1E or 1F of the School Code.

115 ILCS 5/2

21:74 May the employees of an alternative school created under the Safe Schools Law petition for collective bargaining rights?

Yes.

105 ILCS 5/13A-1(m)

21:75 Who is the employer of alternative school employees?

The employer of alternative school employees is probably the regional superintendent of schools, although in specific circumstances the employer may be some other entity (contracted services) or the regional superintendent and some other entity.

105 ILCS 5/13A-6

21:80 Which school employees are covered by the Illinois Educational Labor Relations Act?

The Act covers any school district employee except supervisory, managerial, confidential, short-term, or student employees.

115 ILCS 5/2(b)

21:90 What is a supervisory employee?

A supervisor is any individual having authority in the interests of the employer to hire, transfer, suspend, lay off, recall, promote, discharge, reward, or discipline other employees within the appropriate bargaining unit and adjust their grievances, or to effectively recommend such action if the exercise of such authority is not of a merely routine or clerical nature, but requires the use of independent judgment. The term supervisor includes only those individuals who devote a preponderance of their employment time to exercising such authority.

115 ILCS 5/2(g)

Illinois Department of Management Services, 5 PERI 2012 (IELRB Decision and Order, April 28, 1989)

Virden Community Unit School District No. 4, 4 PERI 1060 (IELRB Hearing Officer, March 31, 1988)

21:100 What is a managerial employee?

A managerial employee is an individual who is engaged predominantly in executive and management functions and is charged with the responsibility of directing the effectuation of management policies and practices.

115 ILCS 5/2(o)

Lincoln Way Community High School District No. 210, 5 PERI 1025 (Executive Director's Recommended Decision and Order, January 11, 1989)

21:110 What is a confidential employee?

A confidential employee is an employee who (1) in the regular course of his or her duties, assists and acts in a confidential capacity to persons who formulate, determine, and effectuate management policies with regard to labor relations, or (2) in the regular course of his or her duties has access to information relating to the effectuation or review of the employer's collective bargaining policies. A third "test" is applicable to employees in not yet formed bargaining units. It involves a determination as to whether there is a reasonable expectation the employees at issue would perform confidential duties in a future collective bargaining process.

An employer is not required to bargain with individuals who receive advance notice of its collective bargaining strategy or labor relations policies, even if such persons do so on a sporadic basis. The purpose of excluding confidential employees is to keep employees from having their loyalties divided between the employer and the bargaining unit that would otherwise represent them. For this reason, under certain circumstances, bookkeepers, technology coordinators, and/or certain secretaries may be excluded from bargaining units in which they would otherwise belong.

Labor board determinations of confidentiality are given great deference by the courts. One court opined that its role was to overturn such decisions only in cases when they are clearly erroneous and "wrong with the force of a five-week old unrefrigerated dead fish."

115 ILCS 5/2(n)

Niles Twp. High School District 219 v. IELRB, 387 Ill. App. 3d 58, 900 N.E. 2d 336, 326 Ill. Dec. 700 (1st Dist 2008)

Board of Education of Glenview Community Consolidated School District No. 34 v. Illinois Educational Labor Relations Board, 374 Ill. App. 3d 892, 874 N.E. 2d 158, 314 Ill. Dec. 248 (4th Dist. 2007)

Support Council of District 39, Wilmette Local 1274 v. Educational Labor Relations Board, et al., 366 Ill. App. 3d 830, 852 N.E 2d 372, 304 Ill. Dec. 122 (1st Dist. 2006)

Danville Community Consolidated School District No. 118, 5 PERI 1084 (IELRB Opinion and Order, April 12, 1989)

Board of Education of Plainfield Community Consolidated School District No. 202, Will and Kendall Counties v. Illinois Educational Labor Relations Board, et al., 143 Ill. App. 3d 898, 493 N.E. 2d 1130, 98 Ill. Dec. 109 (4th Dist. 1986)

21:112 When may a petition to exclude a confidential employee be filed?

A petition to remove a confidential employee from a bargaining unit may be filed at any time.

Niles Twp. High School District 219 v. IELRB, 387 Ill. App. 3d 58, 900 N.E. 2d 336, 326 Ill. Dec. 700 (1st Dist 2008)

21:115 What is a short-term employee?

A short-term employee is one who is employed for less than two consecutive calendar quarters during a calendar year, and who does not have reasonable expectation that he or she will be rehired by the same employer for the same service in a subsequent calendar year.

115 ILCS 5/2(q)

21:120 May educational support employees seek union recognition and bargaining rights under the Educational Labor Relations Act?

Educational support personnel may seek recognition and bargaining rights under the Act provided they are school board employees and not the employees of an independent contractor (except a non-public special education facility). The employees of independent contractors (such as independent bus companies or janitorial service companies) are generally not covered under the Act.

115 ILCS 5/2(b)

Decatur School District No. 61, 3 PERI 1022 (IELRB Opinion and Order, February 10, 1987)

Alpha School Bus Company, 2 PERI 1008 (Executive Director's Recommended Decision and Order, November 7, 1985)

STATUTORY OBLIGATIONS OF EMPLOYERS

21:130 Does the Illinois Educational Labor Relations Act require school boards and their employees to bargain collectively?

The Act requires educational employers to collectively bargain with representatives of duly recognized employee bargaining units. If an appropriate bargaining unit gains voluntary recognition or recognition by election, the employer must bargain with it.

115 ILCS 5/10

21:140 What matters are educational employers obligated to bargain with their employees?

Covered employers are required to bargain collectively with regard to policy matters directly affecting wages, hours, and terms and conditions of employment, as well as the impact thereon, upon request by an employee representative. However, employers are not required to bargain over matters of inherent managerial policy.

115 ILCS 5/3

115 ILCS 5/4

Central City Education Association, IEA-NEA v. Illinois Educational Labor Relations Board and Central City Community Consolidated School District No. 133, 149 Ill. 2d 496, 599 N.E. 2d 892, 174 Ill. Dec. 808 (1992)

Board of Education Decatur District No. 61 v. Illinois Educational Labor Relations Board, 180 Ill. App. 3d 770, 536 N.E. 2d 743, 129 Ill. Dec. 693 (4th Dist. 1989)

Must an employer bargain issues related to pension reform legislation?

In 2013, the General Assembly passed P.A. 98-599, a comprehensive pension reform bill that had an effective date of June 1, 2014. The law was struck down in 2015 by the Illinois Supreme Court. Pension reform in Illinois is controversial and any legislation will face court challenges from many different interest groups. The 2013 legislation contained a new duty to bargain provision that included significant limiting language regarding the obligation to bargain issues arising out of pension reform.

115 ILCS 5/10.5

21:145 May an employer avoid bargaining obligations by assigning a subject of bargaining to a non-bargaining committee for study or resolution?

When an employer assigns a mandatory subject of bargaining to a committee for resolution, the subject is not removed from the realm of collective bargaining — nor is the employer relieved of any bargaining obligations — even though the union agrees to the committee assignment. If both labor and management are represented on the committee to which the subject is assigned, agreements reached by the committee may be contractual unless there is an express waiver by the union to the contrary.

These assignments to committee most frequently occur when difficult and complicated issues (such as health insurance specifications) are being bargained and the issue is deemed too time consuming or complicated for resolution at the bargaining table.

Board of Education of DuPage High School District No. 88 v. Illinois Educational Labor Relations Board, 246 Ill. App. 3d 967, 617 N.E. 2d 790, 187 Ill. Dec. 333 (1st Dist. 1993)

Alton Community Unit School District No. 11 v. Illinois Educational Labor Relations Board, 209 Ill. App. 3d 16, 567 N.E. 2d 671, 153 Ill. Dec. 713 (4th Dist. 1991)

21:150 What are the inherent managerial policies that employers are not required to bargain?

Matters of inherent managerial policy include such areas of discretion or policy as the functions of the employer, standards of services, the overall budget, the organizational structure, and selection of new employees and direction of employees.

A balancing test is used to determine whether a particular subject is more nearly a "wage, hour, or term and condition of employment" that must be bargained, or a management right that need not be bargained.

115 ILCS 5/4

115 ILCS 5/10

Central City Education Association, IEA-NEA v. Illinois Educational Labor Relations Board and Central City Community Consolidated School District No. 133, 149 Ill. 2d 496, 599 N.E. 2d 892, 174 Ill. Dec. 808 (1992)

Board of Education Leroy Community Unit School District No. 2 v. Illinois Educational Labor Relations Board, 199 Ill. App. 3d 347, 556 N.E. 2d 857, 145 Ill. Dec. 239 (4th Dist. 1990) 149 Ill. 2d 496, 599 N.E. 2d 892, 174 Ill. Dec. 808 (1992)

Board of Education Decatur District No. 61 v. Illinois Educational Labor Relations Board, 180 Ill. App. 3d 770, 536 N.E. 2d 743, 129 Ill. Dec. 693 (4th Dist. 1989)

21:155 What is past practice?

The past practices of an employer assist a decision-maker in determining the meaning of ambiguous contract language and may have relevance in determining status quo.

Past practice does not alter contract language and clear contract language is always enforceable, even if there is a past practice to the contrary. Past practice is only grievable if the employer and its union have agreed to a broad grievance definition (this result is best avoided). A past practice must be clear and consistent. When a particular course of conduct has frequent exceptions, it is not a past practice. A past practice requires longevity and repetition and both the employer and the union must know about the practice and accept it.

When an employer seeks to resolve an issue about which the contract is not clear, but seeks to avoid any suggestion that the interpretation is more than an isolated resolution (not part of a past-practice sequence), the best course is to contemporaneously with resolution commit to writing the intention of the parties that the resolution not be used to establish past practice.

Thornton Fractional High School District No. 215 v. Illinois Educational Labor Relations Board, 404 Ill. App. 3d 757, 936 N.E. 2d 1188, 344 Ill. Dec. 431 (1st Dist. 2010)

Vienna School District No. 55 v. Illinois Educational Labor Relations Board, 162 Ill. App. 3d 503, 515 N.E. 2d 476, 113 Ill. Dec. 667 (4th Dist. 1987)

21:160 Is the school board free to make unilateral decisions on matters of inherent managerial policy?

Yes, a school board may make decisions on matters of inherent managerial policy. However, when any such decision affects the wages, hours, and terms or conditions of employment of any employee, the school board may be required to bargain the decision and/or the impact of any decision upon timely request of a recognized bargaining agent.

Whether or not the employer has an obligation to bargain in any given circumstance may be governed by a subjective balancing test. This obligation regarding the impact of managerial policy decisions is called "impact bargaining."

Central City Education Association, IEA-NEA v. Illinois Educational Labor Relations Board and Central City Community Consolidated School District No. 133, 149 Ill. 2d 496, 599 N.E. 2d 892, 174 Ill. Dec. 808 (1992)

21:166 May a school board unilaterally create a new extra duty or job assignment?

Yes. However, the wages to be paid for the new extra duty or new job assignment and the duties attendant to it must be bargained on demand by the exclusive representative. Discussions between the employer and individual employee about wages or duties will likely result in unfair labor practice charges; extra-duty bargaining must involve the employer and the union.

Board of Education of Sesser-Valier Community Unit School District No. 196 v. Illinois Educational Labor Relations Board and Sesser-Valier Education Association, IEA-NEA, 250 Ill. App. 3d 878, 620 N.E. 2d 418, 189 Ill. Dec. 450 (4th Dist. 1993)

21:170 How does bargaining the impact of a decision differ from bargaining the decision itself?

Decisional bargaining requires the employer to bargain with the exclusive bargaining agent over a decision to do something before the decision is made or implemented. Impact bargaining means that the employer is free to make an unfettered decision but is obligated to bargain, on demand, the effects of the decision on wages, hours, and terms or conditions of employment.

Central City Education Association, IEA-NEA v. Illinois Educational Labor Relations Board and Central City Community Consolidated School District No. 133, 149 Ill. 2d 496, 599 N.E. 2d 892, 174 Ill. Dec. 808 (1992)

Berkeley School District No. 87, 2 PERI 1066 (IELRB Opinion and Order, May 30, 1986)

21:180 What rights do support personnel have with respect to the subcontracting of their work?

Subcontracting is the entry into an agreement with an outside contractor to supply work that previously was performed by school district employees. Common subcontracts are for food delivery, janitorial, or bus services.

Before a 2007 change in the statute, a school board could enter into a subcontract subject only to its compliance with the provisions of the Illinois Educational Labor Relations Act and the seniority-layoff provisions of the School Code. After the change in the law, subcontracts occur much less frequently and are much more difficult to effect.

The 2007 amendment to the relevant statute provides that a board of education may enter into a contract with a third party for non-instructional services currently performed by any employee or bargaining unit member or lay off those educational support personnel employees upon 90 days' written notice to the affected employees, provided that a contract cannot be entered into and become effective during the term of a collective bargaining agreement, as that term is set forth in the agreement, covering any employees who perform the non-instructional services; the contract may only take effect upon the expiration of an existing collective bargaining agreement and any third party that submits a bid to perform the non-instructional services must provide the following:

1) Evidence of liability insurance in scope and amount equivalent to the liability insurance provided by the school board pursuant to Section 10-22.3 of the School Code;

2) A benefits package for the third party's employees who will perform the non-instructional services comparable to the benefits package provided to school board employees who perform those services;

3) A list of the number of employees who will provide the non-instructional services, the job classifications of those employees, and the wages the third party will pay those employees;

4) A minimum three-year cost projection, using generally accepted accounting principles and which the third party is prohibited from increasing if the bid is accepted by the school board, for each and every expenditure category and account for performing the non-instructional services;

5) Composite information about the criminal and disciplinary records, including alcohol or other substance abuse, Department of Children and Family Services complaints and investigations, traffic violations, and license revocations or any other licensure problems, of any employees who may perform the non-instructional services, provided that the individual names and other identifying information of employees need not be provided with the submission of the bid, but must be made available upon request of the school board; and

6) An affidavit, notarized by the president or chief executive officer of the third party, that each of its employees has completed a criminal background check as required by Section 10-21.9 of the School Code within three months prior to submission of the bid, provided that the results of such background checks need not be provided with the submission of the bid, but must be made available upon request of the school board.

A contract must not be entered into unless the school board provides a cost comparison, using generally accepted accounting principles, of each and every expenditure category and account that the school board projects it would incur over the term of the contract if it continued to perform the non-instructional services using its own employees with each and every expenditure category and account that is projected a third party would incur if a third party performed the non-instructional services.

Review and consideration of all bids by third parties to perform the non-instructional services must take place in open session of a regularly scheduled school board meeting, unless the exclusive bargaining representative of the employees who perform the non-instructional services, if any such exclusive bargaining representative exists, agrees in writing that such review and consideration can take place in open session at a specially scheduled school board meeting.

A minimum of one public hearing, conducted by the school board prior to a regularly scheduled school board meeting, to discuss the school board's proposal to contract with a third party to perform the non-instructional services must be held before the school board may enter into such a contract; the school board must provide notice to the public of the date, time, and location of the first public hearing on or before the initial date that bids to provide the non-instructional services are solicited or a minimum of 30 days prior to entering into such a contract, whichever provides a greater period of notice.

A contract must contain provisions requiring the contractor to offer available employee positions pursuant to the contract to qualified school district employees whose employment is terminated because of the contract.

A contract must contain provisions requiring the contractor to comply with a policy of nondiscrimination and equal employment opportunity for all persons and to take affirmative steps to provide equal opportunity for all persons.

A board of education may enter into a contract, of no longer than three months in duration, with a third party for non-instructional services currently performed by an employee or bargaining unit member for the purpose of augmenting the current workforce in an emergency situation that threatens the safety or health of the school district's students or staff, provided that the school board meets all of its obligations under the Illinois Educational Labor Relations Act.

The 2007 changes do not apply to non-instructional services of a school district that on August 17, 2007 are performed for the school district by a third party.

105 ILCS 5/10-22.34c

Buckellew v. Board of Education of Georgetown-Ridge Farm Community Unit School District No. 4, 214 Ill. App. 3d 506, 575 N.E. 2d 556, 159 Ill. Dec. 58 (4th Dist. 1991)

Service Employees International Local Union No. 316 v. Illinois Educational Labor Relations Board and Carbondale Community High School District No. 165, 153 Ill. App. 3d 744, 505 N.E. 2d 418, 106 Ill. Dec. 112 (4th Dist. 1987)

21:185 May a school district subcontract for alternative learning opportunities program instructional services?

The Alternative Learning Opportunities Law provides that a school district may contract with a non-profit or for-profit educational entity for the delivery of services, but a school district may have bargaining obligations to a recognized exclusive bargaining representative before it does so. All educational entities providing instructional services for eligible students under this statute must be entities that are recognized by the State Board of Education.

105 ILCS 5/13B-75

21:190 In addition to bargaining a union contract, may a school board be required to bargain during the term of that contract?

During the term of a collective bargaining agreement — absent a broad zipper clause — the school board must, on demand by the exclusive bargaining representative, bargain over wages, hours, and terms or conditions of employment that were not fully bargained during the bargaining of the collective bargaining agreement. This is called "interim bargaining" or "midterm bargaining."

West Chicago School District 33 v. Illinois Educational Labor Relations Board, 218 Ill. App. 3d 304, 578 N.E. 2d 232, 161 Ill. Dec. 105 (1st Dist. 1991)

Waverly Community Unit School District No. 6, 5 PERI 1002 (IELRB Opinion and Order, November 23, 1988)

21:200 What is a zipper clause?

A zipper clause is a form of waiver of a union right to bargain. Specifically, it is a negotiated contract clause under which a union waives its right to engage in mid-term bargaining over mandatory subjects of bargaining. There are two kinds of zipper clauses — broad and narrow.

A narrow zipper clause waives the right to bargain over issues actually negotiated by the parties. A broad zipper clause forecloses bargaining on any issue not included in the contract even if the issue was unknown or not within the contemplation of the parties at the time the contract was signed.

Mt. Vernon Education Association, IEA-NEA v. The Illinois Educational Labor Relations Board, 278 Ill. App. 3d 814, 664 N.E. 2d 1067, 215 Ill. Dec. 553 (4th Dist. 1996)

Board of Regents of the Regency University System (Northern Illinois University), 7 PERI 1113 (IELRB Opinion and Order, October 24, 1991)

East Richland Education Association v. IELRB, 173 Ill. App. 3d 878, 528 N.E. 2d 751, 124 Ill. Dec. 63 (4th Dist. 1988)

Rock Falls Elementary School District No. 13, 2 PERI 1150 (IELRB Opinion and Order, May 14, 1987) aff'd. sub nom.

21:202 Is a waiver or zipper clause a mandatory subject of bargaining?

An employer proposal for a broad zipper clause is a permissive subject of bargaining. The employer may not insist to impasse on a broad zipper clause without committing an unfair labor practice.

An employer proposal for a narrow zipper clause is a mandatory subject of bargaining. An employer may insist to impasse over a narrow zipper clause without committing an unfair labor practice.

A union may voluntarily agree to a broad waiver, but the employer should be cautious because the waiver may be withdrawn unilaterally by the union during an appropriate bargaining period. If the waiver was bargained to neutralize or as a trade for some otherwise consequential language in the collective bargaining agreement, the effect of the removal of the waiver would be to leave the offending language in the contract but without the neutralizing waiver.

Waivers frequently take the form of attempts to exclude contract language from the grievance procedure, side agreements, zipper clauses, and other attempts to avoid bargaining obligations.

Mt. Vernon Education Association, IEA-NEA v. The Illinois Educational Labor Relations Board, 278 Ill. App. 3d 814, 664 N.E. 2d 1067, 215 Ill. Dec. 553 (4th Dist. 1996)

Board of Regents of the Regency University System (Northern Illinois University), 7 PERI 1113 (IELRB Opinion and Order, October 24, 1991)

21:206 May a collective bargaining agreement contain an "election of remedies" clause?

Any clause that limits the rights of employees to file claims should be carefully considered before adoption or inclusion in a collective bargaining agreement. While some "election of remedies" clauses are undoubtedly permissible, others are not. The law is unsettled as to which forms are okay and which are not.

Equal Employment Opportunity Commission v. Board of Governors of State Colleges, 957 F. 2d 424 (7th Cir. 1992)

BARGAINING UNITS

21:210 What is a bargaining unit?

A bargaining unit is a group of employees who have gained recognition, determined an exclusive representative, and have bargaining rights under the terms of the Educational Labor Relations Act.

115 ILCS 5/2(m)

21:220 What is a wall-to-wall bargaining unit?

A wall-to-wall bargaining unit is a bargaining unit composed of both professional and educational support employees. To form a wall-to-wall bargaining unit, both the professional and the non-certificated employees must vote to approve the combined bargaining unit.

115 ILCS 5/7

Riverside-Brookfield Township District No. 208, 5 PERI 1136 (IELRB Decision and Order, July 25, 1989)

21:230 On what basis is a bargaining unit determined to be appropriate?

In determining the appropriateness of a unit, the Educational Labor Relations Board must decide in each case, in order to ensure employees the fullest freedom in exercising the rights guaranteed by the Illinois Educational Labor Relations Act, the unit appropriate for the purpose of collective bargaining based upon, but not limited to, such factors as historical pattern of recognition; community of interest, including employee skills and functions; degree of functional integration; interchangeability and contact among employees; common supervision, wages, hours, and other working conditions of the employees involved; and the desires of the employees.

115 ILCS 5/7(a)

EXCLUSIVE BARGAINING REPRESENTATIVE

21:240 What is an exclusive representative?

An exclusive representative is the labor organization that has been designated by the Illinois Educational Labor Relations Board as the representative of the majority of educational employees in an appropriate unit, or one that has historically been recognized as the representative of an appropriate unit, or one that is voluntarily recognized by an employer upon evidence that the organization has been designated as the exclusive representative by a majority of the employees in an appropriate unit.

115 ILCS 5/2(d)

21:250 How may an exclusive representative gain recognition?

Prior to a 2003 statutory and rules change, elections were conducted by the Illinois Educational Labor Relations Board (IELRB) except in the relatively rare case when the employer voluntarily recognized. Because of the rules change, the majority of initial recognition questions are handled internally by IELRB using card check procedures and the conduct of elections is relatively rare.

A labor organization may gain recognition as the exclusive representative of an employee unit when it is voluntarily recognized by the employer or by a determination by IELRB that the representative represents a majority of the employees in the designated unit or by an election of the employees in the unit. Voluntary recognition is not possible whenever an employee organization has lawfully attained representation rights as the exclusive representative of the employees in the bargaining unit or whenever there has been a valid representation election or a majority interest petition has been dismissed within the preceding 12 months or whenever the proposed bargaining unit would include both professional and nonprofessional employees.

In most cases, the IELRB makes a representation determination (by checking cards filed by the union suggesting a majority of the employees in the proposed bargaining unit desire representation) or the parties waive hearing, enter into a consent agreement, and an election is held pursuant to the consent agreement.

115 ILCS 5/7

80 Ill. Admin. Code 1110.40

80 Ill. Admin. Code 1110.105

County of DuPage v. The Illinois Labor Relations Board, 231 Ill. 2d 593, 326 N.E. 2d 848, 900 Ill. Dec.1095 (2008)

21:255 May the employer appeal a card check representation result?

An employer is not entitled to review a finding of majority support for the union except on the basis of fraud or coercion or appropriateness of the bargaining unit.

County of DuPage v. The Illinois Labor Relations Board, 231 Ill. 2d 593, 326 N.E. 2d 848, 900 Ill. Dec.1095 (2008)

21:260 What ballot choices are required in the election of an exclusive bargaining representative?

An incumbent bargaining representative is automatically placed on any ballot. An intervening labor organization may be placed on the ballot if the intervenor can demonstrate a 15 percent showing of interest. Any other bargaining representative seeking recognition requires a 30 percent showing of interest. In any election the voters must be given the choice of "no representative."

115 ILCS 5/7

115 ILCS 5/8

21:270 How are representation elections conducted?

Representation elections are conducted by secret ballot in accordance with rules and regulations established by the Illinois Educational Labor Relations Board (IELRB). Usually, notice of election announcing the election, noticing election dates, times and places and describing the proposition to be voted on, is posted in prominent places in the school district for 30 days before the election. Absentee ballots are permitted when an individual would otherwise be unable to cast a ballot.

If none of the choices on the ballot receives a majority, a run-off is conducted between the two choices receiving the largest number of valid votes cast in the election. Any party to the election may file objections with the Board alleging improper conduct occurred which affected the outcome of the election. Objections must be received by the Board no later than five working days after the final tally was served on the representatives.

115 ILCS 5/8

80 Ill. Admin. Code 1110.140

80 Ill. Admin. Code 1110.150

21:274 What happens if an employer fails to include all the appropriate names on a representation election voter eligibility list?

The employer is responsible for the submission of a voter eligibility list to the Illinois Educational Labor Relations Board (IELRB) and all interested parties prior to a representation election. If the list the employer submits is incomplete and if the election tally is close, the election results may be set aside by the IELRB.

College of Lake County and College of Lake County Staff Council, Lake County Federation of Teachers, Local 504, IFT-AFT/AFL-CIO, 14 PERI 1095 (IELRB Decision and Order, October 8, 1998)

21:280 What is decertification?

A decertification results when an incumbent representative no longer represents the majority of the employees in the bargaining unit. A decertification petition requires an allegation and showing of interest by at least 30 percent of the employees in the appropriate bargaining unit. An employer cannot instigate or lend support to a decertification petition.

115 ILCS 5/7(c)

80 Ill. Admin. Code 1110.50

80 Ill. Admin. Code 1110.60 et seq.

21:282 How may an employer respond to a decertification question from a bargaining unit member?

An employer may not interfere, restrain, or coerce employees who exercise rights guaranteed by the Illinois Educational Labor Relations Act. The employer should not respond to decertification questions by an employee except to give the employee the phone number of the Illinois Educational Labor Relations Board.

115 ILCS 5/14(a)(1)

District 114 Support Staff IEA-NEA and Fox Lake Elementary School District, 10 PERI 1097 (IELRB Administrative Law Judge, June 14, 1994)

21:290 When may employee representation be challenged?

A petition seeking a representation election may only be filed during certain specified time periods. There is a waiting period after a previous election in a particular bargaining unit before another petition may be filed, and petitions may only be filed during a specified window period during the life of a collective bargaining agreement.

115 ILCS 5/7

80 Ill. Admin. Code 1110.70

21:300 How are election objections filed?

A charge alleging improper election conduct that affected the outcome of an election may be filed with the Illinois Educational Labor Relations Board (IELRB) within five days of the final tally of votes. The IELRB must investigate the allegations, and if it finds probable cause that improper conduct occurred and could have affected the outcome of the election, it must set a hearing on the matter on a date falling within two weeks of when it received the charge.

If the IELRB determines, after the hearing, that the outcome of the election was affected by improper conduct, it must order a new election and must order corrective action that it considers necessary to ensure the fairness of the new election. If it determines upon investigation or after hearing the alleged improper conduct did not take place or it did not affect the results of the election, it must immediately certify the election results.

115 ILCS 5/8

80 Ill. Admin. Code 1110.150

Decatur Federation of Teachers IFT-AFT, AFL-CIO v. Educational Labor Relations Board, 199 Ill. App. 3d 190, 556 N.E. 2d 780, 145 Ill. Dec. 162 (4th Dist. 1990)

Champaign Community Unit School District No. 4, 5 PERI 1124 (Executive Director's Recommended Decision and Order, June 15, 1989)

Centralia School District No. 135, 4 PERI 1094 (IELRB Opinion and Order, February 25, 1988)

NON-UNION EMPLOYEES

21:310 May a contract provision require employees to join a union as a condition of employment?

No. A school board may enter into a collectively bargained agreement that requires all employees covered by the agreement to pay a "fair share" fee, but may not make union membership a condition of employment.

115 ILCS 5/11

Chicago Teachers Union Local 1, AFT, AFL-CIO v. Hudson, 106 S. Ct. 1066, 475 U.S. 292, 89 L. Ed. 2d 232 (1986)

Abood v. Detroit Board of Education, 97 S. Ct. 1782, 431 U.S. 209, 52 L. Ed. 261, reh. den. 97 S. Ct. 2989, 433 U.S. 915, 53 L. Ed. 2d 1102 (1977)

21:320 Must an exclusive bargaining representative represent non-union employees?

An exclusive bargaining representative has "a duty of fair representation" that extends to all members of the bargaining unit, whether the bargaining unit member is a union member or not. If the exclusive bargaining representative fails to provide fair representation for any bargaining unit member, the member has a cause of action against the union.

A union breaches its duty to fairly represent a member where its conduct toward a member is arbitrary, discriminatory, or in bad faith. To be arbitrary the union's behavior must be so far outside a wide range of reasonableness as to be irrational.

115 ILCS 5/3

Nemsky v. ConocoPhillips Company, 574 F. 3d 859 (7th Cir. 2009)

Paxton-Buckley Loda Education Association v. IELRB, 304 Ill. App. 3d 343, 710 N.E. 2d 538, 237 Ill. Dec. 908 (4th Dist. 1999)

NEA, IEA Classroom Teachers Council of District 15 (Kostka), 5 PERI 1067 (Executive Director's Recommended Decision and Order, March 13, 1989)

21:330 What is the difference between fair share, agency shop, and union shop?

Fair share and agency shop are synonymous terms and are permissible under the Educational Labor Relations Act. They are contract provisions that require non-union teachers to pay a representation fee to the union as a condition of employment.

The fair share agreement between a school board and a teachers union may require the non-union member to pay an amount to defray the cost of collective bargaining, contract administration, and union grievance representation. A union may not collect money from non-union members to be used in support of ideological causes that are not germane to its duties as collective bargaining agent. Thus, political action assessments may not be included in fair share fees.

Union shop is a contract provision that makes union membership a condition of employment. A union shop provision is illegal.

115 ILCS 5/11

80 Ill. Admin. Code 1125.10 et seq.

Lehnert v. Ferris Faculty Association, 111 S. Ct. 1950, 500 U.S. 507, 114 L. Ed. 2d 572 (1991) reh. den. 111 S. Ct. 2878, 115 L. Ed. 2d 1044, on rem. 937 F. 2d 608

Abood v. Detroit Board of Education, 97 S. Ct. 1782, 431 U.S. 209, 52 L. Ed. 261, reh. den. 97 S. Ct. 2989, 433 U.S. 915, 53 L. Ed. 2d 1102 (1977)

Chicago Teachers Union Local 1, AFT, AFL-CIO v. Hudson, 106 S. Ct. 1066, 475 U.S. 292, 89 L. Ed. 2d 232 (1986)

21:340 Can an employer exclude a union representative from a grievance adjustment meeting if the grievant is a non-union teacher and so requests?

No. Any individual employee or group of employees may at any time present grievances to the employer and have them adjusted without the intervention of the bargaining representative, provided that the adjustment is not inconsistent with the terms of a collective bargaining agreement then in effect. However, the bargaining representative must be given an opportunity to be present at such adjustment.

115 ILCS 5/3

UNFAIR LABOR PRACTICES

21:350 What is "bargaining in good faith"?

Parties subject to bargaining obligations must meet at reasonable times and confer in good faith with respect to wages, hours, and other terms and conditions of employment, and execute a written contract incorporating any agreements reached. Bargaining in good faith does not require a party to agree to a proposal or to make a concession. The totality of bargaining conduct is examined to determine whether or not any particular bargaining was conducted in good faith.

115 ILCS 5/10

Board of Education of Granite City Community Unit School District No. 9 v. Sered, et al., 366 Ill. App. 3d 330, 850 N.E. 2d 821, 303 Ill. Dec. 16 (1st Dist. 2006) pet. for cert. den. 221 Ill. 2d 631, 857 N.E. 2d 669, 306 Ill. Dec. 270 (2006)

Kewanee Community Unit School District No. 229, 4 PERI 1136 (IELRB Opinion and Order, September 15, 1988)

21:360 What is the remedy for failure to bargain in good faith?

Either the employee representative or the employer may file an unfair labor practice charge with the Illinois Educational Labor Relations Board alleging failure to bargain in good faith.

115 ILCS 5/10

115 ILCS 5/14

Board of Education of Granite City Community Unit School District No. 9 v. Sered et al, 366 Ill. App. 3d 330, 850 N.E. 2d 821, 303 Ill. Dec. 16 (1st Dist. 2006) pet. for cert. den. 221 Ill. 2d 631, 857 N.E. 2d 669, 306 Ill. Dec. 270 (2006)

Thornton Township High School District No. 205, 5 PERI 1134 (Executive Director's Recommended Decision and Order, July 10, 1989)

21:370 What is an unfair labor practice charge?

An unfair labor practice (ULP) charge is an allegation of conduct that is prohibited in 115 ILCS 5/14. There are four elements to a ULP:

The employee engaged in protected union activity;

The employer had knowledge of the protected activity;

The employer took an adverse employment action against the employee; and

The employer's action was motivated by the employer's animus toward the employee's protected activity.

If a prima facie case is established with these four elements, then the burden shifts to the employer to show it had a legitimate reason for the adverse employment action and that it relied on that reason. The employer must show that the employee would have suffered the adverse employment action notwithstanding the union's activity.

115 ILCS 5/14

80 Ill. Admin. Code 1120.10 et seq.

County of Cook v. Illinois Labor Relations Board, 2012 IL App (1st) 111514, 976 N.E. 2d 493, 364 Ill. Dec. 215

21:380 Who may file an unfair labor practice charge?

An unfair labor practice charge may be filed by an employer, an individual employee, or a labor organization.

115 ILCS 5/14

80 Ill. Admin. Code 1120.20 a)

21:390 What are union unfair labor practices?

Employee organizations, their agents or representatives, or educational employees are prohibited from

1) Restraining or coercing employees in the exercise of the rights guaranteed under the Educational Labor Relations Act;

2) Restraining or coercing an educational employer in the selection of his or her representative for the purposes of collective bargaining or the adjustment of grievances;

3) Refusing to bargain collectively in good faith with an educational employer;

4) Violating any of the rules and regulations promulgated by the Educational Labor Relations Board regulating the conduct of representation elections;

5) Refusing to reduce a collective bargaining agreement to writing and signing such agreement; and

6) Refusing to comply with the provisions of a binding arbitration award.

115 ILCS 5/14 a)

21:400 What are employer unfair labor practices?

Educational employers, their agents, or representatives are prohibited from

1) Interfering, restraining, or coercing employees in the exercise of the rights guaranteed under the Illinois Educational Labor Relations Act;

2) Dominating or interfering with the formation, existence, or administration of any employee organization;

3) Discriminating in regard to hiring or tenure of employment or any term or condition of employment to encourage or discourage membership in any employee organization;

4) Discharging or otherwise discriminating against an employee because he or she has signed or filed an affidavit, authorization card, petition, or complaint; or given any information or testimony under the Educational Labor Relations Act;

5) Refusing to bargain collectively in good faith with an employee representative that is the exclusive representative of employees in an appropriate unit, including but not limited to the discussing of grievances with the exclusive representative; provided, however, that if an alleged unfair labor practice involves interpretation or application of the terms of a collective bargaining agreement, and said agreement contains a grievance and arbitration procedure, the Educational Labor Relations Board may defer the resolution of such dispute to the grievance and arbitration procedure contained in said agreement;

6) Refusing to reduce a collective bargaining agreement to writing and signing such agreement;

7) Violating any of the rules and regulations promulgated by the Educational Labor Relations Board regulating the conduct of representation elections; and

8) Refusing to comply with the provisions of a binding arbitration award.

115 ILCS 5/14 b)

21:403 What is anti-union animus?

To support an unfair labor practice charge, anti-union animus must have been a substantial or motivating factor in the employer's decision to make adverse employment decisions.

Anti-union animus may be inferred from a variety of factors, such as an employer's expressed hostility toward unionization together with knowledge of the employee's union activities, proximity in time between the employee's union activities and his or her discharge, disparate treatment of employees or a pattern of conduct that targets a union supporter for adverse employment action, inconsistencies between the proffered reason for discharge, and other actions of the employer and shifting explanations for the discharge.

Thornton Fractional High School District No. 215 v. Illinois Educational Labor Relations Board, 404 Ill. App. 3d 757, 936 N.E. 2d 1188, 344 Ill. Dec. 431 (1st Dist. 2010)

City of Burbank v. Illinois State Labor Relations Board, 128 Ill. 2d 335, 538 N.E. 2d 1146, 131 Ill. Dec. 590 (1989)

National Labor Relations Board v. Wright Line, a Division of Wright Line, Inc., 662 F. 2d 899 (1st Cir. 1981)

21:410 How is an unfair labor practice charge filed?

An unfair labor practice charge may be filed with the Educational Labor Relations Board (IELRB) on forms provided by the IELRB. A charge must be signed and must contain the name, address, and affiliation of both the charging party and respondent. It also must contain a complete statement of facts supporting the alleged unfair labor practice, including dates, times, and places of occurrence of each act alleged and the sections of the Act alleged to have been violated. It must also include a statement of relief sought.

Upon receipt of a charge, the IELRB investigates. If the IELRB determines the charge states an issue of law or fact sufficient to warrant a hearing, it issues a complaint. Thereafter, a hearing is held on the charges and a decision rendered. The parties have the right to various appeals.

115 ILCS 5/15

23 Ill. Admin. Code 1120.20 et seq.

Lake Zurich School District No. 45, 1 PERI 1031 (IELRB Opinion and Order, November 30, 1984)

21:420 Is there a limitations period for unfair labor practice charges?

No order may be issued on an unfair labor practice occurring more than six months before the filing of the charge alleging the unfair labor practice.

115 ILCS 5/15

80 Ill. Admin. Code 1100.30

80 Ill. Admin. Code 1120.20 d)

Charleston Community Unit School District No. 1 v. Illinois Educational Labor Relations Board and Charleston Education Association, IEA-NEA, 203 Ill. App. 3d 619, 561 N.E. 2d 331, 149 Ill. Dec. 53 (4th Dist. 1990)

Wapella Education Association, IEA-NEA v. Illinois Educational Labor Relations Board, 177 Ill. App. 3d 153, 531 N.E. 2d 1371, 126 Ill. Dec. 532 (4th Dist. 1988)

21:430 Must a school board permit union representatives to enter the schools during the school day to meet with school employees?

The agents of an exclusive bargaining representative must be allowed to meet with school employees in school buildings during employee duty-free times.

105 ILCS 5/24-25

IMPASSES AND STRIKES

21:440 What is impasse?

Impasse exists if, in view of all the circumstances of bargaining, further discussions would be futile. Impasse does not exist if there is a ray of hope with a real potentiality for agreement if explored in good faith bargaining sessions. An impasse may exist over a single issue provided it is of such overriding importance that it justifies an overall finding of impasse on all the issues. For an impasse to occur, neither party must be willing to compromise. One party cannot unilaterally establish or create an impasse. Both parties must have the same understanding and find themselves at the same point in negotiations. In examining whether or not impasse has been reached the following factors are examined:

1) Bargaining history;
2) The good faith of the parties in negotiations;
3) The length of the negotiations;
4) The importance of the issue(s) as to which there is disagreement; and
5) The contemporaneous understanding of the parties as to the state of negotiations.

115 ILCS 5/12

American Federation of State, County and Municipal Employees Council 31 v. Illinois Labor Relations Board, 2017 IL. App. (5th) 160229, __ N.E. 2d __, __ Ill. Dec. __ __

Kewanee Community School District No. 229, 4 PERI 1136 (IELRB Opinion and Order, September 15, 1988)

21:445 When may a party's position in bargaining be made public?

A party theoretically can make its offer or bargaining position public at any time. Generally, the parties seek to keep bargaining issues and positions private because making them public complicates the process when false rumors and public pressure interfere with discussions at the bargaining table. The relevant law provides that either party or the mediator may initiate a public posting process 15 days after mediation has begun. Initiation of the process must be filed in writing with the Illinois Educational Labor Relations Board (IELRB) and copies must be submitted to the parties on the same day the initiation is filed with the IELRB.

Within seven days after the initiation of the public posting process, each party must submit to the mediator, the IELRB, and the other party in writing the most recent offer of the party, including a cost summary of the offer. Seven days after the receipt of the parties' offers, the IELRB makes public the offers and each party's cost summary dealing with those issues on which the parties have failed to reach agreement by posting the offers on its website, unless otherwise notified by the mediator or jointly by the parties that agreement has been reached. On the same day of publication by the IELRB, at a minimum, the school district must distribute notice of the availability of the offers on the IELRB website to all news media that have filed an annual request for notices. The parties' offers must remain on the IELRB website until the parties have reached and ratified an agreement. Before a 2013 change in the law, the IELRB posting described above required a declaration of impasse.

115 ILCS 5/12

21:450 What is the difference between a mediator, a fact-finder, and an arbitrator?

All three terms refer to third parties brought into a dispute in an effort to assist in its resolution. A mediator can suggest a resolution to the parties, usually does not make his or her recommendation public, and has no authority to enforce any recommended solution.

A fact-finder also suggests resolutions but usually makes his or her recommendations public. Like a mediator, a fact-finder has no power of enforcement.

An arbitrator makes a formal ruling, makes the ruling public, and has power to enforce the ruling.

Mediation of contract formation disputes is mandatory at the request of either party under the Educational Labor Relations Act; fact-finding and interest arbitration are permissive under the Act.

115 ILCS 5/12

80 Ill. Admin. Code 1130.30 et seq.

80 Ill. Admin. Code 1130.50

21:460 Must a contract bargaining dispute be submitted to binding arbitration?

No. Interest arbitration — the process whereby an arbitrator is employed to resolve differences that arise between the parties in reaching contract agreement — is permissible under the Illinois Educational Labor Relations Act (the parties may agree to it). But it is not required.

Grievance arbitration is a process whereby an arbitrator is employed to resolve differences that arise between the parties in interpreting the meaning of contract language. Grievance arbitration is mandatory under the Illinois Educational Labor Relations Act.

115 ILCS 5/12

21:470 What options are there in the selection of a mediator?

Unless an applicable collective bargaining agreement provides otherwise, the parties to a bargaining dispute have several options in the selection of a mediator. The parties may mutually agree to engage:

1) Any qualified, impartial individual who is mutually acceptable to the parties under terms established by the parties.

2) An individual assigned or selected under the auspices of a private service, such as the American Arbitration Association. Filing fees are often charged, and the mediators selected or assigned charge the parties a per diem fee.

3) A federal mediator assigned by the Federal Mediation and Conciliation Service (FMCS). FMCS does not charge for its services. If either party requests the use of mediation services from the FMCS, the other party must either join in the request or bear the additional cost of mediation services from another source.

The IELRB may invoke mediation at the request of either party or on its own motion after a reasonable period of negotiation and absent agreement by the parties on a mediator. Mediators provided by the IELRB charge the parties a per diem fee.

115 ILCS 5/12

80 Ill. Admin. Code 1130.30

80 Ill. Admin. Code 1130.80

21:480 What is a no-strike clause?

A no-strike clause is a contract provision that prohibits strikes during the term of a contract agreement. A no-strike clause does not prohibit a strike after an agreement expires. The Educational Labor Relations Act requires each collective bargaining agreement to contain a no-strike clause. A no-strike clause may explicitly define the meaning of the term "strike" to prohibit work slow-downs and other job actions during the term of a contract.

115 ILCS 5/10(c)

80 Ill. Admin. Code 1130.70 a)

21:490 When are strikes permitted?

Educational employees are prohibited from participation in a strike except under the following conditions:

1) They are represented by an exclusive bargaining representative;

2) Mediation has been used without success and for employers and exclusive representatives who have used a fact-finder, at least 14 days after the Illinois Educational Labor Relations Board (IELRB) has made public the parties' offers;

3) Any time 15 days after mediation has commenced or impasse has been declared by the mediator or either party (it is unclear in the relevant statute whether or not a declaration of impasse is necessary before a strike can occur and it is unclear whether or not the Kewanee definition of impasse is applicable);

4) Within seven days after the declaration of impasse, each party has submitted to the IELRB and the other party in writing its final offer including a cost summary of the offer and the final offers have been made public by the IELRB. The school board has an obligation to post notice to the public of the availability of the offers on the IELRB website and to notify media that have annual requests for notice.

5) At least 14 days have elapsed since the offers were made public;

6) At least 10 calendar days have elapsed after a notice of intent to strike has been given by the exclusive bargaining representative to the educational employer, the regional superintendent, and the Illinois Educational Labor Relations Board;

7) The collective bargaining agreement between the educational employer and educational employees, if any, has expired or been terminated; and

8) The employer and the exclusive bargaining representative have not mutually agreed to submit the unresolved issues to arbitration.

115 ILCS 5/12

115 ILCS 5/13

80 Ill. Admin. Code 1130.40

80 Ill. Admin. Code 1130.50

Kewanee Community School District No. 229, 4 PERI 1136 (IELRB Opinion and Order, September 15, 1988)

21:495 Must a school make up the school days lost to a teacher strike?

There is no statutory requirement that school days lost to a teacher strike be made up during vacation periods or after the school term would, but for the strike, have ended. Whether school days are made up or lost after a strike is a mandatory subject of bargaining.

The resolution of the issue is generally defined in the agreement that ends the strike. If a school district does not make up strike days, it routinely loses state aid for each day during the strike that school was not in session and for which an educational program was not provided.

21:500 May striking school board employees picket the home of a school board member or administrator?

It is unlawful to picket before or about the residence or dwelling of any person, except when the residence or dwelling is used as a place of business. Peaceful picketing is not prohibited if it is at a place of a meeting or assembly or is on premises commonly used to discuss subjects of general public interest.

720 ILCS 5/21.1-2

GRIEVANCE RESOLUTION

21:510 What is a grievance?

What constitutes a grievance is usually defined in a collective bargaining agreement. Commonly, the definition provides that a grievance is an allegation by an employee, group of employees, or exclusive bargaining representative that there has been a violation of a specific provision of the contract.

Staunton Community Unit School District No. 6 v. Illinois Educational Labor Relations Board, 200 Ill. App. 3d 370, 558 N.E. 2d 751, 146 Ill. Dec. 788 (4th Dist. 1990)

Moraine Valley Community College, 5 PERI 1102 (IELRB Opinion and Order, May 12, 1989)

21:513 How is a grievance processed?

Each collective bargaining agreement contains a grievance procedure which usually includes a limitations period or "time bar" that requires that the complaint be brought to the employer within a mandatory time period. There is usually a required informal discussion between the employee or the union and the employer and then the grievance can be submitted formally in writing by either the employee or the exclusive representative (union).

The grievance is usually processed through a number of internal steps (beginning with the principal, appeal to the superintendent and/or board, e.g.). Ultimately, if the matter cannot be resolved internally, there is available an appeal to final and binding arbitration.

21:520 Must a collective bargaining agreement allow grievance arbitration?

The collective bargaining agreement negotiated between representatives of the educational employees and the educational employer must contain a grievance resolution procedure that must apply to all employees in the unit and must provide for binding arbitration of disputes concerning the administration or interpretation of the agreement.

115 ILCS 5/10(c)

80 Ill. Admin. Code 1130.70 a)

River Grove School District No. 85 1/2, 3 PERI 1019 (IELRB Opinion and Order, January 30, 1987)

21:525 How does a school board challenge a grievance that it believes to be inarbitrable?

An educational employer may refuse to arbitrate a grievance where there is no contractual agreement to arbitrate the substance of the dispute or the dispute is not arbitrable under Section 10(b) of the Illinois Educational Labor Relations Act because the subject matter of the dispute conflicts with Illinois law. The employer may also choose to arbitrate and raise inarbitrability defenses in the arbitration hearing. Inarbitrability arguments concern the arbitrator's (or the Illinois Educational Labor Relations Board's) subject matter jurisdiction to decide the dispute.

In terms of outcome, complexity of defense, or substance of the issues considered, there is little difference in how the employer elects to proceed.

115 ILCS 5/10(b)

Cobden Unit School District No. 17 v. Illinois Educational Labor Relations Board, 2012 IL App (1st) 10716, 966 N.E. 2d 503, 359 Ill. Dec. 182

21:527 Must the school district comply with a request for information the union or a teacher claims is necessary to process a grievance?

A school district must provide information to the exclusive representative to allow the representative to properly perform its duties. That includes supplying information necessary to grievance processing. But information discovery by the exclusive representative may be limited by "bona fide confidentiality concerns articulated by the employer." Such defenses may include production prohibitions contained in the Illinois School Student Records Act.

105 ILCS 10/6

115 ILCS 5/17

State of Illinois v. American Federation of State, County and Municipal Employees Council 31, 2017 Ill. App. (4th) 160827, __ N.E. 2d __, __ Ill. Dec. __

Board of Education of the City of Chicago v. Illinois Educational Labor Relations Board, 2013 IL App (1st) 122447, 3 N.E. 3d 343, 378 Ill. Dec. 63

21:530 What is the difference between interest arbitration and grievance arbitration?

Interest arbitration is a process whereby an arbitrator is employed to resolve differences that arise between the parties in reaching contract agreement. Under the Illinois Educational Labor Relations Act, interest arbitration is permissible (the parties may agree to it).

Grievance arbitration is a process whereby an arbitrator is employed to resolve differences that arise between the parties in interpreting the meaning of contract language. Grievance arbitration is mandatory under the Illinois Educational Labor Relations Act.

115 ILCS 5/10(c)

115 ILCS 5/12

21:540 Which body has jurisdiction to vacate or modify an arbitration award?

The Illinois Educational Labor Relations Board has sole and exclusive jurisdiction to vacate or modify arbitration awards. A school board seeking to appeal a decision of an arbitrator must refuse to comply with the provisions of the arbitrator's award and await an unfair labor practice charge. Circuit courts lack jurisdiction to vacate or modify arbitration awards.

115 ILCS 5/14

115 ILCS 5/16

Board of Education Warren Township High School District No. 121 v. Warren Township High School Federation of Teachers Local 504, IFT/AFL-CIO, 128 Ill. 2d 155, 538 N.E. 2d 524, 131 Ill. Dec. 149 (1989)

Board of Education of Community Unit School District No. 1 v. Compton, 123 Ill. 2d 216, 526 N.E. 2d 149, 122 Ill. Dec. 9 (1988)

21:542 What is the likelihood an arbitration award will be overturned on appeal?

The review standard applied by the Illinois Educational Labor Relations Board (IELRB) and the courts is extremely limited. When considering whether a school board has committed an unfair labor practice by refusing to comply with a binding arbitration award, the inquiry is limited to whether the award was binding, the content of the award, and whether or not the school board has complied with the award.

The IELRB considers whether the award was rendered in accordance with the applicable grievance procedure, whether the procedures were fair and impartial, whether the award conflicts with other statutes, whether the award is patently repugnant to the purposes and policies of the Illinois Educational Labor Relations Act, and any other basic challenge to the legitimacy of the award.

The courts will not reverse the IELRB unless its decision is "clearly erroneous." A decision will be reversed because it is clearly erroneous only if the reviewing court, based on the entirety of the record is "left with the definite and firm conviction that a mistake has been committed." It is not enough to show the arbitrator committed an error; or even a serious error. To overturn the award the challenging party must show there is no interpretive route to the award so that a non-contractual basis can be inferred and the award set aside.

Griggsville-Perry Community Unit District No. 4 v. Illinois Educational Labor Relations Board, 2013 IL 113721, 984 N.E. 2d 440, 368 Ill. Dec. 494

Central Community Unit School District v. Illinois Educational Labor Relations Board, et al., 388 Ill. App. 3d 1060, 904 N.E. 2d 640, 328 Ill. Dec. 451 (4th Dist. 2009)

Board of Education of DuPage High School District No. 88 v. Illinois Educational Labor Relations Board, 246 Ill. App. 3d 967, 617 N.E. 2d 790, 187 Ill. Dec. 333 (1st Dist. 1993)

Board of Education of City of Chicago v. Illinois Educational Labor Relations Board, 170 Ill. App. 3d 490, 524 N.E. 2d 711, 125 Ill. Dec. 211 (1988)

21:544 What is the basis for overturning a Labor Board decision because it violates public policy?

Public policy is determined by the constitution, laws, and judicial decisions, not by the varying opinions of laymen, lawyers, or judges as to the demands or the interests of the public.

Central Community Unit School District v. Illinois Educational Labor Relations Board, et al., 388 Ill. App. 3d 1060, 904 N.E. 2d 640, 328 Ill. Dec. 451 (4th Dist. 2009)

CONTRACTUAL PROVISIONS

21:550 What is the maximum term of a collective bargaining agreement?

A collective bargaining agreement of three years or less is enforceable and authorized under the Illinois Educational Labor Relations Act. Agreements of longer duration are probably enforceable provided an exclusive representative election challenge does not arise during the term of the agreement. A bargaining agreement of less than three years may be extended up to three years if the extension is agreed to in writing before the filing of an election petition.

115 ILCS 5/7

21:560 May a collective bargaining agreement give teachers or other employees more rights than are provided by law?

The parties to the collective bargaining process may implement a provision in a collective bargaining agreement if that provision has the effect of supplementing any provision in any state statute pertaining to wages, hours, or other conditions of employment.

However, the parties may not implement any contract provision that contradicts any such state statute. Whether a contract provision granting employees more rights than are provided by law is legal, therefore, depends upon whether it is construed as supplementary or contradictory to state statutes.

115 ILCS 5/10(b)

21:565 What is a "just cause" provision?

A "just cause" provision in a collective bargaining agreement is a contract clause that limits the employer to the discipline or dismissal of employees only when there is "just cause" to do so. Some "just cause" clauses use synonymous phrases, such as "for good cause shown" or "only for good reasons." A "just cause" provision is enforceable to the extent it is not in violation of, inconsistent with or in conflict with Illinois law.

115 ILCS 5/10(b)

Board of Education of Rockford School District No. 205, v. The Illinois Educational Labor Relations Board, 165 Ill. 2d 80, 649 N.E. 2d 369, 208 Ill. Dec. 313 (1995)

Midwest Central Education Association v. Illinois Educational Labor Relations Board, et al., 277 Ill. App. 3d 440, 660 N.E. 2d 151, 213 Ill. Dec. 894 (1st Dist. 1995)

21:570 May an employee group agree in a collective bargaining agreement to give up some statutory rights in exchange for other rights or money? For example, could a teacher bargaining unit trade tenure for a large salary increase?

No. The parties to a collective bargaining agreement may not effect or implement a provision in a collective bargaining agreement if the implementation of that provision would be inconsistent or in conflict with any statute enacted by the General Assembly.

No provision in a collective bargaining agreement may be effected or implemented if such provision has the effect of negating, abrogating, replacing, reducing, diminishing, or limiting in any way any employee rights, guarantees, or privileges pertaining to wages, hours, or other conditions of employment provided in statute. Any such provision in a collective bargaining agreement is void and unenforceable, but does not affect the validity, enforceability, and implementation of other permissible provisions of the collective bargaining agreement.

115 ILCS 5/10(b)

21:580 May a collective bargaining agreement include a cost of living adjustment (COLA) clause or any other clause that ties salary increases to outside factors?

Yes.

Libertyville Education Association IEA-NEA v. Board of Education, 56 Ill. App. 3d 503, 371 N.E. 2d 676, 13 Ill. Dec. 741 (2nd Dist. 1977)

21:590 Which benefits must be provided employees after expiration of a collective bargaining agreement and before a successor agreement is reached?

The school board must maintain the status quo. An employer's unilateral alteration of prevailing terms and conditions of employment under negotiation during the course of bargaining is an unfair labor practice.

American Federation of State, County and Municipal Employees Council 31 v. Illinois Labor Relations Board, 2017 IL. App. (5th) 160229, __ N.E. 2d __, __ Ill. Dec. __

Vienna School District No. 55 v. Illinois Educational Labor Relations Board, 162 Ill. App. 3d 503, 515 N.E. 2d 476, 113 Ill. Dec. 667 (4th Dist. 1987)

RELATED REQUIREMENTS

21:600 Must a collective bargaining agreement be posted on the school district's website?

Yes. Section 10-20.44 of the School Code requires that the contents of collective bargaining agreement(s) be posted, not just a notice that they exist.

105 ILCS 5/10-20.44

21:620 When must an employer provide an employee with the right to representation?

A member of a bargaining unit must be provided an opportunity for union representation when the employee is engaged in an activity protected by the Illinois Educational Labor Relations Act. In most cases, an employer should err by providing employees more opportunity for representation rather than less. Failure to provide representation often provides a procedural obstacle to obtaining a substantive disciplinary result.

An employee engages in protected union activity only when the employee's actions invoke a right under the law or the collective bargaining agreement. Employees engage in protected activity when involving contractual rights because that activity is a direct extension of collective bargaining.

Speed District 802 v. Warning, 242 Ill. 2d 1292, 95 N.E. 2d 1069, 35 Ill. Dec. 241 (2011)

Ehlers v. Jackson County Sheriff's Merit Commission, 183 Ill. 2d 83, 697 N.E.2d 717 (1998)

Summit Hill School District No. 161, 4 PERI 1009 (IELRB Opinion and Order, December 1, 1987)

National Labor Relations Board v. J. Weingarten, Inc., 95 S. Ct. 959, 420 U.S. 251, 43 L. Ed. 2d 171 (1975)

21:630 Are statements made during a settlement conference to resolve a grievance or unfair labor practice admissible?

Statements made during a settlement conference are inadmissible to prove the validity of a claim or to impeach a prior inconsistent statement or contradiction. Such a statement may be admissible to prove witnesses bias or prejudice or to negate an allegation of undue delay.

Illinois Rule of Evidence 408

County of Cook v. Illinois Labor Relations Board, 2012 IL App (1st) 111514, 976 N.E. 2d 493, 364 Ill. Dec. 215

22: SCHOOL DISTRICTS AND LIABILITY FOR INJURIES

TORT IMMUNITY CONCEPTS

22:10 What is a tort?

A tort is a private or civil wrong or injury, other than a breach of contract, for which the law provides a remedy in an action for damages. The elements of every tort require a duty flowing from the defendant to the plaintiff, a breach of that duty and damages that proximately result.

22:12 What are punitive damages?

Punitive damages are those given in addition to compensation for a loss sustained in order to punish and make an example of the wrongdoer.

25 C.J.S. Damages 2

22:14 What is willful and wanton misconduct?

Willful and wanton misconduct is an intentional act or an act committed under circumstances exhibiting a reckless disregard for the safety of others, such as a failure, after knowledge of impending danger, to exercise ordinary care to prevent it, or a failure to discover the danger through recklessness, or carelessness when it could have been discovered by ordinary care.

The Tort Immunity Act defines willful and wanton misconduct as "a course of action which shows actual or deliberate intention to cause harm or which, if not intentional, shows an utter indifference to or conscious disregard for the safety of others or their property."

745 ILCS 10/1-210

In re Estate of Jeffrey Stewart, 2016 IL App (2d) 151117, 60 N.E. 3d 896, 406 Ill. Dec. 345

Burke v. 12 Rothschild's Liquor Mart, Inc., 209 Ill. App. 3d 192, 568 N.E. 2d 80, 154 Ill. Dec. 80, app. den. 139 Ill. 2d 594, 575 N.E. 2d 912, 159 Ill. Dec. 105, order vac. on reconsideration __ Ill. 2d __, 575 N.E. 2d 1234, 159 Ill. Dec. 174, app. allowed 141 Ill. 2d 536, 580 N.E. 2d 109, 162 Ill. Dec. 483, aff'd. 148 Ill. 2d 429, 593 N.E. 2d 522, 170 Ill. Dec. 633 (1992)

Braun v. Board of Education of Red Bud Community Unit School District No. 132, 151 Ill. App. 3d 787, 502 N.E. 2d 1076, 104 Ill. Dec. 416 (5th Dist. 1986) app. den. 115 Ill. 2d 538, 511 N.E. 2d 426, 110 Ill. Dec. 454 (1987)

Gammon v. Edwardsville Community Unit School District No. 7, 82 Ill. App. 3d 586, 403 N.E. 2d 43, 38 Ill. Dec. 28 (5th Dist. 1980)

22:15 What is the difference between negligence and willful and wanton misconduct?

Ordinary negligence is a failure to exercise that degree of care that the ordinary prudent person would exercise under similar conditions. Willful and wanton misconduct requires an intentional act or an act committed under circumstances exhibiting a reckless disregard for the safety of others.

Mitchell v. Special Education Joint Agreement School District No. 208, 386 Ill. App. 3d 106, 897 N.E. 2d 352, 325 Ill. Dec. 104 (1st Dist. 2008)

Ramos v. Waukegan Community Unit School District No. 60, 188 Ill. App. 3d 1031, 544 N.E. 2d 1302, 136 Ill. Dec. 527 (2nd Dist. 1989)

Lynch v. Board of Education of Collinsville Community Unit School District No. 10, 82 Ill. 2d 415, 412 N.E. 2d 447, 45 Ill. Dec. 96 (1980)

Thomas v. Chicago Board of Education, 60 Ill. App. 3d 729, 377 N.E. 2d 355 (1st Dist. 1978), rev. on other grounds 77 Ill. 2d 165, 395 N.E. 2d 538, 32 Ill. Dec. 308 (1979)

Gerrity v. Beatty, 71 Ill. 2d 47, 373 N.E. 2d 1323, 15 Ill. Dec. 639 (1978)

McCauley v. Chicago Board of Education, 66 Ill. App. 3d 676, 384 N.E. 2d 100, 23 Ill. Dec. 464 (1st Dist. 1978)

Kobylanski v. Chicago Board of Education, 63 Ill. 2d 165, 347 N.E. 2d 705 (1976)

Clay v. Chicago Board of Education, 22 Ill. App. 3d 437, 318 N.E. 2d 153 (1st Dist. 1974)

Mancha v. Field Museum of Natural History, 5 Ill. App. 3d 699, 283 N.E. 2d 899 (1st Dist. 1972)

Woodman v. Litchfield Community Unit School District No. 12, Montgomery County, 102 Ill. App. 2d 330, 242 N.E. 2d 780 (5th Dist. 1968)

Fustin v. Board of Education of Community Unit School District No. 2, 101 Ill. App. 2d 113, 242 N.E. 2d 308 (5th Dist. 1968)

22:18 What is the intentional infliction of emotional distress?

To establish a cause of action for intentional infliction of emotional distress, a plaintiff must prove: (1) the defendant's conduct was extreme and outrageous; (2) the defendant either intended that his or her conduct should inflict severe emotional distress or knew there was a high probability that his or her conduct would cause severe emotional distress; and (3) the conduct in fact caused severe emotional distress.

Intentional infliction of emotional distress does not extend to mere insults, indignities, threats, annoyances, petty oppressions, or other trivialities. The standard is very high. In order to meet the threshold for intentional infliction of emotional distress, the conduct must be such that the recitation of the facts to an average member of the community would arouse resentment against the actor and lead him or her to exclaim "outrageous!"

The courts apply an objective standard taking into consideration including the degree of power or authority which the defendant has over a plaintiff; whether the defendant reasonably believed his or her objective was legitimate; and whether the plaintiff is particularly susceptible to emotional distress because of some physical or mental condition or peculiarity.

Lewis v. School District #70, 523 F. 3d 730 (7th Cir. 2008)

Strasburger v. Board of Education Hardin County Community Unit School District No. 1, et al., 143 F. 3d 351 (7th Cir. 1998)

Public Finance Corporation v. Davis, 66 Ill. 2d 85, 360 N.E. 2d 765, 4 Ill. Dec. 652 (5th Dist. 1976)

TORT IMMUNITIES

22:20 Are there tort liability immunities that apply to school boards?

Neither a school board nor its employees or agents may be held liable for injuries caused under certain conditions specified in the tort immunity section of the statutes.

745 ILCS 10/1-101 et seq.

Arteman et al. v. Clinton Community School District No. 15, 198 Ill. 2d 475, 763 N.E. 2d 756, 261 Ill. Dec. 507 (2002)

Henrich by Henrich v. Libertyville High School et al., 186 Ill. 2d 381, 712 N.E. 2d 298, 238 Ill. Dec. 596 (1999)

22:22 May a school district be liable for negligent supervision of an activity?

The Tort Immunity Act provides that "neither a local public entity nor a public employee who undertakes to supervise an activity on or the use of any public property is liable for an injury unless the local public entity or public employee is guilty of willful and wanton conduct in its supervision proximately causing such injury."

Failure to supervise includes improper supervision. The same statute provides: "Except as otherwise provided (in the Act) neither a local public entity nor a public employee is liable for an injury caused by a failure to supervise an activity on or the use of any public property unless the employee or the local public entity has a duty to provide supervision imposed by common law, statute, ordinance code, or regulation and the local or public employee is guilty of willful and wanton conduct in its failure to provide supervision proximately causing such injury."

When properly raised in failure-to-supervise cases, the immunity provided by The Tort Immunity Act controls over the protections of Section 24-24 of the School Code.

745 ILCS 10/3-108

Doe ex rel. Ortega-Piron v. Chicago Board of Education, 339 Ill. App. 3d 848, 791 N.E. 2d 1283, 274 Ill. Dec. 872, (1st Dist., 2003) aff'd. 213 Ill. 2d 19, 820 N.E. 2d 418, 289 Ill. Dec. 642, (2004)

Henrich by Henrich v. Libertyville High School et al., 186 Ill. 2d 381, 712 N.E. 2d 298, 238 Ill. Dec. 596 (1999)

Grandalski ex rel. Grandalski v. Lyons Township High School District 204, 305 Ill. App. 3d 1, 711 N.E. 2d 372, 238 Ill. Dec. 269 (1st Dist. 1999)

22:24 Under what circumstances may school officials rely upon tort immunity in defense of a bad decision by an employee?

The Tort Immunity Act provides: "... a public employee serving in a position involving the determination of policy or the exercise of discretion is not liable for an injury resulting from his act or omission in determining policy when acting in the exercise of such discretion even though abused." Policy decisions are those that require the public entity or employee to balance competing interests and to make a judgment call as to what solution will best serve each of those interests.

Discretionary decisions are protected; ministerial acts are not. Ministerial acts are performed on a given set of facts in a prescribed manner, in obedience to the mandate of legal authority and without reference to the official's discretion as to the propriety of the act.

The same statute immunizes a school district from liability for an injury resulting from an employee's act or omission where the employee is not liable. The legislative purpose of the Tort Immunity Act is to permit public officials to exercise their judgment in rendering decisions without fear that a good faith mistake might subject them to liability.

To obtain the protection of the statute, the courts have held that the act or omission must be both a determination of policy and an exercise of discretion.

The courts have also held that the negligent performance of discretionary duties does not subject the governmental entity to tort liability, but that the negligent performance of ministerial duties can subject the entity to liability.

Discretionary acts are those that are unique to a particular public office. Ministerial acts are those "which a person performs on a given state of facts in a prescribed manner, in obedience to the mandate of legal authority, and without reference to the official's discretion as to the propriety of the act."

745 ILCS 10/2-109

745 ILCS 10/2-201

In re Estate of Jeffrey Stewart, 2016 IL App (2d) 151117

Albers v. Breen, 346 Ill. App. 3d 799, 806 N.E. 2d 667, 282 Ill. Dec. 370 (4th Dist. 2004) pet. for leave to app. den. 211 Ill. 2d 569, 823 N.E. 2d 962, 291 Ill. Dec. 376 (2004)

Arteman et al. v. Clinton Community School District No. 15, 198 Ill. 2d 475, 763 N.E. 2d 756, 261 Ill. Dec. 507 (2002)

Harrison v. Hardin County Community Unit School District No. 1, 197 Ill. 2d 466, 758 N.E. 2d 848, 259 Ill. Dec. 440 (2001)

Johnson v. Decatur Park District, 301 Ill. App. 3d 798, 703 N.E. 2d 416, 235 Ill. Dec. 67 (4th Dist. 1998)

Snyder v. Curran Township, 167 Ill. 2d 466, 657 N.E. 2d 988, 212 Ill. Dec. 643 (1995)

22:30 May a school district be held liable for civil rights violations?

A school district may be held liable for civil rights violations. An employee or agent of a school district has available a qualified good faith immunity defense. This defense is not available to a school district.

Owen v. City of Independence, 100 S. Ct. 1398, 445 U.S. 622, 63 L. Ed. 2d 673, on rem. 623 F. 2d 550, reh. den. 100 S. Ct. 2979, 446 U.S. 993, 64 L. Ed. 2d 850 (1980)

22:35 Is a school district liable for civil rights violations committed by school district employees?

A public school district is potentially liable when it sanctions or orders the action that results in the violation. A private person acts under color of state law when he or she is a willful participant in joint action with the state or its agents. Violations may be explicitly or implicitly sanctioned by the policy or past practice of a school district. A widespread practice may constitute an official policy with the force of law even though the practice itself is not reduced to written form.

105 ILCS 5/10-20.20

L.P. v. Marian Catholic High School, 852 F. 3d. 690 (7th Cir. 2017)

King ex rel. King v. East St. Louis School District No. 189, 496 F. 3d 812 (7th Cir. 2007)

Spann for Spann v. Tyler Independent School District, 876 F. 2d 437 (5th Cir. 1989)

Pembaur v. Cincinnati, 106 S. Ct. 1292, 475 U.S. 469, 89 L. Ed. 2d 452 (1986)

22:37 Is a school board liable for libelous or slanderous statements made by its employees?

The Tort Immunity Act insulates public entities from liability. A local public entity is not liable for injury caused by any action of its employees that is libelous or slanderous or for the provision of information either orally, in writing, by computer or any other electronic transmission, or in a book or other form of library material.

745 ILCS 10/2-107

Goldberg v. Brooks, et al., 409 Ill. App. 3d 106, 948 N.E. 2d 1108, 350 Ill. Dec. 601 (1st Dist. 2011)

22:50 May a school district be liable for punitive damages?

No, but its school board members and employees may be held liable.

745 ILCS 10/2-102

Collins v. School District No. 189, St. Clair County, 115 Ill. App. 3d 100, 450 N.E. 2d 387, 70 Ill. Dec. 914 (5th Dist. 1983)

LIABILITY OF INDIVIDUALS

22:60 Can a school employee, volunteer, or school board member be held personally liable for an act or failure to act that was done or not done for the benefit of the school?

The school district must indemnify and protect school board members, employees, volunteers, mentors of certified staff, and student teachers against civil rights damage claims and suits, constitutional rights damage claims and suits, and death and bodily injury and property damage claims and suits, including the costs of defense; when damages are sought for negligent or wrongful acts alleged to have been committed in the scope of employment or under the direction of the school board or related to any mentoring services provide to certified staff.

Indemnification and protection extend to persons who were members of school boards, employees of school boards, authorized volunteer personnel, mentors of certified staff, or student teachers at the time of the incident from which a claim arises. No agent may be afforded indemnification or protection unless he or she was a member of a school board, an employee of a board, an authorized volunteer, a mentor of certified staff, or a student teacher at the time of the incident from which the claim arises.

Federal legislation in 2002 contains a broad limitation on liability applicable to professional and non-professional employees who work in schools and individual school board members.

20 U.S.C. 6733 et seq.

105 ILCS 5/10-20.20

745 ILCS 10/1-101 et seq.

Bridewell v. Board of Education of Shawnee Community Unit School District No. 84 of Union, et al. Counties, 2 Ill. App. 3d 684, 276 N.E. 2d 745 (5th Dist. 1971)

22:64 Under what circumstances do school employees or school board members have qualified immunity from liability for civil rights violations?

Governmental officials performing discretionary functions are usually shielded from liability for civil damages insofar as their conduct does not violate clearly established statutory or constitutional rights of which a reasonable person would have known. The contours of the right must be sufficiently clear that a reasonable official would understand that what he or she is doing is wrong.

Baird v. Board of Education for Warren Community School District No. 205, 389 F. 3d 685 (7th Cir. 2004)

Harlow v. Fitzgerald, 102 S. Ct. 2727, 457 U.S. 800, 73 L. Ed. 2d 396 (1982)

Anderson v. Creighton, 107 S. Ct. 3034, 483 U.S. 635, 97 L. Ed. 2d 523 (1987)

22:70 May a school employee, volunteer, or school board member be personally liable for punitive damages?

Punitive damages are intended to punish the party on whom they are assessed. Indemnity and immunity protections provide some protection for public officials from liability for punitive damages in any action arising out of an act or omission made by the public official while serving in an official executive, legislative, quasi-legislative, or quasi-judicial capacity. Employers, however, may be liable for the acts of their agents when the employer authorizes or ratifies a discriminatory act, recklessly employs an unfit agent, or when the agent commits a discriminatory act while employed in a managerial capacity and acting within the scope of his or her authority.

In all other circumstances, school-connected individuals may be liable for punitive damages. Punitive damage awards are rare, however, and are imposed only in instances of extraordinary wrongdoing. The courts consider whether the harm caused was physical as opposed to economic; whether it constituted a reckless disregard for the health and safety of others; if the target of the conduct had financial vulnerability; whether the conduct involved repeated actions or was an isolated incident; and whether the harm was the result of intentional malice, trickery, or deceit or mere accident.

Equal Employment Opportunity Commission v. Autozone, 707 F. 3d 824 (7th Cir. 2013)

105 ILCS 5/10-20.20

745 ILCS 10/2-102

22:75 What are the risks when a school board member exceeds his or her authority?

A school board member who acts outside the scope of his or her authority may be personally liable for his or her wrongdoing.

INJURIES TO EMPLOYEES

22:80 May a school employee sue the school district for a work-related injury?

School employees are subject to worker compensation statutes and may recover only under the provisions of those laws. However, it is sometimes possible to bring related causes of action under the Illinois Human Rights Act or under the grievance procedure contained in a collective bargaining agreement.

820 ILCS 305/1 et seq.

775 ILCS 5/1-101 et seq.

22:90 Does the Occupational Safety and Health Act apply to public school districts?

No. The federal Occupational Safety and Health Act (OSHA) excludes school districts. The Illinois Department of Labor, however, often adopts and enforces OSHA standards.

29 U.S.C. 652 (5)

INJURIES TO STUDENTS

22:100 Under what circumstances may a school employee be held liable for injuries to students while in school?

If an "in loco parentis" relationship is found to exist between an injured student and a defendant school employee, the employee cannot be liable for ordinary negligence. The student can recover only if he or she can prove willful and wanton misconduct. If an in loco parentis relationship does not exist, the employee would be liable for injuries arising out of ordinary negligence, and the school board would be responsible to defend and indemnify the employee for his or her negligent or wrongful acts if they were committed within the scope of employment or under the direction of the school board.

105 ILCS 5/10-20.20

105 ILCS 5/24-24

Sidwell v. Griggsville Community Unit School District No. 4, 146 Ill. 2d 467, 588 N.E. 2d 1185, 167 Ill. Dec. 1055 (1992)

Plesnicar v. Kovach, 102 Ill. App. 3d 867, 430 N.E. 2d 648, 58 Ill. Dec. 616 (1st Dist. 1981)

O'Brien v. Township High School District No. 214, 83 Ill. 2d 462, 415 N.E. 2d 1015, 47 Ill. Dec. 702 (1980)

Thomas v. Chicago Board of Education, 60 Ill. App. 3d 729, 377 N.E. 2d 355 (1st Dist. 1978), rev. on other grounds 77 Ill. 2d 165, 395 N.E. 2d 538, 32 Ill. Dec. 308 (1979)

Kobylanski v. Chicago Board of Education, 63 Ill. 2d 165, 347 N.E. 2d 705 (1976)

Clay v. Chicago Board of Education, 22 Ill. App. 3d 437, 318 N.E. 2d 153 (1st Dist. 1974)

22:105 Does a school district have a duty to protect its students or employees from criminal attack?

The question usually arises in the aftermath of Columbine-like attacks or in the instance of fights or sexual misconduct. Generally, the school district does not have a duty to protect a person from harm unless the harm is reasonably foreseeable and the parties are in one of four special relationships: common carrier and passenger; innkeeper and guest; business invitor and invitee; and/or voluntary custodian and protectee.

The state actor might also be liable where the state places a person in a position of danger the person would not otherwise have faced. To meet this standard, a plaintiff must prove that the state created a danger that the plaintiff faced, its failure to protect the plaintiff was the proximate cause of the plaintiff's injuries, and the state's failure shocks the conscience.

Courts find an official's conduct conscience shocking when it evinces a deliberate indifference to the rights of the individual. "Where circumstances call for hurried judgments in order to protect public safety or maintain public order and thereby render reasoned deliberation impractical, conduct must reach a higher standard of culpability approaching malicious or intentional infliction of injury ..."

Only the most egregious official conduct will satisfy this requirement and usually only where it evinces a deliberate indifference to the rights of the individual.

King ex rel. King v. East St. Louis School District No. 189, 496 F. 3d 812 (7th Cir. 2007)

Jackson v. Indian Prairie School District 204, et al., 653 F. 3d 647 (7th Cir. 2011)

Green v. Carlinville Community Unit School District No. 1, 381 Ill. App. 3d 207, 887 N.E. 2d 451, 320 Ill. Dec. 307 (4th Dist. 2008)

Hernandez v. Rapid Bus Co., 267 Ill. App. 3d 519, 641 N.E. 2d 886, 204 Ill. Dec. 456 (1st Dist. 1994)

22:110 Which employees enjoy the protections of "in loco parentis?"

Teachers and other certificated employees stand in place of parents for students under their supervision and, therefore, cannot be held liable for ordinary negligence. Educational support personnel do not enjoy this defense against ordinary negligence claims.

105 ILCS 5/24-24

22:112 Can a school district assert "in loco parentis" immunity?

Limited immunity under Section 24-24 of the School Code is available only to teachers and other certificated educational employees, not school districts. A school district vicariously benefits when a cause of action predicated on negligence is brought against an educational employee, however.

Sidwell v. Griggsville Community Unit School District No. 4, 146 Ill. 2d 467, 588 N.E. 2d 1185, 167 Ill. Dec. 1055 (1992)

22:114 When is an employee's action deemed to be "within the scope of employment?"

In general (there are exceptions) an employer is not liable for the actions of in employee when the action is committed outside the scope of employment. An act by an employee is within the scope of employment when it is actuated, at least in part, by a purpose to serve the employer. An employee is acting within the scope of employment when the injurious act is incidental to the conduct authorized, or when it furthers, to an appreciable extent, the employer's business. An employer is not liable for an employee's acts committed outside the scope of employment even though the particular injury could not have occurred without the facilities afforded by the relation of the servant to the master.

To illustrate the line of demarcation between inside and outside scope of employment, normally sexual misconduct by an employee committed upon a student victim would be outside the scope of employment. But the conduct probably comes inside the scope of employment if the offender were, for example, a physical care aide charged with assisting the victim in changing clothes and/or toileting and the misconduct occurs while the aide was performing such tasks.

Hansen v. Board of Trustees of Hamilton Southeastern School Corporation, 551 F. 3d 599 (7th Cir. 2008)

Bagent v. Blessing Care Corp. 224 Ill. 2d 154, 862 N.E. 2d 985, 308 Ill. Dec. 782 (2007)

22:140 Does the "in loco parentis" status of teachers extend to activities outside school?

The "in loco parentis" status of teachers is restricted to those activities which are connected to the total school program. It extends to extracurricular activities, but may not extend to other activities that have a more tenuous connection to the total school program.

Stiff v. Eastern Illinois Area of Special Education, 251 Ill. App. 3d 859, 621 N.E. 2d 218, 190 Ill. Dec. 349 (4th Dist. 1993)

Montag v. Board of Education of School District No. 40, Rock Island County, 112 Ill. App. 3d 1039, 446 N.E. 2d 299, 68 Ill. Dec. 565 (3rd Dist. 1983)

Weiss v. Collinsville Community Unit School District No. 10, Madison County, 119 Ill. App. 3d 68, 456 N.E. 2d 614, 74 Ill. Dec. 893 (5th Dist. 1983)

Plesnicar v. Kovach, 102 Ill. App. 3d 867, 430 N.E. 2d 648, 58 Ill. Dec. 616 (1st Dist. 1981)

Lynch v. Board of Education of Collinsville Community Unit School District No. 10, 82 Ill. 2d 415, 412 N.E. 2d 447, 45 Ill. Dec. 96 (1980)

Woodman v. Litchfield Community Unit School District No. 12, Montgomery County, 102 Ill. App. 2d 330, 242 N.E. 2d 780 (5th Dist. 1968)

Fustin v. Board of Education of Community Unit School District No. 2, 101 Ill. App. 2d 113, 242 N.E. 2d 308 (1968)

22:145 What duty does a school district have to a student riding or leaving a school bus?

A school district has a very high duty of care to students while they are riding a school bus. The standard of care is effectively the same as that applied to common carriers. The courts reason that while on a school bus a student cannot ensure his or her own safety and must rely on the school district to provide fit employees to do so. There remains a degree of uncertainty as to whether given the high standard of care, a carrier is responsible for the intentional or criminal acts of its employees when those acts are committed outside the scope of employment.

The duty becomes a duty of reasonable care with respect to the students once they have left the bus and are on their way home. This latter duty means the school district cannot expose the students to unreasonable risks by reason of the school district's selection of bus routes, drop off points, or procedures.

Green v. Carlinville Community Unit School District No. 1, 381 Ill. App. 3d 207, 887 N.E. 2d 451, 320 Ill. Dec. 307 (4th Dist. 2008)

Garrett v. Grant School District No. 124, 139 Ill. App. 3d 569, 487 N.E. 2d 699, 93 Ill. Dec. 874 (2nd Dist. 1985)

Posteher v. Pana Community Unit School District, 96 Ill. App. 3d 709, 421 N.E. 2d 1049, 52 Ill. Dec. 186 (4th Dist. 1981)

Katamay v. Chicago Transit Authority, 53 Ill. 2d 27, 289 N.E. 2d 623 (1972)

Sims v. Chicago Transit Authority, 351 Ill. App. 314, 115 N.E. 2d 96 (1st Dist. 1953), rev. on other grounds 4 Ill. 2d 60, 122 N.E. 2d 221 (1954)

22:147 Are school districts required to provide car seats for children under the age of 8 years?

The Motor Vehicle Code requires that when any person is transporting a child under the age of 8 years in a non-commercial motor vehicle of the first division (a first division vehicle is one designed for the carrying of not more than 10 persons.), any truck or tractor that is equipped with seat safety belts, any other motor vehicle of the second division with a gross vehicle weight rating of 9,000 pounds or less, or a recreational vehicle, the person shall be responsible for providing for the protection of such child by properly securing him or her in an appropriate child restraint system. The parent or legal guardian of a child under the age of 8 years must provide a child restraint system to any person who transports the child.

A sentence that had been in the law from 2004 until 2007, apparently absolving the driver of responsibility if the parent failed to provide a car seat, was removed from the statute effective January 1, 2008.

For purposes of this provision, "child restraint system" means any device which meets the standards of the U. S. Department of Transportation designed to restrain, seat, or position children, which also includes a booster seat.

A child weighing more than 40 pounds may be transported in the back seat of a motor vehicle while wearing only a lap belt if the back seat of the motor vehicle is not equipped with a combination lap and shoulder belt. The statute also provides that in no event shall a person's failure to secure a child under eight years of age in an approved child restraint system constitute contributory negligence or be admissible as evidence in the trial of any civil action.

625 ILCS 25/4
625 ILCS 25/5

22:150 What responsibilities and liabilities do school districts incur when providing medical treatment to students?

When a medical emergency occurs and trained medical personnel are unavailable, teachers standing in loco parentis may render necessary emergency treatment to pupils. Teachers are not expected to possess expert medical knowledge but, rather, to act reasonably and prudently.

745 ILCS 10/6-104 et seq.

22:155 Should a school district create an emergency medical form for students with special needs?

A 2002 amendment to the School Code contains language that encourages school districts to create medical information forms for use by bus drivers and emergency medical technicians "for those students with special needs or medical conditions." The statute does not require that a school district have such a form or request that parents provide information, but a school district's failure to do so when there is a subsequent student injury will present a certain political and probable legal problems for the school district.

The statute provides:

"The form may include without limitation information to be provided by the student's parent or legal guardian concerning the student's relevant medical conditions, medications that the student is taking, the student's communication skills, and how a bus driver or an emergency medical technician is to respond to certain behaviors of the student.

"If the form is used, the school district is encouraged to notify parents and legal guardians of the availability of the form. The parent or legal guardian of the student may fill out the form and submit it to the school that the student is attending. The school district is encouraged to keep one copy of the form on file at the school and another copy on the student's school bus in a secure location."

105 ILCS 5/10-20.35
105 ILCS 5/10-20.36

22:160 If an Illinois public school student is injured on an out-of-state field trip, which state's immunity laws control?

Immunity defenses to tort claims are governed by the laws of the state in which the lawsuit is properly brought.

Nevada v. Hall, 99 S. Ct. 1182, 440 U.S. 410, 59 L. Ed. 2d 416, reh. den. 99 S. Ct. 2018, 441 U.S. 917, 60 L. Ed. 2d 389 (1979)

22:164 If a parent provides a permission slip for his or her child to participate in a school activity, will the school be protected from liability if an accident occurs?

A parent's waiver of liability will not prevent the minor child from bringing suit. While such waivers do not violate public policy in Illinois, they are not favored by the courts and are strictly construed against the benefiting party. A minor does not have capacity to waive liability.

Meyer by Meyer v. Naperville Manor, Inc., 262 Ill. App. 3d 141, 634 N.E. 2d 411, 199 Ill. Dec. 572 (2nd Dist. 1994)

Masciola v. Chicago Metropolitan Ski Council, 257 Ill. App. 3d 313, 628 N.E. 2d 1067, 195 Ill. Dec. 603 (1st Dist. 1993)

22:167 Does tort immunity protect a school district from liability when an injury occurs on a school playground?

Neither a school district nor its employees can be held liable for an "...injury where the liability is based on the existence of a condition of any public property intended or permitted to be used for recreational purposes..." unless the school district or employee has caused the injury by willful and wanton misconduct. Whether or not the property is used for recreational purpose depends upon the character of the property, not the activity performed on it at any given time.

745 ILCS 10/3-106

Arteman et al. v. Clinton Community School District No. 15, 198 Ill. 2d 475, 763 N.E. 2d 756, 261 Ill. Dec. 507 (2002)

Bubb v. Springfield School District No. 186, et al., 167 Ill. 2d 372, 657 N.E. 2d 887, 194 Ill. Dec. 518 (1995)

22:168 Does a school district have liability for failure to provide students with safe equipment?

A school district has a duty to provide safety equipment reasonably necessary to protect against serious, foreseeable injuries. But a school district has tort immunity for negligent discretionary policy determinations.

To the extent a school district frames its defense in the context of its decision to provide or not provide safety equipment it may assert a tort immunity defense.

Under the law at the time of this writing, school districts have broad protection from suit in claims arising out of negligent provision of equipment. It is likely the existing law will be amended to modify the scope of this immunity.

745 ILCS 10/2-201

Arteman et al. v. Clinton Community School District No. 15, 198 Ill. 2d 475, 763 N.E. 2d 756, 261 Ill. Dec. 507 (2002)

22:170 Is there a cause of action for educational malpractice?

Educational malpractice lawsuits have, for the most part, been unsuccessful. There is no recognized duty to educate, the breach of which would create a cause of action.

Donohue v. Copiague Union Free School District, 418 N.Y.S. 2d 375, 47 N.Y. 2d 440 (1979)

SAFETY REQUIREMENTS

22:180 What safety requirements are contained in the School Code to protect persons on school property from injury?

Every student, teacher, and visitor must wear an industrial-quality eye protective device when participating in or observing any of the following courses in public schools:

1) Vocational or industrial arts shops or laboratories involving experience with the following: hot molten metals; milling, sawing, turning, shaping, cutting, grinding, or stamping of any solid materials; heat treatment, tempering, or kiln firing of any metal or other materials; gas or electric arc welding; repair or servicing of any vehicle; and caustic or explosive materials;

2) Chemical or combined chemical-physical laboratories involving caustic or explosive chemicals or hot liquids or solids.

105 ILCS 115/1

22:190 What other statutory safety requirements are imposed on school boards to protect persons from injury while on school property?

School building construction and maintenance are subject to stringent State Board of Education regulations in the Illinois Life-Safety Code. Schools also are subject to the occupational safety standards contained in the Illinois Health and Safety Act and enforced by the Illinois Department of Labor. Other safety standards applicable to schools include various environmental requirements, such as asbestos abatement and safe drinking water, traffic safety, and the common law "duty of care" owed to students while on school premises.

15 U.S.C. 2641 et seq.

105 ILCS 5/2-3.12

820 ILCS 225/1

23 Ill. Admin. Code 180.10 et seq.

Jastram v. Lake Villa School District No. 41, 192 Ill. App. 3d 599, 549 N.E. 2d 9, 139 Ill. Dec. 29 (2nd Dist. 1989)

22:191 What is a school bus?

A school bus is every motor vehicle owned or operated by any public, private, or religious primary or secondary school and/or public, private, or religious nursery school for the transportation of persons regularly enrolled as students in grade 12 or below in connection with any activity of such entity. The definition does not include:

1) A bus operated by a public utility, municipal corporation, or common carrier authorized to conduct local or interurban transportation of passengers when such bus is not traveling a specific school bus route but is on a regularly scheduled route for the transportation of other fare-paying passengers or furnishing charter service for the transportation of groups on field trips or other special trips or in connection with other special events; or being used for shuttle service between attendance centers or other educational facilities;

2) A motor vehicle of the first division; and

3) A multifunction school-activity bus.

625 ILCS 5/1-182

22:192 What are a school district's transportation options?

Every student enrolled in grade 12 or below must be transported in a school bus or a bus operated by a public utility, municipal corporation, or common carrier authorized to conduct local or interurban transportation of passengers when such bus is not traveling a specific school bus route but is on a regularly scheduled route for the transportation of other fare-paying passengers or furnishing charter service for the transportation of groups on field trips or other special trips or in connection with other special events; or being used for shuttle service between attendance centers or other educational facilities or a motor vehicle of the first division for any curriculum-related school activity.

A multi-function school activity bus may not be used to transport schoolchildren to or from a curriculum-related school activity.

"Curriculum-related school activity" includes transportation from home to school or from school to home; tripper or shuttle service between school attendance centers; transportation to a vocational or career center or other trade-skill development site or a regional safe school or other school-sponsored alternative learning program; or a trip that is directly related to the regular curriculum of a student for which he or she earns credit.

Every student enrolled in grade 12 or below who is transported in a vehicle that is being operated by or for a public or private primary or secondary school, including any primary or secondary school operated by a religious institution, for an interscholastic, interscholastic-athletic, or school-sponsored, non-curriculum-related activity that (i) does not require student participation as part of the educational services of the entity and (ii) is not associated with the students' regular class-for-credit schedule must transport students only in a school bus or a bus operated by a public utility, municipal corporation, or common carrier authorized to conduct local or interurban transportation of passengers when such bus is not traveling a specific school bus route but is on a regularly scheduled route for the transportation of other fare-paying passengers or furnishing charter service for the transportation of groups on field trips or other special trips or in connection with other special events; or being used for shuttle service between attendance centers or other educational facilities, a motor vehicle of the first division or a multifunction school-activity bus

This restriction does not apply to any second division vehicle used by any of the above entities for a parade, homecoming, or similar non-curriculum-related school activity.

A first division vehicle is one designed for the carrying of not more than 10 persons. A second division vehicle is designed for carrying more than 10 persons, those motor vehicles designed or used for living quarters, those motor vehicles which are designed for pulling or carrying freight, cargo or implements of husbandry, and those motor vehicles of the first division remodeled for use and used as motor vehicles of the second division.

625 ILCS 5/1-146
625 ILCS 5/1-182
625 ILCS 5/11-1414.1

22:193 What safety standards apply to the construction and operation of school buses?

There are both federal and state rules and regulations that govern school bus construction and safety standards for school vehicles.

49 C.F.R. 571.101 et seq.
92 Ill. Admin. Code 440.10 et seq.
92 Ill. Admin. Code 442.110 et seq.
92 Ill. Admin. Code 444.5 et seq.

22:196 May a school district purchase a 12- or 15-passenger van for use as a school bus?

Under federal law, a school bus is a passenger motor vehicle designed to carry 11 or more persons. Any such vehicle must meet federal bus safety standards. A school district should not purchase, lease, or use a van that is designed to carry 11 or more passengers unless the vehicle meets federal standards, even if state law suggests otherwise. To ignore the federal law will potentially increase the school board's exposure in the event of an accident.

Illinois law defines a multifunction school activity bus (MFSAB) as a school bus manufactured for the purpose of transporting 11 or more persons, including the driver, whose purposes do not include transporting students to and from home or school bus stops. A MFSAB is prohibited from meeting the special requirements for school buses in Sections 12-801, 12-803, and 12-805 and subsection (a) of Section 12 802 of the Motor Vehicle Code.

49 U.S.C. 30101 et seq.
625 ILCS 5/1-148.3a-5

22:198 How may a school district transport students to and from extracurricular activities?

Any school district transporting students in grade 12 or below for an interscholastic, interscholastic athletic, or school-sponsored, non-curriculum-related activity that (i) does not require student participation as part of the educational services of the district and (ii) is not associated with the students' regular class-for-credit schedule or required five clock hours of instruction must transport the students only in a school bus, a vehicle manufactured to transport not more than 10 persons, including the driver, or a multifunction school-activity bus (MFSAB) manufactured to transport not more than 15 persons, including the driver.

A student in grades 9 through 12 may be transported in a MFSAB as defined in Section 1-148.3a-5 of the Illinois Vehicle Code for any curriculum-related activity except for transportation on regular bus routes from home to school or from school to home, provided the driver holds a valid school bus driver permit and the use of a MFSAB is subject to the requirements of Sections 6-106.11, 6-106.12, 12-707.01, 13-101, and 13-109 of the Illinois Vehicle Code.

A school district furnishing transportation for students under the authority of the relevant School Code provision must insure against any loss or liability of the district resulting from the maintenance, operation, or use of the vehicle. The statute contains specific coverage requirements. Such vehicles used to transport students may claim a depreciation allowance of 20 percent over five years as provided in Section 29 5 of the School Code.

105 ILCS 5/29-6.3
625 ILCS 5/1-148.3a-5
625 ILCS 5/6-106.11
625 ILCS 5/6-106.12
625 ILCS 5/12-707.01
625 ILCS 5/13-101
625 ILCS 5/13-109

22:200 What immunities and/or defenses against tort liability would be available to a school board for injuries arising out of violations of statutory safety requirements?

School boards owe a "duty of care" to students, employees, and visitors where the safety of buildings, grounds, and equipment are concerned. The protections of "in loco parentis" are available only where an injury arises from the supervisory duties of a certificated employee, and would not protect the school district where the injury arises, for example, from faulty equipment or unsafe building conditions.

Whether any of the immunities specified in the tort immunity statute would apply to unsafe building conditions would depend upon the facts in each situation.

745 ILCS 10/1-101 et seq.

22:210 What standard of care does a school district owe invitees on school property?

A school district must exercise reasonable care with respect to invitees on school property. Invitees include spectators at athletic contests and parents attending a conference day.

Borushek v. Kincaid, 78 Ill. App. 3d 295, 397 N.E. 2d 172, 33 Ill. Dec. 839 (1st Dist. 1979)

Tanari v. School Directors of District No. 502, County of Bureau, 69 Ill. 2d 630, 373 N.E. 2d 5, 14 Ill. Dec. 874 (1977)

JUDGMENTS

22:230 What manner of payment may a school board elect in paying a settlement or judgment?

If a school board does not pay a tort judgment during the fiscal year in which it becomes final and if, in the opinion of the school board, the payment of the judgment creates an unreasonable financial hardship for the school district, it must pay the balance of the judgment with interest in installments subject to conditions set forth in statute.

745 ILCS 10/9-104

Evans v. City of Chicago, 689 F. 2d 1286 (7th Cir. 1982)

22:240 Is a school district that loses a civil rights suit responsible for paying the attorney fees and expert witness fees of the plaintiff?

The school district defendant would be liable to pay the attorney fees of the plaintiff, but not the plaintiff's expert witness fees.

West Virginia University Hospital v. Casey, 111 S. Ct. 1138, 499 U.S. 83, 113 L. Ed. 2d 68 (1991)

22:250 With what resources does a school board pay settlements and related legal costs?

A school board is authorized to maintain a Tort Immunity Fund and to levy taxes and/or to issue bonds in an amount necessary to pay judgments and related expenses specified by statute.

105 ILCS 5/17-2.5
745 ILCS 10/9-102 et seq.

23: PROPERTY TAX INCOME

AUTHORITY TO LEVY TAXES

23:10 On what property may a school board levy taxes?

A school district may levy on all taxable property within school district boundaries, including property that at the time of the levy was part of the school district but which at a later date in the same tax year was detached.

People ex rel. Nordstrom v. Barry, 11 Ill. 2d 259, 142 N.E. 2d 26 (1957)

People ex rel. Davis v. Spence, 3 Ill. 2d 244, 120 N.E. 2d 565 (1954)

23:20 May vocational education or special education cooperatives levy taxes?

No. However, a special education joint agreement district, composed of one member of the school board of each cooperating district, has the authority to borrow by issuance of bonds or notes. Each member district has an obligation to repay but that obligation does not affect the debt limitation of the member district.

105 ILCS 5/10-22.31

23:30 May a school district levy a personal property tax?

No.

Ill. Const. art. IX, sec. 5(c)

Cherry Bowl, Inc. v. Property Tax Appeal Board, 100 Ill. App. 3d 326, 426 N.E. 2d 618, 55 Ill. Dec. 472 (2nd Dist. 1981)

Central Illinois Light Co. v. Johnson, 84 Ill. 2d 275, 418 N.E. 2d 275, 49 Ill. Dec. 676 (1981)

PROPERTY ASSESSMENTS

23:40 How is property assessed?

The county assessor appraises all real property. Railroad property used for transportation, private car lines, pollution control equipment, and capital stock are assessed by the Illinois Department of Revenue, which certifies these valuations to the county clerk. In some counties, township assessors do the assessments.

The appraisals are subject to appeal by the taxpayer to the county board of appeals. The assessor's appraisals are equalized by the Illinois Department of Revenue. The purpose of equalization is to develop a common level of assessments among counties. (Equalization of assessments is essential to provide an equitable basis for distributing state aid to schools.) The Department equalizes assessments by means of multipliers assigned to each county. The multiplier is applied to all assessments in a county to adjust assessments by a given percentage in order to bring the county level to a specified percentage of fair market value.

In all Illinois counties except Cook, the statutory standard for equalization of property assessments is 33 1/3 percent of fair market value. In September 2008, the Cook County Board set assessments at 10 percent of fair market value for residential property and to 25 percent for commercial and industrial property effective for the 2009 assessment year, thereby conforming the specified levels to the levels actually being assessed.

35 ILCS 200/9-145 et seq.

23:50 How does a school district secure information on the taxable property located within its boundaries?

The county clerk must furnish the school board of any school district, upon request, a certificate showing the last ascertained full, fair cash value of the taxable property of the district. When a school district lies partly in two or more counties, the county clerk of each county in which any part of the district lies must furnish the school board, upon request, a certificate showing the last ascertained full, fair cash value of the taxable property in that part of the district lying in each county.

105 ILCS 5/17-10

Board of Education of Beach Park Community Consolidated School District No. 3, Lake County v. Hess, 140 Ill. App. 3d 653, 488 N.E. 2d 1358, 95 Ill. Dec. 15 (2nd Dist. 1986)

23:55 May a school board intervene if it believes that certain taxable property is under-assessed?

Yes, a school board may challenge any property assessment by filing a complaint with the county board of review within a timeframe specified by statute. Decisions of the county board of review may be appealed to the State Tax Appeals Board and then to the courts, or in some cases directly to the courts on Administrative Review.

35 ILCS 200/16-55 et seq.

35 ILCS 200/16-160 et seq.

TAX INCREMENT FINANCING

23:60 What happens to the value of taxable property in an area that is included in a tax increment financing district?

The equalized assessed valuation of property within a tax increment financing district is frozen at its current valuation insofar as its impact on school district property tax revenue is concerned. Revenue generated by the school district tax levy on any future increase in assessed valuation is paid over to a special tax increment district redevelopment fund controlled by the municipality that created it.

Under provisions of the Real Property Tax Increment Allocation Development Act, revenue derived from future increases in assessed value may be lost to the school district for up to 23 years, depending upon provisions of the municipal ordinance creating the tax increment financing district.

65 ILCS 5/11-74.4-1 et seq.

105 ILCS 5/18-8.05

People ex rel. City of Canton v. Crouch, 79 Ill. 2d 356, 403 N.E. 2d 242, 38 Ill. Dec. 154 (1980)

23:63 What notice does a school district get prior to the creation of a redevelopment area?

If a municipality or a commission adopts an ordinance or resolution providing for a feasibility study on the designation of an area as a redevelopment project area, a copy of the ordinance must be sent to the school district. The ordinance must contain notice of the boundaries of the area; the purpose of the project; a general description of the tax increment allocation financing; and the name, phone number, and address of the municipal officer who can be contacted for additional information. A public hearing is required before a municipality can designate an area for redevelopment.

65 ILCS 5/11-74.4-4.1

65 ILCS 5/11-74.4-5

23:65 May a school district acquire information about the financial condition of a tax increment financing district?

If a majority of the taxing districts represented on the review board in which the redevelopment project area is located request it, the municipality must provide detailed financial information within 180 days after the close of each fiscal year to the taxing bodies as required by statute. The state comptroller's website contains financial information about the district as required by statute. The information is posted not later than 45 days after it is received by the comptroller.

65 ILCS 5/11-74.4-5(d)

23:68 What happens if land in a tax increment financing district is not developed as anticipated?

If a redevelopment project has not been initiated in a redevelopment project area within seven years after the area was designated by ordinance, the municipality must adopt an ordinance repealing the area's designation as a redevelopment project area. The definition of a development project is the existence of a signed redevelopment agreement or expenditures on eligible redevelopment project costs associated with a redevelopment project.

65 ILCS 5/11-74.4-4(r)

TAX LEVIES

23:80 What is a certificate of tax levy?

A certificate of tax levy is a document authorized by formal action of the school board, signed by the president and clerk or secretary of the board, and issued to the county clerk. The document certifies the amount of money necessary in each fund to be levied against the equalized assessed valuation of the taxable property of the school district for a given fiscal year.

105 ILCS 5/17-11

23:90 When is a certificate of tax levy filed?

The certificate of tax levy must be filed with each county clerk on or before the last Tuesday in December annually.

105 ILCS 5/17-11

Board of Education of Community Unit School District No. 16 v. Barrett, 67 Ill. 2d 11, 364 N.E. 2d 89, 7 Ill. Dec. 102 (1977)

23:100 When are property taxes levied and when are they collected?

Taxes that are levied on the current year's budget and filed in December with the county clerk are extended in the spring and usually received by a school treasurer in June and September, after the current school year has ended.

35 ILCS 200/20-50 et seq.

35 ILCS 200/20-130 et seq.

23:110 May a county clerk refuse to extend a school district's taxes if the district does not file required documents within the required time?

The governing authority of each taxing district must file with the county clerk within 30 days of their adoption a certified copy of its appropriation and budget resolutions, as well as an estimate, certified by its chief fiscal officer, of revenues, by source, anticipated to be received by the school district in the following fiscal year. Failure to file the required documents (after timely notice) authorizes the county clerk to refuse to extend the tax levy imposed by the governing authority until the documents are filed.

35 ILCS 200/18-50

23:115 When may a newly combined school district levy taxes?

If the election of the school board of the new district occurs at a regular election and the board of education makes its initial levy or levies in that same year, the county clerk must extend the levy or levies, notwithstanding any other law that requires the adoption of a budget before the clerk may extend the levy. In addition, the districts from which the new district is formed, by joint agreement and with the approval of the regional superintendent of schools, must be permitted to amend outstanding levies in the same calendar year in which the creation of the new district is approved at the rates specified in the petition.

If the election of the board of education of the new district does not occur in the same calendar year that the proposition to create the new district is approved, the districts from which the new district or districts are formed, by joint agreement and with the approval of the regional superintendent of schools, must be permitted to levy in the same calendar year in which the creation of the new district is approved at the rates specified in the petition. The county clerks must extend any such levy notwithstanding any law that requires adoption of a budget before extension of the levy.

105 ILCS 5/11E-100

23:120 If a school district is located in two or more counties, must the school district file a certificate of levy with the county clerk in each county?

When a school district lies partly in two or more counties, the school board, after ascertaining as nearly as practical the amount to be raised by special taxes through levy, is required to prepare a certificate of tax levy for each county in which the district lies and deliver one such certificate to each of the county clerks of the counties that are a part of the district.

105 ILCS 5/17-12

23:130 May a school board amend its tax levy?

Under certain circumstances, a school board may amend its certificate of tax levy to the amount necessary to raise its operating tax rate to the level necessary to qualify for the maximum amount of state aid. However, the general state aid program introduced for 1998-1999 and thereafter does not require a school board to levy a minimum qualifying tax rate to obtain its maximum state aid. Therefore, this statutory provision provides no basis for the school board to amend its tax levy.

105 ILCS 5/17-11.1

105 ILCS 5/18-8.05

105 ILCS 5/18-18.15

In re County Collector of McHenry County, 181 Ill. App. 3d 345, 536 N.E. 2d 1288, 130 Ill. Dec. 77 (2nd Dist. 1989)

23:134 May a school board file an additional tax levy following voter approval of a tax rate increase?

The school board may make an additional tax levy whenever the voters approve a tax rate increase in the educational and/or operations and maintenance fund after the levy has been filed. To do so, the board must approve an additional or supplemental budget by a majority vote of its full membership and file an additional levy for that fiscal year. Because the tax rate is increased with voter approval, adoption of the additional budget and levy probably complies with the Truth in Taxation Act.

35 ILCS 200/18-55 et seq.

105 ILCS 5/17-3.2

In re County Collector of McHenry County, 181 Ill. App. 3d 345, 536 N.E. 2d 1288, 130 Ill. Dec. 77 (2nd Dist. 1989)

23:136 What is the latest date by which a school board may file an amended or additional tax levy?

Assuming that a school board has received voter approval for an increased tax rate or otherwise meets the criteria necessary for an amended levy, the amended certificate of levy must be filed with the county clerk in time to be incorporated in the tax bills without materially impeding the county's ability to extend and collect taxes.

105 ILCS 5/17-3.2

105 ILCS 5/17-11.1

In re County Collector of McHenry County, 181 Ill. App. 3d 345, 536 N.E. 2d 1288, 130 Ill. Dec. 77 (2nd Dist. 1989)

LEVY HEARINGS

23:140 When must a school board hold a public hearing on a proposed tax levy?

A school district proposing to increase its aggregate levy more than 105 percent of its prior year's extension including any amount abated by the taxing district prior to any extension but exclusive of the cost of an election, must publish notice of hearing and thereafter hold a hearing as required by law.

Prior to January 1, 2003, an annual truth in taxation hearing was required for all Cook County school districts on the first Wednesday in December for all high school districts and the first Tuesday in December for all other school districts. This requirement has expired.

Also, a public hearing must be held when a school board intends to amend a certificate of tax levy.

35 ILCS 200/18-55 et seq.

35 ILCS 200/18-72

35 ILCS 200/18-101.1 et seq.

23:145 What happens if a newspaper fails to publish a school district's truth in taxation notice?

A levy of a taxing district is not invalidated for failure to comply with the levy and extension article of the Property Tax Code if the failure is attributable to the newspaper's failure to reproduce the information in the notice accurately or to publish the notice as directed by the taxing district.

35 ILCS 200/18-100

23:150 When must a school board estimate its annual aggregate tax levy?

Not less than 20 days prior to adoption of its aggregate tax levy in school districts outside Cook County and not less than 30 days prior to adoption of its aggregate tax levy in school districts inside Cook County, a school board must determine the amount of money, exclusive of any portion of that levy attributable to election costs, estimated to be necessary to be raised by taxation for that year on the taxable property within its district.

35 ILCS 200/18-60

23:160 What is included in a school board's aggregate levy?

The "aggregate levy" includes the entirety of a board's annual levy except any portion of a tax levy attributable to paying the cost of conducting an election that is required under the general election laws and taxes levied to pay the principal and interest on bonds, notes, and other obligations that were secured by property tax levies and amounts due under a public building commission lease.

35 ILCS 200/18-60

Board of Education of Township High School District 211, Cook County, v. Kusper, 92 Ill. 2d 333, 422 N.E. 2d 179, 65 Ill. Dec. 868 (1982)

PROPERTY TAX RATES

23:170 What amounts may a school board levy in the educational fund, operations and maintenance, fund and transportation fund?

A school district may levy amounts for these funds within the tax rate limits established by law. Tax rate limits for each of these funds, which differ according to type of district, may be increased by referendum.

Further, a cap on property taxes may limit school district levies in these funds in the counties of Cook, DuPage, Kane, Lake, McHenry, Will, and certain other counties that have voted to impose tax caps. The county clerks in these counties may not extend taxes in the aggregate for any taxing district in excess of 105 percent of the previous year's extension or the percentage increase in the consumer price index for the prior levy year (whichever is less). Although some portions of the tax levy are exempted from the cap, the cap can limit the amount of the extension to less than what the authorized tax rate would otherwise produce. In PTELL districts under certain circumstances (where the cap is not exceeded) a particular fund levy can be increased to an amount that would not be otherwise possible without voter approval.

35 ILCS 200/18-185 et seq.

105 ILCS 5/17-2 et seq.

105 ILCS 5/17-4

105 ILCS 5/17-5 et seq.

Board of Education of Auburn Community Unit School District No. 10 v. Illinois Department of Revenue, et al., 398 Ill. App. 3d 629, 941 N.E. 888, 347 Ill. Dec. 19 (4th Dist. 2010)

Board of Education of Batavia v. Cunningham, 346 Ill. App. 3d 1027, 806 N.E. 2d 1219, 282 Ill. Dec. 631 (2nd Dist. 2004)

23:175 What is a tax rate and how is it calculated?

A tax rate in Illinois reflects the dollars levied per $100 of equalized assessed valuation (EAV) of real property. A tax rate is calculated by dividing the dollar amount of the tax levy by the total EAV of the taxing district and multiplying the product by 100. Thus, a levy of $200,000 divided by a tax base of $20 million EAV would produce a tax rate of $1.00 per $100 EAV.

23:180 What are the school district types that distinguish among different tax rates authorized by law?

A "unit school district" provides education in grades K-12. "Dual district" is a term describing either an elementary school district or a high school district. An elementary school district provides education in grades K-8 and a high school district provides education in grades 9-12. Each is called a dual district because both are required in a given geographical area to provide the same range of education as is provided by a unit district.

23:190 What are the maximum allowable tax rates without referendum?

A school board may annually levy a tax not to exceed the maximum rates and for the specified purposes upon all the taxable property of the district at the value, as equalized or assessed by the Department of Revenue, as follows:

1) Districts maintaining only grades 1-8 may levy up to .92 percent for educational purposes and .25 percent for operations and maintenance purposes.

2) Districts maintaining only grades 9-12 may levy up to .92 percent for educational purposes and .25 percent for operations and maintenance purposes.

3) Districts maintaining grades 1-12 may levy up to 1.84 percent for educational purposes and .375 for operations and maintenance purposes. (The school board may raise the permissive rate for operations and maintenance, subject to back door referendum, to .465 percent for the 1991-92 school year and .50 percent thereafter.)

4) All districts may levy up to .075 percent for capital improvement purposes if approved by the voters.

5) Districts maintaining only grades 1-8 may levy up to .12 percent for transportation purposes, except that under certain specified conditions a rate of up to .20 percent is permissible; districts maintaining only grades 9-12 may levy up to .12 percent for transportation purposes; and districts maintaining grades 1-12 may levy up to .20 percent for transportation purposes.

6) Districts providing summer classes may levy up to .15 percent for educational purposes if approved by the voters.

In addition, some school districts are subject to the Property Tax Extension Limitation Law (PTELL). The law effectively imposes a limit on the aggregate tax rate when the current year's tax extension reaches 105 percent of the prior year's extension or the percentage increase in the Consumer Price Index, whichever is less. Beginning in 2017, notwithstanding the provisions, requirements, or limitations in any law, any tax levied for educational purposes by a school district subject to the PTELL for the 2016 levy year or after may be extended at a rate exceeding the rate established for educational purposes by referendum or the School Code, provided that the rate does not cause the school district to exceed the limiting rate applicable to the school district under the PTELL for that levy rate established for educational purposes by referendum or the School Code, provided that the rate does not cause the school district to exceed the limiting rate applicable to the school district under the PTELL that levy year.

35 ILCS 200/18-190 et seq.
105 ILCS 5/17-2
105 ILCS 5/17-3.6
Board of Education of Batavia v. Cunningham, 346 Ill. App. 3d 1027, 806 N.E. 2d 1219, 282 Ill. Dec. 631 (2nd Dist. 2004)

23:193 What are the maximum education fund and operations and maintenance fund rates for a newly created unit district?

If a unit district is being established from an elementary district or districts and a high school district under School Code Article 11E, and the combined rate of the elementary district or districts and the high school district prior to the formation of the unit district is greater than 4 percent for educational purposes or .75 percent for operations and maintenance, then the maximum rates for the unit district are:

For the first year following the formation of the new district, the maximum rate equals the lesser of the actual combined rate of the previous highest elementary district rate and the high school district rate or 6.4 percent for education and 1.03 percent for operations and maintenance.

For the second year after the formation of the new district, the maximum rate equals the lesser of the actual combined rate of the previous highest elementary district rate and the high school district rate or 5.8 percent for education and .96 percent for operations and maintenance.

For the third year after the formation of the new district, the maximum rate equals the lesser of the actual combined rate of the previous highest elementary district rate and the high school district rate or 5.2 percent for education and .89 percent for operations and maintenance.

For the fourth year after the formation of the new district, the maximum rate equals the lesser of the actual combined rate of the previous highest elementary district rate and the high school district rate or 4.6 percent for education and .82 percent for operations and maintenance.

For the fifth year after the formation of the new district and thereafter, the maximum rate is no greater than 4 percent for education and .75 percent for operations and maintenance.

105 ILCS 5/17-3
105 ILCS 5/17-5

23:195 At what rate may a school board levy taxes to pay the principal and interest on bonded debt?

Bonds represent general obligations of a school district. The county clerk levies a separate tax to pay the principal and interest of the bonds of the district without limitation as to rate or amount. Although there is no statutory limit on the tax rate for debt service, school district indebtedness is limited to an aggregate amount for all forms of debt expressed as a percentage of the total value of taxable property in the district.

105 ILCS 5/17-9
105 ILCS 5/19-1

23:200 May a school district levy a tax for special education?

A school board may, by resolution, levy a tax for special education. Dual districts (those maintaining only elementary or only secondary programs) may levy .02 percent. Unit districts (those maintaining programs in grades K-12) may levy .04 percent. The rates may be increased to .40 and to .80 percent respectively with voter approval.

105 ILCS 5/17-2.2a

23:207 May a school district levy a tax for computer technology?

A school district may use the lease tax to purchase computer technology, lease educational facilities, or both. The lease tax rate may not exceed .05 percent, or .1 percent upon approval of the voters. The proceeds of the tax may be used to secure the payment of a lease, lease purchase, or installment agreement.

105 ILCS 5/17-2.2c

23:210 How may a school board levy to support summer school?

A school board may, by proper resolution, cause a proposition to authorize an annual tax for summer school education purposes to be submitted to the voters of the district at a regularly scheduled election. If a majority of the votes cast on this proposition is in favor, the board may thereafter levy the tax as authorized in the referendum to a maximum of .15 percent.

105 ILCS 5/17-2.1

23:220 How much and for what purposes may a school district levy taxes in its tort immunity fund?

A school district may levy whatever amount is required to pay

1) Settlements or judgments for compensatory damages and associated attorney fees and costs as defined in the Tort Immunity Act;

2) Settlements or judgments under the federal Comprehensive Environmental Response, Compensation and Liability Act of 1980 and the Environmental Protection Act, but only until December 31, 2010; and

3) Insurance, individual or joint self-insurance (including reserves), including all operating and administrative costs and expenses directly attributable to loss prevention and loss reduction; legal services directly attributable to the insurance and educational, inspection, and supervisory services directly related to loss prevention and reduction; and participation in a reciprocal insurer including all costs directly attributable to being a member of an insurance pool;

4) The costs, principal, and interest on certain tort immunity bonds; and

5) The cost of certain risk care management programs.

42 U.S.C. 9610 et seq.
105 ILCS 5/17-2.5
415 ILCS 5/1 et seq.
745 ILCS 10/9-102 et seq.

In re Objections to Tax Levies of Freeport School District No. 145, 372 Ill. App.3d 562, 865 N.E.2d 361, 310 Ill. Dec. 37 (2nd Dist. 2007)

In re Consolidated Objections to Tax Levies of School District No. 205, 193 Ill. 2d 490, 739 N.E. 2d 508, 250 Ill. Dec. 745 (2000)

23:221 May a school district pay the portion of administrative salaries and expenses attributable to loss prevention from the tort fund?

Before 1999, some school districts were paying a portion of their administrative costs and other expenses from the tort fund. These payments were justified as "risk management" or "loss prevention." In 1999 the General Assembly amended the statute that allegedly justified the practice as follows:

"...the purpose of this Section is to provide an extraordinary tax for funding expenses relating to tort liability, insurance, and risk management programs. Thus, the tax has been excluded from various limitations otherwise applicable to tax levies. Notwithstanding the extraordinary nature of the tax authorized by this Section, however, it has become apparent that some units of local government are using the tax revenue to fund expenses more properly paid from general operating funds. These uses of the revenue are inconsistent with the limited purpose of the tax authorization. Therefore, the General Assembly declares, as a matter of policy, that (i) the use of the tax revenue authorized by this Section for purposes not expressly authorized under this Act is improper and (ii) the provisions of this Section shall be strictly construed consistent with this declaration and the Act's express purposes."

The practice has continued, largely because the tort levy can be increased without referendum and the risk of challenge had been low. There have been several recent challenges to this practice, however, and boards have not fared well in court. The Second District Appellate Court has held that "risk management directly attributable to loss prevention and loss reduction means more than deliberate actions intended to reduce risk or the performance of duties with care."

The court adopted a four-part test for the propriety of a risk management program:

1) The prior identification and analysis of loss exposures;

2) The selection of techniques to be used to handle each exposure;

3) The implementation of the chosen techniques; and

4) The periodic monitoring of the implementation techniques, including the making of adjustments as appropriate.

To be safe, a school board that contemplates using the tort fund to pay portions of salaries attributable to risk management should be certain that it has adopted an appropriate policy or job description defining the risk management duties and that it pays only such portions of salaries from tort as are attributable to risk management as defined by the four-part test.

Expenditures from the tort immunity fund must be separately identified in the annual report or audit.

745 ILCS 10/9-107

In re Objections to Tax Levies of Freeport School District No. 145, 372 Ill. App. 3d 562, 865 N.E. 2d 361, 310 Ill. Dec. 37 (2nd Dist. 2007)

In re Consolidated Objections to Tax Levies of School District No. 205, 193 Ill. 2d 490, 739 N. E. 2d 508, 250 Ill. Dec. 745 (2000)

23:222 May a school board transfer surplus funds from the tort immunity fund to other school district funds?

No.

105 ILCS 5/10-22.33

REFERENDUM TO INCREASE TAX RATES

23:230 May a school board levy taxes at rates exceeding the maximums authorized by statute?

A school board may levy taxes at rates exceeding statutory maximums only where (a) the statute permits increases by referendum, and (b) voters approve such an increase at a referendum. Statutes permit school boards to seek voter approval to increase maximum tax rates in the education fund, operations and maintenance fund, and transportation fund.

In addition, unit districts may, by school board resolution, raise their authorized rates in the operations and maintenance fund, subject to back door referendum.

A district subject to the Property Tax Extension Limitation Law (PTELL) may use only the referendum options in PTELL to raise more taxes than the cap allows. A PTELL district may not use Sections 18-120 or 18-125 of the Property Tax Code to raise taxes.

A PTELL district may increase the extension limitation as provided in Section 18-205, increase the limiting rate or levy for a new tax rate, both as provided in Section 18-190, or increase the debt service extension as provided in section 18-212.

35 ILCS 200/18-120
35 ILCS 200/18-125
35 ILCS 200/18-190
35 ILCS 200/18-205
35 ILCS 200/18-212
105 ILCS 5/17-3 et seq.
105 ILCS 5/17-4
105 ILCS 5/17-5 et seq.

23:232 May a proposition be put to the voters authorizing, if passed, a temporary tax increase in the education fund?

A referendum to increase the tax rate in the education fund may provide for a permanent tax increase or a tax increase for a limited period of not less than three, nor more than 10 years. Districts subject to the Property Tax Limitation Law (PTELL) may ask voters to increase the limiting rate for one to no more than four levy years. Beginning in 2017, notwithstanding the provisions, requirements, or limitations in any law, any tax levied for educational purposes by a school district subject to the PTELL for the 2016 levy year or after may be extended at a rate exceeding the rate established for educational purposes by referendum or the School Code, provided that the rate does not cause the school district to exceed the limiting rate applicable to the school district under the PTELL for that levy rate established for educational purposes by referendum or the School Code, provided that the rate does not cause the school district to exceed the limiting rate applicable to the school district under the PTELL that levy year.

105 ILCS 5/17-3
105 ILCS 5/17-6

23:235 May property tax limitations be raised by referendum?

Yes. In a school district subject to the Property Tax Extension Limitation Law, a voter-approved tax rate increase raises the aggregate extension base on which the district's property tax limitation is calculated.

Also, voters may approve a cap on property tax extensions that is higher than the cap specified by law — 105 percent of the prior year's extension or the percentage increase in the Consumer Price Index, whichever is less.

35 ILCS 200/18-205 et seq.

Board of Education of Auburn Community Unit School District No. 10 v. Illinois Department of Revenue, et al., 398 Ill. App. 3d 629, 941 N.E. 888, 347 Ill. Dec. 19 (4th Dist. 2010)

Board of Education of Batavia v. Cunningham, 346 Ill. App. 3d 1027, 806 N.E. 2d 1219, 282 Ill. Dec. 631 (2nd Dist. 2004)

23:240 What is a back door referendum?

A back door referendum is the submission of a public question to the voters of a political subdivision, initiated by a petition of voters or residents of the political subdivision, to determine whether an action by the governing body of the subdivision should be adopted or rejected.

10 ILCS 5/28-2
105 ILCS 5/17-2
105 ILCS 5/17-2.2
105 ILCS 5/20-7

23:250 Which school district tax levies are subject to back door referendum?

School district tax levies that are subject to back door referendums under certain circumstances specified in the applicable statutes are the educational fund; operations and maintenance fund; transportation under narrow circumstances in certain elementary districts; funding bonds to pay orders for teachers' wages or other claims; non-high school tuition; and working cash fund bonds.

105 ILCS 5/12-13
105 ILCS 5/17-2
105 ILCS 5/17-2.2
105 ILCS 5/17-5
105 ILCS 5/19-9

TAX ABATEMENTS AND EXEMPTIONS

23:270 May a school district participate in a tax abatement program?

Yes. School districts are among the local governments authorized by law to abate property taxes to help spur commercial or industrial growth. A school board may agree to forgive all or a portion of the taxes on the assessed valuation of new or expanded commercial/industrial property for up to 10 years.

35 ILCS 200/18-45

23:280 Is land owned by a school district subject to the property tax?

All real property is subject to taxation unless a specific statute provides an exemption. Land owned by a school district is generally exempt unless the land "is used with a view to a profit." Property used by the state is not tax-exempt, only property owned by the state. A school's use of lease revenues for school expenses does not make the leased property tax exempt even if the property is owned by the school district if the lease revenues constitute "use with view to a profit."

Land owned by a school district for future expansion is exempt unless the school district leases the land for use for other than public purposes.

35 ILCS 200/15-35(e)
35 ILCS 200/15-60
35 ILCS 200/15-135

Springfield School District No. 186 v. Department of Revenue of the State of Illinois, 384 Ill. App. 2d 715, 893 N.E. 2d 1042, 323 Ill. Dec. 568 (4th Dist. 2008)

Northern Illinois University Foundation v. Sweet, 237 Ill. App. 3d 28, 603 N.E. 2d 84, 177 Ill. Dec. 303 (2nd Dist. 1992)

24: STATE AID AND OTHER SCHOOL INCOME

SOURCES OF INCOME

24:10 In addition to property taxes, what other sources of income are used to support public schools in Illinois?

An Illinois school district derives income from any or all of the following: state aid, both general and special-purpose categorical aid; grants of various types; corporate personal property replacement tax; in some school districts from the county school occupation tax; federal aid in various forms; investment income; fees and charges; insurance proceeds; and gifts. Beginning in 2018, school districts will receive funding based on the evidence-based funding formula.

Other than real estate taxes, state aid represents the most significant source of revenue for Illinois schools, providing a statewide average of more than 30 percent of school district income.

24:20 Where lies the primary responsibility for financing Illinois public schools?

The state constitution imposes upon the state the primary responsibility for financing the public schools. To carry out this responsibility, the state provides various forms of direct financial support and authorizes school boards to levy taxes on property, borrow money, invest idle funds, accept gifts, charge certain fees, and purchase insurance to protect school district assets. The constitutional mandate does not mean that more than 50 percent of the funds needed to finance public education must be derived from state aid.

State law also imposes upon school boards the duty "to provide for the revenue necessary to maintain schools in their districts."

Ill. Const. art. X, sec. 1
105 ILCS 5/10-20.3

24:30 What determines school district income?

A school district's income is affected by each of the following factors:

1) Property values. The total property value in a school district determines how much revenue the district is capable of raising from property taxes. Property values are set by the marketplace and the assessor.

2) Tax rates. Tax rates reflect the dollars levied per $100 of equalized assessed valuation of real property. The rate at which a community taxes itself also reflects its level of effort to support its schools. State law establishes maximum tax rates that may be levied by various types of school districts. Some rates may be raised with voter approval at a referendum. The aggregate tax rate of a school district may be limited if the district is located in a county that is governed by the Property Tax Extension Limitation Law (PTELL).

3) State guarantees. Each year, the state establishes a per-pupil revenue guarantee called the "foundation level." State aid makes up the difference between the foundation level and a school district's "available local resources."

4) Pupil enrollment. School district revenue from state aid increases and decreases in response to changes in student enrollment, as reflected in average daily attendance, because state aid is based in part on the number of students served.

35 ILCS 200/1-1 et seq.
105 ILCS 5/18-9
105 ILCS 5/18-10

STATE MANDATES

24:40 What is a state mandate?

A state mandate is any state-initiated statutory or executive action that requires a local government to establish, expand, or modify its activities in such a way so as to necessitate additional expenditures from local revenues. As a result of the Mandates Act, the state is required to fully or partially fund certain program requirements that are statutorily imposed on units of local government.

30 ILCS 805/1 et seq.

24:50 Are there funding exemptions to the State Mandates Act?

The state is not obligated to pay for a mandate if it

1) Is imposed to accommodate a request from local government;

2) Imposes additional duties of a nature that can be carried out by existing staff and procedures at no appreciable net cost increase;

3) Creates additional costs but also provides offsetting savings resulting in no aggregate increase in net costs;

4) Imposes a cost that is wholly or largely recovered from federal, state, or other external financial aid;

5) Imposes additional annual net costs of less than $1,000 for each of the several local governments affected or less than $50,000 in the aggregate for all local governments affected;

6) Results from legislation enacted by the General Assembly to comply with a federal mandate; or

7) Is specifically exempted from compliance with the Mandates Act by reason of the express terms of the legislation.

Failure on the part of the General Assembly to make necessary appropriations relieves the local government of the obligation to implement a mandate unless an exemption is explicitly stated in the act establishing the mandate.

30 ILCS 805/1 et seq.

30 ILCS 805/8

Board of Education of Maine Township High School District No. 207 v. State Board of Education, 139 Ill. App. 3d 460, 487 N.E. 2d 1053, 94 Ill. Dec. 176 (1st Dist. 1985)

24:55 Is there a process by which a school district can avoid implementation of an unfunded mandate?

No public school district or private school is obligated to comply with the following types of mandates unless a separate appropriation has been enacted into law, providing full funding for the mandate for the school year during which the mandate is required:

1) Any mandate in the School Code enacted after August 20, 2010.

2) Any regulatory mandate promulgated by the State Board of Education and adopted by rule after August 20, 2010 other than those promulgated with respect to section 22-60 of the School Code or statutes already enacted on or before August 20, 2010.

If the amount appropriated to fund a mandate does not fully fund the mandated activity, then the school district or private school may choose to discontinue or modify the mandated activity to ensure that the costs of compliance do not exceed the funding received.

Before discontinuing or modifying the mandate, the school district must petition its regional superintendent of schools on or before February 15 of each year to request to be exempt from implementing the mandate in a school or schools in the next school year. The petition must include all legitimate costs associated with implementing and operating the mandate, the estimated reimbursement from state and federal sources, and any unique circumstances the school district can verify that exist that would cause the implementation and operation of such a mandate to be cost prohibitive.

The regional superintendent of schools must review the petition and must convene a public hearing to hear testimony from the school district and interested community members. The regional superintendent must, on or before March 15 of each year, inform the school district in writing of his or her decision, along with the reasons why the exemption was granted or denied. The regional superintendent must also send notification to the State Board of Education detailing which school districts requested an exemption and the results.

If the regional superintendent grants an exemption to the school district, then the school district is relieved from the requirement to establish and implement the mandate in the school or schools granted an exemption for the next school year. If the regional superintendent of schools does not grant an exemption, then the school district must implement the mandate in accordance with the applicable law or rule by the first student attendance day of the next school year.

The school district or a resident of the school district may on or before April 15 appeal the decision of the regional superintendent to the State Superintendent of Education. The State Superintendent shall hear appeals on the decisions of regional superintendents of schools no later than May 15 of each year. The State Superintendent shall make a final decision at the conclusion of the hearing on the school district's request for an exemption from the mandate. If the State Superintendent grants an exemption, then the school district is relieved from the requirement to implement a mandate in the school or schools granted an exemption for the next school year. If the State Superintendent does not grant an exemption, then the school district shall implement the mandate in accordance with the applicable law or rule by the first student attendance day of the next school year.

If a school district or private school discontinues or modifies a mandated activity due to lack of full funding from the state, then the school district or private school shall annually maintain and update a list of discontinued or modified mandated activities. The list shall be provided to the State Board of Education upon request.

The mandate exemption does not apply to any new statutory or regulatory mandates related to revised learning standards developed through the Common Core State Standards Initiative and assessments developed to align with those standards or actions specified in the state's Phase Two Race to the Top Grant application if the application is approved by the U.S. Department of Education, or new statutory or regulatory mandates from the Race to the Top Grant through the federal American Recovery and Reinvestment Act of 2009 imposed on school districts designated as being in the lowest performing five percent of schools within the Race to the Top Grant applications.

In any instances in which the mandates exemption provision conflicts with the State Mandates Act, the State Mandates Act prevails.

105 ILCS 5/22-60

24:60 Is the state obligated to pay a percentage of school operating costs?

While the Illinois Constitution provides that "The State has the primary responsibility for financing the system of public education," the General Assembly is not obligated to fund the schools at any particular level.

Ill. Const. Art. X, Sec. 1

Carr v. Koch, 2012 IL 113414, 981 N.E. 2d 326, 367 Ill. Dec. 1

Committee for Educational Rights, et al. v. Edgar, 174 Ill. 2d 1, 672 N.E. 2d 1178, 220 Ill. Dec. 166 (1996)

San Antonio Independent School District v. Rodriguez, 93 S. Ct. 1278, 411 U.S. 1, 36 L. Ed. 2d 16, reh. den. 93 S. Ct. 1919, 411 U.S. 959, 36 L. Ed. 2d 418 (1973)

Blase v. Illinois, 55 Ill. 2d 94, 302 N.E. 2d 46 (1973)

McInnis v. Shapiro, 293 F. Supp. 327 (N.D. Ill. 1968), aff'd. *McInnis v. Ogilvie*, 89 S. Ct. 1197, 394 U.S. 322, 22 L. Ed. 2d 308 (1969)

24:62 Is education a fundamental right for purposes of equal protection analysis?

Disparities in educational funding between school districts based on relative property wealth does not offend the efficiency requirement of the education provision of the Illinois Constitution, and the mere mention of educational equality by the framers of the Constitution does not give rise to a constitutional guarantee of fairness and parity in educational funding. The state constitutional right to education is not a fundamental right for purposes of equal protection analysis.

Committee for Educational Rights, et al. v. Edgar, 174 Ill. 2d 1, 672 N.E. 2d 1178, 220 Ill. Dec. 166 (1996)

San Antonio Independent School District v. Rodriguez, 93 S. Ct. 1278, 411 U.S. 1, 36 L. Ed. 2d 16, reh. den. 93 S. Ct. 1919, 411 U.S. 959, 36 L. Ed. 2d 418 (1973)

STATE AID

24:70 What is state aid?

State aid is money provided by the General Assembly to assist in supporting public education. State aid may be categorical or general. Also, some supplemental aid is appropriated to protect school districts against loss of revenue (hold harmless) and, beginning July 1, 1998, to assist districts with high concentrations of poverty-level students. (In prior years, poverty assistance was built into the general state aid formula.). Beginning in 2018, state aid is calculated using the evidence-based funding formula.

105 ILCS 5/18-1 et seq.

24:80 What are the differences between general state aid and categorical state aid?

Categorical state aid is earmarked for a particular purpose and may be used for that purpose only. Categorical and special program grants support special education, transportation, vocational education, school lunches and breakfasts, adult education, textbooks, and programs for students needing remedial help, as well as various school improvement programs for at-risk students.

General state aid, which combines with "available local resources" to provide a minimum foundation level of income per pupil, may be used at the discretion of the school district for any legal school purpose. The computation bases for aid distribution differ for categorical and general state aid.

105 ILCS 5/10-22.20

105 ILCS 5/14B-8;

105 ILCS 5/14C-12

105 ILCS 5/18-1 et seq.

105 ILCS 405/3-1

24:90 What is the source of state aid funds?

General state aid and some categorical aids come from the Common School Fund. This fund consists of moneys appropriated by the General Assembly for the support of common schools. It includes moneys set aside for education from the Retailers' Occupation and Use Tax (sales tax), the Illinois State Lottery, and other sources.

School districts also receive moneys from such sources as the Education Assistance Fund, the General Revenue Fund, and the Driver Education Fund.

20 ILCS 1605/2

35 ILCS 120/1 et seq.

STATE AID COMPUTATIONS

24:100 How is a school district's general state aid computed?

Prior to evidence-based funding and beginning with the fiscal year that started July 1, 1998, general state aid was computed by multiplying equalized assessed valuation by a calculation tax rate (3 percent for unit districts, 2.3 percent for elementary districts, and 1.05 percent for high school districts). The product was added to revenue from the Corporate Personal Property Replacement Tax and the total divided by the best three months average daily pupil attendance to produce "available local resources per pupil." General state aid made up the difference for each pupil between available local resources and the foundation level — $6,119 per pupil in FY 2009-2010 and each year thereafter.

The formula made up the entire difference for any district with available local resources of less than 93 percent of the foundation level. Where local resources represented 93 to 175 percent of the foundation amount, state aid was reduced on a sliding scale. A district with local resources representing 175 percent or more of the foundation level received a flat $218 per pupil.

Prior to legislation enacted in 1997, general state aid computations also included grade-level weightings (i.e., 1.25 for high school students and 1.05 for 7th and 8th graders), as well as a different formula for calculating the local share of the foundation level.

Other factors important in determining a school district's state aid included:

1) Any applicable reductions in a district's equalized assessed valuation (i.e., resulting from the Farmland Assessment Act);

2) The number of special needs students in a district;

3) Whether or not the district participates in a tax abatement or tax increment allocation program under the Real Property Tax Increment Allocation Redevelopment Act;

4) The amount of money a district receives as a replacement for taxes previously received from the corporate personal property tax;

5) The number of days the schools of the district are operating with students in attendance;

6) Whether or not kindergarten students attend school for full-day or half-day sessions; and

7) Whether the schools in the district are recognized by the State Board of Education as meeting state-required standards for recognition.

Illinois school districts have discovered in recent years that the state aid they receive is significantly affected by the amount of money appropriated each year for that purpose by the state. When the annual appropriation is inadequate to meet the funding levels specified by statute, a district's state aid may be pro-rated based on the percentage of funds appropriated.

105 ILCS 5/18-8.05
105 ILCS 5/8-8.15A-8
105 ILCS 5/18-9

24:102 What is the "evidence-based funding formula"?

In 2017, the General Assembly passed a new evidence-based funding formula which is commonly called "Senate Bill 1." At the time this edition of the *Survey* was being updated, in December 2017 and early January 2018, there were no rules to implement the statute and no distributions using evidence-based funding had yet been remitted to school districts. The new legislation will, in 2018, supplant the existing school funding system which is found at 105 ILCS 5/18-8.05 and which will sunset shortly after this edition of the *Survey* is published. References to 18-8.05 remain in this edition because they will be relevant for a short time after its publication.

The evidence-based funding formula is found at 105 ILCS 5/18-8.15. It calculates an adequacy target for each "organizational unit" in the state that considers the costs to implement research-based activities, the unit's student demographics, and regional wage difference. The model calculates each unit's local capacity, or the amount each unit is assumed to contribute towards its adequacy target from local resources. The model calculates how much funding the state currently contributes to the unit, and adds that to the unit's local capacity to determine the unit's overall current adequacy of funding. The model's distribution method allocates new state funding to those units that are least well-funded, considering both local capacity and state funding, in relation to their adequacy targets.

A unit receiving any evidence-based funding may apply those funds to any fund for which that unit is authorized to make expenditures by law.

105 ILCS 5/18-8.05
105 ILCS 5/18-8.15

24:105 May a school district's state aid claim be re-computed after it has been paid?

The State Board of Education has authority to re-compute within three years from the final date for filing of a claim any claim for reimbursement of state aid or one year from the final date for filing of any claim based on evidence-based funding to any school district if the claim has been found to be incorrect. The State Board may adjust subsequent claims accordingly and may re-compute and adjust any such claims within six years from the final date for filing when there has been an adverse court or administrative agency decision on the merits affecting the tax revenues of the school district. No adjustment is made regarding equalized assessed valuation (EAV) unless the district's EAV is changed by the greater of $250,000 or 2 percent.

For requests for re-computation of general state aid claims received after June 30, 2003, that were originally calculated using an extension limitation equalized assessed valuation, a qualifying reduction in EAV is deducted from the extension limitation EAV that was used in calculating the original claim.

Under certain circumstances specified in the statute, re-computation claim adjustments are prorated among districts for a particular fiscal year. If a claim (or a portion of a claim) is approved but not paid in a fiscal year, the unpaid amount may be resubmitted as a valid claim in the following fiscal year.

105 ILCS 5/2-3.33
105 ILCS 5/2-3.33a

24:110 What is the state aid grade level weighting formula?

Prior to fiscal year 1999, pupils in grades pre-K-6 were weighted 1.00; pupils in grades 7 and 8 were weighted 1.05; and pupils in grades 9-12 were weighted 1.25. A school district's pupil count also included weightings for federally defined low-income pupils. All pupil weightings were abolished for FY 1999 and after.

STATE AID PENALTIES

24:140 What is the penalty for failure to have school the minimum number of pupil attendance days?

If any school district fails to provide the minimum number of pupil attendance days, the school district's state aid is reduced by 1/176 or .56818 percent for each day less than the minimum number required by law. The school district may also suffer recognition penalties.

105 ILCS 5/18-12

Cronin v. Lindberg, 66 Ill. 2d 47, 360 N.E. 2d 360, 4 Ill. Dec. 424 (1976)

24:150 What is an "act of God" day?

Under certain circumstances, a school district may receive full state aid even though it has not provided the minimum school term. The State Superintendent of Education may determine that a failure to provide the minimum school term was occasioned by an act of God — or by conditions beyond the control of the school district — which posed a hazardous threat to the health and safety of pupils.

The relevant statute provides that if a school district is precluded from providing the minimum hours of instruction required for a full day of attendance due to an adverse weather condition or a condition beyond the control of the school district that poses a hazardous threat to the health and safety of students, then the partial day of attendance may be counted if the school district has provided at least one hour of instruction prior to the closure of the school district, a school building has provided at least one hour of instruction prior to the closure of the school building, or the normal start time of the school district is delayed.

If, prior to providing any instruction, a school district must close one or more but not all school buildings after consultation with a local emergency response agency or due to a condition beyond the control of the school district, then the school district may claim attendance for up to two school days based on the average attendance of the three school days immediately preceding the closure of the affected school building. The partial or no day of attendance described in this section and the reasons therefore shall be certified within a month of the closing or delayed start by the school district superintendent to the regional superintendent of schools for forwarding to the State Superintendent of Education for approval.

No exception to the requirement of providing a minimum school term may be approved by the State Superintendent unless a school district has first used all emergency days provided for in its regular calendar.

105 ILCS 5/18-12

24:155 May a school district claim state aid if a school building is closed during a public health emergency?

After consultation with a local health department, if a school district closes one or more recognized school buildings, but not all buildings in accordance with Section 18-12 of the School Code, during a public health emergency, as determined by the State Board of Education (ISBE) in consultation with the Illinois Department of Public Health, the district may claim a full day of attendance for those days based on the average of the three school days of attendance immediately preceding the closure of the school building.

Attendance for those days may be claimed only if the school building was scheduled to be in operation on those days. The partial or no day of attendance and the reasons must be certified, as prescribed by ISBE, by the school district superintendent to the regional superintendent of schools within a month after the closing for forwarding to the State Superintendent of Education for approval.

105 ILCS 5/18-12.5

STATE AID DISTRIBUTION SYSTEM

24:160 How are funds from the Common School Fund delivered to school districts?

Funds due local school districts are dispersed by electronic transfer from the state school fund. Beginning July 1, 2002, all payments for school districts, regional offices of education, and other providers entitled to payment under programs administered by the State Board of Education must be dispersed through electronic transfer except as the State Board of Education otherwise directs.

105 ILCS 5/2-3.2a

105 ILCS 5/2-3.116

105 ILCS 5/3-9

24:170 How is state aid distributed when funds appropriated by the General Assembly are not adequate to cover all school district entitlements?

The legislature each year appropriates a specific sum of money to each of numerous programs. If the money appropriated for a particular program — such as pupil transportation or special education — is less than the money required to fully fund the entitlements of all the school districts in the state, the amount of money available is apportioned so that each school district has its aid for that program proportionately reduced.

Historically, the prorating of claims has not been generally applicable to general state aid, because school district entitlements have been based on the amount appropriated.

105 ILCS 5/18-8.05

People ex rel. Carruthers v. Cooper, 404 Ill. 395, 89 N.E. 2d 40 (1950)

24:175 What is a "delayed state aid payment"?

The term describes legislation enacted in 1991 to shift a general state aid payment from the last month of one fiscal year (June) to the first month of the following fiscal year (July). Although action by the Governor has advanced a state aid payment from time to time since then, the 1991 legislation has never been reversed to put payments back on the pre-1991 schedule. The delayed payment amounted to a reduction in general state aid for the 1991-1992 fiscal year.

Beginning with fiscal year 2009, the payment schedule was amended so that payments which had been 1/24 of the total and paid in every month are now 1/22 of the total and paid August through June.

105 ILCS 5/18-11

INVESTMENT INCOME

24:180 How is a depositary for school funds selected?

Trustees of schools in Class II county (Cook) school units, school boards in Class I county (all other counties) school units, and school boards in those Class II county school units that have elected or appointed their own school treasurer shall designate one or more banks or savings and loan associations, situated in the state of Illinois, in which school funds and moneys in the custody of the township treasurer or school treasurer shall be kept.

105 ILCS 5/8-7

24:182 Is a school district required to have an investment policy?

By not later than January 1, 2000 school districts were required to have a written investment policy. The policy must address safety of principal, liquidity of funds, and return on investment. The policy must address the following:

1) A listing of authorized investments;

2) A rule such as "the prudent person rule" establishing the standard of care that must be maintained by the persons investing the public funds;

3) Investment guidelines that are appropriate to the nature of the funds, the purpose for the funds, and the amount of the public funds within the investment portfolio;

4) The policy regarding diversification of the investment portfolio that is appropriate to the nature of the funds, purpose of the funds, and the amount of the public funds within the investment portfolio;

5) Guidelines regarding collateral requirements if any, for the deposit of public funds in a financial institution made pursuant to the Act, and, if applicable, guidelines for contractual arrangements for the custody and safekeeping of that collateral;

6) A policy regarding the establishment of a system of internal controls and written operational procedures designed to prevent losses of funds that might arise from fraud, employee error, misrepresentation by third parties or imprudent action by school employees;

7) The identification of the chief investment officer who is responsible for establishing the internal controls and written procedures for the operation of the investment program;

8) Performance measures that are appropriate to the nature of the funds, the purpose for the funds, and the amount of the public funds within the investment portfolio;

9) A policy regarding appropriate periodic review of the investment portfolio, its effectiveness in meeting the school district's need for safety, liquidity, rate of return, and diversification, and its general performance;

10) A policy establishing at least quarterly written reports of investment activities by the school district's chief financial officer for submission to the school board and superintendent. The report must include information regarding securities in the portfolio by class or type, book value, income earned, and market value as of the report date;

11) A policy regarding the selection of investment advisors, money managers, and financial institutions; and

12) A policy regarding ethics and conflicts of interest.

30 ILCS 235/2.5

24:184 What kinds of investments are lawful for school moneys?

The investment of all public funds is regulated by law. Financial institutions must meet specified standards and obligations. Certificates of deposit, government securities, the commercial paper of private corporations, and interest-bearing bank deposits are among the investment vehicles that are permissible for school funds if they meet specified standards.

In addition, school districts may combine their funds for investment purposes. Township and school treasurers are authorized to enter into agreements of any defined or undefined term regarding the deposit, investment, reinvestment, or withdrawal of school funds, including, without limitation, agreements with other township and school treasurers, agreements with community college districts authorized by the Community College Act, and agreements with educational service regions.

30 ILCS 235/2 et seq.
105 ILCS 5/3-9.1
105 ILCS 5/8-7

24:186 How may earnings from invested school funds be used?

Although moneys from various fund accounts may be combined for investment purposes, the amount of money belonging to each account must be reflected in the records of the treasurer. Interest earned on invested school funds must be credited to the same fund account as the principal that produced the earnings. The resulting interest income may be used for any lawful purpose for which the principal may be used.

105 ILCS 5/8-7
105 ILCS 5/10-22.44

24:188 May school boards invest borrowed funds, such as the proceeds of a bond issue or sale of tax anticipation warrants?

Yes. However, such investments are subject to federal restrictions on arbitrage. The interest earned by an investor on school district debt instruments is treated as tax exempt under federal and state tax codes, which often enables school districts to borrow at lower rates of interest than the rates they earn when they reinvest those funds. In order to retain tax-exempt status, the proceeds of district borrowing must meet certain requirements of the Internal Revenue Code that limit investment earnings for the district.

26 U.S.C. 1233

GIFTS

24:190 May a school district accept a gift, grant, or bequest?

A school district or attendance center may accept a gift, grant, or bequest. If the donor expresses an intention that the property be used for a particular purpose, the school board must effectuate the donor's intention until the school board in its discretion determines it is no longer practical to do so.

105 ILCS 5/16-1

Wauconda Community Unit School District No. 118, Lake County v. LaSalle National Bank, 143 Ill. App. 3d 52, 492 N.E. 2d 995, 97 Ill. Dec. 336 (2nd Dist 1986)

Community Unit School District No. 4 v. Booth, 1 Ill. 2d 545, 116 N.E. 2d 161 (1954)

24:195 May a booster group raise funds for school district programs?

Athletic and band booster groups organized by the parents of participating students exist in many school districts. Such groups may raise and handle large sums of money and may engage in fundraising activities that benefit school programs. There is no statutory authority for the existence of such groups, nor is there any statutory prohibition of them.

But school officials should be wary. Often such groups are loosely organized, lack insurance, lack a corporate structure (more is required than just loosely adopted rules of order), and intentionally or unintentionally hold themselves out to be school organizations.

Contributors may believe school officials have oversight of the group and the school district may encounter public relations problems if contributed money is not appropriately managed. Moreover, such groups may incur liability (for torts, civil rights violations, or for mismanagement) for the school district if school officials do not take care that the group is properly organized and completely separate from the school or, in the alternative, incorporated into the school chain of command and subject to audit and oversight by school officials.

If a booster group is responsible for paying the salary of a person employed to perform extra duties, school officials may lose authority to supervise or discipline the person so employed.

School officials should also be wary that a booster group can be a powerful political force and may have a powerful membership. Any attempt to regulate such a group should consider the politics of the matter.

24:200 May a tax exempt foundation be created to help raise funds for school purposes?

Yes. Although a school district is an eligible recipient of tax deductible charitable gifts, school officials and/or interested citizens also may make a school or school district the beneficiary of support from a tax exempt foundation qualified to accept gifts, donations, bequests, and other contributions.

26 U.S.C. 501 (c)(3)

24:205 May a school group sponsor a raffle or other game of chance in order to raise funds?

The conduct of a raffle is prohibited by gaming laws and is legal only under certain narrow circumstances. A license obtained from a county or municipality is required. Only bona fide religious, charitable, labor, business, fraternal, educational, or veteran's organizations that operate without profit to their members and that have been in existence continuously for a period of five years immediately before the application is made may obtain a license. The Raffles Act contains numerous other restrictions, including limitations on the circumstances under which a minor may participate.

A tax-exempt educational foundation could most likely qualify for a raffle license. However, most booster groups do not qualify for licensure because they lack an appropriate organizational structure.

230 ILCS 15/1 et seq.

24:210 What laws govern the creation and operation of a tax-exempt educational foundation?

In order to acquire tax-exempt status eligible to accept tax-deductible contributions, an educational foundation must be organized as a not-for-profit corporation or as a charitable trust and make application to the federal Internal Revenue Service. In addition, any charitable corporation that solicits contributions in Illinois must register with the Attorney General and file informational returns with the Internal Revenue Service and the Attorney General. A foundation organized as a not-for-profit corporation also must file an annual report with the Illinois Secretary of State.

26 U.S.C. 501(c)3

760 ILCS 55/7

805 ILCS 105/101.01 et seq.

OTHER SOURCES OF INCOME

24:300 How may a school board dispose of school equipment that is no longer needed?

A school board is authorized to sell at public or private sale any personal property either no longer needed by the school district or available through an arrangement under which the personal property may be leased by the district from the purchaser. The school board may adopt a resolution declaring the property surplus and no longer needed for school purposes and may direct the superintendent to sell it. The board may establish a minimum selling price and may specify a public or private sale.

105 ILCS 5/10-22.8

24:310 What is the county school facility occupation tax?

The school facility occupation tax is a sales tax that may be imposed countywide to support school facilities.

A 2007 statute allows a county board to impose a tax on all persons engaged in the business of selling tangible personal property (other than personal property titled or registered with an agency of this state's government) at retail in the county on the gross receipts from sales made in the course of business. The tax proceeds provide revenue to be used exclusively for school facility purposes. The tax may be imposed only in .25 percent increments and may not exceed 1 percent. The tax is not imposed on the sale of food for human consumption that is to be consumed off the premises where it is sold (other than alcoholic beverages, soft drinks, and food that has been prepared for immediate consumption) and prescription and nonprescription medicines, drugs, medical appliances and insulin, urine testing materials, syringes, and needles used by diabetics.

The tax may not be imposed until, by ordinance or resolution of the county board, the question of imposing the tax has been submitted to the voters in the county at a regular election and approved by a majority of the voters voting on the question. Upon a resolution by the county board or a resolution by school district boards that represent at least 51 percent of the student enrollment within the county, the county board must certify the question to the proper election authority in accordance with the Election Code.

A 2011 amendment to the relevant statute removes any authority the county board might have had to withhold a properly certified question from the ballot and requires the imposition of the tax if the voters approve the question.

55 ILCS 5/5-1006.7

105 ILCS 5/3-14.31

P&S Grain v. The County of Williamson, et al., 399 Ill. App. 3d 836, 926 N.E.2d 466, 339 Ill. Dec. 234 (5th Dist. 2010)

25: BUDGETING AND MANAGING SCHOOL FUNDS

THE BUDGET

25:10 What is a school district budget?

Each school board must budget its income and expenses each year and make the budget available for public inspection. A public hearing must be held prior to the adoption of the budget. The budget is the school district's plan for receipt and expenditure of moneys. It is the basis for a school district's tax levy.

The relevant statute requires the budget be balanced, but establishes no penalty for the failure to do so except a requirement that if the budget is not balanced the school district must adopt and file with the State Board of Education a deficit reduction plan to balance the budget within three years.

The board must file with the county clerk within 30 days of their adoption a certified copy of its appropriation and budget resolutions, as well as an estimate, certified by its chief fiscal officer, of revenues, by source, anticipated to be received by the school district in the following fiscal year. Failure to file the required documents (after timely notice) authorizes the county clerk to refuse to extend the tax levy imposed by the governing authority until the documents are filed.

If a school district has a website, it must post its current annual budget itemized by receipts and expenditures on the site and must notify parents and guardians that the budget has been posted and the address of the website.

Beginning in 2005, school districts must submit to the State Board of Education the "annual budget, deficit reduction plans, and other financial information, including revenue and expenditure reports and borrowing and interfund transfer plans, in such form and within the timelines designated by the State Board of Education." The budget must conform to requirements set by the State Board of Education and found at 105 ILCS 5/2-3.28.

35 ILCS 200/18-50

105 ILCS 5/2-3.27 et seq.

105 ILCS 5/17-1

105 ILCS 5/17-1.2

People ex rel. Stanfield v. Pennsylvania Railroad, 3 Ill. 2d 524, 121 N.E. 2d 748 (1954)

People ex rel. Schlaeger v. Belmont Radio Corporation, 388 Ill. 11, 57 N.E. 2d 479 (1944)

People ex rel. Toman v. Siebel, 388 Ill. 98, 57 N.E. 2d 378 (1944)

25:20 What must be included in a budget?

Within or before the first quarter of each fiscal year, a school board must adopt an annual budget that it deems necessary to defray all necessary expenses and liabilities of the district, and which must specify the objects and purposes of each item and amount needed for each object or purpose. The budget is entered on a form provided by the State Board of Education and contains a statement of the cash on hand at the beginning of the fiscal year, an estimate of the cash expected to be received during such fiscal year from all sources, an estimate of the expenditures contemplated for the year, and a statement of the estimated cash expected to be on hand at the end of the year.

The estimate of taxes to be received may be based upon the amount of actual cash receipts that may reasonably be expected by the district during the fiscal year, estimated from the experience of the district in prior years, and with due regard for other circumstances that may substantially affect receipts.

105 ILCS 5/17-1

25:22 When must a school district post employee salaries?

A 2011 amendment to the Open Meetings Act requires that within six business days after an employer participating in the Illinois Municipal Retirement Fund (IMRF) approves a budget, that employer must post on its website the total compensation package for each employee having a total compensation package that exceeds $75,000 per year.

If the employer does not maintain a website, the employer must post a physical copy of this information at its principal office. If an employer maintains a website, it may choose to post a physical copy of this information at the principal office of the employer in lieu of posting the information directly on the website; however, the employer must post directions on the website on how to access that information.

At least six days before an employer participating in IMRF approves an employee's total compensation package that is equal to or in excess of $150,000 per year, the employer must post on its website the total compensation package for that employee. If the employer does not maintain a website, the employer must post a physical copy of this information at the principal office of the employer. If an employer maintains a website, it may choose to post a physical copy of this information at the principal office of the employer in lieu of posting the information directly on the website; however, the employer must post directions on the website on how to access that information.

Total compensation package means payment by the employer to the employee for salary, health insurance, a housing allowance, a vehicle allowance, a clothing allowance, bonuses, loans, vacation days granted, and sick days granted.

The relevant statute is titled "Duty to post information pertaining to benefits offered through the Illinois Municipal Retirement Fund," but appears to require the posting of all relevant salaries (for certified employees and non-certified employees alike).

5 ILCS 120/7.3

25:25 Is there a limitation on the growth of administrative expenditures by a school district?

For the 1998-1999 school year and each year thereafter, school districts are required to undertake budgetary and expenditure control actions so that the increase in administrative expenditures for that school year over the prior school year does not exceed 5 percent.

School districts with administrative expenditures per pupil in the 25th percentile and below for all districts of the same type as defined by the State Board of Education may waive the limitation for any year following a public hearing and by a vote of at least 2/3 of the members of the school board. Other districts may request a waiver if the district's failure to stay within the expenditure limit is beyond the control of the district and the district has "exhausted all available and reasonable remedies to comply with the limitation."

105 ILCS 5/17-1.5

25:27 What happens if a school district does not limit the growth of administrative expenditures as required by law?

If the State Superintendent finds that a school district has failed to comply with the administrative expenditure limitation, the district is notified of the violation and directed to take corrective action to bring the district's budget into compliance. The district has 60 days to provide assurance to the state that appropriate corrective actions have been or will be taken. If the district fails to provide adequate assurance or fails to undertake the necessary corrective action, the State Superintendent may impose progressive sanctions against the district that may include withholding all subsequent payments of general state aid or evidence based funding due the district until the assurance is provided or the corrective action is taken.

105 ILCS 5/17-1.5

25:30 May a school board amend its budget?

A school board may from time to time amend its budget by the same procedure utilized to establish the original budget.

105 ILCS 5/17-1

25:35 What happens if a school district fails to timely adopt a budget?

The failure of a school board to adopt a budget or to comply with Section 17-1 of the School Code regarding the adoption of a budget does not affect the validity of any tax levy of the district that is otherwise in compliance with the law. Except as otherwise provided by law, a school board's adoption of an annual budget is not a prerequisite to the adoption of a valid tax levy and is not a limit on the amount of the levy.

105 ILCS 5/17-1

25:40 How does a school board amend its budget after a tax rate increase has been approved at a referendum for the educational fund or operations and maintenance fund?

Whenever the voters of a school district have voted in favor of an increase in the annual tax rate for educational or operations and maintenance purposes or both at an election held after the adoption of the annual school budget for any fiscal year, a school board may adopt or pass during that fiscal year an additional or supplemental budget under the sole authority of Section 17-3.2 of the School Code. The vote requires a majority of the full membership of the board, any other provision of the School Code notwithstanding.

In such additional or supplemental budget the board must appropriate such additional sums of money as it may find necessary to defray expenses and liabilities of the district to be incurred for educational or operations and maintenance purposes or both of the district during that fiscal year, but not in excess of the additional funds estimated to be available by virtue of such voted increase in the annual tax rate for educational or operations and maintenance purposes or both.

105 ILCS 5/17-3.2

In re County Collector of McHenry County, 181 Ill. App. 3d 345, 536 N.E. 2d 1288, 130 Ill. Dec. 77 (2nd Dist. 1989)

ACCOUNTING PROCEDURES

25:50 What accounting system can a school district use?

A school district may use either a cash basis or accrual system of accounting; however, any board electing to use the accrual system may not change to a cash basis without the permission of the State Board of Education.

105 ILCS 5/2-3.27
105 ILCS 5/10-17

25:60 What is a school district fund?

The Illinois State Board of Education amended the rules governing school district funds in 2008 and 2009. The rules require each school board to use an appropriate set of journals and ledgers for the recording, summarization, and control of transactions and require the use of the double-entry bookkeeping method and a fund accounting system.

Each school board must establish and maintain the number and types of funds necessitated by the nature and scope of its operations. In Tables A through F in Chapter 23, Part 100, of the Illinois Administrative Code, the State Board of Education lists and describes the funds that comprise the various charts of accounts. Each chart of accounts must include at least the following:

1) Fund or fund group (Table A);
2) Balance sheet accounts (Table B);
3) Revenue sources (Table C);
4) Expenditure purposes or functions (Table D); and
5) Expenditure objects (Table F).

Each school board must use the account codes assigned by the State Superintendent of Education. However, any number not listed in the tables cited above may be used if the description falls within the relevant classification. Prefixes and suffixes may also be used, provided that the basic code assigned by the State Superintendent remains discernible for purposes of aggregating and reporting information.

23 Ill. Admin. Code 100.30

25:65 Is there a minimum or maximum fund balance specified in the law?

Illinois law does not establish a minimum or maximum fund balance. Excessive fund balances may encourage tax objections. The Illinois Supreme Court has held that a fund balance in excess of two or three times the annual expenditures in the fund is illegal.

Central Illinois Public Service Co. v. Miller, 42 Ill. 2d 542, 248 N.E. 2d 89 (1969)

25:70 May a school board deposit general state aid in any fund it chooses?

A school district may deposit general state aid in any fund except the working cash fund.

105 ILCS 5/18-8.05 A 4
105 ILCS 5/18-18.15

FUND ACCOUNTS

25:80 What is the educational fund?

The educational fund is used for all transactions not designated to another fund. The educational fund must be used to pay the direct costs of instruction, health, attendance, and lunch programs, and all costs of administration. Certain revenues must be credited to this fund, including educational tax levies, textbook rentals, athletics, and lunch programs.

The salaries of janitors and maintenance employees, and the costs of fuel, lights, gas, water, telephone service, and custodial supplies and equipment must be charged to this fund unless a school board, by resolution, determines to pay such costs from the operations and maintenance fund.

105 ILCS 5/17-2
23 Ill. Admin. Code 100.Tab.A

25:90 What is the operations and maintenance fund?

The costs of maintaining, improving, or repairing school building and property, renting buildings and property for school purposes, and the payment of insurance premiums on school buildings are charged to the operations and maintenance fund. Certain costs that otherwise would be charged to the educational fund may be paid out of the operations and maintenance fund if the school board passes a resolution authorizing the charge.

105 ILCS 5/17-2
23 Ill. Admin. Code 100.Tab.A

25:100 What options does a school board have in paying costs out of the district's operations and maintenance fund?

Any sum expended or obligations incurred for the improvement, maintenance, repair, or benefit of school buildings and property, including the cost of interior decorating and the installation, improvement, repair, replacement, and maintenance of building fixtures; for the rental of buildings and property for school purposes; or for the payment of all premiums for insurance upon school buildings and school building fixtures; or for the purchase of equipment to be used in the school lunch program must be paid from the tax levied for operations and maintenance purposes and the purchase of school grounds.

The board may provide by resolution the payment of all salaries of janitors, engineers, or other custodial employees and all costs of fuel, lights, gas, water, telephone service, and custodial supplies and equipment or the cost of a professional survey of the conditions of school buildings, or any one or more of the preceding items shall be paid from the tax levied for operations and maintenance purposes and the purchase of school grounds in which event such salaries or specified costs, or both, must be so paid until the next fiscal year after the repeal of such resolution.

Expenditures for all similar purposes not specified for this fund are made from the educational fund.

105 ILCS 5/17-7

23 Ill. Admin. Code 100.Tab.A

25:110 What is the transportation fund?

Any transportation operating costs incurred for transporting pupils to and from school and school-sponsored activities and the costs of acquiring equipment must be paid from a transportation fund. The transportation fund consists of moneys received from any tax levy for such purpose, state reimbursement for transportation, all funds received from other districts for transporting pupils, and any charges for transportation services rendered to individuals or auxiliary enterprises of the school.

For the purpose of this fund, "transportation operating cost" includes all costs of transportation except interest and rental of building facilities.

105 ILCS 5/17-8

23 Ill. Admin. Code 100.Tab.A

25:120 What is the long-term debt accounts fund?

Moneys deposited in this fund are the proceeds of taxes levied to pay the principal and interest on outstanding bonds and refunding bond proceeds. A school district may deposit corporate personal property replacement taxes and/or general state aid revenue in this fund and abate a like amount of property tax. Before 2008, this fund was called the bond and interest fund.

23 Ill. Admin. Code 100.Tab.A

25:130 What is the municipal retirement/social security fund?

A municipal retirement/social security fund is created when a school district levies taxes to pay social security or retirement contributions for non-certificated employees.

40 ILCS 5/7-171

40 ILCS 5/21-101

40 ILCS 5/22-403

23 Ill. Admin. Code 100.Tab.A

25:135 What is the fire prevention, safety, environmental, and energy fund?

Under certain conditions specified in statute, a school district may levy for fire prevention, safety, the protection of the environment, energy conservation, handicapped accessibility, or for school security purposes.

105 ILCS 5/17-2.11 et seq.

23 Ill. Admin. Code 100.Tab.A

25:140 What is the capital projects fund?

Before 2008, this fund was known as the "site and construction fund."

New buildings and additions are generally constructed after an election authorizing special financing. The proceeds of each bond issue are placed in this fund to separate these moneys from operating moneys. The special moneys may be spent for purposes specified in the bond issue and on the ballot.

Often the cost of furniture and other equipment needed to open a new building is included in the amount of the bond issue. Those assets are recognized in the capital asset accounts fund. Expenditures that would ordinarily be charged to the educational fund, but that may be charged to the capital projects fund (unless paid before the fund is created) include election expenses, fidelity insurance, architect fees, legal fees for title searches, bond legal opinions, and other administrative costs directly related to the construction project.

Expenditures that would ordinarily be charged to the operations and maintenance fund, but that may be charged to this fund (unless paid before the fund is created) include actual construction costs, builder's risk insurance, land purchase and other site costs, landscaping, parking lots, sidewalks, utility connections, and other items directly related to the construction project.

105 ILCS 5/19-2 et seq.

23 Ill. Admin. Code 100.Tab.A

25:160 What is a capital improvements fund?

Before 2008, this fund was known as the capital improvements fund and is still referred to as the capital improvements fund in the School Code. However, it is referred to as the "capital projects fund" in State Board of Education rules.

With voter approval at a referendum, a school board may create a capital improvements fund, levy an annual tax of up to .075 percent, and accumulate moneys in the fund to be spent only in accordance with purposes set forth in the resolution calling for the referendum and on the referendum ballot.

105 ILCS 5/17-2(4)

105 ILCS 5/17-2.3

23 Ill. Admin. Code 100.Tab.A

OTHER FUNDS

25:170 May a school board create revolving funds?

Revolving funds and petty cash funds exist pursuant to Section 10-20.19(2) of the School Code. State Board of Education rules require each school board to establish by resolution the school board's policy as to the amounts and types of payments that are made from the fund, state the amount at which the fund is established, designate a custodian of the fund, and require that the fund be maintained in compliance with Section 10-20.19 of the School Code and all other applicable statutes.

In the case of a petty cash fund:

1) The resolution must also authorize a check in the amount of the fund to be drawn payable to the designated custodian.

2) Each disbursement must be approved by the signature of a person other than the custodian.

3) Each petty cash voucher must be pre-numbered and each shall be accounted for as having been used, voided, or unused. Each petty cash voucher must also provide for the signature of the person to whom cash is paid.

4) The custodian must attach to each petty cash voucher the receipt for the disbursement made and must note the proper expenditure account code or provide sufficient descriptive information to allow assignment of the correct code.

5) When the larger part of the cash on hand has been disbursed, the custodian must take the paid petty cash vouchers to the person authorized to prepare and issue checks so that the fund can be replenished.

In the case of any revolving fund other than a petty cash fund:

1) The resolution must also provide that the fund be maintained in a bank.

2) The total of all checks written since the last reimbursement plus the bank balance for the checking account must equal the amount set aside for the revolving fund.

3) No check may be issued without presentation of pre-approved documentation for the expenditure, such as a signed voucher, a completed and approved travel request, an approved purchase requisition, an order, or an invoice. The record for each check written must include the expense account code or sufficient descriptive information to allow assignment of the correct code.

4) At regular intervals, the revolving fund must be reimbursed up to its original amount. The check written for this reimbursement must be included on the school board's monthly listing of bills, charging the appropriate expenditure accounts and indicating the recipient and explanation for each revolving-fund check that was issued.

105 ILCS 5/10-20.19(2)
23 Ill. Admin. Code 100.70

25:173 What requirements are imposed on a school district's use of credit cards for certain expenditures or purchases?

If a school board has obtained and issued credit cards or procurement cards for the use of board members, the superintendent, or other district employees or officials to pay certain job-related expenses or to make purchases on behalf of the board or district, or any student activity funds, or for purposes that would otherwise be addressed through a conventional revolving fund, then the board must adopt a written credit card policy that at least

1) Identifies the allowable types of purchases;

2) Provides for the issuing bank to block the cards' use at unapproved merchants;

3) Limits the amount a cardholder can charge in a single purchase or within a given month;

4) Provides specific guidelines on purchases via telephone, fax, and the internet;

5) Indicates the consequences for unauthorized purchases;

6) Requires cardholder to sign a statement affirming that they are familiar with the board's credit card policy;

7) Requires review and approval of purchases by someone other than the cardholder or user;

8) Requires submission of original receipts to document purchases;

9) Forbids the use of a card to make purchases in a manner contrary to the requirements of Section 10-20.21 of the School Code; and

10) Indicates how financial or material rewards or rebates are to be accounted for and treated.

23 Ill. Admin. Code 100.70

25:175 What is the difference between student activity accounts and convenience accounts?

Student activity accounts are those funds that are owned, operated, and managed by organizations, clubs, or groups within the student body under the guidance and direction of one or more faculty or staff members for educational, recreational, or cultural purposes. Examples of student activity accounts include homeroom moneys, yearbook collections, class year accounts, choral and band accounts, class projects, student clubs, student council, and student bookstore moneys.

Convenience accounts are those funds maintained by the local education agency at the request of and for the convenience of faculty, staff, faculty-parent organizations, or similar non-student groups. Examples of convenience accounts include scholarship funds, faculty-parent organization accounts, faculty funds, and employee coffee funds.

Different fund management requirements apply to each type of account.

Funds that are sometimes mistaken as activity funds, but are budgeted district accounts include lunch program, athletic program, building trades program, restricted grants-in-aid from state or federal sources, towel-locker and book rentals, student insurance, and sales of district supplies and services.

23 Ill. Admin. Code 100.70
23 Ill. Admin. Code 100.80

25:180 What control must a school board exercise over funds raised by student organizations?

A school board must take the following actions with respect to each fund:

1) Approve the fund's establishment and purpose;

2) Set policies for students' participation and for supervision by adults;

3) Approve the collection of all moneys;

4) Cause records to be kept that will verify the amounts received and disbursed and the assets on hand;

5) Appoint a treasurer, bonded in accordance with Section 8-2 of the School Code, who will be the custodian of the fund's assets;

6) Determine whether the treasurer will be authorized to invest any of the fund's assets;

7) Designate depositories for cash and any investments;

8) Determine the method of distribution of earnings from investments, if any;

9) Determine whether, and under what circumstances, loans may be transacted between funds;

10) If the relevant activity has been discontinued, or if there has been no activity for one year, transfer money to another activity fund, to the district's funds, or to members of the activity group on a pro rata basis; and

11) Designate the individuals who will have authority to approve written purchase orders or other authorizations that will be required in order to spend funds in instances in which the provisions of Section 10-20.21 of the School Code do not apply and those who will have authority to conduct procurement activities when those provisions do apply.

Each activity group must deposit any funds received from any source with the activity fund's treasurer and obtain a signed receipt identifying the activity fund and the amount. The treasurer of each activity fund must

1) Be the fund's sole custodian;

2) Keep all moneys in a depository designated in accordance with Section 8-7 of the School Code or invest them in conformance with the Public Funds Investment Act (30 ILCS 235) and maintain liability accounts to show the ownership of all assets;

3) Make all disbursements from the fund by a treasurer's check drawn upon the fund;

4) Write checks only when sufficient funds are on hand to cover them;

5) Reconcile the bank and investment balances with the fund's liabilities monthly;

6) Provide to group members and the school board a monthly report that includes a statement of receipts, disbursements, and current balances;

7) Carry the fund's balance over to the next fiscal year unless otherwise instructed by the school board; and

8) Make loans between activity funds, if and as authorized by the board's policy.

If the board subsidizes a portion of an activity fund, that portion must be reported as an expenditure or disbursement against the board's regular budget and as a revenue or cash receipt by the activity fund.

105 ILCS 5/10-20.19(2)
23 Ill. Admin. Code 100.80

FINANCIAL REPORTS AND AUDITS

25:190 What financial reports are required of Illinois school districts?

Prior to December 1 of each year, each school district is required to compile, submit to the State Board of Education and publish in a newspaper of general circulation published in the school district a statement of financial affairs showing the district's revenue, expenditures, and financial condition in a form prescribed by the State Board of Education. The document includes a requirement that each person be listed by name to whom the annual fiscal year gross payment exceeds $2,500.

105 ILCS 5/10-17

25:200 When are school district accounts audited?

Each school district is required to cause an annual audit of its accounts to be made by a person who is lawfully qualified to practice public accounting in Illinois.

A copy of the audit must be provided to the regional superintendent on or before October 15 of each year, or by a time extended by the regional superintendent not to exceed 60 days.

105 ILCS 5/3-7

25:205 What is a school district's fiscal year?

A school district may establish its fiscal year. July 1 to June 30 is commonly selected.

105 ILCS 5/17-1

PURCHASING

25:300 What steps are required to release payment for school district purchases?

When the school board provides the treasurer with evidence that it has formally approved payment, the treasurer releases funds. The school board may provide the treasurer with a certified copy of the minutes of its meeting, reflecting the approval of specific bills approved and the budget items to be debited, or the board may adopt a voucher system or other procedure that meets standards of the State Board of Education.

105 ILCS 5/8-16
105 ILCS 5/10-20.19(1)

25:310 Must a school district list its contracts on its website?

Each school board must list on the district's website, if any, all contracts over $25,000 and any contract that the school board enters into with an exclusive bargaining representative. Section 10-20.44 of the School Code requires that the contents of the collective bargaining agreement(s) be posted, not just a notice that they exist.

Each year, in conjunction with the submission of the Statement of Affairs to the State Board of Education prior to December 1, provided for in Section 10-17, each school district must submit to the State Board of Education an annual report on all contracts over $25,000 awarded by the school district during the previous fiscal year. The report must include at least the following:

1) The total number of all contracts awarded by the school district;

2) The total value of all contracts awarded;

3) The number of contracts awarded to minority owned businesses, female owned businesses, and businesses owned by persons with disabilities, as defined in the Business Enterprise for Minorities, Females and Persons with Disabilities Act, and locally owned businesses; and

4) The total value of contracts awarded to minority owned businesses, female owned businesses, and businesses owned by persons with disabilities, as defined in the Business Enterprise for Minorities, Females and Persons with Disabilities Act, and locally owned businesses.

The report shall be made available to the public, including publication on the school district's website, if any.

105 ILCS 5/10-20.44

25:320 What is an education purchasing contract?

An education purchasing contract is a statewide master contract negotiated by the State Board of Education or its statutorily defined designee. When a school district purchases items supplied as the result of the letting of a statewide master contract, the purchase of such items is exempt from competitive bidding, even if bidding statutes would otherwise apply.

No such contract is a master contract within the meaning of the statute unless the State Board of Education designates it as a master contract.

105 ILCS 5/28A-5 et seq.

25:330 May a school district borrow money to purchase a school bus?

A school district is not authorized to incur debt except when law specifically permits. The School Code allows contracts for the purchase of a school bus to be paid for over such period of time as does not exceed the vehicle's depreciable life. This provision has been widely interpreted to permit seller-financed agreements. It probably does not permit other forms of borrowing for the same purpose.

A school board is authorized to enter into a school bus lease agreement with a term not more than five years. The vote to enter into the lease requires an affirmative vote of 2/3 of the school board.

105 ILCS 5/10-23.4
105 ILCS 5/10-23.4a

25:340 May a school district enter into a multi-year transportation contract with a private carrier?

A school district may enter into a contract for up to three years for transportation of pupils to and from school. The contract may be extended for up to two more years by mutual agreement of the parties and, after that, may be extended on a year-to-year basis.

No contract may be extended on a year-to-year basis if the school board receives a timely request from another interested contractor that a contract be let for bid. A district is not required to respond to such a request more than once every two years. A request is not considered timely unless it is submitted in writing by certified mail addressed to the school board at the administrative offices or any school of the district, or if it is made more than 24 months or less than three months before the expiration of the collective bargaining or other agreement that is in effect at the time the request is made and that governs the terms and conditions of employment of the school bus drivers employed by the district.

105 ILCS 5/29-6.1
105 ILCS 5/29-6.4
625 ILCS 5/6-106.11

25:350 May a school district acquire personal property under an installment contract?

A school district may obtain personal property by lease with or without an option to purchase or under an installment contract. These contracts are sometimes called "lease-purchase agreements." The term of the lease or contract may not exceed five years. The authorizing statute specifies the maximum interest rate. To enter into such a lease requires a 2/3 vote of the school board.

105 ILCS 5/10-22.25a

25:360 May a school district borrow money to purchase computer equipment?

The State Board of Education administers a loan program that allows school districts to borrow money for computer hardware, technology networks, and related wiring. The program does not finance the purchase of software.

Loans are available on a two-year rotating basis — grades 9-12 in fiscal year 2004 and each second year thereafter, grades K-8 in fiscal year 2005 and each second year thereafter. Up to 10 percent of the loan may be used to purchase computer furniture. The repayment period for the loans is three years or less.

In 2005, the legislature repealed the statute (section 2-3.121 of the School Code) that authorized the revolving fund that funded this program and in 2008 removed the statutory reference (in section 2-3.117 of the School Code) authorizing matching grants.

105 ILCS 5/2-3.117a

25:370 May a school district purchase energy saving systems by installment contract?

A school district, area vocational center, or school districts in combination may enter into installment contracts or lease purchase agreements for the purchase and installation of energy conservation measures. There are detailed statutory provisions that govern how such a contract or agreement may be awarded.

Energy conservation means any improvement, repair, alteration, or betterment of any building or facility owned or operated by a school district or any equipment, fixture or furnishing to be added to or used in a building, or facility that is designed to reduce energy consumption or operating costs.

50 ILCS 515/25
105 ILCS 5/19b-1 et seq.

25:372 When must a school district make public its energy audit?

When a school district is contemplating an energy conservation contract under article 19b of the School Code, and if an energy audit was performed by an energy services contractor for the school district within the three years immediately preceding the solicitation, then the school district must publish as a reference document in the solicitation for energy conservation measures the following:

1) An executive summary of the energy audit, provided that the school district may exclude any proprietary or trademarked information or practices; or

2) The energy audit, provided that the school district may redact any proprietary or trademarked information or practices.

The school district may not withhold the disclosure of information related to the school district's consumption of energy, the physical condition of the school district's facilities, and any limitations prescribed by the school district.

The solicitation must include a written disclosure that identifies any energy services contractor that participated in the preparation of the specifications issued by the school district. If no energy services contractor participated in the preparation of the specifications issued by the school district, then the solicitation must include a written disclosure that no energy services contractor participated in the preparation of the specifications for the school district.

The written disclosure is to be published in the Capital Development Board Procurement Bulletin with the Request for Proposal.

105 ILCS 5/19b-5

25:380 May a school district operate an energy generating wind turbine?

The School Code authorizes a school district to own and operate a wind generation turbine farm, either individually or jointly, if it directly or indirectly reduces the energy or other operating costs of the school district.

105 ILCS 5/10-20.42

25:390 When is a Use Tax charged?

A 2003 amendment to the School Code requires, as a condition of any contract for goods and services, that persons bidding for and awarded a contract and all affiliates of the person collect and remit Illinois Use Tax on all sales of tangible personal property to the state in accordance with the provisions of the Illinois Use Tax Act regardless of whether the person or affiliate is a retailer maintaining a place of business in Illinois.

The 2003 amendment also added a requirement that school boards require a certification from bidders that they are not barred from bidding or entering into a contract and allows boards to declare the contract void if the certification is false.

35 ILCS 105/1 et seq.
105 ILCS 5/10-20.21

BIDDING REQUIREMENTS

25:500 When do bidding requirements apply?

A school board is required to let all contracts for supplies, materials, or work involving an expenditure in excess of $25,000 or a lower amount as required by board policy to the lowest responsible bidder considering conformity with specifications, terms of delivery, quality, and serviceability after due advertisement.

However, certain contracts are exempted from competitive bidding requirements, including

1) Contracts for the services of individuals possessing a high degree of professional skill where the ability or fitness of the individual plays an important part;

2) Contracts for the printing of finance committee reports and departmental reports;

3) Contracts for the printing or engraving of bonds, tax warrants, and other evidences of indebtedness;

4) Contracts for the purchase of perishable food and perishable beverages;

5) Contracts for materials and work which have been awarded to the lowest responsible bidder after due advertisement, but due to unforeseen revisions not the fault of the contractor for materials and work must be revised, causing expenditures not in excess of 10 percent of the contract price;

6) Contracts for the maintenance or servicing of, or provision of repair parts for, equipment which are made with the manufacturer or authorized service agent of that equipment where the provision of parts, maintenance, or servicing can best be performed by the manufacturer or authorized service agent;

7) Purchases and contracts for the use, purchase, delivery, movement, or installation of data processing equipment, software, or services and telecommunications and interconnect equipment, software, and services;

8) Contracts for duplicating machines and supplies;

9) Contracts for the purchase of natural gas when the cost is less than that offered by a public utility;

10) Purchases of equipment previously owned by some entity other than the district itself;

11) Contracts for repair, maintenance, remodeling, renovation, or construction, or a single project involving an expenditure not to exceed $50,000 and not involving a change or increase in the size, type, or extent of an existing facility;

12) Contracts for goods or services procured from another governmental agency;

13) Contracts for goods or services which are economically procurable from only one source, such as for the purchase of magazines, books, periodicals, pamphlets, and reports and for utility services such as water, light, heat, telephone, or telegraph;

14) Where funds are expended in an emergency and such emergency expenditure is approved by 3/4 of the members of the board;

15) State master contracts authorized by section 28A of the School Code.

16) Contracts providing for the transportation of pupils, which contracts must be advertised in the same manner as competitive bids and awarded by first considering the bidder or bidders most able to provide safety and comfort for the pupils, stability of service, and any other factors set forth in the request for proposal regarding quality of service, and then price. There is no cause of action against a school board for awarding a pupil transportation contract under this section unless the cause of action is based on fraudulent conduct.

All competitive bids for contracts involving an expenditure in excess of $25,000 or a lower amount as required by board policy must be sealed by the bidder and must be opened by a member or employee of the school board at a public bid opening at which the contents of the bids must be announced.

105 ILCS 5/10-20.21
105 ILCS 5/28A-5 et seq.

25:510 How much time must a school district allow for bidding?

To comply with competitive bidding statutes, each bidder must receive at least three days' notice of the time and place of bid opening. At least one public notice must be given in a newspaper published in the district at least 10 days before the bid date.

105 ILCS 5/10-20.21

25:520 May a school district accept a faxed or emailed bid?

The relevant statute provides that if bidding is required, the bids must be sealed. A 2009 amendment to the bidding statute allows bidding by an electronic process for communicating, accepting, and opening competitive bids. However, bids for construction purposes are prohibited from being communicated, accepted, or opened electronically.

If a school district elects to use an electronic bidding process it must provide for, but is not limited to, the following safeguards:

1) On the date and time certain of a bid opening, the primary person conducting the competitive, sealed, electronic bid process must log onto a specified database using a unique username and password previously assigned to the bidder to allow access to the bidder's specific bid project number.

2) The specified electronic database must be on a network that is in a secure environment behind a firewall; has specific encryption tools; maintains specific intrusion detection systems; has redundant systems architecture with data storage back-up, whether by compact disc or tape; and maintains a disaster recovery plan.

105 ILCS 5/10-20.21

25:530 Under what circumstances can a school district negotiate with more than one bidder after bids have been opened but before a contract has been let?

The desire to negotiate with more than one bidder usually occurs when the school district cannot clearly distinguish the low bid from bids received or seeks to avoid awarding a contract to the low bidder.

When a low bid cannot be distinguished, fault can be found in the way the bid specifications were written. Negotiating with more than one bidder comes dangerously close under any circumstance to a violation of bidding statutes. The safest practice is to reject all bids, rewrite the bid specifications, and rebid.

A school district seeking to avoid awarding a contract to the low bidder must find the bidder irresponsible within the meaning of the statute or award the bid to the low bidder.

A school district may further negotiate price with the low bidder once the low bidder has been identified, but in doing so the school district must be very careful that no material element of the bid specification is changed and that the only matter being negotiated is the price.

105 ILCS 5/10-20.21

720 ILCS 5/33E-12

Acme Bus Corp. v. Board of Education of the Roosevelt Union Free School District, 89 N.Y. 2d 816, 681 N.E. 2d 1304, 659 N.Y.S. 2d 857 (1997)

25:540 Is the letting of insurance contracts subject to competitive bidding?

A school board is required to comply with the competitive bidding provisions of the School Code when awarding insurance contracts. The length of the contract and the facts surrounding its award will determine how soon after the original award the contract must be re-bid. Insurance contracts do not involve the type of professional skills that would except them from bidding requirements.

Self-insurance plans and pools are not subject to bidding requirements.

Compass Health Care Plans v. Board of Education of the City of Chicago and Ted D. Kimbrough, 246 Ill. App. 3d 746, 617 N.E. 2d 6, 186 Ill. Dec. 767 (1st Dist. 1992)

25:550 Must a school board award contracts for architectural or engineering services to the lowest bidder?

No. Professional services are exempted from bidding requirements. When a school board needs architectural, engineering, or land surveying services, the contract must be awarded on the basis of demonstrated competence and qualifications.

Unless it already has a satisfactory relationship with one or more firms, the school board must advertise for (a) statements of interest in a particular project and (b) statements of qualifications and performance data. The school board must evaluate firms submitting these statements and select the top three based on qualifications, ability of professional personnel, past record and experience, performance data on file, willingness to meet time and budget requirements, location, workload, and other applicable factors. The top three firms must be ranked in order of preference.

The school board must attempt to negotiate a satisfactory contract first with the top ranked firm and, if that fails, with the second and third firms, in the order ranked. Another list of three firms may be developed if the board is unable to negotiate a satisfactory contract with one of the first three firms.

50 ILCS 510/1 et seq.

105 ILCS 5/10-20.21

25:552 How must a school board advertise for a new architectural or engineering firm?

The notice provision of the statute requires the following:

1) A notice mailed or emailed to all firms that have a current statement of qualifications and performance data on file;

2) A newspaper advertisement; and

3) A notice on the district's website.

50 ILCS 510/4

25:560 Must contracts to employ construction managers be bid?

The industry practice is to not bid construction manager contracts and to interview for services under the exception to the bidding statute for "individuals possessing a high degree of professional skill where the ability or fitness of the individual plays an important part." It is not the title "construction manager" that allows avoidance of the bidding requirement, but rather the role the construction manager plays in the construction process.

The employment of a general contractor must be bid. The employment of a construction manager may or may not fall within the requirement to bid depending upon the facts regarding the duties to be performed by the construction manager in the contract documents. To meet the professional skill exception, the construction manager should not furnish equipment, building labor, or materials and must serve as an advisor to the owner and have discretion in managing the project.

105 ILCS 5/10-20.21

Shively v. Belleville Township High School District No. 201 and Korte Construction Company, 329 Ill. App. 3d 1156, 769 N.E. 2d 1062, 264 Ill. Dec. 225 (5th Cir. 2002)

East Peoria Community High School District No. 309 v. Grand Stage Lighting Co., 235 Ill. App. 3d 756, 601 N.E. 2d 972, 976 Ill. Dec. 274 (3rd Dist. 1992)

25:570 What may a school board consider to determine whether a bidder is responsible?

A school board may consider any of the following factors to determine if a bidder is responsible:

1) The quality of the work performed on other similar jobs;

2) The financial status of the bidder to assure a financial solvency sufficient to complete the contract;

3) The bidder's quantity and quality of experience on similar jobs;

4) The bidder's reputation;

5) The ability of the bidder to provide a satisfactory performance bond;

6) The bidder's reliability in completing similar contracts under the terms and conditions of those contracts; and

7) The board's past experience with the bidder.

105 ILCS 5/10-20.21

RJB Properties v. Board of Education of The City of Chicago, 468 F. 3d 1005 (7th Cir. 2006)

Compass Health Care Plans v. Board of Education of the City of Chicago and Ted D. Kimbrough, 246 Ill. App. 3d 746, 617 N.E. 2d 6, 186 Ill. Dec. 767 (1st Dist. 1992)

Carlson v. Moline Board of Education School District No. 40, 124 Ill. App. 3d 967, 464 N.E. 2d 1239, 80 Ill. Dec. 256 (3rd Dist. 1984)

Cardinal Glass v. Board of Education of Mendota Community Consolidated School District 289, 113 Ill. App. 3d 442, 447 N.E. 2d 546, 69 Ill. Dec. 329 (3rd Dist. 1983)

Beaver Glass and Mirror Company, Inc. v. Board of Education of Rockford School District No. 205, Winnebago County, 59 Ill. App. 3d 880, 376 N.E. 2d 377, 17 Ill. Dec. 378 (2nd Dist. 1978)

25:580 What recourse is available to an unsuccessful low bidder?

A low bidder who is not awarded the contract may bring suit challenging the award of the contract. In appropriate circumstances, the low bidder may be awarded the contract or may recover money damages or both.

Court Street Steak House v. Tazewell County, 249 Ill. App. 3d 918, 619 N.E. 2d 759, 189 Ill. Dec. 58 (3rd Dist. 1993)

L.E. Zannini & Co. v. Board of Education, Hawthorn School District 73, 138 Ill. App. 3d 467, 486 N.E. 2d 426, 93 Ill. Dec. 323 (2nd Dist. 1985)

Cardinal Glass v. Board of Education of Mendota Community Consolidated School District 289, 113 Ill. App. 3d 442, 447 N.E. 2d 546, 69 Ill. Dec. 329 (3rd Dist. 1983)

25:590 May a school board reject all bids?

Yes.

Premier Electric Construction Co. v. Board of Education of City of Chicago, 70 Ill. App. 3d 866, 388 N.E. 2d 1088, 27 Ill. Dec. 125 (1st Dist. 1979)

25:600 May a school district give preference to local bidders when letting contracts?

If the contract requires competitive bidding, the school board may not give preference to a local bidder.

Doyle Plumbing and Heating Co. v. Board of Education, Quincy Public School District No. 172, 291 Ill. App. 3d 221, 683 N.E. 2d 530, 225 Ill. Dec. 362 (4th Dist. 1997)

Cardinal Glass v. Board of Education of Mendota Community Consolidated School District 289, 113 Ill. App. 3d 442, 447 N.E. 2d 546, 69 Ill. Dec. 329 (3rd Dist. 1983)

25:610 What is the meaning of the term "serviceability" in the bidding statutes?

Serviceability means "durability or usefulness and fitness of the supplies, materials, or work on which bids are solicited." Serviceability does not refer to the service call response time of a bidder.

Doyle Plumbing and Heating Co. v. Board of Education, Quincy Public School District No. 172, 291 Ill. App. 221, 683 N.E. 2d 530, 225 Ill. Dec. 362 (4th Dist. 1997)

25:620 Are there any penalties for improperly influencing the outcome of school district bidding or purchasing procedures in order to favor a local bidder or other favored bidder?

Yes. Any action by a governmental body or employee to knowingly favor or assist any bidder over other bidders may be in violation of laws prohibiting the rigging or rotating of contracts or otherwise interfering with the letting of public contracts. Prohibited actions include the providing of information or criteria to one bidder that is not available to all bidders and the specification of particular subcontractors.

Most violations of the public contracts law are Class 3 or Class 4 felonies carrying fines up to $10,000 and imprisonment ranging from three to 10 years.

720 ILCS 5/33E-1 et seq.

25:630 What options does a school board have when a school building requires emergency repairs?

In the case of an emergency, when the estimated cost to effectuate emergency repairs is less than the amount specified in Section 10-20.21 of the School Code (the bidding statute), the school district may proceed with the repairs prior to approval by the State Superintendent of Education, but must get an estimate as provided in subdivision (2) of School Code section 17-2.11(a) as soon thereafter as may be practical and must also comply with bidding statutes when practical.

If the estimated cost to effectuate emergency repairs is greater than the amount specified in the bidding statute, then the school district must proceed in conformity with the bidding statute and with rules established by the State Board of Education to address such situations. The rules adopted by the State Board of Education to deal with these situations stipulate that emergency situations must be expedited and given priority consideration.

An emergency is a situation that presents an imminent and continuing threat to the health and safety of students or other occupants of a facility, requires complete or partial evacuation of a building or part of a building, or consumes one or more of the five emergency days built into the adopted calendar of the school or schools or would otherwise be expected to cause such school or schools to fall short of the minimum school calendar requirements.

105 ILCS 5/10-20.21
105 ILCS 5/17-2.11

26: SCHOOL BOARD BORROWING AND DEBT

INTERFUND TRANSFERS AND LOANS

26:10 May a school board loan or transfer money among the various funds established by law (e.g. educational fund and operations and maintenance fund)?

A school board may loan or transfer moneys among funds according to statutory provisions specific to each fund. Other loans or transfers are prohibited.

105 ILCS 5/10-22.14
105 ILCS 5/10-22.44
105 ILCS 5/17-2B
105 ILCS 5/20-5
Lutkauskas v. Ricker, 2013 IL App (1st) 121112, 998 N.E. 2d 549, 376 Ill. Dec. 7
People ex rel. Redfern v. Pennsylvania Central Company, 47 Ill. 2d 412, 266 N.E. 2d 334 (1971)

26:20 May a school board permanently transfer money among the educational fund, operations and maintenance fund, and/or the transportation fund?

A school board may transfer funds as listed below provided that

1) A proper resolution is adopted following a public hearing set by the school board or the president of the school board; and

2) The public hearing is preceded by at least one published notice over the name of the clerk or secretary of the board occurring at least seven days and not more than 30 days prior to the hearing in a newspaper of general circulation within the school district setting forth the time, date, place, and subject matter of the hearing and a posted notice over the name of the clerk or secretary of the board at least 48 hours before the hearing at the principal office of the school board or at the building where the hearing is to be held if a principal office does not exist with both notices setting forth time, date, place, and subject matter of the hearing.

Permissible transfers following these procedures are

1) From the educational fund to the operations and maintenance fund;

2) From the operations and maintenance fund to the educational fund; or

3) From the transportation fund to the educational or operations and maintenance fund.

Except during the period July 1, 2003 through June 30, 2016, such a transfer may be made solely for the purpose of meeting one-time, non-recurring expenses.

Except during the period July 1, 2003 through June 30, 2016, any other permanent interfund transfers authorized by any provision or judicial interpretation of the School Code for which the transferee fund is not precisely and specifically set forth in the provision of the School Code authorizing the transfer must be made to the fund of the school district most in need of the funds being transferred as determined by resolution of the school board. Through June 30, 2016, the school board may, by proper resolution, transfer surplus life-safety taxes and interest earnings to the operations and maintenance fund for building repair work. A public hearing and notice are required before the transfer occurs.

105 ILCS 5/17-2A
23 Ill. Admin. Code 100.50
Lutkauskas v. Ricker, 2013 IL App (1st) 121112, 998 N.E. 2d 549, 376 Ill. Dec. 7

26:24 May a school board transfer interest income earned in one fund to another fund?

In certain instances specified in the law, interest income may be transferred from the fund in which the interest was earned to another fund.

Interest earned on the proceeds of the life-safety levy may be transferred to the operations and maintenance fund, but the operations and maintenance tax levy must be reduced by the amount of interest transferred.

Interest income from the debt service levy to pay building, tort immunity, working cash fund, or life-safety bonds may be transferred to any fund. The working cash fund need not be repaid when bond income is transferred.

Interest earned on funds deposited in an insurance reserve fund, or earned on deposits resulting from the tort immunity levy if declared surplus, may be transferred to any fund.

Interest earned on funds deposited in the working cash fund that resulted from the working cash fund levy may be transferred to any fund without repaying the working cash fund.

Through June 30, 2019, the school board may, by proper resolution, transfer surplus life-safety fund interest earnings to the operations and maintenance fund for building repair work. A public hearing and notice are required before the transfer occurs.

105 ILCS 5/10-22.44
105 ILCS 5/17-2.11
105 ILCS 5/20-5
745 ILCS 10/9-107
23 Ill. Admin. Code 100.50

26:25 Are there instances when interest income may not be transferred from the fund in which it was earned?

Yes. Interest earned on deposits resulting from the capital improvements tax levy and interest earned from deposits resulting from the Illinois Municipal Retirement Fund levy must be retained in the fund in which the original deposits were made.

105 ILCS 5/10-22.44
105 ILCS 5/17-2.3

26:30 May a school board transfer money among line items within a fund?

A school board may make transfers between the various items in any fund not exceeding in the aggregate 10 percent of the total of the fund as set forth in the budget.

105 ILCS 5/17-1

26:40 Which interfund loans are permissible?

The following interfund loans are permissible:

1) Operations and maintenance fund moneys may be loaned to the educational fund or transportation fund.

2) Educational fund moneys may be loaned to the operations and maintenance fund or transportation fund.

3) Transportation fund moneys may be loaned to the educational fund or operations and maintenance fund.

4) Working cash fund moneys may be loaned to another fund.

Moneys must be repaid to the loaning fund within three years, except working cash fund loans which must be repaid upon the collection of anticipated taxes. Exceptions to the payment of working cash fund loans exist when tax anticipation notes are outstanding.

105 ILCS 5/10-22.33
105 ILCS 5/20-5

WORKING CASH FUND

26:50 What is a working cash fund?

A school district may create, re-create, or increase a working cash fund by levying up to 5 cents per 100 dollars of equalized assessed valuation. No working cash fund levy is permitted if bonds in the amount of 85 percent of the prior tax extensions for educational purposes have been issued for the working cash fund or if the amount of taxes to be extended will increase the working fund to an amount exceeding 85 percent (125 percent for a financially distressed district) of the taxes last extended for educational purposes.

105 ILCS 5/20-1 et seq.

G.I.S. Venture, et al. v. Novak, 288 Ill. App. 3d 184, 902 N.E. 2d 744, 327 Ill. Dec. 623 (2nd Dist. 2009)

Application of Walgenbach, 166 Ill. App. 3d 629, 520 N.E. 2d 78, 117 Ill. Dec. 88 (2nd Dist. 1988)

Application of Walgenbach, 104 Ill. 2d 121, 470 N.E. 2d 1015, 83 Ill. Dec. 595 (2nd Dist. 1984)

26:60 What is the purpose of the working cash fund?

The purpose of the working cash fund is to enable the school district "to have in its treasury at all times sufficient money to meet demands for ordinary and necessary expenses." Because school revenue is not always received according to schedule, the working cash fund provides a school board with a source of internal borrowing to meet short-term needs and reduce the need to borrow from outside sources that bear interest costs.

105 ILCS 5/20-1

26:70 May a school board abolish a working cash fund after such a fund has been created?

Any school board may abolish its working cash fund, upon the adoption of a resolution so providing, and direct the transfer of any balance in such fund to the educational fund at the close of the then-current school year. Any outstanding loans to other funds of the district must be paid to the educational fund at the close of the then-current school year. Thereafter, all outstanding working cash taxes of such school district must be collected and paid into the educational fund.

105 ILCS 5/20-8 et seq.

G.I.S. Venture, et al. v. Novak, 288 Ill. App. 3d 184, 902 N.E. 2d 744, 327 Ill. Dec. 623 (2nd Dist. 2009)

Bell v. School District No. 84, 47 Ill. 406, 95 N.E. 2d 496 (1950)

26:80 May a school board that has abolished its working cash fund re-create the fund?

Yes.

105 ILCS 5/20-9

AUTHORITY TO BORROW

26:90 Are school boards authorized to borrow money?

School boards may borrow money and issue bonds for various purposes and in various ways specified by law.

105 ILCS 5/10-22.14

26:100 Is there any limit to the amount of money that a school board may borrow?

The maximum debt limitation for a unit district is 13.8 percent of the value of the taxable property located in the school district as determined by the last assessment before the indebtedness is to be incurred. The maximum debt limitation for an elementary district or high school district is 6.9 percent of the value of the taxable property located in the school district.

These debt limits, which apply to the aggregate of most forms of debt, may be increased by referendum or in certain emergency situations. If a school district is certified by the State Board of Education as financially distressed and if the school district meets certain other statutory requirements, it may incur debt beyond the debt limits. Under certain circumstances a school district may incur debt beyond its limits to finance school construction bonds issued in conjunction with a school construction project approved under the School Construction Law.

In addition to the limits on aggregate debt, there are limits to the amounts that may be borrowed against anticipated taxes and state aid.

105 ILCS 5/19-1

People ex rel. Lindheimer v. Hamilton, 373 Ill. 124, 25 N.E. 2d 517 (1940)

SHORT-TERM BORROWING

26:110 What forms of short-term debt may a school board incur in order to meet current operating expenses?

School boards are authorized to issue warrants or notes against anticipated property tax income; issue notes against anticipated state aid and corporate personal property replacement taxes; and to issue general obligation orders in the payment of teachers salaries.

30 ILCS 305/2
105 ILCS 5/8-16
105 ILCS 5/17-16
105 ILCS 5/18-18
105 ILCS 5/32-4.14

26:120 What are tax anticipation warrants?

Tax anticipation warrants are issued in expectation of the collection of taxes and may be issued to the extent of 85 percent of the total amount of the tax levied. The warrants must be repaid upon receipt of tax moneys by the district and bear interest at a statutory rate.

30 ILCS 305/2
105 ILCS 5/17-16
105 ILCS 5/18-8.05

26:130 When may a school board issue tax anticipation warrants?

When there is no money in the treasury of the school district to pay necessary expenses of the district, including amounts necessary to pay maturing principal and interest of bonds, a school board may issue warrants or may provide a fund to meet the expenses by issuing and disposing of warrants, drawn against and in anticipation of any taxes levied for the payment of the necessary expenses of the district, either for transportation, educational, or for all operations and maintenance purposes, or for payments to the Illinois Municipal Retirement Fund, or for the payment of maturing principal and interest of bonds, as the case may be, to the extent of 85 percent of the total amount of the tax so levied.

The warrants must show upon their face they are payable in the numerical order of their issuance solely from such taxes when collected and such taxes are to be set aside and held for their payment.

105 ILCS 5/17-16
105 ILCS 5/18-18

Hamer v. Board of Education of School District No. 113, Lake County, 132 Ill. App. 2d 46, 267 N.E. 2d 1 (2nd Dist. 1971)

26:135 May a school district borrow money from a bank rather than issue tax anticipation warrants?

In lieu of issuing tax anticipation warrants, a school district having a population of 500,000 or less inhabitants may issue notes, bonds, or other obligations (and in connection with that issuance, establish a line of credit with a bank or other financial institution) in an amount not to exceed 85 percent of the amount of property taxes most recently levied for educational, operations and maintenance, transportation, or other tax levy purposes or any combination thereof. This money must be applied to the purposes for which the tax or any combination of the tax may be levied and no other purpose. All moneys so borrowed must be repaid exclusively from property tax revenues within 60 days after the property tax revenues have been received by the board.

In lieu of issuing notes or certificates in accordance with the provisions of the Revenue Anticipation Act or Section 18-18 of the School Code, the school board of a school district other than Chicago may anticipate revenues due in the current fiscal year or expected to be due in the next subsequent fiscal year and issue notes, bonds, or other obligations (and in connection with that issuance, establish a line of credit with a bank or other financial institution) in an amount not to exceed the following:

1) If anticipating revenues due in the current fiscal year, 85 percent of the amount or amounts of the revenues due in the current fiscal year as certified by the State Superintendent of Education or other official in a position to provide assurances as to the amounts; and

2) If anticipating revenues expected to be due in the next subsequent fiscal year, 50 percent of the amount or amounts of the revenues due in the current fiscal year as certified by the State Superintendent of Education or other official in a position to provide assurances as to the amounts.

All moneys so borrowed must be repaid exclusively from the anticipated revenues within 60 days after the revenues have been received.

Borrowing authorized for this purpose must bear interest at a rate not to exceed the maximum rate authorized by the Bond Authorization Act, from the date of issuance until paid.

Prior to borrowing or establishing a line of credit under this provision, the board must pass a resolution authorizing the borrowing or line of credit setting forth facts demonstrating the need for the borrowing or line of credit, stating the amount to be borrowed, and establishing a maximum interest rate limit (as limited by the law) and providing a date by which the borrowed funds must be repaid. The resolution must direct the relevant officials to make arrangements to set apart and hold the taxes or other revenue, as received, that will be used to repay the borrowing.

The resolution may authorize relevant officials to make partial repayments of the borrowing as the taxes or other revenue become available and may contain any other terms, restrictions, or limitations not inconsistent with the law.

There are similar provisions that allow a regional superintendent, special education cooperative, or joint agreement to borrow by establishment of a line of credit.

105 ILCS 5/17-17
105 ILCS 5/17-18
105 ILCS 5/17-19

26:140 How are tax anticipation warrants retired?

Tax anticipation warrants are payable solely from the taxes collected from the levy against which the warrants were issued.

Schreiner v. City of Chicago, 406 Ill. 75, 92 N.E. 2d 133 (1950)

Leviton v. Board of Education of the City of Chicago, 374 Ill. 594, 30 N.E. 2d 497 (1943)

Berman v. Board of Education of the City of Chicago, 360 Ill. 535, 196 N.E. 464 (1935)

People ex rel. Mathews v. Board of Education of the City of Chicago, 349 Ill. 390, 182 N.E. 455 (1932)

26:150 When may a school board issue tax anticipation notes?

A school board is authorized to issue full faith and credit tax anticipation notes as a means of securing operating funds. The issuance of such notes provides an alternative to the issuance of tax anticipation warrants.

Tax anticipation notes are direct general obligations of the school district and the full faith and credit of the school district is pledged for the punctual payment of the principal and interest on the notes. Such notes may be issued in excess of any statutory debt limitation and do not reduce the debt-incurring power of the district. The notes have a fixed maturity date, within two years from their date of issue, and the resolution authorizing their issuance must be filed with the county clerk of each county in which the district is located before the end of the calendar year during which the taxes being anticipated were levied.

No notes can be issued during any fiscal year in which there are tax anticipation warrants outstanding against the tax levied for such fiscal year. Tax anticipation notes may not be issued in an amount exceeding 85 percent of the taxes levied for a specific purpose for the year during which the notes are issued.

30 ILCS 305/2 et seq.
50 ILCS 420/1 et seq.

26:160 For what purposes may moneys received from tax anticipation be used?

Moneys from tax anticipation warrants are in place of the taxes in anticipation of which the warrants were issued. The money may be used only for the purpose for which the taxes were levied.

People ex rel. Mathews v. Board of Education of the City of Chicago, 349 Ill. 390, 182 N.E. 455 (1932)

26:170 What are corporate personal property replacement tax notes?

Corporate personal property replacement tax notes provide a means for a school district to finance anticipated cash flow deficits by issuing notes to anticipate replacement tax revenues. The replacement tax was intended to offset the revenue lost as a result of the abolition of the ad valorem personal property taxes that were abolished by the 1970 Constitution.

Personal property replacement tax notes may not be issued in an amount exceeding 75 percent of the entitlement of replacement taxes for the years anticipated. The entitlement amount must be certified by the director of the Department of Revenue. Personal property replacement tax notes may be issued for the current and next two succeeding calendar years from the time of the issuance of the notes. Notes must have a specific due date not more than 24 months after the date of issuance.

50 ILCS 420/4 et seq.

26:175 What are state aid anticipation certificates?

The school board of any district, by resolution, may borrow against its general state aid entitlement by issuing state aid anticipation certificates. The board may borrow up to 75 percent of its state aid allocation as certified by the State Superintendent of Education, less any funds available for transfer from the district's working cash fund.

However, the total amount of state aid anticipation certificates, general obligation notes, and tax anticipation warrants outstanding for any fiscal year may not exceed 85 percent of the taxes levied by the district for that year. State aid anticipation certificates may be outstanding for no more than 13 months and must be repaid by assigning state aid payments directly to the lender or to a trustee from the regional superintendent.

Proceeds from state aid anticipation certificates may be used only for the purposes set forth in the school board resolution authorizing their issuance.

To deal with the delayed June state aid payment, any district that has reached its maximum short-term indebtedness may borrow up to 100 percent of the state aid payment to be received in July. The certificates must be redeemed no later than August 1 from July state aid payments.

105 ILCS 5/18-8.05
105 ILCS 5/18-18.15
105 ILCS 5/18-18

26:180 What are teachers orders?

Teachers orders are teachers payroll warrants issued by a school district that may be cashed at a bank. By agreement between the school district and the bank, the district will redeem the orders at a future date when tax receipts are received and pay the bank a stipulated rate of interest.

105 ILCS 5/8-16

BOND ISSUES

26:190 What forms of long-term debt is a school board authorized to incur through the issuance of bonds?

A school board may issue bonds as follows:

1) Building and School Site Bonds, with voter approval, for the purchase of a school site; construction of new facilities; equipping the facility; and repairing, remodeling, or adding to an existing facility. School districts participating in vocational education or special education joint agreements may also issue such bonds.

2) Fire Prevention, Safety, Environmental and Energy Conservation Bonds, without voter approval, for the purpose of meeting fire prevention, life-safety, and environmental reasons; to reduce the consumption of energy; for repair of school sidewalks, playgrounds, parking lots, or school bus turnarounds under specified conditions; handicapped accessibility; and/or for school security purposes.

3) Funding Bonds, with voter approval if voters petition for an election (backdoor referendum), to pay for the salaries of teachers or claims against the district when they cannot be paid out of current revenues.

4) Refunding Bonds that are used to pay off outstanding bonds and interest due when funds are not available for payment, or when restructuring of such outstanding bond issues is advantageous to the district.

5) Working Cash Bonds, with voter approval if voters petition for an election (backdoor referendum), for the purpose of creating, recreating or increasing the working cash fund. A district may not issue working cash bonds totaling more than 85 percent of the educational levy, plus 85 percent of the last known Corporate Personal Property Replacement Tax entitlement.

6) Bonds issued without voter approval by a district certified by the State Board of Education as financially distressed.

7) Alternate Bonds require that a revenue source of a specified amount be pledged to the payment of principal and interest, and are subject to a backdoor referendum and are exempt from debt limitation, unless taxes are extended to pay them.

The amount of a public school district's debt is limited by statute.

30 ILCS 350/15
105 ILCS 5/17-2.11
105 ILCS 5/19-1 et seq.
105 ILCS 5/20-1 et seq.

26:200 What is a bond?

A bond is a written certificate or evidence of a debt signed by the president and clerk of the school board to pay a specific sum of money, frequently called the face value, at a fixed time in the future, frequently called the date of maturity, and at a fixed rate of interest.

A bond represents a general obligation of the district. Taxes in an amount necessary to pay principal and interest due each year are extended by the county clerk without regard to the tax rate or amount.

30 ILCS 305/1 et seq.
30 ILCS 345/1 et seq.
105 ILCS 5/17-9
105 ILCS 5/19-2

26:210 What powers do school boards have to borrow money by issuing bonds to pay for real property or improvements?

The powers of school directors and boards of education differ with respect to borrowing money by the issuance of bonds. For the purpose of building or repairing schoolhouses or purchasing or improving school sites, the directors of any school district, when authorized by a majority of the votes cast on such proposition conducted in accordance with the general election law, may borrow money and, as evidence of such indebtedness, may issue bonds, signed by the president and clerk of the board, in denominations of not less than $100 and bearing interest at a rate set by statutory formula.

Any school district governed by a board of education having less than 500,000 inhabitants and not governed by a special Act may borrow money for the purpose of building, equipping, altering, or repairing school buildings; purchasing or improving school sites; acquiring and equipping playgrounds, recreation grounds, athletic fields, and other buildings or land used or useful for school purposes; or for the purpose of purchasing a site, with or without a building or buildings thereon, or for the building of a house or houses on such site, or for the building of a house or houses on the school site of the school district, for residential purposes of the superintendent, principal, or teachers of the school district; and issue its negotiable coupon bonds therefor signed by the president and secretary of the board, in denominations of not less than $100 nor more than $5,000, payable at such place and at such time or times, not exceeding 20 years from the date of issuance (except for bonds issued by a school district as qualified school construction bonds under federal tax law), as the board of education may prescribe, and bearing interest at a rate set by statutory formula, payable annually, semiannually, or quarterly, but no such bonds shall be issued unless the proposition to issue them is submitted to the voters of the district at a referendum held at a regularly scheduled election after the board has certified the proposition to the proper election authorities in accordance with the general election law.

30 ILCS 305/2
105 ILCS 5/19-2
105 ILCS 5/19-3

Wilcoxen v. Board of Education of Canton Union School District No. 66, 116 Ill. App. 3d 380, 452 N.E. 2d 132, 72 Ill. Dec. 200 (3rd Dist. 1980)

Carstens v. East Alton-Wood River Community Unit School District, 27 Ill. 2d 88, 187 N.E. 2d 682 (1963)

26:220 What is the maximum bond interest rate a school board may pay?

The maximum bond interest rate allowable may not exceed the greater of 9 percent per annum or 125 percent of the rate specified in a statutorily designated bond index rate.

30 ILCS 305/2

Bates v. Board of Education, Allendale Community Consolidated School District No. 17, 136 Ill. 2d 260, 555 N.E. 2d 1, 144 Ill. Dec. 104 (1990)

26:230 What is the maximum maturity for a school bond issue?

A school bond issue must have a maturity date not exceeding 20 years from date of issue.

105 ILCS 5/19-3
105 ILCS 5/20-2

26:240 Must a school district abolish its working cash fund to issue working cash fund bonds?

No. A school district may issue working cash fund bonds pursuant to statute in an amount not exceeding in the aggregate 85 percent of the taxes permitted to be levied for educational purposes for the current year plus 85 percent of the school district's personal property replacement tax entitlement. Working cash fund bonds are subject to backdoor referendum.

105 ILCS 5/20-2 et seq.

In re Walgenbach, 104 Ill. 2d 121, 470 N.E. 2d 1015, 83 Ill. Dec. 595 (1984)

26:250 What are tort judgment bonds?

Tort judgment bonds may be used by all types of school districts and the taxes that may be levied for these bonds are not subject to any minimum or maximum rate requirements. Tort judgment bond revenues are used by school districts for the payment of liabilities created by a settlement or a tort judgment, defense costs, to pay liabilities under the Unemployment Insurance Act, Workers' Compensation Act, Occupational Diseases Act, or a risk care management program.

745 ILCS 10/9-105

26:260 May a school board issue bonds to pay teachers orders when the bond issue would exceed the debt limitations established by law?

Bonds issued to pay teachers orders may, when added to other indebtedness of the school district, exceed any statutory debt limit.

105 ILCS 5/19-8

DEBT AND FINANCIAL DIFFICULTY

26:270 What happens when a school board reaches its debt limit?

A school board that has reached its debt limit may continue to incur new debt by issuing orders to pay teachers salaries. Those orders will have first claim on any revenue that becomes available. If funds are not available to cover other types of expenditures, a school board can only take steps to curtail expenditures or increase revenue. The school district cannot close its doors.

Long before a school board's financial situation reaches this point, however, the State Board of Education will intervene and require the local board to adopt a spending plan that is fiscally sound and designed to rid the district of its indebtedness.

105 ILCS 5/1A-8

26:280 When does the State Board of Education determine a school district has financial difficulties?

The State Board of Education, after proper investigation of a school district's financial condition, may certify a district is in financial difficulty when any of the following conditions occur:

1) The district has issued school or teachers orders for wages;

2) The district has issued tax anticipation warrants or tax anticipation notes in anticipation of a second year's taxes when warrants or notes in anticipation of current year taxes are still outstanding or has issued short-term debt against two future revenue sources, such as, but not limited to, tax anticipation warrants and general state aid certificates or tax anticipation warrants and revenue anticipation notes;

3) The district has for two consecutive years shown an excess of expenditures and other financing uses over revenues and other financing sources and beginning fund balances on its annual financial report for the aggregate totals of the educational, operations and maintenance, transportation, and working cash funds;

4) The district refuses to provide financial information or cooperate with the State Superintendent in an investigation of the district's financial condition.

No school district is deemed to be in financial difficulty solely by reason of any of the above circumstances arising as a result of the failure of the county to make any distribution of property tax money due the district at the time such distribution is due; or the failure of the state to make timely state aid (evidence-based funding or categorical payments), or if the district clearly demonstrates to the satisfaction of the State Board of Education at the time of its determination that such condition no longer exists.

The State Board of Education is empowered to require school districts in financial difficulty to develop, adopt, and submit a financial plan within 45 days after certification of financial difficulty. The financial plan must be developed according to guidelines presented to the district by the State Board of Education within 14 days of certification. The guidelines address the specific nature of each district's financial difficulties. Any proposed budget of the district must be consistent with the financial plan approved by the State Board.

A district certified to be in financial difficulty must report to the State Board of Education at such times and in such manner as the State Board may direct concerning the district's compliance with each financial plan. The State Board may review the district's operations, obtain budgetary data and financial statements, require the district to produce reports, and have access to any other information in the possession of the district that it deems relevant. The State Board may issue recommendations or directives within its powers to the district to assure compliance with the financial plan. The district must produce such budgetary data, financial statements, reports, and other information and comply with such directives.

105 ILCS 5/1A-8

105 ILCS 5/1F-1 et seq.

105 ILCS 5/1H-1 et seq.

Innovative Modular Solutions v. Hazel Crest School District No. 152.5, 2012 IL 112052, 965 N.E. 2d 414, 358 Ill. Dec. 343

26:290 Does the State Superintendent have authority to investigate a school district's finances?

The State Superintendent of Education may require a school district to share financial information relevant to a proper investigation of the district's financial condition and the delivery of appropriate state financial, technical, and consulting services to the district if the district has been designated, through the State Board of Education's School District Financial Profile System, as on financial warning or financial watch status; or has failed to file an annual financial report, annual budget, deficit reduction plan, or other financial information as required by law; or has been identified, through the district's annual audit or other financial and management information, as in serious financial difficulty in the current or next school year.

105 ILCS 5/1A-8

27: ILLINOIS HIGH SCHOOL ASSOCIATION

27:10 What is the IHSA?

IHSA is the Illinois High School Association, a voluntary association of Illinois public and private high schools. Unlike the National Collegiate Athletic Association (NCAA), the IHSA operates under color of state law and is a state actor for purposes of civil rights suits. The IHSA is not a public body for purposes of the Freedom of Information Act or the Open Meetings Act.

105 ILCS 25/1 et seq.

http://ihsa.org/AbouttheIHSA/ConstitutionBylawsPolicies.aspx

Better Government Association v. Illinois High School Association, 2017 IL 121124, __ N.E. __, __ Ill. Dec. __

Brentwood Academy v. Tennessee Secondary School Athletic Association, 121 S. Ct. 924, 531 U.S. 288, 148 L. Ed. 2d 807 (2001)

Libby by Libby v. South Interconference Association, 728 F. Supp. 504 (N.D. Ill. 1990)

NCAA v. Tarkanian, 109 S. Ct. 454, 488 U.S. 197, 102 L. Ed. 2d 469 (1988)

Griffin v. Illinois High School Association, 822 F. 2d 671 (7th Cir. 1987)

Menora v. Illinois High School Association, 683 F. 2d 1030 (7th Cir. 1982) cert. den. 103 S. Ct. 801, 459 U.S. 1156, 74 L. Ed. 2d 1003 (1983)

Bucha v. Illinois High School Association, 351 F. Supp. 69 (N.D. Ill. 1972)

Robinson v. Illinois High School Association, 45 Ill. App. 2d 277, 195 N.E. 2d 38 (2nd Dist. 1963) cert. den. 85 S. Ct. 647, 379 U.S. 960, 13 L. Ed. 2d 555 (1965)

Sanders v. Louisiana High School Athletic Association, 242 So. 2d 19 (La. App. 19 70)

27:20 How is the IHSA organized?

The IHSA is governed by a board of 10 directors who are elected to office by the principals of the secondary schools that belong to the IHSA. The state is divided into seven geographical regions and one director from among the high school principals in each region is elected from each region. In addition, three directors are elected at-large. One of the at-large members must be a racial minority and one must be a member of the underrepresented gender, and one must be a member of a private/non-public school.

IHSA Const. art. 1.310 et seq.

27:30 Can the IHSA regulate high school athletic eligibility by the adoption of rules regulating amateur status, extracurricular participation, attendance, transfer, and receipt of benefit?

Yes.

Gaines v. National Collegiate Athletic Association, 746 F. Supp. 738 (M.D. Tenn. 1990)

Banks v. National Collegiate Athletic Association, 746 F. Supp. 850 (N.D. Ind. 1990)

Shelton v. National Collegiate Athletic Association, 539 F. 2d 1196 (9th Cir. 1976)

27:35 May a school or student be punished by the IHSA if a court order sought by the student or school against the IHSA is vacated?

If a student, or a member school otherwise in non-compliance with IHSA rules, participates in an interscholastic contest in accordance with a restraining order, injunction, or other court order against the IHSA or a member school and the order or injunction expires without final determination or is vacated, stayed, reversed, modified, or found to have been entered in error, the contests in which the student participated are subject to forfeit and the school and student are subject to IHSA sanctions.

IHSA By-law 6.022

IHSA By-law 6.023

STANDARDS FOR SCHOOLS

27:40 How is a school's size determined for purposes of its placement in the IHSA classification system?

IHSA's classification system has been controversial and has undergone frequent change. A school's class placement is determined by its student enrollment as reported on September 30 of the preceding school year to the State Board of Education in its Fall Housing Report. A multiplier of 1.65 is applied to all non-boundaried schools. Under specified circumstances a high school's enrollment is subject to adjustment and certain waivers are possible. Member schools may petition the IHSA to play up in classification.

A school may request a classification variance by submitting a request for any given year to the executive director no later than April 1. Variances may be granted for verifiable decreases in enrollment equaling 20 percent or more or when a high school houses out-of-district special education students.

IHSA Administrative Procedures, Guidelines and Policies 18

27:45 What is a non-boundaried school?

A non-boundaried school is any private school, charter school, lab school, magnet school, residential school, and any public school in a multi-high school district that does not accept students from a fixed portion of the district.

IHSA By-law 2.160

27:50 May private or parochial schools become IHSA members?

Private or parochial high schools may be admitted to membership in the IHSA provided the school's financial assistance program complies with IHSA standards and the school complies with all other applicable membership rules. IHSA rules require that financial assistance by parochial or private schools be provided only in cases of economic need or on the basis of academic performance and may not be related to athletic interest or performance.

IHSA Const. art. 1.210
IHSA Const. art. 1.250

27:60 Under what conditions may high schools field cooperative athletic teams or activity programs?

Two or more public high schools may form cooperative athletic teams or activity programs upon approval of the IHSA Board of Directors, provided:

1) The schools are located in the same geographical area;

2) All schools participating in the cooperative are IHSA Class A (in a two-class system) or class 1A or 2A (in a three- or four-class system) schools or, in the event one or more of the cooperating schools is a Class 3A or 4A public school, the cooperative team is for a sport other than boys football or boys or girls basketball. In the event one of the schools involved in the cooperative is a public non-boundary school, that school's actual enrollment, not the multiplied enrollment, is used to determine the eligibility of the cooperative team request; and

3) The cooperative agreement is established for a period of two consecutive years, is approved by the governing boards of all the participating schools, and a joint application is submitted to the IHSA.

Private schools with non-multiplied enrollments of 200 or less also are eligible to form cooperative teams.

The combined enrollment of all the schools involved in a cooperative determines the IHSA classification of the cooperative team.

IHSA By-law 2.030

27:70 Under what circumstances may cooperative agreements be extended?

After completion of two years of approved operation, continuation of the cooperative agreement requires timely notice to the IHSA that will permit the cooperative team to participate for a period of another two years provided the cooperative team continues in its original format with no changes. The cooperative must reapply to the IHSA.

IHSA By-law 2.030

27:80 Under what circumstances are teams eligible to compete in IHSA tournaments?

To be eligible to compete in IHSA meets or tournaments, an established school team must have engaged in at least six interscholastic contests in the sport during the current season (or during the preceding IHSA season in the case of boys baseball, boys golf, boys tennis, girls softball, girls golf, and girls tennis).

Girls participating on a boys team will not satisfy the requirement for entry of a girls team in the state meet, but a girls team competing against boys teams will count toward the six-contest requirement.

IHSA By-law 3.054

27:90 If an IHSA member school participates in an event with a school from another state, or a school not governed by IHSA rules, which rules apply to the event?

IHSA members must abide by IHSA rules in all athletic and non-athletic contests and activities whether with members or non-members of the IHSA. Waiver of eligibility rules is possible only by the IHSA Board of Directors.

IHSA By-law 2.010

27:100 May a school team practice or compete during a teacher strike at the school?

A school that does not have 51 percent of its students in attendance during a strike and that cannot offer a minimum program pursuant to State Board of

Education rules and regulations may not engage in interscholastic activities. The school may host an activity in which the school on strike does not engage.

Practice sessions may be held if they are approved by the local board of education; conducted by personnel meeting IHSA supervision rules; and are conducted in a manner that assures the health and safety of participants. Students from a school on strike may not participate with a team from a school that is not on strike.

The 51 percent rule is applicable to strike situations only and does not prevent interscholastic activities on the same day a school is closed because of holiday, vacation, or emergency day provided school is in full operation on the preceding school day.

IHSA By-law 2.140

IHSA Administrative Procedures, Guidelines and Policies, Number 6

Proulx by Proulx v. Illinois High School Association, 125 Ill. App. 3d 781, 466 N.E. 2d 620, 81 Ill. Dec. 34 (4th Dist. 1984)

SPORTSMANSHIP

27:110 Are there IHSA rules governing sportsmanship?

Yes. Persons found to be in gross violation of the ethics of competition or the principles of good sportsmanship may be barred by the Board of Directors from athletic contests or interscholastic activities.

IHSA By-law 3.141

IHSA By-law 4.061

27:120 May the IHSA penalize a school for unsportsmanlike conduct?

The IHSA executive director has authority to penalize an individual or a school for unsportsmanlike conduct.

IHSA By-law 2.041

IHSA By-law 6.00 et seq.

27:122 What penalty does the IHSA impose if a player is ejected from a game?

If a player is ejected for unsportsmanlike conduct, he or she is ineligible for the next interscholastic contest at that level of competition and all other contests at any level in the interim in addition to any other penalties his or her school or the IHSA may impose.

IHSA By-law 6.011

27:124 What penalty does the IHSA impose if a coach is ejected from a game?

If a coach is ejected for unsportsmanlike conduct, he or she is ineligible for the next interscholastic contest at that level of competition and all other contests at any level in the interim in addition to any other penalties his or her school or the IHSA may impose.

IHSA By-law 6.012

STUDENT ELIGIBILITY

27:130 Does a student have a constitutional right to participate in public school interscholastic activities?

There is no recognized constitutional right to participate in athletics. A student may, however, raise legitimate constitutional issues in the context of a claim addressing a ruling on eligibility by implicating, for example, a constitutionally protected property right, alleging that a particular rule disadvantages a suspect class, or by framing a breach of contract claim.

Monts ex rel. Monts v. Illinois High School Association, 338 Ill. App. 3d 1099, 789 N.E. 2d 413, 273 Ill. Dec. 513 (4th Dist. 2003)

Jordan by Edwards v. O'Fallon Township High School District No. 203 Board of Education, 302 Ill. App. 3d 1070, 706 N.E. 2d 137, 235 Ill. Dec. 877 (5th Dist. 1999)

Kulovitz v. Illinois High School Association, 462 F. Supp. 875 (N.D. Ill. 1978)

Board of Curators v. Horowitz, 98 S. Ct. 948, 435 U.S. 78, 55 L. Ed. 2d 725 (1975)

Colorado Seminary (University of Denver) v. NCAA, 570 F. 2d 320 (10th Cir. 1978)

Bucha v. Illinois High School Association, 351 F. Supp. 69 (N.D. Ill. 1972)

Mitchell v. Louisiana High School Association, 430 F. 2d 1155 (5th Cir. 1970)

27:140 Does an athlete have a cause of action against the IHSA if his or her school is penalized for rules violations and as a result the athlete is unable to compete?

Athletes have attempted to bring lawsuits against the National Collegiate Athletic Association (NCAA) on the premise that a penalty against their school for violation of an NCAA rule has denied them some benefit to which they were otherwise entitled. Usually, the lawsuit alleges violation of a property right, such as loss of opportunity to obtain a professional contract, or an equal protection argument alleging the penalties disproportionately affect some suspect classification of persons. The courts have held that such claims brought by athletes do not rise to the level of a constitutional right invoking due process requirements in connection with an athletic association's imposition of sanctions against a school.

Hawkins v. National Collegiate Athletic Association, 652 F. Supp. 602 (C.D. Ill. 1987)

Justice v. National Collegiate Athletic Association, 577 F. Supp. 356 (N.D. Ariz. 1983)

Colorado Seminary (University of Denver) v. National Collegiate Athletic Association, 570 F. 2d 320 (10th Cir. 1978)

Parish v. National Collegiate Athletic Association, 506 F. 2d 1028 (5th Cir. 1975)

27:150 May graduates or other unattached athletes compete in high school athletic contests?

No.

IHSA By-law 3.023

IHSA By-law 3.050 et seq.

27:160 May a student participate and be eligible in more than one sport at the same time?

Yes.

IHSA By-law 3.050 et seq.

27:170 When are physical examinations required for participation in athletics?

A school must have on file for each student who participates (including practice) in interscholastic athletics a certificate of physical fitness issued by a licensed physician not more than one year preceding practice or participation in any interscholastic athletic contest or activity.

IHSA By-law 2.150

27:175 What is required when an athlete suffers a concussion?

The School Code includes mandatory concussion protocols when a student-athlete suffers a concussion. There are also mandatory educational requirements for athletic trainers.

105 ILCS 5/22-80

27:180 Is a student physical examination by a chiropractor or by spiritual means sufficient for athletic eligibility?

Not unless the spiritual advisor or chiropractor is licensed in Illinois to practice medicine in all its branches.

IHSA By-law 2.150

27:185 Is drug testing of athletes required by the IHSA?

A 2009 law (P.A. 96-132), which was repealed on July 1, 2011, required the Illinois High School Association (IHSA) to enforce a drug-testing program. The law required the IHSA to prohibit a student from participating in an athletic competition sponsored or sanctioned by the IHSA. The IHSA adopted a policy mirroring the requirements of the law and the policy continues in effect. It requires that the following conditions are met:

1) The student agrees not to use any performance-enhancing substances on the IHSA's most current banned drug classes list, and, if the student is enrolled in high school, the student submits to random testing for the presence of these substances in the student's body; and

2) The IHSA obtains from the student's parent a statement signed by the parent and acknowledging that the parent's child, if enrolled in high school, may be subject to random performance-enhancing substance testing; that Illinois law prohibits possessing, dispensing, delivering, or administering a performance-enhancing substance in a manner not allowed by law; that Illinois law provides that bodybuilding, muscle enhancement, or the increase of muscle bulk or strength through the use of a performance-enhancing substance by a person who is in good health is not a valid medical purpose; that only a licensed practitioner with prescriptive authority may prescribe a performance-enhancing substance for a person; and that a violation of law concerning performance-enhancing substances is a criminal offense punishable by confinement in jail or imprisonment.

The IHSA must require that each athletic coach for an extracurricular athletic activity sponsored or sanctioned by the IHSA at or above the 9th-grade level complete an educational program on the prevention of abuse of performance-enhancing substances developed by the IHSA and must require the person to complete an exam developed by the IHSA showing a minimum proficiency of understanding in methods to prevent the abuse of performance-enhancing substances by students.

The Department of Public Health (DPH) provides oversight of the annual administration of a performance-enhancing substance testing program by the IHSA under which high school students participating in an athletic competition sponsored or sanctioned by the IHSA are tested at multiple times throughout the athletic season for the presence of performance-enhancing substances. The IHSA may alter its then current performance-enhancing substance testing program to comply with this subsection. The testing program, by law, must do the following:

1) Require the random testing of at least 1,000 high school students in this state who participate in athletic competitions sponsored or sanctioned by the association;

2) Provide for the selection of specific students for testing through a process that randomly selects students from a single pool consisting of all students who participate in any activity for which the IHSA sponsors or sanctions athletic competitions;

3) Be administered at approximately 25 percent of the high schools in Illinois that participate in athletic competitions sponsored or sanctioned by the IHSA;

4) Provide for a process for confirming any initial positive test result through a subsequent test conducted as soon as practicable after the initial test, using a sample that was obtained at the same time as the sample used for the initial test;

5) Require the testing to be performed only by a performance-enhancing substance testing laboratory with current certification from the Substance Abuse and Mental Health Services Administration of the United States Department of Health and Human Services, the World Anti-Doping Agency, or another appropriate national or international certifying organization; the testing laboratory must be chosen following state procurement procedures;

6) Require that a trained observer, of the appropriate sex, witness the student provide the test sample;

7) Require that the student be chaperoned by a school-designated official from the time he or she is notified of the test until he or she has completed delivering the test sample;

8) Provide for a period of ineligibility from participation in an athletic competition sponsored or sanctioned by the IHSA for any student with a confirmed positive test result or any student who refuses to submit to random testing;

9) Provide for a school or team penalty on a case-by-case basis, to be determined by the contribution of a student with a confirmed positive test result to the team or the school's lack of enforcement of the rules of the testing program or both;

10) Provide for a penalty for any coach who knowingly violates the rules of the testing program; and

11) Require that coaches be responsible for providing a copy of the association's most current banned drug classes list to every high school student participating in an athletic competition sponsored or sanctioned by the IHSA.

Results of a performance-enhancing substance tests are confidential and, unless required by court order, may be disclosed only to the student and the student's parent and the activity directors, principal, and assistant principals of the school attended by the student.

The prohibition does not apply to the use by a student of a performance-enhancing substance that is dispensed, prescribed, delivered, or administered by a medical practitioner for a valid medical purpose and in the course of professional practice, and the student is not subject to a period of ineligibility on the basis of that use as long as the student's coach has provided the student with a copy of IHSA's most current banned drug classes list, the student has consulted with his or her medical practitioner to confirm the valid use of the substance, and the student has notified his or her coach or a school administrator of a prescription for the use of the substance for valid medical purposes. Students that are prescribed such a substance, after receiving a copy of IHSA's most current banned drug classes list, are required to provide notice of that prescription at the time the prescription is issued. Any information concerning a student's use of a performance-enhancing substance obtained by a coach or school administrator is confidential and may be disclosed only to those persons necessary to the determination of eligibility.

The law relieves the IHSA and its directors or employees from liability for damages in connection with the performance of the IHSA's responsibilities under the law unless an act or omission involved willful or wanton conduct.

IHSA Administrative Procedures, Guidelines and Policies, Number 23

27:190 What attendance requirements affect a student's IHSA athletic eligibility?

A student must attend a school and may only represent in interscholastic competition the school the student attends. "Attend" means the student is enrolled at the school, and is taking at, or under arrangements approved by the school, a minimum of 20 credit hours of work for which credit toward high school graduation will be granted by the school upon the student's completing and passing the courses. The school that enrolls the student is exclusively responsible to verify the student's compliance with all of the eligibility requirements of all IHSA rules.

The IHSA Board of Directors has discretion to waive the attendance requirement for the Illinois schools for the deaf or blind. In unit systems having a 6-3-3 or 6-4-2 type of organization, 9th- grade students may participate on senior high school athletic teams at the member high school in the district designated by the board of education, provided:

1) Such participation is approved by the district's superintendent of schools;

2) The senior high school principal certifies the 9th-grade students are eligible under IHSA rules, are students at a junior high school located in the district that supports the senior high school, and are not members of a grade or junior high school team in the same sport; and,

3) The senior high school principal assumes full responsibility for the conduct of these students during all athletic contests in which they represent the senior high school.

Only bona fide students of a member school may participate in a practice session for any interscholastic team sponsored by a member school.

A student must be enrolled and in attendance not later than the beginning of the 11th school day of the semester. Exception may be considered only if written verification that delay in enrollment or attendance is caused by illness of the student or his or her immediate family or by other circumstances deemed acceptable by the board of directors.

Including a student's name on school attendance records for a period of 10 or more school days during any given semester, beginning with the date of the student's first physical attendance and ending with the date of the student's official withdrawal from school, is considered a semester of attendance.

If a student does not attend school for 10 days in a semester, but participates in any interscholastic athletic activity, the student is considered to have completed a semester of attendance, unless withdrawal from school occurs prior to completion of 10 days' attendance and is necessitated by disabling illness or injury that is certified by a physician.

A student may not have any lapse of school connection during any given semester of greater than 10 consecutive school days. Lapse of school connection for greater than 10 consecutive school days shall render the student ineligible for the remainder of the semester. Exceptions may be considered only if written verification that lapse in school connection is caused by illness of the student or his or her immediate family or by other circumstances deemed acceptable to the board of directors.

The absence of a student required by military service to state or nation in the time of any state of national emergency does not affect the student's eligibility.

IHSA By-law 3.011

IHSA By-Law 3.132

IHSA By-law 4.011

Spath v. National Collegiate Athletic Association, 728 F. 2d 25 (1st Cir. 1984)

27:192 Is a home-schooled student eligible to compete in IHSA-sanctioned events?

The relevant IHSA bylaw provides that a student is not eligible "unless the student is enrolled in a school and is taking courses at, or under arrangements approved by the member school, a minimum of 25 credit hours of work for which credit toward high school graduation will be granted by the member school upon the student's completing and passing the courses."

IHSA By-law 3.011

IHSA By-law 4.011

Kaptien v. Conrad School District, 931 P. 2d 1311 (Mont. 1997)

Bradstreet v. Sobol, 650 N.Y.S. 2d 402 (1996)

27:196 Are handicapped students eligible to compete in interscholastic activities?

A child's access to participation in extracurricular activities (including athletics) is protected by Section 504. In January 2013, the U.S. Department of Education Office for Civil Rights issued a guidance letter suggesting that "students with disabilities are not being afforded an equal opportunity to participate in extracurricular athletics in public elementary and secondary schools."

29 U.S.C. 701 et seq.

www.gao.gov/assets/310/305770.pdf

www2.ed.gov/about/offices/list/ocr/letters/colleague-201301-504.html

27:200 How do attendance requirements differ for IHSA programs involving activities other than athletics?

The only differences are for music programs. The IHSA allows grade school or junior high school students to participate with high school musical organizations or ensembles in interscholastic music activities. Joint music curricular programs involving two or more schools are also permitted.

IHSA By-law 4.017 et seq.

27:210 May a student who is absent from school because of illness on the day of an IHSA event participate in the event?

Provided there is no local school rule preventing participation, the student may compete. There is no IHSA rule or bylaw requiring that a student attend school on the day he or she competes in an IHSA event.

27:220 In order to retain IHSA eligibility, what academic requirements must a student meet?

To retain IHSA eligibility, a student must be doing passing work in at least 25 credit hours of high school work per week. Except in the case of a student entering high school for the first time, a student must have received credit for 25 hours of high school work for the previous semester. The work must have been completed in the semester for which credit is granted or in a recognized summer school program that has been approved by the local board of education and for which graduation credit is received. Under narrowly specified circumstances, a student may be granted a waiver reducing the credit hour requirement to 20 hours.

Passing work is defined as work of a grade that if on any given date the student would transfer to another school, passing grades for the course would be certified on the student's transcript to the school to which the student transfers.

Work taken in a junior college, college, university or by correspondence may be accepted for meeting eligibility requirements provided the work is recognized as credit toward graduation from high school by the local board of education.

To retain eligibility, the student must not have graduated from any four-year high school or its equivalent.

IHSA By-law 3.021 et seq.

IHSA By-law 4.021 et seq.

IHSA Administrative Procedures Guidelines and Policies 7

Texas Education Agency v. Stamos, 817 S.W. 2d 378 (Tex. Ct. App. 1991)

Associated Students, Inc. of California State University-Sacramento, et al. v. National Collegiate Athletic Association, 493 F. 2d 1251 (9th Cir. 1974)

Howard University v. National Collegiate Athletic Association, 367 F. Supp. 926 (D.C. D.C. 1973)

27:230 When is eligibility regained after a student has been academically ineligible for a semester?

A student who has been academically ineligible for a semester does not regain eligibility (after satisfactory academic performance) until the first day of the next semester.

IHSA By-law 3.020 et seq.

27:240 What residence requirements affect IHSA athletic eligibility for public school students?

A student is eligible if the student resides full time with his or her parents, custodial parent, or guardian appointed by a judge of a court having jurisdiction; or he or she currently and for the last two years prior to the student's enrolling in high school has lived with another family member or relative who has provided full support and adult supervision for the student as though the family member or relative was the guardian; and the student and the family member or relative live within the boundaries of the attendance area of the high school he or she attends; or the student resides or has attended a minimum of the 7th and 8th grades as a tuition-paying nonresident student in the district in which the high school he or she attends is located; or the student resides full-time with one birth or adoptive parent without assignment of custody or legal guardianship by a court, provided their residence is in the district in which the member school they attend is located and they attended that member school the previous school term. When the State Board of Education grants a waiver for a child of a faculty member to attend a school tuition-free, the student has eligibility at the school where the parent teaches.

In all other cases, the student cannot participate without a ruling by the executive director.

IHSA By-law 3.031 et seq.

IHSA Administrative Procedures, Guidelines and Policies, Number 1

Howard University v. National Collegiate Athletic Association, 367 F. Supp. 926 (D.C. D.C. 1973)

27:242 What residence requirements affect IHSA athletic eligibility for private school students?

A private school student is eligible at the high school in which he or she enrolls provided the student resides full-time with parents, custodial parent, or guardian appointed by a judge of a court having jurisdiction; or he or she currently and for the last two years prior to the student's enrolling in high school has lived with another family member or relative who has provided full support and adult supervision for the student as though the family member or relative was the guardian; and the student and the family member or relative live within the school district in which the high school he or she attends is located; and

1) Within the boundaries of the public school district in which the private high school he or she attends is located;

2) He or she has attended private schools on a continuous basis for the last two consecutive school years before entering high school or for a total of not less than four school years from kindergarten through 8th grade;

3) He or she attends the private member school attended by one or both of his or her parents; or

4) He or she attends a private member school within a 30-mile radius of his or her residence as defined above.

All other residency cases involving students who properly reside full time with a parent or guardian require an eligibility ruling by the executive director.

IHSA By-law 3.032 et seq.

27:244 What residence requirements affect IHSA athletic eligibility for students who attend public schools without boundaries?

A student attending a public member school that does not have a geographical boundary is eligible at the school in which he or she enrolls provided the student resides full time with parents, custodial parent or guardian appointed by a judge of a court having jurisdiction, or he or she currently and for the last two years prior to the student's enrolling in high school has lived with another family member or relative who has provided full support and adult supervision for the student as though the family member or relative was the guardian; and the student and the family member or relative live within the school district in which the high school he or she attends is located; and

1) Within the boundaries of the public high school district in which the non-boundaried public high school he or she attends is located;

2) He or she has attended non-boundaried public schools or private schools on a continuous basis for the last two consecutive school years before entering high school or for a total of not less than four school years from K-8 grade;

3) He or she attends the non-boundaried public school attended by one or both of his or her parents or the current spouse of one of his or her parents; or

4) He or she attends a non-boundaried public member school within a 30-mile radius of his or her residence as defined above.

All other residency cases involving students who properly reside full time with a parent or guardian require an eligibility ruling by the executive director.

IHSA By-law 3.033 et seq.

27:246 Under what conditions are foreign exchange students eligible?

Foreign exchange students enrolled in IHSA-approved student exchange programs and attending school in Illinois are eligible for a maximum period of one calendar year beginning with the date of their enrollment and initial attendance at an IHSA school. To be considered for approval, a foreign exchange program must assign students to schools by a method that insures that no student, school, or other interested party may influence the assignment for athletic or other purposes.

IHSA By-law 3.034.3

IHSA Administrative Procedures, Guidelines and Policies, Numbers 4-5

27:247 Is a student ineligible if his or her parents move during the student's senior year?

A student who has attended the same school for his or her entire high school career, and whose parents, custodial parent, or court-appointed guardian move from the district or community traditionally served by that school following the student's completion of 11th grade, may remain in the member school and retain eligibility regarding residence for the 12th grade, provided the student obtains the approval of the school's governing body and there is no evidence of undue influence to retain the attendance of the student and provided

1) The student, if not yet 18 years of age, resides full-time with the parents, a custodial parent, a non-custodial birth parent or a court appointed legal guardian; or the student, if 18 years of age, continues to reside with parents, custodial parent, a non-custodial birth parent or a court appointed legal guardian, or is accepted for enrollment by the school as a student having reached the age of majority under the laws of the state of Illinois;

2) Such attendance is approved by the board of education or local governing board of the school; and,

3) There is no evidence of undue influence, including but not limited to inducement, remuneration, pressure, promise or provision of special benefits, or any other form of encouragement or persuasion, on the part of any person(s) directly or indirectly connected to the school, to retain the student's attendance.

IHSA By-law 3.034.2

Tennessee Secondary School Athletic Association v. Brentwood Academy, 127 S. Ct. 2489, 551 U.S. 291, 168 L. Ed. 2d 166, (2007)

Monts ex rel. Monts v. Illinois High School Association, 338 Ill. App. 3d 1099, 789 N.E. 2d 413, 273 Ill. Dec. 513 (4th Dist. 2003)

27:248 What eligibility rules apply to special or vocational education students?

A student taking part of his or her work at a special or vocational education center and taking the remaining portion of his or her work at his or her home high school is eligible at the home high school only. A student who takes all of his or her work at a special center may make an eligibility election. Once the election of eligibility at the special center or the home school is made, however, the election may not be changed without loss of eligibility not to exceed one calendar year.

IHSA By-law 3.034.4 et seq.

27:250 What transfer rules affect a student's IHSA athletic eligibility?

The IHSA has complicated transfer rules that have changed frequently over time. The transfer rules consider the child's residence and the residence of his or her parent(s) and guardians as well as changes in the family's financial position and extenuating circumstances.

IHSA By-law 3.040 et seq.

IHSA Administrative Procedures, Guidelines and Policies, Number 1

Tennessee Secondary School Athletic Association v. Brentwood Academy, 127 S. Ct. 2489, 551 U.S. 291, 168 L. Ed. 2d 166, (2007)

Monts ex rel. Monts v. Illinois High School Association, 338 Ill. App. 3d 1099, 789 N.E. 2d 413, 273 Ill. Dec. 513 (4th Dist. 2003)

Beck v. Missouri State High School Activities Association, 837 F. Supp. 998 (E.D. Mo. 1993)

Crane by Crane v. Indiana High School Athletic Association, 975 F. 2d 1315 (7th Cir. 1992)

Griffin High School v. Illinois High School Association, 822 F. 2d. 671 (7th Cir. 1987)

Kulovitz v. Illinois High School Association, 462 F. Supp. 875 (N.D. Ill. 1978)

27:260 What is the age limitation for athletic eligibility?

A student is eligible through age 19, except that if the student will turn 20 during a sport season, his or her eligibility terminates on the first day of the sport season in which he or she will become 20.

IHSA By-law 3.061

Baisden v. West Virginia Secondary Schools Activities Commission, 568 S.E. 32 (W.Va. 2002)

Butts v. NCAA, LaSalle University, 751 F. 2d 609 (3rd Cir. 1984)

Robinson v. Illinois High School Association, 45 Ill. App. 2d 277, 195 N.E. 2d 38 (2nd Dist. 1963) cert. den. 85 S. Ct. 647, 379 U.S. 960, 13 L. Ed. 2d 555 (1965)

27:262 Does the eligibility age limit discriminate against disabled athletes by denying them eligibility?

The age limit requirement probably does not violate either Section 504 of the Rehabilitation Act or the Americans with Disabilities Act. The IHSA age limit is an essential eligibility requirement that has a legitimate purpose in an interscholastic program. Reasonable accommodation does not require an institution to "lower or to effect substantial modification of standards to accommodate a handicapped person."

Baisden v. West Virginia Secondary Schools Activities Commission, 568 S.E. 32 (W.Va. 2002)

Pottgen v. Missouri State High School Activities Association, 40 F. 3d 926 (8th Cir. 1994)

27:270 How does the age limit differ for interscholastic activities other than athletics?

A student may participate in non-athletic activities through age 19.

IHSA By-law 4.041

Robinson v. Illinois High School Association, 45 Ill. App. 2d 277, 195 N.E. 2d 38 (2nd Dist. 1963) cert. den. 85 S. Ct. 647, 379 U.S. 960, 13 L. Ed. 2d 555 (1965)

27:280 How many semesters of athletic eligibility may a student have?

After a student enrolls in the ninth grade, the student is eligible for no more than eight semesters and no more than four school years of competition in any sport. The last two semesters of eligibility must be consecutive; other semesters of eligibility need not be consecutive.

IHSA By-law 3.051 et seq.

Spath v. National Collegiate Athletic Association, 728 F. 2d 25 (1st Cir. 1984)

27:290 How do the semesters of eligibility rules differ for students enrolled in activities other than athletics?

Students participating in interscholastic activities other than athletics need not use their last two semesters of eligibility consecutively, nor do the six-contest rules applicable to team sports apply.

IHSA By-law 4.030 et seq.

BOYS AND GIRLS TEAMS

27:300 Are gender-based rule classifications subject to strict scrutiny?

A classification based on sex is a suspect classification under Illinois law, which, to be held valid, must withstand strict judicial scrutiny. This means that the state must show a compelling state interest to meet the strict scrutiny standard. Gender-based classifications are not a suspect classification under federal constitutional law, and to meet the federal standard such classifications need only serve important governmental objectives and must be substantially related to achievement of those objectives.

Ill. Const. art. I, sec. 18

Craig v. Boren, 97 S. Ct. 451, 429 U.S. 190, 50 L. Ed. 2d 397 (1976)

People v. Ellis, 57 Ill. 2d 127, 311 N.E. 2d 98 (1974)

In re Griffiths, 93 S. Ct. 2851, 413 U.S. 717, 37 L. Ed. 2d 397 (1973)

27:305 May a school eliminate a sport in order to make its total athletic program comply with sex equity rules?

In order to prevail in a suit challenging the elimination of a sport from an educational institution's menu of sports, the plaintiff must show that exclusion from participation in or denial of access to benefits of the athletic program were based on gender, rather than some other legitimate purpose.

Boulahanis v. Board of Regents, 198 F. 3d 633 (7th Cir. 1999)

Gonyo v. Drake University, 837 F. Supp. 989 (S.D. Ia. 1993)

27:307 What factors are considered in determining whether a school has given boys and girls equal opportunities to participate in athletics in compliance with Title IX?

Title IX provides that no person shall be excluded "from participation in, be denied the benefits of, or be subjected to discrimination under any education program or activity receiving federal financial assistance." Federal regulations cover interscholastic teams, clubs, and intramural athletics. They require a school district to "provide equal athletic opportunity for members of both sexes."

In determining whether or not a program is compliant, the U.S. Department of Education considers the following:

1) Whether the selection of sports and levels of competition effectively accommodate the interests and abilities of members of both sexes;

2) The provision of equipment and supplies;

3) Scheduling of games and practice time;

4) Travel and per diem allowance;

5) Opportunity to receive coaching and academic tutoring;

6) Assignment and compensation of coaches and tutors;

7) Provision of locker rooms and practice and competitive facilities;

8) Provision of medical and training facilities and services;

9) Provision of housing and dining facilities and services; and

10) Publicity.

The first factor focuses on accommodation (known as effective accommodation claims) and the remaining factors focus on denial of equivalence in other athletic benefits (known as equal treatment claims). Effective accommodation claims concern the opportunity to participate in athletics, while equal treatment claims allege sex-based differences in the schedules, equipment, coaching, and other factors affecting participants in athletics.

A claimant must allege a systemic, substantial disparity that amounts to a denial of equal opportunity. Disadvantaging one sex in one part of a school's athletic program can be offset by a comparable advantage to that sex in another area.

20 U.S.C. 1681(a)

34 C.F.R. 106.41(a)

34 C.F.R. 106.41(c)

Parker v. Franklin County Community School Corporation, 667 F. 3d 910 (7th Cir. 2012)

Mansourian v. Regents of University of California, 602 F. 3d 957 (9th Cir. 2010)

Communities for Equity v. Michigan Athletic Association, 178 F. Supp. 2d 805 (W.D. Mich. 2001)

Cohen v. Brown University, 879 F. Supp. 185 (D.C. R.I. 1995)

27:310 May a girl compete in a state tournament on a boys athletic team?

Yes, if the following conditions are met:

1) The member school is in compliance with Illinois Sex Equity Rules; and

2) The only team in the sport at the school is a boys team; and the girl participates on the boys team in that sport during the regular season.

Ill. Const. art. I, sec. 18

105 ILCS 5/27-1

IHSA Affirmative Action Policy for Girls on Boys State Series Teams Number 31

27:320 May a boy compete in a state tournament on a girls athletic team?

No.

IHSA Affirmative Action Policy for Girls on Boys State Series Teams Number 31

Petrie v. Illinois High School Association, et al., 75 Ill. App. 3d 980, 394 N.E. 2d 855, 31 Ill. Dec. 653 (4th Dist. 1979)

Massachusetts Interscholastic Athletic Association and Gomes v. Rhode Island Interscholastic League, 469 F. Supp. 659 (D.C. R.I. 1979)

27:330 Does the IHSA regulate regular-season participation of girls on boys teams or boys on girls teams?

No. IHSA rules address only eligibility for the state tournament series.

IHSA Affirmative Action Policy for Girls on Boys State Series Teams Number 31

27:340 May a girl be excluded from a boys team because the sport she wishes to participate in involves contact?

No. The case law and applicable statutes require that if there is no comparable girls team offered by a school, a girl seeking to play on a boys team must be given the opportunity to play even if the sport is a contact sport such as wrestling or football.

Leffel v. Wisconsin Interscholastic Athletic Association, 444 F. Supp. 1117, (E.D. Wis. 1978)

Darrin v. Gould, 85 Wash. 2d 859, 540 P. 2d 882 (1975)

Commonwealth of Pennsylvania by Israel Packel, Attorney General v. Pennsylvania Interscholastic Athletic Association, 18 Pa. Cmwlth. 45, 334 A. 2d 839 (1975)

Brenden v. Independent School District 742, 477 F. 2d 1292 (8th Cir. 1973)

Morris v. Michigan State Board of Education, 472 F. 2d 1207 (6th Cir. 1973)

Gilpin v. Kansas State High School Activities Association, Inc., 377 F. Supp. 1233 (D.C. Kan. 1973)

Bucha v. Illinois High Association, 351 F. Supp. 69 (N.D. Ill. 1972)

Reed v. Nebraska School Activities Association, 341 F. Supp. 258 (D.C. Neb. 1972)

Haas v. South Bend Community School Corporation, 259 Ind. 515, 289 N.E. 2d 495 (1972)

COACHING AND PRACTICING

27:350 Who may be employed as a coach?

To serve a member school as a head or assistant coach, the person must be regularly certified by the Illinois State Board of Education as a teacher, administrator, or school service personnel; be a retired teacher from an IHSA member school; or be college student coaching as part of an official student teaching assignment; or be certified through ASEP, NFHS, or other IHSA board-approved coaches certification program and be at least 19 years of age and be officially employed by the local school board of the member school.

IHSA By-law 2.070 et seq.

27:370 May a student attend an athletic sports camp or coaching school without affecting his or her athletic eligibility?

During the school year a student may not participate in any coaching school, camp, or clinic for any interscholastic sport or that provides instruction in any skill of an interscholastic sport. A coaching school, camp, or clinic is any program sponsored by an organization or individual that provides instruction in sports theory and/or skills that does not culminate in competition and that is attended by more than two persons from the school that a student attends.

Programs that involve only demonstration of skills and sports theory without providing instruction and requiring active participation by attendees are not considered coaching schools. Violation causes ineligibility for a period not to exceed 365 days.

Students may attend a coaching school, camp, or clinic during the summer months provided they do not attend before school is out in the spring or after Saturday of week number four in the IHSA standardized calendar. Such coaching schools, camps, and clinics may be conducted by an individual, group, or a member school and instruction at such program may be provided by any person.

However, in the case of a school-sponsored camp, participation may not be restricted to high school students who have been certified eligible for athletics. Students may participate in school physical conditioning programs and recreational programs. During the school year, students may serve as demonstrators for a coaching school, camp, or clinic conducted exclusively for coaches or officials. Students may participate in one practice session for such event with the instructor for whom they will demonstrate.

IHSA By-law 3.110 et seq.

27:375 May a coach have contact with his or her players during the summer months?

Persons who coach a sport at an IHSA member school may have a maximum of 25 days contact in that sport with students from that school. Students may have a maximum of 25 days of contact per sport with persons who coach that sport at the school they attend during the same time period.

A day of contact is defined as any date on which any coaching or instruction in the skills and techniques of any sport takes place. These limitations apply to all sports except baseball and softball. An exception may be made by the IHSA executive director under the guidelines adopted by the IHSA board of directors for competitions sponsored and conducted directly by the national governing body for the sport.

IHSA By-law 3.153

27:380 May a school have an open gym policy without violating IHSA rules?

Schools may open their gymnasiums or facilities for recreational activities to students or other persons who reside in or outside their district, under the following conditions:

1) A variety of recreational activities are available during the course of the year.

2) There is no coaching or instruction in the skills and techniques in any sport at any time.

3) Participation is voluntary and is not required directly or indirectly for membership on a high school squad.

4) Comparable opportunities are afforded to all participants.

IHSA By-law 3.161

27:390 May a student take private lessons in his or her sport outside the school season from his or her high school coach?

If the lesson program is limited to students from the instructor's school, the lesson program is a form of organizing and practicing the school team and is in violation of the bylaws. If the lesson program also contains students from outside the coach's home school population, the program is permissible, but no lesson group may contain more than two students from the same school.

IHSA By-law 2.090
IHSA By-law 3.114

27:400 May a student tryout for a non-school team during his or her school team's season?

Yes, provided the tryout is exclusively a demonstration of skills with no practice or instruction involved.

IHSA By-law 3.100 et seq.

27:420 May a coach be a staff member at a summer camp?

Yes, provided none of the coach's assignments at the camp involve exclusively students from the coach's school.

IHSA By-law 3.110 et seq.

27:430 May a student who is declared ineligible by the IHSA practice with his or her school team?

Provided there are no local rules to the contrary, the student may practice. IHSA rules prohibit only participation in or dressing for interscholastic competition. An ineligible student may also sit on the bench or perform as a team manager so long as he or she does not dress for the game.

IHSA By-law 3.130

RECRUITMENT

27:440 What is a special recruiting inducement?

It is a violation of IHSA rules to offer a student-athlete any special inducement that is not made available to all applicants who enroll in or apply to a school. A special recruiting inducement includes but is not limited to the offer or acceptance of

1) Money or other valuable consideration by anyone connected with the school;

2) Room, board, or clothing or financial allotment for clothing;

3) Pay for work that is in excess of the amount regularly paid for the work;

4) Free transportation by a school connected person;

5) Residence with any school-connected person;

6) Any privilege not afforded non-athletes;

7) Reduced rent for parents;

8) Payment of moving expenses for parents or assistance with the moving of parents;

9) Employment of parents in order to entice the family to move to a certain community if someone connected with the school makes the offer; or

10) Help in securing a college scholarship.

IHSA By-law 3.072

27:450 Can a school recruit athletes if it provides them no special inducements?

Recruitment or attempted recruitment of athletes is prohibited by IHSA rules. Even when there are no inducements offered, the attempt to encourage any prospective student to attend any member school for the purpose of participating in athletics is a violation of IHSA rules.

IHSA By-law 3.071
IHSA By-law 3.073

27:460 What penalties may be invoked for recruiting violations?

A person found guilty of exercising undue influence to secure or retain the attendance of a student at a member school is ineligible to coach at a member school for one year. Sanctions are also imposed against the school. Persons and or schools may be penalized in the form of written warning, reprimand, and may be required to take affirmative corrective action. The IHSA has authority to suspend or expel a person or school from participation in IHSA activities.

IHSA By-law 6.010

Tennessee Secondary School Athletic Association v. Brentwood Academy, 127 S. Ct. 2489, 551 U.S. 291, 168 L. Ed. 2d 166, (2007)

Monts ex rel. Monts v. Illinois High School Association, 338 Ill. App. 3d 1099, 789 N.E. 2d 413, 273 Ill. Dec. 513 (4th Dist. 2003)

Kulovitz v. Illinois High School Association, 462 F. Supp. 875 (N.D. Ill. 1978)

27:470 May a private school recruit students without violating IHSA rules?

Academic recruitment programs are permitted, as are recruitment programs that are designed to attract students because of a school's overall academic and extracurricular program. There are very specific IHSA rules governing what may and may not be done by a school in a multi-school district or by a private or parochial school in the recruitment of its general school population.

IHSA By-law 3.073

27:480 May a coach initiate contact with a prospective student-athlete?

No. School administrators or other school personnel who are not coaches may, however, initiate contact, provided that the contact is in the context of the enrollment of the student as a prospective student, not a prospective athlete.

IHSA By-law 3.073

27:490 May a coach attend and observe a grade school or unsanctioned athletic contest?

Yes, but the coach may not make improper contact with an athlete at the event.

IHSA By-law 3.073

27:500 May an alumnus or booster group provide financial assistance to needy students?

No direct financial assistance may be provided. Donations may, however, be provided to a school and distributed by the school to students who qualify for financial assistance. Student-athletes may not receive any special consideration in the distribution of financial assistance.

IHSA By-law 3.072

27:510 May a school employee, booster, alumnus, or other individual connected with a school make a home visit to a prospective athlete for recruiting purposes?

No.

IHSA By-law 3.073

NON-SCHOOL EVENTS

27:520 May a student-athlete compete on a non-school amateur team at the same time he or she is competing on a school team in the same sport?

During the school season for a given sport, in a school that maintains a school team in that sport, a student may not participate on any non-school team, nor as an individual unattached in non-school competition, in that given sport or in any competition that involves the skill of the sport in question. Violation results in ineligibility for a period not to exceed 365 days. Exceptions may be made by the executive director under the guidelines by the board of directors for competitions sponsored and conducted directly by the National Governing Body or its official Illinois affiliate for the sport.

A student cannot participate on or practice with any college, junior college, or university athletic team. To be eligible for a school team in a given sport, a student must cease non-school practice and competition in that sport no later than seven days after the date on which the school team engages in its first interscholastic contest in that sport.

During the school year, a person who is a coach in any sport at a member school, may be involved in any respect with any non-school team, only if the number of squad members from his/her school that are on the non-school team roster does not exceed one-half the number of players needed to field a team in actual IHSA state series competition in that sport.

IHSA By-law 3.100 et seq.

IHSA Administrative Procedures, Guidelines and Policies 15

27:530 Does participation in an all-star game affect a student's athletic eligibility?

A student may not participate in an all-star game in basketball, football, soccer, or volleyball during the student's high school career. After completion of a student's athletic eligibility, the student may compete in one IHSA-approved all-star game in that sport.

IHSA By-law 3.120

27:540 Are student-alumni games permitted under IHSA rules?

No. Alumni are not "school groups" within the meaning of IHSA bylaws. A faculty-student game is permissible and such a game does not count against the number of contests to which a school team is limited.

IHSA By-law 2.050

27:550 How many students may participate on a non-school team without violating length-of-season rules?

The limitations are as follows: basketball (five-player), 2 players may participate; soccer (11-player), 5; football (11-player), 5; football (seven-player passing), 3; volleyball (six-player), 2; swimming, 13; track, 17; gymnastics, 9; golf, 2; cross country, 3; wrestling, 5; badminton, 2; bowling, 2; tennis, 2.

IHSA By-law 2.090

27:560 May a student-athlete compete on the same team with a professional athlete?

Yes, provided the student does not receive cash in any amount for winning or placing in competition or merchandise prizes that exceed $75 in fair market value.

IHSA By-law 3.083

STUDENT AWARDS

27:570 May a student-athlete accept a trophy for athletic accomplishment without violation of IHSA rules?

For winning or placing in athletic competition, a student may accept a medal, cup, trophy, or plaque from the sponsoring agent regardless of cost. Schools may provide an individual or teams that win an IHSA state championship, a ring/memento not to exceed $200 in fair market value. Businesses, booster clubs, or other organizations desiring to make contributions toward the purchase of a championship ring/memento must make those contributions to the school.

A student may accept any other award for participation in an athletic contest or for athletic honors or recognition, that does not exceed $75 in fair market value, in the following sports: badminton, baseball, basketball, bowling, cross country, football, golf, gymnastics, soccer, softball, swimming, tennis, track and field, volleyball, wrestling, and any other sport in which the students' school provides interscholastic competition.

A student may receive and retain items of wearing apparel that are worn for non-school athletic competition as part of a team uniform provided for and worn by the student during competition.

A student may accept a school letter regardless of cost.

IHSA By-law 3.080 et seq.

Wiley v. National Collegiate Athletic Association, 612 F. 2d 473 (10th Cir. 1979)

TABLE OF CASES

Listed here are all of the court decisions cited in the text of *Illinois School Law Survey*. Cases are arranged in alphabetical order by name of plaintiff.

Each case listed carries a full legal citation followed by the question number(s) in bold face where the case may be found cited in the text.

Kraut v. Rachford, 51 Ill. App. 3d 206, 366 N.E. 2d 497, 9 Ill. Dec. 240 (1st Dist. 1977) **11:180, 11:220**

Kreimer v. Bureau of Police for the Town of Morristown, 958 F. 2d 1242 (3rd Cir. 1992) **10:400**

Krizek v. Board of Education, 713 F. Supp. 1131 (N.D. Ill. 1989) **17:480**

Krughoff v. Naperville, 68 Ill. 2d 352, 369 N.E. 2d 892, 12 Ill. Dec. 185, (1977) **9:100**

Kulovitz v. Illinois High School Association, 462 F. Supp. 875 (N.D. Ill. 1978) **27:130, 27:250, 27:460**

Kuykendall v. Board of Education of Evanston Township High School District No. 202, 111 Ill. App. 3d 809, 444 N.E. 2d 766, 67 Ill. Dec. 530 (1st Dist. 1982) **16:120, 16:160, 16:170**

L.E. Zannini & Co. v. Board of Education, Hawthorn School District 73, 138 Ill. App. 3d 467 486 N.E. 2d 426, 93 Ill. Dec. 323 (2nd Dist. 1985) **25:580**

L.P. v. Marian Catholic High School, 852 F. 3d. 690 (7th Cir. 2017) **22:35**

Lacks v. Ferguson-Florissant Reorganized School District, R-2, 147 F. 3d 718 (8th Cir. 1998) sugg. for reh. den. 154 F. 3d 904, cert. den. 119 S. Ct. 1158, 526 U.S. 1012, 143 L. Ed. 2d 233 (1999) **17:480, 17:482**

Laine v. Dittman, 125 Ill. App. 2d 136, 259 N.E. 2d 824 (2nd Dist. 1970) **12:125**

Lake County Forest Preserve District v. Northern Trust Bank, 207 Ill. App. 3d 290, 565 N.E. 2d 715, 152 Ill. Dec. 182 (2nd Dist. 1990) **6:290**

Lake Zurich School District No. 45, 1 PERI 1031 (IELRB Opinion and Order, November 30, 1984) **21:410**

Lamb's Chapel v. Center Moriches Union Free School District, 113 S. Ct. 2141, 508 U.S. 384, 124 L. Ed. 2d 352 (1993) **9:432, 14:145**

Lane v. Board of Education of Fairbury Cropsey Community Unit School District No. 3, 38 Ill. App. 3d 742, 348 N.E. 2d 470 (4th Dist. 1976) **19:200**

Laro v. New Hampshire, 259 F. 3d 1 (1st Cir. 2001) **17:900, 17:903, 17:908, 17:910, 17:915, 17:920, 17:925, 17:930**

Last v. Board of Education of Community Unit School District No. 321, Winnebago and Stephenson Counties, 37 Ill. App. 2d 159, 185 N.E. 2d 282 (2nd Dist. 1962) **15:110**

Latham v. Board of Education of Chicago, 31 Ill. 2d 178, 201 N.E. 2d 111 (1964) **2:20, 10:390**

Laukhuf v. Board of Education of School District No. 140 et al, 02 CH 59 (Cir. Ct. of the 11th Judicial Circuit, Woodford County) **6:150**

LaVine v. Blaine School District, 257 F. 3d 981 (9th Cir. 2001) **12:175**

Lawrence v. Texas, 123 S. Ct. 2472, 539 U.S. 538, 156 L. Ed. 2d 508 (2003) **11:430, 17:570**

Layshock ex rel. Layshock v. Hermitage School District, 593 F. 3d 249 (3rd Cir. 2010) **12:145**

Lee v. Weisman, 112 S. Ct. 2649, 505 U.S. 577, 120 L. Ed. 2d 467 (1992) **14:60, 14:61, 14:62, 14:123**

Leebaert v. Harrington, 332 F. 3d 134 (2nd Cir. 2003) **10:10, 14:210**

Leffel v. Wisconsin Interscholastic Athletic Association, 444 F. Supp. 1117, (E.D. Wis. 1978) **27:340**

Lehnert v. Ferris Faculty Association, 111 S. Ct. 1950, 500 U.S. 507, 114 L. Ed. 2d 572 (1991) reh. den. 111 S. Ct. 2878, 115 L. Ed. 2d 1044, on rem. 937 F. 2d 608 **21:330**

Lemon v. Kurtzman, 91 S. Ct. 2105, 403 U.S. 602, 29 L. Ed. 2d 745 (1971), reh. den. 92 S. Ct. 24, 404 U.S. 876, 30 L. Ed. 2d 123 (1971), on rem. 348 F. Supp. 300, aff'd. 93 S. Ct. 1463, 411 U.S. 192, 36 L. Ed. 2d 151 (1971) **14:20, 14:62, 14:123, 14:130**

Lenard v. Board of Education of Fairfield School District No. 112 of Wayne County, 57 Ill. App. 3d 853, 373 N.E. 2d 477, 15 Ill. Dec. 131 (5th Dist. 1978) app. after rem. 74 Ill. 2d 260, 384 N.E. 2d 1321, 24 Ill. Dec. 163 (1978) **16:300**

Lester v. Board of Education of School District No. 119, Jo Daviess County, 87 Ill. App. 2d 269, 230 N.E. 2d 893 (2nd Dist. 1967) **15:10, 16:60, 19:200**

Leventhal v. Vista Unified School District, 973 F. Supp. 951 (D.C. So. Cal. 1997) **6:225**

Leviton v. Board of Education of the City of Chicago, 374 Ill. 594, 30 N.E. 2d 497 (1943) **26:140**

Lewis v. North Clay Community Unit School District No. 25, 181 Ill. App. 3d 689, 537 N.E. 2d 435, 130 Ill. Dec. 368 (5th Dist. 1989) **15:230**

Lewis v. School District #70, 523 F. 3d 730 (7th Cir. 2008) **17:935, 17:940, 22:18**

Libby by Libby v. South Interconference Association, 728 F. Supp. 504 (N.D. Ill. 1990) **27:10**

Libertyville Education Association IEA-NEA v. Board of Education, 56 Ill. App. 3d 503, 371 N.E. 2d 676, 13 Ill. Dec. 741 (2nd Dist. 1977) **21:580**

Lieber v. Board of Trustees of Southern Illinois University, 176 Ill. 2d 401, 223 Ill. Dec. 641, 680 N.E. 2d 374 (1997) **7:80, 7:450**

Lincoln Way Community High School District No. 210, 5 PERI 1025 (Executive Director's Recommended Decision and Order, January 11, 1989) **21:100**

Lindblad v. Board of Education of Normal School District, 221 Ill. 261, 77 N.E. 450 (1906) **2:210**

Lindeman v. Kelso School District No. 458, 127 Wash. 2d 526, 111 P. 3d 1235 (2005) **7:170**

Linke v. Northwestern School Corp., __ Ind. App. __, 734 N.E. 2d 252 (Ind. App. 2000) **12:235, 12:236**

Linwood v. Board of Education of Peoria School District 150, 463 F. 2d 763 (7th Cir. 1972) **12:80, 12:380, 12:460, 12:470, 12:475**

Lippincott v. Board of Education of Community Unit School District No. 5 of Coles County, 342 Ill. App. 642, 97 N.E. 2d 566 (3rd Dist. 1951) **17:160**

Lipscomb v. Sisters of St. Francis Health Services, Inc., 343 Ill. App. 3d 1036, 799 N.E. 2d 293, 278 Ill. Dec. 575 (1st Dist. 2003) pet. for leave to app. den. 207 Ill. 2d 605, 807 N.E. 2d 976, 283 Ill. Dec. 135 (2004) **11:335**

Rice v. Board of Trustees of Adams County, 326 Ill. App. 3d 1120, 762 N.E. 2d 1205, 261 Ill. Dec. 278 (4th Dist. 2002) **6:165**

Richards v. Board of Education of Township High School District No. 201, 21 Ill. 2d 104, 171 N.E. 2d 37 (1960) **15:110**

Richmond v. County Board of School Trustees of Whiteside County, 93 Ill. App. 2d 142, 235 N.E. 2d 657 (3rd Dist. 1968) **8:220**

Righi v. SMC Corp., 632 F. 3d 404 (7th Cir. 2011) **17:905**

Riley v. Elkhart Community Schools, 829 F. 3d 886 (7th Cir. 2016) **14:620**

River Bend Community Unit School District No. 2 v. Illinois Human Rights Commission, et al., 232 Ill. App. 3d 838, 597 N.E. 2d 842, 173 Ill. Dec. 868 (3rd Dist. 1992) app. den. 147 Ill. 2d 637, 606 N.E. 2d 1235, 180 Ill. Dec. 158 (1993) **17:47**

River Grove School District No. 85 1/2, 3 PERI 1019 (IELRB Opinion and Order, January 30, 1987) **21:520**

Riverside-Brookfield Township District No. 208, 5 PERI 1136 (IELRB Decision and Order, July 25, 1989) **21:220**

RJB Properties v. Board of Education of The City of Chicago, 468 F. 3d 1005 (7th Cir. 2006) **25:570**

R.J.J. v. Shineman, 658 S.W. 2d 910 (Mo.App. 1983) **14:225**

Robertson by Robertson v. Granite City Community Unit School District No. 9, 684 F. Supp. 1002 (S.D. Ill. 1988) **13:100**

Robinson v. Illinois High School Association, 45 Ill. App. 2d 277, 195 N.E. 2d 38 (2nd Dist. 1963) cert. den. 85 S. Ct. 647, 379 U.S. 960, 13 L. Ed. 2d 555 (1965) **12:495, 27:10, 27:260, 27:270**

Robinson v. Oak Park and River Forest High School, Board of Education District 200, 213 Ill. App. 3d 77, 571 N.E. 2d 931, 156 Ill. Dec. 951 (1st Dist. 1991) **12:440, 12:470, 12:480**

Rock Falls Elementary School District No. 13, 2 PERI 1150 (IELRB Opinion and Order, May 14, 1987) aff'd. sub nom. **21:200**

Rockford Newspapers, Inc. v. Northern Illinois Council on Alcoholism and Drug Dependence, 64 Ill. App. 3d 94, 380 N.E. 2d 1192, 21 Ill. Dec. 16 (2nd Dist. 1978) **6:35, 7:402**

Rodiriecus L. By Betty H v. Waukegan School District No. 60, 90 F. 3d 249 (7th Cir. 1996) **13:520**

Rojicek v. Community Consolidated School District No. 15, 888 F. Supp. 878 (N.D. Ill. 1995) **20:142**

Rolando v. School Directors of District No. 125, 44 Ill. App. 3d 658, 358 N.E. 2d 945, 3 Ill. Dec. 402 (3rd Dist. 1976) **18:120**

Romer v. Evans, 116 S. Ct. 1620, 517 U.S. 620, 134 L. Ed. 2d 855 (1996) **17:570**

Rosa H. v. San Elizario Independent School District, 106 F. 3d 648 (5th Cir. 1997) **11:418**

Rosenberger v. Rector and Visitors of the University of Virginia, 115 S. Ct. 2510, 515 U.S. 819, 132 L. Ed. 2d 700 (1995) **10:410, 12:130, 14:140**

Rosenfeld v. New Jersey, 92 S. Ct. 2479, 408 U.S. 901, 33 L. Ed. 2d 321 (1972) on rem. State of New Jersey v. Rosenfeld, 303 A. 2d 889 (N.J. 1973) **6:245**

Ross ex rel. Ross v. Board of Education of Township High School Dist. 211, 486 F. 3d 279 (7th Cir. 2007) **13:20, 13:51**

Ross v. May Company, 377 Ill. App. 3d 387, 880 N.E. 2d 210, 316 Ill. Dec. 232 (1st Dist. 2007) **20:142**

Rutan v. Republican Party of Illinois, 110 S. Ct. 2729, 497 U.S. 62, 111 L. Ed. 2d 52, reh. den. 111 S. Ct. 13, 111 L. Ed. 2d 828 (1990) **17:460**

Ryan v. Warren Township High School District No. 121, 155 Ill. App. 3d 203, 510 N.E. 2d 911, 109 Ill. Dec. 843 (2nd Dist. 1987) **4:340**

S-1 v. Turlington, 635 F. 2d 342 (5th Cir. 1981) **13:370**

St. Francis College v. Al-Khazraji, 107 S. Ct. 2022, 481 U.S. 604, 95 L. Ed. 2d 582 (1987) **14:550**

Safford Unified School District No. 1 v. Redding, 129 S. Ct. 2633, 557 U.S. 364, 174 L. Ed. 2d 354 (2009) **12:231**

Sandra T.E., et al., v. South Berwyn School District 100 and Sidley Austin LLP., 600 F. 3d. 612 (7th Cir. 2010) **17:710**

San Antonio Independent School District v. Rodriguez, 93 S. Ct. 1278, 411 U.S. 1, 36 L. Ed. 2d 16, reh. den. 93 S. Ct. 1919, 411 U.S. 959, 36 L. Ed. 2d 418 (1973) **24:60, 24:62**

Sanders v. Louisiana High School Athletic Association, 242 So. 2d 19 (La. App. 1970) **27:10**

Sandholm v. Kuecker, et al., 405 Ill. App. 3d 835, 942 N.E. 2d 544, 347 Ill. Dec. 341 (2nd Dist. 2010) **2:144**

Sangamon County Sheriff's Department v. Illinois Human Rights Commission, 233 Ill. 2d 125, 908 N.E. 2d 125, 908 N.E. 2d 39, 330 Ill. Dec. 187 (2009) **17:505**

Sanguigni v. Pittsburgh Board of Public Education, 968 F. 2d 393 (3rd Cir. 1992) **17:451**

Santa Fe Independent School District v. Doe, 120 S. Ct. 2266, 530 U.S. 290, 147 L. Ed. 2d 295 (2000) **14:55, 14:61**

Sartwell v. Board of Trustees of the Teachers' Retirement System of the State of Illinois, 403 Ill. App. 3d 719, 936 N.E. 2d 610, 344 Ill. Dec. 81 (4th Dist. 2010) **15:766**

Saxe, et al., v. State College Area School District, 240 F. 3d 200 (3rd Cir. 2001) **11:416**

Schaefer v. Board of Education of Arlington Heights School District No. 25, 157 Ill. App. 3d 884, 510 N.E. 2d 1186, 110 Ill. Dec. 155 (1st Dist. 1987) app. den. 116 Ill. 2d 576, 515 N.E. 2d 126, 113 Ill. Dec. 317 (1987) **16:220**

Schafer v. Board of Public Education of School District of Pittsburgh, 732 F. Supp. 565 (W.D. Pa. 1990) **17:180**

Schaffer ex rel. Schaffer v. Weast, 126 S. Ct. 528, 546 U.S. 49, 163 L. Ed. 2d 387 (2005) **13:553**

Scheller v. Trustees of Schools, Township 41 North, 67 Ill. App. 3d 857, 384 N.E. 2d 971, 24 Ill. Dec. 104 (2nd

QUICK REFERENCE INDEX

This index refers to question numbers rather than to page numbers. The reader is cautioned that, where a topic is discussed in a series of questions, only the first question is listed here. The reader often will find additional information under questions immediately following those listed.

The author has tried to make the entries in this index reasonably narrow and detailed. The user who is trying to locate a narrow question of law, therefore, is advised to first look for that specific topic. If that proves unfruitful, look for a broader topic that may lead to a productive area of the text.

- A -

continued

- B –

continued

continued

continued

- D -

continued

- E -

continued

- F -

continued

I

continued

- M -

- N -

- O -

continued

- P -

continued

- Q - R -

continued

continued

continued

continued